American Literary Scholarship

1981

American Literary Scholarship

An Annual / 1981

Edited by James Woodress

Essays by Wendell Glick, David B. Kesterson, Donald B. Stauffer, Robert Milder, Jerome Loving, Louis J. Budd, Robert L. Gale, George Bornstein and Stuart Y. McDougal, Karl F. Zender, Scott Donaldson, William J. Scheick, Kermit Vanderbilt, John J. Murphy, Jack Salzman, Jerome Klinkowitz, Richard Crowder, Lee Bartlett, Walter J. Meserve, John M. Reilly, Jonathan Morse, Marc Chénetier, Hans Galinsky, Gaetano Prampolini, Keiko Beppu, Mona Pers

Duke University Press, Durham North Carolina, 1983

© 1983, Duke University Press. Library of Congress Catalogue Card number 65–19450. I.S.B.N. 0–8223–0552–6. Printed in the United States of America by Heritage Printers, Inc.

This book is dedicated to the memory
of four former contributors
 Rolando Anzilotti (1919–1982)
 Richard Beale Davis (1907–1981)
 Oliver Evans (1915–1981)
 C. Hugh Holman (1914–1981)

Foreword

As Editor J. Albert Robbins announced in the foreword to *ALS 1980*, this is the final volume the present editor will bring out. Henceforth the volumes will be edited by Robbins and Warren G. French. Also next year there will be some changes in contributors: David Kesterson, who has reviewed Hawthorne scholarship, will be replaced by Rita K. Gollin (State Univ. College, Geneseo, N.Y.); George Bornstein and Stuart McDougal, who have collaborated on the Pound-Eliot chapter, will be succeeded by Hugh Witemeyer (Univ. of New Mexico); Kermit Vanderbilt will turn over the 19th century to George Hendrick (Univ. of Illinois); Jack Salzman will be followed by Louis Owens (Calif. State Univ., Northridge); Jonathan Morse will hand over chapter 20 to its former tenant, Michael Hoffman (Univ. of California, Davis). We will have the same foreign contributors as this year, except that Hiroko Sato will alternate with Keiko Beppu in reviewing Japanese scholarship on American literature. To all those contributors retiring from the heavy chore of writing a chapter for this annual I give my thanks, and to the new contributors for next year I extend a welcome.

There is no essay on East European contributions this year. The reason: new governmental policies and pressures in Poland.

There are no innovations in this year's *ALS*, but I have made a more strenuous effort than usual to keep the volume to a reasonable size. Contributors have been instructed to pass silently over trivial or redundant scholarship, but this admonition has not been sufficient, and, as one contributor put it, he had to cut away bone to get his manuscript to fit the space allotted to him. Thus, unless the editor had the strength, the Duke University Press the temerity, and subscribers the wherewithal to cope with a volume running to perhaps 700 pages, it would not be possible to review all the useful scholarship appearing on the subject of American literature in any one year.

Inevitably we miss items that should be reviewed even with a

policy of omitting work of lesser importance. This year the printout
of the American literature section of the *MLA Bibliography* was not
available until mid-August, the date that essays for this volume
were due from contributors, and some items appearing there, which
had been overlooked in our own searches, have been held over until
next year. Others the editor pasted in as inserts in the manuscript of
this volume. More than ever this year, the collecting of material for
review in *ALS* has been a project independent of the work of the
MLA's bibliography committee. Again I urge writers of articles to
send copies or offprints to the appropriate contributor and writers
of books to ask their publishers to forward copies for review.

James Woodress

University of California, Davis

Table of Contents

Key to Abbreviations

Festschriften, Essay Collections, and Books Discussed in More Than One Chapter

America as Utopia / *America as Utopia*, ed. Kenneth M. Roemer (Burt Franklin)

The American Identity / *The American Identity: Fusion and Fragmentation*, European Contributions to American Studies 3, ed. Rob Kroes (Amsterdam: European American Studies Association)

The American Self / *The American Self: Myth, Ideology, and Popular Culture*, ed. Sam B. Girgus (N. Mex.)

American Writers / *American Writers: A Collection of Literary Biographies*, Supplement II, Part 1, ed. A. Walton Litz (Scribner's)

Anglo-American Encounters / Benjamin Lease, *Anglo-American Encounters: England and the Rise of American Literature* (Cambridge)

The Apocalyptic Vision / Lakshmi Mani, *The Apocalyptic Vision in Nineteenth Century American Fiction: A Study of Cooper, Hawthorne, and Melville* (Univ. Press)

Aspects du mal / *Aspects du mal dans la civilisation et la littérature Anglo-Saxonne*, Annales de l'Université de Savoie.

Books Speaking to Books / William T. Stafford, *Books Speaking to Books: A Contextual Approach to American Fiction* (N. Car.)

Brumm Festschrift / *Forms and Functions of History in American Literature: Essays in Honor of Ursula Brumm*, ed. Winfried Fluck, Jürgen Peper, and Willi Paul Adams (Berlin: Erich Schmidt)

Contemporary Drama / *Essays on Contemporary American Drama*, ed. Hedwig Bock and Albert Wertheim (Munich: Max Hueber Verlag)

The Fictional Father / *The Fictional Father: Lacanian Readings of the Text*, ed. Robert Con Davis (Mass.)

Foreigners / Marcus Klein, *Foreigners: The Making of American Literature, 1900–1940* (Chicago)

History of the Novel / Walter L. Reed, *An Exemplary History of the Novel: The Quixotic Versus the Picturesque* (Chicago)

The Life of the Poet / Lawrence Lipking, *The Life of the Poet: Beginning and Ending Poetic Careers* (Chicago)

Literary Democracy / Larzer Ziff, *Literary Democracy: The Declaration of Cultural Independence in America* (Viking)

Literary Romanticism / *Literary Romanticism in America*, ed. William L. Andrews (LSU)

Literature and the Urban Experience / *Literature and the Urban Experience: Essays on the City and Literature*, ed. Michael C. Jaye and Ann Chalmers Watts (Rutgers)

Mythes, Images, et Représentations / *Mythes, Images, et Représentations*, Actes du XIVème Congrès de la Société Française de Littérature Générale et Comparée, Tramés 79 (Paris: Didier)

The New Book on Nature / Robert Nadeau, *Readings from the New Book on Nature* (Mass.)

New England Heritage / *American Literature: The New England Heritage*, ed. James Nagel and Richard Astro (Garland)

Novel vs. Fiction / *Novel vs. Fiction: The Contemporary Reformation*, ed. Jackson I. Cope and Geoffrey Green (Norman, Okla.: Pilgrim Books)

The Past in the Present / Thomas Daniel Young, *The Past in the Present: A Thematic Study of Modern Southern Fiction* (LSU)

Rappaccini's Children / William H. Shurr, *Rappaccini's Children: American Writers in a Calvinist World* (Kentucky)

Riewald Festschrift / *Costerus: From Cooper to Philip Roth—Essays on American Literature Presented to J. G. Riewald on the Occasion of His Seventieth Birthday*, ed. J. Bakker and D. R. M. Wilkinson (Roldopi)

Ruined Eden / *Ruined Eden of the Present: Hawthorne, Melville, and Poe*, ed. G. R. Thompson and Virgil Lokke (Purdue)

Schulze Festschrift / *Studien zur Englishchen Philologie zu Ehren von Fritz W. Schulze* (Tubingen: Narr)

Seeing and Being / Carolyn Porter, *Seeing and Being: The Plight of the Participant Observer in Emerson, James, Adams, and Faulkner* (Wesleyan)

Sport and the Spirit of Play / Christian K. Messenger, *Sport and the Spirit of Play in American Fiction: Hawthorne to Faulkner* (Columbia)

Tomorrow Is Another Day / Anne Goodwyn Jones, *Tomorrow Is Another Day: The Woman Writer in the South, 1859–1936* (LSU)

Traditions / *Traditions in Twentieth-Century American Literature*, ed. Marta Sienicka (Poznán: Adam Mickiewicz Univ.)

Ultimately Fiction / Dennis W. Petrie, *Ultimately Fiction: Design in Modern American Biography* (Purdue)

The Universe of Force / Ronald E. Martin, *American Literature and the Universe of Force* (Duke)

Untying the Text / *Untying the Text: A Post-Structuralist Reader*, ed. Robert Young (Routledge)

Wächtler Festschrift / *Weltsprache Englisch in Forschung und Lehre: Festschrift für Kurt Wächtler* (Berlin: Erich Schmidt)

Wall Street / Wayne W. Westbrook, *Wall Street in the American Novel* (NYU, 1980)

Who Is in the House? / Sally Allen McNall, *Who Is in the House: A Psychological Study of Two Centuries of Women's Fiction in America, 1775 to the Present* (Elsevier)

The Wisdom of Words / Philip Gura, *The Wisdom of Words: Language, Theology, and Literature in the New England Renaissance* (Wesleyan)

Periodicals, Annuals, Series

AAuS / *Americana-Austriaca: Beiträge zur Amerikakunde*

ABBW / *AB Bookman's Weekly* (from merger of *Antiquarian Bookman* and *Bookman's Weekly*)

ABC / *American Book Collector*

AF / *Anglistische Forschungen*

AI / *American Imago*

AL / *American Literature*

ALR / *American Literary Realism*

ALS / *American Literary Scholarship*

AmerS / *American Studies*

AmerSS / *American Studies in Scandinavia*

Amst / *Amerikastudien*

AN&Q / *American Notes and Queries*

AppalJ / Appalachian Journal
APR / American Poetry Review
AQ / American Quarterly
AR / Antioch Review
ArmD / Armchair Detective (White Bear Lake, Minn.)
ArAA / Arbeiten aus Anglistik und Amerikanistik
ArielE / Ariel: A Review of International English Literature
ArQ / Arizona Quarterly
ASInt / American Studies International
AtM / Atlantic Monthly
ATQ / American Transcendental Quarterly
BALF / Black American Literature Forum
BB / Bulletin of Bibliography
Biography: An Interdisciplinary Quarterly
Boundary / Boundary 2: A Journal of Post-Modern Literature
BSUF / Ball State University Forum
Callaloo: A Black South Journal of Arts and Letters
C&L / Christianity and Literature
CB / Classical Bulletin
CEA / CEA Critic
CentR / The Centennial Review
ChiR / Chicago Review
CL / Comparative Literature
CLAJ / College Language Association Journal
CLQ / Colby Library Quarterly
CLS / Comparative Literature Studies
CMHS / Collections of the Massachusetts Historical Society
CollL / College Literature (West Chester State College)
CompD / Comparative Drama
ConL / Contemporary Literature
ConP / Contemporary Poetry: A Journal of Criticism
ContempR / Contemporary Review (London)
CP / Concerning Poetry
CQ / The Cambridge Quarterly
CR / Critical Review (Australia)
CRAA / Centre de Recherches sur l'Amérique Anglophone

CRCL / Canadian Review of Comparative Literature
CRevAS / Canadian Review of American Studies
Crit / Critique: Studies in Modern Fiction
CritI / Critical Inquiry
Criticism: A Quarterly for Literature and the Arts (Detroit)
CS / Concord Saunterer
DAI / Dissertation Abstracts International
DeltaES / Delta: Revue du Centre d'Etudes et de Recherche sur les Ecrivains du Sud aux Etats-Unis (Montpellier, France)
DicS / Dickinson Studies (formerly Emily Dickinson Bulletin)
DLB / Dictionary of Literary Biography
DQ / Denver Quarterly
DR / Dalhousie Review
DrN / Dreiser Newsletter
DSN / Dickens Studies Newsletter
EA / Etudes Anglaises
EAL / Early American Literature
EAS / Essays in Arts and Science
Edda: Nordisk Tidsskrift for Litteraturforskning
EIC / Essays in Criticism
EJ / English Journal
EigoS / Eigo Seinen: The Rising Generation (Tokyo)
Éire / Éire-Ireland: A Journal of Irish Studies
ELH / English Literary History
ELN / English Language Notes
ELWIU / Essays in Literature (Western Ill. Univ.)
EngR / English Record
Enquiry: Research at the University of Delaware
EON / Eugene O'Neill Newsletter
ES / English Studies
ESC / English Studies in Canada (Toronto)
ESQ / ESQ: A Journal of the American Renaissance
EurH / Europäisch Hochschulschriften/Publications Universitaire Européennes/European University Studies

EuWN / Eudora Welty Newsletter
Expl / Explicator
FR / French Review
FSt / Feminist Studies
GaR / Georgia Review
Glyph / Glyph: Textual Studies
GPQ / Great Plains Quarterly
GyS / Gypsy Scholar
HC / Hollins Critic
HCN / Hart Crane Newsletter (now called *The Visionary Company*)
HemR / Hemingway Review
HJ / Higginson Journal (formerly *Higginson Journal of Poetry*)
HJR / Henry James Review
HLB / Harvard Library Bulletin
HLQ / Huntington Library Quarterly
HN / Hemingway Notes
HSE / Hungarian Studies in English
HSL / Hartford Studies in Literature
HSN / Hawthorne Society Newsletter
HTR / Harvard Theological Review
HudR / Hudson Review
IowaR / Iowa Review
JAC / Journal of American Culture
JAF / Journal of American Folklore
JAmS / Journal of American Studies
JBlS / Journal of Black Studies
JEGP / Journal of English & Germanic Philology
JEn / Journal of English (Sana'a University)
JIS / Journal of Indian Studies
JLN / Jack London Newsletter
JNH / Journal of Negro History
JNT / Journal of Narrative Technique
JOHJ / John O'Hara Journal
JPC / Journal of Popular Culture
JW / Journal of the West
KR / Kenyon Review
L&P / Literature and Psychology
Lang&S / Language and Style
LC / Library Chronicle (Univ. of Penn.)
LetA / Letteratura d'America (Rome)
LFQ / Literature/Film Quarterly
LGJ / Lost Generation Journal
LitR / Literary Review (Fairleigh Dickinson Univ.)
LJGG / Literaturwissenschaftliches Jahrbuch in Auftrage der Görres-Gesellschaft

LQ / Language Quarterly (Univ. of South Florida)
LRN / Literary Research Newsletter
LWU / Literatur in Wissenschaft und Unterricht (Kiel)
MarkhamR / Markham Review
MD / Modern Drama
MELUS / MELUS: Journal of the Society for the Study of the Multi-Ethnic Literature of the United States
MFS / Modern Fiction Studies
MHLS / Mid-Hudson Language Studies
MHRev / Malahat Review: An International Quarterly of Life and Letters
MidAmerica: The Yearbook of the Society for the Study of Midwestern Literature
MinnR / Minnesota Review
MissouriR / Missouri Review
MissQ / Mississippi Quarterly
MLN / Modern Language Notes
MLS / Modern Language Studies
MMis / Midwestern Miscellany
Mosaic: A Journal for the Comparative Study of Literature and Ideas
MP / Modern Philology
MPS / Modern Poetry Studies
MQ / Midwest Quarterly
MQR / Michigan Quarterly Review
MR / Massachusetts Review
MSE / Massachusetts Studies in English
MSEx / Melville Society Extracts
MSpr / Moderna Språk (Stockholm)
MTJ / Mark Twain Journal
MTMN / Mark Twain Memorial Newsletter
MTSB / Mark Twain Society Bulletin
MV / Minority Voices
Names: Journal of the American Name Society
N&Q / Notes and Queries
NAR / North American Review
NBR / New Boston Review
NCF / Nineteenth-Century Fiction
NConL / Notes on Contemporary Literature
NEQ / New England Quarterly
NER / New England Review

NewL / New Letters
NewRep / New Republic
NLauR / New Laurel Review
NLH / New Literary History
NMAL / Notes on Modern American
   Literature
NMHR / New Mexico Humanities
   Review
NMW / Notes on Mississippi Writers
Novel / Novel: A Forum on Fiction
NR / Nassau Review
NYH / New York History
NYRB / New York Review of Books
NYTBR / New York Times Book
   Review
Obsidian: Black Literature in Review
   (Fredonia, N.Y.)
OL / Orbis Litterarum: International
   Review of Literary Studies
ON / Old Northwest (Oxford, Ohio)
OPL / Osservatore Politico Letterario
Paideuma: A Journal Devoted to Ezra
   Pound Scholarship
Paragone / Revista Mensile di Arte
   Figurativa e Letteraturg
ParisR / Paris Review
Parnassus: Poetry in Review
PBSA / Papers of the Bibliographical
   Society of America
Phylon: The Atlanta University Re-
   view of Race and Culture
PLL / Papers on Language and
   Literature
PNotes / Pynchon Notes (Brent-
   wood, N.Y.)
PoeS / Poe Studies
PMHS / Proceedings of the Massa-
   chusetts Historical Society
PMLA / PMLA: Publications of the
   Modern Language Association
PMPA / Publications of the Missouri
   Philological Association
Poetica: Zeitschrift für Sprach-und
   Literaturwissenschaft (Amster-
   dam)
PoT / Poetics Today (Tel Aviv)
PQ / Philological Quarterly
PR / Partisan Review
Prospects: An Annual of American
   Cultural Studies
PrS / Prairie Schooner
PVR / Platte Valley Review

QL / Quizaine Littéraire
QQ / Queen's Quarterly
RALS / Resources for American
   Literary Study
RANAM / Recherches Anglaises et
   Américaines (Strasbourg)
ReAL / RE: Artes Liberales
RecL / Recovering Literature: A
   Journal of Contextualist Criticism
Rendezvous / Rendezvous: A Journal
   of Arts and Letters (Idaho State)
Renditions (Hong Kong)
RFEA / Revue Française d'Etudes
   Américaines (Paris)
RJN / Robinson Jeffers Newsletter
RLC / Revue de Littérature Comparée
RLMC / Rivista di Letterature
   Moderne e Comparate (Firenze)
RS / Research Studies (Wash. State
   Univ.)
RSA / Rivista di Studi Anglo-
   Americani (Brescia)
SA / Studi Americani
SAF / Studies in American Fiction
SALit / Studies in American Lit-
   erature (Kyoto)
SAmH / Studies in American Humor
SAP / Studia Anglica Posnaniensia:
   An International Review of English
   Studies
SAQ / South Atlantic Quarterly
SAR / Studies in the American
   Renaissance
SB / Studies in Bibliography
SBHC / Studies of Browning and His
   Circle
SBL / Studies in Black Literature
SCR / South Carolina Review
SDR / South Dakota Review
SELit / Studies in English Literature
   (Japan)
SFS / Science-Fiction Studies
SGym / Siculorum Gymnasium
SHR / Southern Humanities Review
SIH / Studies in the Humanities
SIR / Studies in Romanticism
SJS / San Jose Studies
SLitI / Studies in the Literary Imagi-
   nation
SLJ / Southern Literary Journal
SN / Studia Neophilologica

SNNTS / *Studies in the Novel* (North Texas State Univ.)

SoQ / *The Southern Quarterly*

SoR / *Southern Review*

SoRA / *Southern Review* (Australia)

SoSt / *Southern Studies: An Interdisciplinary Journal of the South* (formerly *LaS*)

Soundings / *Soundings: A Journal of Interdisciplinary Studies*

SpM / *Spicilegio Moderno* (Bologna)

Sprachkunst / *Sprachkunst: Beiträge zur Litteraturwissenschaft*

SR / *Sewanee Review*

SS / *Scandinavian Studies*

SSF / *Studies in Short Fiction*

SSMLN / *Society for the Study of Midwestern Literature Newsletter*

StHum / *Studies in the Humanities*

StQ / *Steinbeck Quarterly*

SwAL / *Southwest American Literature*

SWR / *Southwest Review*

TBA / *Tübinger Beiträge zur Anglistik*

TCL / *Twentieth-Century Literature*

TDR / *Drama Review* (formerly *Tulane Drama Review*)

Thought: A Review of Culture and Idea

TJ / *Theatre Journal* (formerly *Educational Theatre Journal*)

TJQ / *Thoreau Journal Quarterly*

TkR / *Tamkang Review*

TLS / *Times Literary Supplement*

TM / *Temps Modernes*

TriQ / *Tri-Quarterly*

TSB / *Thoreau Society Bulletin*

TSL / *Tennessee Studies in Literature*

TSLL / *Texas Studies in Literature and Language*

TWNew / *Tennessee Williams Newsletter*

TUSAS / Twayne United States Authors Series

TW / *Thomas Wolfe Review* (formerly *Thomas Wolfe Newsletter*)

UMSE / *Univ. of Mississippi Studies in English*

USP / *Under the Sign of Pisces: Anaïs Nin and Her Circle*

VMHB / *Virginia Magazine of History and Biography*

VNRN / *Vladimir Nabokov Research Newsletter*

VQR / *Virginia Quarterly Review*

WAL / *Western American Literature*

WCR / *West Coast Review*

WiF / *William Faulkner: Marterials, Studies, and Criticism* (Tokyo)

WIRS / *Western Ill. Regional Studies*

WLB / *Wilson Library Bulletin*

WMQ / *William and Mary Quarterly*

WSJour / *Wallace Stevens Journal*

WVUPP / *West Virginia Univ. Philological Papers*

WWR / *Walt Whitman Review*

WWS / Western Writers Series (Boise State Univ.)

YER / *Yeats Eliot Review* (formerly *T.S. Eliot Review*)

YR / *Yale Review*

YULG / *Yale University Library Gazette*

ZAA / *Zeitschrift fürr Anglistik und Amerikanistik*

ZAL:A&E / *Zeitgenössische Amerikanische Literatur: Anglistik & Englishchunterricht*

Publishers

AHM / Arlington Heights, Ill.: AHM Publishing Corp.

Alabama / University, Ala.: University of Alabama Press

AMS / New York: AMS Press

Archon / Hamden, Conn.: Archon Books

Arlington / Westport, Conn.: Arlington House

Atheneum / New York: Atheneum Publishers

Barnes and Noble / Totowa, N.J.: Barnes and Noble

Baylor / Waco, Tex.: Baylor Univ. Press

Black Sparrow / Santa Barbara, Calif.: Black Sparrow Press

Bourgois / Paris: Bourgois

Bowker / New York: R. R. Bowker Co.

Bucknell / Lewisburg, Pa.: Bucknell Univ. Press

Burt Franklin / New York: Burt Franklin and Co.

Calif. / Berkeley: Univ. of California Press

Cambridge / Cambridge, Eng.: Cambridge Univ. Press

Chicago / Chicago: Univ. of Chicago Press

City Lights / San Francisco: City Lights

Columbia / New York: Columbia Univ. Press

Copper Canyon / Port Towsend, Wash.: Copper Canyon Press

Cornell / Ithaca, N.Y.: Cornell Univ. Press

Crown / New York: Crown Publishers

Delacorte / New York: Delacorte Press

Delaware / Newark, Del.: Univ. of Delaware Press

Delmas / Ann Arbor, Mich.: Delmas

Didier / Paris: Didier

Doubleday / New York: Doubleday & Co.

Drama Book / New York: Drama Book Specialists

Duke / Durham, N.C.: Duke Univ. Press

Duquesne / Pittsburgh: Duquesne Univ. Press

Elsevier / Utrecht, Netherlands: Elsevier

Erlbaum / Hillsdale, N.J.: Lawrence Erlbaum Associates

Facts on File / New York: Facts on File

Fairleigh Dickinson / Madison, N.J.: Fairleigh Dickinson Univ. Press

Falcon / Sparks, Nev.: Falcon Hill Press

Farrar / New York: Farrar, Straus & Giroux

Fortress / Philadelphia: Fortress Press

Gale / Detroit: Gale Research Co.

Gallimard / Paris: Gallimard

Garland / New York: Garland Publishing Co.

Georgia / Athens: Univ. of Georgia Press

Gordian / Staten Island, N.Y.: Gordian Press

Greenwood / Westport, Conn.: Greenwood Press

Hall / Boston: G. K. Hall and Co.

Harcourt / New York: Harcourt Brace Jovanovich

Harmony / Greenport, N.Y.: Harmony and Co.

Harper / New York: Harper & Row

Harvard / Cambridge, Mass.: Harvard Univ. Press

Hawaii / Honolulu: Univ. Press of Hawaii

Hill & Wang / New York: Hill and Wang

Holt / New York: Holt, Rinehart, and Winston

Holy Cow! / Minneapolis: Holy Cow! Press

Hopkins / Baltimore: John Hopkins Univ. Press

Houghton Mifflin / Boston: Houghton Mifflin

Max Hueber / Munich: Max Hueber Verlag

Huntington / San Marino, Calif.: Huntington Library Publications

Illinois / Urbana: Univ. of Illinois Press

Indiana / Bloomington: Indiana Univ. Press

Japadra / L'Aquila: Leandro Ugo Japadre, Editore

Kansas / Lawrence: Regents Press of Kansas

Kennikat / Port Washington, N.Y.: Kennikat Press

Kentucky / Lexington: Univ. Press of Kentucky

Lang / Frankfurt, Germany: Peter Lang

Little, Brown / Boston: Little, Brown

LSU / Baton Rouge: Louisiana State Univ. Press

McFarland / Jefferson, N.C.: McFarland

McGraw-Hill / New York: McGraw-Hill Book Co.

Mass. / Amherst: Univ. of Massachusetts Press

Methuen / London: Methuen
Miss. / Jackson: Univ. Press of
Mississippi
NAL / New York: New American
Library, Inc.
Nan'undo / Tokyo: Nan'undo
N. Car. / Chapel Hill: Univ. of
North Carolina Press
New Directions / New York: New
Directions Publishing Corp.
New England / Hanover, N.H.: Univ.
Press of New England
N. Mex. / Albuquerque: Univ. of New
Mexico Press
North Point / San Francisco: North
Point Press
NPF / Orono, Maine: National
Poetry Foundation
NYU / New York: New York Univ.
Press
Ohio / Athens: Ohio Univ. Press
Ohio State / Columbus: Ohio State
Univ. Press
Oklahoma / Norman: Univ. of
Oklahoma Press
Oxford / New York: Oxford Univ.
Press
Penn. State / University Park: Penn-
sylvania State Univ. Press
Performing Arts / New York: Per-
forming Arts Journal Publications
Phil. Lib. / New York: Philosophical
Library
Pilgrim / Norman, Okla.: Pilgrim
Books
Pittsburgh / Pittsburgh: Univ. of
Pittsburgh Press
Prentice-Hall / Englewood Cliffs, N.J.:
Prentice-Hall
Princeton / Princeton, N.J.: Princeton
Univ. Press
Purdue / West Lafayette, Ind.:
Purdue Univ. Press
Random House / New York: Random
House
Reidel / Dordrecht, Netherlands:
D. Reidel Publishing GmbH
Rodopi / Amsterdam: Rodopi N.V.
Routledge / Boston: Routledge and
Kegan Paul
Rutgers / New Brunswick, N.J.:
Rutgers Univ. Press

Salem / Pasadena, Calif.: Salem Press
Scarecrow / Metuchen, N.J.:
Scarecrow Press
Schmidt / Berlin: Erich Schmidt
Verlag
Schocken / New York: Schocken Books
Scribner's / New York: Charles
Scribner's Sons
So. Ill. / Carbondale: Southern
Illinois Univ. Press
SUNY / State Univ. of New York
Swallow / Athens, O.: Swallow Press
Tenn. / Knoxville: Univ. of Tennessee
Press
Texas / Austin: Univ. of Texas
Press
Theatre Arts / New York: Theatre
Arts Books
Transcendental Books / Hartford,
Conn.: Transcendental Books
Tulane / New Orleans: Tulane
University Press
Twayne / Boston: Twayne Publishers
Ungar / New York: Frederick Ungar
Publishing Co.
Univ. Microfilms / Ann Arbor, Mich.:
University Microfilms Interna-
national
Universitetsforlaget / Oslo: Uni-
versitetsforlaget / Distributed in
U.S. by Columbia Univ. Press
Univ. Press / Washington, D.C.:
Univ. Press of America
Viking / New York: Viking Press
Virginia / Charlottesville: Univ. Press
of Virginia
Wash. / Seattle: Univ. of Washington
Press
Wash. Square / New York: Washing-
ton Square Press (div. of Simon
& Schuster)
Wesleyan / Middletown, Conn.:
Wesleyan Univ. Press
Whitston / Troy, N.Y.: Whitston
Publishing Co.
Yale / New Haven, Conn.: Yale
Univ. Press
Yamaguchi / Tokyo: Yamaguchi
Shoten
Yoknapatawpha / Oxford, Miss.:
Yoknapatawpha Press

Part I

Part I

1. Emerson, Thoreau, and Transcendentalism

Wendell Glick

Reading each year for the past five the annual corpus of scholarly criticism on Emerson and Thoreau, trying to discern trends, I have been struck by the decline in fault-finding with transcendentalist thought, which must have reached a peak ten years or so ago during the period of intense American social activism. To be sure, there are sporadic analyses of alleged personal hangups, chiefly sexual, and an occasional nonspecialist will deplore the presumed insidiousness of Emerson's teaching of unbridled individualism to American youth, but the total chorus is clearly and increasingly laudatory. The old charges of aloofness, of impractical moonshine and mysticism, are giving way to claims, sometimes by eminent modern philosophers, that Emerson and Thoreau were profound original thinkers, pioneer language theorists, metaphysicians fit for the company of Wittgenstein and Kant. I am aware of one instance even of Thoreau's being taught in the department of philosophy of a major university. The next few years may well be critical ones to new evaluations of American transcendentalism, with poststructuralists and philosophers joining literary scholars in circling Emerson and Thoreau in thickening clouds, present-day deemphasis of the humanities notwithstanding.

i. General Studies, Textual Studies, Bibliography

Alexander Kern's "Coleridge and American Romanticism: The Transcendentalists and Poe," pp. 113–36 of *New Approaches to Coleridge: Biographical and Critical Essays*, ed. Donald Sultana (Barnes and Noble), is a fitting point of departure for a survey of the year's

I acknowledge the aid of Mara Smith in helping me again this year to locate the periodical criticism.—W.G.

criticism on Emerson and Thoreau, since the influence of Coleridge upon American romanticism continues to intrigue scholars. In a brief but thoroughly researched essay, Kern accomplishes more than some books in showing how and why the Coleridgean epistemology was particularly appealing to the major transcendentalists and Poe, who imbibed their Coleridge from James Marsh, adapting it to the American environment. Coleridge, Kern believes, "more than Wordsworth, Carlyle, or any German writer, precipitated American Transcendentalism" (p. 132). Kern's article provides a useful setting against which Philip Gura's two important studies of the interrelatedness of philological with aesthetic, religious, and philosophical thought may be read. In "Language and Meaning: An American Tradition" (*AL* 53:1–21) and *The Wisdom of Words* Gura brings to a new synthesis the philological studies of the past decade or so of himself, Michael West, Barry Wood, John T. Irwin, and others. Gura sees Marsh's *Aids to Reflection* (1829) as diverting American philological study away from both the theological debate over scriptural language and the Lockean epistemology that was the staple of college curricula, directing it toward Thoreau's view that language was one of the keys to man's understanding of the universe. In the final (and for me, the least convincing) chapter of his book, Gura goes so far as to suggest that "the philological explorations into a universal language by Elizabeth Peabody and Henry Thoreau . . . created the possibility for Hawthorne and Melville's symbolistic methods" (p. 169). Gura's is a major contribution and should provoke further studies. Anne C. Rose's *Transcendentalism as a Social Movement, 1830–1850* (Yale) is less seminal. Rose's claim is that the contribution of the American transcendentalists to the refinement of American society between the Revolution and the Civil War was greater than has generally been supposed. Rose's book does not settle the issue; it falls into the trap (it began as a Yale dissertation) of viewing American transcendentalism as largely an overt social movement, as it surely was not, in the sense that the Fourieristic phalanxes and the peace, temperance, and antislavery societies were. A movement, moreover, that included Alcott and Ripley as well as Emerson and Thoreau proved too diverse for Rose, leading her often into a quicksand of half-truths. Two samples: "What the Transcendentalists advocated was no longer Christianity per se but simply religion" and "The Transcendentalists were the philosophers of evangelical Unitarianism who stopped to consider the intellectual issues raised by the movement itself" (p. 38). Bland generalizations aside, and they are far too frequent in this book, the moral character of transcendental social consciousness has been better handled elsewhere than by Rose.

Bernard Rosenthal's *City of Nature: Journeys to Nature in the Age of American Romanticism* (Delaware) attempts a redefinition of the term "nature" as it was used by American romantics. Examining the works of Thoreau and Emerson, Cooper, Hawthorne, and Melville, Rosenthal develops two connotations for the term out of the plethora of 19th-century meanings and finds the two irreconcilable: nature representing "commodity being transformed into civilization" (p. 44), and nature as "the metaphor for a new spiritual mythology" (p. 45). Rosenthal views pre–Civil War American thought as informed by an external journey "into the wilderness from which would emerge nature and the city," and an internal journey "that would lead to nature and the city of the self" (p. 27). "The typology of each journey," he goes on, "presents the wilderness as the trope for fragmentation and the city as the image of order."

The few periodical articles on the Transcendental movement appearing during the year add little to our understanding of the ethos of the age. Sterling F. Delano in *"The Harbinger* Reviews Its Transcendental 'Friends': Margaret Fuller, Theodore Parker, and Ralph Waldo Emerson" (*CLQ* 12:74–84) calls attention to the reactions of Ripley and the Brook Farm group to the writings of Fuller, Parker, and Emerson, who declined to join the community. Delano argues that "too many partially informed students continue to identify Transcendentalism almost exclusively with Emerson and Thoreau" (p. 83) —though the rash of recent books and articles on the minor figures of the movement would seem to contradict him. John Elder in "The Natural History of American Culture" (*NER* 4:152–64) tries with questionable success to fit Emerson and the transcendentalists into his cursory survey of the literature of natural history in America from John Bartram to Thoreau.

I have encountered five new printings during the year of hitherto unpublished primary material, three of them in Joel Myerson's *Studies in the American Renaissance* (Twayne). Larry A. Carlson is editor of "Bronson Alcott's 'Journal for 1837': Part One" (pp. 27–132). Since Alcott's journals are voluminous, it is improbable that they will ever be published in toto, and that being the case the year 1837 seems a good choice for publication of a segment since it was a time of crisis for Alcott and his Temple School and a period critical to the career of Emerson, about whose lectures Alcott has considerable to say. It seems clear also from the 1837 journal why Alcott's "Orphic" flashes were too metaphysical for his age, but it is just as clear that he remained anchored to his "principles." Guy R. Woodall's "The Journals of Converse Francis: Part One" (SAR, 265–343) reveals a less reflective, more orderly mind, recording succinctly events from 1819 to 1824. A Unitarian minister at Watertown, Francis was farther out on the periphery of the Transcendental movement than was Alcott; this, the factual nature of his entries, and the time, before Emerson had become known, make the journal less interesting and less significant than Alcott's. Francis P. Dedmond's " 'A Pencil in the Grasp of Your Graphic Wit': An Illustrated Letter from C. P. Cranch to Theodore Parker" (SAR, 345–57) reproduces in facsimile a 21 January 1848 letter of Cranch to Parker from Rome, complete with ten satirical drawings in the same vein as Cranch's witty cartoon commentary upon Emerson's transparent eyeball. Done at the request of Parker, the drawings reveal a keen satirical talent and make one regret that the many drawings placed by Cranch in Parker's hands have since disappeared. Robert D. Habich prints for the first time "James Freeman Clarke's 1833 Letter-Journal for Margaret Fuller" (ESQ 27:47–56), with entries from 23 April 1833 to 17 May of the same year. Very personal letters (Clarke addresses Fuller as "Margaret"), they comprise Clarke's comments upon his reading (e.g., of *Wilhelm Meister*), reflections upon mutual friends, and criticisms of Andrews Norton's conservatism, which was not to Clarke's more liberal taste. "Emerson's Earliest Extant Letter to Frederic Henry Hedge," ed. Gary Scharnhorst and Ronald Tobias (AL 52:639–42) publishes in its entirety (Rusk had found only a portion) a letter Emerson wrote to Hedge from Bangor in 1834 where Emerson was temporarily filling the Unitarian pulpit. The letter asks Hedge to consider becoming permanent pastor there, which Hedge eventually did.

    Bibliographic aids to the study of the transcendentalists accumulate. Kenneth Walter Cameron in *Parameters of American Romanticism and Transcendentalism* (Transcendental Books) has provided a chronological checklist of 700 or so recently gathered papers of Franklin B. Sanborn, locating each in one of the seven collections of

Sanborn material he has published. Joel Myerson's *Theodore Parker: A Descriptive Bibliography* (Garland) has joined the impressive series of bibliographies of the transcendentalists currently appearing; and Myerson and Philip Gura's *Ralph Waldo Emerson: A Descriptive Bibliography* (Pittsburgh) is also in print. I have examined only the *Parker*, where the entries are complete, chronologically arranged, and easily accessible to the researcher and student. The inaccessibility of the *Emerson* is directly related to the price of $70. I was unwilling to buy it and the publisher to send it. AMS Press is reissuing the Walden Edition (1906) of *The Writings of Henry David Thoreau* and the Centenary Edition (1903–04) of *The Complete Works of Ralph Waldo Emerson*. Since much of the material in both editions has been superseded by authoritatively edited CEAA texts, one wonders why.

ii. Emerson

a. **Life and Thought.** The single most impressive piece of Emerson scholarship to be published this year is by all odds Gay Wilson Allen's *Waldo Emerson* (Viking), a massive volume of 750 pages, 28 chapters, and more than 2,000 notes. Publication of the preface of the biography preceded publication of the book, appearing as " 'Waldo Emerson': Preface to a Biography" in *GaR* 35:297–305. Allen's work now supplants Rusk's as the Emerson biography of standard reference, adding somewhat to the facts of Emerson's life that have emerged in the last 30 years but, more significantly, revealing to us far more fully Emerson the person, Emerson the lover, brother, son, husband, father, friend, and acquaintance of the intellectual community of the Western world, all the while illuminating Emerson the man thinking, struggling for self-understanding and an understanding of his relation to the physical world and to his age. Winnowing Emerson's journals, lectures, and other published works, Allen emerges with a portrait of unusual coherence, depth, and comprehensiveness, undercutting the notion of Emerson's obsolescence and revealing him instead as one in the van of modern discoveries of the subconscious and unconscious, an anticipator of Jung and William James. Encyclopedic as this biography is in its amassing of facts, one's sense of Emerson the person is never lost, unlike the experience of reading Rusk's 1949 biography from which the human being emerges only dimly. I was struck in reading the book with the extent of Emerson's philanthropy on behalf of friends and acquaintances, wholly out of accord with his disparagement of philanthropy in his essays. Even when in financial straits himself, Emerson provided support for the Alcotts, Thoreau, his mother, his brother Buckeley, Ellery Channing, and many more needy friends, in addition to using his good offices in support of Carlyle, Clough, Jones Very, and other struggling writers.

A biography of the magnitude of Allen's can be expected to stimulate reviews that in themselves approach reinterpretations; two, at least, are worthy of comment. Alfred Kazin (*NYRB* 21 Nov.:3–6) in "The Father of Us All" argues that Allen overrates Emerson's poetry (accepting Hyatt Waggoner's view that the best poetry is in the essays) and contends that Emerson's genius lay in his "extraordinary ability to tap his *verbal* unconscious" (p. 6). R. W. B. Lewis in "The Man Behind the Sage" (*NewRep* 185:21–27) uses Allen's book to refute President A. Bartlett Giamatti's "ferocious assault [in his spring 1981 commencement address at Yale] on Ralph Waldo Emerson as the source of everything that is most pernicious and destabilizing in our culture" (p. 21). In response to my request to Giamatti that he permit me to publish his remarks in the *Thoreau Quarterly*, he responded by letter that his "old friend" Lewis had "played up the ferocity of those remarks" and advised me that his comment on Emerson was already in print in *The University and the Public Interest* (Atheneum), where I found it in the chapter "Power, Politics and a Sense of History" (pp. 172–77). I shall leave it to Giamatti to define "ferocity," but it is clear that he is mincing no words when he alleges that "it is Emerson who freed our politics and our politicians from any sense of restraint by extolling self-generated, unaffiliated power as the best foot to place in the small of the back of the man in front of you," and that "Emerson is as sweet as barbed wire, and his sentimentality as accommodating as a brick" (p. 174). And he concludes, "Emerson's views are those of a brazen adolescent and we ought to be rid of them" (p. 177). But Lewis is predictably on the side of Allen, in opposition to such disparagers as Giamatti and Robert Penn Warren. At the same time he declines to side with Harold Bloom, to whom Emerson is "everything that is *American*" (p. 21). Lewis views Emerson as a level-headed thinker for whom metaphysics was reinforced by life and life illuminated by metaphysics. "At 38,000 feet both Giamatti and Bloom may be dead right [he concludes], but at sea level it is Gay Wilson Allen's Emerson that we recognize and need" (p. 27).

I have my doubts that Emerson would recognize himself in Eric Cheyfitz' *The Trans-Parent: Sexual Politics in the Language of Emerson* (Hopkins). Cheyfitz, like Allen, views Emerson's life as a struggle, but as a sexual one between the masculine and feminine elements of the self which he was never able to reconcile. This struggle accounts for (Cheyfitz argues) the pervasive irony and imbalance in his language. Perhaps so, though I for one am unable to follow Cheyfitz in his extrapolation of sexuality from some of Emerson's tropes. For example, what seems to me a casual entry in the journal—"Today came to me the first proof-sheet of 'Nature' to be corrected, like a new coat, full of vexations" (p. 163)—stimulates in Cheyfitz a chain of reasoning that develops into this conclusion: "Put in the crudest terms—terms that Emerson might appreciate, given his suggestive figures and his attraction for and use of common speech—the manly 'whole' that the reader seeks to contemplate is suggested as a womanly 'hole,' an abyss that 'lies under the undermost garment' of the mother and lies to the reader about the fatherly 'Rest or Identity' it represents, luring the reader, seeking certain ground, into a perpetual fall of uncertainty" (p. 165). Apparently, Emerson can't even remark that he didn't like to read proof without revealing that he was "obsessively concerned with . . . language and sex" (p. xi). Luckily, new trousers fit him better than new coats. Erik Ingvar Thurin's *Emerson As Priest of Pan: A Study in the Metaphysics of Sex* (Kansas) attempts to demonstrate a consistent pattern in Emerson's thought by tracing "a number of ways in which his view of sex and polarity affects his account of human relations and the possibility of redemption in this world" (p. xiii). I will not follow the steps of Thurin's argument, which moves coherently from an analysis of Emerson's sexist view of women to Emerson's visualization of a noble human society raised above considerations of sex. Behind all of Emerson's polarities Thurin detects the influence of his immersion in Plato, the result being a "consistent ambiguity" in his thought (p. xiii). Imposing upon Emerson such rigid conceptual structures, as Cheyfitz and Thurin do, obliterates for me the broadly human thinker and writer of Allen's biography.

John Stephen Martin's "Emerson and the Rhetoric of Belief"

(*CRevAS* 12:209–24) is as the title suggests an attempt to reverse the old assumption that for Emerson language followed belief, and to argue instead that Emerson was an innovator whose belief was shaped by language. This in a general sense is the thrust, Martin believes, of a spate of recent studies of Emerson by Kenneth Marc Harris, Joel Porte, David Porter, William J. Scheick, and R.A. Yoder, all of which build to some degree upon Bloom, Bishop, and Waggoner. That these critics would accept Martin's categorization of them is probably questionable, but Martin's voice joins a rising chorus who now argue that for Emerson language determines concepts, words govern one's vision. David Porter's *Emerson and Literary Change* (*ALS 1978*, 8–9) is the most perceptive statement to date, Martin believes, of Emerson's view that "the words that a man uses, determine the world that he sees, and what he imagines he sees, explains the words that he uses" (p. 220). Emerson's rhetoric thus foreshadows "the philosophical position of Post-Modernism" (p. 223). Joseph Kronick's "Emerson and the Question of Reading/ Writing" (*Genre* 14:363–81) views Emerson through the lenses of Freud and Derrida. What emerges is an image of Emerson "as the major American theorist of complicity between reading, writing, and death" (p. 366). If, so the argument goes, "all reading is a kind of quotation" (p. 369), as Emerson wrote, then books are crypts in which the author strives to resuscitate for the reader the thoughts of dead authors. "If 'Words are signs of natural facts,' then they must be metaphors of metaphors. There is no nature, only surplus of dead metaphors" (p. 377). To followers of Derrida this line of reasoning will no doubt prove illuminating; to nonfollowers, sophistry. I am distressed that persons attending the International Conference in American Studies held in Budapest in April 1980 apparently gave serious attention to Maria Ujhazy's "Emerson's Expedient Philosophy" (*ZAA* 29:213–24). It is a mishmash of quotation out of context by an uninformed critic who feels called to warn us to be "chary of Emerson's beguiling style and aware of the pitfalls of his logic and of the expedient fallacies of his philosophy" (p. 224). Ujhazy could profitably study Jeffrey Steinbrink's "The Past as 'Cheerful Apologue': Emerson on the Proper Use of History" (*ESQ* 27:207–21). Steinbrink shows convincingly that what is often construed to be Emerson's categorical rejection of the past and of history is far from a complete rejection: what Emerson warns against is using history as an authoritative key to the present rather than as a source of insight and inspiration. "*Man thinking* is never to compromise his integrity by mindlessly deferring to the past, but neither should he mindlessly dismiss it as irrelevant to his genius" (p. 220). Joel Myerson in "Historic Notes on Life and Letters in Transcendental New England," *New England Heritage,* pp. 51–63, points out that Emerson in formulating his judgment of New England juxtaposed New England life against the English heritage: "Emerson took the best traits of old England and the Puritans, showed why these traits were good ones and also explained why the discarded traits were bad, and forged these traits into an eclectic yet idealized New England character" (p. 61). Larzer Ziff in "Questions of Identity: Hawthorne and Emerson Visit England," *Brumm Festschrift,* pp. 91–102, observes that Americans in Emerson's time not only used England as a point of reference to judge New England, but traveled to England as well to gain a sense of their own identity—to answer Crèvecoeur's question, "What is an American?" What Emerson discovered to be unique about Americans from his English travel was that their sense of self was so firm that they could not conceive "of any external factor which counterbalanced that self, not even the state"; and moreover, as James Baldwin has since put it, that an American is the only person in the world who keeps asking, "What is an American?" And finally, there is the annual essay or two on the perennial subject of Emerson's standoffishness toward organized reform movements. Len Gougeon's "Abolition, the Emersons, and 1837" (*NEQ* 54:345–64) adds nothing new to this well-winnowed issue; its contribution is its revelation of the existence of several new primary documents preserved in the Concord Free Public Library and in the MS collection at the Boston Public testifying to the well-known enthusiasm of Concord residents (among them members of the Emerson family) for Garrisonian abolitionism. Gougeon's "Emerson and the New Bedford Affair" (*SAR,* 257–64) interprets Emerson's refusal to lecture before the New Bedford Lyceum in 1845 because of its "blatant racial prejudice" (p. 262) as an act that would "generally accelerate his long slide into the radical politics of the abolition movement" (p. 257). But the slide was indeed long, and Emerson's reluctance to participate in organizational antislavery continued so

long after 1845 that one must wonder if the New Bedford affair is
the watershed Gougeon makes it out to be. Most of this essay
Gougeon devotes to Emerson's familiar stance of moral suasion.

b. **Emerson's Influence on Other Writers.** This year the favorite is
Frost, but before I summarize the two essays linking Frost with
Emerson, I wish to call attention to a fine study by Carl L. Anderson, "Emerson in Nineteenth-Century Sweden: Liberal Reform, 'Robinson,' and Ellen Key" (*SS* 53:1–19) which for me, at least, breaks
entirely new ground. Anderson shows that Emerson's writings often
served as a standard by which theological liberals measured the
failures of organized religion, not only in America, but in Sweden
also. Translations of Emerson appeared in Swedish as early as 1853
and by the 1860s were being read by Ellen Key and Urban von
Feilitzen, whose correspondence reveals that both were influenced
by Emerson to rebel "against the meaningless forms in which much
of life is conducted" (p. 15). Key repudiated both formal Christianity and supernaturalism. The two essays linking Emerson with
Robert Frost unfortunately do not build on each other, or upon
Darrel Abel's earlier and broadly philosophical studies (*ALS 1978*,
340–41) which reveal Frost to be an empiricist who relies on his own
imagination rather than an Emersonian relying on the Over-soul.
Barbara Glenn has written a stimulating essay, "The Way Up and
the Way Down: A Consideration of Robert Frost in the Context of
Baudelaire and Emerson" (*SoR* 17:142–63) arguing that Emerson
"set the terms of a modern tradition for succeeding generations of
Americans" (p. 142), the "terms" being, according to Glenn, "the
belief that meaning is accessible exclusively in sensation, that meaning resides ultimately in feeling" (p. 143). Unfortunately, 20 pages
is not long enough to establish a thesis so broad. Jay Parini's "Emerson and Frost: The Present Act of Vision" (*SR* 89:206–27) is a more
discriminating piece which examines a dozen or so of Frost's poems
to show that Emersonian presuppositions underlie many of them
and that Frost's poetry "represents a continuing dialogue with his
great predecessor" (p. 226). Parini calls attention to the differences
between Frost and Emerson as well as the similarities: Emerson's
certainty gives way in Frost to a rueful skepticism; "the assumed
benevolence of the Creator seems missing too." Yet both insist on
sense experience as the avenue to truth. Joann Peck Krieg sees a

parallel in Emerson's enthusiastic response to the 1855 *Leaves of Grass* and his response (recorded in his journal) to Spenser's "Muiopotmos, or The Fate of the Butterfly" ("Whitman, Emerson, and Spenser's Loom" [*WWR* 27:163–65]). "Elbert Hubbard, *The Philistine*, and the Legacy of Emerson" (*MarkhamR* 10:33–6) is an influence study that makes a clear case for Hubbard's saturation in Emerson and his promulgating Emerson's ideas in his journal, *The Philistine*, which reached a circulation of 200,000 in 1911. "Henry Adams' Emersonian Education" (*ESQ* 27:38–46) by Jonel C. Sallee broaches the theory that behind *The Education of Henry Adams* there is "a clear Emersonian system of values." The values and the imagery that inform Adams' "Dynamic Theory of History" Sallee discovers in such Emerson pieces as "Circles" and "Fate." The weakness of Sallee's case is that Adams in the *Education* makes only a few passing references to Emerson, at one point even calling him naïf. The similarities between the two men may be hardly more than one would expect to find in two thoughtful persons living in America in the nineteenth century. Since Adams titles one of his chapters in the *Education* "Teufelsdrockh," could Carlyle have been the source of his "Dynamics of History"?

In conclusion, I note two final essays on Emerson, explications of particular works. Gayle L. Smith's "Style and Vision in Emerson's 'Experience'" (*ESQ* 27:85–95) takes its cue from David Porter's valuable *Emerson and Literary Change* (*ALS 1978*, 8–9), where it was argued that the power of Emerson's prose derived from his re-attachment of language to process rather than conclusion. Smith cites dozens of sentences from "Experience" to demonstrate how Emerson's rhetorical patterns of interrogation, causation, fragmentation, interruption, sentence linkage, and so on reflect his belief that "subtle forces, including language itself, predetermine our perceptions, robbing us of genuine contact with reality" (p. 85). Though Smith's adumbration of the obvious in Emerson's syntax sounds at times like the analysis of a freshman theme, her analyses support her reflections on Emerson's conscious and careful use of language. Richard Tuerk's "Mythic Patterns of Reconciliation in Emerson's 'Threnody'" (*ESQ* 27:181–88) has as its thesis that Emerson's use of a succession of myths (of vegetation, of the hyacinth, of metempsychosis) brings him to a final reconciliation with grief at the poem's end, in contrast to the views of Porter, Ronda, and others that the final stanzas are "coerced" (p. 181). "The final reconciliation," Tuerk believes, "is achieved in part through the narrator's recognition that the processes of the natural world . . . are somehow connected with the immortality of the dead beloved" (p. 181).

iii. Thoreau

a. **Life and Thought.** The debate goes on as to what sort of man Thoreau was, and not without rancor. Commenting on volume 1 of the Princeton Edition of Thoreau's *Journal* in the *NYTBR* (20 Dec.: 13) Leon Edel labels Thoreau a "prig"; he can think, he says, of no other word. Robert Erwin in "Reputations Reconsidered: Thoreau" (*Harvard Magazine* 84:57–60) impugns "the reputation, the life, the writing, and the vision of the priggish cookie muncher" (p. 60). Erwin's attack provoked stinging rebuttals in the next issue of the *Harvard Magazine* from Joel Porte and Patricia Caldwell (85:18). Richard Ford in "Country Matters" (*Harper's* July:81–84), commenting on writers who retire to the country to write, finds a lack in Thoreau of "the sense of the lived life" (p. 82), which is precisely what partisans of Thoreau discover in him. These negative views were balanced somewhat by William Howarth's popular "Following the Tracks of a Different Man: Thoreau" (*National Geographic* 159:349–87), which describes narratively Howarth's retracing of Thoreau's journeys to Maine, Canada, Cape Cod, and Minnesota; and by William A. Davis's "Past is Present in Chesuncook," an account of present-day Chesuncook in the *Boston Sunday Globe* (27 Sept. 1981, pp. 57, 62). But the prime counterforce to the negative appraisals is the sole American book devoted exclusively to Thoreau appearing during the year: Edward Wagenknecht's *Henry David Thoreau: What Manner of Man?* (Mass.) (See also chap. 21,*vi.*) "All in all," Wagenknecht believes, "Thoreau is certainly one of the great sons of joy" (p. 24), which did not mean that Thoreau could not be crotchety. Wagenknecht's is possibly the most lucid introduction to Thoreau that we now have. It is conscientiously researched: the 172 pages of text are supported by 25 pages of notes exclusive of the extensive bibliography. Chapter headings follow much the same pattern as in Harding and Meyer's *New Thoreau Handbook* (ALS 1980, 6–7). A personal portrait of Thoreau (chap. 1) is followed by "Others," treating Thoreau's social relationships, "Wider Circles," delineating his attitude toward social and political institutions, "The Seen," describing his views on physical nature, and finally "The Unseen," summarizing his religious beliefs. Wagenknecht's interpretations are by and large the conventional ones. I have two caveats. Locations of quotations in the text are sometimes not given in the notes, e.g., from Sherman Paul on p. 51, Henry James and Charles Ives on p. 95, and from Frederick Garber on p. 150, to cite only a few cases. Moreover, some of the most subtle studies of Thoreau in the past several years are not assimilated into the book at all, for example, Garber's *Thoreau's Redemptive Imagination* (*ALS 1977,* 9) and Stanley Cavell's *The Senses of "Walden"* (*ALS 1972,* 12–13), rpt. 1981. But Wagenknecht is a useful prologue to both Garber and Cavell.

This juncture seems an appropriate place to call attention to the reissuance of Cavell's book (by North Point Press) with the addition of "Thinking of Emerson" (*ALS 1979,* 9) and a new essay, "An Emerson Mood." The neglect of this daringly innovative response to *Walden,* not only by Wagenknecht, but by scholars generally, is baffling and not to the credit of Thoreau scholars. The new *Thoreau Quarterly* (Philosophy Dept., Univ. of Minn.) will devote two issues to reviews by distinguished philosophers and Thoreau scholars of Cavell's study, which labels *Walden* "a work of systematic philosophy" (p. 94). Cavell places Thoreau with Wittgenstein and Kant among Western philosophers: "*Walden,* in effect, provides a transcendental deduction for the concepts of the thing-in-itself and for determination—something Kant ought, so to speak, to have done" (p. 95). If Cavell is right, and his argument is persuasive, Thoreau scholars may soon find themselves sharing their subject with philosophers and theoretical linguists.

"An Emerson Mood," added to the North Point Press edition of Cavell, deals almost as much with Thoreau and Wittgenstein as with Emerson (pp. 141–60). Cavell views them all as "language philosophers" addressing the perception that "our relation to the world's existence is somehow *closer* than the ideas of believing and knowing are made to convey" (p. 145). "I am for myself convinced [Cavell writes] that the thinkers who convey this experience best, most directly and most practically, are not such as Austin and Wittgenstein but such as Emerson and Thoreau" (pp. 145–46). I find this as daring a judgment of the two major transcendentalists as I have read in a long time. Teachers of American literature, and I am one, who have been apologizing for years for the transcendentalists' slipshod metaphysics, will need to rethink their assumptions. Cavell will have to be accepted, or answered.

Michael Meyer enlarges somewhat our knowledge of Thoreau's position with respect to black slavery with his "Thoreau and Black Emigration" (*AL* 53:380–96) by analyzing Thoreau's response to an editorial in the *Wheeling Intelligencer* reacting to John Brown's raid. Thoreau's statement that the editorial was the "most sensible . . . of the apparently editorial articles on this event that I have met with" (p. 381) leads Meyer to ponder whether Thoreau would have favored the systematic expatriation and resettling of blacks as advocated in the editorial. Meyer's conclusion is that he possibly did and that "Thoreau's approval of the *Intelligencer* editorial is startling" (p. 385). But Thoreau did not say that the editorial was "sensible," as Meyer asserts (p. 394); he said that it was the "most sensible" that he had "met with," and his wholesale castigation of the newspapers in "A Plea for Captain John Brown" does not suggest to me his "approval" of the position of any of them. Moreover, if he approved of the Colonization Society's resettlement aims he was strangely silent about it elsewhere, and he had plenty of opportunities to state his position. Walter Harding's "*Walden*'s Man of Science" (*VQR* 57:45–61) makes a case for Thoreau's original contributions to a number of scientific fields. Harding attributes to Thoreau discoveries not only in entomology, ornithology, and botany, but in limnology and geology as well. Richard J. Schneider in "Humanizing Henry Thoreau" (*ESQ* 27:57–71) attempts to find a common purpose and theme in eight recent books on Thoreau by Frederick Garber, Walter Harding, George Hendrick, Richard Lebeaux, Michael Meyer, Mary Elkins Moller, Fritz Oehlschlaeger and George Hendrick, and Robert F. Sayre. Collectively, he argues, they "humanize" Thoreau, demonstrating him to be "an essentially typical nineteenth- and perhaps even twentieth-century man." It is not clear to me what such a typical man would be, but genius is surely atypical. Philip R. Yannella's method as stated at the conclusion of his "Socio-Economic Disarray and Literary Response: Concord and *Walden*" (*Mosaic* 14,i: 1–24) "is one which emphasizes fact over critical imagination, over theory, and as a prerequisite to interpretation" (p. 19). This will turn off most non–social scientists, if they get to the end at all. (How would "Kubla Khan" fare under such a "method"?) But Yannella argues that to judge *Walden* one needs to understand first of all the socioeconomic structure of Concord, and second to ascertain whether Thoreau's depiction of this structure was accurate. His method, he alleges, demonstrates "the need for 'interdisciplinary' study" (p. 19). Concord in Thoreau's time was in "socio-economic disarray" as a consequence of the infusion of Irish immigrants, Yanella observes, and Thoreau's perception of the town's problems was inaccurate and obtuse. Thoreau's "encomiums to frugality" in *Walden* were thus ludicrous as remedial nostrums. So it goes when literature is put to the service of the GNP.

An essay students of Thoreau should not miss is Anthony John Harding's "Thoreau and the Adequacy of Homer" (*SIR* 20:317–32), by far the most subtle study that we have of the penetration of Thoreau's thought and art by Greek consciousness. Harding sees Thoreau's problem as sojourner and writer at Walden to be "how to keep the Homeric model before him, as a measure of the wholeness he is trying to recreate, without insulating his imagination from history . . . to such an extent that he no longer shares common ground with his contemporaries" (pp. 325–26). Deferring his reading of the *Iliad* but keeping it on his table was Thoreau's solution, in other words, expanding "the notion of 'reading' Homer into the seemingly larger one of 'emulation' " (p. 328). With ironic brilliance, Harding argues, Thoreau in "Reading" in *Walden* "turns his advice on how to read Homer into a claim for the primacy of his own text" (p. 332). Viewing a March 1856 Thoreau letter to H. G. O. Blake as an attempt to reassure himself that his imagination was still vital at 38, Richard Lebeaux assigns to Thoreau in " 'Sugar Maple Man': Middle-Aged Thoreau's Generativity Crisis" (*SAR*, 359–77) still another Eriksonian life-stage crisis, to be added to the infantile, childhood, Oedipal, young-man crises explored by Lebeaux in *Young Man Thoreau* (*ALS 1977*, 11). This particular "generativity crisis" came to a head, according to Lebeaux, in 1859 with the death of Thoreau's father. Even "A Plea for Captain John Brown" is construed as "a plea for *Thoreau's* generativity and integrity; it is an attempt to ward off accusations and chronic self-doubts that his life had not been productive" (p. 371). "A Plea" still impresses me as an overflow of moral indignation, and the sugar maple image as no more pregnant with insecurity than hundreds of other images that Thoreau characteristically used.

It is possible to mention but a few of the multitude of short essays appearing in the *Thoreau Society Bulletin*, the *Thoreau Journal Quarterly*, and elsewhere. Robert J. Scholnick in "Titus Munson Coan: An Early Defender of Thoreau" (*NEQ* 54:119–21) notes praise in the *Galaxy* in 1869; the *Thoreau Society Booklet* 31 traces the history of "The Fred Hosmer Copy of a Dunshee Ambrotype of Thoreau," reproducing the ambrotype. Walter Harding in "Thoreau in Emerson's Account Books" (*TSB* 159:1–3) prints all of Emerson's entries from 1838 to 1859 dealing with Thoreau. The record says a good deal about Emerson's benevolent treatment of the younger man. J. R. Audet and Wendell Glick in "The Last Will of Estienne Thoreau" (*TSB* 155:1–4) publish a facsimile and a translation from the 18th-century French of the will of a Jersey ancestor of the American Thoreaus. Richard H. Dillman examines Thoreau's instruction in composition by Edward Tyrell Channing in "Thoreau's Harvard Education in Rhetoric and Composition: 1833–1837" (*TJQ* 13:47–62); Gary Scharnhorst explores in "'He is Able to Write a Work That Will not Die': W. R. Alger and T. Starr King on Thoreau" (*TJQ* 13:1–17) the puzzling shift in Alger's estimate of Thoreau.

b. **Studies of Individual Works.**   The few critical studies of Thoreau's works that appeared during the year are of high quality. Mitchell Robert Breitwieser in "Thoreau and the Wrecks on Cape Cod" (*SIR* 20:3–20) reveals an underlying thematic unity in Thoreau's four *Cape Cod* fragments. Thoreau was writing about writing, Breitwieser believes; *Cape Cod* was Thoreau's "symbolic contemplation of writing and wreck that he was interspersing among his memories of Cape Cod's desolation" (p. 3). Since Thoreau was celebrating wreckage as "a condition of new vision" (p. 6) he could look upon carnage and death with detachment. "*Cape Cod*, the transcript of one man's exemplary encounter with a fierce landscape" is "a traversing through symbols of the distance between sentiment and the intuition of the sublime" (p. 10). Using *Cape Cod* as his source, Peter Balakian published in *Carolina Quarterly* (33:i) "Thoreau at Nauset," a poem which mediates the tension in Thoreau generated by the conflict of his transcendentalism with his Puritan roots. The first extended critical essay on Thoreau's *Wild Apples* that I am aware of is Kevin P. Van Anglen's "A Paradise Regained: Thoreau's *Wild Apples* and the Myth of the American Adam" (*ESQ* 27:28–37). In a very perceptive, carefully structured essay, Van Anglen links *Wild Apples* to *Walden* and *A Week* as another of Thoreau's attempts "to find a new way of writing, a new way to make myth" (p. 29). Thoreau identifies "man's spiritual progress not with the apple trees of Eden or the Hesperides but with the real apple tree found in the fields and forests of his America instead" (p. 32). This essay not only illuminates an individual work, but places it also in the context of Thoreau's major writings. Roland Tissot's "Les douze échos d'économie dans *Walden*" (*EA* 34:32–43) suggests several functions for the lengthy "introduction" ("Economy") of *Walden*, seeing a parallel "avec le premier chapitre de *La Letter ecarlate* de Hawthorne" (p. 43).

Joseph Allen Boone's "Delving and Diving for Truth: Breaking Through to Bottom in Walden" (*ESQ* 27:135–46) is a lucid counter-response to Walter Benn Michaels' "Walden's False Bottoms" (*ALS* 1977, 14) in which Michaels argued that the search for a solid bottom in *Walden* would not succeed. Boone points out that Michaels misreads *Walden* by reducing "what for Thoreau are metaphoric connotations into literal statements of value" (p. 146). Granting that Michaels is correct in warning against searching in *Walden* for a pattern that implies a single meaning, Boone carefully explicates passage after passage from the *Walden* text to demonstrate Thoreau's use of the metaphoric language of digging, mining, burrowing, "to describe the endeavor to penetrate surfaces and gain knowledge of the deeps" (p. 141). Thoreau puts to the same use the metaphors of fishing and cleaving with ax and spade. "The convolutions of his very writing style . . . become for the reader a lesson in how to dip beneath the surface of the literal or apparent in order to 'get at the inside at last'" (p. 135).

iv. Minor Transcendentalists

The absence of books on Margaret Fuller this year stamps the year as unique. Three essays on Fuller appeared, however, two of them filling lacunae in Fuller criticism. Laraine Fergenson's "Margaret Fuller: Transcendental Feminist" (*CS* 15:9–23) is bland, largely biographical as most pieces on Fuller are, and emphasizes Fuller's feminism. The other two essays on Fuller, however, are sharply focused: David M. Robinson's "Margaret Fuller and the Transcendental Ethos: *Woman in the Nineteenth Century*" (*PMLA* 97:83–98) and Albert J. von Frank's "Life as Art in America: The Case of Margaret Fuller" (*SAR*, 1–26). Robinson's essay deals with the significance of *Woman in the Nineteenth Century* as a central transcendentalist document; biographical matter is introduced only to support the central point, that a belief in "self-culture" permeates the transcendentalism of Alcott, Channing, Emerson, and Fuller, that it accounts in part for Fuller's attraction to Goethe, and that Fuller was able to accommodate it to her zest for societal reform. "Fuller, who embodied her ideal in the commitment to self-culture, discovered that self-culture as an end required social reform as a means, that fulfillment of women necessitated the concerted action of women" (p. 96). *Woman*, Robinson argues convincingly, was a "fulfillment" rather than a "repudiation" of transcendentalism (p 95). Von Frank's thesis has its similarities with Robinson's but his canvas is broader: emphasizing the "cultural paucity of her environment" (p. 1), von Frank sees Fuller's life as a "recognition time and again that her finest pleasures in life were all acts of art and imagination, and . . . that her sharpest disappointments came from the failure of her environment to aid and support these acts" (p. 6). Her wanderings were thus searchings for remedies "for the imbalances and distortions of consciousness that her early provincial experience had bequeathed her" (p. 13). Von Frank believes that she achieved a synthesis in late life through looking upon life as art.

    I mention two scholarly works on Lydia Maria Child, realizing that her alignment with transcendentalism was not close. William S. Osborne's *Lydia Maria Child* (TUSAS 380 [1979]) I missed last year; Osborne stresses Mrs. Child's courage and intrepidity as an antislavery partisan and provides in his biography brief, useful critical commentaries upon each of her major works: *Hobomok* (the first novel of miscegenation in America), *The Rebels*, *Philothea*, and *Letters From New York*. The facts of Mrs. Child's active life become clear from Osborne's book, but the reader receives something less than a full sense of her humanity and her personal tribulations. Patricia G. Holland's "Lydia Maria Child as a Nineteenth-Century Professional Author" (*SAR*, 157–67) redresses this imbalance somewhat, since it deals with Child's difficulties as a woman in sustaining a writing career at a time when writers were responsible for merchandizing their own books. Holland contends that Child "never doubted that she had the right to express herself, even though she was a woman and an abolitionist, and her early success opened the way for other women to express themselves" (p. 163).

Andrew Delbanco's *William Ellery Channing: An Essay on the Liberal Spirit in America* (Harvard) amounts to intellectual history from Edwards to Emerson. The book seeks to restore Channing's importance to American thought, to rehabilitate him by demonstrating that he fits into the mainstream of American thought from Edwards to Emerson, as it was perceived by Perry Miller. Delbanco's book is sharply analytical, but is convincing only if one accepts the premise that Miller's definition of the course of American thought from Edwards directly to Emerson is the correct one. If it is, then Channing's Unitarianism has to be viewed as only a tributary to the main channel. But Delbanco wants both to accept Miller *and* to assert Channing's importance, and to effect this end he argues that Channing's late conversion to antislavery activism locates him in Miller's Edwards-to-Emerson current and thus establishes his importance. I doubt if this book will clear the field of those who view Emerson as largely a product of the liberal tradition that Channing led.

We have another book this year on Sylvester Judd, which must be some sort of record for Judd scholarship. Richard D. Hathaway's *Sylvester Judd's New England* (Penn State) is broader in scope, as the title indicates, than Francis Dedmond's *Sylvester Judd* (*ALS 1980*, 19), and it is filled with the minutiae of the daily lives of the Judd family and friends in Westhampton and Northampton, set against the backdrop of the theological tensions of the day, the rise of Unitarianism, and Judd's gravitation into the liberal camp. Hathaway recognizes Judd's literary shortcomings (he sees some merit in Judd's novel, *Margaret*), but he makes an extravagant claim for Judd's representativeness; Judd is seen as "one whose life and works illustrated the intellectual and religious tensions of Emerson's day" (p. 1). I have checked the index of Delbanco's more analytical study of the liberal religious movement in New England and discovered that Judd's name is not even mentioned, though Hathaway claims that Judd looked to "such men [as Channing] for inspiration more

than to Emerson" (p. 227). Hathaway's easy generalizations, moreover, about the tangled intellectual currents of the age are discon-
certing: "Judd's writing was all soul, too often, and Emerson's was
body instinct with soul" (pp. 227–28). Statements of this kind are
not helpful, and this book abounds in them. In "George Partridge
Bradford: Friend of Transcendentalists" (SAR, 133–56) James W.
Mathews raises another forgotten New England liberal to the light.
Mathews' claim is that Bradford's contacts with the great were so
close and numerous that his neglect is "surprising" (p. 133). An excellent schoolteacher, Bradford's students included Lydia Jackson,
George William Curtis, John S. Dwight, Isaac Hecker, Anna Alcott,
and he was a friend of Hawthorne, Emerson, Thoreau, and Alcott.
But as to his "neglect," Mathews' article suggests the reason: he was
a catalyst to the achievements of others. Fordyce Richard Bennett
in "Bronson Alcott and Free Religion" (SAR, 403–21) has narrated
the story of Alcott's relationship to the "Free Religious Association"
from 1865 on, has described in detail the meetings of this ultra-liberal
religious group, and has shown how its hostility toward Christianity
and its drift toward scientific rationalism led to Alcott's disassocia-
tion.

University of Minnesota, Duluth

2. Hawthorne

David B. Kesterson

It was not an outstanding year for Hawthorne studies. "Low-keyed" is the word, especially in comparison with the last few years, which have seen the publication of important and exciting biographical, textual, and critical books. There were no new centenary volumes this year, no *Nathaniel Hawthorne Journal,* and only one noteworthy book devoted entirely to Hawthorne—Claudia Johnson's *The Productive Tension in Hawthorne's Art.* The *Hawthorne Society Newsletter*—containing short articles and notes, bibliography, and abstracts of program papers—came out in the customary two issues; and an important festschrift, *Ruined Eden,* was published in honor of Darrel Abel, containing eight articles on Hawthorne. Moreover, the usual steady flow of doctoral dissertations continued.

If no great strides were made, at least there were some interesting and worthy individual efforts in specialized areas of Hawthorne study: more, for example, on the Hawthorne-Melville relationship, and more on the nature of Hawthorne's artistry. The stories received considerable attention as did *The Scarlet Letter,* but there were few studies that take an overview of Hawthorne's works. It was more a year of specific reactions to particular works, a fact that makes the total productivity appear piecemeal.

i. Texts, Editions, Bibliography, Biography

Textually, little happened this year in Hawthorne studies, though preparation of the letters and re-edited English notebooks continued at Ohio State. One piece of textual criticism deserves mention. Brian Higgins and Hershel Parker's "The Chaotic Legacy of the New Criticism and the Fair Augury of the New Scholarship" (*Ruined Eden,* pp. 27–45) applauds the new wave of American scholarship in effect since the middle 1970s which has spawned "scholarly studies alert to critical implications and critical studies alert to aesthetic implications of scholarly evidence"—the best of the new critical and contextual studies combined. Citing Seymour Gross's and Fredson Bowers' textual decisions on "The Gentle Boy" as examples of the narrow textual criticism of the '50s, Higgins and Parker argue against the notion fostered by W. W. Greg and accepted by Gross and Bowers that the last authorial text is necessarily the best. What was deleted in the 1837 version of "The Gentle Boy," for example, causes inexplicable gaps and awkward passages. Higgins and Parker's chapter should be compared with Parker's 1978 piece, "Aesthetic Implications of Authorial Excisions: Examples from Nathaniel Hawthorne, Mark Twain, and Stephen Crane" in *Editing Nineteenth-Century Fiction* (see *ALS 1980*, 23).

A popular edition of *The Scarlet Letter* and *The House of the Seven Gables* (NAL) is admirably introduced by Hawthorne biographer James R. Mellow. His remarks quite naturally stress biographical background to the composition, characters, and themes of each novel.

Two works mix primary with secondary bibliography. More general in scope is Burton R. Pollin's "A Potpourri of Hawthorne Items in the Contemporaneous Journals" (HSN 7,ii:5–7) in which some 65 allusions to Hawthorne or his works, brief reviews, and reprints of shorter works are gleaned from chiefly American periodicals from the middle 19th century. Buford Jones's "Some 'Mosses' from the *Literary World*: A Critical and Bibliographical Survey of the Hawthorne-Melville Relationship" (*Ruined Eden*, pp. 173–203) includes a valuable appendix, "Melville and Hawthorne in the *Literary World* (1847–1853)," that lists by year some 124 articles and reviews either by or on Hawthorne and Melville. Jones observes that, in keeping with the contemporaneous reputations of each author, 53 of the 67 items in which Melville's name appears were written in 1850 or earlier, while 55 of the 61 that mention Hawthorne appeared in 1850 or following. The listing is revealing and helpful. While Joel Myerson's "The Development of Hawthorne Primary Bibliography" (*Review* [Charlottesville: Univ. Press of Va.] 3:285–300) is not itself bibliography, its intensive review of *Nathaniel Hawthorne: A Descriptive Bibliography* by C. E. Frazer Clark, Jr. (Pittsburgh, 1978) and account of the rise of Hawthorne descriptive bibliography from 1905 to the present is extremely helpful in evaluating developments in this area. On Clark's work proper, Myerson concludes that it is the "best bibliography of a nineteenth-century American author we have."

As for checklists of Hawthorne scholarship, the most current and comprehensive is Buford Jones's "Current Hawthorne Bibliography" (*HSN* 7,i:9–11), containing 60 items (some annotated) of bibliography, editions, books, essays and studies in books, articles, dissertations, and miscellany. C. Hugh Holman and Janis Richardi's "Nathaniel Hawthorne (1804–1864)" in *The American Novel Through Henry James* (AHM, [1979], pp. 56–69) is a revised listing of some 298 textual, bibliographical, biographical, and critical studies. One caveat is that the listing includes no item later than 1973, and most are from the 1960s to 1972. Thus the recent important biographical, critical, and textual works are missing. It is still useful as a general guide, however.

In biography the year offered less by way of new studies than critical reaction to the last few years' prolific work in this area. There was a spate of reviews and essay-reviews especially on the 1980 biographies by Arlin Turner and James R. Mellow, two of the most important being Alexander Welsh's "Lives of Hawthorne" (*YR* 70: 421–30) and Michael J. Colacurcio's "The Sense of an Author: The Familiar Life and Strange Imaginings of Nathaniel Hawthorne" (*ESQ* 27:108–33), which boldly encompasses not only the biographies of Turner and Mellow but recent thesis studies by Baym, Carlson, Dauber, Dryden, Gollin, Stoehr, and Waggoner. Colacurcio rightly singles out a "return to biography" as the major recent trend in Hawthorne scholarship.

New biographical insights are brought to light this year mainly by Rita K. Gollin in "The Hawthornes' 'Golden Dora'" (*SAR*, 393–401) and "The Matthew Brady Photographs of Nathaniel Hawthorne" (*SAR*, 379–91). The former examines the Hawthornes' close association with domestic Dora Golden, who dutifully served the family in Salem from 1846 to 1849 and who won such a warm spot in Hawthorne's heart that he used her as the Dora in "The Snow Image." The latter essay focuses on the circumstances of Hawthorne's being photographed by Brady in Washington, D.C., in March 1862. Gollin reprints the four extant poses, gives vignettes of

Brady and his manager, Alexander Gardner, and tells of Hawthorne's attitude toward the photographical craze of the day. She interestingly concludes that the experience with the Brady studio shows a touch of vanity on Hawthorne's part, a willingness to participate in the "popular practice of promulgating photographs," and his interest as a celebrity in receiving something for nothing (he had been promised a large portrait free). One final biographical essay, "Bold Hawthorne and Rufus W. Griswold" (*UMSE* 1 [1980]:56–57) by J. Lasley Dameron, focuses on Griswold's role in writing the only surviving text of the popular nautical ballad "Bold Hawthorne." By examining other accounts of the cruise of Daniel Hawthorne's ship *True America* and noting major discrepancies between those and Griswold's, Dameron concludes that the Griswold version is inaccurate—that among other things the role of "bold" Hawthorne is played up, possibly because Nathaniel was a rising author whom Griswold "may have wished to bring to the reader's attention."

ii. General Studies

The major book-length study of Hawthorne for the year is Claudia D. Johnson's *The Productive Tension of Hawthorne's Art* (Alabama). Treating selected short stories and all four major novels, Johnson turns new ground by claiming that it was Hawthorne's Puritan forebears and his Protestant contemporaries, especially the "perfectionists," who supplied the "philosophical organicism" that allowed him to resolve the tensions inherent in his chosen vocation. The religious insistence on altruism created in Hawthorne a "productive tension" that "spelled the demise of Hawthorne's belief that art must be artist-centered." It was in theology rather than romanticism, Johnson insists, that Hawthorne found the myths which became "the vehicles for his exploration of his vocation." The "redemptive journey of the good man" becomes to Hawthorne's mind the same as that of the artist: from inward self-destruction (hell) to assimilation with the world outside self, a movement away from passivity and the static forms of art. *The Marble Faun*, Johnson believes, resolves the "warring forces in Hawthorne's philosophy" by depicting art as being regenerative like the soul. Johnson's book is clear and well written, logically and convincingly developed. Special strengths are the expanded definitions of "organicism" and "perfectionism" as they apply to Hawthorne's art and incisive, fresh discussions of the works, even if occasional interpretations invite challenge.

Several articles and chapters point to Hawthorne's attitudes toward everything from romanticism to religious ideology. Arlin Turner and Larzer Ziff examine Hawthorne in relation to America and the past. In "Nathaniel Hawthorne: Questioning Observer and Interpreter of America" in *Literary Romanticism*, pp. 19–37, Turner presents a reflective Hawthorne who thought about America at great length: its past, present, and future, its makeup, its conflicts, its reform movements—all with an eye for showing how "the seeds of one age produce fruit in a later age, that there is no escaping an inheritance, that the sins of the fathers are visited on the sons." Ziff's chapter "The Great Conservative: Hawthorne and America" in *Literary Democracy*, pp. 108–28, undertakes a biographical and critical view of Hawthorne's conservatism in his politics, his feelings for country and democracy, and in his historical themes. In his fiction Hawthorne demonstrated repeatedly, Ziff holds, that America was "shaped by traditional feelings rather than progressive ideas" and that Hawthorne's characters who survive and triumph are those who accept this principle.

The subject of Hawthorne and religion is addressed by John Updike in "On Hawthorne's Mind" (*NYRB* 19 March:41–42). Updike stresses that Hawthorne, though quiet about it, had a strong inner religious conviction. Not that he was conventionally religious: it is a "very vivid ghost of Christianity" that "stares out at us from his prose, alarming and odd in not being evenly dead, but alive in some limbs and amputated in others." Updike's reading of *The Blithedale Romance* as "the most actual, the most nervously alive" is as intriguing as his charge that readers of *The Scarlet Letter* rejoice in Dimmesdale's fall is puzzling. Hawthorne's view of ontology is the chief interest of Jeffrey L. Duncan in "The Design of Hawthorne's Fabrications" (*YR* 71:51–71). Covering the prefaces, sketches, tales, and *The Scarlet Letter*, Duncan presents a Hawthorne beset by the ambiguities of reality. Neither in his prefaces nor autobiographical characters does Hawthorne practice his own dictum, "Be true, be true." Rather, he remains a dissembler who hides behind the design of his fiction because he could never feel comfortable with his own findings about reality. Duncan's article is provocative and challenging. Two other studies of Hawthorne's beliefs, however, are less successful. Lakshmi Mani's chapter "Hawthorne's Apocalypse, a Revelation" in *The Apocalyptic Vision*, pp. 125–206, turns up little new on Hawthorne's theme of the millennium's having to occur within the individual instead of society. Perry D. Westbrook's "Nathaniel Hawthorne" in his *Free Will and Determinism in American Literature* (Fairleigh Dickinson [1979], pp. 29–37) is sound in judgment but sketchy in discussion of Calvinistic determinism in the four major novels. Westbrook concludes that Hawthorne labored under the central paradox of Calvinism: "the paradox of a drastically proscribed liberty of will existing with full responsibility for one's actions."

Continuing the Puritan theme but broadening it to include transcendentalism and sex is William H. Shurr's "Eve's Bower: Hawthorne's Transition from Public Doctrines to Private Truths" (*Ruined Eden*, pp. 143–69), one of three essays this year to deal with Hawthorne and sex. Shurr's thesis is that a sea change overcame Hawthorne during the idyllic years at the Old Manse where, in tending his garden, he defined his position in relation to transcendentalism, the myth of Edenic bliss and the Fall, and his own career as a tale writer preparing to be a novelist. Insightful readings of three pieces in *Mosses* that contain gardens demonstrate that Hawthorne discovered out of the entanglement of Puritan legacy and transcendentalism a "Garden solution" to life's central problem: one can find "personal happiness through sexual liberation." An earlier version of his discussion of "Rappaccini's Daughter" and several other stories, as well as a view of Hester, is found in the introduction and chapter 6 of Shurr's *Rappaccini's Children*. To Shurr "Rappaccini's Daughter" is an allegory of Eden emphasizing that "we are all Rappaccini's children and must deal with this heritage as we can." In other discussions, Shurr reads "The Maypole of Merry Mount" as an index to Hawthorne's views of dark Calvinism and sees Hester Prynne as a symbol of Hawthorne's "ambivalence toward cultural ideals." The only problem with Shurr's argument is a tendency to overstate Hawthorne's dependence on a Puritan construct. Larzer Ziff's chapter "Sexual Insight and Social Criticism" in *Literary Democracy* (pp. 129–45) is discursive and trite in places but still makes the interesting observation that in Hawthorne's fiction, especially *The Blithedale Romance* and *The Scarlet Letter*, "sexually initiated ideas . . . attain fictive embodiment and resonance as they make sex itself symbolic of other concerns." Through Coverdale, for example, Hawthorne moves from "sexual insight to social criticism."

Two psychological studies encompass elements of biography and style. Only one succeeds. Leonard F. Manheim in "Outside Looking In: Evidences of Primal-Scene Fantasy in Hawthorne's Fiction" (*L&P* 31:4–15) takes a Freudian approach in discussing how nearly a dozen of Hawthorne's works present the motif of outside observer and inside observed, with emphasis on the Paul Pry observer figure. Though interesting, the interpretations are shallow and sketchy and there seems little concrete evidence to support the conjecture that primal-scene fantasy experiences of Hawthorne's boyhood shaped his almost neurotic concern with the observer-observed motif. Much more rewarding is John Franzosa's "A Psychoanalysis of Hawthorne's Style" (*Genre* 14:383–409), another chapter in the old story of searching for Hawthorne's personality in his writings. Franzosa believes the closest we can get to Hawthorne is not through thematic or formal analyses of the texts, but through "description of the relationships Hawthorne established between himself and his readers," which were a "series of negotiations" with the changing expectations of his audience over the years. The article is a valuable addendum to the body of scholarship on the prefaces.

Finally, two general studies are more avant-garde. Hawthorne on language and its fictive use is the subject of Roy R. Male's "Hawthorne's Literal Figures" (*Ruined Eden*, pp. 71–92). Challenging, if sometimes abstract, Male's argument places Hawthorne in a context of linguistic theory. By examining *The Scarlet Letter*, Male shows that Hawthorne's use of language is pictorial and masterfully Janus-faced when it comes to balancing literal images and figurative implications. Male's discussion is a timely consideration of Hawthorne and language. On a rather unorthodox topic Christian K. Messenger has written "Hawthorne: The Play Spirit" in *Sport and the Spirit of Play*, pp. 15–37. Spinning off from the central thesis of the book that sport and play "are at the center of our social pattern," Messenger discusses how Hawthorne's depiction of play helped prepare the way for later writers to make fuller-fledged treatment of sport. For Hawthorne play was "suggestive, fascinating, and imaginative," but "never dominant." Hawthorne was the first great American writer firmly to "sense play as a response to the human need to move out of the tormented self." Messenger's chapter is especially illuminating in the discussions of play motifs and imagery in *The Scarlet Letter* and *The Marble Faun*. There is little new in the treatment of *The Blithedale Romance*.

iii. Novels and Longer Works

Most of the year's work is on individual novels, especially *The Scarlet Letter*. An exception is Nina Baym's "The Significance of Plot in Hawthorne's Romances" (*Ruined Eden*, pp. 49–70). Baym takes issue with Darrel Abel's and other New Critics' approaches of the 1950s, which largely ignore plot in Hawthorne's works. Baym insists that all other elements of Hawthorne's fiction are made "orderly and compelling" by the story lines, which "even at their most obscure, provide the impetus that keeps us reading through to the end of the romance." She is at her best on *The Scarlet Letter*; the rest of the essay is weakened by so much quarreling with Abel and the New Critics that other novels suffer from scanty treatment.

Of the year's numerous treatments of *The Scarlet Letter*, two purport to view the origin and genre of this novel in entirely new light. Robert Merrill in "Another Look at the American Romance" (*MP* 78:379–92) argues that Hawthorne's book is not a romance fraught with allegorical implications, but a realistic novel concerned with "the effects of experience on individuals." Though the thesis has some validity, the overall thrust of Merrill's argument is forced and somewhat futile. A new source for the novel is Earl R. Hutchinson, Sr.'s, supposed find in "Antiquity in *The Scarlet Letter*: The Primary Sources" (*HSL* 13:99–110). Hutchinson's discovery, defended earnestly if not wholly convincingly, is that the classical figures Aphrodite and Hetaira Phryne are the main anchors of Hawthorne's novel; they are not just prototypes of Hester and Pearl, but also thematic precursors that convey the idea so central to the novel of "paganism and an earthly, healthy love of life."

There is plenty of grist other than source material for the mills of *Scarlet Letter* critics. In "The Puzzle of Anti-Urbanism in Classic American Literature," an essay in *Literature and the Urban Experience*, pp. 63–80, Leo Marx uses evidence from the novel to show that Hawthorne, along with other classic American writers, was not anti-urban and propastoral. Being a "non-representational" writer, Hawthorne simply chose not to describe the city with the detail of the realist or naturalist. Topography to Hawthorne is a secondary subject or vehicle of the "great central figurative conception whose primary subject, or tenor, is the search for inner freedom and fulfillment." An enlightening discussion, Marx's chapter presents the age-old conflict of town vs. country in a new guise. A shorter version of the essay, entitled "Two Tales of the City: Anti-Urbanism in American Literature," appears in the *New Boston Review* (6,iv:12–13, 14, 16). A fresh slant on gothicism in the novel is Paul Lewis' contribution, "Mournful Mysteries: Gothic Speculation in *The Scarlet Letter*" (*ATQ* 44:279–93). Lewis shows how gothic mystery and stereotypes contribute to "thematic richness" and "complex characterization" of the novel. Specifically, each character, isolated socially and psychologically, "becomes a ghost haunting himself and others," and he or she is either trapped by mystery or can escape it through death or through "profound personal change." Hester is the only one able to experience the change as she grows from her isolation in mystery. A provocative study of the function of Pearl is Leland S. Person, Jr.'s "*The Scarlet Letter* and the Myth of the Divine Child" (*ATQ* 44:295–309). Hawthorne uses Pearl, according to Person, as a redemptive figure symbolic of a breaking away from the past and establishing a better sense of community in the present. But as Pearl leaves Boston and moves to Europe, myth fails to accomplish its purpose and remains outside history. Pearl's "demoniacal artistic vision" is akin to Hawthorne's hell-fired feelings and inspiration as an artist, and thus there is a special affinity for Pearl on Hawthorne's part.

A slightly forced reading of *The Scarlet Letter* to fit a Christian context is James Ellis' "Human Sexuality, the Sacrament of Matrimony, and the Paradox of the Fortunate Fall in *The Scarlet Letter*" (*C&L* 29[1980]:53–60). The gist of the novel is "the working out of Dimmesdale's redemption," and sex and marriage enter with Augustinian overtones as part of the Fortunate Fall concept. Hester, at the end of the novel, is a "kind of female John the Baptist speaking to the women of Boston in anticipation of 'the destined prophetess to come.' " While Thomas L. Hilgers' "The Psychology of Conflict Resolution in *The Scarlet Letter*" (*ATQ* 43:211–24) is good in identifying Dimmesdale's social tensions, there is disproportionate stress on what Hilgers calls the "interpsychic" as opposed to the "intraphysic" conflicts involved. Another mirror image study is Barbara Price's

"Substance and Shadow: Mirror Imagery in *The Scarlet Letter*" (*PMPA* 7:35–38), a fairly conventional analysis that concludes, unsurprisingly, that the distorted image in Hawthorne's fiction is usually a "more accurate representation of reality than is the object itself."

The House of the Seven Gables and *The Blithedale Romance* drew only one substantial article each. For the former it is Michael T. Gilmore's "The Artist and the Marketplace in *The House of the Seven Gables*" (*ELH* 48:172–89). In his view of the "sunny" ending of the novel, Gilmore adopts William Charvat's speculation that Hawthorne simply yielded to the wishes of the reading public. By probing the text of the novel, Gilmore finds considerable evidence of Hawthorne's concern with his relation to the public and with his "priorities as a writer who both craved fame and money" and aspired to be a master storyteller. Displeased with his concession to the reading public, Hawthorne perhaps failed in his declining years because of his "growing alienation from the process of exchange." Another view, albeit brief, of the marketplace and Hawthorne's novel is taken by Wayne W. Westbrook in *Wall Street*, pp. 10–11, where Judge Pyncheon is targeted as the demonic embodiment of the person obsessed by money. He is Hawthorne's "accursed capitalist." Money and finance in Hawthorne's novel are shown to be "as evil and ugly as the organ grinder's monkey that performs under the arched window." The major study of *The Blithedale Romance* relates it to *The Scarlet Letter*. Donald A. Ringe's "Romantic Iconology in *The Scarlet Letter* and *The Blithedale Romance*" (*Ruined Eden*, pp. 93–107) compares the two novels from a standpoint of similar spatial relationships in an effort to prove that *The Blithedale Romance* is not an anomaly in the Hawthorne canon but closely tied to the other works. A more limited, only mildly informative approach to the novel is Edward T. Jones's "Therapeutic Dystopia: A Szaszian Approach to Hawthorne's *The Blithedale Romance* and L. P. Hartley's *Facial Justice*" (*Proceedings [of] Asclepius at Syracuse: Thomas Szasz, Libertarian, Humanist* [Albany: SUNY, 1980], pp. 19–28). A Szaszian perspective on the novel would see Coverdale and Priscilla standing apart from the reforming scheme and thus experiencing more freedom and individuality than the other characters, who represent the more deterministic, controlled theme of the novel. Coverdale is read as "more benign and admirable than he has usually been seen."

The Marble Faun invited three character-theme studies for the year. The most comprehensive is Peter A. Obuchowski's ambitious "Character and Theme in *The Marble Faun*" (*CLAJ* 24:26–41), which sets out to prove that Hawthorne uses the four major characters to "symbolize, simultaneously, a dimension of human experience, an approach to life, and a dimension of art." Since the characters' dominant traits are the "four major dimensions of human experience," they represent a balanced approach of the novel to life and also highlight Hawthorne's artistic theory, which holds that the work of art of highest order must balance harmoniously "the sensual, religious, aesthetic, and moral." A less significant comment on Hawthorne's art is David Downing's "The Feminine Ideal and the Failure of Art in *The Marble Faun*" (*RecL* 9:5–14). Focusing on the power and influence of Hilda as a character representing "faith" rather than "energy" (artistic energy) and Kenyon's surrendering of his artistic ambitions, Downing argues that the last third of the novel charts the breakdown of art. Diane Long Hoeveler's approach to *The Marble Faun*, "La Cenci: The Incest Motif in Hawthorne and Melville" (*ATQ* 44:247–59), concludes that both Hawthorne's and Melville's uses of the Cenci story constitute an "ominous warning to American idealism." History being an "inescapable wheel" that allows only "repetitive variations" of the same themes, Donatello, like Pierre, is doomed to repeat his father's fate as are Miriam and Hilda aspects of Beatrice's history. Though there is nothing new here on Hawthorne and history, the Cenci influence is presented in fresh perspective.

iv. Short Works

The short fiction attracted its usual abundance of criticism, with "Rappaccini's Daughter" and "The Birthmark" drawing most individual attention. Only one article, Richard Harter Fogle's "Art and Illusion: Coleridgean Assumptions in Hawthorne's Tales and Sketches" (*Ruined Eden*, pp. 109–27), treats the tales in general.

Fogle, in keeping with his ongoing work on Hawthorne and the English romantics, identifies Coleridgean elements in the stories and sketches. Not only did Hawthorne have "considerable acquaintance" with Coleridge's prose and poetry and refer to Coleridge several times, Fogle insists, but there is a "pervasive influence of Coleridge's

theoretical criticism upon Hawthorne's literary theory, and even
upon his imagination and sense of unity." Fogle's argument is informative, if occasionally somewhat forced, in drawing direct parallels
between particular phenomena in a Hawthorne story and Coleridgean elements.

Three articles deal with Hawthorne's biographical and historical
sketches. The "Benjamin West" vignette from *Biographical Stories
for Children* is the subject of two examinations by John L. Idol, Jr.
The first, "Why Hawthorne Chose to Write a Sketch of Benjamin
West" (*HSN* 7,ii:4–5), concludes that Hawthorne selected West
over such artists as Copley, Peale, Stuart, or Allston because West's
life set a moral example for children and sketches of West for juve-
niles had already been successfully marketed by other authors. In
"Hawthorne's Biographical Sketch on Benjamin West" (*ReAL* 7,ii:
1–7) Idol posits that in such elements as the artful design of the
frame, the fitting style, and the humor of the sketch Hawthorne
worked to make "the literary quality of the sketch polished, instructive, sensitive, and appealing," thus demonstrating that Hawthorne
adopted high standards even for his early, relatively obscure writings
for children. How Hawthorne combined history with romance is
Robert C. Grayson's focus in "Fiction in Hawthorne's Four Early
Biographical Sketches" (*PMPA* 5[1980]:15–20). Grayson's work is
adequately done, but the view that in his historical works—here "Sir
William Phipps," "Sir William Pepperell," "Mrs. Hutchinson," and
"Dr. Bullivant"—Hawthorne "imaginatively reshaped his data" to
enliven history and used fiction "to elucidate historically revealed
traits of character or a known historical situation" hardly breaks new
ground.

Hawthorne's early stories "The Gentle Boy," "Roger Malvin's
Burial," "My Kinsman, Major Molineux," and "Young Goodman
Brown" received the usual share of attention. Robert Grayson in "The
Identity of the Puritan Minister in 'The Gentle Boy'" (*PMPA* 6:
6–9) names Richard Mather as the prototype for the minister of the
story, a possible, if still somewhat tenuous, connection. More convincing is Sarah I. Davis' source hunting in "Braddock's Defeat and
'Roger Malvin's Burial'" (*HSN* 7,i:6–7) in which Davis identifies
John Galt's *Life and Studies of Benjamin West* as Hawthorne's source
for the idea of the return to bury the dead and "the notion of a
constellation of family relationships." The ending of "My Kinsman,

Major Molineux" is criticized by W. S. Penn in "The Tale as Genre
in Short Fiction" (*SHR* 15:231–41) as being "insincere structurally."
In a puzzling and disputable stand, Penn protests that the "dream
coda" "contradicts the reader's sense of possible endings, adds nothing to the theme, and does not provide a significant aid" to interpretation. The Molineux name game is the concern of Stanford S. Apseloff in "'My Kinsman, Major Molineux': The Family Name" (*HSN*
7,i:6). Apseloff believes the name might stem from "Molinism," the
Renaissance doctrine that man has free will and can perform good
and evil acts. Robin, thus, is confused over which way to turn since
the major is both good and evil, as are the colonists. A novel approach to "Young Goodman Brown" is taken by James L. Williamson in "'Young Goodman Brown': Hawthorne's 'Devil in Manuscript'" (*SSF* 18:155–62). Williamson holds that "The Devil in
Manuscript," written seven months after the appearance of "Young
Goodman Brown," is a gloss on the earlier tale, not only because
of all the demonic figures and imagery in both pieces, but because
the narrator in Brown, a devil-like figure himself, is writing a burlesque on the conventions of authorship in the 1830s. The narrator's
mocking attitude and feigned innocence are a synthesis of the demonic traits of the three other identifiable devil figures in the story.
The other article on "Young Goodman Brown," Frank Shuffleton's
"Nathaniel Hawthorne and the Revival Movement" (*ATQ* 44:311–
23), examines the story's social concerns, specifically its view of the
misguided religious enthusiasm of the early 1830s. The main flaw in
an otherwise judicious article is in Shuffleton's attempt to prove specific influence of Mrs. Frances Trollope's description of a camp
meeting in *Domestic Manners of the Americans* on Hawthorne's depiction of the witch meeting.

Among the later stories, "Ethan Brand" is the subject of Prabhat
K. Pandeya's disappointing "Hawthorne's 'Ethan Brand': Discovering the Unpardonable Sin" (*JEn* 7:134–43), a fragmented, diffuse
look at the story from standpoints of journey symbolism, demonic
elements, laughter, and other isolated motifs. David Cody's "Invited
Guests at Hawthorne's 'Christmas Banquet': Sir Thomas Browne
and Jeremy Taylor" (*MLN* 11[1980–81]:17–26) is a plausible source
study. Hawthorne likely found the skeleton figure for his sketch,
Cody opines, in works by Browne and Taylor since, in an 1841 essay
on Hawthorne, Evert Duyckinck noticed a Hawthornean similarity

to the two authors that probably caused Hawthorne to look deeper
into their works.

"Rappaccini's Daughter" and "The Birthmark" among the later
stories drew most attention. The best article on the former is Seymour L. Gross's "'Rappaccini's Daughter' and the Nineteenth-
Century Physician" (*Ruined Eden*, pp. 129–42). Gross views the
story in relation to the reputation of the medical profession during
Hawthorne's time, demonstrating Hawthorne's criticism of physicians. Hawthorne's dim view of Dr. Rappaccini comes not only
from his personal dislike of physicians, but from "a remarkably precise reflection of the image of the physician in early nineteenth-
century America." A somewhat overinvolved psychological interpretation of the story is offered by Martin Karlow in "'Rappaccini's
Daughter' and the Art of Dreaming" (*HSL* 13:122–38). Karlow
probes the possibilities that the story can be read as a dream in relation to reality, as a dream "in relation to the dark caverns of human
nature," or as an "astonishing prediction of psychoanalytic insights
into dreaming and narcissism." William H. Shurr's Edenic interpretation of the story has already been treated in part *ii*.

The three articles on "The Birthmark" lack distinction. John O.
Rees rides a tired hobbyhorse in "Aminadab in 'The Birth-mark':
The Name Again" (*Names* 28:171–82). Rees's conjecture has it that
the main prototypes for Aylmer's servant are Shakespeare's Caliban
and Goldsmith's lowly minor character in *She Stoops to Conquer*.
Charles L. Proudfit's "Eroticization of Intellectual Functions as an
Oedipal Defence: A Psychoanalytic View of Nathaniel Hawthorne's
'The Birthmark'" (*International Review of Psycho-Analysis* 7[1980]:
375–83) is a Freudian interpretation in the vein of Frederick Crews
and Simon O. Lesser. Though eye-opening to a point, Proudfit's
thesis that "through the art of fiction Hawthorne has given us a masterful description of the eroticization of intellectual functions as a
major defence" founders in its own occasional illogic and jargon.
Finally, an imbalanced treatment of the story results from "'The
Birth-Mark': A Deathmark" by James Quinn and Ross Baldessarini
(*HSL* 13:91–98). The authors spend too much time arguing the
hardly questionable point that Aylmer is a "neurotic and troubled
obsessional soul" and then close with two hasty and undefended
observations about the sexual implications of Georgiana's blemish.

v. Hawthorne and Others

Influence and parallel studies continued at their customary fast pace this year. Most of them deal with Hawthorne and American writers, and more treat Hawthorne in relation to Melville than to any other author. There is noteworthy attention to Hawthorne and modern American writing, however.

David Van Leer takes yet another look at an old familiar subject, Hawthorne and Spenser, in "Roderick's Other Serpent: Hawthorne's Use of Spenser" (*ESQ* 27:73–84). He believes that since Hawthorne's use of allegory, symbols, and plot in "Egotism; or the Bosom Serpent" deviates from the story of the Redcrosse Knight and Una in *The Faerie Queen*, his source, then Hawthorne is probably ironic about Spenserian thematic and artistic parallels and is actually levelling criticism at Spenserian idealism as not being applicable to the times. While incisive on the subject of Hawthorne and Spenser, the article is marred by Van Leer's assumption that Hawthorne would necessarily follow the Spenserian original literally.

While the often-treated subject of Emerson and Hawthorne disappointingly brought only scattered references in Gay Wilson Allen's *Waldo Emerson: A Biography* (Viking) and the topic of James and Hawthorne only one article, the Melville-Hawthorne relationship enjoyed ample coverage. The James-Hawthorne relation has been treated over the last few years largely from the standpoint of the fiction of each, but this year Sarah B. Daugherty in *The Literary Criticism of Henry James* (Ohio), pp. 94–101, explores Hawthorne's influence on James's critical development. Hawthorne's deeper psychology combined with his practice of the romance broadened James's concept of the romance.

The most impressive work on Hawthorne and Melville this year is Buford Jones's "Some 'Mosses' from the *Literary World*: A Critical and Bibliographical Survey of the Hawthorne-Melville Relationship" (*Ruined Eden*, pp. 173–203). The bibliographical portion has already been discussed in part *i*. The essay portion develops two theses: that Melville was so aware by the summer of 1850 that Hawthorne's reputation was eclipsing his own that in "Hawthorne and His Mosses" he wrote to "align his faltering critical reputation as much as possible with the success that Hawthorne had so gradually but irreversibly received," and, second, that much remains to be done on the "seminal influences of each man on the other." Also important is Sidney H. Bremer's "Exploding the Myth of Rural America and Urban Europe: 'My Kinsman, Major Molineux' and 'The Paradise of Bachelors and the Tartarus of Maids'" (*SSF* 18:49–57), a well done, revealing analysis of these stories by Hawthorne and Melville from an antiromantic standpoint that attacks the myth of a rural America "radically different from urban Europe." Disappointing, however, is Sharon Cameron's chapter "The Self in Itself: Hawthorne's Constructions of the Human" in her book *The Corporeal Self: Allegories of the Body in Melville and Hawthorne* (Hopkins), pp. 77–157. Cameron's attempt to show how Hawthorne and Melville each variously allegorize the body to establish ideas of identity and reveal the "philosophical dualism that attends it" bogs down in verbosity, repetition, and obscurity. Moreover, much pertinent Hawthorne-Melville scholarship is ignored.

Turning to the 20th century, two critics present Hawthorne vis-à-vis philosophy and literature abroad. The aim of Benita A. Moore in "Hawthorne, Heidegger, and the Holy: The Uses of Literature" (*Soundings* 64:170–96) is to show how two diverse writers "separated by time, nationality, culture, and mode of discourse" nevertheless converge when they "touch the depths of human experience." She identifies common subject matter in Hawthorne and Heidegger, especially the theme of "the human person encountering 'the other' in experience." Meanwhile, Gretchen Graf Jordan compares Hawthorne and Graham Greene in "Adultery and Its Fruit in *The Scarlet Letter* and *The Power and the Glory*: The Relation of Meaning and Form" (*YR* 71:72–87). Detecting an unsung influence of Hawthorne on Greene, Jordan sorts through parallels and differences between the two novels in arguing convincingly that "the metaphor of adultery and its fruit has served both Greene and Hawthorne well." Parallels are spotted not only between Dimmesdale and the Whiskey Priest, but also in structures and forms of the novels. Jordan wisely handles the Hawthornean elements in Greene as "reminders"—or what Hyatt Waggoner calls Hawthorne's "presence" —rather than definite influence.

Hawthorne's "presence" in modern American writings is the subject of one essay and two "conversations." L. Terry Oggel in "Twin Tongues of Flame: Hawthorne's Pearl and Barth's Jeannine as the

Morally Redemptive Child" (*NR* 4[1980]:41–49) views Pearl as an enigmatic childtype who "rescues adults from deficiencies of thought and errors of perception" similar to John Barth's Jeannine in *The Floating Opera*. The idea of the child of flame adopted by Hawthorne and Barth may have come down via Jonathan Edwards and Emerson, for Emerson's phrase "children of fire" is perhaps an extension of Edwards' reference to children as "heirs of hell." Though an interesting viewpoint, little new light is shed on the function of Pearl in the novel. In two "conversations," one modern author tries to dissociate himself from Hawthorne and his tradition, while another readily parades the influence. Gore Vidal in *Views from a Window: Conversations With Gore Vidal*, ed. Robert J. Stanton (Lyle Stuart [1980], *passim*), while admitting some borrowing from *Our Old Home* in *Burr*, generally faults Hawthorne and the romantic tradition for their limitations. Vidal holds that there is no kinship between him and Hawthorne and other early American writers because of their writing romances, feels that *The Blithedale Romance* fails because Hawthorne did not master an "ironic or a comic style," and generally condemns Hawthorne for having "something awfully wrong with his writing. Partly no ear for dialogue. Partly too much Romance?" Editor Stanton, to the contrary, admits his own fascination with Hawthorne and praises him to Vidal for having a sharp eye: "he was a brilliant observer and his art is rich and deep, especially his descriptive powers." In Charlie Reilly's "A Conversation with John Updike" (*Canto* 3,iii:148–78), Updike openly avows the connection between *A Month of Sundays* and *The Scarlet Letter*. He speaks of having Hawthorne's novel in mind when writing *Month* and says that in fact his novel is a kind of retelling of *The Scarlet Letter*, especially from Dimmesdale's point of view. Calling *The Scarlet Letter* the "first American masterpiece," Updike admires the way it "masterfully considers the problems of religion, the plight of women in general, the problems of a fascinating woman in particular. . . . The more I read it, the more I'm struck by how 'right' everything is." What more fitting way to close discussion of Hawthorne scholarship for the year!

North Texas State University

3. Poe

Donald B. Stauffer

Judging by the number of books and essays I was able to find, Poe studies in 1981 were on the wane; however, significant work continues to be done. The textual chaos of former years is gradually yielding to order with the appearance of new editions of the long narratives and the *Marginalia*. John Ward Ostrom's revised checklist of the letters will also reduce scholars' legwork. Structuralist and poststructuralist critics are continuing to find Poe's texts a rich mine for the development of their theories; in turn, their theories are directing our renewed attention to the centrality of language in Poe's tales and criticism. This is particularly the case in France, where Claude Richard's journal *Delta* has devoted a second entire issue to Poe. Especially good this year were essays by Merrill Maguire Skaggs, Barton St. Armand, and Isabelle Rieusset.

i. Texts, Sources, Influences, Miscellaneous

New editions of *The Narrative of Arthur Gordon Pym*, "The Unparalleled Adventure of One Hans Pfaall," and *The Journal of Julius Rodman* are now available in one volume, *The Imaginary Voyages*, ed. Burton R. Pollin (Twayne). This is volume 1 of a projected Collected Writings of Edgar Allan Poe, in which Pollin intends to continue the work of T. O. Mabbott, whose three volumes of the Collected Works were published by Belknap Press. For this edition Pollin was able to make use of the Mabbott materials now deposited in the University of Iowa library. Pollin displays the encyclopedic knowledge of Poe's life, his sources, and his contemporaries for which he is well known, providing extensive textual and scholarly apparatus, including notes detailing the way Poe used his sources, which in *Pym* amount to almost a fifth of the text. Pollin's rather pedestrian and fact-laden introductions and notes emphasize the historical context, and he is impatient with psychological, oneiric, phenomenological, and sociological interpretations that do not take cognizance of the facts of composition and publication. His choices of copy-texts are wise ones. *Pym*, for example, is based upon the 1838 Harper edition collated with the two installments in the *Southern Literary Messenger*; most previous editions have used, or at least relied heavily upon, Griswold's 1856 edition. Pollin is substantially assisted by Joseph V. Ridgely, who provides background materials from his own projected edition of *Pym* as well as textual variants and other notes for "Hans Pfaall." Ridgely also contributes an introductory essay, "The Growth of the Text," in which he presents a modified view of his and Iola Haverstick's thesis (see *ALS 1966*, 132) that *Pym* was written in stages. He also takes account of the role of the Panic of 1837 in Harper's decision to postpone publication.

Along with a new edition we have an updated bibliography of *Pym*. Frederick S. Frank, "Polarized Gothic: An Annotated Bibliography of Poe's *Narrative of Arthur Gordon Pym*," *BB* 38:117–27, does an excellent job of listing the vast number of articles on what he calls "the most written-about of Poe's tales"—a striking change from 1950, when Auden's edition resurrected an almost totally forgotten novel. The bibliography is divided into three sections: important printings of *Pym* in the 20th century, articles and essays on sources, and analytical and interpretive articles, essays, and dissertations. Books giving extensive treatments of *Pym* are listed in a footnote.

Frederick C. Prescott's *Selections from the Critical Writings of Edgar Allan Poe*, originally published in 1909, has been reissued by Gordian Press with a preface by J. Lasley Dameron and an introduction by Eric W. Carlson. This is currently the only collection in print of Poe's best criticism and Prescott's notes are still useful, especially those making connections between Poe and other romantic writers. Both Dameron and Carlson stress Poe's centrality in the history of literary criticism.

The University Press of Virginia has published a complete edition of *Marginalia* in a handsome volume, edited by the late John Carl Miller. In a brief introduction Miller notes this is the first time all 17 installments have been collected in book form, since early editors, including Harrison, omitted some of them. The text is Poe's original printed text in a "slightly modernized format."

In "Poe's Possible Authorship of 'An Opinion on Dreams'" George E. Hatvary argues for the addition to the canon of a short 1839 essay in *Burton's*. He offers Killis Campbell's "silent acceptance" and certain stylistic qualities as reasons to question Mabbott's rejection of the piece as authentic (*PoeS* 14:21–22). In "Poe's Debt to Scott in 'The Pit and the Pendulum,'" *ELN* 18:281–83, Donald A. Ringe discovers still another source for that tale: an episode in Scott's *Anne of Geierstein*, where sources for "The Raven" and "The Domain of Arnheim" have already been found. Burton Pollin notes a source for a line in "Annabel Lee" in a poem, "Estelle," by Mary L. Lawson, a source annotated by Poe in the Huntington Library copy of the *Broadway Journal* ("From 'Estelle' into 'Annabel Lee': Genesis of a Line," *AN&Q* 19:106–07). Walter Shear detects an influence of Thomas Moore's *The Epicurean* on "The City in the Sea" (*AN&Q* 19:105–06), and Edward W. R. Pitcher has discovered some striking similarities between an 1823 story by Harrison Ainsworth and passages in several of Poe's tales: *Pym*, "The Pit and the Pendulum," and "Landor's Cottage" ("Poe's Borrowings from Ainsworth's 'The Fall of Ohiopyle,'" *AN&Q* 19:4–6).

The growing interest in Poe's influence on Henry James is pursued by Christopher Brown in "Poe's 'Masque' and *The Portrait of a Lady*" (*PoeS* 14:6–8). Brown finds parallels between the descriptions and metaphorical significance of Osmond's Palazzo Roccanera and the pleasure palace of Prince Prospero. D. H. Fussell's "'Do You Like Poe, Mr. Hardy?'" (*MFS* 27:211–24) is an interesting source study that presents "evidence of an underlying similarity of vision and of certain central preoccupations" between the two writers. In addition to influences on his poetry, Fussell finds that Poe's central theme of the lost love provided a basis for Hardy's novel *The Well-Beloved*.

In "E. P. Whipple Attacks Poe: A New Review" (*AL* 53:110–13) Gerald E. Gerber reprints a newly discovered article in the December 1841 *Boston Notion* attacking Poe's "Chapter on Autography."

John Ward Ostrom has consolidated his 1948 checklist of Poe's letters with its four supplements and other unpublished materials to provide a "Revised Checklist of the Correspondence of Edgar Allan Poe" (*SAR*, 169–225). Some 926 items have been chronologically arranged, renumbered, annotated, and indexed. This information, formerly scattered in several places, is now conveniently avail-

able in one. An appendix lists sale prices of letters, the highest price
—$19,500—having been paid in 1929 for the 9 August 1846 letter to
P. P. Cooke.

ii. General Studies

In a wide-ranging study of monograph length Isabelle Rieusset, "Edgar A. Poe, poète de la connaissance," *Delta* 12:35–126, examines
Eureka and other works in the light of Valéry's descriptive phrase,
poet of knowledge. Rieusset looks at several different types of epistemological discourse in Poe's work and matches them in pairs: metaphysical and materialist, idealist and dialectical, phallocentric and
"différence." She shows that in *Eureka* writing and knowledge are
the same, that they cannot be separated, and that the three poles of
meaning (signifier, signified, and referent) are indissolubly linked
into one form—symmetry—which she says is *Eureka's* key concept.
The most interesting and modern point about Poe is his theory that
the real is apprehended as a language, a system of signs, a text to be
read: "The Universe is a Plot of God." For Poe, she concludes, there
is no subject anterior to writing. The subject of the writing exists,
but as an effect of the writing itself: it therefore becomes reflexive,
acting as a mirror of itself (a concept recently developed at length
by John Irwin in *American Hieroglyphics* [*ALS 1980*, 54]). Along
the way, Rieusset also examines the connections between *Eureka*
and the big-bang theory of the universe, the theory of significant
form in "The Purloined Letter," and the phallocentricism of "The
Raven" and the tales with women's names in the title. She is particularly concerned to show that Poe was already a "structuralist"
in his concepts of the function of language. Disorderly and digressive as it is, the study is still full of challenging ideas about the
connections between form and content, the symbolic function of
women, and the role of significant form in Poe's *"écriture."*

Some useful distinctions between science fiction and fantasy are
made by Gwenhaël Ponnau's "Edgar Poe et Jules Verne: le statut
de la science dans la littérature fantastique et dans la littérature de
science-fiction" in *Mythes, Images, et Représentations*, pp. 359–67.
Ponnau's method is to refer to Verne's own distinction between Anne
Radcliffe's "terrible genre," which explains apparent supernatural
explanations, and the pure fantastic of Hoffman, which cannot be

explained by physical causes. Poe is situated somewhere between these two genres, creating a "cold-blooded fantasy" in which supernatural events are apparently explained when actually they are not. This illustrates the different uses to which science is put by the two writers: Verne uses actual scientific facts to project tales of the future based on them, while Poe, whose interest lies elsewhere, is not so careful to use actual facts, as in such fantasies as "Hans Pfaall." In "Usher" Poe provides a number of quasi-scientific explanations for his supernatural events, but the result is not science fiction, since these "facts" merely deepen rather than explain the mystery. Science, then, plays a role in both genres, but in science fiction it provides material support and explanation for the "dream," or the beginning of the action. Ponnau's attempts to define these two genres and distinguish between them are a substantial addition to the growing literature on fantasy and should be read in connection with other theoretical work on the subject, such as that of Tsvetan Todorov.

Perhaps the best place for J. R. Hammond's *An Edgar Allan Poe Companion* (Barnes and Noble) is the bedside table. This pleasant, adulatory guide conveys the author's enthusiasm for his subject and provides chapters on various topics: a sketch of Poe's life; a dictionary of his works arranged by title; four chapters on the short stories, the "romances," (*Pym*, "Balloon-Hoax," "Hans Pfaall"), the essays and criticism, and the poetry; a dictionary of characters and places; and an appendix listing some film versions of Poe's works. As an English writer, Hammond is interesting on the subject of Poe's English connections, particularly the early years in Stoke Newington. The book could be useful to beginning students or Poe fans but is of little interest to scholars. In an essay with a somewhat misleading title, "Poe's Perverse Imp and M. Dupin," *CollL* 8:175–85, Daniel Marder gives a loose biographical interpretation to all of Poe's oeuvre.

iii. Fiction

Both "Ligeia" and "The Fall of the House of Usher" were the subjects of several studies. Claude Richard offers a new reading of "Ligeia" in " 'L' ou l'indicibilité de Dieu: une lecture de 'Ligeia,' " *Delta* 12:11–34. The title refers to the significant recurrences of the letter *L* throughout the tale, but particularly in the closing sentence.

In a close textual analysis he discovers reasons to associate Ligeia with God and with gold, while Rowena is associated with death (or dead) and lead. While the ostensible conflict is between God and death, there is hidden conflict between gold and lead, and god and dead become transformed in their other meanings through the letter *L*. Aside from the alchemical content of the transformation, or "revivication," of lead into gold, Richard suggests that God is himself the letter *L* and that Ligeia is the daughter of God. This is a reading derived from Barthes and Derrida demonstrating the self-contained lexical ingenuity typical of French criticism, and Richard's own conclusion to both the tale and his study is, "c'est toujours le langage qui a le dernier mot." Still its interest goes beyond the wordplay, forcing us to look at some interesting lexical features that lie beneath the surface.

The connection between Poe's aesthetics and his metaphysics is raised again by Maurice J. Bennett in " 'The Madness of Art': Poe's 'Ligeia' as Metafiction" (*PoeS* 14:1–6). With the narrator's reaching after the otherworldly beauty of Ligeia, Bennett carefully documents parallels in Poe's criticism, particularly in such metaphors as the desire of the moth for the star, in an attempt to show the extent to which the tale dramatizes mental processes Poe merely describes elsewhere. In *The Living Dead: A Study of the Vampire in Romantic Literature* (Duke) James B. Twitchell explores the vampire motif in several of Poe's tales. He sees "Berenice," "Morella," and "Ligeia" as tales that use the vampire motif metaphorically as a way to describe the relationship between lovers, in which one party attempts to achieve sexual dominance over the other, and this "bloodsucking" of one by the other seesaws back and forth as the battle rages between them. In "Usher" he acknowledges that vampirism exists in both Roderick and Madeline, as well as in the House itself (as various critics have observed), but offers a suggestion that the narrator himself, as a displaced artist in whom energies are exchanged between the creator and his creation, is also vampiric. Twitchell says that "The Oval Portrait" is Poe's most sophisticated treatment of vampirism, in which the process of creation becomes vampiric, but he dismisses Poe's use of vampirism in "Berenice" as "Gothic stuffing." However, Hal Blythe and Charlie Sweet disagree. In "Poe's Satiric Use of Vampirism in 'Berenice'" (*PoeS* 14:23–24) they see the title character, not the narrator, as the vampire: in his diseased imagination he "sees the passive Berenice in the threatening patterns of the vampire and its spell" and therefore removes her teeth. The authors also suggest that certain features of the tale are satiric.

There is an interesting exchange of views between Patrick F. Quinn and G. R. Thompson concerning Thompson's 1973 reading of "The Fall of the House of Usher" in *Poe's Fiction: Romantic Irony in the Gothic Tales* (*ALS 1973*, 45) in *Ruined Eden*. Quinn throws down the gauntlet in "A Misreading of Poe's 'The Fall of the House of Usher'" (pp. 303–12); the issue is Thompson's contention that Poe's use of the unreliable narrator device creates irony in the tale and that the story is essentially about the mental collapse of the narrator. In a studiously literal reading of the tale Quinn attacks four points in Thompson's argument: his comparison of the appearance of the house to a skull; his three-way connection between the face of the narrator, the facade of the house, and the face of Usher; his attempt to explain that the house's collapse could have resulted from an explosion of gunpowder ignited in the vault by lightning; and his contention that the narrator is mentally unstable and completely untrustworthy. In "Poe and the Paradox of Terror: Structures of Heightened Consciousness in 'The Fall of the House of Usher'" (pp. 313–40) Thompson defends himself by pointing out that he based his own reading on the 30-year-old essay, "A Key to the House of Usher" by Darrel Abel (to whom the festschrift is dedicated). Accusing Quinn of literal-mindedness, he defends his own reading by a detailed examination of the development of the narrator's mental deterioration and finally asserts the need to recognize the essential ambiguity of the tale in Poe's balancing of natural and supernatural elements. Editor Thompson then graciously allows Quinn the last word in a rebuttal, "'Usher' Again: Trust the Teller!" (pp. 341–53). Quinn takes up some of the same points again but concludes that they are as much at odds over their readings of Abel's essay as they are over reading Poe. All three essays are carefully, closely argued, but readers will have to judge for themselves about their validity. Each makes a number of debater's points, but our understanding of the tale is not appreciably advanced by them.

Benjamin Franklin Fisher IV joins those who see the narrator of "Usher" as unreliable, although in his view the unreliability comes from a too easy susceptibility to gothic conventions, or "Germanism." Examining the tale's excesses and incongruities, Fisher concludes that Poe was working on two levels: supplying the mass of credulous readers with the horror they wanted while at the same time burlesquing the outworn props of Germanism, achieving a tale which holds these two opposing aims in balance ("Playful 'Germanism' in 'The Fall of the House of Usher': The Storyteller's Art," *Ruined Eden*, pp. 355–74).

In a study of " 'The Tell-Tale Heart' and the 'Evil Eye' " (*SLJ* 13,ii:92–98) B. D. Tucker returns to the question of why the narrator fixes on the eye of the old man. Like others before him, he notes the connection between evil eye and evil "I," resulting in an emphasis on the narrator's guilt feelings. He goes further, however, to suggest that the haunting, mysterious triangular eye on the reverse side of the Great Seal of the United States may also have inspired Poe; also that there are parallels between the visit of the three men to Abraham in the Book of Genesis and the narrator's account of the three men who discover his deed. Although interesting as insights, these ideas are not developed fully, and the article seems inconclusive.

In an interesting theoretical article that complements other recent criticism of the tales of ratiocination Merrill Maguire Skaggs, "Poe's Longing for a Bicameral Mind" (*SoQ* 19:54–64) modestly but convincingly shows the usefulness of applying Julian Jaynes's two-hemisphere theory of the functions of the brain (*The Origin of Consciousness in the Breakdown of the Bicameral Mind*) to the character of Dupin, with his creative and resolvent sides. Jaynes's theory that the right hemisphere, associated with music, poetry, and the voices of the gods, gave way to dominance by the left hemisphere with its functions of reasoning and an alienating self-consciousness, provides us with another framework for Poe's theories of analysis. Skaggs's exposition of this theory provides a basis for her original reading of "The Purloined Letter," where she sees Dupin as a sinister and threatening superman who is the triumphant rival of his brother, the Minister D——.

Allan G. Smith looks at Poe's use of enigmatic inscriptions or images, such as the word "DISCOVERY" on the sail in "MS. Found in a Bottle," the figure of the cat in "The Black Cat," and the chasms in *Pym*, and argues persuasively that it is more useful in attempting to understand Poe's use of language to use a Saussurean model than to look at Poe as a symbolist like Emerson or Thoreau. Instead of the signifier's referring to some lost natural language, Poe's writing "stresses the emptiness of the signifier and its arbitrary nature, and insists upon an endlessly elusive suggestiveness instead of a possible exactness of articulation" ("'Discovery' in Poe," *Delta* 12:1–10).

The Narrative of Arthur Gordon Pym is the subject of three studies, each using a different approach to arrive at different readings of this "most written-about" tale. Curtis Fukuchi in "Poe's Providential *Narrative of Arthur Gordon Pym*" (*ESQ* 27:147–56) sees Pym's quest for knowledge as a foreordained one, in which he obeys a divine injunction to journey south to learn what Benjamin Morrell, in his *Narrative of Four Voyages*, called "the secrets of the great Creator." Pym is, in Fukuchi's view, an epic or biblical hero who must journey to a wilderness or underworld and return with some form of redemptive knowledge. The novel is therefore to be read as a prophetic text in which Pym "enacts a providential role in a redemptive design for mankind."

Paul Rosenzweig, on the other hand, sees no clear development in Pym, although the novel is still a closely patterned work pervaded by motifs of enclosure. Looking more closely at such motifs than others who have noted them, he is led to conclude that Pym is a static and undeveloped character who is immobilized by his conflicts with an ambiguous and potentially hostile environment. Rosenzweig's method is useful: using a recurring pattern to arrive at latent content—and he arrives at a conclusion different from many of the studies that attempt to see development and design in Pym's journey ("The Search for Identity: The Enclosure Motif in *The Narrative of Arthur Gordon Pym*," *ESQ* 27:111–26).

Stephen Mainville in "Language and the Void: Gothic Landscapes in the Frontiers of Edgar Allan Poe" (*Genre* 14:347–62) notes the presence of frontiers between the conscious and the unconscious, the known and the unknown, subject and object, in Poe's two longer works, *Journal of Julius Rodman* and *Arthur Gordon Pym*. The mysterious cliffs along the Mississippi in *Rodman* present an appearance of meaning but are undecipherable by the narrator, in the same way that the figures in Pym's landscape remain undecipherable to him. Mainville argues along the lines of Jean Ricardou and John Irwin's *American Hieroglyphics* (1980) to conclude that Poe's supernatural landscapes mark a frontier between literal meaning and the uninterpretable, which they both reveal and conceal.

Charles N. Watson, Jr., in " 'The Mask of the Red Death' and

Poe's Reading of Hawthorne" (*LC* 45:143–49) finds enough striking similarities of imagery and theme to conclude that Poe was influenced not only by Hawthorne's "Legends of the Province House" but also by a number of details in "The May-Pole of Merry Mount" and "The Haunted Mind"—the first in its description of a group's retreat to the country to escape the threat of puritanism; the second in its treatment of a dreamlike escape from time.

A stimulating examination of Poe's unstated ideological position, Andrew Horn's "'A Refined Thebiad': Wealth and Social Disengagement in Poe's 'The Domain of Arnheim'" (*ESQ* 27:191–97) shows that Poe was rejecting philanthropy and ignoring contemporary social ills in his depiction of Ellison's extravagant and isolated monument to self. Poe's sense of a frightening social-economic conflict in 19th-century American society prompted him to place in Ellison's hands a powerful solution: to withdraw and "establish a territory within the material world in which only the products of labor but never the laborers themselves may be perceived."

Roland Barthes applies his techniques of decomposition of a text through applying a system of "codes" in his "Textual Analysis of Poe's 'Valdemar'" (*Untying the Text*, pp. 133–61). This is a translation of a 1973 essay that first appeared in France as "Analyse Textuel d'un Conte d'Edgar Poe" in *Sémiotique Narrative et Textuel*, ed. Claude Chabrol et al. (Paris: Larousse).

iv. Poetry

There were only three items on the poetry, but all are worthwhile. Helen Ensley's Poe Society lecture surveys Poe's rhyming techniques and defends his poetry against accusations that it is heavy-handed and full of exaggerated sound effects (*Poe's Rhymes*, Baltimore: Edgar Allan Poe Society). Barton Levi St. Armand has published an excellent re-examination of a well-known poem in "Poe's Unnecessary Angel: 'Israfel' Reconsidered," *Ruined Eden*, pp. 283–302. Contrasting "Israfel" with Emerson's "Uriel," he looks at it in the context of Poe's aesthetic statements. He sees it as a dramatic rather than a didactic poem, in which the poet-speaker confronts the awesome and finally contemptible power of the angel Israfel, who in effect has imprisoned the poet and prevented him from attaining a vision of a hidden or Gnostic God. St. Armand supports this careful and appreciative reading with relevant passages from Gnostic thought.

Finally, a good straightforward analysis of "The Raven" in the context of Poe's other work is provided by Mary Hallab and Christopher Nasaar in "Leonore versus Pallas Athene: A Reading of Poe's 'The Raven'" (*LC* 45:129–42). They see Lenore as the symbol of pure and spontaneous love and the bust of Athene as the symbol of rationalism, which has divided and destroyed the fallen scholar-speaker of the poem—a reading that draws heavily on Richard Wilbur's cosmic myth of the poet in a fallen world.

State University of New York at Albany

4. Melville

Robert Milder

The most satisfying work in this nonvintage year was done on the edges of Melville scholarship and criticism or was published in some of the less-read journals or in other out-of-the-way places. The Gallic invasion continued, with mixed results, the most visible common denominator being an unwillingness or incapacity to write clear English prose. Most other methods were also represented, giving Melville studies the air of a thriving pluralism. Pluralism it is, and thriving it might be if critics gave more thought to what their approaches required. More than one article was compromised by its author's neglecting to ask what he or she meant by a crucial term or what kinds of evidence were pertinent to (say) a reader-response analysis. Other articles were damaged by a faulty sense of how and how far to press an idea, a tendency to inflate a sound but modest point, or an effort to prove what might better have been left to suggestion. The more ambitious essays commonly strained against the limits of the conventional journal form and might have been more effective had they abandoned it entirely, as a few essays actually did. Editors may complain about fragmentary or timid work, but the best critical essay of the year, a 40-page reading of *The Confidence-Man*, could not have been published in any journal of American literature.

i. Bibliography, Biography, Scholarship

Jeanetta Boswell's *Herman Melville and the Critics: A Checklist of Criticism: 1900–1978* (Scarecrow) is a useful bibliography, arranged alphabetically by author, which supersedes the Ricks-Adams bibliography of 1973, though its subject index is less comprehensive. For the first 30 years of the century Brian Higgins' *Herman Melville: An Annotated Bibliography, Volume I: 1846–1930* (Hall, 1979) is still the book to use for its excellent summaries, and Boswell's unan-

notated *Checklist* will have currency only until the second volume
of the Higgins bibliography appears. Gary Scharnhorst's "Addenda
to the Melville Bibliography, 1850–1928" (*MSEx* 47:15–16) uncovers
ten items not included in Higgins' book, six of them contemporary
reviews. And Buford Jones's bibliography of references to or discussions of Hawthorne and Melville in the *Literary World*, appended
to "Some 'Mosses' from the *Literary World*: Critical and Bibliographical Survey of the Hawthorne-Melville Relationship" (*Ruined
Eden*, pp. 173–203), will be of use to anyone who is skeptical of the
commonplaces about Hawthorne and Melville's contemporary reputation and wants to see for himself. The conclusion Jones draws
from his research—that Melville tried to save "his faltering reputation" by aligning himself "as much as possible" with Hawthorne's
solid, if unspectacular success—is debatable, but Jones's essay is full
of suggestions and caveats which ought to be considered by anyone
thinking about the Hawthorne-Melville relationship. A brief but
useful complement to Jones's listing from the *Literary World* is
Daniel A. Wells's "Melville Allusions in *Harper's New Monthly
Magazine*, 1850–1900" (*MSEx* 48:12–13), the first of several pieces
Wells plans to publish on Melville references in late 19th-century
periodicals.

Biographical studies were unusually sparse this year, but for
those who missed what Hershel Parker called "the most important
biographical article that has yet appeared on Melville," *The Endless,
Winding Way in Melville: New Charts by Kring and Carey*, ed. Donald Yannella and Hershel Parker (Melville Society), reprints Walter
D. Kring and Jonathan S. Carey's "Two Discoveries Concerning
Herman Melville" (*PMHS* 87:137–41) along with a foreword by the
editors, an introduction by Kring, and commentary by twelve Mel-
villeans who responded to the question "How does the new evidence
[about Melville's belonging to All Souls Unitarian Church in New
York City and about a marital crisis and his family's suspicion of his
insanity in 1867] confirm or change your sense of Melville and his
family?" The rehabilitation of Lizzie Melville which has been going
on for the last few years continues in Kathleen E. Kier's "Elizabeth
Shaw Melville and the Stedmans, 1891–1894" (*MSEx* 45:3–8). Drawing upon Lizzie's letters to the Stedmans concerning Melville's life
and the republication of his books, Kier sketches not only a loyal and
indefatigable wife but a shrewd manipulator who understood "what

fawning motions to go through in order to get" what she wanted, the recognition of her husband's achievement. If Robert R. Craven is correct in " 'Roger Starbuck' (Augustus Comstock) and *Moby-Dick*" (*MSEx* 48:1–5), a lurid, popularized Melville enjoyed markedly greater success in the dime novels of Augustus Comstock, author of *The Mad Skipper* (1866) and other books, who may also have borrowed his pseudonym from *Moby-Dick*. Lastly, those who see Melville as despondent in his final years will be cheered to know that in 1890 he could recreate the inner man by casting his eye on a nude Diana "aiming her arrow in his direction," when the wind was right, "from her tower crown on Stanford White's gleaming new Madison Square Garden." So, amongst other things, Charles Neumeier and Donald Yannella report in "The Melvilles' House on East 26th Street" (*MSEx* 47:6–8), which gives a partial history of the site.

The major scholarly work of the year, and a solid achievement in any year, is Thomas Farel Heffernan's *Stove by a Whale: Owen Chase and the "Essex"* (Wesleyan), a comprehensive account of the sinking of the whaleship *Essex* in 1820, the fate of its crew, and the various tellings and retellings of the story from Owen Chase's *Narrative* of 1821 through the scholarship and popular redactions of the present. Heffernan reprints Chase's 60-page narrative, along with related documents, and reproduces and transcribes Melville's markings and annotations in the copy of Chase's *Narrative* he acquired through Judge Shaw in April 1851 and used in the composition of *Moby-Dick*. Heffernan is a careful scholar with a gift for animating the past and a judicious sense of what his subject can bear. About Melville himself and his documentable borrowings from Chase he has little to add to the existing record, but his comments on the deeper effect of the *Essex* story upon Melville's imagination are admirable in their perceptiveness and restraint. Students of *Moby-Dick* will be best repaid, however, by those parts of Heffernan's book which have nothing directly to do with Melville but manage to conjure up the epic and human dimensions of 19th-century whaling.

ii. General Studies

Neither of the two books devoted to Melville, Jane Mushabac's *Melville's Humor* (Archon) and Joyce Sparer Adler's *War in Melville's Imagination* (NYU), is a major addition to the Melville shelf. Mushabac's book purports to be about Melville's debt to what Mushabac calls "frontier humor," or "prose humor" (the two are used interchangeably), by which she means a tradition that, "beginning in the Renaissance with the opening of the New World frontier, celebrated a new man, a man of infinite potentials." Since Mushabac's tradition eclectically spans four centuries, three languages, and more genres and philosophical points of view than I would care to count, it is hard to see what links her writers together, aside from the fact that Melville probably read all of them, or why other writers—Swift, for example, or Carlyle—should have been excluded. As it turns out, the tenuousness of Mushabac's thesis doesn't matter very much, for after a perfunctory first chapter she does relatively little with it. What she does do hasn't much order to it, but Mushabac knows how to make a paragraph move and writes with an ingenuous gusto which almost makes one forget that her assortment of bright fragments does not constitute an argument. Adler's *War*, on the other hand, is relentless in its argument, which holds that "'war or peace' is the question that unifies *Mardi* and reveals its hidden design, the center around which the particles in *White-Jacket* revolve, the challenge to man's imagination expressed in *Moby-Dick*, world literature's symbolic poem of war and peace," and so on through *Billy Budd*. "War" would not seem to be a word in much need of definition, but Adler could certainly have profited from asking herself what she meant. In her chapters on *White-Jacket, Battle-Pieces*, and *Billy Budd* (her three best), war means war, or sometimes military discipline; but with *Typee* and *Omoo* it slides over into colonial domination, with *Moby-Dick* it means "Life-hating," with "Benito Cereno" racism, with *The Confidence-Man* racism and genocide, and with *Israel Potter* America's betrayal of the promise of the Revolution. Adler seems unaware that she is talking about many things successively, or that the many might be made into one if she could clarify the relationship between war (an event), oppression (a social condition), and repression (a psychological and cultural condition). Even without this, probably no one would dispute her claim that "Melville's passion against war was a great dynamic in his imagination and a main shaping force in his art" if her "a" weren't continually veering over into a "the." One would gladly make peace with Adler, who is a competent critic with some sensible things to say, but she will accept nothing but unconditional surrender, which means divesting ourselves of everything else we thought Melville was about.

Melville figures largely in two of the most important general books of the year, Larzer Ziff's *Literary Democracy* and Michael Davitt Bell's *The Development of American Romance* (Chicago). Ziff is ambitious and means his book to be the modern complement or successor to *American Renaissance*. Unlike Matthiessen, whom Ziff finds exclusively literary, and Van Wyck Brooks, whom he justly calls vague, Ziff intends to show "the social origins of great writing" and demonstrate "certain *precise* connections, literary as well as biographical, between the American democracy and its first great body of imaginative writing." I emphasize "precise" because Ziff generally doesn't. Ziff writes as fluently as anyone, but his book is the sort that historians will praise for its literary sections and literary scholars for its history, and whose ideal reader is the cultured generalist with no detailed acquaintance with either field. Ziff simply has not taken the trouble to make himself knowledgeable about American history, to think deeply about the relationship of history and literature (let alone about the relationship of both to psychology), or to possess himself of the work of the last decade or so which has transformed the level of discourse in American cultural and literary history. Ziff's chapters on Melville are particularly invertebrate. Yes, *Moby-Dick* is Melville's effort "to shape the democratic audience through writing democratic literature," but one wants to see this idea wrought out, or at least presented within a stronger and more coherent overview of Melville's career than Ziff manages to suggest. The best book on Melville and the American Renaissance is still *American Renaissance*. Bell's *Development of American Romance* is a more sinewy work whose interest is not in romance as a genre or a continuing native tradition but in the activity of "romancing" as it was understood by five 19th-century writers (Brown, Irving, Poe, Hawthorne, and Melville) and their contemporaries. So far as Melville is concerned, Bell's most incisive remarks appear in his application of the sociologists' notion of "deviance" to the situation of the American writer in a "hostile climate." "Deviance" is a loaded word, but as Bell develops them the theories of Howard Becker and Kai Erickson become a promising framework for interpreting the dynamics of Melville's relationship to his audience in a more inward way than William Charvat did in his valuable "Melville and the Common Reader." Unfortunately, as Bell turns from literary history to practical criticism the sophistication and authority of his writing decline considerably and his early insights into Melville's career are lost in a disappointingly narrow discussion of Melville as a "rebel."

One of the most rewarding essays of the year is Merton M. Sealts, Jr.'s "Olson, Melville, and the *New Republic*" (*ConL* 22:167–86), which excerpts passages from the Olson-Sealts correspondence and follows the two men, Olson especially, as they pursue Melville from 1940 through Olson's review of the Mansfield-Vincent *Moby-Dick* in 1952. Olson on Melville is always worth listening to—never more so than here, where he is speaking more unaffectedly than in *Call Me Ishmael*, and where his feeling for this "extraordinary *man*, this phenomenon, HM" and how he may be grasped leads him to impromptu discourses on method. In presenting Olson and letting him speak, Sealts for the most part effaces himself, but he writes with a dramatist's instinct for the play of personality and for the wider meanings of his subject. Without ever telling us so, Sealts has given us an essay on the Scholar, or on two kinds of scholars, the poet-critic and the academician, as well as on (in Olson's words) "the real engagements called for" from anyone working on Melville. In Régis Durand's " 'The Captive King': The Absent Father in Melville's Text" (*The Fictional Father*, pp. 48–72), Melville criticism enters a Lacanian stage. Those who are uncertain what this means might want to preface their reading of Durand with editor Robert Con Davis' "Critical Introduction," which describes Lacanianism as "*a psychoanalytic anthropomorphism of the text*," or a sustained analogizing between Freudian "laws of transformation" and the literary structure of a work of art. Unlike Melville's Freudian biographers, Durand is not interested in how a personal crisis becomes translated into a literary myth but with how "the question of the symbolic father" affects "the narrative momentum and shape" of a work. Thus in *Moby-Dick* the absence of a father expresses itself in a concern "with how things come to life and are produced by a play of forces, in ice breaking and flood subsiding, connections being made and energy doubling back on itself—all of which is to say: without a father, without a clearly identifiable source." There is something to this (which, by the way, as aptly describes Durand's prose as Melville's); the problem with Durand's neo-Freudian phenomenology of style is that it argues away the manifest content of a work (e.g., the voyage in *Redburn* is only "*superimposed* on the inner core" of meaning, Redburn's "hallucination" of the father in Liverpool) and involves Durand in a game of hit-and-run commentary that has no rules. Lacanianism may be a critical approach and a presumption about literary content, but it is not, in Durand at least, a method, though Durand offers some remarkable insights along the way.

Two contributions by Philip F. Gura advance the study of 19th-century language theories as a background for literary interpretation, though students of transcendentalism will profit more from Gura's work than students of the novel. Gura's chapter "Ambiguity and Its Fruits: Toward Hawthorne and Melville" is the least impressive in his otherwise challenging book, *The Wisdom of Words*, partly because "Hawthorne and Melville themselves never were concerned with [the] specific philosophies of language" with which Gura is concerned. This forces Gura to shift from philology, his strength, to epistemology, and to argue that the 19th-century breakdown in religious belief compelled Hawthorne and Melville to develop a new "literary style," which we now call symbolism. Substitute "form" for "style" and you have one of Richard H. Brodhead's theses in *Hawthorne, Melville, and the Novel*. Both arguments are simplistic in their dry historical causality, but Gura's might have yielded something valuable if it had been developed through the close philosophical analysis of style it seems to require, rather than through familiar remarks about epistemological relativism in *Moby-Dick*. Gura's other contribution on Melville, "Language and Meaning: An American Tradition" (*AL* 53:1–21), is an omnibus article which deals with two theorists, semantic philosopher Alexander Bryan Johnson and clergyman Horace Bushnell, and two writers, Melville and Thoreau. Ignoring the advice of Johnson, who warned against taking words for things, Gura fashions his article by creating a thing, a "tradition," from elements which lack demonstrable continuity and have at most a common source in the *zeitgeist* or a certain analogic resemblance: Thoreau in some ways is "like" Johnson, whom he apparently didn't read; Melville has affinities with Bushnell, "although there is no proof that Melville knew Bushnell's work." In his book and article both, Gura has staked out an important subject but has not discovered how best to mine it.

Melville's "British connection" is the subject of Benjamin Lease's chapter on Melville in *Anglo-American Encounters*, a genial bio-graphical-critical study aimed at the general reader and a good book of its kind, but as pertinent for the specialist as Redburn's guidebook to Liverpool. Old-fashioned in a different way is Lakshmi Mani's section on Melville in *The Apocalyptic Vision*, which neglects the relevant scholarship of the last several years and even the standard editions of Melville texts, and which has all the flaws of a dissertation that has not received the editorial advice it needs. One difficulty with the Melville section is that Mani does not seem to know which apocalyptic tradition she wants to talk about. Her opening chapter gives a useful summary of Judeo-Christian apocalyptic thought from the beginnings through the 19th century; but after some dreary, moralistic commentary on Ahab as the Devil's "chosen disciple" and Ishmael as "a Christ figure in his acceptance of God's will," Mani turns her attention to Hindu and Buddhist *avatars*, which occupy the remainder of her discussion of *Moby-Dick* and nearly all of her discussion of *Pierre* and *The Confidence-Man*.

While only illustratively about Melville, Brian Higgins and Hershel Parker's "The Chaotic Legacy of the New Criticism and the Fair Augury of the New Scholarship" (*Ruined Eden*, pp. 27–45) is a valuable handbook about the relationship of historical, biographical, textual, and bibliographical scholarship to criticism. Better yet is Parker's "The 'New Scholarship': Textual Evidence and its Implications for Criticism, Literary Theory, and Aesthetics" (*SAF* 9:181–97), which has the air of a manifesto. If there is a weakness to Higgins and Parker's position, it is the assumption that the New Scholarship (which is not new; Hayford and Sealts have been practicing it for years) is the normative and perhaps the only responsible critical method. Reliable criticism requires reliable texts, but when Parker presses critics to learn the "textual history" of a work, he sometimes means two different things, the history of revision and publication, which helps scholars establish an authoritative text (and critics choose between the rival texts available), and the history of composition, which may be important only to critics concerned with the work as it unfolded in the author's mind. At issue here is what Wellek and Warren long ago called the "ontological situs" of a work of art, or the question of where meaning resides; and once a text has been established, there is no compelling reason why a formalist or a reader-response critic, neither of whom shares Higgins and

Parker's disposition toward authorial meaning, should need to know its genesis. The choice of a critical method is a practical matter which depends, as R. S. Crane said, upon the particular kind of knowledge "we may happen, at one time or another, to want. And who is there with authority sufficient to entitle him to inform critics what [this] must be?" The New Scholarship may be the most promising game in town so long as its practitioners don't oversell it or entangle the exposition of significant textual and biographical evidence with their private interpretation of that evidence, leaving the next generation of New Scholars the unenviable task of separating fact from opinion.

Somewhere, at some time, everyone has read Henry A. Murray's four important essays on Melville—"In Nomine Diaboli," the Hendricks House Introduction to *Pierre*, "Bartleby and I," and "Dead to the World." Now the four have been collected and reprinted in *Endeavors in Psychology: Selections from the Personology of Henry A. Murray*, ed. Edwin S. Shneidman (Harper). A brief introductory note by Shneidman tells of Murray's reading *Moby-Dick* in the 1920s and discovering "the vast mysterious world of the unconscious—a topic that had previously never occupied his mind and subsequently never left it."

iii. *Typee* through *White-Jacket*

In "Montaigne, Melville, and the Cannibals" (*ArQ* 37:293–309), the best of five articles on Melville in the Winter issue of *Arizona Quarterly*, Gorman Beauchamp uses the similarities between Montaigne's discussion of cannibals and Melville's treatment of the natives in *Typee* to remind us that Melville's praise for the noble savage in his first book was a technique for whipping the civilized world's posteriors, not a Rousseauistic statement of belief or a sentiment that grew out of the dramatic situation of the fictional Tommo. Though Beauchamp's main idea owes much to Charles R. Anderson's *Melville in the South Seas*, perhaps his well-drawn parallel to Montaigne will encourage critics to explore the rhetoric of *Typee* and not read the book quite so ingenuously as a novel, a romance, or a fictionalized but lightly veiled expression of Melville's "ideas." Beauchamp remarks Melville's later acquaintance with Montaigne and suggests the possibility of Montaigne's influence in *Typee* but sensibly does not press the point beyond what the evidence warrants. In contrast, Michael Clark in "A Source for Tommo" (*ATQ* 44[1979]:261–64) argues unconvincingly that Melville "named his first protagonist after . . . Philip Freneau's Tomo Cheeki, the Creek Indian who visits Philadelphia"—evidence, Clark says, that "young Herman Melville was aware of the American literary tradition." Another *ATQ* piece, Elmer R. Pry's "*Redburn* and the 'Confessions'" (*ATQ* 43[1979]: 181–88), overlooks the literary meaning of "confessions" and interprets the word from Melville's subtitle as indicating "the mature narrator's personal remorse" for his failure to be "a proper 'brother' to Harry Bolton," a feeling Pry finds responsible for the narrative discontinuities in the book.

A lively example of the newer criticism is Wai-Chee S. Dimock's "*White-Jacket*: Authors and Audiences" (*NCF* 36:296–317), a reader-response essay which argues that Melville's "need for readers" forced him to assume the role of "genial companion" and "ardent advocate" for reform, a role he half-resented and repeatedly undercut through a covert verbal aggression against his audience. Dimock writes intelligently but like many reader-response critics she relies on a handful of impressions and makes her case by lifting passages out of their context without regard to the generic signals that control response. To a literate reader of Melville's time, a character named Cadwallader Cuticle or a chapter entitled "The Good or Bad Temper of Men-of-war's men, in a great Degree, attributable to their Particular Stations and Duties Aboard Ship" (Dimock's examples) would have immediately suggested the flat grotesquery of the comedy of humors or the 18th-century picaresque. No contemporary of Melville's would have responded to them as Dimock does, nor could Melville consciously or unconsciously have conceived them in a spirit of audience-baiting. *White-Jacket* is a more ambivalent book than was once thought, but Dimock's article, which adds measurably to our sense of the book's complexity, might have been even better if the author had reflected more deeply upon her method.

Aside from sections in Adler's and Mushabac's books, the only other writing on the early works is James Duban's "Melville's Use of Irving's *Knickerbocker History* in *White-Jacket*" (*MSEx* 46:1,4–6), which finds a source for "The great Massacre of the Beards" and "Old Ushant at the Gangway" in Irving's story of "old Kildermeester," a soldier who is court-martialed for resisting an order to crop his hair.

iv. Moby-Dick

Though not plentiful, the writing on *Moby-Dick* was varied and without a visible center or a common critical language. The conflict among Quakers between pacifism and justice provides the context for Wynn M. Goering's " 'To Obey, Rebelling': The Quaker Dilemma in *Moby-Dick*" (*NEQ* 54:519–38), a solid essay whose main flaw is a magnification of the Ahab-Starbuck conflict at the expense of Ahab's quarrel with the whale. Goering's *Moby-Dick*, in which "the trying-out of Quaker pacifism is central to the plot," is not quite Melville's, nor does Goering help himself by overstating the prominence of Quaker themes in two of Melville's earlier works, *Mardi* and *White-Jacket*, in order to make *Moby-Dick* "the conclusion of a kind of Quaker trilogy." Like several other articles of the year, Goering's sensible essay would have been stronger if it had respected the limits of its subject. "The 'Nameless Horror': The Errant Art of Herman Melville and Charles Hewitt" (*Boundary* 9[1980]:127–39), by William V. Spanos, is a cant-ridden restatement of the commonplace, its only novelty consisting in its brief coupling of *Moby-Dick* with the paintings of Charles Hewitt. Ahab's mistake, Spanos writes, is that he "reifies the 'errant' temporality—the nothingness—of being, transforms its proliferating difference into Identity, its multiplicity into the One (*Monos*) in order not simply to understand—to comprehend —its elusive mystery, but to gain mastery over—to 'take hold of,' to 'grasp,' (as the etymology of 'comprehend' suggests) its elusive and thus dreadful mystery." Shorn of its linguistic and typographical paraphernalia, Spanos's article is not saying anything essential that has not been said and taught since time immemorial, or at least since R. E. Watters in 1940. Platitude is not the problem with Sharon Cameron's "Ahab and Pip: Those are Pearls that Were His Eyes" (*ELH* 48:573–93), which argues that "the querying of identity is not simply a persistent theme" in *Moby-Dick* but the subject to which its surface meaning "is forced to cede": "What we would comprehend, were we to give ourselves over to its images, is the repetitive and feverish question: of what are bodies made?" Unlike Spanos, Cameron offers an original reading of this "most nervewracking of novels," but unfortunately Cameron's presentation can be discouragingly nerve-wracking itself. Against Spanos' obfuscations and Cameron's joyless turgidity, Paul Brodtkorb's brilliant and jargon-free phenomenological interpretation of *Moby-Dick* (*Ishmael's White World*, *ALS 1965*, 30–31), seems fresher and more contemporary than ever.

One of the sources Olson privately told Sealts was most formative for Melville—Goethe's passage on the "Demonic" in *Truth and Poetry: From My Own Life*—is the subject of Robert Milder's " 'Nemo Contra Deum . . .': Melville and Goethe's 'Demonic' " (*Ruined Eden*, pp. 205–44), a road to Xanadu-ish speculation which (according to the editors of *Ruined Eden*) explores "the mind of Melville and how it processed the texts and experiences that confronted him from *Mardi* to *Moby-Dick*. The result is simultaneously a reading of the presumed Melville behind the text and an interpretation of the more puzzling aspects of *Moby-Dick*," among them the relationship between the different experiential worlds of the book and the link between Ahab's madness and Ishmael's sanity. Another important source, the Prometheus myth, figures centrally in William H. Shurr's section on Melville in *Rappaccini's Children*, pp. 120–40. Citing Emerson's remark that "Prometheus is the Jesus of the old mythology," Shurr discusses *Moby-Dick* as a refraction of the Prometheus story through the medium of American Calvinism, thus bringing together main themes from two recent books, Gerard M. Sweeney's *Melville's Use of Classical Mythology* (*ALS 1975*, 67–68) and T. Walter Herbert, Jr's *Calvinism and "Moby-Dick"* (*ALS 1977*, 56), though Shurr makes little or no use of either work. In "Cetology: Center of Multiplicity and Discord in *Moby-Dick*" (*ESQ* 27:1–13), Robert M. Greenberg argues competently but without much verve that "the aesthetic and philosophical goal of the cetological material is to convey a sense of epistemological fragmentation and disarray." And in a footnote to the "two *Moby-Dicks* theory" which its adherents may be less than eager to accept, "Melville's 'Aristotelian' Carpenter" (*ArQ* 37:310–16), David R. Eastwood finds a symbolic parallel between the carpenter's making a life-buoy out of a coffin and Melville's recasting the "lifeless matter" of his putative first book into the "immortality-preserver" of the finished *Moby-Dick*. This is a nice conceit which ought to have been left at that. A slighter but potentially more valuable piece, June W. Allison's "The Similes in *Moby Dick*: Melville and Homer" (*MSEx* 47:12–15), counts "approximately 805 similes" in Melville's book, more (Allison guesses) than in "any other work written in English." Counting similes may sound as rewarding as picking oakum, but Allison divides her similes into useful categories and shows some sensitivity to how and why Melville employs them. Her conclusion, that Melville's similes make "the prose account as complex, grand, and awesome as its subject," is too broad to be worth very much, but someday someone might take up Allison's work and, by understanding how Melville characteristically used different types of similes, come to see what he intended with a particular local effect and, cumulatively, with whole blocks and patterns of effects. Anyone wishing a copy of Allison's list may receive one from the author for the cost of copying. Lastly, Hallman B. Bryant's "The Anacharsis Clootz Deputation: Chapter XXVII of *Moby Dick*" (*AN&Q* 19:107–09) repeats the Mansfield-Vincent suggestion of 1952 that Melville drew his knowledge of Clootz from Carlyle's *French Revolution*, Bryant adding that Melville's Ahab and Carlyle's Clootz "defied respectively the instituted powers of the universe and the state."

v. Pierre, Israel Potter, The Confidence-Man

After a renaissance in the middle to late 1970s, the writing on *Pierre* seems mostly to have slid back to the forgettable. The best of the year's four articles is Hershel Parker's "Melville and the Berkshires: Emotion-Laden Terrain, 'Reckless Sky-Assaulting Mood,' and Encroaching Wordsworthianism" (*The New England Heritage*, pp. 65–80), a chatty, catch-all essay which extends his important previous work on *Pierre* with two lesser speculations: first, that the Berkshires, not Hawthorne, may have had "the most momentous effect on Herman Melville in the summer of 1850"; and second, that Melville's reading of Wordsworth during or soon after the composition of *Pierre* may have "helped humanize the Berkshires" for him and helped teach him to hear " 'The still, sad music of humanity.' " Between these two biographical suggestions, Parker sandwiches one solid, if slightly worn, critical point: that the Enceladus dream occurred to Melville late in the process of composition and bore upon his own situation, not upon his character's. The achievements of the 1970s were not visible in any of the other writing on *Pierre*. Steve Gowler's "That Profound Silence: The Failure of Theodicy in *Pierre*" (*SHR* 15:243–54) argues that *Pierre* "systematically depicts the failure of all available theodicies—secular as well as Christian—to provide the hero with a frame of meaning sturdy enough to withstand his increasing consciousness of evil." Of what evil? Metaphysical, moral, social, psychological? Gowler never asks, nor does his survey of the discredited Christian and romantic theodicies ever get much beyond the perfunctory. In a different vein, "Pierre's Sexuality: A Psychoanalytic Interpretation of Herman Melville's *Pierre, or, The Ambiguities*" (*HSL* 13:111–21) by Paula Miner-Quinn argues plausibly that Pierre's incestuous relationship with Isabel is never consummated and implausibly, though with some clinical support, that his "downfall . . . is precipitated by deeper psychological dilemmas involving possible impotency and homosexuality." Much sketchier and more amateurish is Diane Long Hoeveler's psychological reading in "La Cenci: The Incest Motif in Hawthorne and Melville" (*ATQ* 44[1979]:247–59), which passes from a standard discussion of *Pierre* as a story of incest and narcissism to some unearned generalizations about 19th-century American culture and Melville's skepticism toward history. There may be a good article somewhere in this, but Hoeveler has not taken the time to write it.

As with *Omoo, Mardi,* and *Redburn,* there was almost nothing this year on *Israel Potter*—sections in Adler and Mushabac, two sensible pages in Bell, and a brief note by R. D. Madison, "Melville's Edition of Cooper's *History of the Navy*" (*MSEx* 47:9–10), which shows that Melville "borrowed heavily" from Cooper's "account of the battle between the *Bon Homme Richard* and the *Serapis.*" Perhaps some of the energy that goes into superfluous commentaries on "Bartleby" might be redirected toward *Israel Potter,* a minor book but also a good one, and much neglected.

One of the more fascinating exercises of the year is Mary K. Madison's "Hypothetical Friends: The Critics and the Confidence-Man" (*MSEx* 46:10–14), a tabulation of who has said what about the identity of the Confidence-Man since Carl Van Vechten unmasked him as Emerson in 1922. Interestingly, of the 101 critics Madison lists, only 16 have held to the "Confidence-Man as Devil theory," though some of these (Elizabeth S. Foster, for example) have been among the book's best. Nonetheless, there is tinder here if anyone cares to start any fires, as someone surely will with the Northwestern-Newberry Edition of *The Confidence-Man* scheduled to appear in 1982.

Perhaps the lesson of Madison's chart is that the Confidence-Man (in Richard Boyd Hauck's words) "is a red herring" whom we "chase until our capacity for perplexity is exhausted and we begin to realize that something else is happening." This at least is Hauck's own starting point in "Nine Good Jokes: The Redemptive Humor of The Confidence-Man and *The Confidence-Man*" (*Ruined Eden*, pp. 245–82), a thoroughly satisfying treatment of Melville's book and probably the finest piece of practical criticism of the year. Hauck's thesis, that the Confidence-Man is not a devil but a devil's advocate who "works to expose his mark's true character," sounds flat in summary; the strength of his essay is its sustained intelligence and its fundamental understanding of the kind of book Melville wrote. Although Hauck does not use the term, he recognizes *The Confidence-Man* as an example of what Northrop Frye called "thematic" literature, or literature in which the characters and events are primarily vehicles through which an author addresses (or chides or cons) an audience. The conclusions Hauck reaches may be no more definitive than a dozen others that might be put forward, but Hauck's method of approaching the book inductively and seeing what is to be seen is a model for lucid, undogmatic criticism, just as his prose represents clean, graceful academic writing as its near best.

If Hauck travels light, Walter L. Reed in "*The Confidence-Man* and *A Connecticut Yankee in King Arthur's Court*: The Novel, the Original, and the New" (*History of the Novel*, pp. 217–31) labors under the double burden of his thesis about the novel since Cervantes and his subthesis about the American novel, which he sees as an extreme case of the novel's antiliterary bias. Lacking a literary tradition of their own, American novelists "were confronted with a need to be more original on one hand, to reach back behind discredited traditions to more archetypal sources of authority, while on the other hand to be more novel in the common sense of the word, more new-fashioned or new-fangled in their evocation of a brave New World." Perhaps so; illustrating a theory of the American novel through *The Confidence-Man*, however, is a little like showing a foreign tourist America by taking him to San Francisco: both are brilliant anomalies. The tradition of the novel may look different when one places Cervantes front and center, but for most readers Reed's example of *The Confidence-Man* will probably seem too quirky to support his thesis and his thesis too cumbersome to do justice to the subtleties of *The Confidence-Man*, though Reed's perceptive chapter is worth studying.

In a "companion-piece" to their earlier article, "Melville's Cosmopolitan: Bayard Taylor in *The Confidence-Man*" (*Amst* 22:286–89), Hans-Joachim Lang and Benjamin Lease in "Melville and 'The Practical Disciple': George William Curtis in *The Confidence-Man*" (*Amst* 26:181–91) dispute the identification of Mark Winsome's disciple Egbert with Thoreau and make a strong but not conclusive case for associating him with George William Curtis, a warm admirer of Emerson and a literary businessman with whom Melville had dealings (he was an editor at Putnam's). What is missing from Lang and Lease's well-researched article is the suggestion of an adequate motive. If Melville was parodying Curtis he was biting the hand that had fed him, and for the most part fed him well, though more needs to be known about "Melville's dealings with editors and publishers during this difficult period of his career," as Merton M. Sealts, Jr., has been reminding us for some time. A source study of a lesser order, but ably managed, is Douglas Robillard's "The Metaphysics of Melville's Indian Hating" (*EAS* 10:51–57), which conjectures that the word "metaphysics" in Melville's chapter title may have been suggested by Charles W. Webber's pseudonymous "The Metaphysics of Bear Hunting: An Adventure in the San Saba Hills." The story appeared in the August 1845 issue of *The American Review*, a Whig periodical then published by Wiley and Putnam which Robillard guesses Melville read "assiduously."

vi. Stories

Despite what William J. Burling calls "a Sargasso Sea of redundancy" in "Bartleby" criticism, there were more essays and notes published on "Bartleby" this year than on Melville's first five books combined. Burling's own "Commentary on 'Bartleby': 1968–1979" (*ArQ* 37:347–54) is a needless addition to Bruce Bebb's " 'Bartleby': An Annotated Checklist of Criticism" published along with Elizabeth Williamson's "Supplement" in *Bartleby the Inscrutable* (Archon, 1979). Burling's "List of Works Consulted" is not anything near comprehensive, nor are his summaries as discerning as those in past volumes of *ALS*.

Economic interpretations of "Bartleby" were still among the most

popular. Marrying William B. Dillingham's disposition to put the
worst face on everything the narrator says and does to Louise K.
Barnett's interpretation of Bartleby as "Marx's alienated worker,"
James C. Wilson in " 'Bartleby': The Walls of Wall Street" (ArQ 37:
335–46) reads Melville's story as "one of the bitterest indictments of
American capitalism ever published" and casts Bartleby as a revolutionary manqué whose "tragedy is that he does not become conscious of the social causes of his alienation" and identify his personal
plight with "the class alienation of the propertyless workers." Less
doctrinaire but also critical of Wall Street is Michael J. McTague's
chapter on "Bartleby" in The Businessman in Literature: Dante to
Melville (Phil. Lib.), which focuses upon "six negative qualities of
business developed . . . by Melville." Written at once for "the literary
scholar" and "the business student," McTague's book will appeal
more to the second group of readers than to the first. In Allan Silver's
"The Lawyer and the Scrivener" (PR 48:409–24), the narrator of the
story is not "an early capitalist" but "a professional gentleman" who
"belongs to a past that is beginning to recede," and who finds himself
through Bartleby in a terrifying modern world where "helping bonds
. . . are potentially limitless because they are no longer set in a
structure of specified obligations." Though Silver's sociohistorical
remarks are not as smoothly joined to his practical criticism as one
would like, his reading of "Bartleby" is a thoughtful alternative to
clumsy quasi-Marxist interpretations like Wilson's; one small weakness is that in taking the narrator for a hero of sorts who "grows in
moral accomplishments to the boundaries of his possibilities and of
ours," Silver is too apt to identify "ours" with the specifically modern,
as if the real achievement of the narrator were to become one of us.
For Walter E. Anderson in "Form and Meaning in 'Bartleby the
Scrivener'" (SSF 18:383–93), "us" is more timelessly human. Unlike many recent critics of the story, Anderson is alive to the narrator's "whimsical sense of humor" and finds him "a considerably
better man than most," while Bartleby represents "the most provok-
ing test of brotherhood one is ever likely to encounter either in fiction
or in life." Anderson's conclusion, that the narrator's failure with
Bartleby signifies our common failure, is a modest but refreshingly
sane one after the harsh treatment the narrator has received of late;
but in hinting several times that the rhetoric of "Bartleby" implicates
its audience in the story, Anderson seems on the verge of an illumi-

nating reader-response analysis he doesn't know quite how to write. Let's hope that whoever does write it is as sensitive to the tone of the narrator's words as Anderson.

Developing an idea from Edwin H. Miller's *Melville*, Robert N. Mollinger in *Psychoanalysis and Literature* (Nelson-Hall), pp. 85–96, reads "Bartleby" as a story "about eating and not eating," or the gratification or frustration of primary needs, with Bartleby starving himself to death to punish the world in general and the narrator in particular for failing to feed him—Bartleby the Anorexic. Rounding out the year's work on "Bartleby" are two briefer pieces. David Jaffé's "*Bartleby the Scrivener*" *and Bleak House: Melville's Debt to Dickens*" (Arlington, Va.: Mardi Press), 15 pp., was anticipated in part by Charlotte Walker Mendez' note of the preceding year, "Scriveners Forlorn: Dickens's Nemo and Melville's Bartleby" (*DSN* 11:33–37), though Jaffé argues for a broader influence and points out that "*Bleak House* was serialized in *Harper's New Monthly Magazine*, to which Melville subscribed." Lastly, aside from some remarks about the "sepia, horsecar Manhattan" of the 1850s and the glass-and-steel city of today, Elizabeth Hardwick's "Bartleby and Manhattan" (*NYRB* 16 July:27–31) is "largely concerned with the nature of Bartleby's short sentences" and will be of interest to admirers of Elizabeth Hardwick.

With one exception, commentary on Melville's other stories was minimal both in number and in quality. Beryl Rowland's "Melville and the Cock that Crew" (*AL* 52:593–606) labors to explain what some readers feel is a shift from realism to fantasy in "Cock-a-Doodle-Doo!" by attributing to Melville's story an interpretive structure which no writer had ever used before "in a secular work of fiction" and which Melville apparently would never use again—the "four-fold method of scriptural exegesis," which in "Cock-a-Doodle-Doo!" becomes a three-fold symbolism (allegorical, tropological, anagogical; "Melville evidently regarded the literal level as unimportant"). The allegorical is also cultivated by Dougas L. Verdier in "Who is the Lightning-Rod Man?" (*SSF* 18:273–79), which sides with those who interpret Melville's salesman as Satan and reads the story as "a mythical account of Man's temptation by the Devil and the eventual triumph of Man over the forces of darkness through faith." Sidney H. Bremer's "Exploding the Myth of Rural America and Urban Europe: 'My Kinsman, Major Molineux' and 'The Paradise of Bachelors and the Tartarus of Maids'" (*SSF* 18:49–57) is a fragmentary piece that shows that Melville's story "weaves a complex web in which parallel, idealized images of a garden city and a rural hamlet strain against—and ultimately give way to—confrontation with the interrelated economic realities of urban commerce and rural industry." More scholarly but only somewhat more satisfying is Timothy Dow Adams' "Architectural Imagery in Melville's Short Fiction" (*ATQ* 44[1979]:265–77), which squanders a good working knowledge of contemporary architectural theory in some piecemeal comments that have the status of a minor footnote—more evidence for one or another well-documented theme or further proof that Melville attended to his craft.

The year's most thoughtful, if trying, essay on the stories is Eric J. Sundquist's "Suspense and Tautology in 'Benito Cereno'" (*Glyph* 8:103–26). The essay is well titled—"suspense" (as in "suspension") suggesting not only the relationship among Melville's characters and the experience of the reader as he reads the story but the mode of Sundquist's criticism itself, a brooding monotone which revolves around its subject like a melancholy art critic circling Laocoon; and "tautology," indicating that after all has been said, one is still a little unsure whether anything has been said. For example: "The comedy that we apprehend [in the shaving scene] is thus a function of both Delano's empty intent and Cereno's failed response, and the precarious standoff or suspension of commanding authorities generated by the events of the story is supported and rendered all the more excruciating by the standoff that takes place in the interrupted function of the comic: the lifting of inhibitions occurs only in the reader, again and again, and yet its very repetition augments the urgency of its constant reformation and dispersal, to the point that one might well speak of the reader's own position as a kind of enslavement or tormented constraint." There is a troubling convergence here of the profound and the banal, as if by sailing west long enough toward the sophisticated play of sensibility one were to end up in the familiar east of New Critical "irony" and "point of view." Sundquist is an original in his unmediated encounter with a text, and if an intense possession of the "quality" of a work is what matters, he is among the saved. But this does not necessarily make his meditations valuable for anyone else to read. Perhaps Sundquist should brood a little on Warner Berthoff's chapter on *Billy Budd* in

The Example of Melville, another exercise in sensibility but also a masterful piece of communication—suspense without tautology. The only other article on "Benito Cereno" is M. E. Grenander's *"Benito Cereno* and Legal Oppression: A Szaszian Interpretation" (*Libertarian Studies* 2:337–42), another reading of Melville's story as an attack on slavery, and one that adds little to previous interpretations aside from the questionable point that what overshadows Benito Cereno at the last is his new-found awareness of what it means to be a slave. In a note on "Benito Cereno" apparently excised from her article (*Expl* 39:33–34), Grenander produces a few more shreds of evidence for the truism that Amasa Delano condescends toward blacks and does not regard them as fully human.

vii. Poetry

There was some solid, unostentatious work written on the poetry this year. Walter Hesford's "The Efficacy of the Word, The Futility of Words: Whitman's 'Reconciliation' and Melville's 'Magnanimity Baffled' " (*WWR* 27:150–55) offers a sensitive reading of both poems and raises larger questions about the poets' "attitudes toward the very foundation of their mutual profession." Hesford knows Whitman and Melville, not simply their poems, and his suggestions ring true. Less speculative but more thorough is Lucy M. Freibert's "The Influence of Elizabeth Barrett Browning on the Poetry of Herman Melville" (*SBHC* 9:69–78), a model in miniature of scholarship done well and claims pressed intelligently with a sense of proportion. Working with "Melville's comments about Browning, his markings and annotations of her poems, and parallel passages in their works," Freibert shows that Browning may have helped Melville at a critical point in his career "when he was struggling to get *Clarel* underway." Broader in scope but also well presented is Basem L. Ra'ad's "The Death Plot in *Clarel*" (*ESQ* 27:14–27), which develops Robert Penn Warren's suggestion that the six deaths in the poem " 'mark the stages of Clarel's education,' " Ra'ad arguing that the "characters who die can be said to disappear from Clarel's sight because their associative or representative meanings become either invalid or impossible for him as alternatives between the polarities of faith and doubt, of ideal and real." The final essay on the poetry, Edward Stessel's "Naval Warfare and Herman Melville's War Against Failure" (*EAS*

10:59–77), discusses the battle of the *Monitor* and the *Merrimac* and the four poems from *Battle-Pieces* it inspired, and asks why the decline of the wooden ship should have called forth "the passionate, almost-thirty-year-long eulogy that Melville gave it." Stessel's answer —that Melville identified the passing of the "unarmored ship" with his own obsolescence as a pre–Civil War "unarmored man" and with the downward course of his literary career—has been suggested before, but his general-reader essay is so engaging one hardly minds.

viii. Billy Budd, Sailor

Despite its inauspicious title, George B. Hutchinson's "The Conflict of Patriarchy and Balanced Sexual Principles in *Billy Budd*" (*SNNTS* 13:388–98) is a fluent, jargon-free essay which aims "to point out thematically significant Greek mythic parallels to the story of Billy Budd and to show how Melville grafted them onto Christian parallels to comment upon sexual alienation and redemption in a fallen world." Untangling a complexly woven myth like *Billy Budd*'s is no easy matter, and in exploring parallels to Iphigenia, Eros, Adam, and Christ, Hutchinson finds himself with more ideas than he can neatly handle. What distinguishes his article is its sense of how the mythic imagination works and its command of the relevant contexts, the late poetry (especially the poem "The New Rosicrucians"), and the Hayford-Sealts genetic text. The result is not absolute clarity or persuasiveness, but one admires Hutchinson's suppleness and scholarly responsibility, qualities rarely seen together.

In the only other full-fledged article on *Billy Budd*, "Captain Vere's Existential Failure" (*ArQ* 37:362–70), James F. Farnham restates the familiar argument that Billy Budd is the victim of Vere's commitment to "measured forms" and his fear of the chaos of uncircumscribed life. Beginning with a loosely existential notion of freedom, Farnham passes from a legal to a moral indictment of Vere's behavior without ever considering Melville's psychological portrait of his Captain, which became more prominent and ambiguous as the manuscript evolved. Altogether, Farnham seems more interested in judging Vere than in understanding how Melville's text asks us to respond to him. William T. Stafford's "Truth's Ragged Edges: Melville's Loyalties in *Billy Budd*—The Commitment of Form in the Digressions" in *Books Speaking to Books*, pp. 105–14, deals briefly with the five sections of *Billy Budd* that follow the hanging scene—"partial truths which distort the whole" but which in their "comprehensive totality" allow us to "begin to conceive the whole." And in a suggestive note (*Expl* 40:30–31), James L. Babin takes up Melville's hint that Claggart might have been a foreigner by birth and conjectures a possible source in the German *Kläger,* "a legal term meaning plaintiff or complainant in a suit" and a close equivalent of "the Hebrew word translated as *satan.*" Thus Claggart's name "suggests not only his role in Billy's fate but also his nature and motivation." Finally, two previously published articles on *Billy Budd* appeared in books: Joyce Sparer Adler's "*Billy Budd* and Melville's Philosophy of War" (*PMLA* 91:266–78; see *ALS 1976,* 57–58) in *War in Melville's Imagination* and Barbara Johnson's "Melville's Fist: The Execution of *Billy Budd*" (*SIR* 18:567–99; see *ALS 1979,* 58) in *The Critical Difference* (Hopkins [1980]).

Washington University

5. Whitman and Dickinson

Jerome Loving

It seems that every year is a Whitman anniversary of one sort or another, and 1981 is no exception according to the editors of *Walt Whitman: The Measure of His Song*. Observing the centennial year of the poet's sixth and final arrangement of *Leaves of Grass*, this collection of essays by carvers of the "new wood" is clearly the year's most interesting contribution to Whitman studies. The choice is more difficult for Dickinson, who received slightly more attention than Whitman (for perhaps the first time since *ALS* began counting). This interest in Dickinson includes two book-length critical studies, but these are of less permanence than *The Manuscript Books of Emily Dickinson*, edited by R. W. Franklin. This much-awaited look into the poet's workshop may well bring the analysis of her work full circle back to the editorial (and critical) dilemma faced by Dickinson's first editors (i.e., what exactly constitutes the definitive version of a Dickinson poem?).

i. Whitman

a. **Bibliography, Editing.** Scott Giantvalley's *Walt Whitman, 1838–1939; A Reference Guide* (Hall) is the major contribution to this area of concern. A secondary bibliography of the first century (and a year) of Whitman scholarship, it even includes as "secondary" items written by Whitman about himself—though the compiler misses a few citations here. The entries are arranged chronologically, with two divisions per year, "one for books, arranged alphabetically by author, [and] one for periodicals, arranged chronologically beginning January 1." Use of the bibliography is facilitated by an index by author, title, and subject. There are, of course, some inconsis-

Preparation of this chapter was facilitated by the research assistance of Susan Roberson.—*J.L.*

tencies in a work of such a wide latitude. The compiler boasts, for example, of including "thousands of items hitherto not included in published bibliographies" and at the same time assures the reader that "items noted as having only incidental mention of Whitman have not been included." But the truth is that many of the "new" items deal with Whitman in only an incidental way. Excess is naturally better than neglect in such a work, however, and generally it can be said that Giantvalley's *Reference Guide* is a worthy contribution to the study of Whitman.

It is also, aside from the quarterly bibliography in the *WWR*, the only contribution to the field of bibliography. Otherwise, mention needs to be made of Harold Blodgett's "Walt Whitman's Poetic Manuscripts" (*West Hills Review* 2[1980]:28–38), which estimates that out of the 426 poems in *Leaves of Grass* (1855–1892) there exist in varying stages of completion "manuscripts for at least two hundred and seventy" poems. One of the original editors of the variorum edition of *Leaves of Grass* (*ALS*, *1980*, 68–69), Blodgett speaks as one "whose hands"—as Hershel Parker lovingly put it in *ALS*, *1976*, 50—"have been soiled in the manuscript collections." Blodgett also gives the story of the distribution of the manuscripts after the poet's death and lists the institutions now holding them in special collections.

b. **Biography.**   Certainly we know more about Whitman's life after the Civil War than before it, but one postbellum area of neglect has nevertheless been the poet's trip out West in 1879. Whitman's journey that year over territory he had traveled vicariously in *Leaves of Grass* is the subject of Walter Eitner's *Walt Whitman's Western Jaunt* (Kansas). The monograph is well written and closely documented. It is particularly important to the biography in showing the discrepancies between the facts of Whitman's actual trip and the romanticized account in *Specimen-Days* (1882). Eitner fills his narrative with a number of interesting items, but the most significant is probably an anonymous interview the aging poet conducted with himself for the St. Louis *Post-Dispatch*. Here Whitman openly accuses the American literary establishment of nepotism, a complaint that echoes the one in his now-famous *West Jersey Press* "release" of 1876. The volume also contains 23 photographs and two maps illustrating Whitman's sojourn.

Further information about Whitman's life can be found in M. Wynn Thomas' " 'A New World of Thought': Whitman's Early Reception in England" (*WWR* 27:74–78). As Morton D. Paley's recent article about the first English edition (*ALS*, *1980*, 69) has suggested, there are still a few gaps in our knowledge of Whitman's British affiliation. Thomas's article presents a letter dated 19 February 1856 to Leigh Hunt from Charles Ollier, which generally praises *Leaves of Grass*. The epistle is noteworthy for a couple of reasons. First, its author was the publisher of (the early) Keats, Shelley, and Lamb; and thus his favorable (albeit private) impression of Whitman's book suggests that the American "language experiment" was attracting serious readers more than a decade before William Michael Rossetti played midwife and nursemaid to *Leaves of Grass* in England. Second, the letter establishes the correspondent's son, Edmund Ollier, as the author of "Transatlantic Latter-Day Poetry." This essay, published in the (English) *Leader* of 7 June 1856, was one of several anonymous reviews that Whitman appended to the second edition of his book. Thomas exaggerates the value of his discovery, however, when he hints that it indicates a correspondence between Whitman and Shelley. And this kind of scholarly "adventurism" doubtless led him to confuse the idealistic persona of *Leaves of Grass* with the political realist who declared in "The Eighteenth Presidency!" (one of the works Thomas examines) that runaway slaves must be returned as long as the Constitution upheld the legality of slavery ("Whitman and the American Democratic Identity Before and During the Civil War," *JAmS* 15:73–93). Although the essay is somewhat useful in its examination of the generally neglected *Drum-Taps*, it is ludicrously naive in its view of Whitman as becoming the Shelleyean poet disenchanted with urban America and its brand of democracy.

Thomas' characterization of Whitman's political posture resembles more that of the poet's friend and champion, the subject of Florence B. Freedman's "W. D. O'Connor: Whitman's 'Chosen Knight' " (*WWR* 27:95–101). Described as the introduction to her biography of O'Connor now nearing completion, the essay reads more like a summary of her subject's life. And if the "introduction" is any indication, the biography will doubtless make claims for O'Connor's importance that have yet to be demonstrated. Central to Freedman's concern is apparently the question of whether this fiery polemicist would have become (without Whitman's cause to preoccupy him) "one of the great writers of his time." In "Whitman's First Funeral" (*WWR* 27:132–34) Freedman notes that both O'Connor and John Burroughs were asked by Whitman's more obsequious advocates (Horace Traubel and Richard Maurice Bucke) to speak at the bard's funeral in 1889 when it looked as though the end was near.

The last piece to be noted in this section concerns both the English and O'Connor, "Walt Whitman's British Connection: Letters of William Douglas O'Connor" (*PBSA* 75:271–300). Skillfully edited and introduced by Randall H. Waldron, the seven letters help to illumine further the background to the first English edition of *Leaves of Grass*. Parts of the letters (which are addressed to Moncure Daniel Conway, the American clergyman who acted as Whitman's literary agent in England; and Rossetti, Whitman's first English editor) have been published before, but the texts were based on copies of auction catalogues. Waldron presents them for the first time in their entirety, basing his texts on the actual manuscripts in the Yale and Ohio Wesleyan collections.

c. **Criticism: General.** Two chapters (15 and 16) are devoted to Whitman in Larzer Ziff's *Literary Democracy*, a literary history and assessment that will probably serve the general reader better than the specialist in one or another of the major writers covered in the volume. On Whitman, Ziff is careless with some biographical facts and occasionally vague in his argument. This is truer with the prewar Whitman, whom he sees as departing from Emerson "in an imagination that gave corporeality to the soul." D. H. Lawrence said almost the same thing and more clearly in *Studies in Classic American Literature* (1923). But the argument gains in strength and originality when Ziff observes that Whitman's concern after the war was less with the "simple separate person" and more with the "swarming collectivity." One regrets only that this most talented chronicler of the 19th-century American scene chose to exemplify his point with a poem first published in 1859—"Out of the Cradle Endlessly Rocking." The Civil War probably had little to do with Whitman's war with himself, which more likely occurred during those dark "Calamus" years of 1857–1859. From that experience the poet realized his true vocation as the singer who fuses Love and Death. Or, as Ziff points out, Whitman learned that the true poet of democracy had to become the poet of Death—had to celebrate the "merge" of the individual with the universal.

Ziff's division of the pre- and postwar Whitman is sharpened a bit in Roy Harvey Pearce's "Whitman Justified: The Poet in 1855" (*Crit I* 8:83–97). The title is somewhat misleading, for Pearce is not pulling up stakes and joining the Malcolm Cowley camp in its preference for the first edition over the third (cf. Pearce's "Whitman Justified: The Poet in 1860" in *The Presence of Walt Whitman* [1962]). Generally, it is "historicism once more," as he now focuses upon the 1855 "Song of Myself" and its preservation in the 1856 and 1860 versions as representative of the poet for whom the "present and the past are inextricably implicated one in the other." The later, postwar Whitman finds himself separated from the past—his "I" apart from the "thou"—and now must consciously explain, really defend, his role as a poet. He stopped doing (Pearce hints in this quasi-structuralist analysis) what his readers often stop doing in their critical approach to *Leaves of Grass*: Whitman stopped living *"nel mezzo del camin."* More (and at times tediously) structuralistic is Donald Pease in "Blake, Crane, Whitman, and Modernism: A Poetics of Pure Possibility" (*PMLA* 96:64–85). A poet of pure possibility avoids the dilemma of the modernist who paradoxically acknowledges the influence of the past by rejecting it. Pease may be offering us a metaphor for authorship that departs radically from Harold Bloom's. For his poet does not engage in oedipal and enceladic battle with the past but rather partakes in a continuous inheritance of the sire's wisdom. And hence the identity of the poet is created in the very act of singing, found suspended somewhere between the "I" and the "you" or the speaker and the reader.

We find in Hyatt H. Waggoner's "Visionary Poetry: Learning to See" (*SR* 89:228–47) both a clarification of Whitman's poetic achievement and a veiled warning to those who seek to interpret Whitman as an Emersonian nihilist. Whitman is one of eight poets Waggoner discusses in his definition and defense of the value of visionary poetry. In his best poetry Whitman found a nature or self that is real and knowable—not simply the by-product of a mind confronting life's endless illusions. For Marc S. Reisch that self was also to be found in the photographs Whitman used in his editions ("Poetry and Portraiture in Whitman's *Leaves of Grass*," *WWR* 27: 113–25). The essay makes a few original observations about the "carpenter" engraving first used in the 1855 edition; otherwise, the general statements about the poet's iconography can be found more clearly articulated in an essay by Gay Wilson Allen (*ALS, 1970,* 70).

Three other articles also look for the elusive Whitman in more quotidian environs. We will find, write Stephen Mainville and Ronald Schleifer, "a strong confluence" of the Understanding and the Reason in the poet's use of printer's jargon ("Whitman's Printed Leaves: The Literal and the Metaphorical in *Leaves of Grass,*" ArQ 37:17–30). For Robert Forrey, we must apply Lacanian linguistics to Whitman's diction to get our answer ("Whitman's 'Real Grammar': A Structuralist Approach," WWR 27:14–24). Forrey's analysis is unfortunately vague, but a more unfortunate "deconstruction" is his gross misrepresentation of F. O. Matthiessen's motives and results in the *American Renaissance* chapter on the poet's "language experiment"—a scholarly disservice compounded by the fact that Forrey's critique is based upon an abridged reprinting of the chapter in question. The title of D. R. Jarvis' attempt to understand Whitman explains his method: "Whitman and Speech-Based Prosody" (*WWR* 27:51–62). More than *only* a "spiritual" father, as Pound put it, of modern American free verse and speech-rhythm experimentalists, Whitman was the first "to isolate the technical and theoretical issues and . . . provide a practical demonstration."

d. Criticism: Individual Works. In a reader-response approach which naturally depends on the word "mediate" (might we ban it from the critical commentary for a year?) to make its point, William Aarnes mounts the argument that through the discontinuous text of *Specimen-Days* Whitman "frees the reader to look beyond the margins of the book" and so to focus on nature firsthand (" 'Cut This Out': Whitman Liberating the Reader in *Specimen-Days,*" WWR 27:25–32). For Bruce Piasecki, the place to find Whitman's real thoughts on nature is *Democratic Vistas*. In an essay that rambles more than the one it discusses ("Whitman's 'Estimate of Nature' in *Democratic Vistas,*" WWR 27:101–12), he finds the poet to be an ecologist of sorts who sees the democratic man as integrating nature, "and in the act, discover[ing] his own integrity." Piasecki, like Reisch, needs to consult an article—this time on Whitman's ecological sense—by Gay Wilson Allen (*ALS, 1979,* 65). In "Making Something of Whitman's 'Miracles' " (*ESQ* 27:222–29) John Gatta, Jr., distorts the Unitarian debate over the miracles question in the 1830s (indulging in a number of platitudes and witticisms about Whitman's "general impatience with sectarian controversy and [his] distinct engagement in New York rowdyism") to argue finally that the poet "remythologize[d] biblical materials cast aside by Transcendentalists in the earlier debate." In an assertion almost as imaginative, Roberts W. French discusses "Song of Myself" as a series of crises in which the poet's "human qualities pose a constant threat to his prophetic role" ("The Voice of the Prophet: Collapse and Regeneration in 'Song of Myself,'" *EngR* 32:2–5). In other words, his democratic pose makes him remote from God and hence the source of his inspiration. This sounds like Emerson, not Whitman. French does slightly better in "Music for a Mad Scene: A Reading of 'To a Locomotive in Winter'" (*WWR* 27:32–39). He sees the poem as divided into two kinds of description—"realistic" and "imaginative." Simply *seen* in the first half, the locomotive is a representation of order and design, but *heard* in the second half, the engine suggests the poet's insistence (in the 1870s after a couple of paralytic strokes) on the power of poetry. "What Whitman hears in that music of the locomotive," French concludes, "is the kind of poetry that Shelley describes in his oxymoronic phrase, 'harmonious madness': a poetry of order, yet inspired beyond the capacities of human design."

French may be seeing what he seeks in the poem, but Gregory M. Haynes admits flat out that "The Dalliance of Eagles" means what it does *not* say ("Reading Whitman's Meanings and 'The Dalliance of Eagles,'" *WWR* 27:159–61). This reader-response examination is cleverer than many, however, in its view of the male eagle's continuing pursuit of the female as "a paradigm of that fluctuating gap between fact and meaning," or of the poet and the natural event he describes. He calls the poem "a type of parable of the act of interpretation." If "Dalliance" is a parable of the artist at his zenith, the first and second "annexes" of *Leaves of Grass* are Whitman's illustrations of the "character of himself in old age"— according to M. Wynn Thomas in "A Study of Whitman's Late Poetry" (*WWR* 27:3–14). Thomas more or less laments that Whitman wrote poetry after his peak, but the critic does perform a service in identifying the finer poems in this group and placing them in both a biographical and critical context. Finally, Louise M. Kawada second-guesses the second guesses in "The Truth About 'A Riddle Song': Another

Venture" (*WWR* 27:78–82). To earlier guesses that "two little breaths" (the clue to the riddle) stands for "Good Cause" and "The Ideal," Kawada suggests that they stand for "the truth." We could wax structuralistic, of course, and venture that the "two little breaths" say what they do not say. Whitman engaged in the same kind of banter when he refused to respond to Traubel's guess, saying, "Horace, I made the puzzle: it's not my business to solve."

e. **Affinities and Influences.** In "The Emersonian Key to Whitman's 'Out of the Cradle Endlessly Rocking'" (*ArQ* 37:5–16) Char Mollison and Charles C. Walcutt argue that Whitman's poem re-enacts the Emersonian aesthetic found in *Nature.* In the absence of historical evidence, their use of Emerson's theory seems arbitrary and imaginative at best. Their three-part division of the point of view in *Nature*, for example, ignores the fact that "Out of the Cradle" is a reminiscence. That is, the poem is not necessarily about the boy's progression toward manhood and therefore like Emerson's progression from the Understanding to the Reason in his perception of nature, but about that discovery of the poet's real vocation—a discovery, incidentally, that is mixed with the kind of pessimism not to be found in *Nature.* The historical support is not much more in evidence in Clarice M. Doucette's "Discovery and Celebration of Self in Montaigne and Whitman" (*WWR* 27:62–70). Suggesting with an undated Whitman fragment in the Berg Collection that Whitman probably knew Montaigne through the writings of Emerson, Doucette argues what her title indicates. But the basis for the comparison is so general as to allow Whitman's identification with just about any important writer who preceded him. A more efficient piece of scholarly spadework can be found in Henry B. Rule's essay "Walt Whitman's 'Sad and Noble Scene'" (*WWR* 27:165–70), which traces the source of Washington's farewell to his troops in "The Sleepers" to an account of the 1783 scene in the diary of Colonel Benjamin Tallmadge. Whitman was probably unaware of his actual source, Rule says, because he got the description from an 1807 biography of Washington which quotes it anonymously. Rule may go too far, however, when he says that Tallmadge's account of the farewell enacted for Whitman "the 'Calamus' emotion in its most intense and pure manifestation."

Whitman's allusions reach back beyond the American Revolution for David W. Hiscoe in "St Paul and Whitman's 'Thorn'd Thumb'" (*WWR* 27:82–86). This image of vexation refers to Paul (Cor. 12:7), and with it Hiscoe suggests that Whitman's statement (in section 42 of "Song of Myself") parallels Paul's "insistence on the necessary place of man's fallen state in any scheme of salvation." The author may be forcing some of the evidence, however, in order to place the poem in what he calls the "biblical culture in which Whitman simmered." Much more arbitrary is Walter Hesford's comparison of a poem from *Drum-Taps* with one from Melville's *Battle-Pieces* in "The Efficacy of the Word, The Futility of Words: Whitman's 'Reconciliation' and Melville's 'Magnanimity Baffled'" (*WWR* 27:150–55). But Anthony X. Marriage is at least orderly in his paralleling of the poet with Baudelaire. In "Whitman's 'This Compost,' Baudelaire's 'A Carrion': Out of Decay Comes an Awful Beauty" (*WWR* 27:143–49), he observes that these poems "resurrect before man's eye the activity of life within death."

The subject of Whitman's influence upon other writers is much in evidence this year. Michael G. Miller finds a possible source for a Dylan Thomas poem in section 14 of the poet's elegy to Lincoln ("Whitman's Influence on Dylan Thomas's 'Poem in October,'" *WWR* 27:155–58). More convincing is Stephen Tapscott's "Whitman in Paterson" (*AL* 53:291–301). It argues that William Carlos Williams employs the image of Whitman at the opening and close of his original version of the poem (books I–V) in order to celebrate a generation of poetry that broke the dominance of iambic pentameter in English prosody ("pater-son"). About the only thing missing from this sound piece of scholarship is acknowledgment of the existence of James E. Miller, Jr.'s *The American Quest for a Supreme Fiction* (*ALS*, 1979, 70), which devotes a chapter to Whitman's impact on Williams' "personal epic." Of much less use is Thomas Becknell's comparison of Whitman and Hamlin Garland. In "Hamlin Garland's Response to Whitman" (*ON* 7:217–35), he sees the middleborder's *Prairie Songs* (1893) as "an antiphony of sorts" to Whitman's call for a literature of the West.

Garland is excluded, naturally, from the array of poets both past and present who acknowledge their debt to Whitman in *Walt Whitman: The Measure of His Song*, ed. Jim Perlman, Ed Folsom, and Dan Campion (Holy Cow!). This response is placed into sharp historical context by Folsom's introductory "Talking Back to Whitman"—an essay that is most informative in its discussion of Whitman's legacy to Hart Crane, Stephen Vincent Benet, Garcia Lorca, Allen Ginsberg, Louis Simpson, and other poets anthologized in the volume. The collection also includes updated assessments of the poet. Ginsberg, for example, blends American slang and myth in his tribute to *Leaves of Grass*, one which suggests he is still prepared to follow the bard through the supermarket. Louis Simpson, on the other hand, is now surly to the poet he addressed so memorably in *End of the Open Road*. Now the "Good Gray" is accused of knowing little or nothing of the nuances of everyday life. "Reading Whitman's poetry," Simpson insists, "one would think that the human race is dumb—and indeed, as he tells us, he would rather turn and live with the animals." Such revisionist nonsense is uncharacteristic of the anthology, however, which reaches all the way back to Emerson in its selection of tributes and apostrophes. The volume also contains 17 not altogether well-known photographs as well as a selective bibliography. *Walt Whitman: The Measure of His Song* measures not only the great shadow that Whitman casts over 20th-century poetry but also the usefulness of the kind of small-press operation that produced this remarkable collection.

ii. Dickinson

a. **Bibliography, Editing.**   Willis J. Buckingham continues to provide us with his comprehensive and annotated accounting in "Emily Dickinson: Annual Bibliography for 1979" (*DicS* 40:71–85).

The event for this year in Dickinson is, of course, the publication of the two-volume *Manuscript Books of Emily Dickinson,* ed. R. W. Franklin (Harvard). It contains the original forty "fascicles" (or packets sewn together by the poet between 1858 and 1863) and the poems belonging to the unbound "fascicle" sheets (numbered fifteen and now called "sets" by Franklin to distinguish them from the sewn material). The edition, handsomely bound, is also equipped with eleven appendixes and three kinds of indexes. Excluded from it, however, are the "unbound" manuscripts Lavinia Dickinson found after her sister's death as well as fair copies of poems sent to friends, for the intention is to present only the manuscripts Dickinson included, or copied as if for inclusion, in her manuscript books. The user of these volumes will notice quickly that Franklin has painstakingly attempted to restore the poems "as closely as possible to their original order" (i.e., to their state before the poet's first editor, Mabel Loomis Todd, mutilated the packets to copy and re-order the poems). This restoration is crucial perhaps to our understanding of the overall structure (if any) of the poet's work. Since she did organize her poetry into "books," we are not amiss to look for some larger pattern that informs her work. Franklin suggests, without claiming too much for the possibility, that the packets might have been intended as "artistic gatherings." But *The Manuscript Books* may also change the way we look at many of the individual poems. It will be more difficult, for example, to consider a variant line in the traditional sense. For seeing it tag right along with the original lines in the "text" seems to tell us that it is part of the whole. In other words, since Dickinson never prepared her poems for publication, the "definitive" edition of poems with variants has to be *the poems with their variants*. This was the way she left them, carefully bound, secured by a locked box, and clearly excluded from the incineration that awaited many of her letters. *The Manuscript Books* suggests that these poems were left penultimate on purpose. That like the tensions of life that animate her best poetry, they could not be finished and still live. Hence, we encounter in Franklin's edition not only modern poems but caricatures of the modern poem. In re-opening (or reconstructing the contents of) that locked box, Franklin may have opened Pandora's box. For in Dickinson's case, the "definitive text" is about as elusive as one of Emerson's Lords of Life.

b. **Biography.** Apparently, the myth was far more enticing than the facts for William Luce in his play about the poet. This is the view of Howard N. Meyer in "A Second Look at *The Belle of Amherst*" (*HJ* 30:3–7; reprinted from *MQ* 21[1980]:365–70). And this is doubtless the reason it achieved such acclaim on Broadway and PBS. In a most entertaining review of the play, Meyer shows how Dickinson and her "mentor" Thomas Wentworth Higginson are not only misrepresented but maligned in the play. The remarks may also be an oblique defense of Higginson, whose true character has been replaced in the play by that of the narrow-minded college professor and editor of the *Atlantic Monthly* (of which he was neither). Higginson is seen as the dupe of a scheming poet (played by Julie Harris) in search of recognition. She is heard to tell Higginson in their

first meeting that she has enough poems for the publication of several
volumes and would "prefer morocco-bound." Not quite as fictional
as Luce is Adalaide K. Morris' "Two Sisters Have I: Emily Dickinson's Vinnie & Susan" (*MR* 22:323–32), which mixes metaphors as
well as biographical facts to suggest that the poet's sister and sister-
in-law represented the two poles of her imagination—the one practical, the other "heavenly" (or "other," with regard to the poetic
quest). Sue is compared to Dante's Beatrice without regard for the
sexual metaphor in the *Vita Nuova*. The question of the gender of
Dickinson's muse is discussed in a larger study (reviewed below),
but Morris' speculation is perhaps occasion to quote George Eliot's
observation in *Middlemarch*: "The text, whether of prophet or of
poet, expands for whatever we can put into it, and even [its] bad
grammar is sublime."

But perhaps the fictions we create are important in the sense
that we have a psychological need for biography or the aesthetic
ordering of life. This is the view of Jonathan Morse in "Memory,
Desire, and the Need for Biography" (*GaR* 35:259–72). Biography,
it might be said, is like fiction—the lie that tells the truth. A biography, Morse concludes, tells us more about ourselves than it does
its formal subject. More to the particulars of the Dickinson biography
is Vivian R. Pollak in "Dickinson, Poe, and Barrett Browning: A
Clarification" (*NEQ* 54:121–24). She argues (against Aurelia G.
Scott's thesis in *NEQ* 16[1943]:627–28) that the poet's mention of
"pearl," "onyx," and "emerald" in an 1854 letter of thanks to Henry
Emmons does not indicate that the gift was a book by Poe but one
by Elizabeth Barrett Browning.

c. Criticism: General. Once Emily Dickinson recognized the de-
privation of life, "the possibility of her art opened out." This is the
basis for David Porter's perceptive study *Dickinson: The Modern
Idiom* (Harvard). Her poetry opened *out* into nothing—the silence
that dramatizes the plight of the modern and postmodern artist.
Porter's argument is best summed up in his insightful reading of
"My Life Has Stood a Loaded Gun": "We confront a poetry of
great strength and no direction." This accounts for the "unanchored
tropism," the modern idiom which marks the end of anecdotal poetry
as it follows language off into obscurity or a loaded silence. This is
an important study of both the well-known poems and those seldom

or never anthologized, which will doubtless force a reconsideration
of Dickinson's most problematic works. Its only weakness is in its
length and occasional redundancy.

Parts of Porter's book are either reprinted or restated in "Emily
Dickinson: A Disabling Freedom" (*MSE* 7–8:80–87) and "Emily
Dickinson: The First Modern" (*NBR* 6:17–19). Also focusing on the
silence in Dickinson is Lisa Paddock, who compares it to the spare,
elemental prose of Hemingway ("Metaphor As Reason: Emily Dickinson's Approach to Nature," *MSE* 7–8:70–79). August J. Fry takes
the poet's "modern idiom" or diction and tries to restore it to the
context of the Calvinistic Connecticut Valley. He argues the already
well-argued point that the poetry springs from Dickinson's clash
with (and ability to accept) the tenets of Christianity ("Writing
New Englandy: A Study of Diction and Technique in the Poetry of
Emily Dickinson" in *Riewald Festschrift*, pp. 21–31). Finally, Willis
J. Buckingham extends Porter's investigation of the poet's diction
to her irregular orthography in "Emily Dickinson's 'Lone Orthography'" (*PBSA* 75:419–35). "In her refusal to edit in conventional
ways," he writes, "the poet appears to leave before her poem is
finished."

The other book-length study of the poetry is by Joanne Feit
Diehl. In *Dickinson and the Romantic Imagination* (Princeton) she
argues that the essential difference between Dickinson and her romantic precursors (Emerson included) is gender. In other words,
we have yet another feminist paradigm to explain Dickinson's obscurity. And this one attempts to answer the question first posed in
The Madwoman in the Attic (*ALS, 1979*, 75–76): "Does [the female
poet] have a muse, and [if so] what is its sex?" She does indeed have
a muse, Diehl responds, and its sex is male. Herein lies the *real*
"anxiety of authorship." Whereas the male poet can finally overcome
the "anxiety of influence" and thus distinguish his own ideas from
those of the composite literary past, the female cannot successfully
woo her muse away from the father. To say it another way, since she
cannot finally make love to her muse without the interference of the
lecherous father (who also desires the poet), she retreats from this
composite "priapic power" into herself. Here she explores a nature
that is beyond the possibilities of the male romantic tradition. Diehl's
argument resembles Homans' thesis regarding "unnamable nature"
(*ALS, 1980*, 83–84), a study that is acknowledged in its dissertation

form. Needless to say, both studies are cleverly articulated. And both
are preoccupied with a theory of authorship to rebut Harold Bloom's
idea that an author "fathers" his text. Diehl's book, however, spreads
the paint a little thin in its application to Dickinson's male precursors.
That is, her metaphor for authorship tends to oversimplify the poetic
process for the male in its generosity to Dickinson and by implication
other female writers. The volume nevertheless deserves careful reading and should spark lively debate. Her thesis is restated with more
direct reference to the Bloomian metaphor in "Dickinson and Bloom:
An Antithetical Reading of Romanticism" (*TSLL* 23:418–41).

Rounding out this category are three studies that appear arbitrary in method. The first uses Nietzsche's analysis of aesthetics (in
The Birth of Tragedy) to discuss the poet's expression of angst in
some of her better-known poems (Dwight Eddins, "Emily Dickinson and Nietzsche: The Rites of Dionysus," *ESQ* 27:96–107). The
next, more subjective and ultimately circular, states that by bearing
pain Dickinson possessed it (Suzanne Juhasz, " 'Peril As a Possession': Emily Dickinson and Crisis," *MSE* 7–8:28–39). The last,
Daniel J. Orsini's "Emily Dickinson and the Romantic Use of Science"
(*MSE* 7–8:57–69), rambles in arguing the obvious—that the poet
discovered the source of revelation in nature.

d. **Criticism: Individual Works.** Besides the analyses of particular
poems in the major studies, article-length discussions of the individual poems abound this year. A few, of course, are myopic in
scope, and others can't see at all. One that implicitly mocks such
analyses as well as the Christian piety and dogmatism that Dickinson
herself often mocked is John Cody's "Emily: Hazards, Billowbees
and Rewards" (*MQ* 22:201–17). In a riotously humorous reading of
"I Never Saw a Moor," the author of *After a Great Pain* (*ALS, 1971*,
71) confesses how it changed the course of his education and his
life. Having encountered the poem on an entrance exam for parochial
high school and explicating it with "sheer disregard for the text" (the
examiner reported), he was denied admission and also four years of
"hazing, no talking in corridors, uniforms, no girls, prayers three
times a day, week-long retreats, mandatory confessions, fasting and
Stations of the Cross during lent, regular diatribes against 'self-
abuse,' High Mass on Holy Days"—in short, the kind of spiritual
orientation that would have probably kept him away from the poet

of Amherst. Brenda Murphy shows even less regard for the text as she misquotes from the Johnson edition to examine Dickinson's images of the wind in " 'Wind Like a Bugle': Toward an Understanding of Emily Dickinson's Poetic Language" (*DicS* 41:26–37).

The attempt to separate Dickinson's reputation from Emerson's continues with George Monteiro in "Dickinson's Select Society" (*DicS* 39:41–43). Monteiro sees the poem "The Soul Selects Her Own Society" as a negative response to the Concordian's pronouncements on the universal sense of friendship in the essay on the subject and in *Nature*: "Taking issue with those who would extol the common virtues of a democratizing society, Dickinson advocates following the aristocratic dictates of the exclusive 'Soul.' " The argument may view Emerson's concept of friendship too narrowly. Indeed, there is a sense of democracy in his concept, but it is best seen in the context of the classical definition of friendship—that the two friends must be equal in talent and virtue. Monteiro also overlooks the fact that friendship for Emerson did not violate the "aristocracy" of the Soul—or, to borrow Whitman's phrase, the integrity of the "simple separate person." For in "Friendship" there is this important caveat: that "the only joy I have in [my friend's] being mine, is that the *not mine* is *mine*." We cannot ignore, of course, the fact that the Dickinson family stood socially above most of the citizens of Amherst and that this sense of superiority probably colored the poet's view of democracy. But Nicholas Ruddick is perhaps too literal in " 'The Color of a Queen, Is This': The Significance of Purple in Emily Dickinson's Poetry" (*MSE* 7–8:88–98). Noting that the color purple appears twice as frequently as white and more often than any other single color word in the poetry, he argues (in purple prose) that "the word 'purple' embraces for the poet such abstract ideas as imperial glory, sovereignty, nobility, queenly dignity, a magnificence that dies at dusk, a culmination at noon, and a revelation at dawn."

Some indication of what is to be expected from Diehl's thesis (discussed above) is to be found in the response to her article in *Signs* (*ALS*, *1978*, 74) which argued that Dickinson had no female precursors in poetry. Maryanne Garbowsky in "A Maternal Muse for Emily Dickinson" (*DicS* 41:12–17) points to the similarity between Harriet Prescott's story "Circumstance" in the *Atlantic Monthly* of 1860 and the Dickinson poem " 'Twas Like a Maelstrom, With a Notch," composed about 1862. The parallel, however, does little to

diminish Diehl's larger claim for Dickinson's "anxiety of authorship."
Another whose scope is too narrow is T. Sciarra, who examines
three poems to find in the phenomenal object counterparts in the
landscape of the mind but who never reveals why this inner search
for reality is peculiar to the woman ("A Woman Looking Inward,"
DicS 39:36–40). The need to invoke gender in interpreting Dickinson also distracts from Jane Crosthwaite's otherwise interesting reading of "Because I Could Not Stop for Death" ("Emily Dickinson's
Ride with Death," *MSE* 7–8:18–27). She suggests that the poem is
not a projection of the poet's death but a record of her encounter
with the fact or inevitability of death and the consequences of that
discovery on the life remaining.

Mechanical at best is James S. Leonard's classification of "about
seven percent" of Dickinson's poems according to their rhetorical
approach in "Dickinson's Poems of Definition" (*DicS* 41:18–25).
And Kathleen E. Kier attempts to rescue J. 183 from the relative
obscurity it may deserve in "Only Another Suspension of Disbelief:
Emily Dickinson's 'I've Heard an Organ Talk, Sometimes'" (*MSE*
7–8:40–48). Saying that the poem is an example of the poet's failure
to respond completely to conventional religious views ("frequently
a bridesmaid, but never the bride of Christ"), Kier compares the
poem to such better known and appreciated "protests" as "The Bible
Is an Antique Volume" (J. 1545) and "'Faith' Is a Fine Invention"
(J. 185). The argument is flawed, however, by the author's failure to
distinguish between "faith" and "intuition." Though neither requires
logical proof, the first results in "belief," the second in (poetic)
"knowledge." According to Myrth Jimmie Killingsworth, Dickinson
expresses in "Who Occupies This House?" a loss or lapse of faith in
the adequacy of metaphorical thinking to probe the mystery of death
("Dickinson's 'Who Occupies This House?'" *Expl* 40:33–35).

The poet's use of birds, bees, or flies is the subject of the last four
inquiries in this section. Thomas W. Ford compares Dickinson's
"These Are the Days When Birds Come Back" to Robert Penn Warren's "Blackberry Winter" to discover in both the poem and the
short story an acknowledgment of the tentative nature of life ("Indian Summer and Blackberry Winter: Emily Dickinson and Robert
Penn Warren," *SoR* 17:542–50). James R. Guthrie finds in her "bird
poems" a personification of the poet as "an insecure person, both in
her life and her art." That is, Dickinson vacillates in these pieces be-

tween the need for privacy and the need for fame as a poet ("The Modest Poet's Tactics of Concealment and Surprise: Bird Symbolism in Dickinson's Poetry," *ESQ* 27:230–37). The poet's use of bees, however, expresses her sexual fantasies and frustrations, according to Lois A. Cuddy in "Expression and Sublimation: More on the Bee in Emily Dickinson's Poetry" (*DicS* 39:27–35). The argument takes too much for granted with regard to Dickinson's attitude toward men and society. Finally, John Rachal in "Probing the Final Mystery in Dickinson's 'I heard a Fly buzz' and 'I've seen a Dying Eye'" (*DicS* 39:44–46) joins the long line of pundits (including the poets John Ciardi and John Crowe Ransom) in examining Emily Dickinson's famous fly. Rachal finds its explanation in the companion poem named in the title of his article. The two poems taken together, he argues, represent the same individual at different stages of life (and death—he adds, noting the clause "when I died" in the first poem).

e. Affinities and Influences.   Concern in this department is rather rigorously confined to the question of the poet's affinity to the Christian scenario. Robin Riley Fast, for example, challenges Barton Levi St. Armand's thesis (*ALS*, 1977, 83) that Dickinson shared the consolation writers' belief in a familiar domestic heaven where one was rewarded for his suffering and self-denial (" 'The One Thing Needful': Dickinson's Dilemma of Home and Heaven," *ESQ* 27:157–69). Rather, Fast argues that Dickinson associated heaven with the concept of home advocated by Emerson and Whitman—i.e., "home" is wherever one finds himself and the vagaries of life. The argument may err on two counts. First, it tends to oversimplify St. Armand's assertion for a "domestic heaven" to suggest that the poet is thought to have shared a sentimental concept; more likely, St. Armand argues for Dickinson's concept of heaven as a sanctuary of sorts from the "harsher [Calvinistic] accents of stressing election and damnation." Second, though the poet no doubt shared her brother's conviction that a Dickinson is "never alone" and thus subscribed to Emerson's (and Whitman's) code of self-reliance, Fast exaggerates the case for the two male poets by depicting them as merrily believing in a world community while Dickinson "wrote as an outsider."

In one of the most interesting studies of the year, George Monteiro and Barton Levi St. Armand measure more accurately the extent to which Dickinson may have subscribed to conventional Christian precepts ("The Experienced Emblem: A Study of the Poetry of Emily Dickinson," *Prospects* 6:187–280). They re-examine representative samples of Dickinson's poetry in the light of the emblem books that conveyed orthodox Protestant belief and argue that such books—especially John W. Barber's *Religious Emblems* (1846) and *Religious Allegories* (1848)—"were not only known to the young Dickinson [but would later] spur and spark her poetic imagination." Their investigation reveals images in the most studied poems that have so far gone unnoticed, but more interesting to me is what their results say about the poet's so-called belief in a "domestic heaven." And it is not altogether apparent exactly where Monteiro and St. Armand stand on the issue. Clearly, their Emily Dickinson is not the one David Porter finds on the edge of the abyss. Rather, their poet found her muse somewhere between "secure piety and insecure poetry." In other words, Dickinson wanted to believe but couldn't finally, and out of this struggle came the tensions that were relieved only in poetry.

Touching on the same argument is Elisabeth McGregor in "Standing with the Prophets and Martyrs: Emily Dickinson's Scriptural Self-defense" (*DicS* 39:18–26). Although many of the illustrations supporting the thesis tend to present Dickinson as a fearful Christian, the final effect is to suggest that the poet's use of the Bible was as much a religious choice as it was a literary one. Jerry A. Herndon would agree in his challenge to Jack L. Capp's conclusion in *Emily Dickinson's Reading: 1836–1886* (*ALS 1966*, 140) that there are no allusions in Dickinson's poetry to the Book of Job ("A Note on Emily Dickinson and Job," *C&L* 30:45–52). But the argument is really one of semantics. It goes without proving, of course, that Dickinson knew the Job story and would doubtless reflect on it in her poetry. Her allusions are nevertheless indirect (as Capps would have it), and this is not disproven by Herndon's comparison of four poems with aspects of the biblical tale.

Two others see Buddhism as important to the poet's contemplation of experience: Sirkka Heiskanen-Makela in "The Poet of Abstractive Consciousness" (*HJ* 28:23–24), and Bonnie L. Alexander in "Reading Emily Dickinson" (*MSE* 7–8:1–17). Finally, Jeanette M. Thomas gives the credit for Dickinson's inspiration back to Emerson. In "Emerson's Influence on Two of Emily Dickinson's Poems" (*DicS* 41:38–42) she sees the difference between "Within My Garden Rides a Bird" (c. 1862) and "A Route of Evanescence" (c. 1879) as evidence of Dickinson's growth from the poet for whom nature is refractory to the Emersonian poet for whom nature is fluid. Although the argument is simplistic in its regard for Dickinson during one of her most vital years as a poet, it does contain an interesting comparison of Dickinson and Emerson in their allusions to *The Tempest*.

Texas A&M University

6. Mark Twain

Louis J. Budd

Because of the publishing schedule, the *ALS* chapters benefit from a time warp. They have a good idea of the shape of the coming year as they size up the one under discussion. For Mark Twain, it's already clear that 1982 will end up richer than 1981. While 1981 deposited some lasting work, there was nothing at book length with one major exception. On the popular level Twain's fame kept riding high. The *Saturday Evening Post* could decide that so thin a sketch as "Journalism in Tennessee" was worth reprinting, and *American Heritage* used some Twain passages on Hawaii as the dressing for early photographs. His career wandered into many attractive places, including the Mississippi Valley of course. Jonathan Raban, having read *Adventures of Huckleberry Finn* in England at age seven, finally navigated from Minneapolis to the Gulf of Mexico while making notes for *Old Glory: An American Voyage* (Simon & Schuster); at least two magazines ran its Hannibal section. As a more lasting booster to popularity, the Mark Twain Boyhood Home Associates have founded *The Fence Painter*, a quarterly newsletter devoted to Hannibal.

Read at a panel for the National Council of Teachers of English, my "Opportunity Keeps Knocking: Mark Twain Scholarship for the Classroom" (*LRN* 6:87–94) urges academics to exploit the fascination with Twain's personality as much as his writings. Further encouragement for researchers comes from Thomas A. Tenney in "Mark Twain: A Reference Guide: Fifth Annual Supplement" (*ALR* 14: 157–94). Still filling in the record, he goes back as far as 1870, though the catchup items get fewer with each supplement. His annotations have steadily grown more helpful because his vast knowledge makes connections that others have missed and enriches his judgments on significance. His introduction again rounds up the news on live projects and hopes. It invites tips on sources for his *Mark Twain: A Documentary Life*, a log of where Twain was, whom he saw, what

he wrote, and what else he did on any particular day. Since the
three volumes are headed for publication in 1986, any help should
be offered soon.

i. Biography

While the *Twainian* continues its recent practice of publishing family
letters, some partly or entirely new, the *Mark Twain Society Bulletin* and the *Mark Twain Memorial Newsletter* keep seining for
local material. For example, *MTSB* 4,i:1,3–4, reprints a newspaper
story on Twain's watching a baseball game in Elmira, and *MTMN*
centers on the Hartford house or, more generally, New England
sources. In *Architectural Review* (London) (169:162–66) Sarah
Bradford Landau inevitably gives most space to photographs of the
house, yet she expertly discusses its construction; cliché-peddlers
should heed her verdict that its "steamboat allusions cannot be substantiated." Twain has always been tugged between objective minds
trying to add information about his life and tastes and the journalists
prowling for a good story. Roy Meador in "Mark Twain Takes on
Classical Music" (*Ovation* 2,i:8–11) claims that the opinions of the
"notorious sage, humorist, and critic of the human species . . . contributed to a broader awareness . . . among citizens who, with few
exceptions, never heard a symphony or an opera." However, Meador
is surprisingly well informed for a throwaway piece. More predictably, the relevant four pages in Irving Wallace's *The Intimate Sex
Lives of Famous People* (Delacorte) are useless except for making
Twainians happy that Twain is included.

In *Mark Twain's Steamboat Years: The Years of Command*
(available from Mark Twain's Boyhood Home, Hannibal, Mo.) Raymond P. Ewing mixes fact, lively fancy, and some dubious authorities
about Twain's few years as a pilot. But Ewing's enthusiasm, which
led him to the scarce drawings and photographs he reproduces,
grows infectious while arguing that Twain learned the profession
most handily and achieved a strong record of employment. Likewise,
*Mark Twain in the "Virginia Evening Bulletin" and "Gold Hill Daily
News": Lampoonery and Buffoonery*, ed. Dave Basso (Falcon),
will sharpen the perspective of anybody trying to comprehend the
Washoe years. It reprints 80 references to Twain by other journalists,
who joked often about his heavy drinking. They also argued, in

effect, that he was already a newsmaker, not just a reporter. Untainted by later jealousy, Dan De Quille in "Salad Days of Mark Twain," *Book Club of California Quarterly News-Letter* (46:34–47) —which reprints a newspaper story from 1893—mostly recalls the practical jokes of their camaraderie in Virginia City. As a small brick in the Chinese wall of his reputation and another perspective on how contemporaries saw him, John Idol in "William Cowper Brann and Mark Twain" (*SwAL* 7:34–37) documents the admiration from a self-advertised iconoclast.

"Why I Killed My Brother: An Essay on Mark Twain" (*L&P* 30 [1980]:168–81) by Forrest G. Robinson is encouraging because, evidently, literary neo-Freudians are now probing individual cases rather than imposing reductionist patterns. It is especially interesting because it takes up not only Twain's weakness for self-recrimination but also the curiously skewed rhetoric of his lament over the death of his brother Henry. Robinson builds a fascinating mirror-within-mirror theory about his repressed hostility toward Henry, who may have maneuvered as a "perverse deceiver," getting Sam into trouble and roiling his conscience while posing as a moral *ingénu*. The chief weakness in Robinson's analysis is a heavy use of Twain's reminiscences, which have so often differed from any hard facts available. Not enough scholars realize (or else can afford to benefit from the fact) that the Mark Twain Papers hold much still undigested family materials.

ii. Editions

The most curious edition of late is *Poor Little Stephen Girard* (Schocken), so handsomely illustrated that its European printing won a prize. Unfortunately, the skit still poses mysteries as to its first appearance (at least seven years before the date of 1880 on the dustjacket), its original title (called "Life as I Find It" in a Charles Neider anthology in 1961), and even its authenticity, though it has the Twainian stamp. Another mystery asks why the Penguin reprint of *Roughing It* did not use the Iowa/California text to benefit from all the collating that once irritated Edmund Wilson. *Wapping Alice* (Friends of the Bancroft Library) resolves a different kind of mystery. Through the introduction and afterword, Hamlin Hill pieces together the documents behind a strange, inept story that no magazine would buy. Hill also speculates convincingly about Twain's sexual attitudes, which determined his handling of the actual situation as well as its fictional version. If the notes of Michael Patrick Hearn add little new to *The Annotated Huckleberry Finn* (Clarkson N. Potter), he does offer some fresh connections to other Twain passages as he tries to fill the four-inch margins for a facsimile of the first British edition.

While there's no need to belabor Hearn's attractive package for bookstores, Peter J. Rabinowitz in "Assertion and Assumption: Fictional Patterns and the External World" (*PMLA* 96:408–19) unwittingly shows the importance of precision about texts. His ambitious essay—which ran, we know, a long gauntlet—borrows *Pudd'nhead Wilson* for an argument that presumes Twain "spent the whole novel building to" the fate of the true Tom or supposed slave. Meanwhile, Hershel Parker in " 'The New Scholarship': Textual Evidence and Its Implications for Criticism, Literary Theory, and Aesthetics" (*SAF* 9:181–97) almost as incidentally uses *Pudd'nhead Wilson* to reprove explicators who do not study the history of a manuscript. Calling Twain himself "shameless," Parker contends that he "put together a book with the least possible effort," failing to reconcile chapters composed out of final sequence under "varying notions of character, plot, and theme." Parker anticipates one rejoinder by asking rhetorically: "Can an author 'will' or 'wish' something he has written earlier to acquire a different meaning or function because he has (without backtracking revision) altered the concept of his characters and plot?" Theorists will attack the implied principle without convincing readers who care more about novels than literary metaphysics.

Of course, the textual event of the year was *Early Tales & Sketches, Vol. 2 (1864–65),* ed. Edgar Marquess Branch and Robert H. Hirst (Calif.) as volume 15 of *The Works of Mark Twain.* Picking up from *ET&S1* (*ALS 1979,* 82–83, 87–88), its 77 main items cover the first 20 months of the San Francisco phase. The appendices, which isolate some soundly attributed but unsigned pieces, exemplify the conservative approach. It adopts as copy-text the first known—to the editors but few other scholars—printing. While Branch and Hirst lay out the revisions definitively, they suppress any urge to improve on the copy-text, even with Twain's blessing. They do supply authoritative headnotes that also become a running analysis of his development; the Jumping Frog materials, naturally the star of the volume, should not distract attention from his dogged struggle to refine his gifts. Overall, Branch and Hirst argue that in 1865 he committed his destiny to the powers and burdens of a professional humorist. Still they leave much for formalist critics to illuminate, and since Twain habitually exploited his personality, biographers will find many leads to his tastes and moods.

iii. General Interpretation

Surprisingly terse for so broad a subject, William H. Shurr in *Rappaccini's Children*, pp. 23–30, searches Twain for "documentary evidence that calvinism was still widespread and deeply rooted in American culture at the turn of the twentieth century." Shurr forcefully expounds both Twain's alertness to the basic imbalance in the creed of Jonathan Edwards and his own tension between a fundamentalist heritage and a rationalist critique of it. By exhausting a more limited point, Thomas M. Walsh and Thomas D. Zlatic won the annual Norman Foerster Prize for the best article published in *American Literature* with "Mark Twain and the Art of Memory" (53: 214–31). Grounded in both classical rhetoric and biographical detail, they build up to the right of theorizing that Twain's efforts at "retention and structuring of knowledge certainly impacted on his ideas and mental processes, reinforcing visualist, quantitative, and sequential habits of mind," habits that encouraged the "spatialized, mechanistic, deterministic and cyclical view of history of his later years." But no précis can match the sophistication of their approach, which leaves even a skeptical reader alerted to an aspect of Twain that has seemed eccentric or naive. Thomas M. Grant in "The Curious Houses That Mark Built: Twain's Architectural Imagination" (*MTJ* 20,iv:1–11) speculates boldly about another aspect that brings uninformed grins—the Hartford residence. After showing that Twain far more often used architecture than the "tank" metaphor to describe the writing process, he develops a shaky correlation between the moods as well as the structure of Twain's major books and his changing attitudes toward his family life. On an already beaten road, James W. Gargano in "Mark Twain's Changing Perspectives on the Past" (SAQ, 80:454–65) sees him, after the modernism of *The Innocents Abroad* and parts of *A Connecticut Yankee in King*

Arthur's Court, as "victimized by a narrowing, constricting ideology of disaster." Gargano's perhaps freshest touch interprets Satan of *The Mysterious Stranger* as man's "self-idealization."

Among the essays with a narrowed focus surely the one most worth hearing would be "Mark Twain and the Mind's Ear" in *The American Self*, pp. 231–39, by Walter Blair, who can mimic the vernacular tone superbly. Blair demonstrates how assiduously Twain revised his pages to transmit oral qualities. In *Black English and the Mass Media* (Mass.) Walter M. Brasch holds just as favorable an opinion but, dazzled, stops with broad praise between long quotations (pp. 99–108). A relief because Twain's eagerness to make money is not excoriated still again, *Wall Street* by Wayne W. Westbrook contrasts Twain with Howells and Henry James to declare him admirable for a "satirical" instead of disdainful or morally outraged treatment of the postbellum mania for speculation (pp. 43–50). Incidentally, Westbrook presents Jim (chap. 8 of *Huckleberry Finn*) as encapsulating the naive investor who gets shorn. My "Color Him Curious about Yellow Journalism: Mark Twain and the New York City Press," *JPC* 15,ii:25–33, centers on his wavering, as a subscriber, between disdain for the latest degree of sensationalism and his taste for lively reporting; beyond that it unaccusingly emphasizes his origins in and canny manipulation of the newspaper world. He has endured harsh judgments, and doubtless more will come if only because his popularity with the current media poses a challenge to born debunkers (like Twain himself).

iv. Individual Works

Perhaps benefiting indirectly from *Early Tales & Sketches*, vol. 1, Twain's briefer pieces got more play than usual. *Critical Approaches to Mark Twain's Short Stories* ed. Elizabeth MacMahan (Kennikat) can enrich the teaching of eight texts through its excerpts from a catholic range of viewpoints. Cut to the pattern of the series, my section in *Critical Survey of Short Fiction* ed. Frank N. Magill (Salem), vol. 6, pp. 2360–65, might help beginners to think harder about four of Twain's best-known stories. For one of them, its sources in local history and legend are collected by Herbert A. Wisbey, Jr. in "The True Story of Auntie Cord" (*MTSB* 4,ii:1,3–5). For another, Gary Scharnhorst in "Paradise Revisited: Twain's 'The Man That

Corrupted Hadleyburg'" (*SSF* 18:59–64) surveys the previous approaches before insisting on *Paradise Lost* as its conscious point of reference. Having insisted, he can claim any departure from Milton as a significant touch rather than having to confront a negative clue. Still he concludes reasonably that Twain, without trying to state a "more systematic theology," allows for "the limited exercise of the human will." As a touch of glory for him by conscious association, Marion B. Richmond in "The Lost Source in Freud's 'Comment on Anti-Semitism': Mark Twain" (*Jour. Amer. Psychoanalytic Assoc.* 28 [1980]:563–74) proves that the essay the elderly Viennese summarized in 1938 but could not identify is Twain's "Concerning the Jews" (1899). For a bonus, Richmond compiles a list of Freud's always favorable references to Twain.

Whatever the going level of interest in Twain's travel books, his earliest one still dominates. Reproducing some of the material that armed a subscription agent, J. Frank Papovich in "Popular Appeal and Sales Strategy: The Prospectus of *The Innocents Abroad*" (*ELN* 18:47–50) charts a "succinct indication" of why that book pleased its audience; however, the come-on, almost catchall anyway, reveals better what its publisher thought would lure buyers ahead of time. Sanford Pinsker in "Mark Twain: The Journalist as Chameleon" (*MTJ* 21,i:15–17) reminds us that its shape-shifting persona did not expect to be watched for consistency through a lengthy session of reading. Also letting sociocultural paradigms alone, Merco A. Portales in "Mark Twain before Raphael's 'Transfiguration'" (*MTJ* 21,i: 7–11) stays within the text and practical biography to rework the idea that Twain, anxious to achieve a distinctive impact, shrewdly made himself "his own best subject." Though headed for a broad principle, Robert Regan in "Mark Twain, 'the Doctor,' and a Guidebook by Dickens" (*AmerS* 22,i:35–55) starts with an alleged instance of direct borrowing to develop a convincing theory about the "symbiotic relationship" between Twain and a crony who was also sending travel letters from the *Quaker City*. Imaginatively building on fact instead of preferences, Regan concludes that Twain's originality overrode any literary sources and that *The Innocents Abroad* fulfilled its promise to examine the Old World on his own terms.

Hamlin Hill's introduction for the Penguin *Roughing It* wanted to avoid the obvious after conceding a "hilariously funny book" that could not "possibly be mistaken for a product of Mark Twain's bitter old age." Always lively and knowledgeable, especially about Twain's ties with various schools of humor, Hill may push inferences too hard in arguing that *Roughing It* already "shows glimpses beneath the surface of the pitfalls of the American Dream and the case history of one victim of its falsehoods." The other American travel book gets its most unifying and subtle reading ever through John R. Brazil in "Perception and Structure in Mark Twain's Art and Mind: *Life on the Mississippi*" (*MissQ* 34:91–112). At times Brazil credits no more than a "precocious, profound intuition that Twain could never quite fathom," but in effect he discovers a rigorous level of Twain's theorizing about a "link" between "linguistic, aesthetic, and epistemological issues" and the "historical origins of Southern culture." Most specifically Brazil's analysis devolves into insisting harder than anybody else that the fulfilled plan for *Life on the Mississippi* reflects the tension between the romantic and pragmatic sides of Twain's genius. The new angle of Fred Durden in "The Aesthetics of Bitterness in *Following the Equator*" (*ALR* 14:277–85) concentrates on rhetorical evidence from the "most contemplative" of the travel books. Durden perceives a strategy of "dialectical contrasts" through which the word-landscapes symbolize humankind's faults. Even after granting that the much later book had the consistency Pinsker disclaims for *The Innocents Abroad*, we still must wonder if ailing and weary Twain intended Durden's examples of mock-eloquence or was grinding out copy as best he could. To be sure, the case goes beyond either-or positions, and *Following the Equator* needs more advocates like Brazil to make sure that any consensus will rest on rich debate.

Huckleberry Finn again lorded over the year's work, surely not a last hurrah with its centennial coming up. At least, the one article dealing with its forerunner made a basic contribution. Phyllis Bixler in "Idealization of the Child and Childhood in Frances Hodgson Burnett's *Little Lord Fauntleroy* and Mark Twain's *Tom Sawyer*," pp. 85–96 in *Research about Nineteenth-Century Children and Books*, ed. S. K. Richardson (Univ. of Ill. Grad. School of Library Sci., 1980), distinguishes the "bucolic" from the "georgian" pastoral in which little adults cooperate demurely with their elders. Infusing the bucolic tradition with enough reality to dispel vapidness, the children in *The Adventures of Tom Sawyer* play at defying grown-up values and thus let us enjoy vicariously their deferring the burdens of responsibility. Bixler impressively invokes classical scholarship and the transatlantic literary tradition, helping also to explain why general readers have always preferred *Tom Sawyer* among Twain's boyhood tales. Nevertheless, *Huckleberry Finn* continues to over-shadow it heavily among academics and writers.

For a highly esteemed novelist, Huck's "floating down the river" ranks among the four dominant images in world literature—Charles Reilly, "An Interview with John Barth" (*ConL* 22:1–23); a brochure service aimed at college registrars employs him as a device to catch attention; a philosophers' debate begun some years ago (*ALS 1977*, 95) over Huck's character, presumably both admirable and unam-biguous, continues in Phillip Montague's "Re-examining Huck Finn's Conscience" (*Philosophy* 55[1980]:542–46). Broad-gauged essays in-clude him as a figure whom their readers would otherwise ask about. Thus, David M. LaGuardia in "The Artist as Orphan: Literature out of Revolution" (*BSUF* 22,iii:4–13) hauls him through the well-worn groove of American yearnings to escape from social pressures. For confronting the newest avant-gardes of criticism, Sheridan Baker in "Narration: The Writer's Essential Mimesis" (*JNT* 11:155–65) bor-rows him to argue that fiction archetypically "imitates a person telling about reality." To bring recognition for a distinctively American genre, John F. Callahan in "Democracy and the Pursuit of Narrative" (*Carleton Miscellany* 18,iii[1980]:51–68) points out in *Huckleberry Finn*, along with *Moby-Dick* and *Invisible Man*, "autobiographical form and technique as a way of insisting that characters take re-sponsibility for narrative" and likewise take a stand on sociopolitical questions. Himself a concerned democrat, Callahan interprets the final evasion sequence as a protest against the ongoing oppression of blacks, supposedly set free by the Civil War.

Any sources for so prestigious a novel are worth hearing about. In "Mark Twain and James W. C. Pennington: Huckleberry Finn's Smallpox Lie" (*SAF* 9:103–12) William L. Andrews nominates a slave narrative as the model for the ploy that keeps the bounty hunters away from the raft. In "The Source for the Arkansas Gossips in *Huckleberry Finn*" (*ALR* 14:90–92) David Carkeet, who classi-fied the book's dialects authoritatively (*ALS 1979*, 89), pretty much proves that the chatter (chap. 42) of Aunt Sally's neighbors was stimulated, perhaps inspired, by a Joel Chandler Harris story. Another expert on the novel's language (see *ALS 1976*, 86–87), Janet

Holmgren McKay in "Going to Hell: Style in Huck Finn's Great Debate" (*Interpretations* 13:24–30) analyzes the rhetoric of the decision
to help Jim instead of obeying conscience (chap. 31). I must guess
she submitted her essay before seeing Henry Nash Smith's *Democracy and the Novel* (*ALS 1978*, 84). However, in studying the passage
appreciatively her sensitivity leads close to Smith's perception that
the debate verges into burlesque. Fine tuning to Huck's undertones
would benefit the critics who have soared high on one or two of his
phrases. Tolerantly, Jesse Bier in " 'Bless You, Chile': Fiedler and
'Huck Honey' a Generation Later" (*MissQ* 34:456–62) bids farewell
to the idea—shocking only yesterday, it seems—that Jim and Huck
have a latent homosexual bond. Yet Bier makes me feel not only old
but also up to date by suggesting that Jim—"there in the all-embracive
womb-like tent on board the raft that floats on the flowing waters"
—is a "presiding mother-image," thus adding a "mythopoeic bisexual
parental figure" to Twain's credit. Indeed, the feminists are ready to
ennoble Jim as a nurturer rather than a surrogate father.

Three articles that place Huck's rhetoric within the movement of
the narrative will sharpen anybody's reading. In " 'I Never Knowed
How Clothes Could Change a Body Before': The Dual Function of
Clothing in *Huckleberry Finn*" (*MTJ* 20,iv:19–20) Jeffrey Sommers,
pointing up some little-noticed passages, contends that Twain handled dress as "both symbolizing the construction of 'sivilization' and
functioning ironically in the constant tension between appearance
and reality." With a potentially major yet simple thesis, Christopher
Sten in " 'When the Candle Went Out': The Nighttime World of
Huck Finn" (*SAF* 9:47–64) argues at length that the moral tone
contrasts firmly according to whether the action unrolls in daylight
or after dark. While sensitizing us to the frequency of the night episodes, he does not ask if they exceed the normal range for a tale of
adventure. Another defender of the evasion sequence, he makes it
exemplify an aspect of the darkness mentality: the assertion of freedom simply for personal benefit or pleasure. More persuasively, Paul
Schacht in "The Lonesomeness of Huckleberry Finn" (*AL* 53:189–
201) reconsiders the passages often expounded to show an outcast's
turning away from human cheer and sociability. Schacht decides that
Huck can healthily enjoy dark, desolate, or threatening scenes such
as a thunderstorm when he feels secure, that is, when with some-

body he likes. The larger point is that—like Twain—he suffers not from a death wish but an incapacity for solitude and needs friendly company. This luminous essay should also serve as a warning to follow the text of *Huckleberry Finn* instead of coercing it.

For a general educated audience, Marcus Cunliffe in "Mark Twain and His 'English' Novels" (*TLS*, 25 Dec. 1981:1503–04) infers that the American, aspiring to succeed Dickens and Thackeray as *the* versatile writer-lecturer-humorist, took up the historical romance to fill out his repertoire. *The Prince and the Pauper* nevertheless somehow surpassed a mob of authors straining to exploit its genre. In passing, Cunliffe digs up a Bulwer Lytton novel as a source for *A Connecticut Yankee*. An authority on Twain and the Bible, Allison R. Ensor in "Mark Twain's Yankee and the Prophet of Baal" (*ALR* 14:38–42) convincingly advances Elijah as a model for Hank Morgan. Several other essays or sections of books echo the prevailing consensus that *A Connecticut Yankee* betrayed Twain into projecting his fears about technology. The best restatement comes from Lee Clark Mitchell in his *Witnesses to a Vanishing America: The Nineteenth-Century Response* (Princeton), pp. 264–67.

Three readings try out other abstractions on *A Connecticut Yankee*, a piece of the Twain puzzle that fits nowhere snugly but looks too important to ignore. Tying it unexpectedly to *The Mysterious Stranger*, Frederick E. Pratter—with "The Mysterious Traveler in the Speculative Fiction of Howells and Twain," in *America as Utopia*, pp. 78–90—finds an early avatar of the dreamers who crusaded in now-forgotten novels of the 1890s. While Hank's optimism does crumble for Pratter too, Philip Traum leaves a margin of hope for perfectibility despite Satan's dystopian truths. After unfurling a formalist banner and next promising to exhibit the "interaction of literary text and historical knowledge," Winfried Fluck—in "The Restructuring of History and the Intrusion of Fantasy in Mark Twain's *A Connecticut Yankee in King Arthur's Court*" (*Brumm Festschrift*, pp. 134–43)—focuses on the contradictions between Hank's ideals and the effects of his actions. Fluck implies that a wiser head could have controlled the results better and assumes, without meaning to sound utopian, that an individual can get material success—and even power —while at the same time genuinely honoring the catchwords of romantic democracy. In the course of elaborating a poetics of fiction that works for current oracles like Borges, Walter L. Reed in *History of the Novel*, pp. 217–31, brackets *A Connecticut Yankee* with Melville's *Confidence-Man* for its interweaving of sets of aesthetic, cultural, and historical contrarities. I wonder if Reed knows that our literary comedians once made histories of England into a subgenre. Also, I wonder if he intended an oxymoron when declaring that Hank Morgan "is Quixote as a hardheaded, scheming adult." In any event, Reed now holds the belt for the most reflexive, multilevel, and cerebral exposition of *A Connecticut Yankee*.

Besides the unintended Rabinowitz-Parker clash, Twain's final long novel inspired only "Disorder and the Sentimental Model: A Look at *Pudd'nhead Wilson*" (*SLJ* 13,ii:59–71) by Adrienne Bond. She enlarges on the "tragic octoroon" sterotypes popular after Dion Boucicault's play (1859), which had a pivotal device close to Twain's. Unfortunately, she respects Twain too much to consider that he might use stock characters either cynically or respectfully rather than satirically. Still, her essay will remain useful for both its literary history and suggestive criticism.

Twain naturally benefits from the intense current speculation about autobiography as a genre. For instance, in "American Autobiography: The Western Tradition" (*GaR* 35:307–17), which makes a persuasive and basic point, Arnold Krupat cannot resist dragging Twain in, with dubious results. More productively, in "Mark Twain's Experiments in Autobiography" (*AL* 53:202–13) Marilyn Davis De-Eulis concentrates on his text rather than its relation to a species. Her thesis is that his background led to pondering about how cold type in arbitrary shapes can evoke breathing emotions and ideas; struggling "to cheat the page into charting a life," Twain devised an "idiom never hand-written but printed and peculiar to autobiography." Some Twainians may demur that she adds profundity to his ad hoc comments; others may stay skeptical that his dictations while lounging in bed had an aesthetic drive. Still, her chain of argument hangs on the mind, countering the pull of *Early Tales & Sketches*.

After the variations from year to year average out, scholarship manages to keep Twain's many sides to the forefront. Maybe his biography most needs refinement after the recent combination of his panache and strongminded interpreters drawing broad judgments. Close analysis of a phase or a particular event will give his mundane problems more weight, surely. Meanwhile, Halley's Comet, returning with the 150th anniversary of his birth (or the 75th anniversary of his death), will keep the melodramatic colors of his legend bright. To meet a second need, the rising zest for theories of humor or comedy should more intently take up Twain, who is after all a leading exhibit.

Duke University

7. Henry James

Robert L. Gale

With the recession and all, the James boom is subsiding somewhat. This year saw only five books and about 90 articles. Although much is of high quality, I judge that the level of excellence does not reach that of several recent years. Again, research on James and sources, parallels, and influence accounts for more work than does any other single category; next comes criticism of individual novels; then, discussion of separate short stories. Considerations of biography and James's nonfictional writings have been minor. My nominees for the "nine best" James critics publishing in 1981 are Sarah B. Daugherty, J. Peter Dyson, Daniel Mark Fogel, Barbara Jensen-Osinski, Anthony J. Mazzella, Ruth Evelyn Quebe, E. A. Sklepowich, Adeline R. Tintner, and Darlene Harbour Unrue. No major surprises were unfurled concerning James's fiction; *The Portrait of a Lady*, *The Golden Bowl*, and "The Turn of the Screw" were the only items discussed extensively.

i. Bibliography, Biography, Letters

"James Studies 1978–1979: An Analytic Bibliographical Study" (*HJR* 2:132–52) by Richard A. Hocks and John S. Hardt concerns books on James, then general articles, essays on single novels, and miscellaneous pieces. The two critics close by praising Adeline R. Tintner, whose solid hundred-plus source-and-analogue essays "make . . . us conscious of James's truly multivarious connections with his cultural milieu, especially in the areas of art and literature." Distinguished bibliographer Madeleine B. Stern in "A Lesson for the Master: A. K. Loring" (*HJR* 2:87–90) shows us that it was Aaron Kimball Loring (Boston publisher of Horatio Alger, Jr., among others) rather than Frank Loring (James family friend and model of William Wentworth of *The Europeans*) who pirated James's short story "A Bundle of Letters" and thus taught the novelist to be more careful about copyrighting in America material first published abroad. In "Mr. James's Daughter and Shakespeare's Sister . . ." (*HJR* 3:59–63) Cushing Strout praises Jean Strouse's 1980 *Alice James: A Biography* except for Strouse's succumbing to Virginia Woolf's notion that if Shakespeare had a brilliant sister she would have become lonely, suicidal, or insane. To make Alice James such a "feminists' . . . ideological heroine," Strouse, according to Strout, inadequately analyzes Alice's hysteria, her passion for her brother William James, her relationship with Katharine Loring, and her "bleak and coercive side" in general. Leon Edel should take careful note of Bernard Richards' violent but justified attack on Edel as editor of James's letters. It appears in a review entitled "Amateurism" (*EIC* 31:61–68). Richards castigates Edel for his "failures to annotate adequately," for silently correcting some slips by James but letting others go, for perhaps inaccurately reading James's handwriting, and for his "slap-dash and perfunctory" indexing. Richards defines "the scale and scope of the [Edel] edition" as "misconceived" and pleads for "a full and scholarly edition" instead.

ii. Sources, Parallels, Influences

Two dozen articles concern James and his possible sources, parallels to elements in his work, and his possible influence on other writers. The gamut spreads from B.C., with Euripides, to the BBC.

Adeline R. Tintner in "Euripides Echoed in James' Fiction" (*ABBW* 24 Aug.:1011, 1012, 1014, 1016) suggests that "the sacred rage," a phrase used nine times in *The Ambassadors*, may derive from Euripides.

Cheryl B. Torsney's essay "Prince Amerigo's Borgia Heritage" (*HJR* 2:126–31) presents evidence that Prince Amerigo of *The Golden Bowl* may have descended from Pope Alexander VI, né Roderigo Borgia. The Prince says that one of his ancestors is " 'the wicked Pope, the monster most of all,' " but without naming him. Both Alexander VI and Amerigo are documented as worldly, materialistic, extravagant, dishonest, deceptive, avaricious, sensual, and treacherous. Torsney too handily explains the Prince's un-Borgian weaknesses on the grounds that his blood, like that of Don Mariano,

an early 19th-century descendant of Roderigo, is anemic through
degeneration.

A. R. Tintner in "An Interlude in Hell: Henry James's 'A Round
of Visits' and *Paradise Lost*" (*NMAL* 5:Item 12) reads James's late
story "A Round of Visits" as his vision of hell, with the New York
skyscraper as source, metaphor, and locus thereof. Further, she identifies parallels between James's hellishly mammoth New York ho-
tels and Milton's tall, twinkling Pandemonium, product of Mammon
and Mulciber. Farfetched? Hell, no. Tintner's "In the Footsteps of
Stendhal: James's 'A Most Extraordinary Case' and *La Chartreuse
de Parme*" (*RLC* 55:232–38) proves that James's early story "A Most
Extraordinary Case" parallels Stendhal's *La Chartreuse de Parme* in
structure, characters, and plot. Less persuasive is her assertion that
James "strew[s] . . . clues throughout the story which would be
reminders of the invoked masterpiece" so as to "get . . . the reader to
do 'his share of the task.'" Surely not one in a thousand readers of
James's weak 1868 tale (if there are a thousand out there) recalls
Stendhal, or needs to. In "Vanda de Mergi and Rose Muniment"
(*Notes et Documents* 7 June:110–12) Tintner proposes Vanda de
Mergi, an invalid in Balzac's *L'Envers de l'Histoire Contemporaine*,
as partial model of Rose Muniment, invalid in James's *The Princess
Casamassima*, in regard to mise-en-scène, physical appearance, curiosity, and propensity to chatter; further, the "charitable and non-
religious" work of the "lay brotherhood" in Balzac's novel leads to
aspects of the "secular brotherhood" in James's "The Great Good
Place." And "Henry James' Balzac Connection" (*ABBW* 27 Apr.:3219,
3222, 3224, 3226, 3228) by busy Tintner shows that Balzac's pension
novels are reflected in James's pension tales—"The Pension Beaure-
pas," "A Bundle of Letters," and "The Point of View"—and also that
Louis Leverett, of the last two tales, and Lambert Strether of *The
Ambassadors* have traits echoing those of the titular hero of Balzac's
Louis Lambert.

In "Toward Daisy Miller: Cooper's Idea of 'The American Girl'"
(*SNNTS* 13:237–49) Mary Suzanne Schriber pays tribute to James
for most fully expressing the concept of the 19th-century American
girl in his "Daisy Miller," even as Schriber mainly praises James
Fenimore Cooper for certain young pre-Daisy heroines. Elizabeth
Keyser's "Veils and Masks: *The Blithedale Romance* and *The Sacred*

Fount" (HJR 2:101–10) offers a valuable but prolix comparison of
two somewhat tiresome novels. The veils in Nathaniel Hawthorne's
The Blithedale Romance and James's The Sacred Fount apparently
conceal the reality of passion, exploitation, fascination with feminine
weakness, and death in life. Hawthorne's Miles Coverdale and
James's unnamed narrator remain uncommitted as their respective
narratives move from comic to elegiac in tone.

In "Gossip and Gothicism in The Sacred Fount" (HJR 2:112–15)
E. A. Sklepowich explicates The Sacred Fount as "a subtle reworking
of the Gothic [novel]." Gothic ingredients such as rape, death, vampirism, abduction, haunted house, vicious "lord of the mansion," and
the Gothic novel itself, James converts into loss of reputation, social
disfavor, the sacred-fount theory, inquisitiveness, British country
house as "crystal cage," narrator-guest as one "himself imprisoned,"
and "supreme fiction of epistemological pursuit, capture, and escape."
Tintner in "Henry James's Mona Lisas" (ELWIU 8:105–08) shows
how James selects from the ambiguous description of Mona Lisa by
Walter Pater in his 1869 Fortnightly Review essay on Leonardo Da
Vinci mainly vampiric traits for the titular heroine of James's 1873
story "The Sweetheart of M. Briseux" but more subtly follows Pater
when limning Angela Vivian, central female in his 1879 Confidence:
she is transformed in the course of the novel from an "ambiguously
sinister, mocking woman . . . into an understanding, altruistic person." (For William Makepeace Thackeray's possible influence on
James, see Jean Frantz Blackall below.)

The most prodigious influence study of the year is James J.
Kirschke's Henry James and Impressionism (Whitston), which
ranges and compares with steady skill. First Kirschke discusses the
main aspects of impressionism in the visual and plastic arts (render
direct and fleeting impressions, paint in the open air, move around
the subject and paint it from different angles, use brushwork which
requires distant viewing, juxtapose colors, present the scene hazily).
Second he reviews major Continental influences (some not very impressionistic) on James's impressionism (especially Flaubert, Turgenev, Daudet, Zola). Third—British and American literary influences
(again, some not very impressionistic, including Ruskin, Pater, Du
Maurier, F. M. Ford, Conrad, Howells, and Crane). Fourth and
most important—impressionism in James's fiction, chronologically
and selectively considered. The first three chapters are so informative

that the fourth would be anticlimactic but for its comparable excellence. James is a detached observer of refined consciousness, foreshortens through selectivity and suggestiveness, records special moments in unique light, heightens by complementary intensity, prefers technique over subject, challenges his audiences to follow internalized action and to solve—or savor—ambiguities. Kirschke relentlessly documents, with more than 800 footnotes, some over a page each; in the process he never hesitates to correct major critics or praise minor ones.

Sharon Dean's essay "Constance Fenimore Woolson and Henry James: The Literary Relationship" (*MSE* 7,iii[1980]:1–9) proves that James was influenced by Woolson. The reverse is too often all that is believed. James modified Woolson's use of ambiguity, narrative techniques, and such themes as loyalty, betrayal, entrapment, and unwitting self-incrimination. Influenced by James's "The Pupil," Woolson's 1894 story "A Transplanted Boy" then influenced *What Maisie Knew*. Her 1882 story "The Street of the Hyacinth" is echoed in James's "The Aspern Papers," which also shows the effects of James's reading of "Miss Grief," Woolson's 1880 story. Lynne T. Hanley in "The Eagle and the Hen: Edith Wharton and Henry James" (*RS* 49:143–53) explains that in calling himself "a poor croaking barnyard fowl" compared with energetically pouncing, eagle-like Edith Wharton, James exaggerated through jealousy both his "preoccupation with theory, aesthetic control, and detachment from life," and her unprofessional commitment to intimacies. In this criticism, Percy Lubbock meanly abetted James. Hanley contrasts James's craft, that of mathematician and architect, with Wharton's, that of dream-gardener and tapestry weaver. Hanley seems predisposed to prefer Wharton. In "Henry James as Roth's Ghost Writer" (*Midstream*, March:48–51) A. R. Tintner offers James's formula for using literary sources: "James's narrative technique . . . was to locate for the reader, in a literary classic within his story, some character or situation taken from it, and then to recreate the form of the classic itself through an original variation on it." In his novel *The Ghost Writer* (1979) Philip Roth follows this plan, names James's story "The Middle Years" as his overt analogue, but then uses James's "The Author of Beltraffio" as covert analogue for good measure.

Elizabeth Steele speculates in "A Change of Villains: Hugh Walpole, Henry James, and Arnold Bennett" (*CLQ* 17:184–92) that

Walpole dedicated his macabre 1942 novel *The Killer and the Slain* to the author of "The Turn of the Screw," not as Leon Edel avers, to equate Walpole's killer (a son figure) and the killer's victim (a father figure), but to equate that victim with Arnold Bennett. Steele bases her hypothesis on questionable evidence, including onomastic. I prefer Edel here: young Walpole oedipally kills the old master. Remember that in Walpole's novel the killer becomes his dead victim (as Edel points out, in *AI* 8[1951]:367, which Steele cites without elaborating). Walpole might not have minded doing so. With "Henry James's *The Outcry* and the Art Drain of 1908–9" (*Apollo*, Feb.:110–12) A. R. Tintner builds on her previous "art-drain" studies (see *ALS 1980*, 105) and notes parallels between J. P. Morgan and Breckenridge Bender of *The Outcry*, between the Duke of Norfolk and James's Lord Theign, King Edward VII and James's "Prince," and between certain real paintings and a few figuring in James's once-popular novel.

Celso de Oliveira reveals in "Carlos Fuentes and Henry James: The Sense of the Past" (*ArQ* 37:237–44) that Fuentes' 1962 *novela corta* entitled *Aura* is loosely patterned after James's "The Aspern Papers" (which Fuentes knew well), with the following parallels: James's Venice (old and new) / Fuentes' Mexico City; Jeffrey Aspern and his papers / General Llorente and his unfinished memoirs; Juliana Bordereau and her niece Tina / the general's widow Consuelo and her niece Aura; and James's unnamed narrator / Fuentes' scholar-editor Felipe Montero. Fuentes' climactic erotic horror is not Jamesian.

Anthony J. Mazzella's "A Selected Henry James Artsography" (*HJR* 3:44–58) is a fascinating list, with pertinent details, of 119 adaptations of 17 novels and 34 short stories by James, according to these categories: dance (1), film (12), opera (6), radio (57), television (39), and spoken-word recording (1). Even more fascinating is Mazzella's "'The Illumination Was All for the Mind': The BBC Video Adaptation of *The Golden Bowl*" (*HJR* 2:213–27). In it Mazzella compares James's novel and the distinguished 1972 BBC television version, written by the late Jack Pulman and directed by James Cellan Jones. The result, a superb piece of film criticism, is a creative act itself, as Mazzella hints in a couple of good asides. He analyzes the TV opening, the conflation of elements from separate fictive scenes into one video scene, Cyril Cusack's modulated voiceovers as the commentary of Colonel Bob Assingham—"the drama within the drama of visual and auditory counterpoint and discrimination"—the choice of background music, the use of silences and symbolic props, and especially the love scene of Charlotte and the Prince. Mazzella quotes generously from the film script.

iii. Criticism: General

The best book this year on Henry James is, I believe, Daniel Mark Fogel's *Henry James and the Structure of the Romantic Imagination* (LSU). It is informed, thorough, and lucid. Fogel feels that James is rooted in the romantic tradition because he dramatizes the quest for experience with a concomitant transformation of the self, because his quest structures are bipolar ("inexperience becomes experience, innocence knowledge, incomprehension insight"), and because his protagonists typically synthesize diversities to achieve "a higher order of rightness"—resulting in a Blakean "organized innocence"—for "humanistic affirmation." Like a good dialectical commentator, Fogel makes skillful use of the best Jamesian critics before him, agreeing and tactfully disagreeing, and as he spirals above and beyond them synthesizing well. *The Awkward Age* is a "paradigm of spiral return," while *The Ambassadors* "embodies James's dialectic, from small stylistic detail to the overall pattern of Strether's development"; *The Portrait of a Lady* displays "James's use of polarities," while both rhetoric and imagery are apt in *The Wings of the Dove*, which also incorporates "the principles of opposition and synthesis in . . . [its] dramatic organization"; finally, early key pieces are "governed . . . by antitheses."

Another significant book is Sarah B. Daugherty's *The Literary Criticism of Henry James* (Ohio). It is the most important study of James's criticism since James E. Miller, Jr.'s *Theory of Fiction: Henry James* (see *ALS 1972*, 98–99). To show the relationship between James's criticism of fiction, drama, travel writing, and poetry by others, and his own writings, Daugherty not only studied all of James's critical pieces but also read the works James comments on. Of the hundred or so authors whom Daugherty's fine index indicates James criticized, the following seem the most essential: Balzac, Cherbuliez, D'Annunzio, Daudet, Droz, Eliot, Flaubert, France, the Goncourts, Hawthorne, Howells, Maupassant, Renan, Sand, Stevenson, Taine, Trollope, Turgenev, and Zola. James sought to blend traditional romanticism and emerging realism, and over the years he grew more tolerant of writers' differing with him both in theory and in practice. Daugherty organized her sprawling data thus: James's early sense of mission; his response to French naturalists; "social novelists"; "psychological novelists" and "romancers"; post-Hawthorne American writers; James's "The Art of Fiction" (a masterly exposition); reviews of poetry and Renan; "Toward a New Perspective" (James growing "more tolerant of aesthetic diversity," arguing for better writing by and about women, fighting against "the decline of the English language"); and re-evaluative chapters. Four last points here: Daugherty writes very well, and her book should prove useful in untold ways, is documented with more than 700 footnotes, and includes helpful translations of all French passages quoted.

The thesis of Alwyn Berland's erudite, dogmatic, overpriced *Culture and Conduct in the Novels of Henry James* (Cambridge) is that James's view of "civilization as culture" had "permeating effects" on his fiction, which concerns his characters as they relate to themselves, each other, society, institutions, and traditions (largely "a nineteenth-century aesthetic tradition" as mainly expressed by Matthew Arnold). Berland considers James's civilization-as-culture "themes and motifs": call to duty vs. call to beauty, innocence and betrayal, getting involved under the guidance of an informed intellect, and renunciation. Berland applies his theory especially to *Roderick Hudson* (America vs. Europe), *The Portrait of a Lady* (the heroine chooses, develops her taste, is betrayed, renounces), *The Princess Casamassima* (culture vs. anarchy), *The Bostonians* (a satire of lives without culture), and *The Ambassadors* (Chad Newsome wants both "culture and . . . acquisitiveness" and hence is "dangerously . . . susceptible," whereas "Lambert Strether's culture is high enough to encompass all of James's ideals of character").

Gerard M. Sweeney in "Henry James and the 'New England Conscience'—Once Again" (*NEQ* 54:255–58) reports that James used the term "New England conscience" as early as 1869 in his story "A Light Man," and not for the first time later, as others have said. The two points of Ellen Tremper's jumbled and mistitled "Henry James's 'The Story in It': A Successful Aesthetic Adventure" (*HJR* 3:11–16) are (1) that Mark Ambient, hero of "The Author of Beltraffio," is a mixture of traits of members of Flaubert's *cénacle* plus James's notion of Paterian aestheticism; and (2) that his "The Story in It" combines Gabriele D'Annunzio's aestheticism minus its delimiting eroticism plus, again, Jamesian aestheticism. And Dorothy Berkson in "Tender-Minded Idealism and Erotic Repression in James's 'Madame de Mauves' and 'The Last of the Valerii'" (*HJR* 2:78–86) explains that three impractical idealists in the two stories are foolish when they prefer pure illusion to sensual reality. Sensuality may be bad, but so is repressing it. Berkson treats "The Last of the Valerii" with special freshness.

The best of James has come in for excellent treatment. Edwin Sill Fussell's "Sympathy in *The Portrait of a Lady* and *The Golden Bowl*" (*HJR* 2:161–66) says that although James criticized Hawthorne, the most assiduous of "American sympathy-mongers," he often uses the word "sympathy" himself. With James it becomes "multifaceted, curious in tone, . . . obscure and confusing." Fussell finds it sad that Isabel Archer of *The Portrait of a Lady* sympathizes so much with others, many of whom are unworthy, but in doing so she achieves a "quiet dignity." Sympathy in *The Golden Bowl* is "comic and pathetic" but "signals tragedy" too. Adam Verver, his daughter, and his grandson form such a sympathetic unit that his wife and his son-in-law decide to form another. Further, Fanny Assingham, "addicted to sympathy," becomes "laughably infatuate." I disagree only when Fussell contends that sympathy is irrational, self-congratulatory, and easily deceived, and that since James sympathizes with Isabel we must too. Clare R. Goldfarb in "Matriarchy in the Late Novels of Henry James" (*RS* 49:231–41) discusses key women in *The Wings of the Dove*, *The Ambassadors*, and *The Golden Bowl*. Mrs. Lowder and Mrs. Newsome are treated first: "Each is a maternal figure who desires unequivocal authority in her real or adopted family as well as in her outside domain. Each one seeks to create a matriarchy which allows no room for dissidents . . . or outsiders." British Mrs. Lowder is materialistic, greedy, inhumane; but Mrs. Newsome, even worse, "is a comment on the worst features of American society." By contrast Maggie Verver and Charlotte Stant in *The Golden Bowl* are active "parents" to passive Adam Verver and Prince Amerigo, since each woman wants control. Maggie pushes Adam from the nest, welcomes the Prince home as prodigal son, will be boss and restore "proper relationships." Charlotte is a poor parent, not wanting either Maggie or the Prince to grow up.

Carl Malmgren's heavy "Henry James's Major Phase: Making Room for the Reader" (*HJR* 3:17–23) shows that in his "major phase" James deliberately bewilders his readers by presenting characters who are uncertain, so as to retreat and thus require reader advancement into his fictive world. Much here is totally obvious though chopped wondrous fine, then jargonized. Thomas M. Leitch adduces evidence in "The Editor as Hero: Henry James and the New York Edition" (*HJR* 3:24–32) to present James as a hero. He revised fiction for the New York Edition "to increase his emphasis . . . on the power of the imaginative consciousness to transform the world through the act of seeing." Revising also represents James's successful effort at making himself into his own "ideal reader."

iv. Criticism: Individual Novels

Criticism of individual novels this year has been held to a minimum except for *The Awkward Age*, *The Ambassadors*, and especially *The Portrait of a Lady*. The few other studies of novels are evenly spread chronologically.

In her "Roderick Hudson: A Centennial Reading" (*HJR* 2:172–98), a wise essay on James's first real novel, A. R. Tintner reviews critical currents in chronological order, sees major changes in 1921, the 1940s, the early 1960s, and again in the 1970s. She then identifies art and literary sources (or at least analogues) for *Roderick Hudson* —in antique sculpture, American painting, Novalis, Wordsworthian nature and Tennysonian "dying," minor French painters, Disraeli, French romanticists, Ariosto, and so on. Best here is Tintner's handling of revisions by James of *Roderick Hudson*: American references are pointed out, Gloriani becomes a superinternationalized cosmopolite, Prince Casamassima is put more firmly in the tradition of Italian art, major-phase imagery increases, and Christina Light's oriental perversity and cosmopolitanism are stressed. In seeking sources and parallels so assiduously, does Tintner ignore coincidence and James's originality too much?

The Portrait of a Lady has been treated to five quite varied essays this year. A. R. Tintner in "The Centennial of 1876 and *The Portrait of a Lady*" (*MarkhamR* 10:27–29) tries with more valor than persuasiveness to show that the function of the one mentioned date— 1876—in the novel may be for irony: in the centennial of America's independence Isabel Archer loses hers. Tintner's essay relates to her earlier "Centennial" reading of "An International Episode" (see *ALS 1979*, 109–10). Michael E. Connaughton in "American English and the International Theme in *The Portrait of a Lady*" (*MQ* 22:137–46) proves that, contrary to his later aim "to achieve a uniform Anglo-American idiom," James in *The Portrait of a Lady* "employs distinctive British and American word usage . . . to create linguistically realistic speech patterns and to support his conception of character." Connaughton considers the speech habits of Lord Warburton, Ralph Touchett and his father, and "the American women [in the novel, who] make both the best [Henrietta Stackpole] and the worst [Isabel] case for James's consciousness of dialect." Darlene Harbour Unrue's "The Occult Metaphor as Technique in *The Portrait of a Lady*" (*HJR* 2:199–203) is a packed little essay showing that James in chapter 42 of the novel uses images of the occult—blight, evil eye, gulf, darkness, shadow, moon—to present a threatened Isabel pivoting between present and past, in the grip of mesmeric, necromantic Gilbert Osmond. J. T. Laird in "Cracks in Precious Objects: Aestheticism and Humanity in *The Portrait of a Lady*" (*AL* 52:643–48) undertakes to correct Dorothea Krook's view that James only tentatively presents the theme of the conflict between the aesthetic and the moral in this novel. Laird shows the significance of two images involving Madame Merle, a porcelain pot (chapter 19) and a porcelain cup (chapter 49). The precious objects appear artistic but their close-up evidence of damage symbolizes "moral flaws."

The "implications" in the title of Ruth Evelyn Quebe's solid essay "*The Bostonians*: Some Historical Sources and Their Implications" (*CentR* 125:80–100) are sexual, political, and cultural ones. Quebe reveals the sources of ex-Confederate lawyer-journalist Basil Ransom's stoical skepticism and relates it to James's "minority cynicism" and espousal of diminished American individualism. She discusses old-fashioned pure, submissive, domestic femininity, as embodied in the early Verena Tarrant, and identifies contemporary forces changing it: materialism, social climbing, sensational journalism, Boston reform movements, and women's-rights associations and conventions. Quebe relates spiritual and quack healing to the Tarrants and offers historical models for the main female characters in *The Bostonians* (Elizabeth Stanton, Susan B. Anthony, Victoria Woodhull, Lucy Stone, and Mary Walker).

Randall Craig offers a hermeneutic reading in " 'Read[ing] the Unspoken into the Spoken': Interpreting *What Maisie Knew*" (*HJR* 2:204–12). Craig too closely equates Maisie with immature readers of the morally fastidious and artistically empty fiction of the 1890s and suggests that James's depiction of his heroine's maturing may imply his hope that his readers will also mature morally and aesthetically. The sensitive girl learns to "read" her various challenges, just as we must learn to "replicate Maisie's interpretive and linguistic proficiency" so as "hermeneutically [to] produce, not romantically consume the text."

The Awkward Age continues to tease critics. The awkwardness discussed by Stuart Culver in "Censorship and Intimacy: Awkwardness in *The Awkward Age*" (*ELH* 48:368–86) is "the sense of a difference between the public form of expression and the essentially private source of its significance." A kind of censorship precedes public representation. French naturalists asked readers to suspend moral judgments as they read amoral, photographic works, but the British sought to carry morality straight through eclectic readings. "The late style is James's attempt to steer between the Scylla of French triviality and the Charybdis of British reserve, to address interesting subjects without disregarding their moral implications." More strained is "The Case for Mrs. Brookenham" by Jean Frantz Blackall (*HJR* 2:155–61), which tries too hard to find virtue in duplicitous Mrs. Brook's wit, imagination, social creativity, and suggestive manners and assumed attitudes. The woman uses these weapons to influence Vanderbank. The critic concludes by touching on James's debt in *The Awkward Age* to William Makepeace Thackeray's *The Newcomes* (see R. D. McMaster's essay on Thackeray and James [*ALS 1978*, 93–94], cited by Blackall).

Joseph Halpern in "Changing Patterns in Henry James" (*SHR* 15:53–66) elaborates on the theory that supposedly inconclusive, plotless fictions by James are "grounded not in change and linear development but in exchange and chiasmus." The best model—but not the only one—to validate this thesis is *The Sacred Fount*, in which "'chiasmus and exchange find their correlative in . . . vampirism," which in James is "one form of . . . symmetry." At the end of the novel the narrator's theory as to the characters' actions is stalemated by Mrs. Brissenden's "counterposed system," and thus a third "plot" is activated in the mind of the reader as he or she tries to resolve James's terminal "nescience, reticence, and ambiguity."

The Ambassadors has occasioned two antitradition essays this year. Paul Rosenzweig in "James's 'Special-Green Vision': *The Ambassadors*" (*SNNTS* 13:367–87) analyzes the novel as an untraditional city pastoral, by virtue of its garden imagery, garden scenes, and "a host of elements and values traditionally associated with the pastoral vision." Lambert Strether's "inaction," James's conveying of a melancholy "sense of time and death," and his hero's ability to associate with a diminished social group all attest to James's respect, however unconscious, for "the pastoral ideal." The novel's style also has pastoral elements: ritualistic meal after garden retreat, "union of art and nature" in congenial setting, heroine resembling rural maiden, flower and color tropes, aptness of indirection in scene rendering, wistfulness consequent on "a . . . sense of loss." Untraditional in a different way is Gordon S. Haight's startling essay entitled "Strether's Chad Newsome: A Reading of James's *The Ambassadors*" in *From Smollett to James: Studies in the Novels and Other Essays Presented to Edgar Johnson*, ed. Samuel I. Mintz *et al.* (Virginia), pp. 261–76. Haight demonstrates that "the real Chad is a very different man from the glamorous youth Strether's romantic imagination has created. . . . In retrospect we realize that Chad was actually ready to go home when Strether arrived. But he was finding it awkward to break away from his mistress, and he meant to use Strether's embassy to help end the liaison, which after three years was beginning to pall."

"An Archetypal Reading of *The Golden Bowl*: Maggie Verver as Questor" (*ALR* 14:52–61) by Clare Goldfarb begins by asserting that we cannot finally judge Maggie but should try to understand her responsibly. Goldfarb sees her as "a heroine whose task it is to go in search of the Grail." Wanting to relate meaningfully to her husband, she ends instead by defining "an identity for her father." Regal, fertility, and sterility imagery coalesces to depict Adam Verver as impotent Fisher King, the Principino as possible royal heir, American City as "a waste land," and Maggie as restorative, chivalric heroine of "ritual and romance." Interesting, but how do Prince Amerigo, Fanny Assingham, and the golden bowl function in this Grail tale?

v. Criticism: Individual Tales

Surprisingly few of James's short stories and nouvelles—only six—were treated to separate essay coverage this year. "The Turn of the Screw" naturally proved most popular, with "The Aspern Papers" and "The Beast in the Jungle" also doing well.

In a major revaluation entitled "The Key to the Palpable Past: A Study of Miss Tina in *The Aspern Papers*" (*HJR* 3:4–10) Barbara Jensen-Osinski reviews work by nine previous critics (commending where she can but stating flatly that Tina Bordereau "is neither so innocent . . . nor so crude and jaundiced as" they variously believe) and then challenges all of us to see (past the psychologically blind and deaf, prejudiced, smug editor-narrator) to heroic Tina. She is astute, uncoy, with a "capacity for wonder," loyal to her aunt Juliana Bordereau and to old Venice, "not to be bought or pushed around," not in love, and trying to be reasonable to opposing people. Contrary and slighter is Barbara Currier Bell's "Beyond Irony in Henry James: *The Aspern Papers*" (*SNNTS* 13:282–93). It is an examination of James's attitude that "problems of epistemology are . . . coextensive with problems of morality," as representatively revealed in "The Aspern Papers." James dramatizes the rightness of our seeking knowledge and identity, as well as the morality of our responsibly doing so, by ironically distorting parallels between elements in the novel and the Garden of Eden story. Juliana Bordereau is an evil divinity; her Venetian garden, ugly; the narrator, not heroic but self-deceivingly satanic; and young Miss Bordereau, frail only at first.

Peter W. Lock in " 'The Figure in the Carpet': The Text as Riddle and Force" (*NCF* 36:157–75) sees "The Figure in the Carpet" as close to absurd if read for meaning but exciting if "tackled as an exercise in production." Lock means "production" in the sense, after recent French literary critics (especially Hélène Cixous), of a "text . . . held to be a discourse perpetually in the act of structuring itself." Lock's plot summary explicates the vital movement of James's text. Lock notes the libidinous terms of James's phrasing of his "quest and transmission" motif, to show Hugh Vereker's "secret . . . as an attracting . . . *force*" which "links all the characters and possesses their lives," even terminating some. Vereker's figure becomes narrator's text becomes James's lethal laugh at critics. Lock neatly suggests that the name Vereker could derive from *vere* (truth) and *ker* (death): the truth about Vereker does not set his admirers free.

"The Turn of the Screw" got five more turns this year. John Harmon McElroy begins "The Mysteries at Bly" (*ArQ* 37:214–36) by dividing the story's critics into apparitionists, hallucinationists, and those who believe "that James intended this novella to be all things to all readers, that no one can be 'really sure of what is happening.'" The more I read about this intriguing story the more I align myself with the third group. Here goes again.

McElroy, after a detailed analysis of the story, concludes that both the governess and Miles are innocent of wrong-doing but fatally "fight . . . each other for their lives." McElroy stunningly suggests that Miles's sin at school was not any variation of depravity but simply a threat to write home about unprincipled school authorities. For whom does the governess write her manuscript?—Linda S. Kauffman theorizes in "The Author of Our Woe: Virtue Recorded in *The Turn of the Screw*" (*NCF* 36:176–92) that it is hopelessly addressed to her uncaring Harley Street employer, whose worshipped image she has largely invented and later "sustain[s] . . . by writing." Thus she converts her passion into literary art, which is helped along by her reading, her frenzied seeing, and her aim to be pleasing in her employer's eye. Kauffman cleverly suggests that "the second narrator is not a man but a woman" who loves Douglas as Douglas loved the governess, who loved her absent employer. Thus the story is one of love as well as of evil. William R. Goetz in "The 'Frame' of *The Turn of the Screw*: Framing the Reader In" (*SSF* 18:71–74) sees "the short 'frame' section that precedes the governess's narrative" as a "scene by means of which James tells us how to read his tale." The frame is an oral introduction of a written text and is spoken to a fatuous, wrongly literal-minded audience which may query Douglas but not the governess. The frame has no close, however; that is, it has no epilogue. In "Atmosphere as Triggering Device in *The Turn of the Screw*" (*SSF* 18:293–99) Fred L. Milne elaborates an insight from Thomas M. Cranfill and Robert L. Clark (see *ALS 1965*, 79) that the governess's seizures come when poor light obscures her vision, and also come during times of silence and chill. Milne asserts that "particular conditions of light and sound . . . *induce* the hallucinations" in the young woman, who, further, is "most susceptible to these atmospheric conditions when in a self-congratulatory state of mind." And Robert W. Hill, Jr., in "A Counterclockwise Turn in James's 'The Turn of the Screw'" (*TCL* 27: 53–71) follows James's prefatory suggestion that readers ought to examine the greatest difficulty in his tale and neglect lesser ones. To Hill, Miles is that greatest difficulty. Building on risky assumptions, Hill offers up Miles as "already . . . informed with carnal knowledge of a nature" beyond the governess's experience either in life or in reading, devilishly attracting the naive young woman, because of precocious sexual desire, into believing in ghosts that he invents.

The neglected short story "The Two Faces" is accorded major, perhaps even definitive treatment by J. Peter Dyson in "Perfection, Beauty and Suffering in 'The Two Faces'" (*HJR* 2:116–25). Dyson regards the story as "a distillation of much that he [James] has been dealing with fictionally over the preceding twenty years and more": oblique vision as aid to perception and consciousness, social signals to depict milieu, talented and histrionic villainess controlling world of nuance, in-but-out observer measuring behavior in light and shade, the "baroque exuberance" of operatic social event with country house as theater and central female as *prima donna assoluta*, social "perfection" as antithesis to beauty (enhanced by suffering), and perfected consciousness vs. unconscious vulnerability.

Janice H. Harris advances an unconvincing theory in "Bushes, Bears, and 'The Beast in the Jungle'" (*SSF* 18:147–54). It is that James's language and imagery in the story suggest that the life of John Marcher, its hero, has "an atmosphere of energy and engagement." Harris admits that in passages which she quotes James may be using irony. (The odd title of the essay was inspired by "certain gestalt perception cards.") Far better is Elizabeth Shapland's "Duration and Frequency: Prominent Aspects of Time in Henry James's 'The Beast in the Jungle'" (*PLL* 17:33–47), which begins with a summary of Gérard Genette's "notions of duration and frequency of events in fiction." Duration concerns relationship of continuation of historical event to that of story event. Frequencies, i.e., relative incidence of story events and story sections reporting them, are singulative (telling event one or *n* times if it happened one or *n* times, respectively), repetitive (telling one event two or *n* times), and iterative (pertinently telling just once events having something in common). Shapland structuralistically applies Genette's notions to extendings and sequencings of the 142 narrative segments in "The Beast in the Jungle." She admits that Genette's conclusions, using Marcel Proust's *A la recherche du temps perdu*, differ from hers, because Proust and James have "thematic differences." She further distinguishes between summary and specific story sequences in James. She offers a table of 23 "macro-sequences" (sequences "regrouped by unity of time"). Types of frequencies "interlock." From this complex essay I conclude that (1) such criticism is virtually useless in enhancing James's reader pleasure, (2) much of it is obvious to one of common sense though it displays impressive jargon, and (3) "many years" and then more years transpire in the course of this still-unravished masterpiece of short fiction.

E. C. Curtsinger, Jr., in "Henry James's Farewell in 'The Velvet Glove'" (*SSF* 18:164–69) wrongly rebukes previous interpreters of the tale and theorizes instead that in the story, about an established novelist's refusal to puff a beautiful neophyte authoress's tawdry work, James offers in the young beauty "the embodied imagination of James's writer" and "the last of a long series of varying portraits of the imagination." Neatly enough adducing evidence from earlier fiction by James, Curtsinger must, to force his reading, disconnect James the realistic narrative voice too thoroughly from James's romantic imagination.

vi. Criticism: Specific Nonfictional Work

Nonfictional works by James were almost totally ignored this year. "The Three Travelers in *English Hours*" (*HJR* 2:167–71) is Leon Edel's introduction to a forthcoming reprint of James's *English Hours*, printed early in sneak-preview fashion. Edel notes that James's English essays reveal the author first as a sentimental tourist in his 20s; second as an observant stranger now in his 30s; third as an older writer, long resident in England and now "alien only in name." Edel analyzes James's awareness of the pluses and minuses of the British social structure, of England's imperial past and present, of London's regions and views. Edel's best touch here is the suggestion that James's ultimate praise of Robert Browning contains James's own credo.

University of Pittsburgh

8. Pound and Eliot

George Bornstein and Stuart Y. McDougal

i. Pound

The explosion in Pound studies that produced 18 books and over 150 other items in the previous two years subsided somewhat in 1981. The resultant pause should allow time for the Poundian virtue of excernment to select the components of a new consensus, one surely more capable if not more comfortable in dealing with *The Cantos*. During this period, Pound scholarship often has turned inward upon itself to gloss and expound Pound's frequently difficult works and their particular tradition. Now that their poet's value is secure, Poundians can look outward again. We need, for example, less mere source study and more use of contemporary concepts of literary influence, less mere explication and more genuinely comparative research. The rich trove of surviving manuscripts still awaits proper utilization. And finally, over half a century after Pound denounced "obstructors of knowledge, obstructors of distribution" for "obscuring the texts," the state of his own texts remains a scandal. The Ezra Pound Literary Property Trust, New Directions, and the scholarly community should cooperate in producing a uniform, reliable edition of the complete works, with variorum readings for the poetry. That way, in the language of the last complete canto, if we cannot make Cosmos, we can still achieve the possible.

a. **Text and Biography.** Unlike past years, 1981 produced no new major volume of Pound's still widely scattered texts. The slender *Ezra Pound: From Syria*, ed. Robin Skelton (Copper Canyon), did appear in an edition limited to 250 copies. It contains halftone reproductions of the original manuscript and much-revised typescript to-

George Bornstein has contributed the section on Pound and Stuart Y. Mc-Dougal the section on Eliot.—*ed.*

gether with an introduction by the editor sketching the history of
Pound's work on this early Provençal adaptation. Scholars unable to
obtain the rare Copper Canyon volume may consult Skelton's " 'From
Syria': The Worksheets, Proofs, and Text" (*MHRev* 59:60–92). Several other pieces made their way into journals. The delayed Ezra
Pound triple number of *Agenda* (17,iii–iv; 18,i:1979–80) opens with
a full draft of Canto 115 partially published earlier. "Some Letters to
William Cookson, 1956–1970" (pp. 5–48) includes numerous facsimiles in late Poundian style on political and literary matters, including the *Confucius to Cummings* anthology. Sprinkled throughout
the issue are reprints of fugitive pieces, mostly prose, of which
"Four Uncollected Literary Essays" (on Lytton Strachey, Arthur
Symons, Harold Monro, and Laurence Binyon) merit most attention.

Brita Lindberg-Seyersted straightens out the text and context of
six previously published "Letters from Ezra Pound to Joseph Brewer"
(*Paideuma* 10:369–82). Brewer, president of Olivet College where
Ford Madox Ford tried to entice Pound to join him, became the unwitting recipient of vintage Poundian abuse: "am writing this to say
AGAIN that *all* you blighted American College Presidents ought to
be boiled in [oil]." Elsewhere, Lindberg-Seyersted sensibly surveys
the difficulties of editing Pound's letters in "A Note on Ezra Pound
as Letter-Writer" (*Edda* 1:59–60). In "Breaking the Silence: the
Interview of Vanni Ronsisvalle and Pier Paolo Pasolini with Ezra
Pound in 1968" (*Paideuma* 10:331–45) David Anderson provides
the text of Pound's responses to questions for an Italian television
documentary. Anderson briefly describes both the circumstances of
the interview and Pasolini's idiosyncratic interpretation of Pound,
which derived Pound's "reactionary ideology" from his "peasant
background."

Biographical contributions focused on two areas—the relation
with H. D. and the charges of treason stemming from the radio
broadcasts. References to Pound dot Susan Stanford Friedman's
Psyche Reborn: The Emergence of H. D. (Indiana). The book
rightly places imagism as only one episode of a distinguished career.
Pound sometimes appears in an unflattering light, particularly in his
incarnation as the dashing young poet George Lowndes in H. D.'s
novel *Her*. Michael King's "Go, Little Book: Ezra Pound, Hilda Doo-
little, and 'Hilda's Book' " (*Paideuma* 10:347–60) has few new facts

but does include a useful biographical discussion of the poems in Hilda's "book."

Of the writers on Pound's wartime broadcasting and subsequent sentence, E. Fuller Torrey in his controversial "The Protection of Ezra Pound" (*Psychology Today* 15:57–62) claims most notice. Himself a psychiatrist at St. Elizabeths, Torrey used the Freedom of Information Act to gain access to pertinent hospital records. According to Torrey, the documents show that Pound was sane rather than psychotic and that Dr. Winfred Overholser orchestrated the protective efforts of both prosecution and defense doctors in a "flagrant example of how psychiatrists can abuse their power." If corroborated, such charges would reshape thinking about the last quarter-century of Pound's life; however, see *Paideuma* 11(1982):188 for a timely caution by Carroll F. Terrell, who has also inspected the files. Whatever their ultimate fate, Torrey's claims do harmonize with Ben D. Kimpel and T.C. Duncan Eaves' treatment of the earlier period before Pound's trial and committal in "More on Pound's Prison Experience" (*AL* 53:469–78). Kimpel and Eaves quote extensively from Army psychiatrists who examined Pound in Italy in concluding that "none of these documents suggests that Pound was 'insane' in the usual sense of that word." The other three pieces offer less drama. Pound's daughter Mary de Rachewiltz tries unsuccessfully to present her father as a martyr to free speech in "Fragments of an Atmosphere" (*Agenda* 17/18:157–70); Richard Reid more candidly marshals quotations from the speeches toward an indecisive conclusion in "Ezra Pound Asking" (*Agenda* 17/18:171–86); and David Feldman, a former guard at the Pisan D.T.C., sketches a vignette of "Ezra Pound: A Poet in a Cage" (*Paideuma* 10:361–65). Finally, Desmond O'Grady's "Ezra Pound: A Personal Memoir" paints an appealing but politically naive picture of the aged poet back in Italy after his release.

b. **General Studies.** Written by British scholars, the two general books this year testify to Pound's growing transatlantic reputation. They differ markedly in value. Alan Durant's *Ezra Pound, Identity in Crisis: A Fundamental Reassessment of the Poet and his Work* (Barnes and Noble) hardly lives up to the large claims of its title. Instead, Durant offers potted summaries of fashionable French theories, particularly those of Jacques Lacan, into which he then forces Pound's career. The premise that "the ubiquitous inscription of the phallus in the *Cantos* and elsewhere in Pound's writing repeats precisely an anxiety about castration" becomes the master theme of Durant's treatment of Pound's poetry, poetics, and politics. Instead of a needed examination of sexuality in Pound's work, *Identity in Crisis* provides a modish fantasy inadequately informed by past scholarship. Had Durant made use, for example, of Richard Sieburth's study of Pound and Remy de Gourmont, William Chace's work on Pound's politics, or Herbert Schneidau and Michael Bernstein's various applications of recent theory, he would not have found many topics in his own volume so previously slighted as he maintains. Combined with frequent misreadings and an often opaque style, the problems in method and research result in a work of little use to Poundians. Durant intends his book "to reveal the shortcomings of Pound's understanding of properties of discourse," but he more often exposes his own.

Ian F. A. Bell does better in his *Critic as Scientist: The Modernist Poetics of Ezra Pound* (Methuen). Starting from Pound's penchant for scientific terminology, Bell largely succeeds in his ambition "to demonstrate the relationship between Pound's use of scientific analogy and the more familiar areas of his critical concerns, and to argue that his efforts to create a poetics informed by the discipline of science were the characteristic gestures of his modernity." Perhaps the greatest strength of the study is its placing of early 20th-century scientific thought in a broader cultural milieu. Familiar figures like Fenollosa and Agassiz appear in a new light, along with a host of more rarely discussed authors like the littérateur Hudson Maxim or the physiologist Louis Berman. Occasionally, Bell's avoidance of direct influence in favor of ideas "in the air" leads to digression or unnecessary detail. Some editorial cutting would have led to a more focused argument, and the concluding meditation on closed vs. open form does not always persuade. But overall, *Critic as Scientist* ranks as the fullest exploration of its subject and establishes Bell as a Poundian worth listening to.

Two established American scholars supply provocative perspectives on Pound in relation to both poetic tradition and contemporary theory. In the Pound chapter of her *The Poetics of Indeterminacy: Rimbaud to Cage* (Princeton) Marjorie Perloff dissociates Pound from the "symbolist" high modernism of Yeats, Eliot, or Stevens. She places him instead in an "other tradition" deriving from Rimbaud and valuing indeterminacy, free play, and concern for poetic surface in a view of poetry as "word-system." Perloff's analogies to montage and to contemporary painting clarify the documentary juxtapositions of the Malatesta cantos and result in a particularly suggestive mapping of "continuities" and "cuts" in Canto 74 from the Pisan sequence. Yet in stressing the poem's self-reflexive concern for its own flat documentary surface, Perloff sometimes confuses its refusal of symbolism with a refusal of presentation or of gesture toward a world beyond itself. Exactly that point underlies Hugh Kenner's distinction between Eliot and Pound: "The Possum in the Cave" in *Allegory and Representation*, ed. Stephen J. Greenblatt (Hopkins), pp. 128–44. Contrasting Pound's pilgrimage to Montségur in the Pyrenees with Eliot's visit to French cave paintings, Kenner emphasizes the insistently mimetic quality by which Pound's words point to a reality verifiable outside the poem. In a fine response to deconstructionist theory, he proposes that we affirm not the metaphysical but rather the physical as a stay against nihilism. A third book, Guy Davenport's *Geography of the Imagination* (North Point), includes welcome reprints of several previously published essays on Pound.

The general articles in journals this year disappoint. The best of them, Ian F. A. Bell's "Pound's Vortex: Shapes Ancient and Modern" (*Paideuma* 10:243–71), may be consulted more conveniently in *Critic as Scientist*. Of the four broad studies in the *Agenda* special issue, Michael Alexander's "Pound's Sense of Humor" (17/18: 122–29) deserves reading as a timely reminder of Pound's comic side. Charles Berezin's "Poetry and Politics in Ezra Pound" (*PR* 48: 262–79) deals more with politics than with poetry. Berezin starts well by exploding many Pound critics' tendency to dismiss or devalue his antisemitism, but the subsequent linkage of that bias with fascism and social credit trails off into a standard left-wing view buttressed mainly by quotation from Engels.

c. **The Shorter Poems and Relation to Other Writers.**   Studies of Pound's lyrics overlapped so often with literary influence this year that the two categories can best be treated together.

The largest body of work concerned the Orient and Pound's career as translator. Of the three essays on Pound's adherence to

Fenollosa's generally rejected notion of Chinese characters as pictographs, Scott Johnson's modest "The 'Tools' of the Ideogramic Method" (*Paideuma* 10:525–32) succeeds best. Johnson helpfully traces the line from the early *Shuo Wen* dictionary and *Liu-shu* etymologies through Robert Morrison's unreliable dictionary to Fenollosa and finally to Pound. Two other commentators try to rescue aspects of Pound's adherence to Fenollosa. In "Kennedy, Fenollosa, and the Chinese Character" (*Agenda* 17/18:220–37) Peter Makin identifies the late sinologist George Kennedy of Yale as the chief nemesis of the Pound-Fenollosa view and uses the *Shuo Wen* dictionary among other documents to reveal inconsistencies in Kennedy's attacks. Makin does succeed in holding open the possibility that a metaphoric process may have affected the original formation of Chinese characters and even their later interpretation, but his own admission that he does "not speak Chinese, or read it without a crib" undermines the authority of his assertions. Akiko Miyake's rambling "Contemplation East and West: A Defense of Fenollosa's Synthetic Language and Its Influence on Ezra Pound" (*Paideuma* 10:533–70) at least has the merit of consulting the manuscript drafts for Fenollosa's original lecture, of which Pound later edited the latter version as the famous essay. Miyake presents Fenollosa's ideas of luminous Chinese language in terms of esoteric Buddhism and Western Hegelianism, which Pound conflated with medieval mystic insights. By the end of her long article she seems to have confused "parallelism" with "defense."

Hiroko Uno's "['Changgan Xing'] by Li Po and Its Translation by Ezra Pound" (*Paideuma* 10: 509–23) presents a paraphrase, character-by-character literal translation, and commentary on the materials behind "The River-Merchant's Wife: A Letter." Whether on formal matters like line division and manipulation of time or semantic ones like the legend behind the "look out" (an allusion to Mt. Looking-Out-For-A-Husband), Uno comments incisively and helpfully. An alternate translation by Xu Qi-Ping appears later in the same issue (10:587–88). Taken together, Nobuko Tsukui's translation of Zeami Motokiyo's Japanese play *Yoro* and Akiko Miyake's accompanying "Commentary" (*Paideuma* 10:383–402) offer a chance to evaluate better Pound's own translation and notes. Lastly in this category, Hans-Joachim Zimmermann's labored but interesting "Ezra Pound, 'A Song of the Degrees': Chinese Clarity versus Alchemical

Confusion" (*Paideuma* 10:225–41) inquires into Chinese and al-chemical backgrounds of Pound's sequence, albeit with little sensitivity to the comic tone.

Studies of Pound's relation to Western tradition run the gamut from classical times to the present. One of the solidest, Edgar M. Glenn's "Pound and Ovid" (*Paideuma* 10:625–34), traces Pound's involvement with the Latin poet from 1902 onward. As opposed to the metamorphic tradition mapped by Sister Bernetta Quinn, Glenn stresses structural correlations between *The Metamorphoses* and *The Cantos* as dramatizing "what the authors perceive in the material that they present." Glenn's useful groundwork whets the appetite for important forthcoming studies by Ronald Thomas and Lillian Feder, both already underway. On a different classical author, Thomas' "The Catullan Landscape in Pound's Poetry" (*ConP* 4,i: 66–78) accurately charts the Catullan landscape of Lake Garda and the village Sirmio from the early verse through *The Cantos*.

The distinguished translator Robert Fitzgerald has written an essay at once graceful and brilliant on Pound's attitude toward his favorite medieval poet and modern translator. "Mirroring the *Commedia*: An Appreciation of Laurence Binyon's Version" (*Paideuma* 10:489–508) sensitively explores Pound's growing enthusiasm for Binyon's work. Clarifying Pound's contribution to the translation and its reception, Fitzgerald reprints part of Pound's previously untranslated review of the *Purgatorio* for an Italian journal. Also dealing with medieval material, Marianne Korn emphasizes the indeterminacy of the author in "Truth Near Perigord" (*Paideuma* 10:571–79).

Two articles illuminate Pound's relation to writers closer to his own time. In " 'What Porridge Had John Keats?': Pound's 'L'Art' and Browning's 'Popularity' " (*Paideuma* 10:303–06) George Bornstein demonstrates that Pound's cryptic association of the murex (a Mediterranean shellfish used to make Tyrian purple dye) with Keats derives from Browning's earlier usage. Both poets saw Keats as the neglected innovator of techniques later popularized by more successful Victorian poetasters. Invoking faint echoes of Masters in Pound's verse, Ian F. A. Bell's "In the Real Tradition: Edgar Lee Masters and Hugh Selwyn Mauberley" (*Criticism* 23:141–54) reminds us of Pound's persistently favorable view of the *Spoon River Anthology*, particularly during the second decade of the century. Bell calls attention to the neglected essay on "Webster Ford" (Mas-

ters' early pseudonym) to indicate how Pound viewed Masters as a
sort of American Villon capable of direct speech and concrete presentation of character.

Pound's influence on later writers continues to draw attention.
Rachael Blau Duplessis' "Oppen and Pound" is the most pertinent
to Pound scholars of the essays in the special George Oppen number
of *Paideuma* (10:i). A forthcoming expanded version of the issue
in book form will complement the similarly produced volumes on
Louis Zukofsky: Man and Poet and *Basil Bunting: Man and Poet*
(NPF). Clark Emery has two poems on Pound, "Father William"
and "St. Elizabeth," in *Paideuma* 10:405–09. Elsewhere, Robert
Creeley's personal statement "Why Pound!?!" appears in *Agenda*
17/18:198–99. Finally, the resourceful editor of *Paideuma*, Carroll
F. Terrell, has announced the formation of a new journal, *Sagetrieb*,
devoted to "major poets in the Pound-Williams tradition."

d. **The Cantos.** The 612 pages of *A Concordance to Ezra Pound's
Cantos* by Robert J. Dilligan, James W. Parins, and Todd K. Bender
(Garland) constitute a welcome though flawed research tool. The
computer-generated text divides into four groupings: English words
and Arabic numbers; "non-English words in the Roman alphabet,
words in the Greek alphabet, and Chinese ideograms"; and word
frequencies first in alphabetical order and then in rank order. The
unclear logic of some editorial decisions deserves attention here
because this book will be widely used. For example, the concordance
prints the 199 uses of "against" but consigns the 93 of "thus" to the
limbo of "omitted words," while needlessly distinguishing the sole
appearance of plain "Alsace Lorraine" from the two of hyphenated
"Alsace-Lorraine." Readers interested in all the appearances of a
proper noun like "Adams" or "Ixotta" will need to consult both the
English and foreign lists for separate references and to remember
that a non-English word like "Argicida" will appear in the English
list if its context is English. On a more basic level, the editors naively
take the 1975 New Directions text as definitive, despite its numerous
misprints and other errors. Had they consulted with Pound scholars,
or even followed Barbara Eastman's list of cruxes in *Ezra Pound's
Cantos: The Story of the Text* (NPF, 1979), the concordance would
be more valuable because more reliable. Although the high cost of
the volume guarantees that it will be consulted only in libraries,

we had best instruct our students both in the use of the concordance and in avoidance of its abuse.

Invention outstrips conviction in the only critical book on Pound's epic this year, Forrest Read's *'76: One World and The Cantos of Ezra Pound* (North Carolina). Read sees *The Cantos* as "an epic of revolution" proferring the "three paideumas" of Eleusis, Kung, and John Adams in a unified world view. The American Revolution presents the master paradigm of the poem, particularly through its great documents—the Declaration of Independence and the Constitution. Read construes his paradigm hermetically through esoteric interpretation of the Great Seal of the United States and the neopagan *Little Review* calendar of 1922. This results in elaborate numerologies and arcana which increasingly strain credulity, as does the acknowledged "paucity" of external evidence. Because the late Forrest Read knew so much about Pound, many byways of his argument elicit interest. But the overall thesis will strike most scholars as eccentric.

The best shorter work on *The Cantos* involves clusters of the longer poem. As in past years, I will simply mention in passing that *Paideuma* prints numerous notes on individual cantos (this year Cantos 13, 52, 74, 75, 81, and 104); in addition, Ben D. Kimpel and T. C. Duncan Eaves gloss Jewish allusions from 35 and 74 in *MP* (78: 285–88) and one to Mozart from 76 in *Expl* (40:43). Neither of the two most general articles carries a convincing new thesis, although Walter Baumann's "Ezra Pound and Magic: Old World Tricks in a New World Poem" (*Paideuma* 10:209–24) contains more incidental illumination than does Peter Revell's wandering and elementary chapter, "Toward the Great Healing: The Cantos of Ezra Pound," in his *Quest in Modern American Poetry* (Barnes and Noble).

Two complementary articles revise previous understanding of Pound's historicism in the Malatesta cantos (8–11). Michael F. Harper's "Truth and Calliope: Ezra Pound's Malatesta" (*PMLA* 96: 86–103) defends Pound's choice of hero. Pound noticed that influential portraits of Sigismundo Malatesta as tyrant, such as Burckhardt's, derived ultimately from the biased account of his great antagonist Pius II; in reaction, Pound ransacked several libraries and used particularly the documents assembled in Charles Yriarte's 1882 *Un Condottiere au xvᵉ siècle* to fashion an alternate view. Harper concludes by cautioning against Riddel's recent deconstruction of so referential a poem into "a signifying machine." In "The Poet as Historian: Researching the Malatesta Cantos" (*Paideuma* 10:283–91) Daniel Bornstein gratifyingly locates Pound's own copy of Yriarte and describes its annotation in a way that generally supports Harper's claims. The author also suggests that Pound drew on the long section on Sigismundo in Broglio di Tartaglia's unpublished *Cronaca Universale*. The pleasing focus of both articles contrasts with the rambling diffuseness of Andrew J. Kappel's "The Reading and Writing of a Modern *Paradiso*: Ezra Pound and the Books of Paradise" (*TCL* 27:223–46), which emphasizes Pound's use of quotation in the later cantos.

The remaining articles may be covered more briefly. Helen M. Dennis' interesting suggestions in "The Eleusinian Mysteries as an Organizing Principle in *The Pisan Cantos*" (*Paideuma* 10:273–82) would have more weight had she consulted Leon Surette's recent *A Light from Eleusis: A Study of Ezra Pound's Cantos* (Oxford, 1979). Of the four pertinent pieces in *Agenda*, Moelwyn Merchant's on "The Coke Cantos" (17/18:76–85) has at least the merit of using letters from Pound to the author to support a study of Cantos 107–109 proposing parallels between Coke's situation in 17th-century England and Pound's in 20th-century America. The best of the other three, A. D. Moody's "Cantos I–III: Craft and Vision" (17/18:103–17) offers a sort of New Critical reading unencumbered by recent research. Finally, Philip Furia's "Pound and Blake on Hell" (*Paideuma* 10:599–601) attributes Pound's treatment of printing in Cantos 14–16 to Blake's description of his own method in *The Marriage of Heaven and Hell*: "by printing in the infernal method by corrosives, which in hell are salutary and medicinal, melting apparent surfaces away, and displaying the infinite which was hid." It is unclear whether the description fits the current state of Pound studies or only their final goal.

ii. Eliot

This year's work on T. S. Eliot showed a sharp increase of interest in his criticism, as well as a continuation of the re-examination of his relationship with romantic and Victorian literature which has been taking place for several years now. No textual work appeared this year, although A. S. G. Edwards identified six published letters of

Eliot's which Donald Gallup had overlooked ("Addenda to Gallup: T. S. Eliot" [*PBSA* 75:93]). In addition, another bibliography of secondary materials appeared: *T. S. Eliot: A Bibliography of Secondary Works*, comp. Beatrice Ricks (Scarecrow, [1980]). Although this book covers more years than Mildred Martin's *A Half-Century of Eliot Criticism* (1972), it is less well organized and ultimately less useful. Essays are grouped by categories (e.g., "Biography," "Drama," "Poetry," etc.) and are listed alphabetically by author within each category. Few works are annotated and, where included, these annotations are exasperatingly brief. The "topical index" is woefully incomplete and even misleading. Works of this sort can be very important aids to students and scholars, but not when compiled in a slipshod fashion. Finally, the quantity of unpublished Eliot material remains vast; one only hopes that a project on the magnitude of the Cornell Yeats Edition will also be undertaken for Eliot (and Pound, whose texts are in even more deplorable condition).

a. **General Studies.** In *Time in the Poetry of T. S. Eliot* (Barnes and Noble), Nancy Gish defines her objectives as an attempt "to clarify the meaning of time as it develops through the poetry and to show that mood, tone and structure as well as theme are largely determined by ideas of time." Gish pursues this familiar subject single-mindedly but fails to uncover much that is new or striking. This study could just as easily have been written 20 years ago, since it takes little account of recent critical or theoretical work. A more ambitious argument for the reconsideration of Eliot's work is made by Frederic K. Hargreaves, Jr., in "The Concept of Private Meaning in Modern Criticism" (*CritI* 7:727–46). Hargreaves attacks as "radically false" an important tenet of modern criticism, "the assertion that poetry is unique in being able to convey meaning which public language is unable to define and which every individual experiences as an inner state of mind." Hargreaves begins with John Stuart Mill's discussion of the "private meaning of poetry" and then considers the development of this notion in the poetry and critical prose of Pound and Eliot. Drawing upon Wittgenstein's argument against the concept of a private language, Hargreaves convincingly challenges this notion and the criticism based upon its acceptance. His essay should provoke controversy and contribute to the ongoing re-evaluation of modernism.

Jewel Spears Brooker tries to counter the assertion that Eliot was
an "elitist" poet in "Common Ground and Collaboration in T. S.
Eliot" (*CentR* 25:225–38). "Eliot required common ground," Brooker
suggests, "because he thought of art as collaboration, and collaboration is contingent upon common ground." Although it is true that
many of the poetic techniques which Brooker cites ("allusiveness,
juxtaposition, fragmentation, multi-perspectivism, deliberately unfinished surfaces") "are comprehensible as stratagems for forcing
collaboration from a reader," this reader can hardly be considered
"common" in Brooker's sense. Eliot may have deplored the "dissolution of common ground" between writer and reader in the 20th century, but that ground had been a high plateau and not an assembling
point of the multitudes.

"Among the modernist poets Eliot certainly had the most sensitive
nose," asserts Harvey Gross in "The Wild Thyme Unseen: Notes on
Mr. Eliot's Remarkable Nose" (*Antaeus* 40/41:459–73). Gross's discussion of the significance of olfactory images in Eliot's poetry is
amusing and informative. His comments on *Four Quartets*, where
he demonstrates how "through oblique reference to sense" Eliot
"makes us know a sudden moment of spiritual insight," are particularly illuminating and more convincing than the connection Anita
Gandolfo proposes between Eliot's use of the "wild thyme" in *Four
Quartets* and the "wild thyme" of Blake's *Milton* ("Eliot's 'East
Coker'" [*Expl.* 39,iv:24–25]).

b. Relation to Other Writers. In "The Unidentified Ghost: Arthur
Hugh Clough and T. S. Eliot's *Four Quartets*" (*Studies* 70:35–54),
Paul Murray attempts to establish Clough's presence throughout
Eliot's writings. Murray takes his cue from a 1940 letter from Eliot
to John Hayward acknowledging the influence of Blake and Clough
on *East Coker*. Even though there is no mention of Clough in Eliot's
collected essays and reviews, and "no immediately obvious allusions
to the Victorian poet or to his work" in Eliot's poetry, Murray identifies echoes of Clough's poetry which, I must confess, resonate more
in his ear than in mine. Roy J. Booth identifies a source for the
question posed in "Burbank with a Baedeker" ("Who clipped the
lion's wings/And flea'd his rump and pared his claws?") in Sir John
Harington's translation of *Orlando Furioso* ("Eliot's 'Burbank' Poem
and Harington's 'Ariosto'" [*N&Q* 28:431]). In "Eliot's 'Cousin

Nancy' and *The Song of Hiawatha*" (*EA* 34:454–57) John O. Rees establishes the presence of humorous echoes of Longfellow's poem in the opening stanza of Eliot's satiric work. J. Pikoulis calls our attention to the juxtaposition of two poems in Palgrave's *Golden Treasury*, Shakespeare's "Full fathom five thy father lies" (titled "A Sea Dirge") and Webster's "Call for the robin-redbreast and the wren" (titled "A Land Dirge"), which ends with the lines "For keep the wolf far hence, that's foe to men/For with his nails he'll dig them up again" ("Palgrave and Eliot" [*N&Q* 28:432]). He conjectures that Eliot's use of these lines in *The Waste Land* may have been suggested by Palgrave, or Palgrave's source, Charles Lamb.

Two essays consider Eliot's reciprocal relations with French literature. J. Barton Rollins examines the "Note sur Mallarmé et Poe" which Eliot published in *La Nouvelle Revue Française* in 1926 and concludes that it recapitulates the view of "metaphysicality" which Eliot had expressed earlier to English audiences in "Andrew Marvell" and "The Metaphysical Poets" ("T. S. Eliot on Mallarmé and Poe" [*MarkhamR* 10:9–10]). Catharine Savage Brosman comments interestingly on Eliot in "Gide, Translation, and 'Little Gidding'" (*FR* 54:690–98). Brosman focuses on "Gide's interest in translation, his acquaintance with Eliot, the circumstances in which this version [published in 1943 in Morocco] was done and its characteristics." She concludes her examination of the translation by commenting that "in general the French text is somewhat more rhetorical, more ornamental and refined than the English." Our understanding of Eliot's poem is enhanced by Brosman's skillful discussion of Gide's problems translating it into French.

Eliot's impact on other writers is the focus of several essays. John L. Idol, Jr., considers Thomas Wolfe's responses to Eliot's work and reputation, arguing that Wolfe and Eliot "often stood closer than Wolfe believed they did" ("Thomas Wolfe and T. S. Eliot: The Hippopotamus and the Old Possum" [*SLJ* 13,ii:15–26]). Idol includes some interesting parodies of Eliot by Wolfe, but his essay suffers from a limited understanding of Eliot's work. The powerful impact of *The Waste Land* on Auden's generation of poets is assessed by John R. Boly in "W. H. Auden's *The Orators*: Portraits of the Artist in the Thirties" (*TCL* 27:247–61). Boly calls *The Orators* "a formidable accomplishment" which put an end "to the era of *The Waste Land*" and made "the lyrical and personal voice available to poets writing about contemporary social issues." In "Eliot's 'Little Gidding' and Lawrence Durrell" (*CLAJ* 24:190–93), John J. Pollock suggests that Eliot was influenced by the younger writer's *The Black Book*, which Eliot had praised in 1938 as "the first piece of work by a new English writer to give me any hope for the future of prose fiction." Although there are "similarities in topic, tone and diction" between *Little Gidding* and the last section of Durrell's novel, these similarities do not support the assertion that "Eliot apparently has borrowed many ideas from Durrell." A more convincing case of "borrowing" is offered by R. F. Bell in "Metamorphoses and Missing Halves: Allusions in Paul Theroux's *Picture Palace*" (*Crit* 22,iii:17–30). Bell convincingly analyzes the impact of *The Waste Land* and in particular Eliot's use of Tiresias on Theroux's recent novel.

c. The Poetry and Plays.   For the second time in recent years, a critic has dared to answer the question never asked in "Prufrock" ("Oh, do not ask, 'What is it?'"): the response given by Michael L. Baumann represents the low point of Eliot criticism this year ("Let Us Ask 'What Is It?'" [*ArQ* 37:47–58]). Baumann asserts that "Prufrock proves to be a false rock, a ninny, incapable of saying—as Sweeney would have said—'Let's have sex!'" and then notes modestly that "all this may be too obvious for words and explain why so few have been expounded on it." Would that there had been even fewer. In marked contrast is William Arrowsmith's "The Poem as Palimpsest: A Dialogue on Eliot's 'Sweeney Erect'" (*SoR* 17:17–68). Arrowsmith's brilliantly engaging dialogue illuminates this "intensely personal" poem which unites "two of the most obsessive themes" of Eliot's poetry, "seduction and abandonment . . . and the death of a father." Arrowsmith demonstrates that the poem contains "not random echoes of fragmentary texts, but an intricately structured arrangement of texts and *topoi* designed to reveal, stratum by stratum, the complex archeology of 'the changing mind of Europe.'" Similarly his dialogue reveals, stratum by stratum, the complex archeology of "Sweeney Erect" and suggests ways of reading other quatrain poems of this period.

Two essayists urge us to reconsider *The Waste Land* on the basis of their own readings of the manuscripts, but neither of these readings is informed by current scholarship. In "Hope and Fear: Tension in *The Waste Land*" (*CollL* 8:21–32), Michael Holt contends that a "major reevaluation of the poem" should be based on what he calls "the paradox of conversion" in the original "Death by Water" section. Holt argues that "Pound's unsympathetic, even caustic attitudes toward Eliot's religious interests were adamant, while Eliot's movement in a religious direction was predictably unstable and confused, resulting in a poem that was too influenced by a critic who did not know what it was about." Holt's own view of "what it was about" is considerably narrower than Pound's and his selective emphasis distorts rather than clarifies Eliot's work. William B. Worthen examines the impact of Joyce's *Ulysses* on *The Waste Land* manuscripts in "Eliot's Ulysses" (*TCL* 27:166–77). Worthen attempts to demonstrate Eliot's use of "Joycean techniques and situations," especially in the early "Tom's Place" and "Death by Water" sections. However, there is a problem here with the chronology, since Eliot certainly wrote the first of these sections before reading the "Proteus" and "Hades" episodes of *Ulysses* in 1919 or the "Circe" and "Eumaeus" episodes in 1921. This important subject still awaits careful and complete treatment.

John Paul Riquelme begins his essay "Withered Stumps of Time: Allusion, Reading and Writing in *The Waste Land*" (*DQ* 15,iv:90–110) with a commonplace: that "Eliot's kind of poetry . . . can be appreciated in the light of the kind of criticism he wrote." It is less easy to appreciate him in the murky light of Riquelme's criticism. The following is typical: "By writing the text the poet achieves a status beyond mortality, creating his linguistic double in the poem, as the poem, and through the poem; that is, as character, speaker and reader of the poem." Inventiveness too often outstrips common sense, and the results add little to our understanding of Eliot's poem.

In a valuable study of "Artful Voices: Eliot's Dramatic Verse" (*Agenda* 18,iv:112–19), A. D. Moody examines the range and variation within Eliot's verse. This verse, according to Moody, can find "appropriate voices for the matter of fact and the metaphysical" and "also acts out their fated relations." Thus, Eliot's verse, "through its variety of modes and styles, can be a theater in itself."

Two essays view the spiritual or supernatural aspects of *The Cocktail Party*. Hildegard Hammerschmidt considers "The Role of the 'Guardians' in T. S. Eliot's *Cocktail Party*" (*MD* 24:54–66). Hammerschmidt suggests that the "guardians" should be viewed as "magicians or even magi, whose workings can be regarded as the execu-

tion of ritual magic." Yet all of the characteristics she attributes to
the magician could also apply to a psychiatrist. Her secular reading
of the play becomes as reductive as the strictly religious ones, and
less convincing. Vimila Rao approaches *The Cocktail Party* "in the
light of the *Bhagavad-Gita*" in an attempt to correct what he perceives to be critics' neglect of Eliot's interest in Eastern thought
("T. S. Eliot's *The Cocktail Party* and the *Bhagavad-gita*" [*CLS* 18:
191–98]). Indeed, many passages in the play are clarified by the comparison. Rao argues further that "the central theme of both Eliot's
play and the *Gita* is that one does not separate religion from secular
life, and one cannot separate action or knowledge from love." This is
a "central theme" in a great many works, and generalizations such as
this only weaken Rao's thesis.

d. **The Criticism.**   This year's work shows a renewed interest in
Eliot's critical writings, particularly in the relationship between
these writings and Eliot's romantic and Victorian precursors. In
T. S. Eliot and the Romantic Critical Tradition (Routledge) Edward
Lobb examines "Eliot's place in the Romantic tradition of historiography and rhetorical persuasion." Lobb bases his discussion in part
on materials that have been insufficiently examined heretofore, in
particular the unpublished Clark Lectures on metaphysical poetry
which Eliot delivered at Cambridge University in 1926. Lobb argues
rightly that these lectures, despite their unevenness, "constitute an
essential part of [Eliot's] work," and by extensive quotation and discussion he familiarizes the reader with this important material. However, Lobb's presentation is inadequately focused. Although he acknowledges that "Romanticism" is "a notoriously protean term," he
never satisfactorily explains what he means by, say, "a Romantic tradition of historiography." This use of undefined terms mars what
could be an important contribution to our understanding of modernism.

    A different view of Eliot's critical stance is presented by Daniel
O'Hara in " 'The Unsummoned Image': T. S. Eliot's Unclassic Criticism" (*Boundary* 9,i:91–124). O'Hara contends that Eliot's criticism
belongs "neither to the Romantic, nor to the pseudo-neo-classic
schools of modern criticism. . . . Rather it continues the elaboration,
the tracing of difference between the two schools right up to the

'post-modern' breaking point." Unfortunately, O'Hara could not argue with Lobb's evidence, and he neglects the earlier work of Kermode and Bornstein. O'Hara's Eliot is the "ironic and self-reflective" poet-critic whose "critical prose and the interpretive play of its characteristic figures of speech enact an ironic allegory of the temporal processes of writing, an allegory that discloses how the ruling frames of reference (or codes) of his modernist understanding work." While O'Hara highlights an important aspect of Eliot's work, his facile "neither/nor" simplifies the tensions informing Eliot's critical development.

David Spurr is also concerned with the relationships between Eliot's criticism and the romantic tradition and it is within this context that he analyzes "the evolution" of a conflict between "a ruling critical faculty in endless dispute with an involuntary creative impulse." In "T. S. Eliot's Divided Critical Sensibility" (*Criticism* 23:58–76) Spurr presents a selective but extremely informative reading of Eliot's essays in which he "focuses less on what Eliot said than on the way he said it, on the theory that structural elements in prose such as shifts in style and patterns of imagery serve as an index to the structure of the consciousness informing them." His results are impressive.

Carol T. Christ probes the relations between "T. S. Eliot and the Victorians" (*MP* 79:157–65). She argues convincingly that "the central critical doctrines Eliot uses to define his early poetic achievement—the reunification of sensibility, the objective correlative, the impersonality of poetry—grow directly out of developments in Victorian poetry." This excellent study should help to redefine the continuities between the Victorian and modern periods. Christ demonstrates that "Eliot shares with the Victorians not only the sense of loss and despair, the anxiety over the roots of faith and cultural unity and identity, but specific poetic strategies as well—the use of symbol, the use of dramatic monologue, of myth, and the transformation of the long poem."

Wendell V. Harris makes a plea for Walter Pater's "contemporaneity" in "The Road to and from Eliot's Place of Pater" (*TSLL* 23: 183–96). Harris attempts to "tease out" the "virtue" of Pater's criticism through a juxtaposition with Eliot, "a juxtaposition Eliot himself authorized by setting in motion, through his essay on Pater, both a dialectic and an infinitely reflective convergence of philosophic tendencies." Harris' uncritical acceptance of Eliot's essay weakens his argument in favor of Pater's importance.

In his survey of "Freud and the Twenties," Paul Schwaber proposes that "by considering *The Ego and the Id* in collocation with *Ulysses* and *The Waste Land,* we will be able to appreciate something important about all three, and something too of the moral bases of creativity" (*MR* 22:133–51). His consideration of Freud's work as "an adaptive and professionally cogent response to the Great War" is more informative than his commonplace comments on Eliot and Joyce.

Walter Benn Michaels' valuable "Philosophy in Kinkanja: Eliot's Pragmatism" (*Glyph* 8:170–202) examines Eliot's "allegiance to a classical conception of philosophy and the beginning of his attempt to break with that conception." Michaels analyzes the development of Eliot's position in detail and concludes that "Eliot's pragmatism is not the link which joins the relative with the absolute; it is instead a way of understanding the identity of relative and absolute and denying them both."

Sheldon W. Liebman remedies the unjust neglect of Eliot's Harvard lectures of 1932–33 in "The Turning Point: Eliot's *The Use of Poetry and the Use of Criticism*" (*Boundary* 9,ii:197–218). Liebman cogently demonstrates that these essays, in which Eliot "raises old critical questions and answers them in a new way," are among "the most interesting and important" of Eliot's critical writings. Liebman suggests that the volume has both a private and a public significance: it is "important not only as a personal testament revealing the extent to which Eliot changed his mind about his own critical principles but also as a public document raising compelling questions about the institution Eliot's critical theory and practice helped to establish: modern literary criticism." The essays which address Eliot's critical work this year suggest that a re-evaluation of "modern literary criticism" has begun with vigor and intelligence.

University of Michigan

9. Faulkner

Karl F. Zender

In the preface to *Alternative Pleasures: Postrealist Fiction and the Tradition*, Philip Stevick says, "Even scholars and aficionados of Joyce, Lawrence, and Beckett must agree that there is a kind of insane redundancy in the enormous commentary appended to them." Whether Faulkner scholars and aficionados would be willing to have Faulkner's name added to this bill of indictment I have no way of knowing; but it is the case that in 1981, for the first time in memory, there was a perceptible slackening in the quantity of work published on Faulkner. Along with this decrease in quantity came a narrowing in qualitative range: there was less unconscionably bad work done in 1981 than in past years, but there were also no startling new departures in critical method, no new bodies of data brought into play, no major stages in the scholarly enterprise brought to completion. Within these limits, though, the year saw a fair amount of good work done. Here I think especially of Noel Polk's edition of the original text of *Sanctuary*, the Tulane/Yoknapatawpha Press edition of *Helen: A Courtship and Mississippi Poems*, the section on Faulkner in Carolyn Porter's *Seeing and Being*, the essays by Robert W. Hamblin and Panthea Broughton in "*A Cosmos of My Own*," Gail L. Mortimer's essay on the theme of absence, and the essays on *Absalom, Absalom!* by Stephen M. Ross and François L. Pitavy. Not a vintage year perhaps, but a good one nonetheless.

i. Bibliography, Editions, and Manuscripts

The publication of important previously unpublished work by Faulkner continued in 1981 with the appearance of *Sanctuary: The Original Text*, ed. with an afterword and notes by Noel Polk (Random House) and *Helen: A Courtship and Mississippi Poems* with introductory essays by Carvel Collins and Joseph Blotner (New Orleans

and Oxford, Miss.: Tulane University and Yoknapatawpha Press).
As its title implies, the first of these two works reprints the version
of *Sanctuary* that Faulkner submitted to Cape and Smith in 1929.
Comparing this version of the novel with the published one affords
a striking object lesson, as Malcolm Cowley said (*NYTBR* 22 Feb.:
9,25), in "how a brilliant technician who happened to be a genius in
other ways could work with disappointing galley proofs, save all the
type that could be saved and come out with a new and more effective
novel." One wonders, though, why the decision was made to publish
the book in a trade edition. *Sanctuary: The Original Text* is not a
bad novel—little that Faulkner ever wrote is bad—but it lacks the
extraordinary drive and intensity of vision of the revised version,
and in places it is quite awkwardly plotted. Useful as *Sanctuary:
The Original Text* will undoubtedly prove to be to scholars, it is
difficult to imagine that it will ever be of much interest to the general
reader.

The second volume mentioned above, *Helen: A Courtship and
Mississippi Poems*, combines previously unpublished and previously
published work in a complex way. As Carvel Collins says in his
introduction to *Helen: A Courtship*, of the 16 poems in the book,
"nine have been found published in some form even if only as a
line or two"; as Joseph Blotner says in his parallel introduction to
Mississippi Poems, both the essay "Verse, Old and Nascent: A Pilgrimage" and eight of the 12 poems that together with the essay
make up the contents of the book were published during Faulkner's
lifetime. Furthermore, the whole of *Mississippi Poems* was published
separately by Yoknapatawpha Press in 1979 (see *ALS 1979*, 136–37).
In one regard, then, this dual volume can be viewed as yet another
addition to the bibliographical mare's nest that is being created by
the piecemeal publication of drafts and completed versions of Faulkner's apprentice work. This ungenerous judgment, though, needs to
be balanced against an awareness of the real merits of the book: not
only does it publish some previously unpublished material, but the
introductions by Collins and Blotner—especially the very long one
by Collins—make valuable contributions to our knowledge of Faulkner's biography and of his literary indebtednesses.

The year also saw the publication of a few short pieces of previously unpublished work. In "A Manuscript Fragment" (*MissQ* 34:
340–41), Gail M. Morrison reprints a six-line passage that appears

on the verso of page 122 of the carbon typescript of *Sanctuary*. As Morrison says, the passage is too brief to allow us to identify its narrator, who could be either Quentin Compson or Horace Benbow. In "Additional Manuscripts of Faulkner's 'A Dead Dancer' " (*SB* 34:267–70), Louis D. Brodsky reprints two draft versions of this early poem from his collection of Faulkner manuscripts, compares these versions with the three contained in the University of Virginia collection, and attempts a conjectural reconstruction of the version that appeared in "The Lilacs," a hand-lettered presentation volume largely destroyed by fire in 1942. Brodsky's other contribution for the year, "The Collector as Sleuthsayer," appeared in "*A Cosmos of My Own*" (pp. 125–48; see section *iii.a*). Brodsky used the title of this anecdotal reminiscence of his adventures as a collector of Faulkneriana once before, for a volume published in conjunction with an exhibition of his collection at Southeast Missouri State University.

Two book-length bibliographical aids also appeared in 1981: Thomas E. Dasher's *William Faulkner's Characters: An Index to the Published and Unpublished Fiction* (Garland) and Beatrice Ricks's *William Faulkner: A Bibliography of Secondary Works*, Scarecrow Author Bibliographies, No. 49 (Scarecrow). The first of the two, which is based on Dasher's University of South Carolina dissertation, is designed to replace the various existing character indices, all of which are now about twenty years old. Though some of these earlier guides—most notably Robert Kirk's *Faulkner's People*—have substantially more merit than Dasher attributes to them in his introduction, still the time is ripe for a new one, and Dasher is to be commended for having done a good, careful job of filling the need. The central advantage of his index over its predecessors is its greater range: in addition to indexing the work by Faulkner that has appeared in print since the publication of the earlier indices (including some items, like *Sanctuary: The Original Text*, that were still in press at the time Dasher was doing his work), Dasher indexes some still-unpublished stories in the University of Virginia collection. His book also includes, as the predecessor volumes do not, separate lists of all significant unnamed characters, and of all named literary, biblical, historical, and mythical figures. In one important regard, though, scholars may find *William Faulkner's Characters* a vexatious book to use. In listing the presumed advantages of his book over its predecessors, Dasher says that "no names are inferred from one work to another." This scarcely seems to be an advantage, for what it means in practice is that critics interested in tracing a recurrent character through Faulkner's oeuvre cannot turn to the master index at the back of *William Faulkner's Characters* with any assurance that all of the appearances of a particular character will be gathered together under a single heading. For example, the "Eustace" whom Bayard Sartoris declines to hit in *Flags in the Dust* because he is crippled is listed under "Eustace" in the master index; but the "Eustace Graham" who appears, similarly handicapped, in *Sanctuary* is listed under "Graham, Eustace." An extreme of sorts is reached in this disinclination to infer names from one work to another in the case of Faulkner's two self-references in his fiction: one is indexed under "Faulkner" and the other under "Faulkner, Bill."

Whatever obstacles *William Faulkner's Characters* may place in the way of our use of it, though, it is a model of clarity in comparison with Beatrice Ricks's *William Faulkner: A Bibliography of Secondary Works*. Though Ricks does not mention her *terminus ad quem* in her very short introduction, comparing her book with the last few volumes of *ALS* suggests that her coverage extends through the end of 1978. Had her book been well done, then, it might have constituted a welcome supplement to Thomas L. McHaney's *William Faulkner: A Reference Guide*, which ends its coverage with 1973. As it is, though, severe organizational problems make Ricks's volume an unworthy companion to McHaney's. For example, Ricks divides "Works"—one of her four main categories—into eight subcategories; but one of these, "Novels and Stories," contains nearly 95 percent of the listings in the section, and two of the others—"Awards" and "Collections of Manuscripts and Materials"—scarcely seem to be logical subdivisions of "Works." Even more troublesome than the book's illogical organization of its contents is the capricious way in which Ricks assigns items to categories. The subcategory of "Works" entitled "Speeches" has in it only eight entries and includes none of the critical discussions of the Nobel Prize Acceptance Speech, most (but not all) of which are instead listed under "Awards." The subcategory entitled "Collections of Manuscripts and Materials" contains a listing for an article in the University of Virginia student newspaper announcing the publication of Joseph Blotner's *William Faulkner's Library: A Catalogue* but does not contain a listing for the catalog itself, which is instead listed under "General Criticism" (as is Joan St. C. Crane's and Anne E. H. Freudenberg's *Man Collecting*). All in all, this book makes me yearn for an updated version of McHaney's *Guide*.

The remaining items in this category can be briefly treated. *The Faulkner Newsletter & Yoknapatawpha Review* (Yoknapatawpha) began publication on a quarterly basis at the beginning of 1981. This chatty, informally written newspaper combines information for book collectors with quasi-scholarly reviews and notes and occasional letters of inquiry from Faulkner scholars. The annual Faulkner issue of *Mississippi Quarterly* continues to publish a survey of Faulkner scholarship somewhat like this one. It should be noted that the editorship of the *Mississippi Quarterly* review has passed from Thomas L. McHaney to Dianne L. Cox, and that the new editor has apparently decided to base the final draft of the review more exclusively on the written evaluations submitted by the individual members of the Faulkner Scholarship Survey Committee than did McHaney. The effects of this change are to increase the degree of variation in coverage and in standards of judgment from section to section of the review and to lessen the ability of the committee to comment on interconnections between different aspects of the year's work. The *Mississippi Quarterly* survey for 1980 covers approximately half the number of items covered in *ALS 1980*.

ii. Biography

Little significant work on Faulkner's biography appeared during 1981; what there is is headed by Thomas L. McHaney's short life of Faulkner in James B. Lloyd's *Lives of Mississippi Authors, 1817–1967* (Miss.). McHaney's brief life of course makes no claim to originality, but I draw attention to it here because the volume of which it is a part contains a wealth of information about other Mississippi writers whose lives impinged upon Faulkner's. The only item of direct biographical pertinence to appear during the year is "No Pistol Pocket" (*SoR* 17:358–65), another in the continuing series of Jim Faulkner's reminiscences of life in Oxford in the 1930s. "No Pistol Pocket" is strong in anecdotal value but contains little information about Faulkner.

A work that falls far short of the promise contained in its topic is

Dennis W. Petrie's *Ultimately Fiction.* This book, which is based on Petrie's Purdue University dissertation, examines a number of modern literary biographies in terms of their artistic merits and demerits; it contains a long chapter (pp. 59–110) on Joseph Blotner's *Faulkner: A Biography.* Though the idea of examining the design of Blotner's book is a good one, Petrie provides us with no new grounds for judgment. At one point he says, "I have . . . taken the authenticity of Blotner's presented materials for granted; aside from one reviewer who cites (without furnishing even one example) 'a disturbingly high incidence of errors in copying' of documents . . . , no one has given me reason at this point to doubt their integrity." One may note in passing that James B. Meriwether's 1975 *Mississippi Quarterly* review-essay, which Petrie does not list in his bibliography, cites chapter and verse in discussing Blotner's errors; more importantly, the scholarly self-indulgence implied by Petrie's statement vitiates many of the criticisms that he directs at Blotner. He objects, for example, to Blotner's circumspect treatment of Faulkner's relationships with Meta Carpenter, Jean Stein, and Phil Stone without ever pausing to ask what constraints Blotner was under when writing about these matters.

iii. Criticism: General

a. **Books.** The year saw the publication of two books of general criticism, one collection of essays, and seven books in which Faulkner's fiction receives amounts of discussion varying from a few pages to several chapters. Though both John Pilkington's *The Heart of Yoknapatawpha* (Miss.) and Victor Strandberg's *A Faulkner Overview: Six Perspectives*, National University Publications: Literary Criticism Series (Kennikat) have some good things to say, neither is a truly significant advance in our understanding of the fiction. In organization and coverage, Pilkington's book resembles the various critical surveys produced during the 1950s and 1960s, in that it focuses on the major novels and devotes a chapter of commentary to each of them. In his introduction Pilkington acknowledges this resemblance and then raises the question of why we need yet another general survey of the main novels in the canon. The answer he gives —that new insight into Faulkner's biography and changes in critical fashion necessitate periodic re-evaluations of Faulkner's fiction—is an entirely respectable one, but unfortunately his study neither draws on the recent biographical work in any substantial way nor reflects the revolution in critical methodology that has taken place over the last 20 years. Instead, Pilkington revisits the thematic and structural issues addressed by Brooks, Vickery, Waggoner, and Millgate but without exhibiting the breadth of knowledge and acuteness of perception of these critics.

The other book-length study, Strandberg's *A Faulkner Overview*, is a mixed bag. The volume combines three previously published essays (see *ALS 1965, 1975, 1980*) with three new ones; the new ones are "Music: Faulkner's 'Eroica,'" "Liebestod: The Lessons of Eros," and "Transition: From Freud to Marx." "Liebestod" is the strongest of the three because in it Strandberg has a relatively fresh body of data with which to work. Though marred by occasional unconvincing generalizations about male-female differences, this essay is valuable for its shrewd insights into the patterns of behavior underlying Faulkner's relationships with women. "Transition" is also a strong essay, one in which Strandberg applies a wide-ranging knowledge of Freud and a less wide-ranging but still commendably broad knowledge of Marx to Faulkner's fiction. The third essay, "Music," suffers from many of the difficulties that confront writers who seek to frame comparisons between literature and music. Though elsewhere in *A Faulkner Overview* Strandberg shows that he has read Meta Carpenter's *A Loving Gentleman* carefully, he does not mention her assertion (which receives independent verification in Faulkner's *Paris Review* interview) that Faulkner really didn't care very much for music.

The collection of essays that appeared in 1981, "*A Cosmos of My Own*," ed. Doreen Fowler and Ann J. Abadie (Miss.) is the seventh in the series of proceedings of the annual Faulkner and Yoknapatawpha Conference. Of the 11 essays in the volume, seven are on general topics; I will discuss these seven here and reserve the other four for the appropriate categories elsewhere in the chapter. The evidence afforded by the last few volumes of proceedings convinces me that the Faulkner and Yoknapatawpha Conference has replaced the on-again, off-again Faulkner session at MLA as the most important public forum for the discussion of Faulkner's work. This year's volume of proceedings strengthens me in this opinion, for three of its essays on general topics are of high value, and the other four, though not as significant, are nonetheless provocative and interesting.

Heading the list of essays of high value is the lead essay in the volume, Robert W. Hamblin's "'Saying No to Death': Toward William Faulkner's Theory of Fiction" (pp. 3–35). In Hamblin's view, "the key to Faulkner's theory of fiction is to be found in his statement . . . that writing was his way of 'saying No to death.'" Faulkner says "No," according to Hamblin, by placing memory and imagination into contention with time; the whole aim of his art is to keep "the beloved lost object alive" and thus to defy mutability. This is a plausible view, and Hamblin advances it with intelligence, sensitivity, and insight. When he says, though, that Faulkner's frequent depictions of memory as "burden rather than delight" are of little importance, he dismisses too quickly an important aspect of his subject. Like many of his contemporaries, Faulkner willingly engaged in the deconstruction of the Wordsworthian dream of redemptive memory; and like many of them too, he later found himself needing to reconstruct the sanctuary he had helped to overthrow. Had Hamblin asked himself how and why Faulkner's artistic uses of memory and imagination change as his career advances, he could have substantially improved an already strong essay.

The second and third of the three important general studies in "A Cosmos" are linked essays by Panthea Broughton. In "The Cubist Novel: Toward Defining the Genre" (pp. 36–58) Broughton takes on the ambitious task of defining a new genre in which to locate Faulkner's fiction. The attempt, though forcefully argued and often illuminating, strikes me as being somewhat supererogatory. Broughton attempts to justify it by noting that the "standards of plausibility, continuity, and unity" implicit in prevailing definitions of the novel are more appropriate to 19th-century fiction than they are to the fiction of the modernist era. She recognizes, of course, that this insight has not been vouchsafed to her alone, but her review of recent attempts to expand narrative theory to fit modernist and postmodernist practice is curiously foreshortened. She mentions Scholes's and Kellogg's *Nature of Narrative*, Guerard's *Triumph of the Novel*, Rabkin's *Narrative Suspense*, and some handbooks of literature; she does not mention Barbara Hardy's *Tellers and Listeners*, Tzvetan Todorov's *Poetics of Prose*, Gérard Genette's *Narrative Discourse*, or any of the numerous essays on narrative theory that have appeared in such journals as *New Literary History* and *Critical Inquiry* in the last few years. Every critic clears a space in which to speak in her own way, of course, and I do not mean to imply that Broughton is obliged to refer to any one in particular of the books and journals I have just mentioned. Her turning aside from this whole body of exciting work, though, has the unfortunate effect of diminishing the theoretical reach of an otherwise interesting and well-informed essay.

Once Broughton turns to practical criticism, as she does in "Faulkner's Cubist Novels" (pp. 59–94), the issue of her theoretical reach becomes less important than the question of how successful she is in illuminating Faulkner's fiction. She is very successful indeed—largely, I suspect, because she is really less interested in locating Faulkner's fiction in a new genre than she is in analyzing some central aspects of his artistic development. She argues, very convincingly, that in the 1920s Faulkner underwent a three-stage development which recapitulated in miniature the historical movement from romanticism to realism to modernism; one of the central effects of this development, Broughton says, is a shift on Faulkner's part from expressing desire, to examining it, to creating it in his reader. This consistently stimulating essay merits comparison both with David Minter's analysis of the significance of Faulkner's shift from poetry to prose in *William Faulkner: His Life and Work* (Hopkins [1980]) and, to anticipate a bit, with Jay Martin's analysis of the psychodynamics of Faulkner's early career in " 'The Whole Burden of Man's History of His Impossible Heart's Desire': The Early Life of William Faulkner" (*AL* 53[1982]:607–29).

The remaining four essays on general topics in *"A Cosmos"* can be briefly treated. Like Broughton in her second essay, James B. Carothers takes a developmental approach in "The Myriad Heart: The Evolution of the Faulkner Hero" (pp. 252–83), as he seeks to identify the changing meaning that the concept of heroism held for Faulkner as his career advanced. Unfortunately Carothers combines this promising method with a persistent overvaluation of Faulkner's later, more communally oriented works. The second of the remaining general essays, Charles H. Nilon's "Cooper, Faulkner, and the American Venture" (pp. 168–98) is a solid but unremarkable comparison of Cooper's and Faulkner's depictions of aristocratic characters. The last two general essays are both by Ellen Douglas, a Mississippi novelist. "Faulkner's Women" (pp. 149–67) is a somewhat selective survey of Faulkner's female characters that conducts us to familiar conclusions about Faulkner's misogyny. "Faulkner in Time" (pp. 284–301) is an anecdotal account of the changing impact— ranging from substantial to none whatsoever—that Faulkner's fiction had on Douglas at different times in her life.

The books in which Faulkner receives varying amounts of attention differ widely in approach, focus, and value. Far and away the strongest of the group is Carolyn Porter's *Seeing and Being*. This intelligent, absorbing, and sensitive study analyzes the situation of the participant-observer in works by Emerson, James, Henry Adams, and Faulkner; in the widest reach of its ambition it seeks to create an alternative, basically Marxist in its orientation, to the widely held view that the distinctive character of American literature lies in its attempt to exempt the individual from history. The Faulkner section of the book (pp. 207–76) concentrates on the relation of the reader to Faulkner's depictions of his characters' efforts either to transcend time or to submerge themselves in it. Porter's argument is not without some problems, mainly because of her failure to come to terms with the implications of her association of reading with hearing rather than sight. More than in its analysis of particular themes and motifs, though, the strength of Porter's book lies in the strong challenge it mounts to Cleanth Brooks's denial of a specifically southern significance for Thomas Sutpen's career. Using Faulkner's family history and the writings of Eugene Genovese and C. Vann Woodward as a basis, Porter constructs a convincing view of Sutpen as a figure representative of the entrepreneurial ambitions prevalent both in the South (in its actuality, not its mythic self-representation) and in America at large in the 19th century.

Two books that appeared during 1981 discuss the place of sport in Faulkner's fiction. One of them, Robert J. Higgs's *Laurel & Thorn* (Kentucky), contains only a brief, unfocused discussion of Labove in *The Hamlet*, but the other, Christian K. Messenger's *Sport and the Spirit of Play*, has significant things to say not only about Labove but about Ike McCaslin and Bayard Sartoris. Messenger's comparison of Ike McCaslin and Hemingway's Santiago is informed with a judicious sense of the difference between Faulkner's capacious, play-oriented view of sport and Hemingway's more restricted view of it as a form of competition; and his comparison of Robert Cohn and Labove as satires of the type he calls the "School Sports Hero" juxtaposes two seemingly dissimilar figures in a surprising but illuminating way. Also of considerable value is John H. Schaar's "Community or Contract? William Faulkner and the Dual Legacy" in *The Problem of Authority in America* (Philadelphia: Temple Univ. Press, pp. 93–111). Schaar, a noted political scientist, uses the concepts and language of his discipline to good effect in this thoughtful reconsideration of the main theme of "The Bear."

Two essays that promise but unfortunately do not deliver a fresh view of Faulkner's fiction appear in *The Fictional Father*. The subtitle of this volume—*Lacanian Readings of the Text*—leads one to expect a series of applications of Lacan's ideas to works of literature; but though André Bleikasten tries to meet this expectation in "Fathers in Faulkner" (pp. 115–46), he fails to go much beyond the insights afforded us by more traditionally oriented character analyses. Part of the difficulty here, I suspect, is that Bleikasten underestimates the depth of Faulkner's commitment to the dream of self-creation. Though he acknowledges the presence of a desire for autogenesis, as he calls it, in Faulkner's fiction, Bleikasten does not accord it the same degree of imaginative authority as he does Faulkner's representations of the symbolic father. The effect of his orientation is to turn the works he considers into a rather predictable series of patternings out of the ubiquitous triumph of the father. The problem presented by the second essay on Faulkner in *The Fictional Father* —John T. Irwin's "The Dead Father in Faulkner" (pp. 147–68)— does not lie in its content, which is as exciting as it ever was, but in its provenance. This essay is an almost verbatim reprint of a long section from Irwin's *Doubling and Incest / Repetition and Revenge* (Hopkins, 1975). Readers who discovered this fact in mid-stride, as I did, may wish to join me in feeling a bit disgruntled.

The two remaining items in this category may be briefly treated. Alan Holder's *The Imagined Past* (Bucknell) contains two chapters on Faulkner: "The Doomed Design: William Faulkner's *Absalom, Absalom!*" (pp. 53–72) and "An Odor of Sartoris: William Faulkner's *The Unvanquished*" (pp. 73–91). Both are literate and thoughtful, though not particularly original, studies of the place of history in Faulkner's fiction. Holder displays an unfortunate tendency to construct reductive interpretations of Faulkner's intentions and then to claim that Faulkner's departures from them are a result of his somehow overriding his own desires. Despite the inclusion of Faulkner's name in its subtitle, Gregory L. Lucente's *The Narrative of Realism and Myth: Verga, Lawrence, Faulkner, Pavese* (Hopkins) contains only a brief discussion of the "Flem in Hell" episode in *The Hamlet.* Lucente argues that Faulkner intermingles mythic and realistic effects as a way of creating aesthetic distance in his readers.

b. **Articles.** A story, perhaps apocryphal, has it that Aldous Huxley once looked out a car window at a California rice field and said, "This reminds me of H. G. Wells's mind: miles and miles wide and an inch deep." Many of the articles on general topics that appeared in 1981 remind me of H. G. Wells's mind. Two welcome exceptions are Gail L. Mortimer's "Significant Absences: Faulkner's Rhetoric of Loss" (*Novel* 14:232–50) and Wesley A. Kort's "Social Time in Faulkner's Fiction" (*ArQ* 37:101–15). Mortimer's essay, which should be compared with Stephen M. Ross's "Evocation of Voice in *Absalom, Absalom!*" (see section *vi.*), is a trenchant and closely reasoned analysis of the "dialectic between flowing and control that comes from [Faulkner's] alternately focusing upon and eradicating boundaries between words and, by extension, the concepts they signify." Kort's essay is less contemporary in its critical orientation than is Mortimer's, but it is no less strongly argued. Kort advances the view that the most important kind of time in Faulkner's fiction is social rather than personal or natural, and that Faulkner uses it to depict "the separation of social change from social structure." Though there are moments, such as the Easter service in *The Sound and the Fury*, when this separation is resolved, these moments are not, in Kort's view, powerful or inclusive enough to rescue the society Faulkner depicts from its temporal confusion; they instead serve as "points from which the social time characteristic of Yoknapatawpha can be judged as unfortunate."

Another essay that is an exception to the characteristic diffuseness and shallowness of the year's articles on general topics is James G. Watson's "Literary Self-Criticism: Faulkner in Fiction on Fiction" (*SoQ* 20:46–63). This analysis of reflexivity in Faulkner's fiction begins with some promising comments on *The Sound and the Fury* but then quickly turns to a discussion of *Mayday*, "Black Music," "Afternoon of a Cow," and "Portrait of Elmer." The effect of this selection of texts is to suggest—wrongly I think—that Faulkner addresses reflexive concerns only in his peripheral writings.

Beyond Watson's essay the Wells effect exerts its dominance. Both William Winslow's "Modernity and the Novel: Twain, Faulkner, and Percy" (*GyS* 8:19–40) and Alma A. Ilacqua's descriptively titled "From Purveyor of Perversion to Defender of the Faithful: A Summary of Critical Studies on Faulkner's Theological Vision" (*LQ* 20:35–38) take on subjects far too large for their length. Similarly diffuse and shallow are Norman Rudich's "Faulkner and the Sin of Private Property" (*MinnR* 17:55–57) and Marjorie B. Haselswerdt's "I'd Rather Be Ratliff: A Maslovian Study of Faulkner's *Snopes* [*sic*]" (*LitR* 24:308–27). Rudich's essay is the only one on a general topic in a supplement to the *Minnesota Review* otherwise devoted entirely to interpretations of *Absalom, Absalom!* (see section *vi*); like the other essays in the supplement, Rudich approaches Faulkner's fiction from a Marxist perspective. In her essay Haselswerdt marches purposefully through the Snopes trilogy, matching Faulkner's depictions of Ratliff up against the elements of Abraham Maslow's concept of the self-actualizing individual; but she never establishes an independent perspective from which to judge the worth of Maslow's ideas or their value as aids to literary analysis.

iv. Criticism: Special Studies

a. **Ideas, Influences, Intellectual Background.** The year saw the publication of eight studies of influences on Faulkner's fiction, half of them broadly based and the other half narrowly focused. The best of the four broadly based studies, Martin Kreiswirth's "The Will to Create: Faulkner's Apprenticeship and Willard Huntington Wright" (*ArQ* 37:149–65), traces the influence on Faulkner's early criticism and poetry of Wright's *Creative Will*, a book scholars have long known Faulkner to have read. Kreiswirth's claims for Wright's influence on Faulkner are temperate and carefully supported by evidence; he is especially good on a somewhat incidental topic, the relationship between Swinburne's "Hermaphroditus" and Poem XXXVIII of *A Green Bough*. Two of the other three broadly based studies are also of some worth. Jeffrey J. Folks's "William Faulkner and the Silent Film" (*SoQ* 19:171–82) is a restrained and sensible examination of the influence of the silent film on Faulkner's self-conception (as a Chaplinesque tramp) and on his themes and techniques. As is so often the case with influence studies, though, phenomena that might well be simultaneous effects of an unknown cause are here sorted into a cause-and-effect pattern that accords with the critic's predilection. The third broadly based study consists of one chapter and part of another in William Stafford's *Books Speaking to Books* (N. Car.). Stafford examines Jake Barnes, Nick Carraway, and Benjy Compson as examples of a type he calls "The Innocent Narrator"; he concludes that Benjy is in some ways a parody, and in others an extension, of the earlier exemplars of the type. Despite its title, the fourth and last study in this group, Edward J. Piacentino's "No More 'Treachy Sentimentalities': The Legacy of T. S. Stribling to the Southern Literary Renascence" (*SoSt* 20:67–83), does not attempt to trace influences but instead merely suggests that affinities exist between Stribling's subject matter and Faulkner's. These affinities, such as they are, have long been familiar to Faulkner scholars.

Three of the four narrowly focused influence studies provide convincing arguments in favor of their attributions. Francis S. Heck's "Faulkner's 'Spotted Horses': A Variation on a Rabelaisian Theme" (*ArQ* 37:167–72) argues plausibly for the influence of Rabelais' "Dingdong's Sheep" on the "Spotted Horses" episode in *The Hamlet*. Stephen R. Portch's "All Pumped Up: A Real Horse Trick in *The Hamlet*" (*SAF* 9:93–95) finds a source for the horse-inflation episode in the same novel in a book that was advertised in the Oxford *Eagle* in 1910. In "Wilbur Daniel Steele's Influence on William Faulkner's Revision of 'Beyond' " (*MissQ* 34:335–39), Hassell A. Simpson points to a number of striking similarities between "Beyond" and Steele's prize-winning short story, "Can't Cross Jordan By Myself." Simpson argues that Faulkner deliberately used Steele's story as a model when revising "Beyond" in order to improve his story's marketability. The remaining study of a purported influence on Faulkner is not convincing. In "William Faulkner's 'The Rosary' and Florence L. Barclay" (*SSF* 18:445–47), Jeffrey J. Folks cites only tenuous resemblances in support of his argument that Faulkner's early prose sketch entitled "The Rosary" is a deliberate parody of Barclay's sentimental novel of the same name. Only one study of Faulkner's influence on another writer appeared in 1981. Susan H. Tuck's "House of Compson, House of Tyrone: Faulkner's Influence on O'Neill" (*EON* 5:

10–16) uses Judith Wittenberg's study of the influence of *Mourning Becomes Electra* on *Absalom, Absalom!* (*MissQ* 33[1980]:327–41) as a point of departure for an argument that a reciprocal relationship exists between *The Sound and the Fury* and *Long Day's Journey into Night*.

b. **Style and Structure.** A neglected item from 1980 heads the three-item list of studies of Faulkner's style (there were no studies devoted specifically to the structure of Faulkner's novels). In "Faulkner in French" (*CRCL* 7[1980]:223–35), Frederic Grover and Harriet Mowshowitz subject Maurice Coindreau's translation of *The Sound and the Fury* to careful scrutiny and conclude that the time has come for a new translation. Though they are duly appreciative of the importance of Coindreau's pioneering effort, Glover and Mowshowitz show convincingly that his translation suffers from "too much intellectuality [and] an excessive clarification of the original text." The two other studies, J. E. Bunselmeyer's "Faulkner's Narrative Styles" (*AL* 53:424–42) and Bruce Southard's "Syntax and Time in Faulkner's *Go Down, Moses*" (*Lang&S* 14:107–15) both use the language and concepts of linguistics and examples from *Go Down, Moses* in analyzing Faulkner's style. Bunselmeyer's aim is to distinguish between a "contemplative" and a "comic" Faulknerian style; he says the first of these is characterized by "comparisons, negative comparisons, or-clauses, doubled modifiers, and appositives" and the second by right-branching syntactic patterns. Though Bunselmeyer clearly shows that the styles he describes can be used to achieve the effects he attributes to them, he does not show that they are limited to these effects. I wonder, for example, what an analysis of *Sanctuary* would reveal about the relationship between right-branching patterns and literary effect in Faulkner's fiction. Southard's essay also begins with a discussion of right-branching patterns, but this is merely a point of departure for a discussion of what Southard calls "center embedding," a stylistic technique that he says Faulkner uses when he wishes to suggest a suspension in the flow of time. Both of these essays would have benefited from attention to Richard Poirier's discussion of the style of *Go Down, Moses* in *A World Elsewhere*.

c. **Race.** The decline in interest in Faulkner's treatments of racial themes that I noted in *ALS 1980* reversed itself in 1981 with the

appearance of three studies of the subject. Though the most extensive of the three, Lee Jenkins' *Faulkner and Black-White Relations:
A Psychoanalytic Approach* (Columbia), was savaged in the one
review I happened to read, it strikes me as a book not entirely unworthy of attention. Certainly it is not without serious flaws: Jenkins
is inattentive to important previous work on his subject, makes factual errors, employs an orotund, abstract style, and displays a tendency (despite protestations to the contrary) to convert Faulkner's
novels into case studies. But against these weaknesses should be
balanced his sometimes sophisticated use of psychological concepts,
his willingness to challenge prevailing interpretations of Faulkner's
fiction, and, most importantly, his evenhanded analysis of the limits
of Faulkner's imaginative engagement with the southern black experience. This last matter is something that we Faulkner critics
probably need to be reminded of from time to time. Why this is so
can be seen if Jenkins' book is compared with Charles H. Nilon's
"Blacks in Motion" ("*A Cosmos*," pp. 227–51), a study of Faulkner's
use of images of motion in his depictions of black characters. At one
point, Nilon says "whether a [black] character remains relatively in
control of his movement and free to make his own quest or whether
he is pursued and killed as Will Mayes is in 'Dry September' is perhaps not significant." A reader fresh from Jenkins' book will perhaps
be less comfortable with a statement of this sort than he might otherwise be. The last item in this section is Ladell Payne's *Black Novelists
and the Southern Literary Tradition* (Georgia). This modest but
worthwhile study argues that black and white southern writers share
a common tradition and literary heritage—a position so unexception-
able as scarcely to need to be argued, were it not for the ways in
which the study of black literature has been politicized in the last
few years. In the course of his book, Payne makes some useful comparisons between James Weldon Johnson's *Autobiography of an Ex-
Coloured Man* and *Absalom, Absalom!* and between Richard Wright's
Native Son and *Light in August*.

v. Individual Works to 1929

With the exception of the publication of previously unpublished
poetry (see section *i*), no work on the early prose and poetry, *Soldiers' Pay*, or *Mosquitoes* appeared during the year. The year did see

the appearance, though, of three studies of *Flags in the Dust* and of five studies of *The Sound and the Fury*. In "Keats's Hyperion Myth: A Source for the Sartoris Myth" (*MissQ* 34:325–33) Linda E. Mc-Daniel continues the investigation of Keats's influence on *Flags in the Dust* that she began last year with "Horace Benbow: Faulkner's Endymion" (*MissQ* 33[1980]:363–70). As was the case with her earlier essay, McDaniel's attempt to trace influences is rather schematically done. The second item on *Flags*, John Earl Bassett's "Faulkner, Sartoris, Benbow: Shifting Conflict in *Flags in the Dust*" (*SoSt* 20:39–54), is one of three essays on the theme of family conflict published by Bassett during the year. This one has an intriguing thesis. Bassett argues that "*Flags in the Dust* is a bifurcated novel," one in which "the tension between the two Bayards [is] replaced by the counterpoint of young Bayard and Horace"; this shift in focus, he says, reflects the shift Faulkner himself was making in the late 1920s from being "a vagabond child of World War I" to being "a more resigned, middle-class, married, perhaps limited, craftsman." Though the position Bassett advances is not entirely consistent with the chronology of Faulkner's career, it nonetheless merits consideration. The third and final item on *Flags*, William T. Going's "Faulkner's *Flags in the Dust*" (*Expl* 35:37–39), argues on the basis of verbal similarities that Faulkner may have derived the title of his novel from Father Abram J. Ryan's "The Conquered Banner," a sentimental poem frequently printed in school anthologies in the South around the turn of the century.

The list of items on *The Sound and the Fury* is headed by a complex and stimulating, though somewhat puzzling, essay by Warwick Wadlington entitled "*The Sound and the Fury*: A Logic of Tragedy" (*AL* 53:409–23). If I understand him correctly, Wadlington is saying that Faulkner creates the tragic dimension of *The Sound and the Fury* by standing the modern denial of the possibility of tragedy on its head. In contrast to many essays on Faulkner, this one would have benefited from being ten or so pages longer. A second essay of merit on *The Sound and the Fury* is Martin Kreiswirth's "Learning as He Wrote: Re-Used Materials in *The Sound and the Fury*" (*MissQ* 34:281–98). In this essay Kreiswirth draws together the evidence, hitherto scattered throughout a number of earlier studies by various critics, in support of the view that Faulkner's technical innovations in *The Sound and the Fury* derive from his prior experimentation in such works as *Soldiers' Pay*, "The Kingdom of God," and *Flags in the Dust*.

The three remaining items on *The Sound and the Fury* are of less interest. Linda Kauffman's comparison of Faulkner and Dickens in "The Letter and the Spirit in *Hard Times* and *The Sound and the Fury*" (*MissQ* 34:299–313) is competently written and argued but conducts us to already-known conclusions about "the supremacy of truth over fact, heart over head, spirit over letter" in Faulkner's fiction. Thadious M. Davis' "Jason Compson's Place: A Reassessment" (*SoSt* 20:137–50) is a somewhat contentiously argued reminder of the role played by traditional southern concepts and values in Faulkner's characterization of Jason Compson. The last of the 1981 essays on *The Sound and the Fury*, John Earl Bassett's "Family Conflict in *The Sound and the Fury*" (*SAF* 9:1–20), is not comparable in quality to his analysis of the same theme in *Flags in the Dust* (see above). Bassett begins this rather inconclusive essay by saying that he will use biographical information to construct a reading of *The Sound and the Fury*, but he doesn't really do so; instead, he reads backwards from the novel to an assertion that sibling rivalry and a sense of maternal betrayal were important aspects of Faulkner's childhood, and then forward from the assertion to the novel again.

vi. Individual Works, 1930–39

As has come more and more to be the case in the last few years, the majority of the attention paid to the great fiction of the 1930s was devoted to *Absalom, Absalom!*: of the 21 essays to be discussed in this section, 12 are on this novel. *As I Lay Dying*, by contrast, was the subject of only two essays in 1981. John Earl Bassett's "*As I Lay Dying*: Family Conflict and Verbal Fictions" (*JNT* 11:125–34) is the third of Bassett's three studies of the theme of family conflict; it more closely resembles his essay on *The Sound and the Fury* than it does his study of *Flags in the Dust* (see section *v*). Here, as in his *The Sound and the Fury* essay, Bassett purports to be reading the novel in relation to Faulkner's life, but he does not bring enough biographical information to bear to create a fresh interpretation. The other study of *As I Lay Dying*, Robert J. Kloss's succinctly titled "Faulkner's *As I Lay Dying*" (*AI* 38:429–44), is a Freudian analysis of the "this stands for that" variety. Though Kloss makes interesting use of Freud's essay on the fantasy of a child being beaten, his case as a whole is not convincing.

One of the three items I wish to discuss on *Light in August* appeared in 1980. Timothy P. Martin's "The Art and Rhetoric of Chronology in Faulkner's *Light in August*" (*CollL* 7[1980]:125–35) is a thoughtful and basically well-written study of the relationship between *fabula* and *sujet* in the novel. Also of value on *Light in August* is Peter L. Hays's "Hemingway, Faulkner, and a Bicycle Built for Death" (*NMAL* 5:Item 26). In this brief note Hays links the image of death arriving on a bicycle in "The Snows of Kilimanjaro" to Percy Grimm's adventures on a two-wheeler and to Hemingway's own earlier bicycle imagery; he concludes, quite sensibly, that the image in "Snows" is a natural outgrowth of Hemingway's earlier work, though perhaps modified by Faulkner's use of the same motif. In the remaining item on this novel, "Faulkner's Debt to Keats in *Light in August*: A Reconsideration" (*SoRA* 14:161–67), Richard Pascal insists on a distinction without a difference. He takes previous commentators to task for implying that Faulkner slavishly imitates Keats and says that he will instead look at how the two writers differ in their use of the same imagery; as his quotations from other critics indicate, though, this is pretty much what the other students of the topic have been doing right along.

The 12 essays to appear on *Absalom, Absalom!* during 1981 are headed by three of real distinction. In "The Evocation of Voice in *Absalom, Absalom!*" (*ELWIU* 8:135–49), Stephen M. Ross adds another fine study to his distinguished series of investigations of the metaphor of voice in Faulkner's fiction (see "The 'Loud World' of Quentin Compson" [*SNNTS* 7(1975):245–57] and "'Voice' in Narrative Texts: The Example of *As I Lay Dying*" [*PMLA* 94(1979): 300–310]). "The Evocation of Voice" marks a real advance in our understanding of Faulkner's depiction of the narrative process in *Absalom, Absalom!* Where previous critics have by and large been content to see in the novel an affirmation of the power of the imagination to create reality, Ross goes a significant step further. "The pertinent inquiry," he says, "is not how story-telling can (or cannot) achieve truth, but how this novel's evocation of an imagined past exposes usually buried assumptions about how fiction's discourse can (or cannot) represent reality." At the heart of *Absalom, Absalom!*,

Ross says, is "an essential paradox of verbal representation: the words that evoke a world also defer its presence." This is heady stuff, Derrida made practical as a way of understanding fundamental aspects of the novel's narrative technique.

A second essay of real worth on *Absalom, Absalom!* is François L. Pitavy's "The Gothicism of *Absalom, Absalom!*: Rosa Coldfield Revisited" (*"A Cosmos,"* pp. 199–226). This is a full, rich essay. In addition to providing us with an illuminating discussion of the specifically gothic elements of *Absalom*, Pitavy uses Gérard Genette's distinction between "story," "narrative," and "narration" to examine Rosa's narrative and to show that it, no less than Shreve's and Quentin's, contains its essential truth. He also offers valuable insight into Rosa's characterization as a poet and into Sutpen as an image of the artist, and he makes some telling comments about the importance of absence to Rosa's conception of desire. (Pitavy's treatment of this last topic should be compared with John T. Matthews' comments on it in "The Marriage of Speaking and Hearing in *Absalom, Absalom!*" [*ELH* 49(1980):575–94].)

Maxine Rose's "Echoes of the King James Bible in the Prose Style of *Absalom, Absalom!*" (*ArQ* 37:137–48) is a less ambitious essay than either Pitavy's or Ross's, but in its own way it rivals both of them in value. Drawing on Bishop Lowth's and T. J. Robinson's analyses of the form of Hebrew poetry, Rose constructs a thoroughly convincing demonstration of the influence of Old Testament rhythms on the prose style of *Absalom, Absalom!* Two other essays on *Absalom*, though not of the first rank, also make valuable contributions. Deborah Robbins' "The Desperate Eloquence of *Absalom, Absalom!*" (*MissQ* 34:315–24) is an insightful but somewhat underdeveloped essay on the relationship between speech and personal identity in the novel. Robbins is right to say that "to assume the role of teller is to make a claim to identity, while to surrender that claim is a small death"; but she concludes rather too quickly that "*Absalom, Absalom!* ends with the failure of the search for coherence through speech." We have learned so much about reflexivity in *Absalom, Absalom!* in the last few years that R. Rio-Jelliffe's "*Absalom, Absalom!* as Self-Reflexive Novel" (*JNT* 11:75–90) is largely old news. The essay is useful, though, for Rio-Jelliffe's careful determination of who actually narrates the different chapters of the novel.

Four essays on *Absalom, Absalom!* appeared in a special supplement to the Spring 1981 issue of *Minnesota Review.* Like the essay by Norman Rudich mentioned above (see section *iii.b*), these essays all take a Marxist approach to the study of Faulkner. The best of the four is John McClure's "The Syntax of Decadence in *Absalom, Absalom!*" (pp. 96–103). This brief essay offers some valuable insights into the relationship between style and meaning in the novel. Starting from the idea that Faulkner's characters are "deeply damaged people, and one manifestation of the damage they have suffered is the way they speak," McClure argues that the desire to remain locked in reverie is almost as strong in the novel as is the urge toward disclosure. Another essay of some value is Leon S. Roudiez' "*Absalom, Absalom!*: The Significance of Contradictions" (pp. 58–78). Roudiez traces an interesting linkage between the "ambiguous social liberalism" of the early years of the Great Depression and Faulkner's characterization of Thomas Sutpen, but he largely vitiates his central argument about the significance of contradictions by not attending to any of the recent good work on the novel.

Unfortunately the other two *Minnesota Review* essays are exercises in dogmatic Marxism. One of them, Gaylord C. Leroy's "Mythopoeic Materials in *Absalom, Absalom!*: What Approach for the Marxist Critic?" (pp. 79–95), is a rather jazzily written, condescending consideration of what the Marxist critic should do about Faulkner's unfortunately retrograde view of history. The other, Norman Markowitz' "William Faulkner's 'Tragic Legend': Southern History and *Absalom, Absalom!*" (pp. 104–17), is a savage attack on Faulkner by a Marxist historian. As far as Markowitz is concerned, the only reason Faulkner's novels are highly valued is that "the academic establishment . . . have placed [*sic*] Faulkner in the upper reaches of their literary Pantheon and have stubbornly kept him there." It is extremely irritating to watch the literary critics at the symposium striving in the discussion period afterward to understand, to *sympathetically* understand, this contemptuous dismissal of our greatest writer and of their own profession.

For various reasons, the remaining three items on *Absalom, Absalom!* all fail to provide much insight into the novel. In " 'Be Sutpen's Hundred': Imaginative Projection of Landscape in *Absalom, Absalom!*" (*SLJ* 13,i:3–14) Thadious M. Davis observes that *Ab-*

salom, Absalom! can be distinguished from Faulkner's other major novels by the spareness and infrequency of its landscape descriptions. Rather than pursue the interesting question of why this is so, Davis chooses to expand the category of landscape to unworkable dimensions by including in it descriptions of characters and physical structures and the "landscapes" of Quentin's and Rosa Coldfield's minds. Allan Chavkin's "The Imagination as Alternative to Sutpen's Design" (*ArQ* 37:116–26) is a conventional paean to the power of the imagination to create reality in the novel. Finally, Thomas E. Connolly's "Point of View in Faulkner's *Absalom, Absalom!*" (*MFS* 27:255–72) is a reductive analysis of the function of point of view in the novel. Connolly unfairly accuses Faulkner of oversights and inconsistencies and often finds only limited justification for the novel's complex narrative strategies.

The year also saw the publication of two studies of *The Unvanquished,* but unfortunately neither of them has much new to say. The chapter on *The Unvanquished* in Thomas Daniel Young's *The Past in the Present,* pp. 25–45, is an elegantly written but old-fashioned discussion of the place of traditional values in the novel. The second item, Warren Akin IV's " 'Blood and Raising and Background': The Plot of *The Unvanquished*" (*MLS* 11[1980–81]:3–11) assesses the strengths and weaknesses of the plot of the novel according to conventional criteria. Akin says that the plot is a partial success.

The remaining two items in this section attest to the recent growth of interest in Faulkner's work as a screenwriter. In *The Road to Glory* (So. Ill.) Matthew J. Bruccoli reprints Joel Sayre's and Faulkner's 1935 draft screenplay for a movie directed by Howard Hawks. The volume contains an interesting afterword by George Garrett; Garrett writes about the screenplay with a craftsman's eye, showing how Sayre and Faulkner stretched the conventions of the World War I movie to the point where they could accommodate some elements at least of Faulkner's vision of reality. The screenplay itself contains some interesting anticipations of *A Fable.* The second item on Faulkner as a screenwriter, Peter Hogue's "Hawks and Faulkner: *Today We Live*" (*LFQ* 9:51–58), is more concerned with the completed movie than with either Faulkner's screenplay or "Turnabout," the story on which the screenplay is based. Hogue concludes, oddly, that *"Today We Live* is not at all 'Faulknerian,' even though it remains remarkably faithful to Faulkner's story."

vii. Individual Works, 1940–49

Other than Heck's and Portch's influence studies (see section *iv.a*) and Southard's study of style in *Go Down, Moses* (see section *iv.b*), only two studies appeared during 1981 on the fiction of the 1940s, both of them on *Go Down, Moses*. Daniel G. Ford's "Mad Pursuit in *Go Down, Moses*" (*CollL* 7:115–26) is a very uneven essay. Scattered among its awkward constructions, forced observations, and naive uses of previous commentary are some astute comments about the imagistic and thematic interconnections among the seven sections of the novel. Karl F. Zender's "Faulkner at Forty: The Artist at Home" (*SoR* 17:288–302) examines *Go Down, Moses* in relation to Faulkner's life and seeks to show that a number of the novel's characters are authorial surrogates.

viii. Individual Works, 1950–62

The most ambitious study of the fiction of the last decade of Faulkner's career to appear during 1981 is Noel Polk's *Faulkner's "Requiem for a Nun": A Critical Study* (Indiana). Anyone who is at all conversant with Faulkner scholarship knows of its profound indebtedness to Polk. In the perspicacity with which he has selected projects on which to work and the extraordinary energy with which he has brought them to completion, he has shown himself to be one of the premier representatives of the second generation of Faulkner scholars. This book, which originated in Polk's University of South Carolina dissertation and has been some ten years in the making, is clearly intended to be his critical *chef d'oeuvre*. In it, Polk proposes to effect a revolution in our understanding of *Requiem for a Nun* and especially in our assessment of its characters. In his words, his aim is to prove that "Nancy's murder of Temple's baby . . . is the act of a madwoman and not of a saint; that Nancy's and Stevens' stated motives are not necessarily their real ones; that Stevens is not at all out to 'save' Temple but rather to crucify her; and that Temple rather than Nancy is at the moral center of the novel."

Unfortunately the case Polk presents is not convincing. Most of its difficulties are implicit in the statement of purpose quoted above. For one thing, as Polk himself suggests from time to time, our present understanding of the novel and its characters is considerably more complex and various than his statement would have us believe: it is surely significant, for example, that almost all of the quotations he cites in support of his claim that the Augean stable of criticism on *Requiem* needs to be swept clean are taken from reviews and quite early works of criticism. Also troublesome is the inhibiting effect that his decision to give his book such a strong argumentative orientation has on its range and variety. *Faulkner's "Requiem for a Nun"* contains some good things: an occasional new context in which to view an element of the novel, a good reading of the prose interchapter entitled "The Jail," and, as Floyd C. Watkins observed in his review of the book (*AL* 54[1982]:134–35), a reflective last chapter in which Polk allows himself to take a more relaxed view of the moral issues raised by the novel than the one he permits himself to take in the body of his book. But such incidental virtues are surprisingly rare for a book so long in the making. It is as if Polk's decision to align himself with what L. C. Knights once called the adversary school of criticism afflicted him with a case of tunnel vision, leaving him unable to see any features of the novel not directly germane to the case he was trying to build.

Most troublesome of all, though, is Polk's failure to make the interpretation he advances anything more than an obverse reflection of the one he wishes to deny. He is surely right to say that *Requiem for a Nun* deserves our serious attention; but along with our attention, it deserves a fresh point of view as well, one that breaks free of the game of critical handy-dandy in which characters are shuttled back and forth between the categories of hero and villain, justice and thief. "Saint" and "madwoman" are equally unsatisfactory designations for Nancy Mannigoe because each excludes a significant aspect of the combination of Faulkner's intentions and our reactions that constitutes the novel's field of meaning. Faulkner begins *Requiem for a Nun*, as he did *Light in August*, with a seemingly inexplicable murder; but here, in contrast to the earlier novel, he does not then give us the psychological and sociological information we need to have if we are to arrive at a satisfactorily complex understanding of the murderer's motives. In part this is so, as Polk rightly emphasizes, because Faulkner is more interested in exploring the effect of the murder on his other characters than he is in explaining its cause. But Faulkner's indifference to establishing a plausible context in which to view the murder suggests that it may also have contained a deeper, more private significance for him. Perhaps this is the place to start, rather than at that later point in the critical process where we assign labels to characters: who (or what) did Faulkner kill in *Requiem for a Nun?* and why?

The next item I have to consider—the two-volume *"A Fable": A Concordance to the Novel* (Univ. Microfilms)—is another product of Polk's labors. As was the case with last year's concordance to *The Sound and the Fury*, textual editing for the *Fable* concordance was done by Polk, with Kenneth L. Privratsky, his co-editor, providing technical and administrative assistance. The new concordance gives every appearance of maintaining the high standards of the past volumes in the series, but as I contemplate it, I find myself thinking back to a meeting several years ago of the Faulkner Concordance Advisory Board, at which I and several other people argued in favor of work beginning soon on a concordance to *Absalom, Absalom!* The response we were given—that the text of *Absalom* is unreliable and hence the novel should be given a lower priority than others in the canon—evidently carried the day. However unreliable the text is, though, it is good enough to convince reader after reader that *Absalom* is the greatest novel ever written by an American and to lead increasing numbers of people to want to study the novel and to write about it. A concordance to *A Fable* is of course most welcome; but soon, please, *Absalom?*

The only other work on *A Fable* to appear during 1981 is Doreen Fowler's "The Old Verities in Faulkner's Fable [*sic*]" (*Renascence* 34:41–51). Fowler provides an interesting comparison of the depictions of individuals and communities in *A Fable* with those in Faulkner's earlier fiction. As is often the case with studies of *A Fable*, though, Fowler's examination of the novel itself is somewhat impeded by her eagerness to repudiate earlier harsh judgments of its worth. The only other essay to appear on the fiction of the last decade is James B. Carothers' "The Road to *The Reivers*" (*"A Cosmos,"* pp. 95–124). Like Carothers' "The Myriad Heart" (see section *iii.a*), this essay takes a developmental approach to its subject, but does so in a way that tends to overvalue the late novels.

ix. The Stories

The one substantial study of the short stories to appear during 1981 is Hans H. Skei's *William Faulkner: The Short Story Career* (Oslo: Universitetsforlaget). This book, which is based on Skei's University of Oslo dissertation, is a survey of Faulkner's career as a short story writer, with particular emphasis on genetic and textual issues. Though Skei displays a wide-ranging knowledge both of the stories themselves and of the critical commentary and scholarship they have generated, problems in organization and exposition seriously limit the book's usefulness. The remaining three items in this category are all studies of individual stories. In "Tomorrow and Tomorrow and Tomorrow" (*SoQ* 19:183–97) Jack Barbera examines the relationship between Faulkner's story "Tomorrow" and the television play and movie that Horton Foote adapted from it. Barbera concludes that the movie script preserves the tone and outlook of the story, even though it makes major changes in the plot. The remaining two studies, both by M. E. Bradford, are more concerned with advancing a theory of politics and culture than with explicating Faulkner's fiction. In "Family and Community in Faulkner's 'Barn Burning'" (*SoR* 17:332–39) Bradford uses Sarty Snopes's rebellion against his father as a point of departure for an argument that "the moral life is finally a question of internal choice." Bradford's second essay, "Faulkner's 'A Courtship': An Accommodation of Cultures" (*SAQ* 80:355–59), is in part directed toward holding "the Indian leaders responsible for the decline of the red man and his replacement by new settlers of European stock."

University of California, Davis

10. Fitzgerald and Hemingway

Scott Donaldson

Two long-awaited publications, Carlos Baker's selection of Hemingway letters and Matthew J. Bruccoli's substantial Fitzgerald biography, constituted the major news of the year. Though there were also three critical books on Hemingway, the most significant work probably came in two articles which used structuralist and semiotic methods to examine stories from *In Our Time*. Once again, Fitzgerald criticism concentrated primarily on *The Great Gatsby*, and there was not much of it.

i. Bibliography, Letters, and Biography

Bruccoli's *Some Sort of Epic Grandeur: The Life of F. Scott Fitzgerald* (Harcourt) is more a highly useful collection of information, virtually an encyclopedia, than a conventional literary biography. The emphasis throughout is on Fitzgerald as a dedicated professional writer. The book contains little literary criticism and less about Fitzgerald's personality. Yet what it does provide will prove of value to all Fitzgerald scholars, for in its 624 pages Bruccoli has assembled a great many details unavailable to or unnoted by previous biographers. He also includes in full measure various documents—letters, tapes, reviews—previously printed but scattered among several volumes, and corrects some persistent misconceptions, among them the notion of Fitzgerald as inspired amateur. Authoritative in style, the book invades the minds of both Fitzgeralds without compunction but does not allow for much growth in Fitzgerald's thinking.

Richard L. White's unsophisticated survey of seven good and bad biographies (prior to Bruccoli's) in "F. Scott Fitzgerald: The Cumulative Portrait" (*Biography* 4:154–68) concludes that the appeal of the writer derives from a combination of his accessibility—our sense that he is somehow one of us, though a genius—and the poignancy of his life and work. Scott Donaldson's "The Political Development of F. Scott Fitzgerald" (*Prospects* 6:313–55) contradicts the image of Fitzgerald as intellectual naif through an extensive survey of his political ideas, tracing them from relative indifference in the 1920s through a period of Marxist sympathy in the 1930s to final maturity of judgment during the Hollywood years.

The collected verse in Fitzgerald's *Poems 1911–1940*, edited by Bruccoli with a fine introduction by James Dickey (Gale), proves two things: (1) he was not a good serious poet because, as Dickey notes, his lyric gift was "deeply embedded in a sense of drama" and depended on situations in which the drama had been built up "by the preceding interactions between people," and (2) he was a clever writer of light verse who was not jesting when he suggested that he might have followed the same path as Cole Porter or Lorenz Hart.

In his 1954 "The Art of the Short Story," printed in its entirety for the first time (*ParisR* 23:85–102), Ernest Hemingway addresses the reader as "Jack," attacks other writers, and dons a cloak of infallibility himself. Even in this vein, however, he has important things to say about several of his stories and about the issues of omission and invention. Far more significant, of course, is the publication of *Selected Letters 1917–1961* (Scribner's), which opens perspectives on Hemingway as a personality that could only be hinted at by critics and biographers previously reduced to paraphrasing language which lost its flavor in the process. With minimal notation but liberal cross-referencing to his definitive biography, Baker has chosen to print about ten percent of the available Hemingway letters. This judicious selection reveals the author's egotism and nastiness and belligerence as well as his tenderness and sensitivity and humor. Hemingway did not write much about his work, unfortunately, except to supply word counts of his daily production. The subjects, instead, are fishing and shooting, bullfighting and war, gossip and above all the self. Toward the end the letters, like the published prose, get duller and longer, then lapse into paranoia.

Kenneth S. Lynn's "Hemingway's Private War" (*Commentary* 72,i:24–33) suggests both what can and what should not be done with these letters. Beginning with the presumption that the correspondence can help elucidate Hemingway's stories, Lynn proceeds to some fascinating if eccentric conclusions. He sees "The End of Something" as Hemingway's trying out in fiction the idea of divorce, and "Indian Camp" as related to his being absent when his first son was delivered. Such interpretations sometimes strain against the evidence to make a psychological point, as in Lynn's linchpin argument that "Big Two-Hearted River" is less about the war than Ernest's ongoing quarrel with his mother.

Correspondence provides the evidence for two notes of biographical interest. Ray Lewis White documents through letters Sherwood "Anderson's Private Reaction to *The Torrents of Spring*" (*MFS* 26: 635–37). The reaction was mild. Anderson twice invited the younger writer to visit him on his farm in Virginia after learning of the 1926 parody and announced his intention to visit Paris—and Hemingway —later in the year. Edward F. Stanton's constructive "The Correspondent and the Doctor: A Spanish Friendship" (*HemR* 1,i:53–55) traces the relationship between Hemingway and Dr. Juan Madinaveitia of Madrid.

In "On Aprocryphism" (*ParisR* 23:280–301) Martha Gellhorn, who has for so long kept silence about her years with Hemingway, launches a largely convincing attack on the credibility of Stephen Spender and (especially) Lillian Hellman where anecdotes involving the Spanish Civil War are concerned. Gellhorn labels these writers, and others whose tales tend to build themselves up at the expense of Hemingway, as "apocryphiars." In a response (same issue: pp. 304–06), Spender attempts to deflect such charges. Delving further back into Hemingway's career are two notes about the beginnings in Paris. Scott Donaldson's "Gertrude Stein Reviews Hemingway's *Three Stories & Ten Poems*" (*AL* 53:114–15) locates and reprints the first known review of Hemingway's first book. Jacqueline Tavernier-Courbin's "The Paris Notebooks" (*HemR* 1,i:23–26) inventories and describes 28 notebooks Hemingway kept during the 1920s in Paris.

"Hemingway Manuscripts: Talks Given at MLA" (*HemR* 6,ii: 2–19) includes Tavernier-Courbin's "The Manuscripts of *A Moveable Feast*" and Donaldson's "The Case of the Vanishing American and Other Puzzlements in Hemingway's Fiction" as well as Michael S. Reynolds' "Words Killed, Wounded, Missing in Action." Reynolds focuses on apparent mistakes, particularly deletions Hemingway did not want made, in *Sun* and *Farewell*; Tavernier-Courbin presents an excellent overview of the way *Feast* was edited after the author's death, with special attention to four omitted chapters; Donaldson notes a number of confusions and contradictions in the stories. Is a carefully edited standard text called for, as both Reynolds and Donaldson propose? No, according to Robert E. Gajdusek's "On the Definition of a Definitive Text: Hemingway" (*HemR* 1,i:18–22), which maintains that "the errors are of a sort that really could not have been missed by the Hemingway we know, and that is a far greater argument for leaving them intact than is our own confusion . . . ."

ii. Criticism

a. **Full-Length Studies.**   There are three books of uneven merit on Hemingway, none on Fitzgerald. *Ernest Hemingway: The Papers of a Writer*, ed. Bernard Oldsey (Garland) reproduces the essays—some of them first-rate—presented at the opening of the Hemingway collection. (See *ALS 1980*, 175, for comments on these essays, which first appeared in a special number of *CollL*.) Wirt Williams' *The Tragic Art of Ernest Hemingway* (LSU) goes skimming through the novels and some of the stories in search of support for the view that his fiction moved progressively toward "highly self-conscious tragedy." Equally self-conscious, Williams contends, was Hemingway's use of musical structures to unify the novels; he finds musical forms and symbolic resonances everywhere, not always convincingly. Moreover, the book tends to overvalue work that best fits its thesis. *Across the River* is called, despite its false notes, "a composition of awesome plan and singular beauty." Reynolds' valuable *Hemingway's Reading, 1910–1940* (Princeton) supplies an inventory of books owned or borrowed up to 1940, followed by an index which segregates them into such dominant categories as biography, military history, and poetry, and is preceded by an opening chapter which demonstrates how readable academic prose can be in recounting two tales of scholarly detection: how Reynolds unearthed the reading lists used at Oak Park High School in 1917 and how he was thwarted by various state departments in his attempt to see the library at the Finca Vigia in Cuba.

b. General Essays. A fine article previously unreviewed here is Fay T. Greenwald's "Fitzgerald's Female Narrators" (*MHLS* 2[1979]: 116–33), which asserts that Rosemary and Cecilia fail as narrators where Nick succeeds since they are too immature, too emotionally tied to the protagonist, and neither perceptive nor innocent enough to judge as well as observe the action. Christian K. Messenger's *Sport and the Spirit of Play* deals at length with both Fitzgerald and Hemingway (as well as with Lardner and Faulkner). In examining Fitzgerald's depiction of the "School Sports Hero," Messenger traces the degeneration of romantic football heroes into brutal Tom Buchanans and complicated Dick Divers. Hemingway, on the other hand, considers sport an agonizing struggle in which a "competitor stands alone, physically exposed" to danger, pain, and even death in a ritual that sometimes approaches the sacred. Ronald J. Gervais' wide-ranging and literate "The Trains of Their Youth: The Aesthetics of Homecoming in *The Great Gatsby*, *The Sun Also Rises* and *The Sound and the Fury*" (*AAus* 6[1980]:51–63) asserts that memories of homecoming give Nick, Jake, and Quentin the "deepest sense they have of their own lives."

The best of four philosophically oriented studies of Hemingway is Richard C. Gebhardt's "Hemingway's Complex Values" (*HemR* 1,i:2–10). This significant article, which leads off the initial number of the *Hemingway Review*, attacks the critical tendency to characterize his world-view either as nihilistic or as optimistic. Hemingway's pilosophy is more complex than that: often, Gebhardt observes, his fiction simultaneously denies and affirms traditional values. Anders Breidlid's thorough if not especially original "Courage and Self-Affirmation in Ernest Hemingway's 'Lost Generation' Fiction" (*Edda* 2[1979]:279–99) finds existential affirmation in the fiction. Hemingway's protagonists are not "lost," Breidlid concludes, because "they reject surrender as a possible alternative in times of ultimate crisis." Olga Eugenia Flores's rather pedestrian "Eros, Thanatos and the Hemingway Soldier" (*ASInt* 18,iii–iv:27–35) traces the progress of Frederic Henry and Robert Jordan from the isolated world of Thanatos to that of Eros, where, paradoxically, they find both individuality and communion. An interesting letter from Mary Hemingway enlivens Gerald Locklin and Charles Stetler's "Ernest Hemingway: 'Best of all he loved the fall' " (*HN* 6,ii:20–24), an exercise in rescuing Hemingway from what the authors maintain is a widespread belief that he was a "despoiler of nature."

c. Essays on Specific Works: Fitzgerald. Two articles on *The Beautiful and Damned* (a novel which will bear much more examination) and one on *This Side of Paradise* complement the usual pieces on *Gatsby*. Lynn Haywood's "Historical Notes for *This Side of Paradise*" (*RALS* 10[1980]:191–208) meticulously glosses a wealth of dated or obscure references in Fitzgerald's first novel. Some of the references, as to Aaron Burr, hardly need explaining, but many, as to Clara Shanafelt, certainly do. George J. Searles's "The Symbolic Function of Food and Eating in F. Scott Fitzgerald's *The Beautiful and Damned*" (*BSUF* 22,iii:14–19) marshals an impressive body of evidence for his thesis that Fitzgerald as moralist used discussion of eating habits to discredit Anthony Patch and his companions, and to symbolize their decline. Somewhat less convincingly, Ronald J. Gervais' " 'Sleepy Hollow's Gone': Pastoral Myth and Artifice in Fitzgerald's *The Beautiful and Damned*" (*BSUF* 22,iii:75–79) sees the principal characters as "haunted by the loss of a mythical rural paradise"; the novel, he asserts, is "torn between the pastoral impulse as neurotic withdrawal or as fulfillment of a basic human need for order and stability."

Patricia Pacey Thornton explores the "twinship" of three sets of couples in "Sexual Roles in *The Great Gatsby*" (*ESC* 5[1979]:457–68) and identifies Fitzgerald as a leading chronicler of redefined sexual roles. "The Fitzgerald here is a mirror looker, an egotist, and chooses the girl for her possession of qualities that he, himself, does or would like to possess." Susan Resneck Parr's "Individual Responsibility in *The Great Gatsby*" (*VQR* 57:662–80) moves from two telling insights—that Nick Carraway expects honesty from men but not from women and thus covers his own behavior and Gatsby's with a false facade of integrity—to the less persuasive conclusion that Fitzgerald shared his narrator's moral confusion. Though unsophisticated in handling biographical data and careless in referring to the text (Daisy is reported as telling Gatsby that "Rich girls don't marry poor boys"), Tim Sherer's "Midwestern Influences in F. Scott Fitzgerald's *The Great Gatsby*" (*SSMLN* 11,ii:9–22) takes a fresh tack by regarding Gatsby as less a romantic visionary than a child of his midwestern background driven by perseverance, individualism, and hopefulness.

There are two good notes on *Gatsby*. Bruce Bawer's first-rate " 'I Could Still Hear the Music': Jay Gatsby and the Musical Metaphor" (*NMAL* 5:Item 25) admirably shows how musical references work to contrast "Gatsby's romanticism with the world's reality." Carla Micklus' "Fitzgerald's Revision of *The Great Gatsby*: The Creation of a Textual Anomaly" (*AN&Q* 19[1980]:21–24) regards Nick's early remark that "men who had cared for" Daisy were singularly attracted by her voice as "inexplicable" unless Nick had himself loved her or known someone who did very well. The apparent anomaly Micklus accounts for by a careful textual examination of the shift from a third-person narrator, in the 1923 working draft, to the first-person Carraway of the finished novel. Two other notes discuss possible influences. Jon Bakker's "Parallel Water Journeys into the American Eden in John Davis's *The First Settlers of Virginia* and F. Scott Fitzgerald's *The Great Gatsby*" (*EAL* 16:50–53) draws a doubtful comparison between the ending of *Gatsby* and a passage near the end of Davis' 1805 novel: in each the vision of an earthly paradise is compromised by suggestions of "postlapsarian loss and death." The last word on *Gatsby* comes from Elizabeth Evans' slight but graceful "Opulent Vulgarity: Ring Lardner and F. Scott Fitzgerald" (*NConL* 10,i [1980]:2–3); which suggests that Gatsby's shirt scene may derive from a related display in Lardner's *The Big Town*.

Garry N. Murphy and William C. Slattery's important "The Flawed Text of 'Babylon Revisited': A Challenge to Editors, a Warning to Readers" (*SSF* 18:315–18) proves beyond question that one paragraph in the description of Charlie's taxi ride from the Ritz to the left bank should be omitted. The cut makes sense of the passage, and Fitzgerald wanted it made. Ronald J. Gervais somewhat unconvincingly argues in "A Miracle of Rare Device: Fitzgerald's 'The Ice Palace'" (*NMAL* 5:Item 21) that the story has been too narrowly construed, since it achieves "a Coleridgean synthesis of opposites for a brief and wondrous moment."

d. Essays on Specific Works: Hemingway. The first of two good articles on Hemingway's novels, Warren Wedin's persuasive and original "Trout Fishing and Self-Betrayal in *The Sun Also Rises*"

(*ArQ* 37:63–74) attributes Jake's "flat and uninspired" account of the fishing trip to Burguete to his distress about Brett and Cohn. The five days in Burguete are thus seen not as an idyllic interlude but a link in the chain of Jake's progressive disillusionment. The other major essay, Joyce Wexler's "E.R.A. for Hemingway: A Feminist Defense of *A Farewell to Arms*" (*GaR* 35:111–23), offers a welcome corrective to denigrations of Catherine Barkley. She is "neither demeaned nor idealized," Wexler asserts, but presented as the kind of brave and loving person that Frederic eventually becomes. Three notes are also concerned with the novels. Robert McIlvaine's "Robert Cohn and *The Purple Land*" (*NMAL* 5:Item 8) uncovers parallels between W. H. Hudson's work and *Sun*. Carolina Lawson Donadio's more extensive "Hemingway, Stendhal and War" (*HN* 6,ii:28–33) proposes that the retreat from Caporetto was influenced by the depiction of the battle of Waterloo in *The Charterhouse of Parma*, a novel Hemingway admired. Edward R. Stephenson's overlong "The 'Subtle Brotherhood' of Crane and Hemingway" (*HemR* 1,i:42–52) points to connections between "The Open Boat" and *The Old Man and the Sea*, the closest being a common "empathetic approach to the world."

By far the most significant critical articles on Hemingway were those by Robert Scholes and David Lodge, each of which employed contemporary critical techniques to arrive at fresh insights. Using the diegetic process to investigate "A Very Short Story," Scholes's "Decoding Papa: A Hemingway Story as Word and Text," a chapter in his *Semiotics and Interpretation* (Yale), pp. 110–26, excellently illustrates the usefulness of the semiotic approaches. Though the style of the story seems almost to "efface itself" through a fairy tale beginning and a third-person narration, it only wears "a mask of pseudo-objectivity." The text is the product of "a double motivation. It wants to be art, to be a work [in the New Critical sense]. But it also wants to rewrite life . . . ." Scholes judiciously brings biography to bear on his conclusions only after he has arrived at them. Lodge's brilliant and extremely suggestive "Analysis and Interpretation of the Realist Text: A Pluralistic Approach to Ernest Hemingway's 'Cat in the Rain'" (*PoT* 1,iv[1980]:5–19) uses the tools of "narratology," the poetics of fiction, and rhetorical analysis to shed light on this puzzling story. Besides demonstrating that Hemingway's stories are particularly well adapted to interpretation through a combination of critical methods, essays like these two—written with clarity and sensitivity—go far toward bringing formalist and structuralist modes into harmony.

Two closely reasoned notes deal with other Hemingway stories. In "The Look of Hemingway's 'In Another Country' " (*SSF* 18:309–13) Colin S. Cass maintains that the motif of looking at walls and out of windows helps to tie together a story which otherwise seems divided between the American soldier and the Italian major. Paul R. Jackson concludes in "Hemingway's 'Out of Season' " (*HemR* 1,i:11–17) that confusion about the story derives from a shifting point of view.

As usual, "Macomber" received a good deal of attention. John J. McKenna and Marvin V. Peterson's well-informed "More Muddy Water: Wilson's Shakespeare in 'The Short Happy Life of Francis Macomber' " (*SSF* 18:82–85) shows how risky it is to assume, because the quotation about owing God a death is spoken by one of Shakespeare's fools, that Wilson's use of the quote is meant to discredit him. Robert E. Fleming's "When Hemingway Nodded: A Note on Firearms in 'The Short Happy Life' " (*NMAL* 5:Item 17) points out that Hemingway was in error about Wilson's rifle generating a "muzzle velocity of two tons," since velocity is measured in feet per second. In an ingenious attempt to solve the question of Margot's complicity in her husband's death, Jerry A. Herndon speculates in " 'Macomber' and the 'Fifth Dimension' " (*NMAL* 5:Item 24) that the objective tone of "Mrs. Macomber, in the car, had shot at the buffalo . . ." reflects the technical testimony Wilson will deliver at the inquest, not the actual truth of the matter. John J. Seydow's "Francis Macomber's Spurious Masculinity" (*HemR* 1,i:33–41), which derives most of its evidence from sources outside the story, advances the unlikely view that Macomber does not achieve manly courage at the end but dies full of foolish illusions. Finally, Harbour Winn's "Hemingway's African Stories and Tolstoy's 'Illich' " (*SSF* 18:451–53) proposes that both "Macomber" and "Snows" "build . . . upon" Tolstoy's story yet remain uniquely Hemingway's.

Peter Hays also addresses the issue of borrowings in "Hemingway, Faulkner, and a Bicycle Built for Death" (*NMAL* 5:Item 28). Percy Grimm pursues Joe Christmas on a bicycle in *Light in August* (1932); bicycle policemen serve as harbingers of death in "Snows" (1936). Did Hemingway borrow? No, Hays decides: the writers read each other's work and were not unduly influenced thereby. Jayne A. Widmayer's "Hemingway's Hemingway Parodies: The Hypocritical Griffon and the Dumb Ox" (*SSF* 18:433–38) a rare examination of the 1951 "Good Lion" and "Faithful Bull" fables, regards them as "satiric attacks on pretentiousness and affectation" directed at least in part at *Across the River*.

e. **Dissertations.** In a reversal of the ratio of the past few years, there were four on Fitzgerald and two on Hemingway. Perhaps the most promising among several interesting subjects is "America Revisited: History and Setting in the Works of F. Scott Fitzgerald" by Elizabeth June Silver.

College of William and Mary

Part II

11. Literature to 1800

William J. Scheick

This year studies of Colonial and early National literature spoke in several voices. While many evinced a subdued monotone or echoed the expressions of others, editors spoke the loudest. Large editorial projects, some more useful than others, included the writings of Anne Bradstreet, Edward Taylor, Benjamin Franklin, Native American captives, and prerevolutionary women poets. The most urgent voices this year argued for a keener sensitivity to Jonathan Edwards' intellectual indebtedness and to Charles Brockden Brown's philo-aesthetic achievement.

i. Puritan Poetry

The puzzling manner and organization of a long poem by Edward Taylor received attention in Dennis H. Barbour's "*Gods Determinations* and the Hexameral Tradition" (*EAL* 16:213–25) and George Sebouhian's "Conversion Morphology and the Structure of *Gods Determinations*" (*EAL* 16:226–40). Barbour, who in passing misquotes Milton, details how Taylor's emphasis on the Westfield community, his use of a colloquial style, and his reliance on an impressionistic approach to Genesis depart from hexameral tradition. More interested in the "affective structure" of *Gods Determinations*, Sebouhian discloses an organizational principle in the poem modeled on Taylor's view of the underlying pattern of conversion. Sebouhian presents a thoughtful case well summarized in an outline appended to his essay.

Beyond a doubt the appearance of *The Unpublished Writings of Edward Taylor* (Hall) in three volumes represents not only a fitting conclusion to many years of dedicated work by editors Thomas M. and Virginia L. Davis, but also a valuable contribution to studies of Taylor's work. This contribution includes (1) a careful edition of Taylor's church records, sermons, and verse heretofore virtually inaccessible; (2) meticulous textual apparatuses; (3) a wealth of new data on the gathering of the Westfield church, on the influence of James Fitch on the Westfield creed, on Taylor's extensive and inflexible communal authority, and on the dates of as well as the ideas behind the evolution of Solomon Stoddard's thoughts about conversion and open admission to the Lord's Supper. Concerning the poet more personally, the Davises offer inviting speculations on Taylor's move to Westfield as a re-enactment of the Puritan migration to New England, the chronology of the types of poetry he wrote during his life, the importance of his metrical paraphrases of the Psalms in Hebrew, and the isolation of the elderly poet from the tragedy of the failed Puritan undertaking. In short, *Unpublished Writings* is exemplary, informative, impeccable, and handsome.

In the editorially conservative *The Complete Works of Anne Bradstreet* (Twayne) editors Joseph R. McElrath and Allan P. Robb concede that the first publication of Bradstreet's poetry was unauthorized, based in fact on an incomplete manuscript. They also admit that the poet revised later, but they are nonetheless convinced that the first edition is probably closer to authorial intent. If their claim evokes an image of crystal-ball vapors, their book is certainly palpable. More than half of this 578-page work is painstakingly devoted to emendations of copy-texts, textual notes, press variants, errata, variations in the manuscripts, and explanatory notes—all of which implicitly warns scholars to be chary about relying on any given version of a poem by Bradstreet. A sensible, nonpolemical conclusion, however, appears in " 'No Rhet'ric We Expect': Argumentation in Bradstreet's 'The Prologue'" (*EAL* 16:19–26), in which Jane Donahue Eberwein follows the poet's attempt to demarcate and resolve antithesis by at once emphasizing discrepancies and intimating unity.

Bradstreet and Taylor, among a host of other poets, appear in "Seventeenth-Century American Poetry: A Reference Guide Updated" (*RALS* 10[1980]:121–45), in which Catherine Rainwater and William J. Scheick present an annotated bibliography of scholarship, written from 1971 to 1980, on American colonial verse.

ii. Puritan Prose

Not only Puritan verse but also Puritan prose, particularly histories and sermons, repeatedly depict the world as a theater and the individual as a character in a cosmic drama with tragic overtones. This assertion, the thesis of Paul Sorrentino's "God's Cosmic Drama: Christian Tragedy in the Puritan Vision of Life" (*Soundings* 63 [1980]:432–50), finds scant explicit textual support, evinces no awareness of well-known Puritan attitudes toward the stage, and evades any clarifying sense of the concept of tragedy. Confronted with so much absence, Sorrentino's voice interprets implicit "dramatic potential" in the works of several writers, including Thomas Hooker, Benjamin Colman, and Jonathan Edwards, all of whom are nonchalantly bunched under the monolithic heading "Puritan." In contrast, prose writings by Colman, Daniel Neal, Thomas Prince, Nathaniel Appleton, and Thomas Foxcroft receive more careful attention in Bruce Tucker's "The Reinterpretation of Puritan History in Provincial New England" (*NEQ* 54:481–98). Tucker convincingly documents how the accommodation of liberty of conscience (as set forth in the Charter of 1691) softened the Puritan tradition of the Great Migration, a subtle change eliciting in writers an ambivalence evident, for instance, in the exhortative yet open-ended conclusions of several colonial New England histories.

The first of these histories is treated in Floyd Ogburn, Jr., *Style as Structure and Meaning: William Bradford's Of Plymouth Plantation* (Univ. Press). According to Ogburn, at the intrasentence level Bradford's history exhibits a reliance upon binary stress, connectives, coupling, phrase repetitions, analogies, alliteration, assonance, and parallel structures; whereas at the intersentence level the work exhibits (besides all the features of the intrasentence level) an alternation of the image of Pilgrims from subject to object as well as a movement in general from the visible to the invisible to, again, the visible. Ogburn's transmutation of old-fashioned *explication de texte* into a trendy variety of *démographie de texte* is less *nouveau* than *absence d'esprit*. His analysis of style exaggerates, forcing his categories to contain more than they permit. Moreover, to assert that Bradford's style becomes "a unified and coherent structure" amounts to a short-circuiting of terms. In spite of the title of his book, Ogburn has nothing to say theoretically about literary structure or style; he uses the words in a nontechnical sense startlingly out of phase with the demographic methodology of his study. Apparently Ogburn means to say that the sentence, not (as he says) style, forms a radical structural component in Bradford's work. Even so, a leap of faith is requisite to Ogburn's concluding observation that the intra/inter-sentence patterns of the history are "most probably conscious on the part of Bradford." More satisfying by far, if not always convincing, is Karl Keller's thoughtful discussion of the literary patterns of a second-generation descendent of Bradford's religious heritage. In "The Loose, Large Principles of Solomon Stoddard" (*EAL* 16: 27–41) Keller notes how Stoddard, through the conscious art of equivocation, extended the rhetoric of Puritan doctrine to include what it was traditionally designed to exclude.

Rhetoric, style, and structure in the writings of the son of Stoddard's most outspoken adversary concern Gustaaf Van Cromphout in "*Manuductio ad Ministerium*: Cotton Mather as Neoclassicist" (*AL* 53:631–79). Cromphout instructively discerns in Mather's book a tripartite structure exemplifying a Cartesian geometrical mode of writing. Also, Cromphout remarks, although Mather never escaped his relish for a baroque style, he became steadily more interested in neoclassical literary principles. A better-known work by Mather receives attention in Jane D. Eberwein's "'Indistinct Lustre': Biographical Miniatures in the *Magnalia Christi Americana*" (*Biography* 4:195–207), which I was unable to see. And in "Cotton Mather's Pharmacy" (*EAL* 16:42–49) Mitchell Robert Breitwieser reasonably suggests links between Mather's medical theories and his theology.

A Mather opponent, John Leverett, figures in Norman Fiering's "The First American Enlightenment: Tillotson, Leverett, and Philosophical Anglicanism" (*NEQ* 54:307–44). Fiering persuasively documents how John Tillotson provided, by means of disciples like John Leverett, a major influence on the first American Enlightenment, a time when Christian thought changed, particularly concerning nature as revelation and human reason as autonomous. These changes can be gauged, Fiering observes, in the lucidity, simplicity, and common-sense style of Enlightenment prose by Leverett and others. While Leverett was president of Harvard and even much later, students practiced another mode of prose; in "A Source for Eighteenth-Century Harvard Master's Questions" (*WMQ* 38:261–67) Minor Myers, Jr., discloses that Thomas Johnson's *Quaestiones Philosophicae* provided a source for student presentations of the *quaestio* at commencement, an observation raising the possibility that this practice was often only an academic exercise informed by a prepared syllabus.

Thinking about Harvard generated bitter thoughts in Mather's mind, especially while Leverett was, as Mather phrased it, the "pretended president." Doubtless Mather would be similarly outraged by a recent attempt to reattribute a book generally thought to have been written by his grandfather, John Cotton. In "Dissension at Quinnipiac: The Authorship and Setting of *A Discourse About Civil Government in a New Plantation Whose Design Is Religion*" (*NEQ* 54:14–32) Bruce E. Steiner determines that John Davenport, not John Cotton, wrote a work in 1639 refuting arguments against the restriction of civil power to church members; Steiner does not speculate on the oddity that this work was published for the first time 24 years after it was written. Davenport, Cotton, and other Puritan ministers have distorted current scholarship on antinomianism, explains Amy Schrager Lang in "Antinomianism and the 'Americanization' of Doctrine" (*NEQ* 54:225–42). Antinomianism, Lang contends, endorses not an assertion of self, but its denial; its deviant elevation of the private nature of grace corresponds to the deviant emphasis of traditional puritanism on an ultra-Calvinistic sanctification of individual endeavor. If for Lang mainstream puritanism and antinomianism share a greater affinity than heretofore detected, for James P. Ronda puritanism and Native American traditions were more compatible than scholars have remarked. In "Generations of Faith: The Christian Indians of Martha's Vineyard" (*WMQ* 38:369–94) Ronda focuses on Experience Mayhew's *Indian Converts* as an example of this cultural interface.

iii. The South

In "Robert Beverley Assailed: Appellate Jurisdiction and the Problem of Bicameralism in Seventeenth-Century Virginia" (*VMHB* 88 [1980]:415–29) Jon Kukla gives a timely warning to historians and literary critics to be tentative in commentary on *The History and Present State of Virginia* until Beverley's printed and manuscript sources are better identified. In an effort to provide a source for understanding 17th-century legal problems concerning land in the South, the late Richard Beale Davis edited a pertinent document in "William Fitzhugh and the Northern Neck Proprietary" (*VMHB* 89:39–43).

iv. Edwards and the Great Awakening

Recently a few scholars have insisted on the need to revise our current impression of Edwards' originality, but to date nothing on this subject compares to Norman Fiering's *Jonathan Edwards's Moral Thought and Its British Context* (N.Car.). Its occasionally irritating hubris aside, Fiering's meticulously detailed and wide-ranging book anatomizes Edwards' sources (especially writings by Nicolas Malebranche, Samuel Clarke, and William Wallaston), counters the identification of a mystical strain in Edwards' work, questions the textual reliability of *Charity and Its Fruits,* and importantly revises the claim that Edwards restored the capricious *Deus absconditus* of early Calvinism, when in fact this image of the deity is not characteristic of Calvin or Edwards, who was the most rationalistic of the Puritans in his emphasis on an inherent divine order and harmony. Fiering pinpoints where Edwards' expression of ideas about conscience and about a sense of natural beauty corresponds to the prevalent 18th-century development of a psychology independent of ethics and theology. Fiering's inquiry results in a valuable revisionist systematization of Edwardsean thought that is not reductive but traces, vis-à-vis drifts and inconsistencies, an evolving ideological configuration. As a foundation for this study Fiering has written another long, important book; mentioning Edwards and the Mathers, among others, *Moral Philosophy at Seventeenth-Century Harvard: A Discipline in Transition* (N.Car.) cogently details the emergence in colonial New England of a new moral philosophy which was not American in origin but an amalgamation of Protestant divinity, Augustinian and Cartesian psychology, neo-Platonism, and traditional classical and scholastic ethics.

Moral philosophy figures as well in Conrad Cherry's *Nature and Religious Imagination: From Edwards to Bushnell* (Fortress, 1980), which remarks an imaginative response to nature in Edwards' private and public writings. This response, Cherry explains, utilizes the images of nature less as literal "signs" or as indices to a didactic moralism (as they become for Edwards' New Divinity disciples) than as "symbols" re-presenting the meaning of the reality they signify. In order to move the hearer from sensuous experience (nature as sign) to spiritual knowledge (nature as symbol) Edwards carefully implanted images in his writings, (in Cherry's opinion) the only deliberately planned device in Edwards' sermons. The "images" of a booth, a sickness, an experience in a pasture, and a closet, according to Paul David Johnson in "Jonathan Edwards' 'Sweet Conjunction'" (*EAL* 16:270–81) are four turning points in the "Personal Narrative." If Johnson finally resorts too often to his own imagination to make a case for this organizational feature, he certainly sheds some light on the function of and relationship among segments of the narrative. The interaction of imagery, myth, and society receives attention in *Realtà e Immagine: l'estetica nei sermoni di Jonathan Edwards* (Japadre), a study written in Italian by Marcella de Nichilo, who perceives a parallel between Edwards' use of revolutionary aesthetics and the rise of revolutionary self-awareness in the American colonies.

Interest in a different sort of pattern informs "Jonathan Edwards' Change of Position on Stoddardeanism" (*HTR* 74:79–99), in which John F. Jamieson probes two implicit factors in Edwards' eventual break from his grandfather's practice of open admission to the Lord's Supper: Stoddardean practice was latently Arminian and it encouraged an easy moralism antithetical to the experiential piety associated with primitive Christianity. A summary of the social history of Stoddardean Northampton and of Edwards' difficulty coming to terms with liberal societal change during his ministry there appears in Patricia J. Tracy's *Jonathan Edwards, Pastor: Religion and Society in Eighteenth-Century Northampton* (Hill & Wang, 1980).

The extensive critical debate over Edwards' response to Stoddard can be surveyed in M. X. Lesser's *Jonathan Edwards: A Reference Guide* (Hall), an annotated bibliography composed of good abstracts, impressive coverage, and a judicious introduction reviewing trends in Edwardsean studies. Unfortunately, Lesser misses "Review of 'Edwards on the Affections'" (*Christian Review* 6[1841]:492–506), the absence of which gives the impression that of Edwards' works only *Freedom of the Will* attracted attention in 1841. A contemporary poetical response to Edwards is featured in "'How Will the Heart Endure': Robert Lowell on Jonathan Edwards" (*SAQ* 80: 429–40) by Andrew Hudgins, author of a poem on Edwards published last year (see *ALS 1980*, 202).

By the time of Edwards' senior year at Yale, according to Fier-

ing's revision (above), Samuel Johnson had resigned his tutorship
and so apparently little influenced Edwards' thought. Johnson's own
ideas are elucidated by Peter N. Carroll, whose *The Other Samuel
Johnson: A Psychohistory of Early New England* (Fairleigh Dickinson, 1978) presents an interesting biography of its subject. Occasionally Carroll's psychoanalytic interpretations seem excessive—e.g.,
construing Johnson's characterization of the Great Awakening as an
"epidemical frenzy" to reveal a subliminal expression of a fear of
his own hidden passions; sometimes Carroll invests intense personal
psychological value for Johnson in utterly commonplace conventions
or traditions. Carroll also fails to explore Johnson's writings in any
detail, an oddity calling attention to itself all the more because Carroll is quick to posit absolute validity to anything Johnson says about
himself. Nevertheless, Carroll's book provides a useful and not purely
adulatory introduction to a neglected figure in colonial studies.

Other neglected authors have their say in Pattie Cowell's edition
of *Women Poets in Pre-Revolutionary America, 1650–1775: An Anthology* (Whitston), a carefully compiled long work with informing
introductions and notes. This anthology certainly fills a gap in our
appreciation of colonial women poets, whose work will now be more
readily accessible for any attempt at revising or broadening our overview of prerevolutionary literature. Incidentally, Cowell indicates
that Hannah Griffitts' manuscripts exhibit emendations and that the
author adopted the pseudonym "Fidelia," facts which indeed answer
the question concerning her identity as a poet that I raised last year
(*ALS 1980*, 211–12) as a result of Linda Kerber's mistaken attribu-
tion to Griffitts of a poem by Jonathan Odell.

v. Franklin, Jefferson, and the Revolutionary Period

In *The Autobiography of Benjamin Franklin: A Genetic Text* (Tenn.)
editors J. A. Leo Lemay and P. M. Zall adhere to a holograph manuscript exhibiting final authorial revisions and, in their opinion, they
correct more than fifty substantive errors in the Yale edition. Lemay
and Zall argue that an outline, which Franklin basically followed in
the autobiography, proves that the work was conceived of as a whole;
this authorial self-consciousness underlies the editors' aim in the new
edition to preserve everything Franklin originally wrote, canceled,

added, or revised in his autobiography. Several points made in the introduction to this edition are repeated, with a minor supplemental speculation about a particular revision, in J. A. Leo Lemay's "Franklin's Own Story" (*Enquiry* 1,iv:7–11).

A latter-day Augustinianism in the *Autobiography*—i.e., a self-consciousness concerning the spiritual hazards of literary authorship —is discussed in "The 'Author' of Franklin's *Autobiography*" (*EAL* 16:257–69) by Philip D. Beidler: "for Franklin the man, the underside of a refreshing candor often reveals itself as an almost compulsive need to confess to sharp dealing and a host of other mortal defects; while, for Franklin the author, wit and literary play continually call into question the validity and worth of literary endeavor itself." Less insightful, Tom Bailey's "Benjamin Franklin's *Autobiography*: The Self and Society in a New World" (*MQ* 22:93–104) focuses on Franklin's displacement of selfish private values by cultural goals and of subjectivity by controlled public language. Excessive trust in the public language of newspapers is lampooned in a Franklin story, the origins of which are traced by David M. Larson in "Eighteenth-Century Tales of Sheep's Tails and One of Benjamin Franklin's 'American Jokes' " (*PQ* 59:242–47).

Franklin was "the greatest man and ornament of the age and country in which he lived," remarked Thomas Jefferson, whose biography Dumas Malone has been writing for more than thirty years. *Jefferson and His Time: The Sage of Monticello* (Little, Brown), the sixth and final volume in the series, offers a very readable account of Jefferson's last years, especially of his renewed friendship and correspondence with John Adams. (Parenthetically, a Latin epitaph for John Adams by an unidentified author appears in Leo M. Kaiser's "Epitaph for a Founding Father" [*CB* 57:61–62].) A document edited by Frank L. Dewey in "Thomas Jefferson and a Williamsburg Scandal" (*VMHB* 89:44–63) discloses Jefferson's arguments in a divorce suit before a Virginia general court in 1773. Just as his views on divorce reveal the influence of legal texts, Jefferson's ideas about agrarian life were informed by literary texts. In "The American *agricola*: Jefferson's Agrarianism and the Classical Tradition" (*SAQ* 80:339–54) Douglas L. Wilson traces Jefferson's idealization of rural life to the image of the noble husbandman in Virgil's *Georgics*. Jefferson's own image is the concern of "Discovering Jefferson in the

People's Republic of China" by John Israel and Steven H. Hockman (*VQR* 57:401–19).

"I was once sincerely affectioned towards him," Jefferson wrote about a famous political rival, whose writing receives attention in Charles L. Cohen's "The 'Liberty or Death' Speech: A Note on Religion and Revolutionary Rhetoric" (*WMQ* 38:702–17). The combination of the biblical imagery of Jeremiah and the revolutionary rhetoric of "Cato" suggest to Cohen that Patrick Henry's speech, as we now know it, is the product of several hands, a collaborative effort exemplifying the importance of religion as well as of politics in the literature of the revolutionary period. Religion-engendered expectations figure too in a seriocomic discourse on tragicomedy and didacticism in drama; the discourse (1755), apparently the first sustained colonial commentary on drama, is edited by Robert Micklus in "Dr. Alexander Hamilton's 'Modest Proposal' " (*EAL* 16:107–32). Satire in the life of another Hamilton is discussed in Walker Lewis' "Andrew Hamilton and the He-Monster" (*WMQ* 38:268–94). This 21-page satire (1726) unfairly slandering Hamilton, Lewis speculates, was written by Sir William Keith, governor of Pennsylvania at the time.

The ambiguity of a mildly satiric undercurrent informs "Crèvecoeur's James: The Education of an American Farmer" (*JEGP* 80:552–70), in which David Robinson makes a good case for reading *Letters of an American Farmer* as an account of the education of its narrator, whose optimism by the end of the work is tempered by tragic experience but is also reasserted in the untested vision of a "still simple people"; the narrator's expression of changing values, particularly concerning black slaves and Native Americans, bestows a thematic integrity to *Letters*. Ambiguity in a poem by a former slave interests James A. Levernier in "Wheatley's 'On Being Brought from Africa to America' " (*Expl* 40:25–26), which detects the poet's linguistic subversion of her apparent surface endorsement of the view that slavery was necessary to the Christianization of blacks. In "The Figure of Columbia: Phillis Wheatley Plus George Washington" (*NEQ* 54:264–66) Thomas J. Steele indicates that the personification of Columbia derives from 18th-century presentations of Apollo (poetry) and of Athene (strategy). And, finally, William H. Robinson has produced *Phillis Wheatley: A Bio-Bibliography* (Hall), an attempt to spotlight errors in currently prevalent notions about Wheatley.

vi. The Early National Period

Christian tradition, through the filter of personal religion, informs 17 previously unpublished works in "The Private Poems of Mercy Otis Warren" (*NEQ* 54:199–224) edited by Edmund M. Hayes. Financial rather than religious anxiety is the subject of "Jeremy Belknap: Man of Letters in the Young Republic" (*NEQ* 54:33–53), in which George B. Kirsch reviews Belknap's uncertain literary career and rehearses at some length our present assessment of *The Foresters.*

The financial disorder undercutting Belknap's dream of a literary career was apparently symptomatic. For, according to Patricia Cline Cohen in "Statistics and the State: Changing Social Thought and the Emergence of a Quantitative Mentality in America, 1790–1820" (*WMQ* 38:35–55), economic realities undermined a more pervasive early national vision of order; in the 1790s statistical gazetteers and almanacs, designed to make fact eliminate factionalism, provided a means for integrating the political ideas that fostered a homogeneous racial order with the economic realities that eroded faith in this evolving order. A pertinent tension informs the literature of this period, observes William Hedges in "The Old World Yet: Writers and Writing in Post-Revolutionary America" (*EAL* 16:3–18). Hedges focuses on incompletions in the writings of the Federal period, works agitatedly brooding as much on the past as on the future and mirroring social as well as literary insecurity.

vii. Brown and Contemporaries

Not only in the Federal period, argues Mukhtar Ali Isani in "The 'Fragment' as Genre in Early American Literature" (*SSF* 18:17–26), but throughout the 18th and early 19th centuries incompletion characterizes American fiction. Often this fiction, the offspring of European moral tales dramatically presenting some didactic subject, commences *in medias res* and appears to be a climatic extract of some vague larger narrative.

Narrative incompletion emerges as a central topic in *Critical Essays on Charles Brockden Brown*, ed. Bernard Rosenthal (Hall). No average collection of articles, Rosenthal's book presents six discussions of Brown's work published during the 19th century and nine contemporary essays printed for the first time, followed by a selective bibliography by Charles A. Carpenter—a bold and rewarding combination of the earliest and most recent commentary on Brown. Rosenthal's essay, the carefully reasoned "The Voices of *Wieland*" (pp. 104–25), argues that Brown's romance is an intentionally polemical work refuting morality based on any variety of religious thought; *Wieland* conveys this message principally by seeming to provide explanations while never really illuminating for Clara or for the reader, who insists on answers, the central question of whether Carwin caused Wieland to commit murder; in the elliptical style of this romance details of narrative matter less than their implications, a pattern indicative of the inexplicable nature of truth in human experience. Substantiation for Rosenthal's interpretation appears as well in "On Rereading *Wieland*: 'The Folly of Precipitate Conclusions'" (*EAL* 16:154–74), in which Cynthia S. Jordan cogently remarks Brown's deliberate frustration of the reader's anticipation of what constitutes an ending. Teeming with coincidence and corresponding to Clara's father's imperfect tale and her brother's unfinished book, *Wieland's* failure to achieve narrative closure suits a work in which reality remains inscrutable and the narrator remains unreliable.

Concern with reader response informs other essays in the Rosenthal collection. In "The Problem of Origination in Brown's *Ormond*" (pp. 126–41) William J. Scheick concludes, vis-à-vis Jacques Derrida and Michel Foucault, that the narrative manner of *Ormond*—self-referentiality, framing, nonlinear eventuation, doubling of character traits and circumstances, naming, and repetition of plot elements—keeps the reader epistemologically uneasy, just as this story told by a friend who is always distant from the place of events in the novel objectifies how everyone stands at a distance from his or her origins; by means of this manner fact and fiction transubstantiate in *Ormond*, as unknown extrinsic natural causality transposes with indefinable, self-originated motives. Similarly in "Narrative Unity and Moral Resolution in *Arthur Mervyn*" (pp. 142–63) Emory Elliott charts the unsettling effect of Brown's management of the reader, who must rethink the narrative in terms of complex moral issues and who, finally, is not invited by the author to give a verdict in an implicit moral debate concerning Mervyn's tragically limited character: "Neither picaresque saint nor complete confidence man, Mervyn, a name suggestive of Everyman, is a symbol of the amoral, unschooled but intelligent individual struggling to survive in the social turmoil of the post-revolutionary age." Paul Witherington in "'Not My Tongue Only': Form and Language in Brown's *Edgar Huntly*" (pp. 164–83) also focuses on Brown's deliberate use of an experimental fictional form composed of a cumulative style to probe ethical ambiguities, thereby impressing upon readers the impossibility of revealing truth; consequently loose ends, doubts, and lack of closure in *Edgar Huntly* parallel the pattern of the protagonist's experience of potential beginnings repeatedly culminated in denials of the possibility of enlightenment. Pertinent too is "Charting the Hidden Landscape: *Edgar Huntly*" (*EAL* 16:133–53), in which George Toles insightfully observes how the wilderness, depicted in shadowy outline, objectifies the theme of concealment in the romance; the remoteness of the wilderness intimates a hidden energy, and its persistent elusiveness, always on the verge of revelation, *appears* to be intentional and, consequently, evokes fear from as well as entraps the pursuing mind.

What Toles, Witherington, Elliott, and Scheick interpret as Brown's epistemological aesthetic technique, Nina Baym attributes to ineptitude. In the only dissenting essay in the Rosenthal collection, "A Minority Reading of *Wieland*" (pp. 87–103), Baym accuses scholars of overrating Brown's work, the abundant technical mismanagement of which suggests its author merely sought to benefit financially from the popular fictional genres of his day. *Wieland* certainly evinces difficulties, whether authorially directed or misdirected; but Baym ambushes her argument most evidently when she dismisses Brown's portrait of Clara on the basis of its incompatability with others' descriptions of her. These descriptions cannot be used as an objective measure of anything in the text because they are selectively filtered through Clara's first-person narrative, which itself as a dramatization cannot be equated literally with Brown's view of the protagonist. In the history of fiction, inconsistencies often function within such a narrative framework to violate readers' conditioned expectations and, particularly, confidence in the reliability of narrative voice, of "managing" author, and of interpreting reader. This trait figures in James R. Russo's "'The Chimeras of the Brain': Clara's Narrative in *Wieland*" (*EAL* 16:60–88). Russo, who at times too eagerly leaps to dubious conclusions, believes that Clara lies even more than she herself knows, that a far-from-innocent Clara imparts an inconsistent narrative because her insanity prevents her from differentiating fact from dream, memory from experience. Clara's narrative, according to A. Carl Bredahl, Jr., in "The Two Portraits in *Wieland*" (*EAL* 16:54–59), contains two references to portraits, the land and water imagery of which objectify the interaction of interrogative and declarative language in Brown's text; the paintings and the text reveal a shift toward empiricism, even though the conclusion of the romance suggests a submission to external and arbitrary authority.

The debate on Brown's contribution to American literature is broadened in Charles E. Bennett's essay in Rosenthal's collection: "Charles Brockden Brown: Man of Letters" (pp. 212–23), which describes the novelist's literary activity during the ten years following the completion of his romances. Brown's last two novels, notes Sydney J. Krause in "*Clara Howard* and *Jane Talbot*: Godwin on Trial" (pp. 184–211), should be read in tandem because the arguments in *Clara* transform *Jane* into a consideration of alternative moral precepts, especially apropos the concept of selflessness in William Godwin's *Political Justice*. The influence of Godwin as well as of Mary Wollstonecraft in one of Brown's earliest writings is remarked by Cathy N. Davidson in "The Matter and Manner of Charles Brockden Brown's *Alcuin*" (pp. 71–86), suggesting that Brown's use of dialogue to raise questions and to present characters deserves more attention than the ambiguity implicit in his attitude toward the issue of women's rights. Women dominate in "'My Good Momma': Women in *Edgar Huntly* and *Arthur Mervyn*" (*SAF* 9: 33–46), in which Leland S. Person, Jr., makes a case for detecting Brown's unconscious ambivalence toward family relationships (particularly the wife-figure) and his evasion of this problem through art. But according to George M. Spangler in "C. B. Brown's *Arthur Mervyn*: A Portrait of the Young American Artist" (*AL* 52:578–92) art hardly served Brown as a refuge; Mervyn, who in Spangler's view never explicitly wants to be a writer, functions as a "latent image" of, or surrogate for, Brown's ambivalence over his dream of economic security, his moral concerns, and his compulsion to tell stories. Spangler's emphasis on fragmentation of authorial purpose closes with our opening remarks on generic fragmentation in 18th-century American fiction and on inconclusive narrative manner in

Brown's romances—in short, a substantial round of scholarship this year on Brown's aesthetic of the insubstantial.

viii. Miscellaneous Studies

Puritans Among the Indians: Accounts of Captivity and Redemption, 1676–1724, ed. Alden T. Vaughan and Edward W. Clark (Harvard) presents good editions, informative notes, and a useful bibliography. Its editors reasonably contend that the close involvement of the clergy in the composition of early captivity narratives resulted in a distinctive focus on the image of the family and reinforced the influences of the spiritual autobiography, the sermon, and the jeremiad; later these narratives exhibit a greater generic self-consciousness marked by embellishment of plot and the transformation of the female protagonist from a resilient and resourceful person to a stereotypical and passive mother-figure. Not physical captivity of settlers by aborigines but the spiritual captivity of Native Americans by colonial religion is the subject of J. William T. Youngs, Jr., in "The Indian Saints of Early New England" (*EAL* 16:241–56), the appendix of which attributes a work to Thomas Shepard. Searching the textual periphery of works by Roger Williams, Thomas Mayhew, and John Eliot, Youngs discovers that Puritan ministers tended to overlook the social or material advantages underlying the conversion of individual Native Americans to Christianity. What many ministers could not overlook, according to William S. Simmons in "Cultural Bias in the New England Puritans' Perception of Indians" (*WMQ* 38:56–72), was a structural model informing their belief that Native Americans were bewitched and worshipped devils; Puritan adherence to this devil-and-witchcraft interpretation of Native American culture intensified rather than diminished over the years.

A structural model of another kind surfaces in "New England and the Challenge of Heresy, 1630 to 1660: The Puritan Crisis in Transatlantic Perspective" (*WMQ* 38:624–60), in which Stephen Foster argues that rather than manifesting a cultural decline, New England puritanism maintained a basic integrity through ongoing institutional redefinitions over the years; this process of compromise and partial reformation, moreover, mirrored the improvisational manner of English puritanism before its transplantation to the New World.

Selections from some of the earliest encounters with the New World have been republished in *Hakluyt's Voyages*, ed. Richard David (Houghton Mifflin). Modernized in spelling, punctuation, word forms, and place names, this collection of representative passages is judiciously designed for a general audience. Scholars, however, will benefit from its illustrations, maps, observations on historical, economic, and navigational background, glossary, and inclusive index. Noteworthy too is the editor's mention in passing of covert rivalry and contrapuntal voices in the narratives.

"May not a man have several voices, Robin . . .?" If collectively the many critical voices this year on the New World were not especially profound, they were nonetheless on the whole respectably helpful. And here let my voice conclude where Arthur Barlow's begins in his report on Virginia in 1584: "we hope your wisdom will be satisfied; considering that as much by us hath been brought to light as by those small means . . . we had could any way have been expected or hoped for."

University of Texas at Austin

12. 19th-Century Literature

Kermit Vanderbilt

The quality of scholarship in 1981 on the major-minor authors of the century can be rated high average. The few peaks of excellence are celebrated here, and several of the misadventures are reported in a season that has been more than abundant once again. Anyone who has read or will read the bulk of this year's studies must be heartened by the many voices of our literary past that continue to be considered seriously and reassessed from a broad range of scholarly interests and critical approaches. Relatively few of the contributors to this year's explication and criticism succumb to imitating a modish system, school, or method. Disciples of Northrop Frye or the deconstructionists have been silent. Propp is ritually cited once but not really appropriated, so to speak. There are, however, two ventures into audience response, one into semiotics, and here and there an inescapable reliance on Freud, a touch of the existential, and a vestige of recently flourishing feminism. Most of these few articles happily possess a vitality missing in the usual formula-restricted exercise. Jargon, consequently, has been mainly reduced to clinkers like "insightful," "informed by," "in terms of," and some few other moldy usages. The profession, in fact, can take pride in the directness and clarity of expression in most of the current scholarship. We might now encourage a grace and liveliness of style as well, with undisguised literary pleasure allowed, so that our days and nights of prodigious reading in each other's work may become more recreational. Many a chapter-contributor to *ALS*, past and present, will, I suspect, understand and cheer such a proposal.

i. General Studies

Two somewhat complementary books on 19th-century religious-philosophical debate, one early and the other late, are among the notable scholarly efforts of the year. David S. Reynolds' *Faith in Fiction: The Emergence of Religious Literature in America* (Harvard) is the first survey of the religious fiction of some 250 American writers from 1785 to 1850. Reynolds also casts a preliminary look at colonial origins and a parting glance at the postbellum religious novels. He helpfully organizes the central chapters of this rather punishing assignment to illuminate an entire phase of American cultural history and literary expression. Hardly to be read for an evening's pleasure (slightly more wit is necessary), *Faith in Fiction* will stand as a workmanlike reference source valuable to historians and literary scholars alike.

The nagging philosophical ambiguities neatly avoided by Reynolds' religious fictioneers help to establish the context of Harold Kaplan's *Power and Order: Henry Adams and the Naturalistic Tradition in American Fiction* (Chicago). Though his best chapters are on Adams, Kaplan prepares the philosophic ground in two introductory chapters on the naturalistic ethos and the dialectic of nature's power vs. the action of human will to order and control. He traces these ideas in the Deists, Emerson, Marx, Hegel, and other sources. The ambivalent Adams envisioned a resolution in which man, through a truly civilized education, might wrest "both power and order from nature's 'insanity of force.'" Kaplan views Adams' philosophical crisis largely in the perspective of "naturalistic politics," a contradictory dualism where man is, in one regard, merely "instrumental and passive" in the face of nature's fatalistic energies as they evolve in the history of races, classes, and nations. At the same time, the individual may learn how to conform to the will of history and become a responsible actor and judge in what then becomes an ethical drama of international politics no longer dehumanized or inevitably apocalyptic. Or so can go one paraphrase of Kaplan's grappling with the Virgin-and-Dynamo configurations.

Kaplan then pursues the implicit contradictions of amoral determinism and human agency in American naturalism (parallel to Walcutt's "divided stream") beyond Adams to Norris, Crane, and occasionally later moderns. He reads *McTeague* and *The Octopus* in the light of a proposed formula of naturalistic fiction that includes (1) the pathos of characters unjustly victimized, (2) their abstracted condition amid forces social, biological, and racial, and (3) a violence melodramatic, apocalyptic, perhaps avoidable, but when closest to the vitalist forces of nature, possibly redemptive. In this last regard, he goes on to reinterpret *The Red Badge of Courage* as Crane's affirmation of the vitalist cult. Henry Fleming discovers a transcendent " 'battle brotherhood' " after the release of primitive instincts lifts him to a metaphysical imperative and he realizes the virtues of power latent in sacrifice, suffering, group discipline, and a Nietzschean "redemptive or cathartic violence." Like the best readings of Crane's novel, Kaplan's is as debatable as it is suggestive.

Anne G. Jones's *Tomorrow is Another Day* begins, coincidentally, with Reynolds' final writer, Augusta Jane Evans, author of *Beulah* (1859). Adopting a firmly biographical approach to uncover the tensions in the fiction, Jones presents single-chapter interpretations of Evans, Grace King, and Kate Chopin. The common theme uniting the trio is the fictionalized quest for the feminine inner or "under" self. In each instance, the journey is abortive, either because of capitulation to "patriarchal values" (Evans), or the power of black-white conventional roles (King), or in Chopin's *The Awakening*, because Edna's awareness of male-female dualities has produced an explosively divided self. Two diverging roads open before her, one "the ultimate isolation of death" and the other "the deathly assimilation into a society that will not permit Edna to have 'my own way.' " In the continuing debate over Chopin's heroine, Jones clearly sides with the existential view that Edna's suicide is a final gesture of ethical choice: "acting in the best way she has discovered to feel power without harming others, she swims into the sensuous sea."

ii. Irving, Cooper, and Their Contemporaries

After a year's hiatus, the Irving Complete Works (Twayne) are once again on track with John H. McElroy's edition of *The Life and Voyages of Christopher Columbus*. Published in early 1828, the *Columbus* brought Irving popularity and academic honors at a time when he was uncertain and depressed in his writing career and sorely needed the success. It came after two years of astonishing activity as Irving, unable to interest a publisher in a translation of Navarette's volumes on Columbus, had become a biographer overnight. During ten weeks of research in Spanish documents, he wrote 700 pages, then switched off to draft his *Conquest of Granada*, and returned to revise and double the *Columbus* manuscript the next year. McElroy closely recounts these *Columbus* years. He also ranges far beyond them in a remarkably prolix and redundant introduction (80 pages, 154 footnotes). The editorial apparatus alone runs to nearly 600 pages.

Similarly elaborate are the contexts that Wayne R. Kime provides in the 80-page introduction to his two-volume edition of Irving's *Miscellaneous Writings, 1803–1859* (Twayne). Perhaps Irving's own easy flow of ink infects his editors, though the equally fluent Howells receives an average of 15 pages in the compressed introductions to the new Indiana edition. As I have suggested before (*ALS 1979*, 198–99), the Irving volumes occasionally lack a disciplined and co-ordinating editorial hand. Their primary value to future scholars, however, is beyond question, and Kime's two volumes offer a new horn of plenty, stocked full of Irving's poems, plays, and prose writings, published and unpublished.

This wealth of Irving documents has mounted in yet another volume this year, *Journals and Notebooks: Volume II, 1807–1822*, ed. Walter A. Reichart and Lillian Schlissel (Twayne). (For Nathalia Wright's vol. I:1803–1806, and Reichart's vol. III:1819–1827, see *ALS 1969*, 167; and *ALS 1970*, 181.) The introduction to this volume is sensibly limited to a dozen pages, with editorial energies saved for the labor of annotating Irving's pocket-sized, often pencil-smudged notebooks. Contents range from laundry lists to données, and from a density of travel impressions to felicitous phrasings to be used in later work (though Irving seems not to have recovered very many). Imaginative scholars who will be profiting from these new resources should extend special thanks to Reichart and Schlissel for the sacrifice of eyesight that must have accompanied the skillful editorial deciphering of Irving's topsy-turvy and deteriorated notebook entries.

A new Irving book by Mary W. Bowden (TUSAS 379) departs slightly from the Twayne format by relating biographical data to the works discussed in each chapter. She also approaches the writings by joining theme and imagery to character types American, American-regional (especially New York), English, and European. The result is a pleasant, orderly tour through Irving country and one of the better monographs in the series, perhaps because hers is an author who fully deserves book-length analysis.

A quartet of essays brings new interest to some of Irving's most familiar pages. Robert A. Ferguson attributes the vitality of the Knickerbocker *History* to Irving's creative release of early frustrations, as well as "vocational daydreams" of law and the military. The later Rip and Ichabod stories echo the animus toward republican culture and the legal profession, and while Geoffrey Crayon's "muted tones are harder won and based upon a deeper understanding," Ferguson judges Knickerbocker's voice to be "more clearly original, creative, and authentic" ("'Hunting Down a Nation': Irving's *A History of New York*" [*NCF* 36:22–46]).

The other three articles treat those two later tales of *The Sketch Book*. In "'Rip Van Winkle' as Bawdy Satire: The Rascal and the Revolution" (*ESQ* 27:198–206) William P. Dawson speculates that the source of the tale which the credulous Knickerbocker passes on to Crayon is none other than Rip himself, who has fashioned an innocent self plagued by a shrewish wife. But Irving implies, through sexual images and puns, that Rip, the great favorite of local housewives, has irresponsibly deserted his wife and spent 20 years as a rascal libertine. His career is thus a fable concurrent with Irving's satire of revolutionary independence and republican unrestraint. At the end, however, Rip lives comfortably at home without his former bonds of union, parallel to an America rid of England and perhaps to Irving's own fondly re-embracing the new nation (current Jeffersonian democracy notwithstanding) after his recent residence abroad. Edward F. Pajak has similar enjoyment in "Washington Irving's *Ichabod Crane*: American Narcissus" (*AI* 38:127–35). Like Dawson, he notices Irving's narrative layers, this time moving us into levels of consciousness beneath rationality to the worlds of Freud's "uncanny" and Ovid's Narcissus (glossed by Otto Rank) where Ichabod dwells amid "repressed infantile complexes, such as those involving castration and womb fantasies." Amateurs can take it from there—the punishing headless horseman, the apparitions and shadows of Sleepy Hollow, Ichabod's insatiable orality and unmet Oedipal needs—but they will enjoy Pajak's ingenious reading of the entire story.

Barry Gross treats "Rip" and "Sleepy Hollow" together as parables of change that illustrate Irving's conflicting views toward a fixed past (burden or ballast?), "metamorphosing" present, and unknowable future. This sober essay is sensible enough until Gross is betrayed into an analogy with Fitzgerald's historical imagination. He admits that Ichabod Crane, of course, lacks a Platonic vision. But isn't there something Gatsby-like in his voracious pursuit of Katrina Van Tassel? (See "Washington Irving: The Territory Behind" [*MarkhamR* 10:4–9].)

The second installment of *The Writings of James Fenimore Cooper* (SUNY) matches last year's with another pairing of a Leatherstocking novel with a European travel book. *The Pathfinder* is edited by Richard D. Rust, his copy-text essentially the newly discovered manuscript which, in James Beard's words, forms "the crowning jewel of the Barrett Cooper Collection" at the University of Virginia. Rust also reproduces two manuscript pages of Cooper's tiny script which caused so many compositor misreadings, now corrected in Rust's edition. The copy-text accommodates Cooper's alterations in the first-edition proofs, as well as corrections in the second (Putnam, 1851) edition. Rust's "Historical Introduction" is a rudimentary account of the composition, publication, and reception, nicely compressed into 11 pages. The companion volume is *Gleanings in Europe: Italy*, the introduction and explanatory notes by John Conron and Constance A. Denne, with text established by Denne. Like the Switzerland volume last year, this one includes handsome illustrations to accompany Cooper's sketches, which, at their best, say the editors, are poetically superior to the Swiss scenes. But a "pictorial intensity of landscape" is less sustained in these later gleanings even though Cooper is consciously following the picturesque manner of William Gilpin. The copy-text is established from the printing deposited for copyright in the National Library of Scotland (set from the unlocated manuscript) together with the emendations in Cooper's corrected proofs.

Cooper editors and scholars gathered with nonspecialists for a third summer conference at Oneonta in 1980, the papers edited once more by coordinator George A. Test: *James Fenimore Cooper: His Country and His Art* (Oneonta: SUNY College). The interest of this new round of papers is continuous with the Cooper Edition. Thomas Philbrick ("Cooper in Europe: The Travel Books," pp. 1–8) explains the choice of publishing the well-known Leatherstocking novels in tandem with the usually unpublished European *Gleanings*, establishes the travel series in the perspective of Cooper's career ("the product of that interim period when he wrote no novels"), and likens Cooper's American expression of an "intensely political intelligence" in Europe to Tocqueville's gleanings in America during the same period. Constance A. Denne's "Cooper in Italy" (pp. 19–23) might easily have been a lazy duplicating of her editorial introduction to the Italian *Gleanings*; instead, she gives a crisp recasting, together with an enthusiastic, though undefended, conclusion that neither Hawthorne, Howells, nor James "would surpass Cooper either in his response to the grace of Italian life and the beauty of the country or in the ardour of his recollections." In her second paper, "Cooper's Use of Setting in the European Trilogy" (pp. 52–70), Denne maintains, again with insufficient analysis, that in *The Bravo*, *The Heidenmauer*, and *The Headsman* Cooper's settings are consistently intrinsic to his artistic design and symbolize all of his thematic concerns.

Among the four other papers, Warren S. Walker demonstrates the nature of "Cooper's Fictional Use of the Oral Tradition" (pp. 24–39), chiefly in folk types, the supernatural, and three categories of folk speech—dialect, proverbs, and naming. A secondary bibliography is appended. Leonard R. N. Ashley then explores the fuller importance of names: "The Onomastics of Cooper's Verbal Art in *The Deerslayer* and Elsewhere" (pp. 40–51). In his use of place-names, the Indian naming system, satirical appellations for New England characters, and animal epithets "honorific or derogatory," Cooper enriched the moral and historical content of his fiction. Walker returned to speak on "Cooper's Yorkers and Yankees in the Jeffersonian Garden" (pp. 71–80), a valuable exposition of Cooper's Jeffersonian sympathy with the superior pastoral and aristocratic virtues of an enlightened gentry in his native state, together with his private antagonism toward Yankee interlopers who were not seamen or fervent patriots. Educated liberal activists—lawyers and journalists —were Cooper's least welcome Yankee settlers in upper New York. Finally, in a related paper, "James Fenimore Cooper and the Apocalypse" (pp. 82–91) Lakshmi Mani shows the tension between the dream of a millennial Jeffersonian Eden and the motifs of apocalyptic doom in the Leatherstocking novels and *The Crater*.

Other work in Cooper this year ranges from the labored and un-original to Dennis W. Allen's closely reasoned and convincing "'By All the Truth of Signs': James Fenimore Cooper's *The Last of the Mohicans*" (*SAF* 9:159–79). Cooper advances his conflict of civiliza-tion vs. wilderness by way of "semiotic differences between white and Indian cultures," between language and nonverbal signs. Where the linguistic does enter into Indians' expression, Cooper suggests that their language is superior to white speech and books, the word closer to the thing and person. Further, the whites do not realize that to alter Indians' words is to alter their traditions, weaken the stability of their culture, and vitiate their linguistic constructs of "truth." Jane P. Tompkins also reinterprets the cultural mixture of Mohicans in "No Apologies for the Iroquois: A New Way to Read the Leatherstocking Novels" (*Criticism* 23:24–41) and defends Cooper as a social critic. We should understand that his characters, as in *Mohicans*, behave within an abstract, carefully composed alle-gorical romance of cultural "miscegenation," discord, masquerade, and isolation. Leland S. Person, Jr., treats *Home as Found* as the pivotal work in an Otsego trilogy, standing between the early *Pioneers* and late *Deerslayer*. Natty of *The Pioneers* becomes the posthumous presiding spirit of pristine and ecologically healthy Otsego in this middle novel, but Cooper "records the failure of its characters' effort to invoke" that spirit "as a shaping force in the American present." He was therefore impelled in *The Deerslayer* to relegate "both his landscape and his hero to an isolated realm of myth and prehistory" ("*Home as Found* and the Leatherstocking Tales" [*ESQ* 27:170–80]).

Finally are two articles of more general scope. Mary S. Schriber's "Toward Daisy Miller: Cooper's Idea of 'The American Girl'" (*SNNTS* 13:237–49) moves along redundantly to an obvious con-clusion that Cooper's ideal heroines combine American freshness with the best kind of European social polish; still, it is gratifying to read new appreciations of his less familiar heroines: Eve Effing-ham, Lucy Hardinge, Mary Monson, and Anna McBain. We return to the utterly familiar with Nelson Van Valen in "James Fenimore Cooper and the Conservation Schism" (*NYH* 62:289–306). Cooper's sharply ambivalent treatment of Judge Temple, we are informed, has not been generally recognized. Like the preservationist Natty, the judge is shocked by the pioneers' wholesale destruction of natural resources, yet he completely embraces their enterprising utilitarian spirit. An historian, Van Valen does not cite any articles in literary scholarship pertinent to Cooper's divided loyalties.

Among Cooper's lesser contemporaries, Paulding is the beneficiary of a reading by Leland Person, "James Kirke Paulding: Myth and the Middle Ground" (*WAL* 16:39–54) that recalls the serious attention Parrington once paid these frontier romances *Koningsmarke*, *Westward Ho!*, and *The Dutchman's Fireside*, though Person directs his interest to frontier myth rather than politics and satire. More exactly, he discovers in Paulding, as opposed to Cooper, that frontiersmen and genteel heroes share each other's diverse attributes, resulting in "an alternative myth of the wilderness—a fable of initiation whose goal is a compromise between the too often exclusive claims of the wilderness and civilization." The expected footnote to Leo Marx's pastoral "middle landscape" never appears. In a different vein, Patricia G. Holland describes the typical publishing difficulties of the American woman writer, her instance being "Lydia Maria Child as a Nineteenth-Century Professional Author" (*SAR*, 157–67).

Simms squeezes in this year among the frontier humorists, thanks to Mary Ann Wimsatt's "Native Humor in Simms's Fiction and Drama" (*SAmH* 3:158–65). Despite Trent, Erskine, and Quinn to the contrary, there is sufficient humor in Simms when one tallies up his frontier con men, hunting yarns, and Crockett materials. In the same journal, which one assumed to be defunct (the present issue is dated January 1977), Richard B. and Dean M. Hauck recount their "Panning for Gold: Researching Humor in the *Spirit of the Times*" (*SAmH* 3:149–57). Though much of its humor is fool's gold, the *Spirit* is a rich source of cultural history, valuable for sports, theatre, and book reviews even of Melville's work. It is also indispensable to our tracing the development of writers like G. W. Harris and Charles Noland. Indeed, Lorne Fienberg undertakes precisely that challenge in "Colonel Noland of the *Spirit*: The Voices of a Gentleman in Southwest Humor" (*AL* 53:232–45). Plantation owner, lawyer, politician, and journalist, Noland was a prolific contributor to Porter's elitist *Spirit*, usually extolling the cultivated life-style of the sporting southern gentleman. Later, he felt the urge to depict more of southern life and created the boisterous Pete Whetstone and the ruder Jim Cole. Their humorous actions and vernacular, in sketches framed by a superior narrator, influenced other humorists. And so, too, did Longstreet's ventures in the same mode, William E. Lenz reminds us in his well-informed but unsurprising "Longstreet's *Georgia Scenes*: Developing American Characters and Narrative Techniques" (*MarkhamR* 11:5–10).

iii. Popular Writers of Mid-Century

Increasingly rare is the scholar who braves ridicule to justify the art of Longfellow's popular rhymings. Hans-Joachim Lang and Fritz Fleischmann pool their courage to that purpose in " 'All This Beauty, All This Grace': 'The Building of the Ship' and Alexander Slidell Mackenzie's 'Ship' " (*NEQ* 54:104–18). They contend that Longfellow built his poem with unusual care. Not a "weak and vaporous concoction," it abounds in "precisely rendered details" strategically borrowed from his acquaintance Mackenzie's essay, "Ship," in Francis Lieber's *Encyclopedia Americana*. A difficult companion essay now remains to be written, showing that Longfellow's Sea-of-Life, Ship-of-State poem is not, in fact, a vade mecum of notorious clichés. Meanwhile, M. E. Grenander escorts us to the adjacent world of Holmes across the Charles, where we meet yet another instance of the Autocrat's timeless wisdom. When he explains to his table auditors that John speaking to Thomas becomes three people (the real John, his own ideal John, and Thomas' ideal John) addressing three Thomases (with parallel identities), the sensible Autocrat anticipates in lucidly simple fashion the elaborately codified transactional analysis of today's Harry S. Sullivan, Eric Berne, and Thomas Harris. After reading Grenander's parallels in "Doctors and Humanists: Transactional Analysis and Two Views of Man" (*JAC* 3:470–79), one imagines the constrained tolerance with which the Autocrat might have endured the plonking jargon of Messrs. Sullivan, Berne, and Harris while they designate the same modes of experience, internalized roles, and ego states as "parataxic," "syntaxic," "exteropsychic," "archeopsychic," and so on.

For Stowe enthusiasts, the main excitement this year is the appearance of Ann Douglas' attractive paperback edition of *Uncle Tom's Cabin*, an initial volume in the Penguin American Library, John Seelye the general editor. Douglas uses the first-edition text established by Kenneth Lynn (Harvard, 1962). Her introduction is distinguished for a culminating discussion of Stowe's "art of controversy." Stowe attained her special power when she discovered the voice and matter appropriate to an American woman writer. Not only did she unite political and religious themes peculiar to the era, but she blended the comic and tragic within factual and romantic elements of the slave narrative. In the meantime, Douglas' previous writing on Stowe and other feminine writers of the middle decades has come under the disapproving scrutiny of Jane P. Tompkins, "Sentimental Power: *Uncle Tom's Cabin* and the Politics of Literary History" (*Glyph* 8:79–102). To Tompkins, the sentimental novel written by, for, and about women deserves admiration rather than Douglas' apology and rebuke. This popular genre was "remarkable for its intellectual complexity, ambition, and resourcefulness." She wisely supports this impassioned claim with the example of *Uncle Tom's Cabin*, "a political enterprise, halfway between sermon and social theory, that both codifies and attempts to mold the values of its time." Theodore H. Hovet's less polemical "Modernization and the American Fall into Slavery in *Uncle Tom's Cabin*" (*NEQ* 54:499–518) holds Stowe's masterwork in equal esteem. Hovet interprets George Harris' northern Quaker home as Stowe's ideal society of organic relationships ordered and nourished by feminine domestic values. By contrast, Tom witnesses on the industrialized plantation the disorderly and acquisitive "entropic world of Legree's megamachine." The geographical movement of the novel gives dramatic power to the contrast: the river, a "symbol of the centrifugal force of modern economic growth," becomes the commercial artery of Tom's journey southward into "a symbolic fall from an unchanging Eden toward the dead, materialistic, and mechanized world at the end of the river." Like Douglas' and Tompkins' essays, Hovet's is provocative and highly recommended.

Michael K. Simmons locates Anglo-Saxon prejudices in popular fiction that are not unlike Norman Smith's discovery of Mexican stereotypes last year (*ALS 1980*, 226). WASP nativism between 1860 and 1900 was reflected and reinforced in a wide variety of dime-novel plots and characters. In stories of the Revolutionary War, plain-folk Americans triumphed over sinister British aristocrats. On the western frontier, nature's white noblemen routed savage redskins. Freedmen were patently inferior and steadfastly loyal to their former white rulers. Chinese were devious orientals in pigtails, their English speech incomprehensible, while Italians were "partners in crime and dark deeds" with these " 'Chinks.' " This pop-lit racism, expecially in its anti-oriental cast, helped to shape an imperialist mentality at the turn of the century. (See "Nationalism and the Dime Novel" [*StHum* 9:39–44].)

Concluding this section are the new contributions to our appreciation of Horatio Alger, Jr., by the productive Gary Scharnhorst, author of the corrective recent biography (*ALS 1980*, 225). This year, with Jack Eales (and an introduction by Alger's erratic early biographer Herbert R. Mayes), he has compiled *Horatio Alger, Jr.: An Annotated Bibliography of Comment and Criticism* (Scarecrow). Scharnhorst also contributes several minor items this year, two of which deserve brief notice. In "Had Their Mothers Only Known: Horatio Alger, Jr., Rewrites Cooper, Melville, and Twain" (*JPC* 15: 175–82) he shows Alger's explicit links and argues his implicit debts to the three notables. "Demythologizing Alger" (*MarkhamR* 10:20–27), by contrast, points ahead to the legend associated with Alger in the 20th century. Scharnhorst identifies the ups and downs of Alger's posthumous reputation and speculates on the historical causes.

iv. Local Color and Literary Regionalism

Subsequent to the work on Simms and the Southwest humorists, mentioned earlier, studies in regional literature are less plentiful this year. Perry D. Westbrook's book on Jewett and her New England contemporaries, *Acres of Flint* (Scarecrow, 1951), has been reissued with slight revisions to emphasize feminine authorship. The bibliography is also updated. John C. Hirsh's "The Non-Narrative Structure of *The Country of the Pointed Firs*" (*ALR* 14:286–88) is a note—for the rare teacher of this novel, a crib-note—with a chart to illustrate the double movement between the Todd chapters and the Outsider chapters which gives tension and a realization of provincial values in the world of Dunnet Landing. But a decade of shorter fiction helped to condition this ethical and historical sense in *Pointed Firs*, says Charles W. Mayer in a first-rate essay, " 'The Only Rose': A Central Jewett Story" (*CLQ* 17:26–33). Jewett was more than a nostalgic guardian of customs and memories of the past. She suggests that the past can be debilitating and destructive if it does not enrich our life in the present "by helping us to seal the bond between generations and make commitments of the heart."

Two other books on regionalism this year are also reprintings. Last year's special issue on Cable in the *Southern Quarterly* (see *ALS 1980*, 228–29) is now *The Grandissimes: Centennial Essays*, ed. Thomas J. Richardson (Miss.). R. Bruce Bickley, Jr., has edited *Critical Essays on Joel Chandler Harris* (Hall) to accompany his earlier *Reference Guide* and Twayne monograph on Harris (for both, see *ALS 1978*, 214). One of the most useful in this critical series, Bickley's collection is widely ranging and judiciously assembled. To the 46 reviews of Harris' books and the 15 reprinted critical essays, Bickley adds three new essays he commissioned, thus stimulating Harris studies. Joseph M. Griska, Jr., analyzes Harris' psychological depression (after paternal desertion) and its effects on his literary ambition: " 'In Stead of a "Gift of Gab" ': Some New Perspectives on Joel Chandler Harris" (pp. 210–25). Florence E. Baer writes on the " 'Accidental Folklorist' " (pp. 185–95). And Louis J. Budd in a major essay, "Joel Chandler Harris and the Genteeling of Native American Humor" (pp. 196–209), looks at the total career that began with a salutary apprenticeship in Old Southwest journalism. Harris learned from Longstreet, Thompson, and other humorists how to manage a "mixing of classes, and the clashing of standards in mores or behavior" that give a moderately gritty tension and conflict to his fiction of blacks and whites. But his genteel middle-class reading public valued him as a benign humorist, and he responded to their perception by muffling his irony, resisting tragic overtones, idealizing womanhood, and avoiding radical or bitter treatment of race and society. Nevertheless, Budd defends the total career, for Harris "helped to reinvigorate the vocation of authorship in the postbellum South" and forged "a main link in the received tradition."

Griska shapes a second essay this year out of his continuing research in Harris' letters: "Uncle Remus Correspondence: The Development and Reception of Joel Chandler Harris's Writing, 1880–1885" (*ALR* 14:26–37). In these crowded years, Harris gathered Remus materials, acquired books on folklore, worried about his illustrators and literary techniques, and consistently belittled his achievement when praised by admirers like Mark Twain, R. W. Gilder, and R. H. Stoddard. In view of Griska's psychological probing in the previous essay, he is oddly silent on reasons for Harris' compulsive self-criticism here.

In an article notable for incisive conclusions as well as dangling participles, Mary Jo Bratton compresses her considerable research into "John Esten Cooke and His 'Confederate Lies'" (*SLJ* 13,ii:72–91). Cooke boasted a modest postwar fortune from writing "Confederate lies," but Bratton bids us substitute "myth" for "lies." She traces the complexity of regional and war experience out of which this native West Virginian of yeoman-democratic origins concocted a postwar myth of gallant southern Cavaliers caught in an heroic, irrepressible conflict. Cooke viewed his success ironically for good reason. Privately, he reckoned the Civil War a grubby affair. And his Confederate "lies" were even more popular in the North, where readers delighted in his divided-loyalty families and his portrayal of the Union's vanquishing romantically worthy, aristocratic heroes. Cooke knew that royalty-hankering Americans do not pay to read about the Common Man.

The Western Writers Series (WWS), published by Boise State, gave us three substantial pamphlets this year, an annual harvest that may not be matched in quality in future years when some of the dubious "Forthcoming Titles" appear. Ideally suited to the series format is Christer L. Mossberg's *Scandinavian Immigrant Literature*, a compact overview of the midwestern subculture that produced some 80 novels and short-story collections. Written in Danish, Norwegian, or Swedish, usually by male amateurs who were actual immigrants—farmers, journalists, schoolteachers, and ministers—and published by local newspaper or church presses, this fiction typically grew out of the authors' epistolary experiments. What then followed was a highly patterned fiction with a "dual-world orientation." Mossberg abstracts eight persistent themes in immigration plots and the subsequently "complex, often ambivalent, response to farmsteading," and then discusses the work of representative authors.

The other pamphlets take us to the Far West. Robert E. Fleming surveys the career of Charles F. Lummis with a fine sense of elaborating the separate endeavors. Lummis began as a peripatetic columnist and city editor for the Los Angeles *Times*, followed by free-lance writing wherein he discovered his authentic talent as an historian of the Southwest. He did not disguise an archeologist's love of the region and folklorist's sympathy with the people of the various subcultures. And he gave the same energy and compassion to his editing *The Land of Sunshine* (retitled *Out West*) at the turn of the century, when he published Jeffers, Austin, and Rhodes and crusaded to restore the California missions and protect the rights of the American Indian.

A less ardent crusader but more gifted author had left the Far West shortly before Lummis arrived. This was the colorful and erratic pioneering geologist Clarence King. Peter Wild sketches the undisciplined life of the "hedonistic nomad" whose brilliant failures seemed the stuff of American fable to Henry Adams and other friends. Wild duly tends to the sporadic writings, including a volume of poems privately printed. But the value of his pamphlet rests in an excellent 13 pages on King's youthful literary achievement, *Mountaineering in the Sierra Nevada*.

v. Henry Adams

The seemingly boundless implications of Henry Adams' thought and sometimes labyrinthine art provide again an ample source of scholarly delight and analysis. Outside belles lettres (though he also attracts our interest therein) Adams now seems indisputably the reigning genius of our modern literary history. This year, a potpourri of studies, none of major consequence, light up his many-sided genius. The most ambitious, after Harold Kaplan's pages in *Power and Order* discussed earlier, is Carolyn Porter's "Henry Adams: The Posthumous Spectator," chapter 6 in *Seeing and Being*. The *Education* supports her general thesis that capitalism causes the alienated reification of self. With Adams, the process is predictably complex, his third-person "mannikin" a detached "register" of the century's "accelerated motion and force"; but the "impotent spectator" also becomes a "complicit participant" who wishes to exert will and influence on the deterministic sequence of force he is discovering in history. In his last phase, Adams' "effort to teach reaction . . . constitutes a final effort to exert influence."

In four articles Adams is studied in the company of varied figures of the age: scientists, Emerson, brother Brooks, and Henry James. Paul J. Hamill, "Science as Ideology: The Case of the Amateur, Henry Adams" (*CRevAS* 12:21–35), employs Thomas Kuhn's "paradigms" of scientific thought to explain Adams' pessimism. (For David Marcell's different approach using Kuhn, see *ALS 1979*, 211.) Scientific discovery excited his imagination, but he never understood the critical process of scientific theory and advance. So "every

paradigm shift was a crisis of faith" for Adams the amateur, and
"paradigm failure . . . became the central paradigm of his interpretation of history." On the other hand, Adams viewed himself the superior of the overly naive Concord romantics, though he was solidly
indebted to their leading sage, according to Jonel C. Sallie's "Henry
Adams' Emersonian Education" (*ESQ* 27:38–46). In the *Education*
Adams shows a "thorough absorption" of the notion in "Circles" that
a "strong, perceptive individual center of consciousness" propels our
circular growth, and the corollary premise in "Fate" that the force of
that private vision can break through the circumference of fate.

Katherine L. Morrison corrects the impression of fraternal sym-
biosis in "A Reexamination of Brooks and Henry on John Quincy
Adams" (*NEQ* 54:163–79). Henry was impressed by *The Law of
Civilization and Decay* (1895) but soon lost respect for Brooks and
rebuked him particularly for an adulatory manuscript on their presidential grandfather. While Henry was not much influenced by his
younger sibling, neither did his trenchant criticism seem to ruffle
Brooks, whom Morrison presents as a distinctly thick-headed ideo-
logue. Henry's letters to his brother, tartly seasoned with invective
against Brooks, America, and the universe, are delicious to reread.

Democracy is illuminated in a comparison with *The Bostonians*
by Michael Kreyling in "Nationalizing the Southern Hero: Adams
and James" (*MissQ* 34:383–402). Adams' portrait of Carrington
seems a nostalgic unionizing of Quincy and Mount Vernon, but Basil
Ransom (who was probably germinating for James when he read
Democracy in Adams' home) resists "conversion into a national
type," remaining in James's conception "a point of focus in an ongoing cultural process." Adams' other novel receives a routine feminist gloss in Harriet F. Bergmann's "Henry Adams's *Esther*: No
Faith in the Patriarchy" (*MarkhamR* 10:63–67). An "extraordinary
emphasis on gender and sex roles" in *Esther* "is Adams's way of
forcing the reader to pay attention to the multiplicity of fronts on
which Esther's battle with the patriarch must be fought." She comes
to rely on her own reason and power to escape the institutionalized
force of a masculine and clerical tradition.

These essays on Adams combine with criticism of the recent past
to make a gathering so plentiful that one is startled to realize that
no collection has appeared until now. Earl N. Harbert's *Critical
Essays on Henry Adams* (Hall) becomes a companion to his *Refer-*

ence Guide (see *ALS* 1978, 215). Half of the reprinted essays are by Blackmur, Samuels (2), Levenson (2), and Harbert (2). The only review is Mrs. Humphrey Ward's *Fortnightly* piece inferring Adams' authorship one year after *Democracy*. A single commissioned essay is by Margaret J. Brown, "Henry Adams: His Passage to Asia" (pp. 243–57). To the question, "What was [Adams] seeking in the thought and art of the Orient?" she concludes, after a rather disorganized excursion through abundant data, that he sought "a unifying system of belief." Unfortunately, what he *found* was too various to be so easily capsulized.

vi. Realism and the Age of Howells

William Alexander's *William Dean Howells: The Realist as Humanist* (Burt Franklin) and a further volume of letters in the Selected Edition were the chief publications on Howells in a year that was also graced by an unusually interesting variety of lesser studies. Alexander's Howells has already arrived at maturity in *A Modern Instance*. In theory and practice over the next dozen years, he moves toward a doctrine of "realism" infused with "humane and democratic values." Much of Alexander's tour through this major period of Howells' career, conducted amid the novels and letters but also in the poems and essays, is not markedly original, nor does he update a manuscript completed for the most part by the early 1970s. Still, the book is reliable and absorbing in his account of Howells' enlarging social vision as a novel writer and humanist in a turbulent era made more harrowing by the torments of his personal life. Within John Crowley's categories of Howells' modern critics (see *ALS* 1979, 212) Alexander is decisively a "revisionist" rather than "revivalist."

Volume 4 of the *Selected Letters* (Twayne) enters the later phase of Howells' career, which neither Alexander nor Kenneth Lynn and other critics and biographers have discovered especially compelling. Howells' creative decline has seemed not only remarkably prolonged but also somehow patternless. The editors of the current volume of letters have selected, grouped, and annotated a far-flung correspondence from 1892 to 1901, to suggest that there is both biographical interest and pattern here. The groupings are introduced and annotated by Thomas Wortham, Christoph K. Lohmann, and David J.

Nordloh, with textual editing by Lohmann and Jerry Herron.
Whether they have rejected letters crucial to a new portrait of the
elderly Howells in his full complexity will be decided by his next
industrious biographer. (See my comments in *ALS 1979*, 212–13, on
sensitive correspondence in the Huntington Library essential to the
biographer of Howells.)

The welcome attention to Howells' later creative work continues
this year, especially as he shifted toward what editors Wortham and
Nordloh term a more sustained "delineating the enigmas of subjective reality and the intricacies of human psychology." One early result was a blank-verse play in three acts (1900), the subject of Valden
Madsen's "Autobiographical and Mystical Elements in Howells's
The Mother and the Father" (*RS* 49:46–54). Madsen does little probing of any subtleties in the obvious autobiographical relevance to
Winny Howells in the plot—the parents are emotionally dependent
on each other during the growth, marriage, and death of a daughter
—but he is helpful on Swedenborgian being, nonbeing, and "correspondences" embedded in Howells' dialogue.

Shortly after his verse-play, Howells wrote one of his strongest
psychological novels, and this year it receives the most perceptive
reading yet in John W. Crowley's excellent "Howells and the Sins
of the Father: *The Son of Royal Langbrith*" (*ON* 7:79–94). Crowley
concisely draws the chief parallels with *The House of the Seven
Gables* and then demonstrates Howells' greater psychological insight
into the moral theme shared with Hawthorne, "the effect of the past
on the present." Thanks to an emerging sophistication in turn-of-
century psychoanalysis, Howells was able to explore the influence
of Royal Langbrith's "evil" upon the unconscious motivation of various characters in his lifetime as well as on others who survive him.
When Langbrith's psychically burdened son finally realizes the truth
of his deceased father's villainy, Howells has fully developed both
the moral and psychological riddles of the novel and resolved them:
"Those who have discovered their unconscious springs of motivation
are henceforth responsible for their actions. Those who remain passive in self-knowledge of unconscious evil become its agents."

George Arms continues this discussion of Howells' psychological
approach to moral and spiritual concerns in the early years of the
present century. But first, he charts the earlier varieties of religious
experience, as Howells internalized the Christian moral code of

Swedenborgians, Quakers, transcendentalists, and perhaps Methodists. Then came Tolstoi, the "religious Marxism" of Gronlund, and the political platform of the Christian socialists. Arms proposes that a combination of tolerant fascination and tough wariness on matters of belief and agnosticism, "a committed but objective curiosity not unlike that of William James," most nearly describes the attitudes that Howells ultimately brings to religious experiences in his literature and life. (See "Some Varieties of Howells' Religious Experience" in *The American Self*, pp. 76–87.)

Howells' earlier work is reinterpreted in a final trio of essays. Henry Nash Smith reads *Their Wedding Journey* as an early effort to merge the ideal with commonplace, democratic, "real" materials: "Fiction and the American Ideology: The Genesis of Howells' Early Realism" (*The American Self*, pp. 43–57). Basil March lectures his bride and the reader on this new aesthetic of the commonplace, but his images do not work, his ideal-poetic associations are half-hearted, and an assumed and genteel superiority to fellow passengers undercuts his (and his creator's) announced commitment to a democratic ideal. Smith's keen analysis of the text is enriched by historical and literary knowledge and the careful style which have made his criticism a model for successive generations of scholars. He will no doubt allow an aging former student to argue, however, with an apparent simplifying of Howells' response to a middle-class, "functionally aristocratic" social ideology in America. The ambivalent "Howells Agonistes" who has emerged in the scholarship of the past 15 years was not "systematically blind" but, instead, uncomfortably sensitive to the contradiction between his theoretical "doctrine of equality" and his cultivation of quasi-aristocratic tastes and amenities.

Pertinent to the next two essays is Smith's further contention that Howells viewed Anglo-Saxon America to be "a providentially ordered historical scheme which would lead, indeed was leading, toward a millennial consummation." For all his conventional racism, Howells was probably not quite so unequivocal and steadfast an evolutionist. Or so the returns from only his first two major novels of the 1880s would indicate. Jane Marston, who has recently completed her dissertation (Vanderbilt) on "The Influence of Evolution on the Fiction of William Dean Howells" (*DAI* 42,iv:1636A), elucidates an entire complex of themes on progress, design, chance, moral choice, complicity, and the after-life in "Evolution and Howellsian Realism in

The Undiscovered Country" (*ALR* 14:231–41). Howells did achieve, it seems, a philosophical optimism in *The Undiscovered Country*, but one must strain to discover its recurrence in the darker *A Modern Instance*. Ellen F. Wright bravely undertakes that strenuous mission. In "Given Bartley, Given Marcia: A Reconsideration of Howells' *A Modern Instance*" (*TSLL* 23:214–31) she argues that we have no reason to consider Howells unhappy about the state of American society at that time. Marriage is his central metaphor of American civilization, and the elder Gaylords' marriage is "passable," the elder Hallecks' "very good," and the Athertons' "excellent." Howells does not attribute Bartley and Marcia's unhappy marriage to any deterioration of American social and moral values; the cause is in themselves, in flaws of their character. Elsewhere in the novel, Howells shows the reader a prevailing justice in American law, ethical conscience in journalism, and no evidence of an overall decline in religion. Also thriving in Howells' America are close family ties, suggestively drawn in Marcia's closeness to her father (!), her resemblance to her mother, and the promise that daughter Flavia is growing to be like her mother. Aside from Wright's questionable internal reading of her selective evidence, one misses a larger external framework here, the historical and biographical data germane to a serious discussion of a novelist's complicated moral and social attitudes. On the credit side, Wright is well worth reading on Clara Kingsbury and the Atherton marriage.

John W. De Forest reappears this year in an edition of *Critical Essays* in the G. K. Hall series. James Gargano gathers up reviews of the 11 novels from *Seacliff* to *A Lover's Revolt* (including comment by Howells and James) and reprints five scholarly interpretations in the present century. In a helpful introduction he distills his years of studying De Forest but then concludes on the counterproductive note peculiar to Hall and Twayne writers on the lesser figures: he raises a sophisticated doubt that any lasting interest will be sustained in most of the undoubtedly minor legacy of his author. He goes even further with this denigration in an original essay for the collection, "*Kate Beaumont* and the Omnipresent Narrator" (pp. 164–72), hoping to convince any unbelievers that De Forest's novel, despite minor virtues, is a "failure." All of its defects flow from "the ubiquitous authorial presence," and besides, De Forest's novels generally are superficial, containing "little of horror and less of joyous exhaltation. Rather than refine, subtilize, or re-create extremes of feeling, he prefers to rationalize, sentimentalize, or moralize." A second essay previously unpublished is William J. McGill's more appreciative "The Novelist as Bureaucrat: The Structure of De Forest's *A Union Officer in the Reconstruction*" (pp. 173–81), a first attempt to define the "ordering principle" of the six magazine pieces that De Forest rearranged into a ten-chapter manuscript never published as a book until 1948 (Yale). McGill paraphrases the logical continuity of this informal record of De Forest's term as a subassistant commissioner for the Freedman's Bureau in South Carolina. McGill does not, however, set forth the structural integrity of separate chapters and distinct chapter groupings that more closely defines the literary shape of these recollections.

A truly minor author, who is nonetheless interesting as a transitional figure, is memorialized, with appended bibliography, by Robert J. Scholnick: "Between Realism and Romanticism: The Curious Career of Eugene Benson" (*ALR* 14:242–61). Holding to prewar values of individualism and solitude, Benson was repelled by postwar materialism and assailed the prudery and bloodless decorum of American life and literature. His critical essays for *Galaxy* appeared well before Whitman's *Democratic Vistas* installments in that journal. Benson concluded his journalistic career in the 1870s and then lived as an artist, poetaster, and Italophile in Venice, where his home inspired James's setting for *The Aspern Papers*. Benson's amalgam of realism and romanticism reappears under a different guise in "Helen Hunt Jackson: Docudramatist of the American Indian" by Michael T. Marsden (*MarkhamR* 10:15–19). Within the sentimental tradition adopted for *Ramona*, Jackson injected a serious political purpose. Through the passionate love of her white and red characters, she not only suggested a "passion for unity with her fellow human beings" but also produced "a fictional docudrama of 'fiery truths' which she thought would focus the national spirit on the Indian problem."

vii. Fin-de-Siècle America: Stephen Crane and the 1890s

The annual season of Crane studies may be described as a slight sprinkle with no thunder. Alan R. Slotkin detects a "Dialect Manipulation in 'An Experiment in Misery'" (*ALR* 14:273–76) in which

Crane's correspondent-observer begins his night in the Bowery with a "dialectal norm." Through a growing involvement in the life of the poor, he has adopted by morning some of the usages of New York's miserables. Slotkin makes a necessarily slim case out of a very compressed tale. Robert A. Morace is more ambitious, giving us over three pages of documentation in 38 footnotes to buttress his essay, "Games, Play, and Entertainments in Stephen Crane's 'The Monster'" (*SAF* 9:65–81). Despite the promise of his title, there is not much fun in Morace's plausible but painfully argued theory that "a complex of metaphoric games, entertainments, and play-like behavior . . . underlies the meaning of the story and serves to unify its various parts."

A further pair of articles and two rather elaborate notes complete this year's slight falling off in explications of Crane. For Ronald E. McFarland, the metaphor of the Swede's transit through the storm "'as if he carried sails'" after his fight at Scully's has brought to mind the parallel with Odysseus, a more gracious guest who also received greater respect as the potentially informative and dangerous stranger. Because the well-meaning Scully, the bartender, and the others violate this classic hospitality code, they are all responsible for the Swede's death ("The Hospitality Code and Crane's 'The Blue Hotel'" [*SSF* 18:447–51]). Thomas L. Kent, however, stresses the uncertainty in the characters' "perception about proper codes of behavior" in the same story, and indeed the overall "epistemological uncertainty" there and in "The Open Boat" that Crane has "generated for both the reader outside the texts and the characters within the texts." In a supplementary note elsewhere, he moves the inquiry to *Red Badge*, where the audience is granted a fuller understanding of the unexpected than are the characters; but the reader is still uncertain of Crane's mode and meaning. Kent suggests that Crane's universe is "more than apathetic or even antagonistic: it is unknowable." Earlier scholarship has inspected most of this ground through such old-fashioned formulae as "variations of perspective" and "deterministic irony," but Kent stimulates some profitable reflection in "The Problem of Knowledge in 'The Open Boat' and 'The Blue Hotel'" (*ALR* 14:262–68) and "Epistemological Uncertainty in *The Red Badge of Courage*" (*MFS* 27:621–28).

Stimulating, too, is Robert Shulman's "*The Red Badge* and Social Violence: Crane's Myth of America" (*CRevAS* 12:1–19). Shulman introduces his reading with a well-documented summary of contemporary social violence. He then speculates that the "pervasive smoke, chaos, killing, irrationality and fear" occasioned by the war "machine" in *Red Badge* translate into metaphors that work "in a deep and subtle way" to reveal a critical reaction toward America's urban-industrial society. Coming in the wake of his arresting title and thesis, this interpretive procedure seems impeccable, and one feels that here is a major article. But then several nagging questions refuse to go away. Where is the clinching evidence that Crane was in fact profoundly affected by these current instances of social violence? If indeed he were, how are we to be convinced that he then devised this fiction as a bifocal treatment of the Civil War *and* the 1890s? And why is his central consciousness in *Red Badge* a countrified youth who has never experienced an urban-industrial America but "all his life" has dreamed of the blood and fire of war?

Like Crane, Norris again has attracted a band of admirers to his virtually inexhaustible vein of sources and elusive meanings. One apparent source, lying in full view, is a finding that many a scholar's dreams are made on. Resting for years next to the title card of Norris' *The Octopus* in the Bancroft Library is John R. Robinson's *The Octopus* (1894), a muckraking exposé of railroad companies, including Norris' "Pacific and Southwestern Railroad" (the Southern Pacific). Glen A. Love and David A. Carpenter set forth Norris' plausible debts in the numerous parallels: title and central image, short-haul rates, cost claims, sudden rate changes, alternate trading with the Orient, a corrupted democracy, personal dishonor, and an aroused new progressive spirit ("The Other Octopus" [*ALR* 14: 1–5]).

Richard A. Davison's "Frank Norris and the Arts of Social Criticism" (*ALR* 14:77–89) is equally convincing on the way Edwin Markham's "The Man with the Hoe" and the famous painting by Millet that inspired the poem are paralleled in *The Octopus* with Presley's poem and the painting in Cedarquist's art collection. Norris, like his character Shelgrim, preferred the painting over the bleeding-heart poem and, Davison concludes, there is considerable ambivalence in Norris' treatment of tasteful entrepreneurs like Cedarquist and Shelgrim in particular and capitalist wealth in general.

John Schroeder links the author of *McTeague* and the Bard of Avon through four leading motifs inspired, respectively, by *Two*

Gentlemen from Verona (Friendship Triumphs Over Love), *A Mid-summer Night's Dream* (Love's Awakening in the Animal Man), *The Merchant of Venice* (The Miser's Loss), and *Othello* (The Husband's Revenge). While one cannot be certain that "The Shakespearean Plots in *McTeague*" (*ALR* 14:289–99) may not be a hoax enjoyed at the expense of Norris' source-hunters, the Titania-Trina line in the novel ("'a fairy queen enamored of a clown with ass's ears'") leaves no doubt that one play, at least, had occurred to Norris.

How successfully did Norris shape his source-laden fictions into coherent art? Robert E. Morsberger replies that Norris did not weld his materials into philosophical unity in a work like *The Octopus*, but his private inconsistencies and contradictions typify America's own confusions in ideology and purpose at the turn of the century. In *The Octopus*, Presley is both the romantic and would-be realist, Vanamee the mystic who opposes God, farmer-plutocrats are victims of plutocracy, the environment produces a Victorian saint (Helma Tree) and a street-walker (Minna Hooven), impersonal naturalism is incongruously wed to a transcendental pantheism, and so on ("The Inconsistent *Octopus*" [*WAL* 16:105–13]). Robert Micklus does not regard Norris' "philosophical 'fuzziness'" (echoing Warner Berthoff's judgment) to be as serious a defect as his "facile abandonment of the most difficult question the novel poses: . . . what should the farmers have done to redress their wrongs?" In "Ambivalent Warriors in *The Octopus*" (*WAL* 16:115–23) Micklus ranks the "observers" and "participators" separately and concludes that Cedarquist might have become Norris' representative man, blending the ideal vision of a Vanamee with a participator's concern and then pressing to a workable solution of the farmers' dilemma.

Edwin H. Miller in "The Art of Frank Norris in *Vandover and the Brute*" (*MarkhamR* 10:56–63) reads the posthumous novel in somewhat less Freudian terms than he read *McTeague* (*ALS 1979*, 219), but he basically repeats the approach by establishing a design of symbolic details (13 in all) which he isolates in the early railroad scene and then illustrates through the rest of the story. Joseph R. McElrath, Jr., also builds on his previous labors (see *ALS 1979*, 218) in *Frank Norris: The Critical Reception*, which he edits with Katherine Knight in the American Critical Tradition series of Burt Franklin, volumes designed to reprint, excerpt, or summarize every known review of the selected authors' works. McElrath introduces the volume with an interpretive summary of Norris' reputation, which began to rise only slightly after *The Octopus.* Substantial acclaim followed his death and then subsided; his posthumous tales, criticism, and *Vandover* did not awaken any real literary interest in the apathetic audience before the Great War.

More than adequate critical attention was paid six authors whose unmistakably minor status was at one time not so obvious. Joseph McElrath in "Richard Harding Davis's *The Boys in the Adariondacks*" (*ALR* 14:195–215) reprints some juvenilia by the 16-year-old Davis which forebodes the archly satirical tone and heroic vein of the fiction in the 1890s. Frank R. Stockton receives the minor-author treatment at its best from Henry L. Golemba (*TUSAS* 374), who describes the middle-brow female audience Stockton courted (and whose genteel prejudices he easily shared). They probably never suspected that Stockton's aesthetic was dark-tinged and that it sometimes tempted him in the direction of corrective satire and an outlook not dissimilar to Mark Twain's. One of the period's most popular figures is celebrated in a 536–page memorial volume, *An F. Marion Crawford Companion* (Greenwood), in which John C. Moran compiles a biographical and literary chronology; glossaries of Crawford's literary circle, fictional geography, and characters; plot synopses; and selected quotations from the works. Guy Szuberla's "Henry Blake Fuller and the 'New Immigrant'" (*AL* 53:246–65) is a useful study of the pull between "assimilationist and restrictionist" attitudes toward immigration in Fuller's life and fiction. In *Finley Peter Dunne* (*TUSAS* 402) Grace Eckley struggles without eminent success to organize the opinions of Dooley, to understand Dunne in contexts of literary history and humorous modes, and to account for something meaningful in the later career, given the hiatus from 1915 to 1926 and then a final decade of good living after a legacy from the millionaire Whitney. Finally, Bill Nye, whose humor influenced Dunne, is intelligently interpreted in David B. Kesterson's monograph (*TUSAS* 403). Kesterson emphasizes Nye's versatility as a writer of fiction, poetry, plays, journalism, and historical burlesques; the range of his frequently complex humor, rooted in the incongruities of the commonplace and laced with elements of the cynical, ironic, horse-sensical, clownish, dark, and idiotic; and his ten years on the platform circuit with and without the hard-drinking James Whitcomb Riley.

Three scholars dominated the year's work on Chopin and Bierce. Joyce Dyer alone published four articles on Chopin, one of some consequence and all of them evincing proof that the professor need not perish who comes hungrily to Chopin's banquet of generally unsampled short fictions. In "Kate Chopin's Sleeping Bruties" (*MarkhamR* 10:10–15) Dyer chides those who have appropriated a "feminist" Chopin. Her men in various stories are also awakened, and both sexes, for Chopin, "are complex creatures who have no choice but to discover their passion in spite of risks, confusion, and guilt." Dyer considers a maturely awakened male in "Gouvernail, Kate Chopin's Sensitive Bachelor" (*SLJ* 14,i:46–55). Though Gouvernail figures only briefly as one of nine guests at Edna's birthday party, his "past history and characterization become truly significant to the thematic, emotional, and imaginative experience" of *The Awakening*. My reservation about the aesthetic "experience" afforded by the brief appearance of Chopin's "repeating characters," as they were discussed previously by Patricia Lattin (*ALS* 1979, 220–21), holds in the present case.

Dyer's "The Restive Brute: The Symbolic Presentation of Repression and Sublimation in Kate Chopin's 'Fedora'" (*SSF* 18:261–65) is a tidy reading of this fictional gem, although the attentive reader with only hearsay knowledge of Freud will not need Dyer's help. But her "Night Images in the Work of Kate Chopin" (*ALR* 14:216–30) is a valuable survey of a central "indicator of the variety and growth of Chopin's symbolic method." By *The Awakening*, night not only helps to express the inarticulate domains of sex and the heart in the Chopin characterization, but has now become, like the mythic sea, "a more elaborate symbol for spiritual and sexual mystery."

Emily Toth also interprets traditional elements used by the unconventional Chopin. In "Kate Chopin and Literary Convention: 'Désirée's Baby'" (*SoSt* 20:207–08) Toth alerts us to Chopin's subtle variations on the stock characters in the usually female tragic mulatto convention wherein "racial inheritance determines character." Chopin illustrates instead (with Cable and Faulkner) that "society's reaction to race" shapes character, and she also slyly reverses the sexual roles. The tale becomes "a political analysis of slavery . . .

grafted upon literary convention as a vehicle." Eerily echoed here are the articles on Stowe and Jackson previously discussed.

Lawrence I. Berkove, the most active student of Bierce, gives us a trio of articles on the journalist, social thinker, and writer of fiction. "The Man with the Burning Pen: Ambrose Bierce as Journalist" (*JPC* 15,ii:34–40) sketches the career which began in San Francisco during the late 1860s when the early Bierce defended social pariahs and set his talented " 'burning pen' " against demagogues, bigoted clergy, and "hypocrisy, cant, and all sham." He never retreated from this opinionated courage, even at the end of the century when he opposed the popular imperialism of Hearst, his long-time boss. (Berkove has more to say on Bierce, Hearst, and the war in his introduction to *Ambrose Bierce: Skepticism and Dissent: Selected Journalism from 1898–1901* [Delmas, 1980], an edited volume that arrived too late for notice in *ALS 1980*.) Probably congenial to Hearst, however, were Bierce's conservative satires of utopian thought and experimental communities in California. Berkove concludes "The Impossible Dreams: Ambrose Bierce on Utopia and America" (*HLQ* 44:283–92) with a tart summation his author would have enjoyed and endorsed: "To Bierce, indulgence in utopian schemes was the irrationality of folly but belief in the tenets of republican democracy was the madness of hubris."

A light moment during the Hearst years happened at San Francisco's Cliff House in 1891 when a beautiful young admirer of Bierce's fiction mistook his table companion, W. C. Morrow, for her idol, lured Morrow away, praised his work, and finally punctuated the glowing speech with a warm kiss. Morrow wrote an account of the amusing occasion for the *Wave* of 7 March 1891, and Berkove now reprints it in " 'A Strange Adventure': The Story Behind a Bierce Tale" (*ALR* 14:70–76). A week after, the *Examiner* published Bierce's fictional version of the mistaken identity, "An Heiress from Redhorse." The story gives rare evidence that "Bitter Bierce" had concealed from his devoted readers a talent for whimsical romantic comedy.

San Diego State University

13. Fiction: 1900 to the 1930s

John J. Murphy

The major authors of this period continue to receive comparatively generous attention, although most book-length studies in 1981 were devoted to such minor figures as E. R. Burroughs, Don Marquis, Mary Johnston, and Dubose Heyward.

Two general studies approach several writers from economic perspectives. Wayne W. Westbrook's *Wall Street* traces high finance and big business themes of novelists from Melville to Bellow and contains background information on the robber barons and financial titans that inspired their villains and heroes. Of particular significance is the generous treatment given the neglected David Graham Phillips, whose good guys–bad guys Wall Street formula in *The Master-Rogue* and *The Deluge* is reminiscent of the dime Western. Westbrook also considers Sinclair's *The Metropolis* and *The Money-changers* as exposés, lawless and amoral dimensions of London's Wall Street in *Burning Delight*, Wharton's drama of Fifth Avenue's defeat by downtown business and finance in *The House of Mirth* and *The Custom of the Country*, and Dreiser's Cowperwood as "a direct descendant in fiction of Hawthorne's evil capitalist, Judge Jaffrey Pyncheon." An excellent essay by George M. Spangler, "Suicide and Social Criticism: Durkheim, Dreiser, Wharton, and London" (*AQ* 31[1979]:496–516), evaluates the suicides in *Sister Carrie, Martin Eden*, and *The House of Mirth* according to Emile Durkheim's 1897 study *Suicide*, which posits self-destruction as the result of alienation during times of rapid economic flux. Citing Dreiser's insight that people are materialistic because they are lonely, Sprangler groups Hurstwood and Lily Bart as alienated by material loss and unsuccessful attempts at recovery, and Eden, ironically, by material gain—"the Horatio Alger story inverted, gone sour, its hero ending in self-destruction."

In "Murder Trials, Murder, and Twenties America" (*AQ* 33:163–

84) John R. Brazil uses Zane Grey's fiction and Dreiser's *An American Tragedy* to consider public and professional preoccupation with
murder trials during an era when violent crime seemed to threaten
traditional assumptions about individual freedom. Grey's work, like
detective fiction of the time, challenged its classical origins (*The
Virginian*) by emphasizing violence and murder as norm rather
than exception. Dreiser's novel reflects his engagement with "the
same issues . . . that were central to westerns and detective stories,
. . . an anxiety about the status of the individual and the infrastructure of individualism."

i. Theodore Dreiser

The event of the year in literary scholarship on this period was the
publication of the "Pennsylvania Edition" of *Sister Carrie*, the combined effort of editors James L. W. West III and Neda M. Westlake,
with John C. Berkey and Alice M. Winters serving as historical editors. Using Dreiser's manuscript as copy-text and eliminating most
of the significant cuts and revisions advised by Arthur Henry and
Sarah White Dreiser, approximately 36,000 words are restored, and
Dreiser's revised endings of the last two chapters replaced with his
original endings. The result is a bleaker, more deterministic work
than the one originally published by Doubleday and Page in 1900,
a deeper, more troubled Carrie, and more believable characteriza-
tions of Ames, Drouet, and Hurstwood. Included is a fine essay "*Sister Carrie*: Manuscript to Print" by West, Berkey, and Westlake
detailing Dreiser's inspiration for the novel, his method of composition and revision, his relationship with Henry and marriage to Sarah
(Jug), their subsequent involvement in the project, Dreiser's trouble with Doubleday, and Heinemann's British edition. Berkey and
Winters provide maps of Dreiser's Chicago and New York, and photographs and historical notes indicating Dreiser's penchant for historical accuracy and method of using real people and places, generally aiding our understanding of the era of the novel. West's textual
commentary explains that substantive changes introduced by the
author on the manuscript have been respected and indicates revisions
on the manuscript and typescript by Henry, White, and Dreiser.
Textual apparatus includes lists of selected emendations in the copy-

text, textual notes, block cuts made by Henry and accepted by Dreiser, chapter titles, Dreiser's revised endings for chapters 49 and 50, and White's subsequent revision of 50. Penguin Books "copublished" the Pennsylvania *Sister Carrie* with a helpful introduction by Alfred Kazin (pp. vii–xvi) summarizing much of the commentary from the major edition and claiming that the restored novel is "a different book, fuller, less cruel, more recognizably Dreiser's own work." In "*Sister Carrie* Restored" (*DrN* 12,i:1–8) Richard W. Dowell comments on the increased culpability of Hurstwood and believability of Ames in the new edition and emphasizes our completer picture of the seamier side of Chicago and "valuable opportunity to study [Dreiser's] tendencies and eccentricities regarding sentence structure and punctuation." In a note concerning the original publication of *Sister Carrie*, "*Sister Carrie* Again" (*AL* 53:287–90) Christopher P. Wilson theorizes that Doubleday and Page saw potential in Dreiser but failed to promote his first novel in order to establish him before bringing out anything so controversial; however, Dreiser rejected the concept of "orderly progression of publication as regards novels." The only attention *Sister Carrie* received outside its appearances in print was Laurel T. Hatvary's note "Carrie Meeber and Clara Maugham" (*NMAL* 5:Item 26), which compares the heroine of Margaret Drabble's 1967 novel of contemporary London life, *Jerusalem the Golden*, to Dreiser's heroine in that both conceive the city as a glittering opportunity to compensate for deprived, inexperienced, country childhoods.

An American Tragedy was the subject of three brief articles. Carla Mulford Micklus explores Dreiser's antithetical version of the American Adam in "*An American Tragedy*; or, The Tragedy of the Adamic Myth" (*ALR* 14:9–15). Clyde Griffith is bound to rather than emancipated from his past and relies on luck and chance rather than self. By making Clyde insecure rather than self-reliant and also representative of the actual American existence, "Dreiser explodes the myth of the American Adam." Related in theme is Eugene L. Huddleston's "*Herndon's Lincoln* and Theodore Dreiser's *An American Tragedy*" (*MQ* 22:242–54), which sees Dreiser as "consciously or unconsciously mocking the Alger-like rise of Lincoln," demonstrating the role of circumstances in shaping success. Finally, in "Dreiser in Japan" (*DrN* 12,i:9–11) Kiyohiko Murayama credits recent Japanese recognition of Dreiser to the popularity of *A Place in the Sun*, the film version of *Tragedy*, and discusses plans for a 20-volume limited edition of the works.

An excellent consideration of the Cowperwood novels is Jack E. Wallace's "The Comic Voice in Dreiser's Cowperwood Narrative" (*AL* 53:56–71), which dismisses traditional views of Cowperwood's story as a *de casibus* tragedy by stressing its comic structure and ironic voice. Modeled as much after capitalist Joseph G. Rabin as after Charles T. Yerkes, Cowperwood is a financier of the "newer and quicker order, exotic and fleshy," challenging "the standard conservative and socially well-placed rich." Dreiser's intention was "a Darwinian romance of the 'bohemian' financier and his role in the building of a great city." His numerous sexual exploits merely reflect his economic triumphs, and his final defeat illustrates the principles of laissez-faire necessary for natural balance in the economic system. On a more pedantic note, George Arms provides a useful time chart for Dreiser's last novel in "*The Bulwark*: A Chronology" (*DrN* 12,ii[1980]:10–14). Helene Keyssar's "Theodore Dreiser's Dramas: American Folk Drama and Its Limits" (*TJ* 33:365–76) reminds us of a neglected, imaginative dimension of Dreiser while crediting the failure of his plays to their violation of American middle-class presumptions. The central images of "The Girl in the Coffin," "Old Ragpicker," and *The Hand of the Potter* challenge our preconceptions of what should be depicted on stage and admitted about life.

There were two discussions of Dreiser and philosophy. Ronald E. Martin devotes his long final chapter to the novelist in *The Universe of Force*, pp. 215–55. Martin sees Dreiser as the literary "apotheosis" of the force concept of Herbert Spencer, John Fiske, and others, and traces his constant if haphazard philosophical research (fictionalized in *The "Genius"*) from the rejection of his father's fundamentalism to his own murky aesthetic response to an unknowable ultimate universe. The psychology of forces he adopted to explain the situations and motivations of his characters sometimes merely amounted to a new myth and frequently resulted in the awkward and ridiculous. Martin's analyses of these novels and *The "Genius"* are important, as is his portrait of an artist whose force "theory" depended on feelings and developed from sources as diverse as Darwin and Mary Baker Eddy. Of lesser significance is Marguerite Tjader's "Dreiser's Investigations of Nature" (*DrN* 12,ii[1980]:1–9), which calls attention to Dreiser's unfinished *Notes on Life* in the files of the University of Pennsylvania (selections published by Alabama in 1974). These notes and essays reveal the novelist's interest in the nature writings of Thoreau, Maeterlinck, and Jean Henri Fabre, and his constant search "for the force behind the fact, the whole picture of life."

Dreiser the artist is the subject of Joseph Kwiat's "Theodore Dreiser's Creative Quest: Early 'Philosophical' Beliefs and Artistic Values" (*ArQ* 37:264–74). Kwiat describes the novelist's developing attitude toward his art, from interest in depicting life's spectacle to compulsion to translate life. Dreiser's awareness of the visual arts, especially the postimpressionists, indicates concern with form and artistic rationale. Two items of minor biographical interest were Philip L. Gerber's "Dating a 'Letter to Louise'" (*DrN* 12,i:12–17), which places undated correspondence with Louise Campbell during the writing of *The Stoic*, and Vincent Fitzpatrick's "Gratitude and Grievances: Dreiser's Inscriptions to Mencken" (*DrN* 12,ii:1–16), which attempts with limited success to use inscriptions exchanged between the writers as a barometer of their friendship.

Critical Essays on Theodore Dreiser (Hall) edited by Donald Pizer provides a usable, helpful survey of reviews and articles, although unlike other volumes in this series it contains no original work and an introductory note rather than a full essay. Pizer indicates three overlapping phases in Dreiser criticism: in the first, Mencken and Sherman debated the validity of Dreiserian naturalism, the second concentrated on philosophical and political inconsistencies with Matthiessen defending and Trilling opposing, and the third or scholarly phase includes contributions by Elias, Walcutt, Kazin, and others. Pizer restricts this volume to "the best criticism of Dreiser's fiction" and has "not attempted to represent the full extent of Dreiser 'negative' criticism."

ii. Willa Cather

Although there were no new editions or book-length studies of her works, Cather claimed the lion's share of major articles reviewed in this chapter. Of primary significance are several essays in a special number of *Prairie Schooner* (*PrS* 55,i&ii) honoring veteran Cather critic Bernice Slote. In "Willa Cather—A Pioneer in Art: *O Pioneers!*

and *My Ántonia*" (pp. 141–54) Susan J. Rosowski applies a theory of response to the landscape involving loss and recovery of the self and emphatic union with space to explain Cather's approach to Nebraska in these novels. While Rosowski achieves some clarification of Cather's descriptive method, she serves the novels less well than she serves the thesis applied to them. Judith Fryer's "Cather's Felicitous Space" (pp. 185–98) is a similar attempt to intellectualize Cather by applying a set thesis, in this case Gaston Bachelard's *The Poetics of Space*, to the protagonists of *The Song of the Lark*, *The Professor's House*, and *Death Comes for the Archbishop*. An interesting contrast is managed between Thea Kronborg's emergence from and Godfrey St. Peter's retreat to intimate space. Fryer concludes that through Archbishop Latour, Cather achieves intimacy in the vastness of the desert, successfully balancing inner and outer landscapes. John J. Murphy parallels Cather's Western novels and Cooper's Leatherstocking and Littlepage series in "Cooper, Cather, and the Downward Path to Progress" (pp. 168–84). Surveying these works from the perspective of frontier development phases popularized by Turner, Murphy concludes that both novelists saw the business ethic and destruction of heroic context as the outcome of the American experience. There is little new in this conclusion; however, the detail with which the comparison is managed is contributive, as is the consideration of *A Lost Lady* with the pro-aristocratic Littlepage novels. In a significant if unnecessarily obscure article "Willa Cather's *Lucy Gayheart*: A Long Perspective" (pp. 199–209) Paul Comeau makes some important observations about this neglected novel, that it is "a philosophical work in which . . . the processes of art and life are shown to be the same creative process of memory." Through these combined processes Lucy is "ultimately transformed from a sentimental, suffering young woman into a beautiful idea." Cather's response to New Mexico is compared with Paul Horgan's in Robert F. Gish's "Paul Horgan and the Biography of Place" (pp. 226–32). Both writers identified with Archbishop Lamy as one who derived education from the cultural expressions of the East and Europe and felt exile in the West. Finally, Paul Olson's "The Epic and Great Plains Literature: Rølvaag, Cather, and Neihardt" (pp. 263–85) makes a valid case for Cather's dependence on the *Aeneid* if one can swallow the provincial claim that the sodbusters' unique brush with heroism somehow exempts their literature from the rest

of America's. Olson's balancing of episodes from Virgil's epic and
My Ántonia is the most detailed aspect of his essay. He sees Cather's
final preference for the *Georgics* as a response to the rootlessness
and chauvinism of World War I America.

The western aspect of Cather is continued in Fred Erisman's
informative "Western Regional Writers and the Uses of Place," part
of a special literary issue of *Journal of the West* (19,i[1980]:37–44).
Although flawed by an attempt to establish the uniqueness of the
West (for which Erisman is forced to enlist the support of Maine's
Sarah Orne Jewett and Mississippi's Eudora Welty), the article succeeds in clearly distinguishing regional from local-color writing and
sees Cather as key among western writers in establishing links between the region and the world, particularly her justification of the
city in the West through Chicago and Lincoln settings. "Until the
city develops, with its synthesis of large and small, native and foreign, the region remains only a place. Once the city takes root, it
contributes to the final growth and development of the locale, linking that specific place, once and for all, with the universal currents of
human life." In "The Mesa Verde Story and Cather's 'Tom Outland's
Story'" (*NMAL* 5:Item 9) John J. Murphy examines Cather's use of
western lore in the second book of *The Professor's House*. Comparison of the Wetherill "discovery" of Mesa Verde and Outland's of
Blue Mesa reveals Cather altered facts to add meaning to her narrative.

Three articles were devoted to psychological dualism in Cather.
Susan J. Rosowski's "The Pattern of Willa Cather's Novels" (*WAL*
15:243–63) surveys all the novels from the perspective of personal
and second selves, concentrating on *O Pioneers!*, *The Song of the
Lark*, and *The Professor's House*. Although failing to clarify Alex-
andra Bergson's discovery of her second self and neglect and subsequent realization of her personal self through obvious Whitman
references in *O Pioneers!*, Rosowski does manage to develop aspects
of this novel other critics have not. The emotional emptiness at the
conclusion of *Song* fails to fit her thesis, however; and the analysis
of *House* remains sketchy. Dorothy Van Ghent's treatment of divided selves in her Minnesota pamphlet on Cather (1964) might
have helped. In "Willa Cather's Women" (*SAF* 9:261–75) Rosowski
continues the two-selves pattern with more success, restricting her
thesis to women characters, to how "a woman encounters contradic-

tions between the human pattern of two selves and cultural myths that would limit her to only one of them." In *My Ántonia* and *A Lost Lady* Cather filters her women through the expectations of male consciousness, while *My Mortal Enemy* views a woman through the eyes of a woman. "Old Mrs. Harris" is a woman whose creative self is expressed in family relationships. A clearer and more significant view of dualism in Cather, Michael A. Klug's "Willa Cather: Between Red Cloud and Byzantium" (*CRevAS* 12:287–99) analyzes several novels (primarily *The Song of the Lark, The Professor's House,* and *My Ántonia*) as reflecting a conflict between individual and collective drives in American life and in the American artist. Klug's treatment of *My Ántonia* is particularly illuminating: Jim and Ántonia, each representing opposing sides of this conflict, must go separate ways to pursue individual destinies and to be true to each other. In this separation we see the impossibility in Cather and in American life of "reconciling the demands of personal ambition and the claims of love."

Two major articles focus on individual novels. In "Euripides' *Hippolytus* and Cather's *A Lost Lady*" (*AL* 53:72–86) John J. Murphy examines the play as a possible source for the novel, which he sees as "a particular variation of some materials of the *Hippolytus,* and as such a provocative indication of Cather's creative process." In each case a young male characterized by sexual problems and self-love espouses ideals of Artemis-like purity as protection from Aphrodite and sex. Murphy sees Cather's use of the limited male consciousness in this and other novels as essential to her social criticism. Paul Comeau concentrates on *One of Ours* in the final part of "The Fool Figure in Willa Cather's Fiction" (*WAL* 16:265–78). Using the early story "Lou, the Prophet" as an archtype, Comeau discusses Crazy Ivar in *O Pioneers!,* Tillie Kronborg in *The Song of the Lark,* and Mahailey in *One of Ours* in terms of their insight into eternal things, their support of the hero, and the context in which each functions. *One of Ours* is seen as a turning point in Cather's fiction; in a world of lapsed values the protagonist rather than a minor character becomes the fool figure—a Don Quixote preserving ideals society has abandoned.

Contributive if less significant are two comparative studies. Michael Peterman's "The Charm of Willa Cather's *My Ántonia* and

W. O. Mitchell's *Who Has Seen the Wind*" (*Mosaic* 14:93–106) stresses positive views of mortal life and the benefits of nature as points of comparison. Peterman considers the use of melodrama by both authors and briefly indicates differences. In " 'Presumptuous Girls' of Cather, Dreiser, and James" (*PVR* 9:83–95) John J. Murphy compares Thea Kronborg of *The Song of the Lark* with the heroines of *Sister Carrie* and *The Portrait of a Lady*. "While Dreiser emphasizes Carrie's material success as much as her mind, James stresses the inner life of Isabel Archer, although material fortune is essential to its development. Cather's [novel] combines this increased scope of activity with an intensity of self-realization reminiscent of James' narrower sphere."

Finally, three articles survey Cather's career and critical reception. Peter Benson's "Willa Cather at *Home Monthly*" (*Biography* 4:227–48) gives the history of the short-lived Pittsburgh women's magazine young Cather came from Nebraska to edit. Benson argues that Cather's art "germinated within the strictly defined genres of nineteenth-century popular journalism." His summaries of her *Home Monthly* pieces have little value beyond the context he establishes for them, however, and he should be informed that *all* the stories she wrote for the magazine appear in the 1970 edition of *Collected Short Fiction, 1892–1912* (Nebraska). In a fine essay "Willa Cather's Nostalgia" (*RS* 49:23–34) Marilyn Arnold uses the early stories "Eleanor's House" and "On the Gull's Road" and the late "The Old Beauty" to argue that Cather was not as uncomplicatedly nostalgic as some have made her out to be. Arnold uses the portraits of Sarah Jewett, Mrs. Fields, and Flaubert's niece in *Not Under Forty* to establish that even in this defensively senior collection Cather betrayed admiration for people who live vitally in the present. "Failure to see this double thrust in Cather's work," Arnold notes significantly, "has led some readers to assume that every point-of-view character speaks for the author, or that every character given to nostalgia represents her unqualified attitude." Barry Gross's "Willa Cather and the 'American Metaphysic' " (*MidAmerica* 8:68–78) is a complaint about the neglect of Cather by the generations subsequent to hers. He accuses the critical establishment of sexist bias and cites the hostile reception of *One of Ours*. A weakness in Gross's argument is his total neglect of Cather criticism of the last fifteen years.

iii. Jack London and Edgar Rice Burroughs

Among the considerable activity on London during 1981 was the appearance of Lawrence Teacher and Richard E. Nicholls' excellent one-volume paperback collection *The Unabridged Jack London* (Running Press). Divided into "Yukon" and "Sea" sections with helpful commentaries before each novel and group of shorter pieces, the volume includes nine Klondike articles and stories previously uncollected. The text followed in each case is of the first printing, with corrections kept to a minimum. Nicholls' brief but informative introduction stresses the contradictory nature of London's tumultuous career and the creative perspective he gained from his Klondike experience.

Two of the year's several articles on London are devoted to his philosophy. Of particular significance is "Jack London: Radical Individualism and Social Justice in the Universe of Force," an extensive chapter in Martin's *The Universe of Force*, pp. 184–214. Martin considers London typical of the "advanced" mind of his day, a product of Spencer, Haecker, Darwin, Marx, Nietzsche, and others. London's unique synthesis of the philosophies he found attractive sustains popular works like *The Sea-Wolf*, which depicts the superman coping with natural forces as well as the destructive nature of the superman in a social context. Martin's discussions of this novel and *Martin Eden* ("a version of the whole sailor-to-sage period of London's own life"), according to his force thesis, are thorough and sensible. He observes that London deviated from Spencer in embracing socialism and revolution as the culmination of socioeconomic forces. Of less importance is Anthony J. Naso's "Jack London and Herbert Spencer" (*JLN* 14:13–34), which views London's variations on Spencer as more intentional than unorthodox. Although Naso's concluding section somewhat contradicts his earlier analysis of love elements in *The Call of the Wild* and *The Sea-Wolf*, his essay is worth comparing with Martin's and begins with a helpful summary of the philosopher's views.

A more practical London is the subject of Susan Ward's "Jack London and the Blue Pencil: London's Correspondence with Popular Editors" (*ALR* 14:16–25). Ward reviews the letter collections at the Huntington and New York Public libraries for instances of London's capitulating to editors in matters of subject, plot, length, brutality, politics, language, and sex. While Ward wants to excuse what seem like "errors in artistic judgment," she is forced to admit that for London money took precedence over art and that his attitude toward editors was "pragmatic in the extreme."

Three articles considered single works. In "Land Dogs and Sea Wolves: A Jack London Dilemma" (*MR* 21[1980]:569–93) Abraham Rothberg examines *The Sea-Wolf* as a paradigm of London's conflicting component egos. The effeminate Van Weyden must shackle and bury Wolf Larson to suppress homoerotic desires and express his love for Maud. The fascination of Rothberg's insight is not in the two men's representing London's opposing selves, but in their becoming id and super-ego for each other. Charles N. Watson argues convincingly in "The Composition of *Martin Eden*" (*AL* 53:397–408) that London conceived the novel to end with suicide, that speculations of critics Walker and Calder-Marshall that London hastily terminated the novel for financial reasons are based on a letter by his wife's aunt, who had read only five chapters of the manuscript and theorized about the ending to the *Pacific Monthly*. London's autobiographical travel narrative of his voyage through Polynesia and Melanesia is the subject of David Allison Moreland's "Jack London's *The Cruise of the Snark*" (*JLN* 14:86–104). Moreland gives a detailed synopsis of the voyage and explains how it at once flattered London's ego as romantic adventurer and made him aware of his human limitations.

An important discussion of several works is "The Novels of Jack London" (*JLN* 14:48–71), a chapter from a book-in-progress by Stoddard Martin. Martin considers cook Thomas Mugridge as Nietzschean Underman in *The Sea-Wolf* and in relation to the outcasts in *The People of the Abyss*. "*The People* reflects London's shift of attention from the issue of man's struggle with the forces of nature to that of man's struggle to live decently with other men." Christian socialism in *The Iron Heel* is treated in detail, as are superman aspects of its hero. Perhaps Martin's major contribution is analyses of fantasy elements in *The Star Rover* and stylistic modernism and interior monologues in *The Little Lady of the Big House*, a novel he sees as an experiment in the genteel tradition. Gordon N. Blackman, Jr., concludes the second half of "Jack London: Visionary Realist" (*JLN* 14:1–12) with a survey of London's didactic socialistic science fiction ("the low ebb of London's talent") and better-quality evolutionary fiction, designating *The Scarlet Plague* and *The Star Rover* in the latter category as "among his finest works." Blackman speculates that London's evolutionary story "When the World Was Young," appearing 14 months before Edgar Rice Burroughs wrote the first Tarzan episode, "may have inspired the creation of Tarzan."

The Tarzan books themselves are the subject of *Tarzan and Tradition: Classical Myth in Popular Literature* (Greenwood), a successful attempt by classicist Erling B. Holtsmark to demonstrate the classical origins of the series. Holtsmark finds numerous instances of polarity, chiasmus, and parallelism (characteristics of Greek and Latin style) in Burroughs' prose and generously illustrates techniques like ring composition, synkrisis, and simile in Homer before applying them to the Tarzan novels. Holtsmark's treatment of the animals in Tarzan's world as Burroughs' "innovative departure" from the use of gods in ancient literatures is perhaps the most absorbing aspect of his study. Burroughs' interest in the Romulus and Remus story and knowledge of the *Odyssey* lead to an evaluation of Tarzan according to Somerset's elements of heroic biography and to the conclusion that the classical contribution to Burroughs' hero is "by far the most pervasive and authoritative one." The final and somewhat repetitious chapter considers themes, the most important of which is Burroughs' qualified Darwinianism. While man's spiritual or moral evolution parallels his physical evolution, civilization also "brutalizes and emphasizes the vast gulf between man's apparently (that is, externally visible) advanced stage of evolutionary developments and the truly (that is, internally real) primitive moral sensibility he displays."

iv. Edith Wharton and Sinclair Lewis

Considering recent attention given Wharton by R. W. B. Lewis, Cynthia Wolff, and Elizabeth Ammons, 1981 was an off year. Joan Lidoff's "Another Sleeping Beauty: Narcissism in *The House of Mirth*" (*AQ* 32:519–39), the only article approaching major significance, is heavy-handed in its attempt to satisfy the interdisciplinary requirements of the journal. Lidoff's point that Wharton's sexual fears imprison Lily Bart in narcissism could have been made without so much "psychology." Lily's difficulties with adult responsibility are traced to a need for mother-love she shared with her creator. Although "Wharton is able to tap the well of childhood narcissism and use those resonant feelings to create a brilliantly memorable character," she cannot create a fictional structure to develop that character into "a responsible adult of moral dimensions—a tragic heroine." Adeline Tintner's Wharton contribution to *The Lost Tradition: Mothers and Daughters in Literature*, ed. Cathy M. Davidson and E. M. Broner (Ungar, 1980), "Mothers, Daughters, and Incest in the Late Novels of Edith Wharton" (pp. 147–56), approaches the novelist from a similar biographical angle. The presumption that every problem handled in a novel represents the novelist's own has become a bothersome commonplace in much "sisterhood" criticism, and Tintner is best when avoiding it in admirably comparing Grace Aquilar's *The Mother's Recompense* to Wharton's examination of the role of the mother in a world of lapsed values in her novel of the same name and subsequent *Twilight Sleep*. However, the essay seems to blur the connection between the incest theme and that of untraditional self-definition.

In "The Eagle and the Hen: Edith Wharton and Henry James" (*RS* 49:143–53) Lynne T. Hanley takes an informative as well as amusing look at the celebrated friendship in which James played the fainting damsel to Wharton's "heroic rushes." As artists, however, these roles were reversed; he shaped and controlled his material while hers was shaped by outward circumstances and the wills of her fictional characters: "the woman interacts, records, and receives, the man commands, dictates, and constructs." The distinctions Hanley sees in Wharton's method, her use of time, history, and circumstance in motivation, and the value she placed on verisimilitude make this a noteworthy if minor article. Also helpful is "Botanical Language in Edith Wharton's *The House of Mirth*" (*NMAL* 5:Item 3), in which Martha R. Langley recognizes fashionable New York as the hothouse outside of which its lilies cannot survive.

In "Sinclair Lewis, Stuart Pratt Sherman, and the Writing of *Arrowsmith*" (*RALS* 9:24–30) Fritz H. Oehlschlaeger includes four previously unpublished Lewis letters from the Sherman collection at the University of Illinois written in response to Sherman's evaluation of Lewis after Wharton rather than Lewis won the 1920 Pulitzer

Prize. Lewis felt that *Arrowsmith* would be his best effort so far and
was anxious to satisfy Sherman's request for "a hero qualified to
register in some fashion the results of his own request for the de-
sirable." An awarded rather than missed prize is the subject of David
D. Anderson's "Sinclair Lewis and the Nobel Prize" (*MidAmerica*
8:9–21). Anderson concludes that the reasons for Lewis' receiving
the prize were other than literary and quotes the secretary of the
Swedish Academy praising Lewis for catching America during its
coming of age, "still in the turbulent years of adolescence." Lewis'
place in American literature is also other than literary, says Anderson; "his works are neither poetry nor drama; they are history, sociology, psychology." In "Love Is More Than the Evening Star: A
Semantic Analysis of *Elmer Gantry* and *The Man Who Knew Coolidge*" (*American Bypaths: Essays in Honor of E. Hudson Long*, ed.
Robert G. Collmer and Jack W. Herring [Baylor, 1980], pp. 145–66)
Gary H. Mayer uses semantic concepts to belabor the obvious in
proving that Elmer Gantry and Lowell Schmaltz (who never knew
Coolidge) are, respectively, hypocrite and boor, and misses an opportunity to explore Lewis' comment on the American public's susceptibility to rhetoric.

The most interesting essay on Lewis is James B. Carothers' comparison of *Main Street* and Philip Roth's *When She Was Good*,
"Midwestern Civilization and Its Discontents: Lewis's Carol Ken-
nicott and Roth's Lucy Nelson" (*MMis* 9:21–30). Carothers tries to
establish (perhaps not explicitly enough) the existence of "an important change in the psychology of character and place in the
American novel." Freudian by artistic instinct rather than intention,
Lewis has his heroine's sexual fears, the result of her relationship
with her benign father, turn her from her husband and toward the
community, where she achieves identity and partial fulfillment.
Roth's Lucy, similarly hampered by her violent father but unable
to face herself or seek an outlet in community, dies in a snowstorm.
Lewis' arbitrary fictional structure supports heroic possibilities,
whereas Roth depicts the inevitable fate of a woman destroyed by
her inability to cope with the world outside her own mind. Finally,
in "Lewis' *Babbitt*" (*Expl* 39:39–40) Robert L. Gale feels that the
reference to Dante's *Inferno* during the Babbitts' alcoholic party
might inform the urban maze Babbitt wanders without guidance.

v. Sherwood Anderson and Midwestern Writers

Diligent champion of Sherwood Anderson and midwestern literature, David D. Anderson has assembled a representative selection of essays in *Critical Essays on Sherwood Anderson* (Hall). In the introduction, "Sherwood Anderson and the Critics" (pp. 1–17), Anderson traces the author's critical reception from the publication of *Winesburg* to the devastating estimates of Cleveland B. Chase and Irving Howe, and the more scholarly ones of younger critics who see Anderson's later work as important to his literary development. The first of three original articles in the collection, Roger Bresnahan's "'An Aching, Hurting Thing': The Aesthetic of Ritualistic Reenactment" (pp. 235–41), considers Anderson's mission as a writer to shape his material in such a way as to rescue his subjects from meaninglessness. Anderson is able to give life structure by "reenacting the miserable events of people's lives, by retelling their tales of loneliness and frustration." The other two articles concern Anderson's women. Nancy Bunge reviews *Beyond Desire, Kit Brandon, Dark Laughter,* and *Winesburg* in "Women in Sherwood Anderson's Fiction" (pp. 242–49), an excellent summary of the role of maternal women berated by their antitraditional sisters in rescuing men from our machine-dominated society. After a somewhat plodding beginning, Marilyn Judith Atlas' "Sherwood Anderson and the Women of Winesburg" (pp. 250–66) manages to become a significant study of Anderson's sympathy for women forced to live within a system cruel and destructive for them. Atlas sees Anderson as incapable in *Winesburg* of satisfactorily portraying an active, creative woman able to define herself other than in her relationship to a man. Similar concerns occupy Sally Adair Rigsbee in "The Feminine in *Winesburg, Ohio*" (*SAF* 9:234–44), helpful in exploring the unity of Anderson's collection. Rigsbee argues that conventional sexual mores and marriage in a society like Winesburg suppress women's natural instincts for love and self-actualization and force men to deny the feminine in themselves. The conclusion of "Sophistication" suggests that *Winesburg* is "intended to be a prophetic statement about the quality of the relationships of men and women in the modern world."

There were several items of biographical nature. In "'Borne Back

Ceaselessly Into the Past': The Autobiographical Fiction of Sherwood Anderson" (*MMis* 9:54–60) Roger J. Bresnahan explains that Anderson's growing distance from his early experiences as well as his general mellowing improved his work after the failure of *Windy McPherson's Son*. In *Winesburg* his memories were successfully modified by his imagination; in *Tar: A Midwest Childhood* he was able to treat the topic of fatherhood without bitterness. David D. Anderson's "Sherwood Anderson and Edmund Wilson" (*SSMLN* 11,i:33–48) notes Wilson's fondness for Anderson yet inability to penetrate his "cornfed mystic" manner or understand the compassion behind his reluctance to commit himself less than completely to promoting communism among workers. The death of a friendship is the subject of Ray Lewis White's "Anderson's Private Reaction to *The Torrents of Spring*" (*MFS* 26:635–37), the other half of his 1967 note (*MFS* 13:261–63) on Hemingway's response to his parody of Anderson. White now supplies Anderson's reaction to the younger writer's patronizing tone, concluding with Anderson's version of the termination of their friendship. Finally, Hilbert H. Campbell traces the decline of Anderson's reputation during the 1930s as reflected in the sales of the nine books controlled by Viking Press in "Sherwood Anderson and the Viking Press, 1925–1941" (*RALS* 10:167–72).

Three brief notes examine individual stories. In "The Identity of Anderson's Fanatical Farmer" (*SSF* 18:79–82) Robert Sykes tries to prove through some surprising parallels that Joseph F. Glidden, an inventor-farmer of DeKalb, Illinois, was the basis of Anderson's portrait of Jesse Bentley in "'Godliness." Mark Savin argues in "Coming Full Circle: Sherwood Anderson's 'The Egg'" (*SSF* 18:454–57) that the hyperbole and anecdote in the son's story of his father's ambition is "as much a repetition of his father's acts as it is a remembrance of them." The implications of the egg are examined by Patrick and Barbara Bassett in "Anderson's 'The Egg'" (*Expl* 40:53–54). For the father, eggs "represent the concrete manifestation of his personal failures; for the narrator . . . eggs represent cosmic failure, that is, the futility of life itself."

Works by Booth Tarkington and Homer Croy were given attention in two minor essays. Douglas A. Noverr considers the extension of the urban city and loss of the secure, knowable center in "Change, Growth, and the Human Dilemma in Booth Tarkington's *The Magnificent Ambersons*" (*SSMLN* 11,i:14–32). Despite his failure to clarify the interconnection of Tarkington's many themes, Noverr manages to distinguish Isabel as an integrating factor and the most magnanimous of Ambersons, the salvation of her son during the cultural decline of the industrial age. In a review of regional fiction, "Three Generations of Missouri Fiction" (*MMis* 9:7–20), David D. Anderson surveys the career of Homer Croy, author of 16 books, including *They Had to See Paris*, the vehicle for Will Rogers' first talking picture. Croy's *West of the Water Tower* and *R.F.D. No. 3* "suggest a continuum in the making of a Midwestern myth . . . of the search for success." Anderson considers such success struggles as extensions of the heritage of the hometown to the region and the nation rather than as revolts from the village.

vi. John Dos Passos and Upton Sinclair

The year's major contribution on Dos Passos, Robert C. Rosen's *John Dos Passos: Politics and the Writer* (Nebraska), makes use of the journalistic and historical writings and correspondence (some unpublished) to explain Dos Passos' political views at each stage of his career. Although Rosen's focus is "primarily literary" and his study includes analyses of the major fiction, its effect is that of a running commentary on world and national situations that propelled Dos Passos' radicalisms. Rosen sees Dos Passos' championing of individual freedom as the consistent factor behind his fluctuating political allegiances and as related to the conflict between the privileged aesthete he was and the social critic he tried to be as well as to his efforts to "declass" himself as a writer, resulting in the camera-eye technique in *U.S.A.* The quality of Dos Passos' art was inconsistent, however, declining after *U.S.A.* and touching bottom in the self-pity of *The Great Days* and grotesque caricature of Communists in *Most Likely to Succeed*. Rosen shows how Dos Passos' need for a utopia where life was respected rather than degraded led him from an idealized Spain to an earlier America and into the historical research which produced his biography of Jefferson. Despite the somewhat repetitive nature of Rosen's study and this reviewer's feeling that the author had not thoroughly digested the materials, his use of the unsuccessful stage dramas and summaries of scattered magazine and newspaper essays to trace the political thought give his study significant value.

In "The Anarchist Theme of John Dos Passos's *Three Soldiers*" (*MarkhamR* 10:68–71) Ellwood Johnson concludes that Dos Passos' depiction of the political struggle toward anarchy and freedom is more psychological than ideological. Musician John Andrews' quest for psychological freedom is symbolized by musical motifs in his mind: "His habit of composing music in his head reflects the opposition in himself of the sentient, the collective, and the anarchistic."

Besides consideration in Westbrook's study referred to in my introduction, criticism on Sinclair was confined to a few items in the *Upton Sinclair Quarterly*. In "From West Point Cadet to Presidential Agent: 'Popular Literature' Elements in Upton Sinclair" (4,iv[1980]: 13–19) Dieter Herms attempts to link the early cadet stories to the *World's End* series through middle-class ideology, narrative patterns, and characterization. Of particular interest is Herms's view that similarities between the Superman comic strip and the Lanny Budd plots reside in the pulp fiction these cadet stories represent. Sinclair's unpublished 1953 novel is the subject of Andre Muraire's "Dear Diary: The Unpublished *Zillions*" (5,i:3–6), which blames inferior narrative technique and the characterization of Effie Burnham, the author's mouthpiece, for Sinclair's failure to interest a publisher. Muraire feels the novel has value as indicator of Sinclair's growing use of positive female characters and obsessive fear of desire and the disorder of self-revelation. Four excerpts from *Zillions* follow the essay. Of biographical interest is Irving Stone's recollection of his falling out with Sinclair after his wife interfered with their plans for a proposed biography ("Irving Stone Recalls Upton Sinclair: An Interview," 5,iii:4–12).

vii. Ellen Glasgow and Southern Writers

Revised for coherence, the year's most ambitious effort on Glasgow, Daphne Athas' " 'The Beauty' in *The Sheltered Life*—A Moral Concept" (*SAQ* 80:206–21), would be a major essay on the best of the Queenborough novels. Citing for contrast South American novelist Gabriel Garcia Marquez' *One Hundred Years of Solitude*, in which The Beauty has social and metaphysical rather than moral dimensions, Athas sees *The Sheltered Life* as a classic in an American tradition including Tennessee Williams' *The Roman Spring of Mrs. Stone* and Kurt Vonnegut's *Slaughterhouse-Five*, in which beauty is personalized and/or associated with morality. Glasgow's Beauty, Eva Birdsong, represents an aesthetic and moral ideal created by the attitudes of the people of her dying class and embodying joy, passion, nobility, pride, surprise, savagery, gallantry, character, and queenliness. Glasgow depicts the stripping down of the Beauty, "the unbandaging of a mummy." Removal of the final wrap, Eva's shooting of her philandering husband, seen as "melodramatic" and, in tone, "Aesopian," nevertheless works—the ugliness ascribed to a technologically changing society is acknowledged in Beauty herself. Primarily a review of *Barren Ground*, Linda W. Wagner's appreciative "Ellen Glasgow: Daughter as Justified" (*The Lost Tradition*, pp. 139–46) briefly compares mother-daughter relationships in that novel, *Virginia*, and *Life and Gabriella* before concentrating on Dorinda Oakley's struggle to define herself in other ways than subservience to a male. Wagner feels that because of the brilliance of Glasgow's portrayals we respond with compassion rather than resentment to the devoted but offending mothers who school their daughters in self-sacrifice. Finally, the *Ellen Glasgow Newsletter* (14:11–14) published a "substantive portion" of Glasgow's correspondence with James Branch Cabell from the Cabell Library, Virginia Commonwealth University. D. A. Yanchisin selects 16 brief items tracing the developing friendship to the point of Glasgow's dependence on Cabell for advice and editorial chores. Of particular interest are items indicating his considerable help in preparing her book of prefaces, *A Certain Measure*, for publication.

Glasgow's neglected Virginia compatriot is the subject of C. Ronald Cella's *Mary Johnston* (TUSAS 411). Achieving fame with *To Have and To Hold*, a romantic adventure set in colonial Jamestown and replete with Cooperian Indians, Johnston proved a serious historical novelist in *Lewis Rand*, a tale of ambition and reconciliation set in Jeffersonian Virginia. Cella feels that her handling of the Civil War and portrait of Stonewall Jackson make *The Long Roll*, an apology for the Confederate cause, her most significant effort. In *Hagar*, the story of a contemporary woman's struggle for independence and self-fulfillment, Johnston proved unsuccessful in combining the roles of novelist and feminist advocate. Although her withdrawal into mysticism and belief in reconciliation and universal absorption precipitated her decline, she managed to reclaim her powers and integrate her transcendentalism with the best aspects of her historical Virginia novels in *The Great Valley*. Cella's study is an admirable one of the detrimental effects of "causes" on a novelist's career.

The Civil War also inspired the most ambitious effort of the subject of William H. Slavick's *Dubose Heyward* (TUSAS 392), a writer caught between the myth-making of Thomas Nelson Page and the renascence of the late 1920s. Slavick's study is a good example of how a minor figure can be viewed with significance, for Heyward's failure to recognize the injustice of the racial situation in his native Charleston dramatizes the limiting consequences of aristocratic caste. However, Slavick sees *Porgy* and *Mamba's Daughters* as deeply sympathetic to the conditions of blacks caught between primitive instincts and adjustment to the white world. Heyward's consciousness of his own ambivalence surfaces in the situation of the hero of *Peter Ashley*, who allows his feelings for Charleston to seduce him into entertaining the notion of humane slavery and giving up a writing career to espouse the Confederate cause. Despite occasional incoherence, perhaps due to awkward condensing to satisfy Twayne's format, components such as his analysis of *Porgy* from novel to play to opera *Porgy and Bess* place Slavick's volume above the introductory level of many in this series.

viii. H. L. Mencken and Don Marquis

Two articles touched significantly on Mencken's attitudes. In "H. L. Mencken's *Venture into Verse*" (*SAQ* 80:195–205) Robert F. Nardini speculates that Mencken's later belief that poetry is an inherently inferior form of expression might be traced to his early verse-making experience. Mencken's adolescent verses reveal romantic Victorian and Baltimore burlesque-house influences and would prove an embarrassment to the man who sat in judgment upon the work of gifted poets. Edward A. Martin examines Mencken's attitude toward women in his somewhat rambling "H. L. Mencken and Equal Rights for Woman" (*GaR* 35:65–76). Martin feels that Mencken often hid his sympathy for the woman's movement in "male locker-room" rhetoric because he valued the approval of the male world and because his attitude toward women was somewhat contradictory. His affection for his mother preserved the double standard in his sexual behavior, although his own preference for a career in belles lettres over traditional male pursuits led him to identify with the plight of intelligent women in conflict with roles imposed upon them.

In an appreciative new foreword to a re-issue of Guy J. Forque's *Letters of H. L. Mencken* (Northeastern) Daniel Aaron recalls Mencken's campaign against the old-stock literary establishment and his defense of Dreiser and others considered dangerous. The selected letters provide little insight into the private man but help explain why and how he acquired his reputation and literary force. Of particular interest considering the new Pennsylvania *Sister Carrie* is Mencken's correspondence with the man he dubbed the Hindenburg of the American novel.

A literary jack-of-all-trades most successful as columnist is the subject of Lynn Lee's *Don Marquis* (TUSAS 393), a careful introduction to a humorist at his rare best "on a level with Thurber, Perelman, Benchley, or E. B. White." Remembered primarily as creator of the Archy and Mehitabel series collected in three volumes from newspaper columns, Marquis aimed higher, wrote serious plays and stories, and died before completing his self-proclaimed masterpiece *Sons of the Puritans*, a revolt-from-the-village novel published posthumously in its unfinished state. Although Lee sprinkles his study with generous quotations to prove the significance of several Marquis endeavors, he is forced to admit lack of originality as the reason for their oblivion. Marquis' subjects and views were frequently Twain's; his short story structures were O. Henry's; his serious plays were either derivative or superseded before they appeared. Only Archy and Mehitabel, *Prefaces*, and *The Almost Perfect State*, all drawn from newspaper columns, succeeded in capturing America's literary, social, political, and religious foibles benignly but pointedly during the first quarter of the century. However, Lee is convincing that these are indicative enough of their time to make his study at least a minor contribution.

ix. Ole Rølvaag and Western Writers

Christer Lennart Mossberg's introduction to Rølvaag in *Scandinavian Immigrant Literature* (BSU Western Writers Series 47) is the most general of three considerations of *Giants in the Earth*. Mossberg relates this novel to the others in the trilogy as a tragedy of Americanization dramatizing the "tension between a positive view of history as progress and a negative one viewing history as decline" by fragmenting the pioneer world into conflicts between people and nature, men and women, wilderness and culture, and so on. Per Hansa dies, contends Mossberg, because the need for his optimistic pioneer energy is replaced by the need for the social and cultural ties Beret embodies. In *Peder Victorious* and *Their Father's God* the conflict between Beret and her son replaces the earlier one with her husband, and the inevitable consequence is rootlessness and alienation, loss of native language, religion, family heritage. A similar view of fragmentation and loss occurs in Paul Olson's previously cited *Prairie Schooner* article: "What Rølvaag does in *Giants* is to display heroic accomplishments of the old saga variety as impossible on the frontier because its competitive ethos of individual prosperity, fairy palaces, and super-whitewashed walls separate the hero from his community and make of the heroic an expression of a private autonomous self tied to no community and directed by divinity." While acknowledging the "Norwegian literary and cultural matrix in which *Giants* was formed," Dick Harrison places it squarely within "the mythic spirit of the American West" in his comparative study "Rølvaag, Grove, and Pioneering on the American and Canadian Plains" (*GPQ* 4:252–62). Unlike Frederick Philip Grove's Manitoba prairie novel *Fruits of the Earth*, in which colonizing is a practical affair threatening to extinguish spiritual contact with the natural environment, *Giants* is preoccupied with emotional, moral, and spiritual problems arising from the encounter between civilized man and savage wilderness.

The formula Western is Gary Topping's concern in "The Rise of the Western" (*JW* 19,i[1980]:29–35). After crediting Owen Wister with originating the model (with the help of Cooper and the dime novelists) and Zane Grey with turning it into a formula, Topping discusses the contributions of cowboy Eugene Manlove Rhodes, who depicted the cattle kingdom with historical accuracy and added the murder mystery to the formula, and Bertha M. Bower, who captured the actual speech characteristics of young cowboys. In rather backhanded fashion, Frederic Schiller Faust (Max Brand) is credited with turning the Western formula into a business. William A. Bloodworth, Jr., concentrates on Faust in "Max Brand's West" (*WAL* 16: 177–91). While Faust's ransacking of European sources and commitment to action diverted attention from the historical West, his unorthodox use of classical, Celtic, and Germanic myth and folklore seldom opened up new meanings, merely providing raw materials to sustain his incredible pulp productivity. Bloodworth concedes, however, that Faust's lack of feeling for the West and failure to extend its popular significance might be credited with pruning from the formula historical nostalgia, superfluous landscape descriptions, and hackneyed themes of regeneration. In "Civilization as Emasculation: The Threatening Role of Women in the Frontier Fiction of Harold Bell Wright and Zane Grey" (*MQ* 22:346–60) Fritz H. Oehlschlaeger considers the role of audience demand on the development of the formula. Wright's *The Shepherd of the Hills* and *When A Man's A Man* and Grey's *Riders of the Purple Sage* and *Heritage of the Desert* satisfied a predominantly male audience by confirming its prejudices against women. Both writers associate women with civilizing influences threatening the primitive world and view submission to domineering women as emasculation. Women must be broken like horses; their true satisfaction lies in submission to their red-blooded mates. In her appreciative "Zane Grey and the High School Student" (*EJ* 70,viii:23–29) Carol Gay recommends several Grey novels for their philosophical, historical, and language values.

x. Gertrude Stein

All of the few miscellaneous items on Stein are of interest. In "Gertrude Stein's Sense of Oneness" (*SWR* 65:1–10) Mary Allen sees Stein's unsatisfactory relationship with her parents and her need to determine her own identity in a large family as instrumental in making her a dissident voice celebrating 20th-century fragmentation: "In an age of cynicism, Stein rejoices in the potential of the *one*," whether the individual person, single word, or single object. "Melanctha" warns the individual of the dangers of love and, speculates Allen, might be read as a study in latent lesbianism; *Tender Buttons* attests to the value and integrity of the single word and object, and Stein's fondness for detective fiction is for delaying the connection of events, keeping them separate as long as possible. A refreshing aspect of this article is Allen's ability to discover biographical dimensions without the surfeit of psychological baggage characterizing many similar efforts. Significant if less successful is

Marianne De Koven's "Gertrude Stein and Modern Painting: Beyond Literary Cubism" (*ConL* 22:81–95), which universalizes the implications of Stein's method. In trying to distinguish between words and paint in qualifying Stein's method, De Koven strays into a discussion of Derrida's *Of Grammatology* and works by Julia Kristeva and other feminists in order to associate Stein with the revolt against a patriarchal, linear, symbolic writing culture by a matriarchal, nonlinear, presymbolic one. De Koven concludes that Stein shared with Picasso a common, liberating vision rather than a common method.

In what is labeled a note and should be an article, Brooks Landon's " 'Not Solve It But Be In It': Gertrude Stein's Detective Stories and the Mystery of Creativity" (*AL* 53:487–98) examines *Blood on the Dining-Room Floor* as an attempt to find the central unifying mystery among seemingly unrelated events in the summer of 1933. Solicitous of her audience for the first time, "fearful of disappointing it, but equally fearful of losing her independent identity in attempting to please it," Stein used the detective genre to approach the conflict between human nature, which demanded explanations, and the human mind, concerned with existing, pure creativity, and essences. *Blood* thus prepared her for her most sustained explanatory works, most notably *The Geographical History of America*. Finally, in what is in actuality a note, "Gertrude Stein Reviews Hemingway's *Three Stories & Ten Poems*" (*AL* 53:114–15), Scott Donaldson reprints Stein's review, presumed never published but found among the Hemingway papers in the J.F.K. Library. Stein favored the poems and advised Hemingway to "stick to poetry and intelligence and eschew the hotter emotions and more turgid vision" of the fiction.

Merrimack College

14. Fiction: The 1930s to the 1950s

Jack Salzman

i. "Art for Humanity's Sake"—Proletarians and Others

As was the case last year, several important volumes appeared in 1981 which add considerably to our understanding of the climate of the 1930s. Perhaps the most interesting of these is *One Third of a Nation: Lorena Hickok Reports on the Great Depression*, ed. Richard Lowitt and Maurine Beasley (Illinois), a volume devoted to the confidential reports which Lorena Hickok prepared in 1933 and 1934 "on conditions in the United States, as the administration of Franklin D. Roosevelt grappled with the problems associated with providing relief to victims of the Great Depression." Of great interest, too, are a couple of reprints of books originally published in 1941: John F. Day's description of life in the coalfields of eastern Kentucky in the 1930s, *Bloody Ground* (Kentucky) and *Wyoming: A Guide* (Nebraska), one of the volumes in the WPA's American Guide Series.

Two books devoted to film should prove to be of considerable value. In *The Hollywood Social Problem Film: Madness, Despair, and Politics from the Depression to the Fifties* (Indiana), Peter Roffman and Jim Purdy provide a fairly comprehensive overview of the cycles and patterns of the "Problem Film," in which they examine "the relationship between political issues and movie conventions, between what happened in American society and what appeared on the screen." More specialized is William Alexander's study of *Film on the Left: American Documentary Film from 1931 to 1942* (Princeton), which may not be the most elegantly written of works but is one of the most important additions we have had in recent years to an understanding of the culture of the 1930s.

Of great value, too, though a work of a very different kind, is *DLB*, volume 9 (see also chap. 22). Extended biographical and critical essays are offered on a number of major figures of the period covered here—Cozzens, Farrell, Miller, O'Hara, Steinbeck, West, and

Wolfe, for example—but of far greater help to the student of the period will be those essays on the lesser-known writers: Algren, Barnes, Cantwell, di Donato, Fuchs, Gold, Halper, Herbst, Sandoz, Stribling, and Young, among many others. Unfortunately, the "many others" does not include such writers as Conroy, Dahlberg, Maltz, Roth, and Trumbo, and the omissions are not insignificant.

Some of the writers not included in the *DLB* are at least touched upon by Marcus Klein in *Foreigners*. Although Klein begins his study in 1900, much of the book is concerned with the 1930s. And if there is little in Klein's study that is new, his argument is clearly and simply stated: American literature of the 20th century has been created "by people who have known themselves to be marginal Americans, sometimes by an act of imagination and sometimes by right of birth." If the children of the Mayflower tended to invent Western culture, Klein writes, the children of the immigrants "tended to invent America."

One of the earliest novels to deal with the life of America's Italian immigrants was *Christ in Concrete* (1939) by Pietro di Donato, the subject of Michael D. Esposito's "Pietro di Donato Reevaluated" (*Italian Americana* 6[1980]:179–92). Another writer to receive individual attention is Granville Hicks, the subject of Terry L. Long's *Granville Hicks* (TUSAS 387). Long may be right when he says that his study "should be very useful to anyone who wishes to know what Granville Hicks was about during his long career," but Hicks was "about" much more than this brief and somewhat heavy-handed volume suggests.

a. **James Agee.**   Of the five works to appear about Agee this year, three are of some real interest. In "Agee's Skepticism About Art and Audience" (*SoR* 17:320–31) Victor Kramer concerns himself with Agee's frequently expressed skepticism about the possibilities of language. *Famous Men* is seen by Kramer to be "a sustained example of Agee's combination of self and particular events observed," while *A Death in the Family* "can be thought of as a continuation of Agee's dual awareness: his desire to write, but his definite skepticism about how this could be accomplished." J. A. Ward in "*A Death in the Family*: The Importance of Wordlessness" (*MFS* 26: 597–611) also concerns himself with Agee's sense that "all language is more or less false to its subject" and argues that in *Death* it is the nonverbal elements that "produce its major themes and interior structures." Robert MacLean's focus is somewhat different: in "Narcissus and the Voyeur: James Agee's *Let Us Now Praise Famous Men*" (*JNT* 11:33–52) he contends that "Voyeurism is not only the source of Agee's guilt in *Let Us Now Praise Famous Men*, it is a major preoccupation in his *oeuvre*, ubiquitous to the extent that it assumes the proportions of a metaphysics, or more properly, of a critique of metaphysics."

Warren Eyster's "Conversations with James Agee" (*SoR* 17:346–57) is disappointing because it tells us almost nothing about Agee. Disappointing, too, is the only book about Agee to appear this year, Mark A. Doty's *Tell Me Who I Am: James Agee's Search for Selfhood* (LSU), which argues that "Agee's search for meaning focused on his need to find an approving earthly/heavenly father, his quest for a religious consciousness, and his self-destructive search for death." It is all too simple, even simplistic: there is much more to Agee and his art than Doty's brief book even begins to hint at.

b. **John Steinbeck.** This was not a particularly productive year for Steinbeck scholarship. *Steinbeck Quarterly* published a number of essays, but as usual the quality varies greatly. *StQ* 14,i–ii is devoted to the 1979 MLA Steinbeck Society meeting papers on "Mapping *East of Eden*," ed. Robert DeMott. In addition to DeMott's " 'Culling All Books': Steinbeck's Reading and *East of Eden*" (pp. 40–51) there are papers on such matters as the original manuscript of *Eden* (pp. 14–23), the critical reception of the novel (pp. 6–13), and "Alienation in *East of Eden*: 'The Chart of the Soul' " (pp. 32–39). DeMott also contributes an essay on *East of Eden* to *StQ* 14,iii–iv, "Cathy Ames and Lady Godiva: A Contribution to *East of Eden's* Background" (pp. 72–83), in which he suggests that part of the inspiration for Cathy's role came from Steinbeck's reading of Raoul Faure's novel *Lady Godiva and Master Tom*. The issue also includes pieces on "Steinbeck's Vanderbilt Clinic" (pp. 70–71), Kiyoshi Nakayama's "Steinbeck Criticism in Japan: 1978–1979" (pp. 105–11), and two essays on *Grapes of Wrath*: Reloy Garcia's "The Rocky Road to Eldorado: The Journey Motif in John Steinbeck's *The Grapes of Wrath*" (pp. 83–93) and Mimi R. Gladstein's "Ma Joad and Pilar: Significantly Similar" (pp. 93–104).

Grapes of Wrath is also the subject of two of the other four essays

254   Fiction: The 1930s to the 1950s

to appear on Steinbeck this year: Christopher L. Salter's "John Steinbeck's *The Grapes of Wrath* as a Primer for Cultural Geography" in
*Humanistic Geography and Literature: Essays on the Experience of
Place*, ed. Douglas C. D. Pocock (Barnes and Noble), pp. 142–58,
and Paul McCarthy's "The Joads and Other Rural Families in Depression Fiction" (*SDR* 19,iii:57–68), in which the Joads are compared with other farming families in such novels as Jack Conroy's
A World to Win, Frederick Manfred's *This is the Year*, and Fred
Rothermell's *The Ghostland*. Both are rather inconsequential studies,
as are the other two essays to be considered here. In " 'I Never Returned as I Went In': Steinbeck's *Travels with Charley*" (*SWR* 66:
186–202), Barbara Reitt acknowledges that *Travels* is a potboiler,
but she warns that it would be a mistake to ignore the book "for
both the circumstances surrounding its composition and its content
and structure reveal much about Steinbeck as a writer." Just what
it does reveal about Steinbeck as a writer, however, is never made
very clear. Ronald Scheer in "Steinbeck into Film: The Making of
Tortilla Flat" (*WVUPP* 26:30–36) does make all too clear just what
he has to say about the novel-into-film: the "movie seems true to the
spirit and intent of what Steinbeck wrote," and "each tells the story
in the way it knows best, which is not the same way."

c. **Conroy, Dahlberg, Farrell, and Roth.**   The four writers to be
considered here continue to receive less critical attention than they
deserve. Jack Conroy, for example, is discussed in only one work,
David Anderson's "Three Generations of Missouri Fiction" (*MMis*
9:7–20), in which *The Disinherited* is considered to be the best
novel to come out of the turmoil of the 1930s, and unlike most of
the other proletarian novels of the time it "is not apart from the
mainstream of American life and literature; it is part of it."
     Edward Dahlberg also attracted the attention of only one critic
this year, but Carol Shloss's "*Because I Was Flesh*: Edward Dahlberg and the Rhetoric of American Identity" (*MR* 22:576–84) is
one of the most substantial works yet to appear about Dahlberg.
Shloss argues that Dahlberg "found the origin of his own ability to
write in the 'gallant desperation' of a lady barber, and by idealizing
her, has at once articulated the one great imaginative preoccupation
of his life and extricated himself from it." And although *Because I*

Was Flesh does not belong firmly in the tradition of proletarian naturalism, it nevertheless must be placed in the "literature of revolt against the illusions of American civilization."

James T. Farrell receives occasional mention in Robert J. Higgs's *Laurel & Thorn: The Athlete in American Literature* (Kentucky), but the discussion of such stories as "Pat McGee," "The Echo of Fame," and "Joe Eliot" is limited primarily to plot summary. A more interesting and valuable publication by far is the Arts End Books edition of *Eight Short Short Stories & Sketches* by Farrell. None of the stories or sketches is more than four pages long; chronologically they range from Farrell's first published story in 1929, "Slob," to a 1971 satire of André Malraux, "A Picnic in the Steppes," and two of the pieces—"Pepper" and "Story About a Door"—never have been published before. There are only 19 pages in this handsome little volume, but Farrell's voice is heard distinctly on each page. Not so the voice of Henry Roth, which gets lost in Wayne Lesser's "A Narrative's Revolutionary Energy: The Example of Henry Roth's *Call It Sleep*" (*Criticism* 23:155–76). Lesser sets out to show how "the process of cultural identification functions within the narrative's struggle among its deconstructive and productive impulses." For, "In the struggle between the text's competing modes of understanding—one grounded in aesthetic and social convention, the other in the movement of the tropological discourse—a reconstitution of the relations among author, text, and reader takes place." Lesser, sad to say, could be writing about any book. For him, *Call It Sleep* is just "a case in point." This is the kind of criticism that destroys the heart and purpose of literature.

ii. Social Iconoclasts—Salinger and West

Two of the three pieces to appear on Salinger this year make note of the apparent decline of critical interest in his work. Part of the decline, John Wenke suggests in "Sergeant X, Esmé, and the Meaning of Words" (*SSF* 18:251–59), may be due to Salinger's own public silence—a silence which "may well have evolved from the conviction that deeply-felt human emotions need no expression—a position implied by the successful aesthetic resolution of 'For Esmé—with Love and Squalor.' " It is a story, Wenke contends, which "embodies a beautiful, if tenuous, example of how individuals might pass through squalor to love, achieving meaningful, redemptive expression, even though the successful uses of language are a constant reminder of its general failure." Richard Allan Davis also is concerned with the slowing down of published commentary on Salinger and in "Salinger Criticism and 'The Laughing Man': A Case of Arrested Development" (*SSF* 18:1–15) begins by offering a delineation of the decline in Salinger criticism through 1975. (Although the article has just appeared, it seems to have been written in 1976!) He then offers a reading of "Laughing Man," which he sees as a story of two neophytes—the narrator and John Gedsudski—who struggle in their initial encounters with the mysteries of sex and adult responsibilities. Davis concludes, rather unconvincingly it seems to me, that "If the Gedsudskis of this world do not radiate ultimately positive values, it is because they are doomed to reside in a perennially arrested state where values are not so much childlike as childish." In the third piece to be considered here, "J. D. Salinger's Tribute to Whit Burnett" (*TCL* 27:325–30), Craig Stolz comments not upon the decline of critical attention paid to Salinger but upon Salinger's own reluctance to publish. Despite this reluctance, Stolz notes that in 1975 Salinger did publish a 500-word "salute" to Whit Burnett, which is "a significant addition to Salinger's canon, for it reinforces in prose Salinger's ideas about writing, teaching, and academic approaches to literature which readers have until now been able only to infer from Salinger's fiction."

Although each of the three pieces on West to be discussed deals with a different work, each is concerned with a mode of adaptation. In "'Human Need' in *The Day of the Locust*: Problems of Adaptation" (*LFQ* 9:22–31) Jerome Raff focuses upon the difficulties of adapting West's novel into a film, not the least of which is that "one of the moral premises of the novel is that movies can be life-destroying, so that to make a film of it may be to undercut some of the values essential to the content." Gary Scharnhorst in "From Rags to Patches, or *A Cool Million* as Alter-Alger" (*BSUF* 21,iv[1980]:58–65) directs his attention to the connection between Horatio Alger and *A Cool Million*, which contains "the most notorious use of Alger as a political symbol." According to Scharnhorst, West, believing Alger to be his own best parodist, "obtained copies of several Alger novels in the fall of 1933 and deliberately constructed his patchwork parody from altered and re-arranged fragments of them." In all, over a fifth of *A Cool Million* "is vintage Alger, only slightly modified." And in "Jamesian Psychology and Nathanael West's *Miss Lonelyhearts*" (*SJS* 7,iii:80–86) Carroll Schoenewolf considers the influence of James's *Varieties of Religious Experience* on *Miss Lonelyhearts* and concludes that West not only took from James a psychology for his main characters and a psychological structure for the novel as a whole, but that West's protagonist "is a modern priest whose religious experience is at best meaningless, so far as his suffering parishioners are concerned, and at worst, evil."

iii. Expatriates and Emigrés

a. **Henry Miller and Anaïs Nin.** Although neither of the two pieces to appear about Miller deal specifically with his fiction, both are of sufficient interest to warrant mention here. Lawrence Clark Powell offers an interesting account of his friendship with Miller in "Remembering Henry Miller" (*SWR* 66:117–28), while Barbara Kraft's "A Conversation with Henry Miller" (*MQR* 20,ii:45–58) is an edited transcript of a 1979 conversation in which Miller speaks candidly about several writers, ranging from William Carlos Williams to Jean Paul Sartre to Allen Ginsberg.

Nin is one of three writers discussed by Sylvia Paine in *Beckett, Nabokov, Nin: Motives and Modernism* (Kennikat). Paine apparently began her study "hoping to find out why literature matters so much" and chose to study "modernist" writers because "Modernist art assumes" a "spiritual and moral role." In an opening chapter Paine considers "the unity of the two moving forces of art, the sensuous and the transcendent." Individual chapters are then devoted to the three writers, and in the chapter on Nin (pp. 72–93) Paine focuses her attention largely upon *Seduction of the Minotaur* and *Collages* in an attempt to show that insofar as Nin's characters "exist in and beyond themselves at once, they inhabit a realm of being which imagination realizes in art and makes palpable through the interpenetration of art with its audience." And, Paine concludes, "whatever the critical evaluation of her art, Nin achieves an indisputable triumph at the end of her life. She succeeds in reaching an audience and in outreaching herself, liberating herself through a humanistic love that informs and surpasses her art." But despite its

adulation of Nin, I suspect that Paine's chapter will be of little
value to the student of Nin's work: there's little in the chapter that's
very new or very interesting.

Of greater value to the Nin student, I think, is *USP* 12,iii–iv,
which contains "Blurbs by Anaïs Nin: Part Two" (pp. 1–8) compiled
by Richard R. Centing, Centing's Sixth Supplement to Rose Marie
Cutting's *Anaïs Nin: A Reference Guide* (pp. 18–24), and "The
Erotica of Henry Miller and Anaïs Nin: A chapter from the Memoir
of G. Legman" (pp. 9–18). For financial reasons *Under the Sign of
Pisces* will cease publication with this issue. But the indefatigable
Richard R. Centing, who has done as much as anyone to promote
the study of Nin's work, has announced that he will both publish
and edit *Seashore: The Anaïs Nin/Henry Miller Journal*. The first
issue will appear in 1982, and the advance copy which I have had
an opportunity to examine makes it clear that *Seashore* certainly
will be as valuable as *Under the Sign of Pisces* and perhaps even
more so, since it formally will be devoted to studies not only of Nin
but Henry Miller too.

b. **Vladimir Nabokov.**   This has been another good year for Nabokov studies. Certainly the most important volume to appear is the
collection of Nabokov's *Lectures on Russian Literature*, ed. Fredson
Bowers (Harcourt). Gogol, Turgenev, Dostoevski, Tolstoy, Chekhov,
and Gorki are the writers discussed in these lectures, and suffice it
to say that this volume is no less fascinating or important to the student of Nabokov than last year's *Lectures on Literature*. A work
that should also prove to be of considerable interest is Ellen Pifer's
Nabokov and the Novel (Harvard, 1980), which not only is one of
the most intelligent studies we have of Nabokov's fiction but is also
one of the most lucidly written. Pifer addresses herself to those
critics who laud Nabokov's genius for language but "regard his verbal pyrotechnics as evidence of the aesthete's shallow psychology."
Her intention is to demonstrate "that even the most intricate of Nabokov's artifices reflect the author's abiding interest in human beings,
not only as artists and dreamers but as ethical beings subject to
moral law and sanction." It is a most challenging and stimulating
study.

If Sylvia Paine's chapter on Nabokov in *Beckett, Nabokov, Nin*,
pp. 48–71, fails to add to what already has been written about Nabo-

kov, Daniel Albright's chapter in *Representation and the Imagination: Beckett, Kafka, Nabokov, and Schoenberg* (Chicago), pp. 52–94, is as stimulating a discussion as Pifer's. Of the four artists he treats in his study of representation and the inexpressible, only Nabokov "believed that the goals of traditional fiction were neither trivial nor impossible, and he left portraits of vigorous, sane, and successful artists, ambitious but not overreaching—notably Shade in *Pale Fire* and Fyodor in *The Gift*. But many of his most probing and memorable studies concern men who live in falsely invented worlds, atrocities extorted from nightmares." Less elegantly written and somewhat less imaginative, Paul Bruss's section on Nabokov in *Victims: Textual Strategies in Recent American Fiction* (Bucknell), pp. 33–97, nevertheless offers interesting readings of *Lolita*, *Pale Fire*, and *Ada* in the context of Bruss's exploration of the strategies whereby three very different writers—Barthelme, Kosinski, and Nabokov—"create fiction against the grain of their profound sensitivity to the insufficiency of all human texts."

Of the several articles on Nabokov to appear this year, two focus on *Lolita* and two upon *Ada*. In "The Speech Ritual as an Element of Structure in Nabokov's *Lolita* (*DR* 60:605–21), James R. Pinnells examines *Lolita* to show "how skilfully Nabokov ritualizes dialogue to achieve specific effects in the novel," as well as to show how he uses ritualized dialogue "to define and intensify the two realities that come into collision in this work: Humbert's solipsism and what Nabokov calls 'average reality'." The other piece on *Lolita* is much less ambitious: in "Nabokov's *Lolita*" (*Expl* 39,iv:41–43) Pekka Tammi is content to offer an explanation for a passage from Turgenev's *Home of the Gentry*, which had not been satisfactorily explained in previous studies. Also to be found in *Expl* (39,iii:46–47) is "Nabokov's Ada" by J. E. Rivers and William Walker, which offers an explanation for Nabokov's use of the German word *Knabenkrauter*. A more substantial work is Beverly Lyon Clark's consideration of "Contradictions and Confirmations in *Ada*" (*CollL* 8,i:53–62), which concludes that in *Ada* Nabokov forces us to reevaluate the nature of reality: "Within the book Van's world is reality. And outside the world of the book, as we see how *Ada* twists and realigns our commonly-agreed-upon realities, we recognize how indistinguishable fantasy and reality are, how subjective and imaginative any version of reality must be."

Nabokov's short stories are the subject of three articles. Ellen Pifer writes about "Locating the Monster in Nabokov's 'Scenes from the Life of a Double Monster'" (*SAF* 9:97–101), in which she notes that "The essential singularity of human life, the isolation necessary to the growth of consciousness, is the constant theme in Nabokov's fiction," and nowhere is this more evident than in "Double Monster." Another "constant" theme is the subject of John V. Hagopian's "Decoding Nabokov's 'Signs and Symbols'" (*SSF* 18:115–19), which contends that "Displaced persons and madmen are recurrent themes in Nabokov's fiction, and both are central to his early—and best—short story, 'Signs and Symbols'." David Eggenschwiler is less concerned with dominant themes than he is with the literary effects of Nabokov's allusions. Of all of Nabokov's works, only *Lolita* and *Ada* have received thorough annotation. Yet, Eggenschwiler argues in "Nabokov's 'The Vane Sisters': Exuberant Pedantry and a Biter Bit" (*SSF* 18,i:33–39) that in "The Vane Sisters" Nabokov "uses literary and historical lore with such precise irony that one cannot understand the main techniques of the work without becoming a diligent pedant, following up its allusions and joining in one of the cleverest contests ever played among author, narrator, and reader."

Lastly, it must be noted that the two numbers of *VNRN* (vi and vii) continue to provide the student of Nabokov's work with a most valuable reference tool. In addition to news items, works in progress, bibliographies, and abstracts of papers and dissertations, *VNRN* (7:25–32) includes "From a Family Album," five previously unpublished photographs taken about 1897 and supplied to the Nabokov Society by the novelist's sister. The photos make for a most intriguing gathering and give added importance to the newsletter.

iv. The Southerners

a. **Robert Penn Warren.**   The major addition to Warren scholarship this year, beyond question, is James H. Justus' *The Achievement of Robert Penn Warren* (LSU). Justus acknowledges that the temptation for everyone who has written about Warren is to analyze those themes—such as his most "perdurable theme—self-knowledge"—and moral situations that constitute the "massive centrality of an entire corpus." And although Justus too succumbs to the temptation, he has tried "to emphasize the *ways* by which we become aware of such themes and situations, the technical accomplishment of their rendering that alone justifies our thinking of Warren as a literary artist." His premise is stated simply and explicitly: he has written about Warren from the belief "that his work derived in large measure from the cultural circumstances of place and time in his career." It is shaped by Warren's being "both a border southerner and a transregional intellectual; the values of the country and small town, including the tangled benefits of social cohesion and Christian assumptions about the nature of man, are often seen in conflict with the values of a life governed by art and the academy." All aspects of Warren's writings are covered in this massive study, with Part Four devoted to "The Lying Imagination: Warren the Novelist" (pp. 157–316), which in turn is divided into three sections: Politics and Morals, Romance and History, An Art of Transparency. *The Achievement of Robert Penn Warren* surely is one of the best, perhaps is *the* best, study we have of Warren; it is quite an achievement in its own right.

Although they pale somewhat next to the study by Justus, there are three other books published this year which will be of considerable value to the Warren enthusiast. Neil Nakadate has edited a volume entitled *Robert Penn Warren: Critical Perspectives* (Kentucky), which reprints a number of well-known essays on Warren's fiction, a new essay by Nakadate, "Identity, Dream, and Exploration: Warren's Later Fiction" (pp. 175–89), and includes a list of Warren's published works from 1920 to 1980 as well as a checklist of critical works on Warren's writings. (It must be noted, however, that the value of the book is undermined somewhat by the ugliness of the production job, a rarity for the University Press of Kentucky.) Another collection, this one in Hall's Critical Essays on American Literature series, is edited by William Bradford Clark. In addition to the articles and essays on Warren's fiction and poetry, Clark also reprints several reviews and Richard B. Sale's "An Interview in New Haven with Robert Penn Warren" (pp. 81–107). And, finally, there is Charles Bohner's revised edition of his Twayne study, *Robert Penn Warren* (TUSAS 69), originally published in 1964 and now brought up to date.

Rather surprisingly, there are only a few individual essays to report this year. Although 1981 marks the 35th anniversary of the

publication of *All the King's Men* and Warren wrote an essay for
the anniversary edition of the novel, which appeared in *NYTBR* (31
May:9,39–92) as "In the Time of 'All the King's Men,'" there is
nothing else on Warren's most popular novel but some comments by
James A. Grimshaw, Jr., in "Some Observations on Robert Penn
Warren's Bibliography" (*KR* 2,iii:19–30), who contends that too
many critics "emphasize the political at the expense of other aspects
of the novel," and Thomas Daniel Young's "The Awful Responsibility of Time: Robert Penn Warren's *All the King's Men*" in his
The Past in the Present, pp. 65–85, in which Young argues that "*All
the King's Men* is not only the best political novel in American literature, but it is one of the most profound fictive studies of modernism." The only other essays that need to be noted here are Thomas
W. Ford's "Indian Summer and Blackberry Winter" (*SoR* 17:542–
50), a comparison of "Blackberry Winter" and Dickinson's "These
are the Days when Birds Come Back," and Richard G. Law's "*At
Heaven's Gate*: 'The Fires of Irony,'" (*AL* 53:87–104), an interesting
look at Warren's second novel, which Law sees as being "probably
the best record of Warren's early struggle to assimilate the aesthetic
ideas of his age; in it—perhaps because they are only partly mastered
—the ideas and techniques which inform his later work are highly
visible."

b. **Allen Tate, Caroline Gordon, and T. S. Stribling.** The most important work to appear about Tate this year, and indeed for all too
many years, is *The Republic of Letters in America: The Correspondence of John Peale Bishop & Allen Tate*, ed. Thomas Daniel Young
and John J. Hindle (Kentucky). The correspondence extends from
1929 until 1944 (when Bishop died) and not only provides the
reader with a record of the friendship between the two, but, more
to the point, is filled with telling comments both about their own
work and about many of their contemporaries. Young also includes
a chapter on *The Fathers*, "The Gaping Abyss: Allen Tate's *The
Father's*" in *The Past in the Present*, pp. 47–63, in which he argues
that *The Fathers* suggests that "the imperfections that will destroy
the antebellum southern society are unalterably at work even before
the civil war begins." C. Hugh Holman, on the other hand, contends in "*The Fathers* and the Historical Imagination" (in *Literary*

Romanticism, pp. 80–93) that "*The Fathers* is an American *Bildungs-roman* with a spectator-narrator who is the ultimate subject of the book and who experiences the events of history—in particular those of southern history—in such a way that those historical events become his instructors in finding a way of life." But Alan Holder in his study of *The Imagined Past: Portrayals of Our History in Modern American Literature* (Bucknell) writes in "Antebellum Rootness: Allen Tate's Images of the Old South" (pp. 92–124) that there are important breakdowns in the distinction between the Buchans and the Poseys, and that too much in the novel "should strike us as sleight-of-hand rather than as a genuine illumination of history."

Although Donald E. Stanford pays tribute to Caroline Gordon upon news of her death, "Caroline Gordon" (*SoR* 17:459–60), there is only one significant item to report this year: *The Collected Stories of Caroline Gordon* (Farrar), which is the first time all of her short fiction has been brought together in one volume and includes three stories which have been previously uncollected. Robert Penn Warren provides a brief but elegant introduction in which he writes that Gordon's stories "are dramatic examples of man in contact with man, and man in contact with nature; of living sympathy; of a disciplined style as unpretentious and clear as running water, but shot through with glints of wit, humor, pity, and poetry."

Little has been written about T. S. Stribling during the past few years, but there are three pieces to report this year. Edward J. Piacentino is the author of two articles about Stribling: in *SoSt* (20: 67–83) he writes about "No More 'Treachy Sentimentalities': The Legacy of T. S. Stribling to the Southern Literary Renascence" and in "Babbittry Southern Style: T. S. Stribling's *Unfinished Cathedral*" (*MarkR* 10:36–39) he suggests that *Babbitt* and *Elmer Gantry* had a marked influence on the writing of *Unfinished Cathedral*. Anne French Drake also writes about *The Unfinished Cathedral*—as well as *The Forge* and *The Store*—in "'Love ought to be like religion, Brother Milt': An Examination of the Civil War and Reconstruction Trilogy of T. S. Stribling" (*SLJ* 14,i:24–35), in which she concludes that "Stribling's South is a land divided against itself. His white men dispense with their religious impulse, and exploit their black brothers. The destruction of the South is hastened by the aid of the North, but finally blame must be laid on the South itself."

c. **Katherine Anne Porter and Carson McCullers.** Certainly the
most important work to appear about Porter in the year after her
death is Enrique Hank Lopez' *Conversations with Katherine Anne
Porter: Refugee from Indian Creek* (Little, Brown). Based in large
part upon taped conversations, this volume, we are told, was undertaken with the understanding that it would be at least in part "an
autobiographical recollection that would stand for her life" since
Porter apparently never intended to write an autobiography. Yet, as
Lopez acknowledges, what he finally offers the reader is "the revelation of the life perceived by the subject, not always the life that was
led." Lopez never does explain why he did not take it upon himself
to clarify for the reader the distinction between the two and to supply
the facts where fiction took over. Had he done so, an important volume would have become an even more valuable one. Indeed, in
"Katherine Anne Porter and the South: A Corrective" (*MissQ* 34:
435–44) Jan Nordby Gretlund, who sets out to correct a good number
of misconceptions about Porter's life—convinced "that a more reliable
K. A. Porter biography can prevent some of the common misreadings
of her fiction"—begins by noting that the "recent publication of
Enrique Hank Lopez's inaccurate and unreliable *Conversations with
Katherine Anne Porter* makes my corrective crucial for future K. A.
Porter scholarship." Another aspect of Porter's "life" is touched
upon by Sonia Gernes in "Life After Life: Katherine Anne Porter's
Version" (*JPC* 14:669–75), in which she notes that Miranda's story
"fits almost perfectly the pattern of 'death experiences'" traced by
Raymond A. Moody, Jr., in his study *Life After Life* and contends
that "What Porter has given us in *Pale Horse, Pale Rider* may, in
fact, be less of an allegory than a rare subjective experience, recorded long before current research on the subject, of what it is like
to 'die'." However dubious that contention may be, the actual death
of Porter brought forth a tribute from Donald E. Stanford in the
pages of *SoR* ("Katherine Anne Porter," 17:1–2).

There is only one piece on Carson McCullers to report this year.
In "An Existential Everyman" (*WVUPP* 27:82–88) Mary Etta Scott
takes exception to the "darkly pessimistic" reading of *Clock Without
Hands* offered by most critics and contends that, like Everyman, J. T.
Malone searches for his salvation and when he finds his own self
it is an existential victory—"and that, indeed, according to Carson

McCullers may be the only salvation modern man is capable of achieving."

***d.* Eudora Welty.** Welty scholarship continues to proliferate, although the quality of the work being produced is not of equal value. Elizabeth Evans' *Eudora Welty* (Ungar), the only book-length work to appear this year, should prove to be of greater interest to the person just coming to Welty rather than to the scholar and critic. Evans' study is a volume in the Modern Literature Series and it has all the earmarks of such a book. There is much enthusiasm and admiration, but the insights remain very much on the level of telling the reader that "Although she can write anywhere, Miss Welty prefers to write at home—the most convenient place for the early riser that she is" and that the two words which best characterize "The High Art of Eudora Welty" are love and integrity. Nor is Alan Holder's chapter on Welty, " 'It Happened in Extraordinary Times': Eudora Welty's Historical Fiction," in *The Imagined Past* (see *iv–b*) much better. Holder rightly notes that those works of Welty's which refer to the Natchez trace, including *The Robber Bridegroom*, "constitute a category of 'historical' fiction in the Welty canon whose qualities have not been adequately defined," but in fact Holder adds little to what already has been written about the works he ponderously discusses.

The Robber Bridegroom is also the focus of articles by Warren Akin IV and Lisa K. Miller. In *"The Robber Bridegroom:* An Oedipal Tale of the Natchez Trace" (*L&P* 30[1980]:112–18) Akin sees the story as presenting "a psychological drama in which characters and actions represent projections of a child's mind as she or he grapples with the emotional changes that lead to maturity," while Miller considers "The Dark Side of Our Frontier Heritage: Eudora Welty's Use of the Turner Thesis in *The Robber Bridegroom*" (*NMW* 14:18–25), in which she contends that Welty's novella "Combines the linear movement described by Turner and the cyclic repetion seen by Welty." The only other novel of Welty's to be discussed this year is *The Optimist's Daughter*, which Robert L. Phillips argues in "Patterns of Vision in Welty's *The Optimist's Daughter*" (*SLJ* 14,i:10–23) is, at least in its revised form, "one of the most significant and clear statements that Welty has made about the nature of vision."

Four essays are devoted to four different stories by Welty. W. U. McDonald, Jr., writes about "Artistry and Irony: Revisions of 'Lily Daw and the Three Ladies' " (*SAF* 9:113–21), a story which he finds to be both more comic and more richly ironic in its revised version. McDonald also studies the text of "Petrified Man," and in "Published Texts of 'Petrified Man': A Brief History" (*NMW* 13:64–72) concludes that the definitive text of "Petrified Man" has yet to be printed. Suzanne Marrs examines "The Conclusion of Eudora Welty's 'First Love': Historical Backgrounds" (*NMW* 13:73–78) which, she notes, clearly is based upon fact, and a knowledge of Aaron Burr and of Natchez enhances our understanding of Welty's purpose in the story. And in "When Gratitude Is No More: Eudora Welty's 'June Recital' " (*SCR* 13,ii:62–72) Marilyn Arnold offers a consideration of the work, which "may well be the best thing Eudora Welty has ever written," a "remarkable exploration of the meaning of human relationship within a context of surface order and subsurface disorder."

Finally, attention must be called to Jo Brans's "Struggling Against the Plaid: An Interview with Eudora Welty" (*SWR* 66:255–66) and to the two issues of *EuWN* 5,i and ii), which maintain the high level of the earlier numbers. The second issue marks the completion of five years of publication for the newsletter. In that time it not only has become an invaluable work for Welty enthusiasts but has managed to maintain a level of excellence that clearly makes it one of the best research tools of its kind.

e. **Thomas Wolfe.** This year's most substantial addition to Wolfe scholarship is John Hagan's "Structure, Theme, and Metaphor in Thomas Wolfe's *Look Homeward Angel*" (*AL* 53:266–85). Hagan addresses himself to the prevailing notion that Wolfe's first novel is mere formless autobiography. Although he agrees that the pattern of the book is not the tightest, he nevertheless believes that "organic unity, formal cohesion, and thematic control of a larger and looser kind—of a sort to be found, for instance, in *Moby-Dick*, *Bleak House* and *War and Peace*—are demonstrably present." Accordingly, Hagan sets out to show "how the novel's various themes, images, and symbols are integrated in a rich, complex, many-layered whole, and reach their appropriate culmination in the brilliant and extremely moving last chapter." Of somewhat less interest is John L. Idol, Jr.'s "Thomas Wolfe and T. S. Eliot: The Hippopotamus and the Old

Possum" (*SLJ* 13,ii:15–26), a consideration of Wolfe's use and abuse of Eliot: "Even though the distance between them was not so great as Wolfe evidently thought it was, even though the space diminished through the years . . . Wolfe remained firm in his vitalism, his determinism, his actualism, the belief that all reality is in motion. Eliot, as a royalist and Anglo-Catholic, created a rub that Wolfe could not ignore or pardon."

In "A Bibliography of Books with Selections by Thomas Wolfe" (*BB* 38:194–208) Morton I. Teicher presents 339 citations of books that include selections by Wolfe. The period covered is from 1930 to 1980, with the exception of one entry from 1924; two items which appeared in 1981 are listed in an addendum. Additional bibliographical material is to be found, as usual, in *Thomas Wolfe Review* (formerly, *Newsletter*). Both numbers (5,i and ii) contain "The Wolfe Pack: Bibliography," and *TWR* (5,i) also includes Theodore V. Theobold's "Additions to Wolfe Bibliography" (pp. 42–50), which seeks to fill gaps in Elmer D. Johnson's 1970 *Thomas Wolfe: A Checklist*. Other pieces to be found in *TWR* include Richard Walser's "The McCoy Papers" (5,i:1–6), Jerry L. Rice's "Thomas Wolfe and the Carolina Playmakers" (5,i:7–17), Richard S. Kennedy's "Thomas Wolfe at New York University" (5,ii:1–10)—a chapter cut from Kennedy's *The Window of Memory*—Richard J. Willis's "Thomas Wolfe's Hollow Men" (5,ii:31–36), and John L. Idol's "Fame and the Athlete in Wolfe's Fiction" (5,ii:38–43). Both numbers of *Thomas Wolfe Review* contain information about meetings of the Thomas Wolfe Society—as well as just about everything else pertaining to Wolfe. It continues to be a splendid publication.

Less splendid, from every point of view, is the matter of John Halberstadt and the Houghton Library. For those interested in following the controversy, the following items should be noted: Halberstadt's "Who Wrote Thomas Wolfe's Last Novels?" (*NYRB* 19: March 51–52); Richard S. Kennedy and John Halberstadt, "Crying Wolfe: An Exchange" (*NYRB* 16 July:50–51); John Halberstadt, "The Thomas Wolfe Controversy" (*WLB* 56:282–83, 316–17).

v. Humorists, Critics, and Others

James Thurber does not appear here very often but this year there are two works to report: a not-too-stimulating consideration by St.

George Tucker Arnold, Jr., of Thurber's animals, "Stumbling Dog-
tracks on the Sands of Time: Thurber's Less-than-charming Animals, and Animal Portraits in Earlier American Humor" (*MarkR*
10:41–47), and a very stimulating and entertaining volume, *Selected
Letters of James Thurber*, ed. Helen Thurber and Edward Weeks
(Little, Brown), a collection of more than a hundred letters—and 35
drawings—covering the period from 1935 to 1961.

Two pieces have been published about Edmund Wilson this year,
and although neither deals with *Memoirs of Hecate County*, they
are being noted here because Wilson continues to attract relatively
little attention: George H. Douglas writes about "Edmund Wilson:
The Man of Letters as Journalist" (*JPC* 15:78–85) and Brian Gallagher about "'Incurably History-Minded': Edmund Wilson as
Writer" (*MarkR* 11:17–20). If anything, Conrad Aiken's fiction has
fared even less well than Edmund Wilson's, so it is good to be able
to note the appearance of Mary Martin Rountree's "Conrad Aiken's
Heroes: Portraits of the Artist as a Middle-Aged Failure" (*SLitI* 13,ii:
77–85). Rountree points out that the bulk of Aiken's fiction "springs
from his deep preoccupation with the form and substance of his own
life, not because of his inability to free himself from his own egocen-
trism but because of the philosophical point of view on which he
bases his theory of art and fiction." In his portraits of the artist, "the
voice of defiance predominates over accents of resignation and despair"; Aiken's artists "gain the kind of self-knowledge that makes
possible the creation of an enduring art."

Finally, Jane Bowles, who is little read but who has been attracting the attention of feminist critics, is the subject of a fine biography
by Millicent Dillon, *A Little Original Sin: The Life and Work of Jane
Bowles* (Holt). The work receives less attention than the life, but
many readers may find Dillon's account of the life sufficiently compelling to want to read at least some of the work. The same, I suspect,
will not be the case with those who read Joseph Lovering's Twayne
volume on *Gerald Warner Brace* (TUSAS 384). Brace has received
the scantest of attention from critics, and this pedestrian study will
do little to alter the situation. The same is true of Fred Chappell's
"The Seamless Vision of James Still" (*AppalJ* 8:196–202), which also
is well intentioned but never rises much above that level to give the
reader a sense of Still's artistry.

vi. Popular Fiction

a. **Best-Sellers.** Although none of the writers in this section have been the subject of a major study this year, several have been accorded serious attention. Erskine Caldwell, for example, is the subject of a volume, *Critical Essays on Erskine Caldwell*, ed. Scott MacDonald (Hall). Not only is this the first collection of criticism ever published on Caldwell, but it is a most valuable volume. MacDonald reprints numerous reviews of Caldwell's fiction, essays by such critics as Kenneth Burke (pp. 167–73), Malcolm Cowley (pp. 198–200), and W. M. Frohock (pp. 201–13), and introductions which Caldwell wrote to several of his novels; MacDonald also provides the reader with an overview of the development of Caldwell scholarship as well as "An Evaluative Checklist of Erskine Caldwell's Short Fiction" (pp. 342–60). This volume really is a model of its kind. The two other works to be noted are of considerably less scope but are not without interest. Jac Tharpe offers excerpts from a 1971 "Interview with Erskine Caldwell" (*SoQ* 20:64–74) and Guy Owen concerns himself with "Erskine Caldwell's Other Women" (*NLauR* 10,i [1980]:7–14) in an attempt to show that the Darling Jills and Ellie Mays notwithstanding, "Caldwell often draws sympathetic portraits of women, treating them with dignity and respect—especially if they are young or black."

James Gould Cozzens' *Ask Me Tomorrow* is the subject of two essays: Colin S. Cass's consideration of "Cozzens's Debt to Thomas Dekker in *Ask Me Tomorrow*" (*MarkR* 11:11–16) and Irving Malin's poorly written but nonetheless interesting discussion of "The Education of Francis Ellery" (*JOHJ* 4,ii:32–38), in which he argues that in the novel "obsession" and "conservatism" are at war; "their battle is, indeed, the vital struggle of Ellery's education." But a more significant contribution to Cozzens scholarship than either of these essays is Matthew J. Bruccoli's *James Gould Cozzens: A Descriptive Bibliography* (Pittsburgh), another attractively produced volume in the Pittsburgh Series in Bibliography. This is the first descriptive bibliography of Cozzens's work, and it lists many previously unrecorded items. Because Cozzens frequently revised his books when new editions were being set, Bruccoli includes textual collations of the first American editions against the first English edition and of the first American edition against the latest American edition. In all, Bruccoli continues to serve Cozzens well.

The appearance of Malin's essay on Cozzens in the pages of *John O'Hara Journal* notes a change in its policy. Because of the lack of critical works being written about O'Hara, the journal is being opened to critical articles on 20th-century American writers and poets and also will include original poetry and fiction. Articles on O'Hara, of course, will continue to be published, as is witnessed by the publication of Nancy Walker's "'All that you need to know': John O'Hara's Achievement in the Novella" (*JOHJ* 4,i:61–80), Charles W. Bassett's "O'Hara and History" (*JOHJ* 4,ii:8–12), and Philip B. Eppard's "Bibliographical Supplement: Addenda to Bruccoli" (*JOHJ* 4,ii:59–61), a listing of addenda and corrigenda to Bruccoli's 1978 *John O'Hara: A Descriptive Bibliography*.

Margaret Mitchell also attracted the attention of more than one critic this year. In "'My Dear, I Don't Give a Damn': Scarlett O'Hara and the Great Depression" (*Frontiers* 5,iii[1980]:52–56) Marian J. Morton notes that like much of the popular culture of the 1930s, *Gone With the Wind* "was a defense of tradition and a covert attack on the pursuit of wealth"; and, whatever her intention may have been, "Mitchell created in Scarlett a heroine whose painful choices between new and old roles, between earning money and maintaining custom, were precisely those which faced millions of American women in the 1930's." Dieter Meindel, concerned that a book which succeeded in fulfilling a morale-building purpose in war-torn Europe has never really been accepted as a work of art in this country, offers "A Reappraisal of Margaret Mitchell's *Gone With the Wind*" (*MissQ* 34:414–34). And in "Margaret Mitchell: The Bad Little Girl of the Good Old Days," chapter 8 (pp. 313–50) of her study *Tomorrow Is Another Day*, Anne Goodwyn Jones offers one of the most sustained *and* substantial discussions we have of both Mitchell and *GWTW*, of which she writes: "If there is a winner in *Gone With the Wind*, it is the 'old days.' Fight as the four major characters do to find a way to live in the new, and different though their tactics may be, all are finally defeated. Scarlett and Rhett come closest to inventing a new pattern of life; but they so deeply incorporate contradictory elements of the old, particularly those that defined men and women, that they both are doomed to failure. Perhaps this is what makes the novel both peculiarly southern and internationally popular."

Pearl Buck is the subject of two inconsequential articles—Yu Yuh-chao's "Chinese Influences on Pearl S. Buck" (*TkR* 11,i[1980]: 23–41) and G. A. Cevasco's note about "Pearl Buck's Best Books" (*NMAL* 5:Item 19)—while George Greene offers an interesting consideration of "An Ethics for Wagon Trains: Thornton Wilder's *The Eighth Day*" (*QQ* 88:325–35). More substantial, however, are the two works which conclude this section: John Malcolm Brinnin's portrait of Truman Capote, "The Picture of Little T. C. in Prospect . . ." in *Sextet: T. S. Eliot & Truman Capote & Others* (Delacorte), pp. 3–96, and James R. Giles's Twayne volume devoted to *James Jones* (TUSAS 366), the first book-length study of Jones's fiction, which focuses upon two themes—"the evolution of a soldier and the sexual immaturity of American males"—and sees Jones as "a writer's writer, one of the most human of persons."

b. **Western Fiction.** Mari Sandoz is the writer of Western fiction who attracted the most attention this year. In addition to Rosemary Whitaker's "A Bibliography of Works by and About Mari Sandoz" (*BB* 38:82–91)—which attempts to provide a complete listing of the published works; reprintings as well as the initial publications of short works; published biographical and critical articles; unpublished research papers and theses—there are two articles which should be noted: Whitaker's consideration of "Violence in *Old Jules* and *Slogum House*" (*WAL* 16:217–24) and Fritz O. Berger's more substantial discussion of "The Art of Mari Sandoz's 'The Smart Man'" (*SDR* 19,iv:65–75).

The popular Luke Short receives his first book-length study in Robert L. Gale's Twayne volume *Luke Short* (TUSAS 368). While Gale ignores Short's short stories, he does discuss the 51 novels—dominated by the "pragmatic optimism of his composite hero: such a man sees what must be done, then does it"—and provide a chronology and bibliography; but Gale does little with his own prose to make me think that his study "will send seasoned old Short addicts back to their easy chairs and recruit a million young new ones." Nor is it likely that John Caldwell's pamphlet on *George R. Stewart* (WWS 46) will attract many new readers to Stewart; but for those who know nothing about Stewart this short volume does provide a convenient overview of his career. Frederick Manfred surely is a better-known novelist, though he continues to attract less critical attention than one might expect. "Manfred's Elof Lofblom" (*WAL* 16:125–34), Nancy Nelson McCord's consideration of *The Choke-cherry Tree*, Manfred's "Early autobiographical examination of heroism," is therefore a most welcome addition to the literature.

Most welcome, too, are the three novels reprinted by the University of Nebraska Press: Mari Sandoz' *Slogum House*, Walter Van Tilburg Clark's *The Track of the Cat*, and Jack Schaefer's *Monte Walsh*, which includes an introduction written by Schaefer for the Bison Book Edition.

c. Detective Fiction. This has been another good year for Raymond Chandler and Dashiell Hammett. Chandler, in particular, has fared well, thanks in large part to the publication of *Selected Letters of Raymond Chandler* (Columbia). Chandler's biographer, Frank Mac-Shane, here offers hundreds of letters, many long, informative, and most interesting, which more than support MacShane's contention that the letters document "a sad but decent life" as well as the "achievement of one of the finest letter writers American literature has produced over the last two hundred years." If Jerry Speir's *Raymond Chandler* (Ungar) pales next to the *Selected Letters* the reason has more to do with the exceptional quality of the *Letters* than with any particular failure of Speir's. Indeed, his *Raymond Chandler* is one of the best studies we have of Chandler's work. The seven novels are discussed at some length, the short stories are given adequate attention, Speir provides an extensive bibliography, and almost all that he writes centers on Marlowe, whose very centrality "can be seen as explanation for Chandler's popularity and for his artistic success." But that very centrality "is also a measure of his failure," for "Marlowe is finally too stylized a creation to permit growth and development." A final work to be mentioned here is Randall Maiver's "Raymond Chandler's Self-Parody" (*ArmD* 14:355–59), which takes exception to some of MacShane's observations in his *Life of Raymond Chandler* and notes that Chandler's humor and self-parody are stylistic reminders "of the fact that a whimsical artist stands only a little behind the tough-guy narrator."

The major work to appear about Hammett is Richard Layman's *Shadow Man: The Life of Dashiell Hammett* (Harcourt). Layman tells us more about Hammett's life than has been previously known, his works are discussed at some length, an appendix includes not only a list of Hammett's works but also his testimony before U.S. Second District Court Judge Sylvester Ryan. The one serious problem with Layman's *Life* is that there is little here but the facts; as Layman rightly notes in his preface, his *Life* "is an amalgam of factual information, and the impression of many people who knew Hammett." What is missing is that quality of a person's life which we cannot get from the facts but without which the facts seem almost irrelevant. Not irrelevant, but not of great consequence either, are the two other pieces on Hammett to be reported here: Christopher Bentley's "Murder by Client: A Reworked Theme in Dashiell Hammett" (*ArmD* 14:78–79), which suggests that the murder of Spade's partner in *The Maltese Falcon* was adopted from an earlier Hammett story, "Who Killed Bob Teal?" and David Glover's "The Frontier of Genre: Further to John S. Whitley's 'Stirring Things Up: Dashiell Hammett's Continental Op'" (*JAmS* 15:249–52), which contends that a convincing reading of Hammett's fiction will depend upon a more definitive sense than we now have of "what constitutes the detective genre and just how inclusive we should take it to be."

Hammett and Chandler also figure prominently in two other works on detective fiction to appear this year. In his first-rate consideration of the detective story's popularity, *The Pursuit of Crime: Art and Ideology in Detective Fiction* (Yale), Dennis Porter devotes much attention to both Chandler and Hammett, who not only "have made important contributions to the dark myth of the unredeemable city," but who, by introducing their hard-boiled social pessimism into the sphere of a popular genre, remind us that America "has lacked a theory of society that regarded the city as its normal focus and center." And in "'Realistic' Crime Fiction: An Anatomy of Evil People" (*CentR* 25:101–32) Edward A. Nickerson examines the villains in the works of Hammett, Chandler, and Ross Macdonald and concludes that the three have "set forth, in their portrayals of villainy and the milieu which sustains it, a serious indictment of a whole society." Moreover, "they have offered their readers only a small portion of hope, because their heroes of detection win only temporary victories over these formidable adversaries."

d. **Science Fiction.** Surprisingly, there is little to report here this year. The one exception—one is tempted to say, *of course*—is Isaac Asimov, who has put together three volumes: *Change! 71 Glimpses*

of the Future (Houghton), *In the Beginning . . .* (Crown), and
Asimov on Science Fiction (Doubleday), the last an especially important volume since Asimov has not yet written a book *about* science
fiction.

Hofstra University

15. Fiction: The 1950s to the Present

Jerome Klinkowitz

"What this country needs," a Saul Bellow character advises, "is a good five-cent synthesis." Happily scholars of contemporary fiction have begun work in this direction, and though the prices are sometimes breathtaking ($57.50 for one of the books below) this sudden movement toward comprehensive and comparative judgment is welcome in an area too often Balkanized by factional disputes. In 1981 a remarkable number of both veterans and newcomers have presented wide-ranging assessments incorporating such earlier issues as "postmodernism" and "innovation" within genuinely synthetic treatments of the post-1950 period in fiction.

Consequently this chapter cannot comment on everything published, for that alone would fill the entire *ALS*. Therefore routine analyses whose titles are self-explanatory within *MLAB* will not be exhumed for autopsy. Only those books and essays which break new ground or indicate important trends will be mentioned here.

i. General Studies

Seven major books, including several from important critics whose thoughts on contemporary fiction at large have been long awaited, distinguish 1981 as a good year for syntheses. Ranging from theory through literary history and analysis to sustained interviews, these seven make a considerable resource shelf for future scholars who may wish to locate a particular writer or style.

Christine Brooke-Rose's *A Rhetoric of the Unreal* (Cambridge) presents itself as a rhetoric of innovative fiction, revising Wayne Booth's axioms in the face of the "reality crisis" which has reshaped literature in our time. Her approach, however, is to favor novels which escape the thematic confines of this philosophical problem while still employing all the techniques of realism—in other words what she determines to be the science fiction of Kurt Vonnegut and Joseph McElroy. The former is satiric, the latter poetic; but the achievement of each depends upon an inversion (rather than a replacement) of conventional aesthetics. No far-reaching experimentation here: even the supposedly radical innovations of John Barth, Thomas Pynchon, and Ronald Sukenick are shown to be a form of closet Aristotelianism in their metafictional imitation of imitations of action.

Alan Wilde's *Horizons of Assent: Modernism, Postmodernism, and the Ironic Imagination* (Hopkins) and Philip Stevick's *Alternative Pleasures: Postrealistic Fiction and the Tradition* (Illinois) more willingly acknowledge a rupture in literary history sufficient to reorder the rules. Wilde reaches back to the high and late modernism of Ford, Woolf, and Isherwood to establish how "the modernists proved incapable of either accepting chaos or of denying it," while postmodernism "fulfills the blocked energies inscribed in the modernist crisis." How does "modernism release its humanity"? The works of Donald Barthelme, Max Apple, and Renata Adler shift the terms by claiming "Man is not incarnated in his body; he *is* body, his sexual self, finally an object, a thing." Therefore what earlier writers lamented, these figures celebrate. This is *generative irony* which, instead of rejecting the world, "enters into a relationship with the ordinary" which seemed so threatening before. There is great capital to be made here for the innovative work's essential objecthood; but instead Wilde contradictorily demands a mythic substructure for his style of post-modernism, rejecting the surfiction of Raymond Federman and Ronald Sukenick in favor of the smoothly humanistic optimism of Apple and Adler, or (more defensibly) the madly affirming comedy of Stanley Elkin.

Stevick's book is more aggressively disruptive in its choice of quality literature: given his belief that style can become the stuff of fiction, he favors the pyrotechnics of Leonard Michaels, Donald Barthelme, and Robert Coover over the good-news storytellers Wilde promotes. Metafictions and surfictions are, in his synthesis, not pointless indulgences but rather word-objects which are resolute in their intention "not to make a world" and therefore heedful of postmodernism's suspicion of all constructions. This new fiction "is satire without an object," a style which demonstrates the fictive impulse without satisfying (and therefore compromising) its human goal.

Jack Hicks's *In the Singer's Temple* (N.Car.) is a reductively organized yet very successful attempt to cover all the bases: innovative metafiction (Barthelme), black prose (Ernest Gaines), women (Marge Piercy), Jewish-American fantasy and terror (Jerzy Kosinski), and countercultural protest (Ken Kesey and Richard Brautigan). Part of Hicks's thesis is that "American fiction has fractionated into its primary ingredients," each representing a different departure from realism. Yet America's culture is still evident in these fictions; what is different are the "unique modes of perceiving and responding" to it. Personal subcultures of one sort or another—certainly a reflection of the day's social upheavals—become the basis for this willful fragmentation, which Hicks explains quite well as the aesthetic of our age.

The evolution of scientific thought, from Werner Heisenberg through Niels Bohr, is another useful paradigm for fiction's radical change. There has been an "emotional resistance" to each transformation, argues Robert Nadeau in *The New Book on Nature,* largely because the comfortably Western thought pattern of either/or is here supplanted by a new logic for which fictional conventions have yet to be invented. Hence we have John Barth's struggle with "the indeterminacy of nature's processes," John Updike's joy in "the dynamic interplay between seemingly irreconcilable particulars in thought," Thomas Pynchon's entropy, Tom Robbins' creative use of style to alter content, Don DeLillo's "renewed awareness of the denotative aspect of language," and Kurt Vonnegut's invention of a nonlinear structure to express these ideas and more.

Surprisingly, only one American critic has tried the French approach to "texts," and with an ever-so-delicate use of Roland Barthes's terminology Paul Bruss establishes a useful hierarchy which shows just how fiction is evolving. *Victims: Textual Strategies in Recent American Fiction* (Bucknell) takes Vladimir Nabokov's work as the modernist measure for subsequent advances by Barthelme and Kosinski. Modernists, for all their innovations, usually assumed that language served narrative structure; Barthelme turns that axiom around to create a multi-textuality whose anti-authoritarian posture reflects the social spirit of his times. Bruss offers fine readings of *Snow White* and *The Dead Father* without reducing them to satires; indeed, their lack of a central subject makes them satires of the satiric impulse itself. In *Steps, Cockpit,* and *Blind Date* Kosinski ranges farther to make the reader create the text; even then, Kosinski is more interested in the processes of fiction than in its content, despite his realistic techniques.

Together these first six books do much to establish a canon of works and a feasible theory behind it—two problems which have dogged previous, less complete studies. The year's most important contribution, however, is the book of original interviews compiled by Heidi Ziegler and Christopher Bigsby, *The Radical Imagination and the Liberal Tradition* (London: Junction Books). These conversations were conducted to form a thesis, that the moral fiction/truth-seeking criticism espoused by John Gardner and Gerald Graff has been challenged by the achievements of fiction writers themselves. The ensuing dialogue qualifies as solid scholarship, for Ziegler and Bigsby's mastery of the material is complemented by the eloquence of their subjects (many of whom are graduate-trained practicing critics themselves). Barth, Barthelme, Coover, Elkin, Gardner, William H. Gass, and John Hawkes are the Americans who face the two alternatives to the dilemma of language being a closed, ultimately nonreferential system: ironic (language as an end in itself) or utopian (the leap of faith to a perfect unity of word and thing). In this context Barth is eager to recommend himself as "a perfectly stock bourgeois liberal humanist with the addition of what I think of as some version of the tragic view" which he then analyzes within his novels through *Letters*. Barthelme as always resists attempts to make him a satirist, countering that his intent is "to make a picture" whose meaning will be just as evident yet equally untranscribable as music. Coover, who privileges the creative imagination, is relentless in his pressure which "slowly breaks down moral assurance and a controlled social and aesthetic texture." Elkin explains how things are better "when you make stuff up," while Gardner takes the more serious view that in "telling the world how to be" an artist rightly equates himself with the priest. Gass defends the "solidity of language" and shows how there can be "no poetry but in things." Hawkes adds considerable biographical and analytical support to the widely perceived shift in his fiction after 1960—a transition to comedy which he insists "hasn't lessened the power of the nightmarish aspects of my work." Including similarly analytical interviews with British authors Malcolm Bradbury, John Fowles, Doris Lessing, Iris Murdoch, and Angus Wilson, this collection begins the necessary work of relating transatlantic innovations. A less critically ambitious but extremely helpful interview collection which leans more to younger and more radical British writers but which also contains brilliant interviews with John Gardner, John Hawkes, Grace Paley, and Ishmael Reed has been prepared by Alan Burns and Charles Sugnet under the title *The Imagination on Trial* (London: Allison and Busby; U.S. distribution by Schocken). The thesis here is that certain writers are in tune with the philosophical, techno-logical, and sexual readjustments of their times (notably Paley and Reed), while others encourage "reactionary nostalgia for a caste system, particularly among professors and intellectuals who want to see themselves as the last leisured class, an aristocracy of taste." Sugnet's introduction is especially canny and lucid, coolly evaluating the complex forces at work as contemporary fiction is made.

Ziegler (from Würzberg) and Bigsby (East Anglia) are mem-bers of an international consortium of scholars organized by André LeVot, Gerhard Hoffman, and Ihab Hassan; meeting regularly in the U.S., France, Germany, and Italy, these figures are combining the best of European and American approaches to forge a newly re-sponsible criticism, evident in the interview volume and in the new Contemporary Writers Series announced by Methuen (co-edited by Bradbury and Bigsby). Because of this movement readers may have to watch London, Paris, Frankfurt, and Milan for the most substan-tial work in English on Bellow, Barthelme, Brautigan, Gass, and Kosinski.

One contemporary scholar admirably independent of both the conservative and radical camps is Thomas LeClair, and two of his essays indicate a promising direction. LeClair's standards are simply those of excellence and range: "If we know reality by our fictions," he comments, "they had better be good and they had better be big." Hence his preference is for the uniquely massive tomes of Joseph McElroy (*Lookout Cartridge*), Don DeLillo (*Ratner's Star*), William Gaddis (*JR*), Joseph Heller (*Something Happened*), Robert Coover (*The Public Burning*), and John Barth (*Letters*). In complementary essays he answers first the conservative detractors (Alfred Kazin, John Gardner) and then the innovative boosters (Richard Koste-lanetz, Jerome Klinkowitz) with arguments calculated to support his own seven writers' "massiveness and reassertion of literature's force." In "The Best American Fiction: Which Contemporary Novel-

ists Will Still Be Read in the New Millennium?" (*Lone Star Review*,
monthly supplement to the Dallas *Times Herald*, June: pp. 3, 8)
LeClair admires his seven because "They catalogue the realities other
novelists leave out." "Avant-Garde Mastery" (*TriQ* 53:259–67) schematizes a contrast between mechanistic science and contemporary
systems theory to create a model within which McElroy & Co. fit:
the unmaking of language, mind, and book in order to "remake
everything." *The rhetoric of excess* is LeClair's name for their fictive
approach, which he feels is justified because in our world "The
closer you get, the less you see." A third essay, "Missing Writers"
(*Horizon* 24,x:48–52), links the self-imposed solitude of Pynchon,
Gaddis, and DeLillo with J. D. Salinger's, with the difference that
the writers of excess refuse to "waste words" in public because their
writing itself borders on the extreme. (LeClair's closer studies of
Gaddis and Heller are noted in *vii* below.)

   The recent American short story is treated in two brief overviews.
In his introduction to *Prize Stories of the Seventies From the O.
Henry Awards* (Wash. Square) William Abrahams notes that while
none of the winners treated either of the decade's two most important events—Vietnam and Watergate—nevertheless the spirit of these
affairs is evident throughout the stories he read, namely: "the ever-
widening gulf between public and private experience, between the
language of politicians and the language of artists," and so forth.
Why did the short story thrive in such a climate of nihilism? "Perhaps because writers, turning to the privacy of individual experience for their subject, managed not to be bogged down in stereotypes
of gloom and doom; perhaps because . . . comedy has been rediscovered as a means of expressing (and surviving) some of the bleaker
truths about human experience." Walter Allen's *The Short Story in
English* (Oxford/Clarendon) chooses to emphasize derivations instead: Bernard Malamud's grafting onto his own prose immigrant
Yiddish rhythms, images, and mannerisms; John Updike's and John
Cheever's adoption of a *New Yorker* style of moralism; and Joyce
Carol Oates's Chekhovian summation of life.

   Metaphors—some old, some new—continue to be helpful in pic-
turing contemporary fiction. In an expansion of his classic *The Absurd Hero in American Fiction* (*ALS 1966*, 168) David Galloway
finds that "absurd thought" is even more vigorously pursued "through
the mazes of meta-fiction and post-modernism." For their part, John

Updike has grown since 1966 while Saul Bellow has declined. Countering LeClair, Galloway argues that the finest work has been the shortest—too much of *Humboldt's Gift* is "pompous, overbearing, diffuse," while the complexities of William Styron's *Sophie's Choice* are too extreme for the novel's structure to bear. Neil David Berman's *Playful Fictions and Fictional Players: Game, Sport, and Survival in Contemporary American Fiction* (Kennikat) combines the sophistications of game/play theory with the actualities of popular sports to show how contemporary novels collapse the dualism between work and play, whether for boxing (Leonard Gardner's *Fat City*), football (Peter Gent's *North Dallas Forty* and Don DeLillo's *End Zone*), basketball (Lawrence Shainberg's *One on One*), and baseball (Robert Coover's *The Universal Baseball Association*). For Ihab Hassan, the city is a useful metaphor for his favorite subject, the gnostic transcendence by mind; behind its gritty facade the city of Ralph Ellison's *Invisible Man*, Saul Bellow's *The Adventures of Augie March*, and Thomas Pynchon's *The Crying of Lot 49* is the "agent of all our transformations," an image of "total control" ("Cities of the Mind, Urban Words: The Dematerialization of Metropolis in Contemporary Fiction," in *Literature and the Urban Experience*, pp. 93–112).

The importance to fiction of concerns within the publishing industry is one final trend to emerge this year. *Granta* (iv) features seven pieces on this topic, including a long interview with David Godine (pp. 125–40) detailing just how the economics of his business help determine the style of what is published. At the other end, writers tend to be subservient to these demands, resulting in what Brigid Brophy calls "The Economics of Self-Censorship" (pp. 63–74). In "The End of a Gentleman's Profession" (pp. 75–84) John Sutherland examines these economics from the inside, especially as regards the newly reorganized British-American book trade. Sutherland's own *Bestsellers* (Routledge) further ties market considerations to the ideology of fiction publishing, which is keyed to "popular needs"—whether these needs are responded to or created by the very types of books sold.

There is, of course, a sociology of interest wherever people work together, and the resultant politics have been studied in the past for the publishing industry by Richard Kostelanetz and now within the National Endowment for the Arts by Hilary Masters in "Go Down

Dignified: The NEA Writing Fellowships" (*GaR* 35:233–45) with a
reply by director David Wilk (pp. 246–56). That the grants business
influences by exclusion the study of fiction has long been Kostelanetz' argument, whose closely researched book *The Grants Fix*
was announced for 1981 but then inexplicably withdrawn by its
publisher. Co-editor Richard Ziegfeld has brought to the *DLB Yearbook: 1981*, ed. with Karen L. Rood and Jean W. Ross (Gale) a
sophisticated understanding of the literary business from both sides
of the desk and includes essays such as Larry McCaffery and Sinda
Gregory's on Robert Coover (pp. 34–43), which measures the influence of corporate meddling (the classic case is Coover's *The Public Burning*, the devastating economics of which not only changed
the novel but affected Coover's subsequent living and writing habits
as well). Ross includes her own essays on the politics of "The American Writers Congress" (pp. 3–8) and the hornets' nest stirred up by
Bryan Griffin's recent attack on fiction's contemporary pantheon in
" 'Panic Among the Philistines,' " (pp. 9–18). Even the lowly English
department cannot enjoy its personality wars and endless meetings,
it seems, without shaping the course of American fiction: Stephen
Wilbers' *The Iowa Writers' Workshop* (Iowa) describes the academic politics which created the unique program and then kept it
to its conservative course.

ii. Saul Bellow and Other Jewish-American Writers

Although publication of *The Dean's December* will stir critical activity, Bellow's seven-year silence has given scholars a chance to
catch up; hence there is little new work to report on. The Nobel
laureate's new novel, however, is distinguished by extreme petulance
with both Poland (fictionalized as Romania) and Chicago (its most
Augie Marchian self), and therefore an eerily perceptive study of
the first eight novels titled "Bellow's Crankiness" (*ChiR* 32,iv:92–
107) by Howard Eiland deserves special mention. Bellow is self-
consciously cranky, Eiland stresses, and from *Dangling Man* to
Humboldt's Gift that orneriness "emerges increasingly bold and
complex." The purposes it serves, however, explicate what many
critics have pondered in Bellow's work: "an obsessive distrust of
bourgeois self-fashioning," the "underground idealism" always present as an alternative to "the disease of self-consciousness," and the

grotesque abstraction of woman as the figure of each man's hope. By the time of *Herzog* this impulse becomes self-parodic, with gratifying results, and although deliberately weakened in the cases of Artur Sammler and Charlie Citrine it still provides for "a more ambiguous dominion of the heart." Whether this Marchian quality is enhanced or contradicted by Bellow's newest cranky protagonist, Albert Corde, may be decided in future studies.

Helpful reinterpretations of major novels are offered by Bruce Michelson in "The Idea of *Henderson*" (*TCL* 27:309–24) and Michael G. Yetman in "Who Would Not Sing for Humboldt" (*ELH* 48:935–51). Michelson argues that *Henderson the Rain King* has been underevaluated partly because of Bellow's cautionary disclaimer in "Deep Readers of the World, Beware!" but also because of the novel's multiform structure, which presents several themes (American identity, mentality, and world role) pluralistically; these components of the imaginative life do come together in the "turbulent, consummate scene" of the bear-on-the-rollercoaster (i.e., blamelessness in the face of life's immensities, a theme Michelson might also find in John Irving's novels of bears and mayhem). Yetman's thesis, that *Humboldt's Gift* celebrates "that special exuberance of spirit" which in romantic theory "accompanied the self-creating, sometimes self-obliterating activity of the poet," posits Humboldt as the creator of Citrine; the argument, however, is obscured by a bizarre style of language which can only be a sick parody of the Paris–New Haven studies Johns Hopkins has been publishing. Our nomination for the most preposterous syntax of the year is Yetman's expository advice that "To find a poet young Citrine to the Big Apple first came in 1938 from Madison, Wisconsin, where he was a student."

Solidly good books on Bernard Malamud and Philip Roth help fill the gap left by Bellow studies this year. Iska Alter's *The Good Man's Dilemma* (AMS) examines Malamud as a social critic, drawing on the relation of individual to community in the novels through *Dubin's Lives*. Among Jewish-American writers who have developed in other directions, Malamud has "continued to be a humanistic spokesman, albeit a frequently disappointed one in recent years, for responsibility, compassion, and goodness in a world spinning out of control with frightening speed." His lyrical realism is "the fictive analog to the Chasidic belief that the mystical connection to God" is found in quotidian participation, not ascetic isolation. The Ameri-

can dream, contrasting paradigms of success, the American West as
Eden, minorities, women, art—these are the concerns against which
Malamud tests his protagonists. All can be corrosive factors, especially where a moral approach guarantees material failure. Yet
the author's understanding of this paradox gives humanistic strength
to his struggles for integration with society.

Philip Roth's novels also treat a wide expanse of contemporary
America, but showing how what Alter calls his "self-absorption"
works is the subject of Judith Paterson Jones and Guinevera A.
Nance's excellent *Philip Roth* (Ungar). Roth places the highest pre-
mium on the differences between his "written and unwritten worlds."
At its broadest gap one finds Alexander Portnoy, at the narrowest
Neil Klugman of *Goodbye, Columbus*, and shuttling between those
extremes has shaped Roth's career—both in how his books are written
and how they are received. Through all the novels there is a battle
for control of reality, whether it be simple adolescent self-determination or "coming to terms with the self in the process of resisting what
others perceive one to be." At bottom, Roth's business is the expansion of moral consciousness, and his various approaches have resulted
in novels at times fabulous, at other times realistic. Jones and Nance
emphasize that had Roth not written *Portnoy's Complaint*, the balance in his work would be quite different and that ever since doing
it the author has been striving to "get beyond" that book. Yet it remains his calling card and is one of the central texts for Maurice
Charney's *Sexual Fiction* (Methuen). In *Portnoy* the self-definition
is on the immediately post-pubescent level, which without the coun-
terweight of such works as *The Ghost Writer* and "Defender of the
Faith" makes Roth seem much less the writer than he is. Helping
with this more positive balance is Adeline R. Tintner's "Henry James
as Roth's Ghost Writer" (*Midstream*, Mar.:48–51). Roth's novel acknowledges the influence of James's story "The Middle Years," but
Tintner shows how it is really "The Author of Beltraffio" which supplies the novel's main plot. More than a simple borrowing, this use
of the master stylist indicates Roth's control of the "loose baggy
monster" his full-length fiction used to be—and in the process his
better management of previously foregrounded obsessions.

Holocaust studies, which have flourished, are extended this year
with an unusual and revealing twist. On the side of orthodoxy,
Dorothy S. Blick's *Immigrant-Survivors* (Wesleyan) agrees with

Sidra DeKoven Ezrahi and others that writers such as Malamud, Bellow, I. B. Singer, Susan Fromberg Schaeffer, and Arthur Cohen discard naturalism in favor of a new idealism more suitable to the absurdly unreal circumstances of the holocaust, which she acknowledges has spawned a new subgenre of Jewish-American writing. A new slant, however, comes from Melvin J. Friedman, whose "Recent New England Fiction: Outsiders and Insiders" (*New England Heritage*, pp. 167–82) reveals that among all the major writers now living in the Northeast it has been the two urban exiles—Malamud and Roth—who have most directly used the leafier region in their works; in *Dubin's Lives* New England provides the one satisfactory home for "this diaspora urban Jew," while *The Ghost Writer* takes the "Arcadia" of Henry James's *The American Scene* for its thematic resolution.

iii. Flannery O'Connor, William Styron, Walker Percy, and Other Southern Writers

Flannery O'Connor's letters are providing a rich resource for those who wish to track further the ambivalences in her work. In "Flannery O'Connor's Double-Edged Satire: The Idiot Daughter versus the Lady Ph.D." (*SAF* 9:17–25) Martha Chew uses this correspondence to study the contrasts between "Good Country People" and "The Life You Save May Be Your Own"; stupid timidity or foolish rebellion hurt each character, the composite of which may be O'Connor herself. Also of note is B. W. Telford's "Flannery O'Connor and the Social Classes" (*SLJ* 13,ii:27–40), in which characters' reactions to "distinctive class structure" provide the basis for the author's rich satire, comic irony, and moral humor.

To a revised and enlarged edition (see *ALS 1975*, 351–52) of *The Achievement of William Styron* (Georgia) editors Robert K. Morris and Irving Malin add considerations of *Sophie's Choice* and of Styron's career. An interview with Morris centers on this recent novel, as does Richard Pearce's superb "Sophie's Choices" (pp. 284–97). Pearce shows how, for the novel itself and within the scope of his career, Styron has tried to "approach what is beyond the limits of the human imagination"—a better defense of *Sophie's Choice* than the knee-jerk praise for "a testament of affirmation" which other critics use to create *de facto* masterpieces (banning such phrases would make much scholarship unpublishable). In "Styron's Fiction: Narrative as Idea" (pp. 124–46) Philip W. Leon charts Styron's development through the shifting narrative focus of *Lie Down in Darkness*, the narrative transfer from one character to another in both *The Long March* and *Set This House on Fire*, the division of Nat Turner "into narrator and actor with diction appropriate to each role," and Sophie's telling of her own story (yet in a way which strongly influences the auctorial character Stingo). In periodicals *The Confessions of Nat Turner* still inspired the best work, including Arthur D. Casciato and James L. W. West III's "William Styron and *The Southampton Insurrection*" (*AL* 52:564–77), which establishes Styron's care with historical sources, and James R. Huffman's "A Psychological Redefinition of William Styron's *Confessions of Nat Turner*" (*LitR* 24:279–307), a psychological defense of Nat's integrity (and of Styron's avoidance of racism).

Walker Percy continues to interest Panthea Reid Broughton, whose "Walker Percy and the Innocent Eye" (*Literary Romanticism*, pp. 94–108) argues that each of his protagonists reclaims a connective vision of self and world; against a more contemporary sense of isolation and abstraction Percy expresses romantic wonder. "Walker Percy: The Novelist as Poet" (*SoR* 17:164–74) is John W. Stevenson's treatment of the writer's "sovereign sense of seeing," aptly expressed by his open, gentle, curious, and sympathetic narrators. This special vision is reflected in poetic language which employs both intensification and compression. Personal meaning is at the center of two more predictable surveys: Jan Nordby Gretlund's "Walker Percy: A Scandinavian View" (*SCR* 13,ii:18–27), which draws parallels to a Kierkegaardian transcendence of despair amid the world's trivia, and Thomas Daniel Young's analysis of *The Moviegoer* (in his *The Past in the Present*, pp. 135–66), which concludes that Percy cares less for a restoration of nature and the past than for individual salvation.

Beyond the generally recapitulative studies of Percy's *Lancelot* is William James O'Brien's investigation of its many allusions to Dante's *Inferno*, an approach which shows there is more to the protagonist than the author's self-characterization ("Walker Percy's *Lancelot*: A Beatrician Visit to the Region of the Dead," *SHR* 15: 153–64). How Percy only partially overcomes his previous "equivocation" and "indecisiveness" is shown by Doreen A. Fowler in "Answers and Ambiguity in Percy's *The Second Coming*" (*Crit* 23,ii:13–23). Ever the articulate spokesman for his own and others' works, Percy grants important interviews to Gretlund ("Interview with Walker Percy in his Home in Covington, Louisiana, January 2, 1981," *SCR* 13,ii:3–12) and to Laura Whitney Hobson ("The Study of Consciousness: An Interview With Walker Percy" (*GaR* 35:51–60). Gretlund covers the novels through *The Second Coming*, probing for debts to Kierkegaard and eliciting comments on Percy's ever-neurotic female characters. Hobson's piece moves almost directly to the author's work-in-progress, *Novum Organum*, "a collection of essays on language, mass communication, and psychiatry." Here will be found Percy's model for "a radical science" suited to the unique nature of human consciousness.

Even for a writer so complex as Percy there is much redundant scholarship; a review desk such as *ALS*'s might well plead for studies of younger southern writers, who in the wake of so much work on O'Connor & Co. have been sadly neglected. Patricia V. Beatty adds a welcome essay on Georgian-Floridian Harry Crews ("Body Language in Harry Crews' *The Gypsy's Curse*," *Crit* 23,ii:61–66); the problem is that Crews's world (boxing in this novel and rougher sports elsewhere) is far from pious, making easy shortcuts to "affirmation" impossible. Neither can such facile analyses be made for the more formally innovative fiction which comes from the South, and exploring the "enormous and disturbing energy" of one such writer is the task John Ditsky undertakes in "Further Into Darkness: The Novels of Cormac McCarthy" (*HC* 18,ii:1–11). Time, dialogue, setting, imagery, and narrative flow in the four novels are the elements which make McCarthy's work speak more by style than by theme alone.

iv. Older Realists: Mary McCarthy, Lionel Trilling, Truman Capote, and Shirley Jackson

William Hardy's *Mary McCarthy* (Ungar) justifies its strongly biographical approach by showing how class stratification is an important satiric element in her work. McCarthy's tendencies are toward the essay even within her most successful fiction, which uses caricature rather than characterization for its most typical effect. Edward Joseph Schoben, Jr., in *Lionel Trilling: Mind and Character* (Ungar) takes a more psychological approach, claiming that Trilling was less the intellectual and more the frustrated novelist, a theme which shows itself in *The Middle of the Journey* where the course of honor yields only "inaction." This same "wish versus the world" informs Trilling's criticism as well.

It is worth noting that only introductory series such as Ungar's and Twayne's have been treating novelists of this older realistic school, the higher-powered scholarship apparently having had its say. Nevertheless, there is reason to consult Kenneth T. Reed's *Truman Capote* (TUSAS 388), for Capote's balance of sensibility with style has taken on even more importance in his recent work. Death has always charmed this writer, for where else can one find such final resolutions to the problems of good and evil? That Capote's search for accommodation still partakes of mystery makes Reed's study a worthwhile enterprise.

Shirley Jackson is an equally rich writer, inspiring Dennis Welch's "Manipulation in Shirley Jackson's 'Seven Types of Ambiguity'" (*SSF* 18:27–31); this new reading suggests that the protagonist is not taken advantage of but rather helps take advantage of others. "Details . . . attentiveness, word choice, and timing" indicate the subtlety of Jackson's intended ambiguity.

v. The Mannerists: John Updike and John Cheever

One of the very best books yet written on John Updike also covers the large part of his canon other scholars neglect: poetry, essays, drama, and short fiction. Donald J. Greiner's *The Other John Updike* (Ohio) does more than fill this gap, for its careful analysis of the five story collections through *Museums and Women* not only establishes Updike's unique manner but also answers the familiar complaints about his fiction in general: that it forfeits substance for the superficial effects of style. What makes the stories special? "Persistent desire and enticing memory" are the matters of substance some critics cannot see, Greiner argues; mastery of these interests demands that the writer favor rhythm and mood over character and action, lyrical meditation over conventional plot. "The danger is that silence may facilitate forgetfulness," and in the face of this dilemma "Updike offers a vocabulary" which replaces grandly dramatic action with "understated epiphanies," substitutes mundane experiences for emotional intensity, and builds his stories so that their effect is achieved by "quiet insight" rather than by sudden endings. *The DLB Yearbook: 1980* includes Greiner's useful update (pp. 107–16), extending his analysis through *The Coup, Too Far To Go*, and *Problems*. One of Greiner's latter points, how the stories in the two recent collections "round out one distinct phase of Updike's involvement with themes of family life," is treated in detail by Jane Barnes in "John Updike: A Literary Spider" (*VQR* 57:79–98). The past, as Greiner would agree, is Updike's text for study—not just to regulate the conflict between illusion and reality but as a discipline for knowing how to act in the future. A brief but important note by Albert E. Wilhelm ("Updike's Revisions of *Rabbit, Run,*" *NMAL* 5:Item 15) establishes how style and theme interact: amidst the imagistic and linguistic "enhancement" of language in the novel's second edition can be found thematic revisions which make the minister, Jack Eccles, even more of a failure. Philip Seib's interview "A Lovely Way Through Life" (*SWR* 66:341–50) captures Updike's conversational charm and also notes the fact that his play *Buchanan Dying* began as "my attempt at a political novel"; there will be none other in the wake of *The Coup*.

John Cheever's death in 1982 will call forth many retrospective studies, but substantial scholarship this year was limited to Francis J. Bosha's excellent compilation of works by and about him, right down to major newspaper reviews (*John Cheever, A Reference Guide* [Hall]), and to Glen M. Johnson's "The Moral Structure of Cheever's *Falconer*" (*SAF* 9:21–31), which argues that this novel "develops a version of this Christian pattern of redemption, seeking salvation as its culmination." Only understanding and positive action can counter the effects of sin; once that is accomplished, both God and novelist can shed their grace on Cheever's protagonist.

vi. Newer Realists: Joyce Carol Oates, John Gardner, and Others

With Oates scholarship in a momentary lull, Christina Gillis makes the most of one short story in " 'Where are you going, where have you been?': Seduction, Space, and a Fictional Mode" (*SSF* 18:65–70); physical space is seen to mirror private space as an "innocent" passes to the outer world, and—as one might suspect—Oates describes the entrance into this second world as violent, aggressive, and fearful. That everything we already know about Oates is present in one previously uncriticized story is Keith Cushman's conclusion in "A Reading of Joyce Carol Oates's 'Four Summers'" (*SSF* 18:137–46). Sanford Pinsker's "Speaking About Short Fiction: An Interview with Joyce Carol Oates" (*SSF* 18:239–43) elicits Oates's comment on something new: her "current fascination with the phenomenon of *time*—I seem to want to tell a story as if it were sheer lyric, all its components present simultaneously."

Shorter works by John Gardner—the novella *Grendel* and "The King's Indian"—are equally attractive to the relatively few scholars in his camp this year. In "Blakean Sources in John Gardner's *Grendel*" (*Crit* 23,i:57–66) Michael Ackland identifies borrowings and emphasizes that Blake's "highly pictorial imagination affords a wealth of related images conveying the quintessence of fallen existence or what he termed man's eternal sleep," a posture Gardner's work expresses well. Elzbieta Foeller's "John Gardner's Tale 'The King's Indian' as a Fabulation based on the 19th-Century Literature Tradition" (*Traditions*, pp. 81–89) not only identifies sources in Coleridge, Melville, and Poe, but shows how Gardner is more of a fabulist than his own *On Moral Fiction* might care to admit. The only hotter topic among the controversies surrounding Gardner in recent years has been "plagiarism," and in "*The King's Indian*: Gardner's Imp of the Poeverse" (*NMAL* 5:Item 2) Ted Billy places paragraphs from Poe side-by-side with Gardner's work. Any indictments? As Billy concludes, "it is evident that Gardner has picked Poe's pocket." Still, Gardner continues as a sharp-tongued defender of his own work and critic of others'; Per Winther's "An Interview with John Gardner" (*ES* 62:509–24) ranges through comments on philosophy in novels, psychology as fictional therapy, literary influences, metafictional techniques (including some fancy dodging on *The King's Indian*), and Christianity.

What the lesser-known and often more adventurous new realists are doing has prompted several good essays. In "Thomas Berger's *Little Big Man*: Contemporary Picaresque" (*Crit* 23,ii:85–96) Richard A. Betts shows how this tradition shapes Berger's imaginative perception of both novelistic form and historical material. That James Dickey is up to something less "romantic" and more "postmodern" is R. E. Foust's deduction in "*Tactus Eruditus*: Phenomenology as

Method and Meaning of James Dickey's *Deliverance*" (*SAF* 9:199–216). Samuel Coale presents a fine introduction in "'A Quality of Light': The Fiction of Paul Theroux" (*Crit* 22,iii:5–16), where the "drastic changes" within contemporary cultures and manners lead to a new style of realistic fiction. "Metamorphoses and Missing Halves: Allusions in Paul Theroux's *Picture Palace*" (*Crit* 22,iii:17–30) is Robert F. Bell's account of how the novelist juggles internal and external identities as a way of playing a "dizzying confidence game" with the contrary elements of art and life. Robert Abel conducts "Jay Neugeboren's Second Life: An Interview" (*LitR* 25:5–20) with an eye toward the writer's fifth novel, *The Stolen Jew*, emphasizing Neugeboren's success with "a certain texture, a certain 'specific gravity,' a certain depth at any given moment."

vii. Innovative Fiction

More than half of the specialized books and essays published this year on contemporary fiction treat those innovators who have radically and self-consciously departed from the styles and conventions of their predecessors, studies of whom were discussed in sections *ii–vi* above. That all the general works of 1981 (as discussed in section *i*) also focused exclusively on the innovative fictionists suggests that in terms of academic interest they may well have become the mainstream. Curiously, the most recent annal in this history of literary disruption shows evidence of an indirect return to realism—yet with as profound a difference as between a super-realistic canvas by Richard Estes and a painting by Homer or Corbet. For the very newest writers, two decades of experimentation with irrealistic techniques have made the once-simple mechanics of narrative realism an issue of great controversy and sophistication.

a. **Theoretical Overviews.** As 1981 was the year for grand syntheses in general studies of contemporary fiction, so too did it spawn several key investigations of innovative writing itself. The most important of these is Charles Russell's anthology *The Avant-Garde Today* (Illinois), which as an introduction to his long-awaited study of the avant-garde collects several dozen short texts, each prefaced by his ongoing theoretical discussion of how their formal self-reflexion and thematic disruptions "are evidence of the same avant-garde spirit that has influenced Western writing for 125 years." The innovations of Raymond Federman, Clarence Major, Alain Arias-Misson, Amiri Baraka, and Marvin Cohen (who are the American writers most completely represented) fit this mode of social criticism, which Russell sees as a "larger questioning of this culture's values and stability." Russell's categories explore the scope and progression within the contemporary scene, from Uneasy Activisim and Ambiguity of Personal Perspective through Violence, Fragmentation, and Restriction to an Aesthetics of Play and Disruption and a full analysis of the resultant Social Text.

Another key anthology, Raymond Federman's *Surfiction: Fiction Now and Tomorrow*, which in its first edition collected 19 mostly original critical essays on the subject (see *ALS 1975*, 332), has been reprinted (Swallow/Ohio) with the addition of Federman's important new essay "Fiction Today or the Pursuit of Non-Knowledge" (pp. 291–311). Following Russell, Federman argues that "Contemporary works of fiction are often experienced with a certain anxiety, not because they threaten to extinguish the short story or the novel as recognizable genres, but because they challenge the traditional bases of both cultural and aesthetic judgment." For the innovationists themselves there is the dilemma of making human statements in a world whose aesthetic has eclipsed the familiar forms of rationality; here is the "crisis of knowledge" which has generated new fictive forms—singled out are John Barth, Ronald Sukenick, Walter Abish, and as always Federman's own mentor Samuel Beckett, in whose work access to the truly human is typically reinvented: "Reduced to non-sense, non-signification, non-knowledge, the world is no longer to be known or to be explained, it is to be LIVED, to be experienced as it now re-appears in the new fiction, but no longer as an image (a representation) or an expression (vague feelings) of what we thought it was, but as a newly invented, newly discovered reality, a purified reality." Russell and Federman have identified the consequences of fictive disruption: for the author an energetically reinvented world, and for the established culture an insidious threat to its own systems of compromise. Jackson I. Cope calls this process "The Contemporary Reformation," the title and concern of his own chapter (pp. 1–8) in his and Geoffrey Green's anthology of original essays, *Novel vs. Fiction*; he also prints Federman's "What Are Experimental Novels and Why Are There So Many Left Unread?" (pp. 23–31), which examines the painful literary and academic politics which derive from this condition. That innovative fictionists and their critics are routinely denied support from the establishments they seek to change is documented by Richard Kostelanetz, whose *Autobiographies* (Santa Barbara and New York: Mudborn Press/Future Press) details the problem as he constructs "a new genre of objectively documented autobiography."

There is, of course, another side to the story, this year amply presented by Marc Chénetier in "'Even Posthumanists Get the Blues': Contemporary American Fiction and Its Critics; A Lament and a Plea" (*The American Identity*, pp. 345–62). Chénetier regrets the "surrender to irrationalism" which has pitted Ihab Hassan against "dialectics in favour of an all-embracing eclecticism" and Federman and Klinkowitz against "authoritarian models" with which conventionally realistic fiction has "become confused." The temptations are "synthetic, cybernetic, and mystical," Chénetier claims—"the politics of the last ten years have proved so disastrously inadequate to the problems at hand that there appears a general redistribution of longings and desires along a prophetic line at best, a mistily mystic one at worst, a general 'return to God as the fiction least likely to disappoint.'" For his part Chénetier questions Sukenick and anarchism and urges a moderative social vision, a posture the more radical Americans he describes would find lacking according to the sensual energies they feel are so essential to a new world.

Far from the madding crowd of postmodernist debate are three brief essays which describe specific formal advances among the innovationists. Annie Dillard's "Contemporary Prose Styles" (*TCL* 27: 207–22) contrasts the "plain" and "fancy." Among the latter may be found "fine writing" and "crank narrators," the effect for each of which depends upon a self-conscious use of voice (examples run from Nabokov to Woody Allen). "Clean prose" on the other hand descends from Chekhov and Hemingway through Robbe-Grillet to as plain a stylist as Wright Morris. Jerome Klinkowitz examines the application of Joseph Frank's principles in "The Novel as Artifact: Spatial Form in Contemporary Fiction" in *Spatial Form in Narrative*, ed. Jeffrey R. Smitten and Ann Daghistany (Cornell), pp. 37–47. Writers such as Sukenick, Abish, and Gilbert Sorrentino disregard the linear and push spatial reality into the text itself, so that "instead of being in a sense invisible, leading the reader immediately to the represented reality, the words in contemporary fiction become their own reality," making fiction less dependent upon the temporally organized world. "Innovative Uses of Some Traditional Comic Techniques in the American Novel of the Sixties" (*Traditions*, pp. 9–21; repr. *JOHJ* 4,ii:46–57) is Zoltán Abádi-Nagy's survey of "the comic perspective peculiar to the sixties" and evidenced in novels by Barth, Pynchon, Barthelme, Hawkes, Kesey, Vonnegut, and others; the argument here complements Federman's, Russell's, and Kostelanetz', for as Abádi-Nagy observes from Hungary, "the thwarted bitterness about a baffling American reality inaccessibly withdrawn behind the jungle of proliferating and manipulated appearances was a feeling not at all unjustified in the America of the fifties and sixties, in an age of political witch-hunts and assassinations."

b. **Early Innovators: Jack Kerouac, Terry Southern, William Eastlake, Paul Metcalf, and Hubert Selby.**   Groundwork for the mid-1960s' formal and thematic explosion was laid in the decade previous by writers now acknowledged as underground pioneers (even though some, such as Eastlake and Metcalf, have continued publishing into the 1980s). Jack Kerouac's masterpiece is given full study by Tim Hunt in *Kerouac's Crooked Road* (Archon/Shoe String); the classic American motifs of *On the Road* are traced through the book's textual evolution, with the author's later work *Visions of Cody* being seen as a fifth and final version of the novel.

Terry Southern is one of Maurice Charney's thematic trailblazers in *Sexual Fiction* (Methuen), which sees *Blue Movie* and *Candy* as virtual catalogues of mock-erotic techniques. In "William Eastlake's First Novel: An Account of the Making of *Go in Beauty*" (*WAL* 16:27–37) Don Graham sorts through editorial correspondence and first serial publications to establish the changes between stories and novel which produce the same "tactical problems [of] diverse thematic and structural energies" solved in Eastlake's later works.

Paul Metcalf and Hubert Selby are subjects of the second number (vol. 1) of John O'Brien's important new periodical *The Review of Contemporary Fiction*; bibliographies, memoirs, and interviews form the complement for thorough scholarly essays by Michael Stephens, Robert Buckeye, and others; the magazine also includes a few reprints such as Sorrentino's classic essay on Selby from *Kulchur*.

c. Ken Kesey, Joseph Heller, Kurt Vonnegut, and Richard Brautigan. Not only full biographical and critical explications but also substantial reinterpretations of Ken Kesey's work are offered by Barry H. Leeds in *Ken Kesey* (Ungar). The beleaguered heroism of *One Flew Over the Cuckoo's Nest*, the novel which for many critics has made Kesey a single-book author, is here amplified by an excellent analysis of *Sometimes a Great Notion* where "for every hero in the scheme of this book, there is a monster." Leeds has also followed the underground serial prepublication of Kesey's third novel, *Seven Prayers by Grandma Whittier*, which re-establishes the "richness of extended metaphor and the intense subjectivity" of Chief Broom's narration in *Cuckoo's Nest*, which was itself surely one of the technical coups which signaled the beginning of flamboyant yet accessible experimentation in fiction of the 1960s.

Joseph Heller's *Catch-22* is also a 1960s milestone, and scholarly interest in his later books bears out its critical importance. Heller's second novel is a key work in the canon of excess, which Thomas LeClair sees as the strongest contemporary style ("Joseph Heller, *Something Happened*, and the Art of Excess," *SAF* 9:245–60). In tandem with his general essays described in section *i* above, LeClair argues here that the best new fiction has "an unsettling massiveness or multiplicity of implication that exceeds the norms of conventional fiction," thus qualifying Bob Slocum's story as one of Roland Barthes's "texts of bliss" (novels which discomfortably unsettle the reader's cultural assumptions rather than enhance them). In *Something Happened* Heller is deliberately redundant, just as Pynchon is purposely overloaded; LeClair adds William Gaddis to this group by praising *JR* for its similar informational excess as discussed in section *d* below. Richard Hauer Costa's "Notes from a Dark Heller: Bob Slocum and the Underground Man" (*TSLL* 23:159–82) makes a reductive connection with Dostoevsky, that the protagonist's fears are more justifiably of threats from within himself than from without. Even more reductive is Charles Berryman's "Heller's Gold"

(*ChiR* 32,iv:108–18), which argues that in *Good as Gold* the author has refined his contradictory senses of comedy and mockery to "come home" to the Jewish-American family novel.

Dostoevsky may not shed new light on Heller, but he does on Kurt Vonnegut, as Donald M. Fiene demonstrates in "Elements of Dostoevsky in the Novels of Kurt Vonnegut" (*Dostoevsky Studies* 2:129–42). Fiene assembles a wealth of biographical and textual material not only to make the connection but to show how Vonnegut's vision is similarly "chiliastic" (the theological belief that Christ will rule on earth for one thousand years). More familiar but still valuable studies which extend conventional analyses of the various novels are Richard Giannone's "Violence in the Fiction of Kurt Vonnegut" (*Thought* 56:58–76) and C. Barry Chabot's "*Slaughterhouse-Five* and the Comforts of Indifference" (*ELWIU* 8:45–52). The most reliable critic for Vonnegut's recent work has been Peter J. Reed, whose update in the *DLB Yearbook: 1980* (pp. 116–20) relates the "sermons" of *Palm Sunday* and the public spokesmanship in *Jailbird* to Vonnegut's more familiar style. *Twentieth-Century American Science-Fiction Writers* (see chap. 22) includes Robert Group's treatment of Vonnegut's SF elements (part 2, pp. 184–90), which are more comic than strictly subgeneric; on the other hand Vonnegut's "war novel," *Slaughterhouse-Five*, is less about combat than science.

Brautigan studies too are in a lull, but 1981 produced at least one essay which ranks among the most important. Never an easy author to categorize, Richard Brautigan has since 1971 compounded the problem by "projecting the outlines of various established forms upon his own," from romances, Westerns, and mysteries to detective thrillers. To determine just how much Brautigan considers "form to be an essential part of meaning" Charles Hackenberry examines the subgeneric implications of the first of these experiments in "Romance and Parody in Brautigan's *The Abortion*" (*Crit* 23,ii:24–36).

d. **John Barth, Thomas Pynchon, John Hawkes, and William Gaddis.** These power-hitting innovationists, often ranked together in the heart of contemporary fiction's batting order because of their deep intellectual strength, inevitably produce the highest box score in scholarship. Not to say there is not a certain exasperation—in the shortest academic essay on record, "On John Barth" (*IowaR* 12,i: 147), Oliver Steele sets this sentence on an otherwise blank page:

"In his new novel, *Letters*, John Barth shows that he has thoroughly assimilated his previous work and made it his own." *Letters* is, however, of use to several critics and to Barth himself, who in "An Interview with John Barth" (*ConL* 22:1–23) tells Charlie Reilly that its epistolary form was in "the farthest corner of his imagination" from the human voice experiments of *Lost in the Funhouse*; also included are helpful notes on "The Literature of Exhaustion" and "The Literature of Replenishment." Randolph Runyon uses *Letters* as epilogue material in his *Fowles/Irving/Barthes: Canonical Variations on an Apocryphal Theme* (Miami/Ohio State); noticing that Goethe's *Werther* also contains 88 letters, he points out, "can bring to the surface qualities that weren't realized before." In "Barth, *Letters*, and the Great Tradition" (*Novel vs. Fiction*, pp. 95–115) Max F. Schulz gleefully finds that "Barth has just finished laughing away the self-reflexive Modernists of the twentieth century with his conception of an epistolary novel" where creative self-questionings are deliberately left behind.

What Barth has presumably abandoned, however, still interests scholars. From the earlier works we see Thomas Daniel Young using the loss of identity in *The End of the Road*, as a nihilistic contrast to Walker Percy's *The Moviegoer* (*The Past in the Present*, pp. 167–89), Walter L. Reed hinging his concluding contrast of the quixotic and the picaresque on *The Sot-Weed Factor* (*History of the Novel*), and Inger Christensen choosing *The Sot-Weed Factor* and *Giles Goat-Boy* as examples of aesthetically argumentative metafiction as opposed to Laurence Sterne's jesting and Vladimir Nabokov's synthesizing of art and science in *The Meaning of Metafiction* (Universitetsforlaget). That the innovative fiction of *Lost in the Funhouse* does demand a wholly new style of reader response is shown in two insightful essays, "The Siren in the Funhouse: Barth's Courting of the Reader" (*JNT* 11:64–74) by Carol Schloss and Khachig Tölölyan, and "John Barth's Four-and-Twenty Golden Umbrellas" (*MQ* 22:163–75), in which Jeff Rackham characterizes Barth as "another author like Henry Fielding, willing to step in and instruct us" as Fielding does.

"No More Sea Changes: Hawkes, Pynchon, Gaddis, and Barth" (*Crit* 23,ii:48–60) is John Z. Guzlowski's contribution to the belief that innovative fiction has caused a radical disruption in theme as well as in technique. *Death, Sleep and the Traveler, The Crying of*

Lot 49, The Recognitions, and *The Floating Opera* challenge the "traditional attitude toward the sea and the unconscious that it often represents"; there is no "sea change" in these novels where the whole idea dissolves into parody since inner self is less important than the phenomenology of surface. Hawkes figures twice in *Novel vs. Fiction*: as part of Geoffrey Green's "Relativism and the Multiple Contexts for Contemporary Fiction" (pp. 33–44) where *The Lime Twig* "functions as a depiction of an author actively wrestling with the inherent conventions of his genre," and in Donald R. Wineke's "Comic Structure and the Double Time-Scheme of Hawkes's *Second Skin*" (pp. 117–32). Wineke admits that Hawkes tends to parody conventions but insists that comedy is just as important, especially since the novel's complex temporal structure lets romantic claims be made convincingly. To this thesis Paul Witherington presents a perfect companion essay; his "Character Spin-Offs in John Hawkes's *Second Skin*" (*SAF* 9:83–91) shows how secondary characters mirror the deep sexual conflicts between Skipper and his children.

William Gaddis is one of Thomas LeClair's "novelists of excess," and while LeClair has used Roland Barthes's theories of textual bliss and pleasure to investigate Heller's *Something Happened,* this somewhat more elusive novelist prompts the critic to try a bit of reception theory (though only in its broadest reader-response applications). "In *JR*," he argues, "the quality and quantity of [Gaddis'] prose shift the reader from the conventional question—what will happen to these characters?—to a different kind of curiosity: what kind of system is this?" Gaddis is much more than the parodist or comedian, for his novels "deform at length various stylistic and formal properties" in such a way as to "require readers to question traditional principles of selection, arrangement, and imitation" ("William Gaddis, *JR*, & the Art of Excess," *MFS* 27:587–600).

Thomas Pynchon's novels, the scholarship on which may soon require its own *ALS* chapter, turn out to be fair game for reader-response studies, which this year constitute the most enlightening work. Thomas H. Schaub's *Pynchon: The Voice of Ambiguity* (Illinois) shows how Pynchon implicates the reader in his thematic and stylistic strategies; the novels may well be books of wisdom not for what they say but for how they change our ways of thought. Pynchon's voice "fills the world it describes instead of attempting to speak to us from a Jamesian vantage outside," which is one of Le-Clair's principles of excess. How such behavior "steadfastly rebuffs" the reader in his or her attempt to conventionally trace meanings is explained by John M. Muste in "The Mandala in *Gravity's Rainbow*" (*Boundary* 9,ii:163–79). Bernard Puyfhuizen looks at Pynchon's well-plotted geographical movements of outlandishly drawn characters and concludes that a radical "dislocation of reading" is the author's goal and that unless we submit to a Barthesian "bliss" we misread the text ("Starry-Eyed Semiotics: Learning to Read Sloth-rop's Map and *Gravity's Rainbow*," *PNotes* 7:5–33). Terry P. Caesar's "A Note on Pynchon's Naming" (*PNotes* 5:5–10) suggests that Pynchon's necessarily frivolous naming is an act he "performs upon his characters" which in turn reminds readers that these figures are blatant artifices.

It is therefore understandable that Pynchon's critical readers delight in collecting and comparing arcana, for it is all quite literally important; *PNotes, NMAL*, and other journals are filled with interesting tidbits too numerous to mention here. One trend is that *The Crying of Lot 49* receives almost as much attention as *Gravity's Rainbow*, including Charles Baxter's "De-faced America: *The Great Gatsby* and *The Crying of Lot 49*" (*PNotes* 7:22–37), which parallels each novel's treatment of the "tremendous burden on the individual's ability to 'read' his own past" when epochs change, and Gene H. Bell-Villada's account of what this novel owes to Jorge Luis Borges (*Borges and His Fictions* [N.Car.], pp. 269–71). Key ideas such as entropy and order come up all the time, but there is always room for an even closer reading such as David Seed's "Order in Thomas Pynchon's 'Entropy'" (*JNT* 11:135–55). There is a running debate as to whether Pynchon writes science fiction: Richard Alan Schwartz says yes ("Thomas Pynchon and the Evolution of Fiction," *SFS* 8: 165–72); Mark Siegel says no ("Thomas Pynchon and the Science Fiction Controversy," *PNotes* 7:38–42). And finally there is the New England Calvinism at the center of Pynchon's vision, a topic introduced by Scott Sanders in 1974 and this year extended by Andrzej Kopcewicz in "Elements of Puritanism in Pynchon's *Gravity's Rainbow*" (*Traditions*, pp. 133–45), in which the emphasis is on "a way out," and by the one new essay in Richard Pearce's solid collection, *Critical Essays on Thomas Pynchon* (Hall): Marcus Smith and

Khachig Tölölyan's "The New Jeremiad: *Gravity's Rainbow*" (pp. 169–86), a magnificently documented study of parallels with "the old Puritan Jeremiad" as described by Perry Miller and Sacvan Bercovitch.

e. Donald Barthelme, Jerzy Kosinski, Robert Coover, William H. Gass, and Other Innovators. In addition to their importance for the book-length syntheses described in section *i* above, Barthelme, Kosinski, and Coover have become the subjects of individual books (Tony Tanner is now at work on Gass). Lois Gordon's *Donald Barthelme* (TUSAS 416) is a scholastically thorough and critically excellent study of the novels and stories through Barthelme's most recent collection, of new work, *Great Days*; indeed, the book's value is its commitment to analyze not just a few of the stories (as have previous critics with their own points to make) but virtually all of them (Gordon's index of story references alone runs three double-columned pages). Nor is a thesis imposed; instead, Gordon lets the largest concerns of Barthelme's age take shape as cogent considerations within his art—principally "the role of language in human experience" but also the inverted roles of life and art in our media-ized society.

Elsewhere, the welcome addition of European theory to the field has produced some interesting readings of Barthelme's *The Dead Father*. A logical target for the French Freudians who follow Jacques Lacan, this novel provides Robert Con Davis matter for his own chapter, "Post-Modern Paternity: Donald Barthelme's *The Dead Father*" (pp. 169–82), in his original anthology *The Fictional Father*. "Barthelme's novel forces one to rediscover how to read a novel," Davis says (as do most other critics this year); Lacanian theory comes in when we look at Barthelme's ruptured narrative and dislocated lines of dialogue which "suggest an a-linear model of behavior foreign to the rational economies associated with paternal authority." Freud's dead father represents "the process of internalizing symbolic authority as conscience," implying a conventional form which Barthelme's fiction overthrows. In the year's best essay on Barthelme, Janusz Semrau takes the same novel as a test for the author's widely scorned "communicative capacity" and shows that by applying Jonathan Culler's structuralist model of "naturalization" (in particular "utilization by recovery") Barthelme not only is eminently readable but also does yeoman service in the reconstructing of traditional norms ("Donald Barthelme's *The Dead Father*: An Attempt at Naturalization," *Traditions*, pp. 221–36). Barthelme cannot let fathers rest, and neither can critics; Margaret M. Hallissy presents a fine comparative reading of "Barthelme's 'Views of My Father Weeping' and Dostoyevsky's *Crime and Punishment*" (*SSF* 18:77–79). Barthelme's own briefly cited comments on "distillation" and parodic reinvention (pp. 15–16) are part of David W. McCullough's valuable *People, Books, & Book People* (Harmony).

Kosinski, who at this writing is at the center of a controversy concerning accusations that he has falsified his biography and paid to have his novels ghost-written, is the subject of biographical and stylistic adulation in Byron L. Sherwin's *Jerzy Kosinski: Literary Alarmclock* (Chicago: Cabala Press). Sherwin bases his analysis of the novels on Kosinski's remarkable life story and proceeds through an analysis of his philosophies of art and self to conclude with a very apt consideration of what Kosinski admits (both in interviews and within his novel *Blind Date*) is a direct borrowing from Jacques Monod: that no plot can be imposed upon existence, and that attempting to live by systems (whether keyed to past or future) deprives us of the only reality which exists: the present moment. Kosinski is particularly eloquent on this point in his brief conversation with David W. McCullough (*People, Books, & Book People*, pp. 99–101). What even his detractors admit is a masterpiece is given further study in Geoffrey Galt Harpham's "Survival In and Of *The Painted Bird*" (*GaR* 35:142–57); the boy survives because he can face experiences without emotion, a condition Kosinski explains in his *Notes of the Author*. Kosinski himself has become scandal-sheet material thanks to his recent Hollywood experiences, as writer (for the screenplay of *Being There*) and actor (in Warren Beatty's *Reds*); what the outrageous film ending of director Hal Ashby's *Being There* does to Kosinski's original novelistic intention is explored by Robert F. Wilson in *"Being There" (Film Literature* 9:59–62).

One of the finest contributions to innovative fiction scholarship is Richard Andersen's *Robert Coover* (TUSAS 400). The issues discussed here are metafiction, fabulation, disruption and enhancement of tradition, social responsibility, history, and myth—a veritable catalogue of what is central to the fiction of our time. Coover's special talent for humor throughout this enterprise, Andersen suggests, is what makes his work specially effective; if history is to be "reworked," the comic perspective seems essential. Andersen acknowledges a unique critical debt to Larry McCaffery, who has emerged as not only the ablest Coover critic but also this reclusive author's closest and perhaps sole confidant; to the *Novel vs. Fiction* collection McCaffery contributes "Robert Coover on His Own and Other Fictions" (pp. 45–63), a wide-ranging interview which covers the inspiration for *The Origin of the Brunists* and Coover's treatment of Richard Nixon as a central character in *The Public Burning*. McCaffery's Coover update in the *DLB Yearbook: 1980* (pp. 34–43) includes analysis and editorial history of this latter novel plus the four shorter booklets Coover has published since. Robert B. Siegle agrees that Coover reinvents not only history but man's reading of it, which reader-response analysis can further elucidate ("Coover's 'The Magic Poker' and the Techniques of Fiction," *ELWIU* 8:203–17). Reader-response criticism finds Coover's fiction essential to textual re-education, as witnessed by its utility for Horst Ruthrof's *The Reader's Construction of Narrative* (Routledge).

Worthy of special attention are the American Audio Prose Library's (Columbia, Mo.) taped interviews and readings by Coover, William H. Gass, and Stanley Elkin. The extent to which language can point to itself (rather than to a conventional referent) is James Phelan's interest in *Worlds From Words* (Chicago); Gass's *Willie Master's Lonesome Wife* is the text which has the "capacity to generate multiple meanings and to make us aware of the arbitrary and interconnected codes that govern all uses of language," most emphatically where Gass's stylistics say more about themselves than about their subject.

That most radical of contemporary experimentalists, John Cage, is given a full review by Harriet Zinnes in "John Cage: Writer" (*HC* 17,vi:1–12), with emphasis on his aesthetic of randomness. The other innovationists are treated best in the *DLB* yearbooks. Noteworthy are Larry McCaffery's, Welch D. Everman's, and John O'Brien's respective major essays on Jonathan Baumbach (pp. 127–34), Federman (pp. 195–201), and Sorrentino (pp. 310–14) from the 1980 volume and Sinda J. Gregory and Larry McCaffery's introductory piece on Jerry Bumpus (pp. 168–76) from 1981. McCaffery's "Raymond Federman and the Fiction of Self-Creation" (*Par Rapport* 3–4:31–44) is a paracritical response to the fiction and supporting theory through *The Voice in the Closet*. As a warning to mariners, a notice should be posted regarding Timothy Dow Adams' *DLB Yearbook: 1981* essay on Sukenick (pp. 251–55), which mistakes biographical facts and unfairly assumes that most other critics favor Sukenick's early work above his more recent fiction.

f. Robley Wilson, John Irving, and Other Experimental Realists. "That the current vogue in realistic fiction is something other than a reaction against the full-blown, anti-mimetic experimentalism of the 1960's" is Jerome Klinkowitz' thesis in "The Experimental Realism of Robley Wilson, Jr." (*Crit* 22,iii:88–94), a perspective which applies to a broad range of writers who have come to prominence within the past ten years. For Wilson, experimental realism involves using the conventions of realism not as transparent signifiers but rather as opaque things in themselves. The progressively radical extension of this technique can be seen in Klinkowitz' subsequent investigations: "Stephen Dixon: Experimental Realism" (*NAR* 266,ii: 54–56), "Walter Abish and the Surfaces of Life" (*GaR* 35:416–20), "Kenneth Gangemi" (*American Book Review* 3,iii:12–13), and "Postcards From Thomas Glynn" (*Par Rapport* 3–4:26–30).

The most widely read of the experimental realists is John Irving, and the structural complexity of his work is examined by Michael Priestly in "Structure in the Worlds of John Irving" (*Crit* 23,i:82–96) and by Randolph Runyon in *Fowles/Irving/Barthes* (Miami/Ohio State). Priestly finds that Irving's characters wish to order the universe as novelists do—structure is ordering, and order is everything. Runyon makes fine use of incremental self-reference in *The Water-Method Man* and *The World According to Garp* as part of his larger thesis that reading widely separate texts with one's mind on a certain perspective (here the Book of Tobit from the Old Testament Apocrypha) reveals "a unity they had not revealed before, both in themselves and among each other." Johan Thielemans pushes Irving's work even further, showing "that between the fields of mimesis and irrealism there need not be a radical abyss" ("*The World According to Garp* or Postmodernism as a Tradition," *Traditions*, pp. 253–63). Irving's own thoughts on his novels' themes (vio-

lence, the sheltering family, cultural dispersion) are capsulized in
Alvin P. Sanoff's "A Conversation With John Irving" (*U.S. News &
World Report* 26 Oct.:70–71).

That Thomas McGuane reached a turning point in both his literary career and fictive style with the novel *Panama* is Larry McCaffery's thesis in *DLB Yearbook: 1980* (pp. 67–70). Guy Davenport's
second collection of stories attracts Robert A. Morace's attention
in "Invention in Guy Davenport's *Da Vinci's Bicycle*" (*Crit* 22,iii:
71–87); Davenport, Morace reports, is the single experimentalist
John Gardner admires in *On Moral Fiction* and belongs there because
of his search for affirmative human values. Central to the understanding of this whole new way of combining self-conscious style with
moral substance is Davenport's massive *The Geography of the Imagination* (North Point), 40 essays on a variety of subjects yet touching
upon the central issue of artistic self-creation.

viii. Subgenres

a. The New Journalism. In recent decades the conventions of journalism have been challenged as thoroughly as those of fiction, and
John Hellmann's *Fables of Fact: The New Journalism as New Fiction*
(Illinois) makes a convincing argument that the same cultural
change triggered each disruption. "Fiction is the literary form most
concerned with interior consciousness," Hellmann explains, "while
journalism is that most concerned with public fact. New journalism
attempts to deal with a world in which the latter has, at an un-
assimilable pace, entered the former." Norman Mailer shows how
literature can deal with "the great events and issues of a world in
which even the concept of reality has been doubtful"; further along
in the New Journalism's development Hunter S. Thompson endows
his narrative with its own textual reality; Tom Wolfe has been best
at perceiving and creating patterns in a fragmented society; and at
the radical extreme Michael Herr in *Dispatches* creates "an intensely
self-reflective work in which the act of writing as much as that of
traveling forms a fable of self-discovery." Because its sound analyses
are combined with such helpful correlations to the larger culture
and its styles of fiction, Hellmann's study is the definitive word on
the New Journalism.

Tom Wolfe's creatively fictional use of American manners and any number of Vietnam reports continue to dominate studies of the New Journalism. Wolfe's attempt at a comprehensive theory behind his method is given full analysis by David Lodge in *Working with Structuralism* (Routledge), a predictably insightful book which also deals with broader questions in contemporary literary history. Peter McInerney's " 'Straight' and 'Secret' History in Vietnam War Literature" (*ConL* 22,ii:187–204) singles out Herr's *Dispatches* as one book which celebrates "the fictive character of historical reconstructions"; there is a great difference between "story" and "history," McInerney believes, as indicated by the tensions between Ron Kovic's *Born on the Fourth of July* (which "does not recognize the fictive character of [its] historical reconstruction") and Philip Caputo's *A Rumor of War* (which does).

b. **Science Fiction.** For a review of the *DLB*'s *Twentieth-Century American Science Fiction Writers,* see chap. 22. Mark Rose's *Alien Encounters* (Harvard) offers good readings of the standard SF classics in the process of defining the genre, to the point that this book surpasses its predecessors in terms of supportive analysis. One of Rose's subcategories is given exhaustive study by Rosemary Jackson in *Fantasy: The Literature of Subversion* (Methuen); the complement here to seminal works by Eric Rabkin and Tzvetan Todorov is that Jackson uses psychoanalytic theory to explore both earlier SF classics and very recent mainstream developments by Barthelme, Pynchon, and Coover.

Single-author studies are again the almost exclusive province of the Ungar "Recognitions" series: Timothy O'Reilly's *Frank Herbert,* Lucy Menger's *Theodore Sturgeon,* and Barbara K. Bucknall's *Ursula K. LeGuin,* which are here ranked in descending order from the genuinely insightful to the routinely recapitulative. A noteworthy shorter study is John Grigsby's "Asimov's *Foundation* Trilogy and Herbert's *Dune* Trilogy: A Vision Reversed" (*SFS* 8,ii:149–55), which argues that Herbert as "a literary-romanticist philosopher" patterned his own trilogy on Asimov's by alternately following and reversing various ideas about civilization and religion.

c. **Women Writers and Women in Fiction.** Once again, many women writers and their critics have preferred to let the work of evaluation take place within the mainstream. There are, however, several studies whose necessary sexual politics make them appropriate for special classification. Prominent among these are Maurice Charney's *Sexual Fiction* (Methuen), Elaine Showalter's "Rethinking the Seventies: Women Writers and Violence" (*AR* 39:156–70), and Sally Allen McNall's *Who Is in the House?* Charney sees Gael Greene's *Blue Skies, No Candy* as satire of the "performative, consumerist values" which have replaced eroticism in sexually oriented fiction; Erica Jong's *Fear of Flying* is read more simply as a mirror image of *Portnoy's Complaint* (the forbidden as attractive). Showalter's essay sees a more seriously violent style of male sexuality rampant, in which "Control, autonomy, possibility are mocked by the avenger's fist, or phallus, or knife" (the prime text here is Judith Rossner's *Looking for Mr. Goodbar*); there is even a new subgenre, "intruder novels," typified by Diane Johnson's *The Shadow Knows*. McNall notes that for the past two centuries of fiction heroines have struggled between dependence and independence, and argues that unresolved crises associated with the preconscious developmental tasks of individuation, acceptance of the shadow self, and adjustment to the countersexual self are behind it all. Readers are themselves subject to the same divisions which such unresolved developmental tasks create and find in such fiction a momentary healing.

Eclipsing the critics' boundaries this year are Shirley Ann Grau, Grace Paley, and Joan Didion. Paul Schlueter's excellent *Shirley Ann Grau* (TUSAS 382) explains how typifying Grau as a southern writer is equally limiting, for her complementary senses of power and of love transcend regional considerations; also to be faulted is her characterization, which Schlueter finds weak. In "Mrs. Hegel-Shtein's Tears" (*PR* 48:217–23) Marianne DeKoven argues that Grace Paley is something of an experimental realist who can "reconcile the demands of avant-garde or postmodern form for structural openness and the primacy of surface with the seemingly incompatible demands of traditional realist material for orchestrated meaning and cathartic emotion." Without Yeats's line "Things fall apart; the center cannot hold," articles like Victor Strandberg's "Passion and Delusion in *A Book of Common Prayer*" (*MFS* 27:225–42) could not exist; but neither could Joan Didion's fiction, and Strandberg demonstrates perfectly how her feeling for "the emergence of sexual adventurism as a final bastion of meaning in modern life" creates both a novelistic and journalistic vision.

d. Native Americans and Western Fiction. Per Seyersted, notable for his pioneering work on Kate Chopin, has conducted "Two Interviews with Leslie Marmon Silko" (*AmerSS* 13:17–33), which include comments on her "technical skill as a storyteller as a birthright," early reading influences, and the special pressures brought upon her and other Native Americans' works by the fame of "People like [Jerome] Rothenberg and Gary Snyder" who have "perfected the 'white shamanism' movement."

Two white males who've resisted the call to medicine-manhood are Benjamin Capps and Larry McMurtry—Archer County, Texas, natives who use that region's past and present for both substance and form in their work. Ernest B. Speck's *Benjamin Capps* (WWS 49) stresses Capps's historical achievements within the tradition of realism, while Raymond L. Neinstein's "Afterword" to the University of New Mexico Press reissue of *All My Friends Are Going to Be Strangers* notes the "elegaic" trend in this and McMurtry's five previous books as he successively casts off the contemporary materials of his formation as a writer (mythic horsemen, small-town claustrophobia, and various young adult Texan problems in the worlds of intellect, art, and academe). *All My Friends*, Neinstein shows, is "a regional novelist's farewell to regional literature" and a prolegomena to his subsequent novels, which look eastward in both theme and technique.

University of Northern Iowa

16. Poetry: 1900 to the 1940s

Richard Crowder

The American Council of Learned Societies *Newsletter* 32 (Summer–Fall 1981):17–33 announced its ACLS fellowships and grants-in-aid for 1980–81. Of the 223 awards in various categories, only one went for a subject covered in this chapter—only one, a critical biography of Robert Frost, proposed by William H. Pritchard, professor of English at Amherst College. The year 1981, however, was a good year for scholarship on poets of the first four decades of this century. There were critical books on Marquis, Masters, Winters, H. D., and Moore plus volumes of reprinted essays on Crane, Cummings, Frost, and Stevens. There were letter collections of Bynner, Bishop and Tate, and Frost, and two biographical works each on Frost and Sandburg. It was a lean year for Stevens scholarship, with no book-length studies at all, but for Williams there was Paul Mariani's big biography, easily the most impressive contribution of the year to this area. Dissertation writers also were active, as 36 dissertations were recorded in *DAI* 41,vii–xii, and 42,i–vi, entirely or in part devoted to the poets of this chapter: one each on Lizette Woodworth Reese, Donald Davidson, MacLeish, Winters, Cummings, Charles Reznikoff, Vachel Lindsay, Bishop, Tate, Louise Bogan, Jeffers; four on Frost, five on Crane, ten on Williams, and 13 on Stevens.

i. General Studies

Of four articles of more or less general coverage, one is a narrative in *MMis* 9:43–53 entitled "Harriet Monroe, Margaret Anderson, and the Spirit of the Chicago Renaissance." The author retells the story of the founding of *Poetry* and plays up Monroe's pique at not being recognized by either Babette Deutsch or, even more, Margaret Anderson, the editor of *The Little Review.* "Monroe represented balance and Anderson represented exuberance." Whereas Monroe's chief loyalty was to Chicago and to the journal that supported the renaissance, Anderson appears to have been loyal to the principle of human growth. The two of them differed in age, "in vision, in sensibility, and in style." This account shows us another side of the complexity of the Chicago literary scene after 1912.

James Thorpe in *Gifts of Genius: Treasures of the Huntington Library* (Huntington, 1980) describes briefly in his last chapter, "Frontiersmen of the Spirit: Four Masters of Twentieth-Century Literature," the life and personality of Stevens (pp. 205–09) and of Conrad Aiken (pp. 210–13) as related to the library holdings of the work of these poets and their friends. For example, Thorpe quotes Stevens' "The World as Meditation" "reproduced from Stevens's own copy of the *Hudson Review* for 1952, where it first appeared in print." The author also comments with pride, "There are sixty-five valuable letters from Eliot to Aiken in our collection." These are not scholarly passages, but statements echoing the pleasures of a dilettante.

Peter Revell's *Quest in Modern American Poetry* (Barnes and Noble) develops the theme of seeking for (not necessarily the finding of) restored meaning and harmony in the chaotic world that science and philosophy have left us with. His first chapter paints Walt Whitman as a great American, but holding theories and beliefs no longer valid. The author points to the influences both direct and indirect of psychologist Sigmund Freud and philosopher Henri Bergson.

Then in chapters roughly chronological in order of composition Revell close reads long poems by five of our major poets of the modern period. Aiken's *The Divine Pilgrim* is quite clearly Freudian. *The Cantos* of Ezra Pound and T. S. Eliot's *Four Quartets* are anti-Freudian. (Eliot's work draws from Bergson, though it goes beyond the Frenchman into timelessness.) H. D.'s *Trilogy* (*The Walls Do Not Fall, Tribute to the Angels,* and *The Flowering of the Rod*) is deeply Freudian though with a Christian bias. Williams rejects Christianity for the material world with no reliance whatsoever on metaphysics. Because of his theme and scheme Revell omits consideration of Robinson, Crane, Frost, Jeffers, and other interesting figures of the modern period, but there are enough insights and coverage in this book to give one solid point of view of our poetry in the first half of the 20th century.

A short readable account of contact with American poets (and an artist, Georgia O'Keeffe) is the English poet Charles Tomlinson's *Some Americans: A Personal Record* (Calif.) The opening chapter, "Beginnings," is of special interest here. The author details his gradual introduction to such poets as Moore, Stevens, Crane, and Williams. In sharp, telling phrases he is able to mirror his reaction to these older poets. He has been happy to emulate "the three-ply cadences" and "measure" of Williams. (By "measure" he means "those structural principles that subsist in the language of poetry when one has abandoned traditional metrics.") In Winters the man, he was surprised to find not only the expected "dignity and dimension" but also "a capacity for friendship." He was pleased to learn of Moore's tremendous admiration for John Ruskin. ("He knew everything, didn't he!") In Crane's "Voyages" he admired the division between precise evocation and synesthesia. Stevens' "Thirteen Ways of Looking at a Blackbird" opened up for him a possible release from "rather predictable stanzas." *Some Americans* makes a good and profitable evening's read.

ii. Mencken, Marquis, Rodenburg, and Bynner

H. L. Mencken was a very bad poet. His first book was a volume of admittedly "horrible" teen-age verse influenced by Victorian romanticism and burlesque shows. In all probability the author tried to suppress the book, though it is now a collector's item, one copy recently bringing $3,250 at auction. Robert F. Nardini describes this phenomenon in "H. L. Mencken's *Ventures in Verse*" (*SAQ* 80:195–205).

Lynn Lee's *Don Marquis* (TUSAS 393) devotes a few chapters to the columnist's verse, chiefly the books about Archy and Mehitabel. "Archy is the artist encased in a roach's body who feels superior to much of his current environment. Mehitabel makes few distinctions between individuals in her pursuit of life and love." Lee says the two creatures defy classification but are successful because Marquis used "techniques common to American humor." Their creator could, in the words of E. B. White, "be profound without sounding self-important, or even self-conscious." As poet in other areas Marquis was good at comedy, not so good, for the most part, at noncomic verse (readable and competent but not gifted). Marquis as columnist, novelist, short story writer, and playwright is beyond the scope of our comments.

A minor addition to the roll of Illinois poets is the blind Louis William Rodenberg (1891–1966), who relied for subject matter on the memory of scenes of his boyhood and the accounts of his mother. Forty poems have been privately published in *Poetical Writings*; others are still in manuscript. At his death he left about $4,000 for the publication of 38 more poems. "Pieces in the Quilt" (written in the 1940s) is more than 300 lines long, of which Walter B. Hendrickson has made an extensive analysis in "Louis William Rodenberg, An Illinois Poet" (*WIRS* 4:176–91). The author recognizes that the poems are not great but argues that they recreate late 19th-century midwestern farm life with sensitivity and faithfulness.

Witter Bynner's poems are not conceded to be first rate, but as a person he was delightful and articulate. His *Selected Letters*, well chosen and skillfully edited by James Kraft (Farrar), give an account of the man's life and picture him as guileless, loyal, and sensitive. He makes interesting though not very profound comments on his own work and the work of his contemporaries (e.g., Millay and Amy Lowell). Withal, Bynner was an extremely intelligent, cultivated man, and his letters are highly readable and totally charming and graceful.

iii. Sandburg, Masters, Bishop, Tate, Winters, Jeffers, and Long

Lilla S. Perry met Carl Sandburg in Saratoga Springs in 1918 at a library meeting and invited him to Los Angeles. Subsequently the poet made frequent visits to California to give programs. Mrs. Perry's *My Friend Carl Sandburg*, ed. E. Caswell Perry (Scarecrow), is an anecdotal recounting of the author's contacts with the poet. It relies on 147 of Mrs. Perry's letters (Rare Book Room, Univ. of Ill.) and her extensive collection of newspaper clippings as well as her journal entries. Except for the personal details (often tiresome) the book adds little to our understanding of Sandburg as man and poet. Equally slight is Norman Corwin's *Date with Sandburg* (Calif. State Univ., Northridge: Santa Susana Press). Corwin was the compiler of *The World of Carl Sandburg, A Stage Presentation* (1961), which starred Bette Davis.

Of background interest to readers of Edgar Lee Masters, Hermann R. Muelder's "The Naming of Spoon River" (*WIRS* 4:105–14) contains no direct mention of the famous *Anthology* except to say that Masters' poetry has made Spoon River "widely known." Ian F. A. Bell says that Pound admired *Spoon River Anthology* and even echoed Masters' "directness and simplicity." "In the Real Tradition: Edgar Lee Masters and *Hugh Selwyn Mauberley*" (*Criticism* 23: 141–54) Bell cites a number of passages in *Mauberley* that quietly follow the Masters rhythm, the unornamented particularities, and what Alice Corbin Henderson called the "sense of tragedy." Especially thus characterized are the war poems in the Pound work.

Ronald Primeau has given an extended critical look at Masters' total literary output, the more than 50 books he published from 1915 to his death in 1950 and even the posthumous works. *Beyond "Spoon River": The Legacy of Edgar Lee Masters* (Texas) assumes in general a sympathetic view. The author paints the poet's classical background enriched by a lifetime of omnivorous reading, finding in Masters an astute critical sense without a fondness for critics, in many of whom Masters thought he discovered malice and even stupidity. Contrary to general unconsidered opinion Masters continued to protect and praise his native Midwest. Further, he was an especial foe of formalism, snobs, and the imitators of Europe.

Primeau studies with care the profound influence on the poet of Greek culture and of German, Goethe in particular, and of Emerson and Whitman. Among British poets Masters proves to have been particularly interested in Shelley and Browning. This book, thoughtful and broad-ranging, places much more emphasis on the influences than on the poems themselves. What needs to be done now is to use this research in a thorough reading of the works themselves. If taken seriously, Primeau's book could do for Masters after *Spoon River* what the poet could not do for himself, lift his reputation to a much higher level in American literary history than it has so far achieved.

The Republic of Letters in America: The Correspondence of John Peale Bishop and Allen Tate, ed. Thomas D. Young and John J. Hindle (Kentucky), is divided chronologically into three sections. The first, 1929–34, presents the letters exchanged in France (and Tate's letters to France after his return to America). They are statements of encouragement and of precise, concrete criticism of two intelligent southerners' work, recording in addition their concerned distrust of utopian remedies for the social and economic ruin of the time. The next section, 1934–39, reflects the changes of place for the two— for Tate, Tennessee, North Carolina, New Jersey; for Bishop, Connecticut, Louisiana, Massachusetts. The letters continue (though less frequently) the mutual close reading of each other's essays and poems. The last section, 1939–44, covers the years of World War II to Bishop's death in April 1944. The entire collection is civilized in the highest sense. Tate wrote Bishop in 1933 that in critically approving excellent writing he was doing only his "simple duty by the republic of letters (a kind of republic that can't exist in a political republic)."

In a special issue of 300 pages *Southern Review* (17:681–982) pays homage to Yvor Winters with 19 essays by as many hands. There are reminiscences by Thom Gunn and Turner Cassity. There are papers presented at a critical symposium at the South Atlantic MLA in November 1979, including contributions from Donald E. Stanford, Albert Guérard, Donald Davie, and Ashley Brown. In addition a sheaf of essays deals with a variety of subjects such as the link with the English Renaissance, the relation to Mallarmé, the style, the verse experiments, a reading of "To the Holy Spirit," and numerous others. The entire issue is a fine tribute to a poet of undeservedly limited readership.

Elizabeth Isaacs discusses briefly Winters' life, personality, and stance as critic in *An Introduction to the Poetry of Yvor Winters* (Swallow); then she turns to the poetry, heretofore neglected more than the criticism. In his poems she sees him as a strictly virtuous man, using a concept both moral and rational to hold the poetic elements together aesthetically. She examines the details of his themes, content, forms, tone, imagery and symbols, diction and syntax, and concludes with a 50-page section explicating 20 of the poems. She writes a simple, clear, unpretentious prose and accomplishes her purpose: to *introduce* the reader to Winters' poetry.

Frederic I. Carpenter's "The Inhumanism of Robinson Jeffers" (*WAL* 16:19–25) considers "inhumanism" as both negative (philosophy) and positive (poetic idea). The author follows the term from medieval literature through 20th-century thinking (both secular and religious), which was anathema to Jeffers. In *Robinson Jeffers*

Newsletter 58 and 59 are published various items of specific interest to Jeffers scholars. An article by Robert Zaller, "The Birth of the Hero: Robinson Jeffers' *The Tower beyond Tragedy*" (58:5–16), concludes: "But it was not for Jeffers to rest content with a single ascent of the mountains of mystical peace. The serpent whose fatal bite signifies 'less than nothing' to Orestes is Jeffers' reminder to himself that no philosophy can render him finally invulnerable, that no renunciation of desire in the mind can kill it in the flesh." *RJN* 59:18–33 preserves a record of the friendship between two of our poets. Arnold T. Schwab, in "Jeffers and Millay: A Literary Friendship," has brought together letters, telegrams, and records of visits for his purpose. Supporting items include favors, exchanges of books, introductions, and other symbols of attachment.

Robert Burlingame has analyzed James H. Maguire's selection of 40 poems by Haniel Long (1888–1956) written between 1920 and 1945 and now collected under the title *My Seasons*. In "Haniel Long: His Seasons" (*SWR* 66:21–38) the author indicates that these are only a few of Long's total output and quotes the poet as to his purpose: to "create/A place of peace, in the world's shift and smother." According to Burlingame, if this poet of the Southwest was not great, he at least wrote some very good lines which should not be disregarded.

iv. Crane, H. D., Moore, Lowell, Cummings, MacLeish, and Robinson

Alan Trachtenberg has assembled *Hart Crane: A Collection of Critical Essays* (Prentice-Hall), just what the title suggests, a group of scholarly studies that have appeared elsewhere. Students of Crane will find this grouping serviceable. The entire subject and argument of Alfred Hanley's *Hart Crane's Holy Vision: "White Buildings"* (Duquesne) would have rubbed William Carlos Williams the wrong way as not "in the American grain." But Crane's temperament was quite opposite to Williams'. (Williams avoided Crane's acquaintance until only a couple of years before the younger poet's suicide.) It is reflected in the renaming of *HCN* as *The Visionary Company*.

Using music as an analogue, Michael Sharp calls attention to the similarity in structure between Crane's *The Bridge* and Vincent

D'Indy's *Istar Variations*. Both compositions begin with complex variations and end with a simple statement of theme. *The Bridge* moves through initial complexities to the concluding harmonies of "Atlantis." "Theme and Free Variations: The Scoring of Hart Crane's *The Bridge*" (*AN&Q* 81:197–213) proceeds to point out Crane's deep interest in the music of Bloch, Ravel, Scriabin, and other contemporary composers and discloses analogies with and echoes of music throughout the eight "movements" of the poem. For example, "Cape Hatteras" is a nocturne; "The Tunnel" is a variation on the dark night of the soul; " 'Atlantis' is an evening serenade which courts the ideal." Sharp has written an ingenious and useful essay.

John Montague's *The Rough Field* and Crane's *The Bridge* attempt to solve several similar problems concerning a sense of place embodying "the natural consciousness at a particular time" (Crane, America in the 1920s; Montague, Ireland in the 1960s). Crane uses the symbol of Brooklyn Bridge in much the same way Montague employs his family's heritage, Garvaghey ("rough field"). Woman as symbol is also useful to both men: Crane, Pocahontas as sexual object; Montague, various women as sufferers and firebrands. Both works weave together old-world and new-world strands. Sidney B. Poger makes these comparisons in "Crane and Montague: 'The Pattern History Weaves'" (*Éire* 16,iv:114–24).

Helge Normann Nilsen follows up last year's book, *Hart Crane's Divided Vision* (*ALS 1980*, 367–68), with a brief study of the way the poet "tried to embrace and render the contemporary American scene in a creative act of selfless love," with results that are "fragile, daring and vulnerable." Nilsen's essay is titled " 'Surrender to the Sensations of Urban Life': A Note on the Poetry of Hart Crane" (*EA* 34:322–26). Allen Grossman uses the four-line "The Return" (one of the final poems) as a highly important review of Crane's "myth and life." "Crane was not merely a poet: he was a man of unmistakable gifts who risked everything upon poetry, who had for whatever reason no other means of presence in the world, and whose art therefore attests a perilous extremity of concern unaccountable except on the hypothesis of a life at stake." Grossman finds in his work "the ways in which poetry can and cannot effect human purposes." This essay, "Hart Crane and Poetry: A Consideration of Crane's Intense Poetics with Reference to 'The Return'" (*ELH* 48:841–79), is rich in compact detail, explications, and linkages inseparable from now on from a full reading of Crane.

The New York artist Marsden Hartley (with both his painting and his verse) was particularly influential in Crane's aesthetic growth, says Robert K. Martin in "Painting and Primitivism: Hart Crane and the Development of an American Expressionist Esthetic" (*Mosaic* 14,iii:49–62). Touched by both postimpressionism and expressionism, Crane felt akin to Hartley's interest in the Indian of New Mexico —his harmony with nature and his frank sensuality. In believing that painting is a spiritual art, Crane found fellowship not only with Hartley but through him with Wasili Kandinsky.

Timothy W. Crusius seeks to establish Kenneth Burke as a poet of "artistic integrity and unity" and to relate the poems to Burke's other writings. Among other points he pictures the poet's comic strategy as "athletic," complex, and self-aware. In "Kenneth Burke on his 'Morbid Selph': The Collected Poems as Comedy" (*CEA* 43, iv:18–32) he shows how Burke turns "language upon itself" for the final "pragmatic freedom" of comedy, a countering of "counternature" and its burdens. This is an interesting study of an apparently underrated poet.

The work of two important women poets is brought to the fore this year. *Psyche Reborn: The Emergence of H. D.* (Indiana) is feminist but not shrill. Susan Stanford Friedman divides H. D.'s development into an epic artist into two parts: the role of psychoanalysis and that of religion. She explores the poet's experience with Freud, with whom she enjoyed arguing as artist against scientist, as woman against man. The chapters on the occult and the mystic analyze her own woman-centered mythmaking and her confrontation of the patriarchal tradition. A brief introduction presents biographical details relevant to the study as a whole. Friedman's work is a strong contribution to the growing movement placing H. D. where she should be —in the center of modernist poetry.

Friedman with Rachel Blau DuPlessis puts H. D.'s colloquia with Freud under a microscope in " 'Woman Is Perfect': H. D.'s Debate with Freud" (*FSt* 7:417–30). The authors explain the poet's not publishing "The Master" as honoring Freud's dictum that she must keep her identities separate. Not until the years of World War II, when she was writing *Trilogy*, did her identity as poet-priestess reach full fruition. Whereas in the suppressed "The Master" she had showed an "impulse to prophesy a vision of woman which can counter the 'man-strength' of patriarchy," in *Trilogy* she dared the role of prophet that Freud, now dead since 1939, had been convinced she should repress.

Written in 1920 after her Imagist period was over, the poet's "Helios and Athene" was generated by a trip to Greece at the willing expense of Bryher (Winifred Ellerman), her long-time companion. Adalaide Morris in "Reading H. D.'s 'Helios and Athene'" (*IowaR* 12,ii–iii:155–63) asserts that, as opposed to the "objectivity" of the Imagist poems, this undertaking "is impassioned mythology and history, biography and psychology, esthetics, epistemology, and metaphysics," as difficult as the poet's late long works. Packed with esoteric references, it is totally informed with "the possessed/possessing powers of imagination." Morris guides the reader carefully through the labyrinthine complexities of a poem that leads eventually and inevitably to *Trilogy* and *Helen in Egypt*.

The other woman, Marianne Moore, has had more attention over the years than H. D. This new book, *Marianne Moore: Imaginary Possessions* by Bonnie Costello (Harvard), criticizes Moore's "structures, images, and modes of representation." Its various chapters explain the functioning of symbolism in her poetry; her "capacity for fact" in description; her battle against complacency ("sweetened combat" that converts "anxiety to gusto"); her delight in brightness, play of colors, and changes of form and shape. They also consider form as argument and the poet's reliance on the visual arts. The last chapter studies three of her critical essays in detail as examples "of her predilection for and strategy of indirection." The "Epilogue" presents Moore as a staunch American. Costello's strategy is based on extended analyses of several poems. (She devotes eight and a half long pages to "Poetry.") For the most part the chapters are absorbing in their attention to detail. The author points out a need for "a truly complete edition of Moore's poems" and generously indicates new routes of investigation that other scholars could well undertake. "Moore scholarship is in its infancy." Costello's book is to be highly recommended to devotees of the poetry of this century.

"Amy Lowell and the Orient" by Michael Katz (*CLS* 18:124–40) offers biographical details linking Lowell with the Far East and analysis of the techniques of Oriental verse that Lowell absorbed from a study of Japanese art, her discussion of Oriental poetry with such persons as Pound and John Gould Fletcher, and her translation of Chinese poems with Florence Ayscough. In 1918 she met A. Edward Newton, a manufacturer of electrical equipment in Philadelphia and an aficionado of English literature, who had built up a fine library and was contributing fascinating essays to *Atlantic Monthly*. Housed in the Houghton Library, their correspondence extends from 23 December 1918 to 11 March 1925, two months before Lowell's death. Maxwell Luria has introduced readers to the letters, full of literary gossip and spicy judgments, in "Miss Lowell and Mr. Newton: The Record of a Literary Friendship" (*HLB* 29:5–34).

Norman Friedman admits that Cummings had a great influence on his life. In "Knowing and Remembering Cummings" (*HLB* 29: 117–34) he traces his relationship with the poet from his own high school days in Brooklyn in the 1940s through his days as a graduate student at Harvard and his first full-time job, teaching at the University of Connecticut, and on at last to the beginnings of Friedman's second book on Cummings, published in 1964 (*ALS 1964*, 186–87) after Cummings' death in 1962. This is an intimate and warm-hearted memoir. In an altogether different vein Richard D. Cureton has given us another of his linguistic-aesthetic studies drawn from his 1980 Illinois dissertation (*ALS 1979*; 320–21 and *ALS 1980*, 359). "E. E. Cummings: A Case Study of Iconic Syntax" (*Lang&S* 14:183–215) demonstrates in detail how iconic syntax was joined with orthographic and phonetic structures to show how fully Cummings perceived the world. The author studies a good many poems to point up the contribution of "syntactic icons" to literary technique, stylistics, and literary criticism, first grouping them into three large classes —quantity, quality, and relation, each of these then examined for their spatial and temporal characteristics. Cureton's work underscores the importance and richness of the typology of syntactic icons as a forceful means of stylistic analysis. This is a bold pioneer study in the growing tradition of linguistics.

The eighth volume in *The American Critical Tradition*, ed. M. Thomas Inge (cf. Linda Wagner's *Robert Frost* reviewed in *ALS 1977*, 356), *E. E. Cummings: The Critical Reception*, ed. Lloyd N. Dendinger (Burt Franklin) opens with an examination of the critics' attitudes toward the typography, the lyricism (and associations with Elizabethan and romantic poetry), as well as the often derisive and amused reviewers' tone in considering language and style. The first review is dated 10 May 1922; the last, 19 July 1959. (Some books received little or no critical attention at all.) Each of the 16 volumes by Cummings is given a section which ends with a checklist of reviews in addition to those quoted in the section. Like the others in this series the book should be extremely helpful in providing the researcher the extant comments ready to hand (both sound and shallow) from the newspapers and periodicals current with the publication of the books.

Richard Meryman's "Archibald MacLeish: The Enlarged Life" (*Yankee*, Jan.: 72–77, 116–118) records an interview made up largely of autobiographical recollections—life at Hotchkiss, Harvard, and Yale, in Massachusetts and Paris—and pictures of people MacLeish knew, especially Frost, who "always felt perfectly free and easy about saying what he pleased to me. And I was always careful never to say what I pleased to him." MacLeish intended his epic *Conquistador* to start a movement away from Eliot's despair and nostalgia toward a "communal heroism." Hence his effort to restore traditional epic values. In "The Problems of Modern Epic: MacLeish's *Conquistador*" (*PLL* 17:292–306) Michael Cavanaugh examines the poet's prose of this period to show that *Conquistador* is far more controversial than it might appear. The poet felt that the world after 1929 needed a poetry less "fine" than, say, Eliot's. Cavanaugh insists that *Conquistador* is not a celebration of the Spanish conquest, but an example of "the American metaphor" of the journey to the West; in fact, "the victory sometimes (often) seems to defeat itself." In this poem MacLeish was "urging a reluctant generation to travel into a 'new age.'" He wanted to enrich the nostalgia of Eliot by acts and attitudes of heroism.

Ronald E. McFarland sees linkages and parallels between poems of two unlikely yokefellows—an idle courtier of Charles I and, 300 years later, a quiet, industrious New Englander of Puritan stock. He makes his comments in "Some Observations on Carew's 'Song' and Robinson's 'For a Dead Lady'" (*MarkhamR* 10:29–32). That Isolt and Tristram hold approaches to love basically different from those of society in general is the unsurprising thesis of S. L. Clark and Julia N. Wasserman in "'Time Is a Casket': Love and Temporality in Robinson's *Tristram*" (*CLQ* 17:112–16). The authors indicate that even Andred and Mark recognize the difference. For society love is limited by time; though the love of Tristram and Isolt occurs in time, it goes beyond time. Isolt of the White Hands cannot appreciate this attitude: she can only wait in time and "cannot go beyond it." For Isolt of Ireland and for Tristram the death of their bodies is not the end of their love (they believe).

v. Frost

Edward Connery Lathem (with the help of R. H. Winnick) has reduced to one volume the three-volume life of Frost produced by Lawrance Thompson and Winnick (*ALS 1966*, 190; *ALS 1970*, 288–89; *ALS 1977*, 356). The task has involved cutting, splicing, and slightly altering the wording of the original where unavoidable. With footnotes omitted, paragraphs joined, and transitions sometimes changed, the book has lost Thompson's flavor, though the essential facts are still presented. Not for scholars, the book will no doubt prove sufficient for the general reader. It is called simply *Robert Frost: A Biography* (Holt). Still another examination of the poet's life is found in Natalie S. Bober's *A Restless Spirit: The Story of Robert Frost* (Atheneum), its theme reflected in the title. A children's book, its style is unfortunately plodding in contrast to the Frost quotations it introduces. A warm-hearted prologue is by Robin Hudnut, a granddaughter of the poet.

Robert Frost and Sidney Cox: Forty Years of Friendship ed. William Evans (New England) is a collection of 134 letters exchanged between the frequently cantankerous and contentious poet and his ever-faithful adorer, a college teacher. They often differed, but they were always friends, thanks, one is inclined to think, to the long-suffering character of Cox. The first letter is from Frost in England the day after Christmas 1912. The last one is from Cox from Dartmouth College dated 22 September 1951. A "Coda" presents 13 letters from Cox's widow and an editor at New York University Press, wrapping up the story of the Frost-Cox connection. A solidly compiled index is a godsend in tracking down details otherwise lost. Evans also quotes a long family letter (19 Feb. 1916) from Cox describing in detail a poetry reading by Frost the professor had arranged in Schenectady in "Frost's 'Sound in Sense' and a Popular Audience" (*AL* 53:116–23). Frost made an extremely favorable impression on his sympathetic audience.

In "Robert Frost and the Imagists: The Background of Frost's

'Sentence Sounds'" (*NEQ* 54:467–80) John F. Sears re-emphasizes
that Lowell and Pound both found many Imagist qualities in the
early Frost, but Frost himself refused to join their movement, for he
felt that the Imagists were too narrow in scope. He briefed Louis
Untermeyer on his theory of "sentence sounds," and Untermeyer in
turn developed Frost's differences from the Imagists, who, because
they attempted to describe his work in their own terms, caused him
to articulate and even exaggerate his own theories concerning the
importance of tones as well as of images of sight. His continuing
insistence on meter and rhyme also set him off from the Imagists.
The New England Heritage is a collection of ten essays read at a
conference at Northeastern University in May 1980. Samuel French
Morse contributed "Robert Frost: Society and Solitude" (pp. 131–
43), stating that Emerson's *Nature* gave Frost many ideas, though
Emerson tended to drift toward universals and the ideal, whereas
Frost looked to self, to the actual and specific. Both writers favored
affirmation, though for Frost affirmation was often only a temporary
warding off of disorder. An Emerson passage on picking apples in
"Intellect" is astonishingly close to Frost's famous poem. Several
parallels with Emerson's thought, indeed, light up this essay. Jay
Parini also writes of these two poets. In "Emerson and Frost: The
Present Act of Vision" (*SR* 89:206–227) he maintains that despite
"Frost's rugged singularity" his poetic images are from "the romantic
mainstream." Both Frost and Emerson were inclined to move "from
description to revelation." Though Frost was more ironic than Emerson (as is almost any 20th-century poet), Emersonian echoes abound.
Both poets considered their first duty to be vision, the firm fixing of
the eye on the image.

Priscilla M. Paton examines particularly "Mowing," "After Apple
Picking," and "Birches" to see how Frost confuses fact and dream in
eventually coming to knowledge. Her essay is entitled "Robert Frost:
'The fact is the sweetest dream that labor knows'" (*AL* 53:43–55).
Darrel Abel looks at the inimical side of nature as a dominant theme
throughout Frost's work. "'Unfriendly Nature' in the Poetry of Robert Frost" (*CLQ* 17:201–10) shows that, beginning with "The Demi-
urge" and other early poems, mountains, rocks, and "headlong brooks"
are the source of New England character as the poet sees it. He is
sure, however, that man will continue to endure and absorb the
obstacles nature presents and be all the stronger for it.

Always the gamesman, Frost often used the sonnet structure while pretending his poem was not a sonnet. So says Oliver H. Evans in " 'Deeds That Count': Robert Frost's Sonnets" (*TSLL* 23: 123–37). He points out Frost's "behavior" in composing sonnets, e.g., "Hyla Brook" with 15 lines, "Evening in a Sugar Orchard" with 17, and even "There Are Roughly Zones" with 21. In all these, and other similar variants, rhyme and syntax both make the poem integrated and provide the expected stasis and release. Though Frost surrendered the formalities of the conventional sonnet in these cases, he maintained its chief characteristics and structure in such a long poem as "Not to Keep" (22 lines).

The essays of a symposium of well-known critics and Frost scholars have been edited by Earl J. Wilcox for the Winthrop Studies in Major Modern Writers. In *Robert Frost: The Man and the Poet* (Rock Hill, S.C.: Winthrop College) Cleanth Brooks looks at a number of nature poems and concludes, somewhat differently from Abel, that the poet has neither reverence for nor fear of nature. "Man's gift of consciousness actually separates him from her and his fellow creatures." Guy Rotella sees "The Oven Bird" as exploring "making and meaning" and "poetic limits and possibilities." As poem it struggles "between fiction making and the anti-fictive." John F. Sears argues that in Frost the upright "posture is the physical revelation of a psychological or spiritual state rather than its metaphorical equivalent." Donald J. Greiner uses Frost's "An Old Man's Winter Night" and Stevens' "A Rabbit as King of the Ghosts" to picture, on the one hand, the fear-ridden loneliness of old age and, on the other, the imagination as cure for such pressures. Laurence Perrine concludes his study of sound and sense by analyzing minutely the two-line "The Span of Life," a "superior" poem. These are only five of the dozen commentators in this lively book.

Peter L. Hays admits that "All Revelation" is not among Frost's best poems but is nevertheless worth the trouble of careful reading. For Hays the poem is an accurate description of a television picture tube with electrons playing on crystals and bringing out images of stars and flowers. It is critical of "those who take their knowledge of nature indirectly from television." The article is entitled "Frost and the Critics: More Revelation in 'All Revelation' " (*ELN* 18:283–90).

Maurice Legris in "The Joyful Killer of 'The Witch of Coös' " (*SIH* 9:30–32) sees a crowning irony in the last-minute revelation of the family name, Lajway, a French-Canadian corruption of Lajoie. A man named Joy had killed his wife's lover (the woman herself had not) and had taken pleasure in the act. Fritz H. Oehlschlaeger contradicts the opinion of such critics as Richard Poirier and Frank Lentricchia in proposing to read the grief of the dead child's mother in "Home Burial" as "tragic perceptiveness rather than mental sickness or masochism." In "Tragic Vision in Frost's 'Home Burial'" (*BSUF* 22,iii:25–29) the author maintains that the bereavement teaches the mother that human beings are ultimately isolated and separate. "Amy may, in fact, be mad, but such madness is that of the tragic figure raging against an arbitrary universe."

Haj Ross has contributed "Robert Frost's 'Out, Out—': A Way In" to *Crossing the Boundaries in Linguistics*, ed. Wolfgang Klein and Willem Levelt (Reidel). Ross admits disarmingly to his "apprenticeship as an anatomist of poems" and to the possibility of error in his judgments, but he hopes with experience for deeper maturity. He looks at the piece, typically, as organism, gestalt. Having divided the poem into four sections, he shows that each has its distinctive punctuation and thematic content. He studies the exercise of "negation," the function of conjunctions and verbal forms. He understands that understatement and the New England setting heighten the impact. This is not a bad beginning for the modest Ross.

In quite a different vein Barbara Glenn takes her text from Heraclitus in "The Way Up and the Way Down: A Consideration of Robert Frost in the Context of Baudelaire and Emerson" (*SoR* 17:142–63). Almost all major poets of the past hundred years, she maintains, have seen existence in terms of the opposition of mind and body, including Charles Baudelaire, Ralph Waldo Emerson, and Frost. All three of these poets agree, however reluctantly, "that meaning resides ultimately in feeling." Frost (our focus) rejected the ideal but instead pursued meaning through sensation. Even in intellectual action he found "spiritual lust that is like the physical." Like Baudelaire, Frost found that meaning is at best tenuous: "After Apple-Picking," "To Earthward," and "The Most of It" show the reader how appalling the world actually is.

vi. Williams

Without denying the value of the new books on H. D., Frost, Moore, Winters, and the others, we must declare the most significant volume (for our chapter) published in 1981 to be *William Carlos Williams: A New World Naked* by Paul Mariani (McGraw-Hill). Not to read it carefully would be to omit the cement holding together the super-structure of our period. A huge book (770 pages of main text and 120 pages of front and back matter, including many notes as full and vital as the text itself), it is filled with all imaginable detail, making the poet a fully human being. Though a fascinating chronological account of the "local" in Williams' life, it also explicates the key poems, relating them to the writer's experience, his determination to pare the language down to its core, his aesthetic convictions, and his burning, burrowing vision of the New Jersey environment and its people among whom he deliberately chose to spend his life.

The style is energetic and on the whole skillful, though there are frequent misspellings, evidence of unalert proofreading, occasionally incorrect facts. In spite of these disturbing flaws, however, the book is powerful, even monumental. The author pictures fully the excitement and nourishment of Williams' literary world. He details how the medical profession nurtured the poet in spite of its frequent interference with his writing. He tells of the relationships with artists, musicians, and other writers, especially the friendship with Pound. He bars no holds in recounting the pushes and pulls of Williams' sexuality. And always, as a modern Boswell, he brings us the portrait of an outspoken American, sensitive and tough, compassionate and heroic, with a work schedule too heavy and an income too limited. But Mariani hears a recurring message from the sage to the disciples: "take the search for a new line seriously and listen long and hard to the speech patterns about [you], the pace and pauses, and risings and fallings of speech heard every day." This book is not to be confused with Mariani's earlier *William Carlos Williams: The Poet and His Critics* (ALS 1975, 383–84). It belongs with the best American literary biographies.

Hugh Kenner reviews the Mariani book, adding insights and memories of his own. The incidents recorded in "Breaking the Line: The Bard of Newark's Department Stores" (*Harper's*, Dec.:54–56) support our recognition of the elderly poet's persistence and dedication. Of a bottle of brandy: "His right arm was near-paralyzed and it would be up to me to measure out amber drops older than I was." Williams barked out warning and injunctions that made the visiting Kenner nervous: "Careful, careful"; then "More! More!" At work:

"He grasped the wrist of his right hand with his left, steered the fore-finger over a key, and let it drop." Kenner's observations and anec-dotes further fill out the already incredibly full Mariani book.

Donald C. Gallup relates many adventures and misadventures in "The William Carlos Williams Collection at Yale" (*YULG* 56:50–59). Gallup and Norman Holmes Pearson were chiefly responsible for the first editions and many important papers now in the Beinecke Library. Bryher (H. D.'s great and good friend) made disparaging remarks about Williams in her memoir. For this breach the poet and his wife Floss held Pearson responsible and refused to see him any more. Gallup finally "received" the promised materials from Floss only after her husband's death. John C. Thirlwell, granted a five-year "non-exclusive authorization" for use of Williams materials in writing a biography, at length himself very much disturbed the poet and Floss, who did not see him again. This arrangement, however, as well as succeeding problems, created added confusion and com-plication to gathering in materials for Yale, which now owns, never-theless, a very large collection of Williams' writings.

In addition to his influence on Crane, Marsden Hartley was a friend of Williams. Christopher J. McGowan parallels Williams' own paucity of reputation in 1921 with the painter Hartley's utter neglect by the American public. Neglected artists, however, can give each other support, rejuvenating their creativity and imagination, as the author points out in "William Carlos Williams' 'The Great Figure' and Marsden Hartley" (*AL* 53:302–05). Another friendship with an artist is delineated by William Marling in "A Tense, Inquisitive Clash: William Carlos Williams and Marcel Duchamp" (*SWR* 66:361–75), in which the poet is disclosed as himself finding a strong link between his own work and the point of view of the painter: (1) inconsistency (contradictions) as a positive virtue and an ironic defense against the worship of "fixed positions," and (2) eroticism ranging "from voyeurism to exhibitionism." A reader needs to know the work of Duchamp in order to understand *Kora in Hell*. Williams' *Autobiography* (1951) emphasizes the "rude awakening" with which the French artist shocked America. This is the second study in a year of the Duchamp connection (see *ALS 1980*, 371).

The recently renamed *William Carlos Williams Review* 7 offers several substantial articles by specialists in this poet, especially

Thomas Cole's recollections in "Remembering Williams and Pound" (7,ii:4–20) and Eleanor Berry's "Williams' Development of a New Prosodic Form—*Not* the 'Variable Foot,' but the 'Sight Stanza' " (7,ii: 21–29). This issue is worth a close look. *William Carlos Williams: The Attack from the Present* (Middlebury Coll., 1980) compiled by Robert Buckeye and Fran Naramore, is a catalogue of a Williams exhibit and a bibliography of Williams manuscript materials in the Abernethy Library of American Literature.

In *Iowa Review* (11,ii–iii[1980]:48–67) Ann W. Fisher examines an early Williams item (about 1905) never completed, never titled, in which the poet used autobiographical material, but was really writing about language, the direction he soon chose to follow explicitly. "William Carlos Williams' *Endymion* Poem: 'Philip and Oradie' " traces his venture "into the Keatsian realms of the egotistical sublime" and his continuing maturity leading to "The Wanderer" (1917), his first important poem, "the story of growing up."

Stephen Tapscott details the function of Whitman in opening Book I and closing Book IV of *Paterson*, beginning with a "historical-geological giant" hovering over Paterson and ending with a Whitman-inspired figure turning to the open road "of the American poem itself." In "Whitman in Paterson" (*AL* 53:291–301) the author shows how Williams establishes the link between his own modern search and "the difficult beginnings that his image of Whitman represents."

Williams' play with words gives *Paterson* organization and a manner of progression that threatens ultimate silence or, surprisingly, a concealing "welter of words." Williams goes beyond mere punning, however, into "metathesis ('warped/wrapped') and voicing/devoicing." Philip Furia's "*Paterson's* Progress" (*Boundary* 9,ii:31–49) provides many instances of "verbal play" as the mode of keeping the poem moving—for example, an insistent pun on "mottled/molten" and the related "mauled." Here the author compares Williams with the painters Jackson Pollock, Juan Gris, and Picasso, whom he admired.

D. Hurry shows how much Williams admired Freud's work. Rather than "encouraging some crude decoding process" the poet employed in *Paterson* "the power and process of dream symbolism." Hurry's "The Use of Freudian Symbolism in William Carlos Williams' *Paterson*" (*L&P* 31,i:16–20) emphasizes that the principal means of "structuring and signification" in the long poem came from the poet's understanding of the basis of *The Interpretation of Dreams* as "No ideas but in things."

In gestalt psychology an analysis of perception pictures how all parts depend on each other and interact structurally. Williams worked at the idea of "contact," all the way from a connection with actual soil to the soldier's "field of action." Dawn Trovard in "Perceiving Gestalt in 'The Clouds' " (*ConL* 22:205–17) shows how ordinary things and animals in turn give order to the flux of the imagination. For the poet, thought structure and materials work together to illuminate; in terms of gestalt psychology, structure contributes a "perspective, orientation, or characterization upon the figure or thematic focus of the poem." "No ideas but in things" says it all. Williams seeks to make a unity of all, to see "the whole in the present moment."

David L. Green pursues much the same theme in " 'The Comedian as the Letter C,' 'Carlos,' and 'Contact' " (*TCL* 27:262–71). He comments on the fascination for both Williams and Stevens of "the relationship between reality and imagination." From the beginning, though, Stevens failed to see that Williams was completely involved not only in the dirt of New Jersey but in his own experiences, not only with the outside world but with his inner resources. "At the heart of Williams' poetics" was "the belief in the necessity of creating new forms" (a theme Mariani stresses time and time again in *A New World Naked*). The meaning of these forms neither could Stevens grasp "nor Crispin embody."

Harold Fromm attacks Charles Altieri's lengthy "commentary, analysis and hypothesis" about the importance of Williams' "This Is Just to Say," a "frail little piece" at best. Is this exercise not, he wants to know, a game for professionals, nothing that the common reader can hope to appreciate? "Literary Professionalism's Pyrrhic Defense of Poesy" (*CentR* 25:435–47) is a timely corrective for the onslaughts of such French theorists as Jacques Derrida. In other words, what good do they do?

Herbert Liebowitz has given us a preview of part of a book he is completing on the general subject of American autobiography. In " 'You Can't Beat Innocence': *The Autobiography of William Carlos Williams*" (*APR* 10,ii:35–47) he considers, among other details, Williams' continuing effort to link his practice of medicine with the writing of verse and emphasizes the often strained but generally fruitful friendship with Pound. He also comments that "What works for the relatively simple cellular structure of his imagistic poems and modest lyrics is inadequate for the complex physiology of an auto-biography (or epic poem)."

vii. Stevens

Stevens and Williams are also the subjects of an article by Donald Gutierrez, "Circular Art: Round Poems of Wallace Stevens and William Carlos Williams" (*CP* 14:53–60). He notes that "Anecdote of the Jar" and "The Dance" record phenomena available as "magi-cal circles" for anyone who feels that immortality concerns activities as aesthetically and humanly fundamental as organizing and enjoy-ing space, even though the dance will end in separate lives and the jar can be lost or ignored.

"Art as a Cry Against Extinction in the Poetry of Wallace Stevens" (*WSJour* 5:37–42) is the subject of an article by James S. Leonard and Christine E. Wharton, who see "Domination of Black" and "The Snow Man" as different settings for the same "movement toward annihilation." An indifferent universe is symbolized by the continu-ing motion of clouds in "The Death of a Soldier." The authors find in several other poems reminders of the inevitable movement toward death. Though images of sterility are prominent, a poem, nonethe-less, "can momentarily fix mortality and counter with its cry—its constructive, cadenced human voice." (Is there not something Fros-tian in this concept?)

Doris L. Eder's "Two Views of Terra Infidel: 'Sunday Morning' and 'Esthétique du Mal'" (*WSJour* 5:23–41) states that the two poems find "the health of the world sufficient to withstand pain and suffering" without the solace of religion. Whereas the author thinks "Sunday Morning" is "the greatest poem of earth of the century," she sees the more difficult "Esthétique du Mal" as a proclamation of Stevens' firm belief that poetry has the power to replace "empty heaven and its hymns."

Janis P. Stout advises reading Stevens' "The Comedian as the Letter C" first as a story and only then as a study of poetic sensibility or even the unfolding of poetic history. In "Stevens' 'Comedian' as Journey Narrative" (*CP* 14:31–52) Stout finds Crispin's travels indebted to three journey patterns in American literature: exploration, quest, and the home-seeking journey. The narrative itself is American in quality: the places are identifiable and the brash tone is colloquial and familiar. In addition to the journey structure Stevens fits his story to the patterns of American history: movement from Europe to the Atlantic coast of North America and then into the raw interior. The details are concrete; the poet has avoided abstract theory.

Rajeev S. Patke lays out the correspondences between John L. Stephens' *Incidents of Travel in Central America, Chiapas, and Yucatan* (1841–43) and three of Wallace Stevens' poems: section 3, "It Must Give Pleasure" from "Notes toward a Supreme Fiction," "The Worms at Heaven's Gate," and a typescript (at Yale) of a passage eventually omitted from "The Comedian as the Letter C." The author points out the predominance of the letter C in Stephens' writing while admitting that acquaintance of our poet with *Incidents of Travel* must at present remain hypothetical, though he is known to have owned a copy. This article, "Stevens and Stephens: A Possible Source" may be found in two places: *AL* 53:306–13 and *WSJour* 5: 17–22.

An example of Roy Harvey Pearce's "continuity of American poetry" is found in the influence of Thoreau on three admittedly selective passages from Stevens: "Looking across the Fields and Watching the Birds Fly," canto xxxiii of "The Man with the Blue Guitar," and "Credences of Summer." This is the subject of Errol M. McGuire's " 'A Mythology Reflects Its Region': Stevens and Thoreau" (*WSJour* 5:56–67), which indicates the similarity and actual identity in language and ideas between the two writers.

Marie Boroff continues to pursue interests developed in *Language and the Poet* (*ALS 1979*, 312) in "Sound Symbolism as Drama in the Poetry of Wallace Stevens" (*ELH* 48:914–34). She considers in several poems the function of groups of consonant and vowel sounds as "a sort of phonetic repertory company, whose members are again and again subjected to type-casting." Stevens had the incomparable capacity for performing magic tricks by producing "many colored silken streamers and then, with a flick of insouciance, spiriting them back into his sleeve." This is an imaginative and indispensable study first delivered (in a slightly differing version) as a lecture at the Wallace Stevens Birthday Celebration in Chapel Hill in 1979.

Stevens frequently heightens and intensifies the relationship of reality and artifice by making reality a "trick of the eye." In "Stevens' Trompe l'Oeil: Visual Comedy in Some Short Poems" (*WSJour* 5:3–10) Fred Miller Robinson explains how in "Study of Two Pears" the pedantic lecturer's objectivity is a deception and the "conclusion the grandest deception" ("The pears are not seen/As the observer wills"). Robinson discusses four other poems, including the difficult "What We See Is What We Think," the title being contradicted by the final line, "Since what we think is never what we see," indeed a *trompe l'oeil*.

Stephen Crites has published his lecture, "Wallace Stevens's Necessary Angel," delivered at the American Academy of Religion in New York in 1979 (*Soundings* 64:298–309). Explaining that he is one of few angelologists left in the field of theology, Crites uses "Angels Surrounded by Paysans" as base for his comments on reality and imagination. For Stevens the "paysans" are reality, "but then there is the angel," both resident and foreign: "the earth is unimaginable without him: not conceivable without him."

A contribution to the "Communications" department of *WSJour* 5 (68–79), Douglas E. Airmet's "An Ordinary Essay" takes off from a statement in the "Adagia" of *Opus Posthumous* (1957), p. 161: "Weather is a sense of nature. Poetry is a sense." Airmet argues that Stevens was not so much interested in the concrete poem as in the sense of poetry it conveyed. The author draws examples from many poems to show the poet's view of "absolute mysticism" in the thing observed, which "depends absolutely on the imagination," in which sense "it is a sense." Stevens' permeating use of the metaphor of departure, the taking-off from the thing, amounts to "enlightenment, release."

Allan Chavkin's "Wallace Stevens' Romantic Landscape, Notes on Meditation: 'No Possum, No Sop, No Taters'" (*WSJour* 5:53–45) suggests that the crow in the final lines of the poem is a kind of role model for man—a determined survivor in the midst of a malevolent universe. Chavkin generously cites other critics with diverse interpretations of this passage but concludes for himself that Stevens is saying that man owes it to himself to "come to terms with the darkest recesses of his being." David Lehman claims that in Stevens man distrusts action: with minor exceptions "there is nothing he can do/ To alter the ego of the age." Lehman also studies the poet's fondness for negative expressions, useful among other functions in warning an "observer against seeing things as they might be." Finally the author sees an identity between "the philosopher in Stevens" and "the poet in Freud." They both, for example, approve of "Nietzsche's exposé of the tyranny of heaven." Whereas, however, Stevens makes reality abstract "by placing it in his imagination," Freud places the imagination in reality. These ideas are found in Lehman's "Three Meditations on Wallace Stevens" (*Shenandoah* 32,ii:85–101).

A. Walton Litz participated in the celebration at the Library of Congress of the hundredth birthdays of Vachel Lindsay and Wallace Stevens by delivering a lecture on *Wallace Stevens: The Poetry of Earth* (Library of Congress). Litz argues that in the final analysis Stevens was a very democratic poet. Toward the end he joined Frost, Williams, and John Crowe Ransom in writing of a single time and place (what Williams would call the "local"). Litz follows Stevens' career with characteristic clarity, concluding by discussing the poet's final commitment to his adopted state of Connecticut.

Milton J. Bates has given us three articles on Stevens this year. "Stevens in Love: The Woman Won, the Woman Lost" (*ELH* 48: 231–55) traces the poet's courtship of Elsie Kachel, whom he married in 1909. The article quotes extensively from his love letters and cites his guises and disguises, his way of using his imagination to combat the daily realities. It contrasts the secrecy of the birthday poems of 1908–09 with that trait in the poems intended for a more sophisticated audience in the 1940s and 1950s. Beginning around 1913 the Interior Paramour supplanted the country girl Elsie as the poet's muse, but Stevens was never completely at ease with the post-decadents, though their influence drew him out of the somewhat naive control exercised by Mrs. Stevens. Bates restores the purposely neglected "Red Loves Kit" as affording "a rare peek into Stevens' dressing room." Stevens' growth as poet from 1904 through the early years of his marriage makes us question whether he dwelt more on the actual winning of Elsie or on the later loss of her as emotional partner as she became his Interior Paramour.

Bates's "Stevens as Regional Poet" (*WSJour* 5:32–35) uses the same idea as does Litz in *The Poetry of Earth*: poems written in the 1940s find their locale in specific places in eastern Pennsylvania, e.g., Ephrata, the Oley Valley, the Schuylkill. In "The Countryman" Stevens wrote of his native territory using, however, the idiom of an outsider. "His soil is the poet's intelligence—provided the poet is simultaneously the intelligence of his soil." The third article is entitled "To Realize the Past: Wallace Stevens' Genealogical Study" (*AL* 52:607–27). Not until the last 15 years of his life did the poet take an interest in his family tree, but in 1941 he began amassing reams of genealogical information. Poems and essays reflected more and more the "hereditary lights" which he now pursued "with a renewed sense of destiny."

It was Stevens' practice to fragment experience as a lawyer to make it more manageable, not so disturbing. John Constable makes this observation in "Wallace Stevens: Poetry and Personality" (*SoRA* 14:36–48), in which he argues that the poet was consistent in limiting his contact with other poets to exchange of letters and in remaining an isolationist in politics. He rarely left home in Hartford. Constable concludes that the life of the poet cannot be separated from his poem. Biographical details are indispensable to understanding the work. Even in Hartford "The carefully protected distance between office and study in Stevens' life is the same that exists between the eye and the objects it perceives."

Though not a European traveler, Stevens had an affinity for transatlantic writers. Glen McLeod's "Stevens at the Front: 'Lettres d'un Soldat' " (*WSJour* 5:46–55) uses a translation of the World War I letters of Eugène Emmanuel Lemercier and Stevens' selection from 17 poems based on the letters and now preserved by A. Walton Litz in *Introspective Voyager* (*ALS* 1972, 336–37). Stevens depended here more on a literary source than in any other of his poems for chronological structure and the "inspiration" for the poems themselves. His intent was to summarize in poetry all the letters in Lemercier's book. He felt an affinity with the Frenchman's love of painting, music, and good imaginative writing. Composing war poetry per se did not interest Stevens, and indeed these poems failed because he tried to make the soldier and the poet one. This article is instructive with relation to the poet's problems prior to *Harmonium* (1923).

Another foreign relationship was with the Dublin poet and art critic Thomas McGreevy, one of Stevens' "most stimulating" friends during the last years of his life. In "The Irish Connection: Wallace Stevens and Thomas McGreevy" (*SoR* 17:533–41) Peter Brazeau records that, after McGreevy had sent Stevens a copy of his *Poems* in the spring of 1948, the two writers exchanged about 60 letters. When they finally met in New York in January 1954, the Irishman

found the American "absolutely charming" and McGreevy seemed
to Stevens "a contemporary Whitman."

Robert Buttel's " 'Knowledge on the Edges of Oblivion': Stevens'
Late Poems" (*WSJour* 5:11–16) discloses in half a dozen poems how
the poet, though highly aware that his life was ending, pushed "beyond the border of death" or admitted its finality or "searched for
some continuum between life and death." Thus to the very end of
his life he was creating quietly intense and powerful work. Another
article about the poet's closing work is Janet McCann's " 'The Celestial Possible': Wallace Stevens' Last Poems" (*SWR* 66:73–82).
Whereas the earlier work is set in earlier seasons (the spring of
Harmonium, Transport to Summer, and *The Auroras of Autumn*),
The Rock is marked by poems of winter with a hint of spring returning. Moreover, the idea of "the celestial possible" maintains that the
mind can merge with the world, eliminating the necessity of symbols,
for "metaphor is the result of incomplete knowledge." (Stevens argued with Williams on this point.) The last poems are powerful, as
Buttel also points out: they celebrate "the mind's potential and destiny."

Peter L. McNamara has issued a second edition of his *Critics on
Wallace Stevens* (Univ. of Miami) nine years after the first (*ALS
1972*, 337). It reflects the great amount of Stevens scholarship in the
interim.

Purdue University

17. Poetry: The 1940s to the Present

Lee Bartlett

Next year will mark the 20th anniversary of *ALS*, and looking back through earlier versions of this chapter, I find it rather poignant to recall Theodore Roethke's remark that our culture would rather print a book about poetry than a book of poems. In *ALS 1963* Oliver Evans covered poetry from the 1930s to the present in just 11 pages. Only five years later, A. Kingsley Weatherhead's essay was twice as long, though much of his analysis concerned work on Williams and Stevens. In 1975 Linda Welshimer Wagner managed to review the year's work in 20 pages, though she was forced to relegate Stevens to chapter 16. Currently, while this chapter now covers only poets born after 1900 (thus excluding both Williams and Stevens), it runs to the maximum number of pages our editors, even in their good-hearted patience, can allow. Less than 20 years ago, Evans read for his essay about 10 books and 20 articles; this year I've faced over 45 books and 100 articles.

i. Groundwork

There were two studies of the range of postmodern American poetry this year, one exceptional, the other a disappointment. Cary Nelson's *Our First Last Poets* (Illinois) is a balanced discussion of the "conflict between poetic vision and historical reality" in American poetry over the last 20 years. Nelson argues that "the interplay between poetry and history" in our nation which culminated in Whitman's Civil War poetry was repeated in the poetry which emerged from the war in Vietnam. During the 1960s, he feels, all public discourse became a "mode of deception," and not even poetry escaped with its innocence. Even the most "open" poetry, the most non-self-conscious and non-ironic, still had to contend with readers who had a basic distrust of language. The situation was further complicated for poets because in America our "great myths" are public ones, tied to our experience as a people, our historical situation. Thus the poetry of the Vietnam War (and he means here not so much that overtly political poetry by veterans collected in books like *Winning Hearts and Minds* and Michael Casey's *Obscenities* as work by major poets on the homefront) had to "contend with its coeval public history and court its own formal dissolution." Nelson sees in Theodore Roethke a "polarized poetics of nature," as he sets the fact of open space against that of enclosure. Both aspects of this poetics symbolize kinds of death (the field through "overextension," the greenhouse through claustrophobia), yet each is always a "rite of passage toward rebirth." As Roethke's poetry matures, it moves toward a reconciliation of this polarity, a movement which culminates in the poet's most fully realized long poem, "North American Sequence." Here, in a poem "grounded in loss and failure," Roethke accepts the "cultural pressure behind his art" and thus anticipates the work of the subsequent generation.

Nelson continues with chapter-long discussions of four central figures of that generation—Galway Kinnell, Robert Duncan, Adrienne Rich, and W. S. Merwin. The intervening ten years of "deflating history" since Roethke's long poem, he argues, explain the "far more obsessive and fatalistic" tone of Galway Kinnell's *Book of Nightmares*; further, Kinnell's primary object has been to achieve a "poetics of death that is at once graphic, mystical, and sensual" and therefore sets itself over against Whitman's "attempt to make death culturally specific" through "communality." In his extended analysis of Robert Duncan's aesthetics of process (reading a number of poems from *Bending the Bow* and *Opening of the Field*), Nelson finds a "relation between history and poetry in which terror and beauty are joined." He discusses Adrienne Rich's career of "false starts, reversals, and continual indirection" which has resulted in two distinct voices: the polemical and the introspective. Finally, he examines the later poetry of W. S. Merwin which, as it "ruthlessly deconstructs its own accomplishments," manages to capture "history's powers of dissolution."

In *Our First Last Poets* Nelson writes well, argues closely, and convinces. He obviously cares greatly for the work he discusses (though he is not awed by it), and his individual essays on Roethke, Kinnell, Duncan, Rich, and Merwin are certainly some of the best criticism we have had yet on those poets.

In contrast to Nelson's book, Roberta Berke's *Bounds Out of Bounds: A Compass for Recent American and British Poetry* (Oxford) need not detain us, as this slim volume is really nothing more than a summing-up of countless older studies of postmodern verse in English (by Malkoff, Rosenthal, and Rexroth, for example) or the appropriate chapter in the more recent *Harvard Guide*. Berke neglects many major poets and oddly mentions only a very few American women writers. This book will have some use as an introduction for undergraduates to various movements and trends—the Beat Generation, Black Mountain, the New York Poets—but our students should be warned to proceed with caution.

Is the sky falling? In his rather controversial *The Place of Poetry* (Kentucky) Christopher Clausen thinks so. Clausen's primary subject is the history of the "conflict over whether poetic or scientific discourse" is finally more suitable to the modern world. Although the topic is, of course, an old chestnut, Clausen does manage to warm it up as he summons an impressive amount of evidence to support his basic contentions—that the audience for poetry has just about disappeared in our century (at least, he argues, in America) and that this has been caused by poets' gradual denial of their responsibility as a moral force in culture. When a version of one of Clausen's chapters, "Poetry in a Discouraging Time," was first published (*GaR* 35:703–15), a number of writers were invited to respond ("The Place of Poetry: A Symposium," pp. 716–56). While a few more or less agreed with Clausen (Malcolm Cowley, for example, charmingly asked, "Who or what except a computer's memory bank could remember ten consecutive lines of John Ashbery?"), most did not. Donald Hall's rejoinder, "Poetry, Popularity, and the Golden Age" (pp. 721–25), pointed out that in fact poetry is as popular now in America as it ever was—that readings are often very well attended and that many poetry books actually sell quite well; further, and after reading Clausen's brief I must agree, Hall feels that while Clausen's historical analysis is in places brilliant, one has the sense from the start that he simply does not *like* contemporary poetry.

In a related project, Karl Elder asked 40 poets each to write a 500-word statement discussing "the future of poetry," and he prints 22 of these in *Seems* (No. 14). Strangely, no statements by female poets are included, though the brief essays which do appear here are fairly interesting. They range from Philip Dacey's call for a new poetic "heroism" to combat "The Reigning Style, which is a kind of No-Style," to Paul Zimmer's reminder that poets must be content to "be secret and exult."

Four other exciting books by Marjorie Perloff, Mary Ann Caws (author of two), and Guy Davenport, while not devoted exclusively to this area, were published this year and deserve at least brief mention here. Marjorie Perloff's *The Poetics of Indeterminacy* (Princeton) fascinatingly argues that there are "two separate though often interwoven strands" in modernism—the symbolist mode, which runs from the romantics through Eliot to Lowell, and the "anti-Symbolist" mode "of literalness and free play," which has its source in Rimbaud. It is this second strand, this "other tradition" of indeterminacy, that Perloff takes as her subject. Her first six chapters examine Stein, Williams, Pound, and Beckett as writers in the Rimbaud tradition. In her seventh, " 'Mysteries of Construction': The Dream Songs of John Ashbery" (mentioned in last year's *ALS*), Perloff senses that "not *what* ones dreams but *how*" is Ashbery's primary subject, reading several of Ashbery's poems rather closely. Her final chapter, " 'No More Margins': John Cage, David Antin, and the Poetry of Performance," discusses Cage's "lecture poems" and Antin's "talk poems" as works in the antisymbolist tradition. While this final chapter is fairly convincing given the system she has developed, Perloff's comments on Antin (whom she very much admires) are an example of a first-rate critical intelligence worrying over a second-rate poetic project; once we understand the *theory* behind Antin's current work (and Perloff's elucidation is very articulate), we are left with the "talk poems" themselves. Perloff feels we reject the poems because they are somehow "formless," that they "even avoid that last stronghold of contemporary free verse—lineation." This is, however, simply a straw man. I think most readers' negative response to Antin's "talk poems" is due to the fact that the poems are finally rather boring—not in conception, but in execution. Further, some readers might have trouble with Perloff's sense of the indeterminate itself as they proceed through her study, a difficulty which stems from her notion of indeterminacy as a fixed property of a *text* rather than our *response* to a text. Even so, *The Poetics of Indeterminacy* is a learned and challenging book, one bound to generate considerable discussion.

Mary Ann Caws in her *A Metapoetics of the Passage: Architectures in Surrealism and After* (New England) deals in essence with "the interrelations of act and image" as revealed through the metaphor of "passage" in French poetry, though she does give a brief reading of James Merrill's "The Mad Scene" as an example of the surrealist project. Like many surrealist poems, Caws explains, "The Mad Scene" begins with "an announcement of repetition," while its movement is effected through a series of "verbs of seeing and non-perception." Again, while Caws's second book, *The Eye in the Text: Essays on Perception, Mannerist to Modern* (Princeton), focuses primarily on French surrealist poetry in its attempt to outline the relationship between "an outer object and an inner seen," the text and the act of reading, it also refers briefly to both John Ashbery and Robert Creeley as poets for whom this question is a central concern. In any case, surrealism has become a permanent element of American poetry, and both of these studies provide very useful field guides.

Finally, *The Geography of the Imagination* (North Point) collects 40 of Guy Davenport's occasional pieces. Being a gathering, the book really has no central thesis, though the individual essays (including articles on Jonathan Williams and *Poetry*) are endlessly intriguing. Davenport's "Olson" (which is really the yoking together of two earlier essays) remains one of the best yet on the poet, combining a moving memoir of sorts with a gloss on "The Kingfishers." This later commentary is particularly penetrating, as Davenport ranges widely—from the observation that Olson's use of the slash (as in "shd/") is based upon a misunderstanding of Pound's source (John Adams) to a brief meditation on the "ideogrammatic method." Of all critics now writing, Davenport must rank with Hugh Kenner as one of those most influenced by the tradition of high modernism; like Kenner, as he moves effortlessly through literature, art, and the history of ideas, both his intelligence and style emerge as signal.

The history of poetics is a history of issues, and this year there are a number of interesting articles concerning general problems in postmodern American poetics—the image, morality, the poetic sequence, and translation. The image (its definition, its function, its importance) has held a central place in our criticism since Pound. Robert Pinsky's *The Situation of Poetry* (1977) was in the main an attack on our preoccupation with the object. Arguing that because we can never present experience through the abstraction of language, Pinsky privileged discourse over image, pronouncing the notion of the concrete in poetry a fiction. In "The Attack on the Image" (*Field*

25:67–81) Jonathan Holden attempts to refute Pinsky's position, explaining that most human experience is in fact referential ("that many feelings of familiarity . . . are not *imposed* upon the world of language: they are endemic to it"; that imagery is, "in itself, a kind of language") and that Pinsky misunderstands the convention of the present tense, which is not a "kind of 'naive' directness and immediacy" but a way of dramatizing "the shock of dawning ethical self-consciousness." I am not in sympathy with Pinsky's attacks on Roethke, Kinnell, and Bly, and perhaps thus I find myself drawn to Holden's response. Fortunately, however, as readers we don't have to choose between Kinnell's *Book of Nightmares* and Pinsky's own *An Explanation of America*—we can, and do, have them both.

Interestingly, in a second essay, "The Abstract Image: The Return of Abstract Statement in Contemporary American Poetry" (*NER* 3: 435–49), while he doesn't reverse himself exactly, Holden carefully covers his flank. Here he argues that two "strands of poetic diction" have entered contemporary poetry through surrealism—the "archetypal" (or deep image, which he disparages) and that which makes the "abstractions particular." He calls this second strand "Ashberian" (seeing in Ashbery's work more than in anyone else's the normalization of the "abstract image in the contemporary literary milieu") and he finds this an advance. Further, a piece like Ashbery's "A Tone Poem" "assumes value primarily as a thing-in-itself precisely because it is not set in one-to-one correspondence with a particular experience as referent." *Field* (vol. 24) continues with its "Twenty Years of the Image: A *Field* Symposium," running four short pieces by Donald Hall, Robert Bly, Russell Edson, and Marvin Bell.

John Hollander's "A Poetry of Restitution" (*YR* 70:161–86) addresses the "moral dimension" of contemporary poetry, meditating on "three very consequential poems" by James Merrill, John Ashbery, and A. R. Ammons. When Hollander speaks of morality in poetry, he does not mean to confuse it with rhetoric for, he argues, the contemporary poem does not "urge" but rather teaches by "mythographic means." Merrill's early "The Mirror" is a meditation on that poetry which teaches us about "time, space, and reflections"; Ashbery's "Soonest Mended" is a poem "of being forty-two or forty-three," teaching us "the limits to the possibility of rescue"; Ammons' dedicatory "I Went to the Mountain" is "representative of the American poem of longing for natural power." Hollander's readings of the individual poems are interesting, though it seems to me that the thesis of his long essay offers nothing really new. In "The Pursuit of Suffering" (*Antaeus* 40–41:427–41) Daniel Halpern discusses the paradoxical tradition of romantic love in literature, briefly reading poems by Anthony Hecht, Adrienne Rich, and Louise Bogan as examples of ways contemporary poets deal with loss.

In "The Modern Sequence and Its Precursors" (*CL* 22:308–25) M. L. Rosenthal and Sally M. Gall argue that "the modern sequence is the decisive form toward which all developments of modern poetry have tended." Set against the epic, the sequence seems, they point out, to cry out for subjectivity, while solving the problem of the "encompassment of disparate and often powerfully opposed tonalities and energies," which is beyond the lyric. Rosenthal and Gall trace the development of the form from Poe and Emerson through contemporary poets, and while they make some convincing observations, the topic is obviously too large for this brief article. A full-length study—on the order of that by James E. Miller, Jr., *The American Quest for a Supreme Fiction* (1979)—is needed.

Ezra Pound's *Cathay* and "The Seafarer" established the modern idea of translation for American poets, that is the privileging of sense or tone over literal accuracy. If the translator proceeds as a scientist, Ben Belitt has argued, if "a simplistic semantics and a misguided analogy with scientific method" leads him "to identify the truth of a poem substantially with its 'words' and its 'intent,'" he will end up with a "science fiction of translation." Rather, he must give a "pulse to his language," must "make a poet's demands on the emerging English rather than a pedant's or a proctor" in some Intermediate Original. Rehearsing clearly this basic argument, Tess Gallagher's "Poetry in Translation: Literary Imperialism or, Defending the Musk Ox" (*Parnassus* 9,i:148–67) addresses "the high spirit of adventure afoot in the field of translation in America now" from the perspective of a reader whose only "second language" is poetry. Examining a number of poems by Anna Akhmatova, Osip Mandelstam, Cesare Pavese, and others, rendered into English, Gallagher argues that although we are often unqualified to judge "fidelity" to the original, it is the quality of the poem in English which finally matters. She concludes by noting that the great rise in quality of translations we have witnessed in the past few years is attributable to the fact that more and more first-rate poets are working at translation. As if to support Gallagher's contention, *Ironwood* (9,i:11–21, 40–51) published this year Gregory Orr's edition of transcripts from a 1977 Academy of American Poets symposium on "Chinese Poetry and the American Imagination," with contributions by Kenneth Rexroth, Gary Snyder, Hans Frankel, Stanley Kunitz, David Lattimore, Jonathan Chaves, W. S. Merwin, James Wright, Robert Bly, and Yip Wai-lim.

Two special issues of journals—*Tri-Quarterly*'s "Freedom in American Art and Culture" and *Michigan Quarterly Review*'s "The Automobile in American Culture"—provided a forum for speculations in this area. In "Leaving the Atocha Station: Contemporary Poetry and Technology" (*TriQ* 52:165–81) Daniel Guillory muses that we are living in the first "generation of technical language," that poetry and technology share a "common cultural ancestry," and that since the turn of the century the "marriage of art and technology has produced the most characteristic icons of our civilization." For Guillory, John Ashbery is perhaps the "most difficult and rewarding of practicing poets," and he asks (after reading "Leaving the Atocha Station") whether or not "artistic use of language can be pushed any further without destroying the last vestige of semantic content." In "Control, Freedom, and the Appetite for Poetry" (pp. 197–205) Robert Pinsky writes a "personal essay" outlining his invitation "by chance to think of himself as more historically determined" than he had before during his 1981 visit to the University of Warsaw during the general strike. Closing the volume, in "Letters" (pp. 278–84) Marvin Bell, John Cage, Nikki Giovanni, J. V. Cunningham, Denise Levertov, and David Ignatow reply to a questionnaire sent by editor Jonathan Brent, asking them to meditate on the usual sort of "poet-in-the-world" questions—identification of our most serious political/social/economic problems, the extent of the artist's proper engagement, and so forth. Laurence Goldstein's charming "The Automobile and American Poetry" (*MQR* 19:619–38) looks at a number of poems about the American phaeton, believing that as "interpreters of the latent meaning of things" poets are uniquely qualified to provide "prescriptions for the car's use." Goldstein explains that Karl Shapiro's "Buick" and "Auto Wreck" are probably our two most often anthologized flivver poems, while William Stafford's "Traveling Through the Dark" is the most widely reprinted contemporary poem, and that both "set up in deadly opposition the automobile and the natural creation to which man belongs." Continuing his discussion of "the poetry of automotive consciousness," he makes reference to petrol pram poems by Allen Ginsberg, Galway Kinnell, J. D. Reed, and Joyce Carol Oates.

A third special issue, *Iowa Review*'s 380-page "Extended Outlooks: The *Iowa Review* Collection of Contemporary Writing By Women" (12,ii–iii) edited by Jane Cooper, Gwen Head, Adalaide Morris, and Marcia Southwick, offers a wealth of fine poetry and short fiction. Additionally, in "On Ruth Stone" the number includes brief prose appreciations of an accomplished "lost woman writer in contemporary America," Ruth Stone, by Sandra Gilbert, Wendy Barker, Tillie Olsen, and others.

In an essay on Harold Bloom, Jerome Rothenberg argues that "the arrogance of criticism prospers, even fattens, on the silence of the poets over whom it means to tyrannize. It is an illusory fatness, anyway, & there does come a time when some of us who make poetry are moved, for one reason or another, to break the silence and respond in kind." And when poets do speak out—as in Pound's *ABC of Reading*, Eliot's *Selected Essays*, Olson's *Human Universe*—we often have charted for us the central aesthetic (and often political) issues of the day. This year we have four major prose collections by poets (Thomas Merton, Denise Levertov, Donald Hall, and Jerome Rothenberg), as well as a number of volumes in Michigan's ongoing Poets on Poetry series, taking up Rothenberg's challenge.

Of the four collections, *The Literary Essays of Thomas Merton* (New Directions) is by far both the longest (over 550 pages) and, at $40.00, the most expensive. The book is edited by Brother Patrick Hart, who was Merton's secretary at the Abbey of Gethsemane in Kentucky, and it contains all of Merton's literary criticism. In his introduction Hart explains that Merton wasn't a literary critic in the usual sense (he means, I think, a scholar), but rather that his "essays tended to coincide with his usual Sunday afternoon conferences at the Abbey of Gethsemani" during his last years there; this helps explain their "conversational, tentative, and provisional" tone. General readers will find Merton's seven essays on Albert Camus probably the most rewarding, while readers of contemporary poetry will be interested in Merton's comments on Edwin Muir and Louis Zukofsky, as well as his five fascinating essays on poetry and creativity. While

it is unlikely that Merton will ever be considered a poet of the first
rank, his place in the corpus of American religious writing is secure,
one which *The Literary Essays*—with its evidence of a wide-ranging
and sensitive intelligence and high moral sense—can only reinforce.

As poets, critics, memoirists, and teachers, Denise Levertov and
Donald Hall have been at the center of much of American poetry
for the past three decades. Levertov collected her early prose writings on poetry in *The Poet in the World* (1973), and this year she
has collected essays and notes written since then in *Light Up in the
Cave* (New Directions). The book opens with three previously unpublished short stories, continues with essays on craft and politics
and poetry, and concludes with memoirs of Muriel Rukeyser, Herbert Read, Robert Duncan, and others. Of note is Levertov's "Rilke
as Mentor," in which she describes her own experience with the work
of the German poet, arguing that his currently pervasive influence
is not in style or technique, but in a "sense of aesthetic ethics," a
belief in the sacred nature of the poet's vocation. Although a few
of the pieces—like "The Nature of Poetry" and "News that Stays
News"—are too underdeveloped to be of much more than casual
interest, others—like "An Approach to Public Poetry Listening," "On
the Function of the Line," and a series of essays on political poetry
—are as important as Levertov's earlier "Notes on Organic Form."
To Keep Moving (Geneva, N.Y.: Hobart & William Smith Colleges
Press) collects 20 of Donald Hall's critical essays and introductions
written between 1959 and 1969.

Jerome Rothenberg's *Pre-Faces & Other Writings* (New Directions) is a major collection of the poet's prose, centering primarily
on ethnopoetics. The book opens with a long interview with Rothenberg by William Spanos, which focuses on oral poetries, then brings
together Rothenberg's "pre-faces and manifestos," essays on poetics,
commentaries from his various anthologies, a final short interview, a
bibliography, and a good index. This year two commentators have
questioned Rothenberg's approach: William M. Clements ("Faking
the Pumpkin: On Jerome Rothenberg's Literary Offenses," *WAL*
14,iii:193–204) convincingly outlines four major problems with
Shaking the Pumpkin, all born of Rothenberg's changing "his sources'
words in order to reenforce his own ideas about the material," while
in "Pale or Darkened Moons in the Firmament of Reason" (*Parnassus*
9,i:269–83) Michael Heller concurs, seeing both *Technicians of the*

Sacred and *A Big Jewish Book* as culminations of a "technocratic shamanism," which is merely "another one of our flights from the present." Clements and Heller are articulate in their presentations, and I think their arguments would stand up in court. Still, if Rothenberg is a charlatan he is a good one, and if what he says isn't quite true, it should be. *Pre-Faces*, whose topics range from an exchange between Rothenberg and Robert Creeley on the nature of the deep image to Rothenberg's preoccupation with primitive poetries and the problems of translation, is a rich and stimulating book.

The University of Michigan Press's Poets on Poetry series, primary source collections of interviews, articles, and reviews by well-known contemporary poets, adds four new volumes this year. Richard Kostelanetz' *The Old Poetries and the New* and Louis Simpson's *A Company of Poets* are model volumes—each is over 300 pages and Kostelanetz' includes an index (a feature unfortunately lacking in the other books in the series). Kostelanetz' shots at various magazines like *Poetry* (which "has probably done more to hinder the development of American Literature" than any other journal) and *American Poetry Review*, as well as at Halpern's and Field's anthologies, are engaging, as are his extended pieces on sound and concrete poetry; Simpson's more traditional pieces—autobiography, reviews of contemporaries, essays on influences, and essays on poetics—demonstrate a reserved and balanced judgment that we must value. John Haines's *Living Off the Country* deals in the main with questions of the relationship of place to poetry, while Philip Levine's *Don't Ask*, besides having a charming title, contains seven interviews with the poet which taken together cover pretty much all aspects of his life and art. While the 12 volumes in the series vary in quality, all usefully pull together much hard-to-find material of great value.

Kostelanetz also discusses his intention "to extend poetry and fiction into other media and, conversely, to discover how other media could best be used for publishing poetry and fiction" in "Writing Extended" (*ComP* 4,ii:1–51). And finally, in "On Current Unstated Assumptions About Poetry," three more poets have their say, as *CritI* (7,iv) publishes three short talks by Seamus Heaney, Robert Pinsky, and Thomas Parkinson.

Bradford Morrow and Seamus Cooney have completed a first-rate work of scholarship in their long-awaited *A Bibliography of the Black Sparrow Press* (Black Sparrow). John Hollander published a very brief (54-page) prosody handbook this year, *Rhyme's Reason* (Yale). The book is much too compact to replace either Karl Shapiro's *A Prosody Handbook* or Paul Fussell's *Poetic Meter and Poetic Form*, though Hollander's discussion of various aspects of formal verse is peppered with witty asides and entertaining examples written by the poet specifically for this occasion. A useful handbook for poetry writing workshops. Robert Hass is also interested in prosody in "Listening and Making" (*Antaeus* 40–41:488–509), a lively essay on rhythm. In "The Process of Revision: Turning an Old Poem into a New One" (*ConP* 4,i:401–45) Lewis Turco, whose *Book of Forms* remains a standard text, briefly comments on the revision process, using five drafts of his poem "The Last Schooner" as examples.

Finally, the year saw one new journal of note, and the reprinting of issues of another. Clayton Eshleman and Robert Kelley's *Caterpillar* magazine ran to 20 issues and was a seminal journal of the late 1960s. Now Eshleman (with Kelly listed as a contributing editor) has revived a version of the magazine for the 1980s, *Sulfur*. If the first two issues which appeared in 1981 are any indication, *Sulfur* will be a major postmodern publication. Besides publishing poetry, Eshleman devotes a fourth of each of the first two issues to "The Letters of Edward Dahlberg and Charles Olson," ed. Paul Christensen (see section *iii*), and issue 2 carries a fascinating short piece by Hayden Carruth on contemporary prosody. Hobart and William Smith College Press's decision to reprint the entire run of Robert Bly's *The Fifties* and *The Sixties* magazine is commendable; looking through the first two issues reprinted this year, I find that most of the poetry has aged well, as has Bly's wit in his various asides and "awards." Also, had I a need to be reminded of Bly's role as a tireless translator and champion of other poets' work, these numbers of the journal would do the trick.

ii. The Middle Generation

In a 1972 review of the posthumous publication of Theodore Roethke's notebooks, *Straw for the Fire*, Karl Shapiro (with his usual light-hearted cynicism) noted that in our culture "one can discern a certain trajectory in the poetic career. Following Recognition by the poet's peers, which is really all that matters, there is (1) Cult, (2) Boom, and (3) Racket . . . Sylvia Plath is in Phase 2, while

Roethke is being shunted from 2 to 3." Eventually, the poet "returns to mere Recognition where, *mutatis mutandis*, his best poems will be embalmed and treasured up in the best anthologies." And, one might add, handbooks. With the publication this year of five full-length guides to Roethke, Lowell, Jarrell, and Shapiro himself, we might sense that the major "middle generation" poets have settled into "mere Recognition."

a. **Theodore Roethke.** Lynn Ross-Bryant argues that Roethke's poetry emerges "out of the slime, out of the primordial unity that human beings leave" in their struggle toward individuation in her *Theodore Roethke: Poetry of the Earth . . . Poet of the Spirit* (Kennikat). She begins her discussion with *The Lost Son* (feeling the earlier *Open House* to be experimental and tentative), and reading many of the major poems through *The Far Field*, she sees Roethke's achievement residing in "moments of affirmation of shared life that are grounded in the given, immanent world." Following the pattern of most Twayne volumes, George Wolff's *Theodore Roethke* (TUSAS 390) is a chronological survey of Roethke's life and work, giving brief explications of many of the poems which Wolff attempts to place in their proper "sequences." Unlike Ross-Bryant (whose thought has been influenced by Whitehead and Jung), Wolff has no particular thesis; rather, he prefers to discuss various aspects of the poet's concerns, including the death of his father (which symbolized for him the "painful absence of God"), "the differences between union with nature and union with a woman," and the suggestion in his late work of a "turn toward Christianity." Neither of these studies opens much ground unexplored in Jay Parini's *Theodore Roethke: An American Romantic* (1979), though in their sensitive readings and sensible conclusions, both offer fairly thorough overviews of Roethke's poetry.

Additionally, in her "Self-Poesis in Roethke's 'The Shape of Fire' " (*MPS* 10:121–35) Susan R. Van Dyne sees that poem as "the culmination of Roethke's first thrust beyond his more rational, traditional lyrics of the green house into the more hazardous regions of the subconscious," while M. L. Lewandowska examines Roethke's *Praise to the End!* in "The Words in Their Roaring: Roethke's Use of the Psalms of David" in *The David Myth in Western Literature*, ed. Raymond-Jean Frontain and Jan Wojcik (Purdue, 1980). Last,

Ronald E. McFarland's brief "Roethke's 'Epidermal Macabre'"
(*ConP* 4,ii:16–22) discusses the influence of Richard Lovelace on the
first stanza of Roethke's early poem.

b. **Robert Lowell.**   Burton Raffel's *Robert Lowell* (Ungar) is, amaz-
ingly, the first study of the entire scope of Lowell's work—poetry,
translations, and drama. After a brief chapter tracing Lowell's life,
Raffel devotes three chapters to the poetry: reading the first three
books (*Land of Unlikeness, Lord Weary's Castle,* and *The Mills of
the Kavanaughs*), he finds them generally unsatisfying—formally impressive, but often confused and strained; *Life Studies,* Raffel feels,
is Lowell's "best book," and part 4 of that volume contains "perhaps
the best of Lowell's poems, 'Skunk Hour'"; *For the Union Dead* "is
not so much a bad book as a tired one," while *Near the Ocean* is
"competent" though "derivative"; *Notebook,* in its hammering "away
in the almost monomaniacal single-form approach," is unimpressive,
though *Day by Day* contains nine interesting poems, "new in the
sense that they seem to take new approaches to the creation of poetry." In chapter 5 Raffel discusses *Imitations,* whose free-verse
poems, he argues, are superior to Pound's "translations," though inferior to Galway Kinnell's (he interestingly sets a passage from Kinnell's rendering of Villon next to Lowell's version). Finally, Raffel
concludes with a brief analysis of Lowell's plays, of which he finds
Phaedra the most successful. In his study of Lowell, Raffel doesn't
depart much from the standard criticism, and he therefore adds little
new to our understanding. *Lowell* is, however, a clear and balanced
examination of the life and work of one of our major poets, and as
an introduction it is highly recommended.

In his lucid discussion of poetic careers, *The Life of the Poet,*
Lawrence Lipking rejects the deconstructionist attempt to "render
poems anonymous" for, he convincingly argues, "poems themselves,
above all, declare the life of the poet." In his final chapter, "Endings,"
Lipking briefly reads Lowell's later work as a repudiation of the
earlier, "the wax and honey of a mausoleum," which kept him "pris-
oner." Along the same line, Carol Lee Saffiot's "Between History and
Self: The Function of the Alexander Poems in Robert Lowell's *History*" (*MPS* 10:159–71) sees *History* as an exploration of the self for
which "historical events provide both instrument and specimen"; the

figure of Alexander "serves as the epitome of the tension between self and history." In "Magna Mater" (*Cumberland Journal* 14:3–38) Frank Allen meditates on Lowell and Gary Snyder in terms of "commemoration of the father" and "reverence for the mother." Finally, Jackson G. Barry's "Robert Lowell's 'Confessional' Image of an Age: Theme and Language in Poetic Form" (*ArielE* 12,i:51–58) argues that "Memories of West Street and Lepke" and "Man and Wife" (*Life Studies*) incorporate Lowell's "personal images of an age . . . in a particularly reverberant structure of thematic and linguistic textures"; this is achieved through a series of contrasts between the 1940s and the 1950s.

c. Randall Jarrell, Karl Shapiro, John Berryman. In addition to Wolff's *Roethke*, two other Twayne volumes appeared on these poets this year, Sister Bernetta Quinn's *Randall Jarrell* (TUSAS 398) and Joseph Reino's *Karl Shapiro* (TUSAS 404), and like Wolff's book, both of these studies survey the range of their subjects' work. Quinn obviously feels Jarrell to be a major poet, and her discussion of his poetry, prose, and translations is sympathetic. In her two most interesting chapters, she examines a number of the poet's poems on art (including "The Old and the New Masters," Jarrell's "most comprehensive pictorial analogy"), and paraphrases reminiscences of Jarrell by a number of the poet's former students. In his discussion of Karl Shapiro's "three interrelated facets . . . the prize-winning poet, the exasperating literary critic, and the unabashed autobiographer," Reino argues that four strands are evident in the poet's work: "Fugitive ironies, Beat rebellions, Confessional dispositions, and finally sentimental romanticism." His assessment of Shapiro is much more mixed than Quinn's of Jarrell, as he concludes that the poet's "equivocation, balancing acts, and clever sleights of hand" at times provide his work with a real intensity, though often undercut its "consistency." The year's three articles on Jarrell and Shapiro include George V. Griffith's brief note on "The Death of the Ball Turret Gunner" (*Expl* 40:62), which reads the poem as an ironic commentary on two New Testament injunctions, and Philip L. Gerber's interview with Shapiro in "Trying to Present America" (*SHR* 15:193–208), focusing on such questions as influences, prosody, and the Jewish poet in America. Further, in "Signing the Syllables: The Poetry of

Karl Shapiro" (*SCR* 14,i:109–20) Richard Jackson uses Derrida,
Ricoeur, and Jakobson in his attempt to describe what he feels has
been Shapiro's primary poetic "strategy": "to expose our critical emphasis on the representationality of poetry."

Three articles appeared on John Berryman this year, all centering
on *The Dream Songs*. In " 'I Am Feeling Double': Duality and Dialectic in *The Dream Songs*" (*MissouriR* 4,ii:93–110) Andrew Hudgins is interested in the structuring principle of the long poem, seeing
it as "the dialectic of opposites which do not resolve," as Henry
fluctuates between "genius" and "insanity." Jerry McGuire's "John
Berryman: Making a Poem of the Self" (*MPS* 10:174–89) briefly
looks at the whole of Berryman's work as an "enactment of multiple
self," immersing itself "in any number of intense, discontinuous,
momentary" circumstances; this is most apparent, of course, in Berryman's long poem. In "John Berryman and the Art of *The Dream
Songs*" (*ChiR* 32,iv:34–43) Dona Hickey argues the poem succeeds
due to Berryman's "extraordinary sensitivity to the diversity of English sentence patterns." She examines (with examples) Berryman's
"syntactic surprises," his register (he "experiments with all sorts"),
lexis (strange collocations, puns, and so forth), ellipsis (Berryman
"leaves a lot to the reader's imagination"), and intonation, among
other facets of the poem's lexicology.

d. Richard Wilbur, Elizabeth Bishop. Finally, two notes on Richard Wilbur and one on Elizabeth Bishop are of interest. In "October
Maples, Portland' " (*Expl* 40:60–62), Helen Dry argues that two
paradoxes in Wilbur's poem "reinforce the suggestion that natural
beauty may purify and redeem," while in "Wine, Women, and Wilbur: 'A Voice From Under the Table' " (*NMAL* 5:Item 27) Charles
Sanders sees Wilbur's voice to be both that of the "sot" and that of
the "seer-sorcerer of song." Again, in "A Hol(e)y Communion: Elizabeth Bishop's 'A Miracle for Breakfast' " (*NMAL* 5:Item 14) Charles
Sanders suggests that Bishop's poem depends upon two "ancient
Christian parables" for its "modern 'parable'-montage" quality. Additionally, Wesley Wehr provides a number of comments by Bishop
made in 1966 in "Elizabeth Bishop: Conversations and Class Notes"
(*AR* 39:319–28), while in "Poetry and the World" (*Antaeus* 40,i:
474–87) Robert Pinsky reads Bishop's "In the Waiting Room" and

"Crusoe in England" as examples of the necessity for isolation from "the social, worldly world, in order not to be lost in it."

iii. A Kind of Field

a. **Charles Olson.** In 1974 a special issue of *Boundary 2* edited by Matthew Corrigan was devoted to Charles Olson, and since that time there has been an explosion of both critical and archival work on the poet. While no major full-length study appeared this year, two collections of letters were added to the Olson canon, and a number of excellent articles by leading Olson scholars were published.

Olson introduced himself to Edward Dahlberg in August of 1936, and the two men corresponded extensively until their final falling-out 19 years later. Paul Christensen (whose own *Charles Olson* is a seminal critical study of Olson's poetry and poetics) has undertaken the editing of these letters for Clayton Eshleman's new journal, *Sulfur.* Following a clearly written introduction by Christensen, which sets the letters in context, *Sulfur* 1 prints the surviving letters from 1939 to 1948 (pp. 104–68); *Sulfur* 2, the voluminous correspondence between 1949 and 1950 (pp. 65–166); and next year's *Sulfur* 3 promises to run the remainder of the letters. Most interesting in the first two sections are the writers' discussions of the publishing scene, their comments on Melville, and Dahlberg's assertion that he's "read no modern book since *Call Me Ishmael*" for the moderns "are not my food; my rapture and my eden are in the ancients." Christensen's editing seems sure, though the absence of notes is, given both men's allusiveness, unfortunate.

George F. Butterick continues his major project of editing the Olson–Robert Creeley letters with volume 3 of *The Complete Correspondence* (Black Sparrow). This selection again includes only a few months' letters (21 September–7 November, 1950), though it runs to well over 150 pages (we can see why the series of letters is finally expected to fill at least ten volumes). Unlike Christensen, Butterick again provides notes, and these are a great help, as the letters cover a wide range of subjects, including poetry and prose by both men, Pound, Williams, Cid Corman, and Olson's sense of "Space. SPACE. I spell it large because it comes large here. Large, and without mercy." Drawing on his own correspondence with Olson (to be published soon by Wisconsin), Merton M. Sealts discusses Olson's attitude toward Melville and the state of Melville criticism (c. 1950) in his "Olson, Melville, and the *New Republic*" (*CL* 22: 169–86).

The Fall 1980 *Iowa Review* featured a Charles Olson "Festival" with articles by George Butterick, Robert Creeley, and Sherman Paul. In "Charles Olson and the Postmodern Advance" (pp. 4–27) Butterick clearly traces the development of the idea of the postmodern in Olson's thought. Although Arnold Toynbee used the term "postmodern" as early as 1946, Butterick suggests that Olson was the "first to use it in its current application, and the first to use it repeatedly if not consistently." Creeley's " 'An Image of Man . . .' Working Notes on Charles Olson's Concept of Person" (pp. 29–43) makes several fascinating observations on Olson's methodology, sense of history, and influences in notes toward a discussion of the poet's "book of the body." In "Birds, Landscape, Place, Cosmicity" (pp. 45–61) Sherman Paul continues his work on Olson with a meditation on the poet's achievement, one "of the highest order because, in his concern with cosmology and psychology (his studies in myth join both), he transvalues our primary conceptions of nature and self and gives us a new ontological possibility." As the bird is always in motion and thus defines itself, so too the poet is a poet only when, as Creeley has pointed out, he is writing poems; and like the bird, which "is exemplary because it makes a shelter of such inhospitable materials," the poet transforms landscape and the facts of history into a new "cultural geography."

Olson's interest in C. G. Jung is briefly examined in two pieces in *Spring: An Annual of Archetypal Psychology and Jungian Thought* (1979). In "Poetry and Psyche" (pp. 93–101) Charles Boer argues that Olson is separated from his other, more self-destructive contemporaries by a "unique sense of 'ego' in poetry," his adoption of an "archetypal perspective" wherein poetic perception is seen as "unmediated (immediate) by a subjectivist ego." Jed Rasula's "Charles Olson and Robert Duncan: Mythologistical Grounding" (pp. 102–17) sees the struggle of Olson's *Maximus* and Duncan's "Passages" at least in part an attempt to overcome "the fatal dilemma inherent in speaking of history *or* myth." I'm not sure I agree with Rasula's assertion that the work of Olson and Duncan is the *first* "whose interest in myth reflects the motivations of the soul rather than the exercise of a class privilege"; what of Rilke, for example, or Jeffers? Still, the paper interestingly concludes that Olson and Duncan represent "a major poetic adjustment to the fact of myth as an archetypal condition and not as the reflection of classical education."

Last, the second (and final) installment in Ralph Maud's survey of "Charles Olson: Posthumous Editions and Studies" appeared in *WCR* (15,iii:37–47) this year. Maud's brief comments on books by Charles Boer, Ann Charters, Robert von Hallberg, Sherman Paul, Paul Christensen, and Michael Scoggan are useful, but he is best in his extended discussion of Butterick's fine *Guide to the Maximus Poems*, wherein he offers a number of addenda and corrections.

b. Robert Creeley, Edward Dorn, Robert Duncan, Denise Levertov. Sherman Paul's *The Lost America of Love: Rereading Robert Creeley, Edward Dorn, and Robert Duncan* (LSU) is a difficult book to assess, as it is not strictly speaking a developed work of criticism but rather a book of meditations on the order of Creeley's own *Daybook*. Paul explains that the volume, a sequel to his *Olson's Push*, is a reading of "younger poets of Olson's generation of poets who were closest to him and shared his adventure." He calls his discussions of Creeley, Dorn, and Duncan "open, serial," as he has here in essence made notes on his "rereadings" of these three poets from 1977 to 1979. The Creeley chapter opens with comments on the poet's relationship to Whitman, deals with the influence of Williams, reads poems from *For Love* and *Presences*, then concludes with comments on *Later*; in his notes on Dorn, Paul again considers the influence of Whitman in his analysis of Dorn's poetry from the early chapbooks through *Slinger*, as well as the centrality of geography in the poet's work; finally, Paul takes Duncan's sequences from the "H. D. Book" (in which Duncan uses a similar "open" technique in his rereading of H. D.) as a graph for examining *The Truth & Life of Myth*, *The Opening of the Field*, and *Bending of the Bow*. While it might rightly be argued that *Lost America* is really merely notes toward a draft of a book Paul might have written, I am attracted to its form. Further, though the study is occasionally a little hermetic, Paul is a sensitive reader, and many of his observations (especially his recurrent attempts to locate these poets in "the Green American Tradition") are quite illuminating.

Edward Dorn's first book, *The Newly Fallen*, appeared in 1961,

and through the 1960s and early 1970s Dorn gathered almost a cult
following as his readers tracked his work from little magazine to small
press book and chapbook publication. With the publication of Dorn's
Collected Poems and the complete *Slinger*, however, more general
critical interest in his poetry has seemed to awaken, and this year
in addition to Paul's notes, Michael Davidson has published a major
article on the poet's masterwork, "To Eliminate the Draw: Edward
Dorn's *Slinger*" (*AL* 53:442–64). Davidson traces Dorn's geography,
the lore and exploitation of the American West, to Olson's "Bibliography on America for Edward Dorn," an eclectic essay in which Olson advises the younger man in the formation of "a methodology for
studying and presenting historical data in some determinate relation
to one's immediate concerns." In his reading of *Slinger* Davidson
makes some interesting points, relating the Slinger to Howard
Hughes (one "maintains cycles of acquisition and warfare," the other
"deconstructs the rhetoric upon which these cycles are based"),
remarking on his essential anti-Cartesian ontology, and concluding
that at its most fundamental level, *Slinger* provides us with a comprehensive look at post-1945 language. Dorn is a poet who will progressively demand more of our attention, and Davidson's articulate
piece should serve for some time as an introduction to Dorn's mysterious galaxy. A second article, "Edward Dorn: 'This Marvellous
Accidentalism'" (*Boundary* 9,ii:51–80) by Robert von Hallberg,
focuses on Dorn's political poetry, work derived from Olson's "commitment to didactic, discursive poetry." Von Hallberg reads a number
of Dorn's best shorter poems, as well as passages from *Slinger*, demonstrating how, while the poet's work is "more intelligently political
and more sensitive to wide complicity than that of any of his American contemporaries," it manages through "analytical cool" to "generate new groupings," taking "poetry toward a more human engagement."

Robert Duncan discusses his relationship to Olson ("I played
heretic often to Olson's position"), his homosexuality ("the fact that
I didn't have inbilt [*sic*] any religious or negative formulation about
homosexuality meant that my poetry didn't have to be overt"; additionally, the poet describes a falling-out with John Crowe Ransom
during which Ransom says in a letter that homosexuals "should be
castrated"), his poetics ("I go by a series of omens . . . of compelling
directions that certain things are no longer"), and the genesis of

"Often I Am Permitted to Return to a Meadow" in a major interview with Jack R. Cohn and Thomas J. O'Donnell (*CL* 21[1980]:513–48).

Finally, in his "Denise Levertov, Robert Duncan, and Allen Ginsberg: Modes of the Self in Projective Poetry" (*MPS* 10:200–40), William Aiken begins with a seeming paradox—the close friendship between Levertov and Duncan, and their mutual respect and influences, yet the profound differences "in appearance, technique, content and aim" of their poetry. After closely reading through a number of each writer's poems, Aiken decides that Levertov is an "organic imagist" while Duncan is "best understood as an allegorist." In part 2 of his article, Aiken somewhat confusingly shifts to a discussion of poetry by Levertov and Duncan (and here he adds Ginsberg to his argument) occasioned by the Vietnam War in an analysis of "To Stay Alive," "Passages 26" and "27," and "Wichita Vortex Sutra." While his comments here generally add nothing new to Mersmann's *Out of the Vietnam Vortex* or Nelson's chapter on Duncan in *Our First Last Poets*, Aiken's sense that Ginsberg is able to resolve in his work "that rare integration of visual and aural, phenomenal and personal attentions" that has eluded both Levertov and Duncan is in his essay fairly well substantiated.

c. **George Oppen.** With the publication of Mary Oppen's *Meaning a Life: An Autobiography* (1978) and the poet's own most recent volume, *Primitive*, there has been a revival of interest in the work of George Oppen, signaled this year by *Paideuma*'s special issue (10,i) dedicated to the poet and edited by Burton Hatlen. The first section contains rather slight appreciations of Oppen's achievement by David Ignatow, Charles Tomlinson, and others. More substantially, in "The Periplum" Paul Aester writes "A Few Words in Praise of George Oppen" (pp. 49–52), wherein he observes that Oppen's task has "never been to make pronouncements about the world," but rather to "discover it"; in " 'At Least Not Nowhere': George Oppen as a Maine Poet" (pp. 53–58) Constance Hunting reads Oppen's "Maine poems" as examples of the poet's "making" his geography; Rachel Blau Duplessis' major article "Oppen and Pound" (pp. 59–83) explores at length the critical relationship between the two men, interestingly arguing that in their "objectivist poetics" the two generally agree, while in the practice of that poetics "they divide"; finally, in "Third Phase Objectivism" (pp. 85–89) Ron Silliman discusses what he senses is "objectivism's third or renaissance phase, from 1960 onward," marked by the resurgence of interest in Zukofsky, Bunting, and both Oppens. "The Gallery" includes reproductions of five photographs of George and Mary Oppen taken by Richard Friedman in 1980 (pp. 92–96), while "The Explicator" offers Cid Corman's "The Experience of Poetry" (pp. 99–103) and David Mc-Aleavey's "Unrolling Universe: A Reading of Oppen's *This In Which*" (pp. 105–28). Corman briefly examines three of Oppen's poems from *Primitive* which, he feels, demonstrate "marvellous security" and Shakespearean "persuasion"; McAleavey gives us an extended (and difficult) analysis of Oppen's 1965 volume, finding the poet's primary desire ("that of achieving an immediate, reciprocal relation with the world") to be at great odds with his "self-consciousness." In "The Biographer" Eliot Weinberger ("A Little Heap for George Oppen," pp. 131–36), Jane Augustine ("Mary Oppen: Meaning a life," pp. 137–40), Donald Powell ("'At the Time of the Rogue's First Flood' —A Life Together," pp. 141–42), Michael Heller ("For George Oppen," pp. 143–47), and Dan Gerber ("Of Fathers," pp. 149–51) all add to our knowledge of Oppen's life with a series of articles and memoirs. Finally, in "The Bibliographer" David McAleavey has provided a detailed checklist of the works of Oppen (pp. 155–69) to close the volume.

Of even more importance is *George Oppen*, ed. Burton Hatlen, the third volume in the National Poetry Foundation's Man and Poet series. As Hatlen points out in his introduction, the collection "is not, repeat NOT" a reprinting of the *Paideuma* issue, but rather consists of 514(!) pages of primarily new material. Like NPF's volumes on Bunting and Zukofsky its contents are divided into four sections —"The Milieu," "The Method," "The Canon," and "The Testament"— with essays by John Peck, Eric Mottram, Eric Homberger, Marjorie Perloff, Michael Andre Bernstein, and many others. Some readers are bound to find irony in the publication of a volume of criticism on a poet which runs to about double the number of pages of his *Collected Poems*, an irony which is not lost on Hatlen himself. Others might argue that Oppen's achievement simply doesn't merit such a monument. To both I suggest that they reserve judgment until reading in this collection; like the previous Man and Poet volumes, *George Oppen* is not only a study of an individual poet which is unlikely to be surpassed, it charts modern and postmodern issues—both aesthetic and political—which remain central to our art and our time.

"Political Commitment and Poetic Subjectification: George Oppen's Test of Truth" comes under Norman M. Finkelstein's scrutiny this year in *CL* (22:24–41). Finkelstein notices that while Oppen and his "fellow objectivists" were followers in the established tradition of high modernism in terms of style, Oppen took a left-wing, activist stance foreign to the modernist sensibility. He convincingly argues (through both biography and text) that Oppen's primary shift from the Pound/Williams influence in the extremely objectivist *Discrete Series* to the more subjective post-1950s poems was motivated by a necessary "subjectification in explicitly moral terms" of imagism and objectivism.

iv. The Autochthonic Spirit: Allen Ginsberg, Gary Snyder, Lawrence Ferlinghetti, Gregory Corso, William Everson, Jack Spicer

Almost perversely, at a period in which interest in the writers of the Beat Generation/San Francisco Renaissance seems—at least in terms of conferences, readings, course offerings, and book sales—at its height, for the first time in over a decade almost no new work was published on these poets this year.

Lee Bartlett's *The Beats: Essays in Criticism* (McFarland) anthologizes essays on Beat poets, most of which have been previously published: John Clellon Holmes's "Unscrewing the Locks: The Beat Poets" (pp. 5–13), Albert Gelpi's "Everson/Antoninus" (pp. 40–52), L. A. Ianni's "Lawrence Ferlinghetti's Fourth Person Singular and the Theory of Relativity" (pp. 53–65), James Breslin's "Allen Ginsberg: The Origins of *Howl* and *Kaddish*" (pp. 66–89), Thomas S. Merrill's "Allen Ginsberg's Reality Sandwiches" (pp. 90–106), Barbara Christian's "What Happened to Bob Kaufman" (pp. 107–14), Thomas Parkinson's "The Poetry of Gary Snyder" (pp. 133–46), Robert Kerns's "Clearing the Ground: Gary Snyder and the Modernist Imperative" (pp. 147–64), and Geoffrey Thurley's "The Development of the New Language: Michael McClure, Philip Whalen, and Gregory Corso" (pp. 165–80). *The Beats* concludes with an afterword reprinting two of Everson's seminal essays—"Dionysus and the

Beat Generation" and "Four Letters on the Archetype" (pp. 181–94)—which examine these poets from a Jungian point of view. Finally, the editor has provided an extended annotated bibliography of both primary and secondary material.

Mark Johnson draws a parallel between D. H. Lawrence's "argument for a poetry of the immediate present" and Ginsberg's poetics, arguing that (contra Mark Schorer) such a notion does not mean lack of a disciplined poetry in "Discovery as Technique: Allen Ginsberg's 'These States'" (*ConP* 4,ii:23–45). Johnson examines various passages from Ginsberg's long poem, concluding, not surprisingly, that "the seminal point is that the poem's form is determined by something interior and alogical."

In "Where We Might Meet Each Other: An Appreciation of Galway Kinnell and William Everson" (*LitR* 24:355–70) Joe Marusiak reads these poets' "retrospective" volumes, *The Avenue Bearing the Initial of Christ Into the New World* and *The Veritable Years*, as highly successful struggles with "questions of perception and expression and significance." Of Everson's collected Catholic poetry (written as Brother Antoninus) in particular, Marusiak feels that the work is a treatment of "the self in agonized, lonely, sometimes frenzied search" in which it "becomes clearer that the achievements of image and sound are every bit as profound and affecting as the statements on personal need."

The publication of *The Collected Books of Jack Spicer*, edited with a long commentary by Robin Blaser (Black Sparrow, 1975), made Spicer's work readily available, while *Boundary 2*'s special Spicer issue two years later marked the first major collection of academic criticism on the poet and generated wider interest (as in the case of *Boundary 2*'s Olson issue) in his work. In this year's "Jack Spicer's Ghosts and the Gnosis of History" (*Boundary* 9,ii:81–100) Norman M. Finkelstein laments the fact that despite explication of his individual works, no "unified attempt has been made to place Spicer in a genuinely historical perspective." Finkelstein takes Yeats as Spicer's "greatest precurser," seeing the poet's verse as "a synthesis of interior (i.e. Romantic) and exterior (i.e. Modernist/Objectivist) modes of poetic discourse." This clearly argued essay on a poet Finkelstein takes to be the only postmodern American "poetic theorist" who stands perhaps beyond Olson is a solid contribution.

v. Dream of a Common Language

a. **Sylvia Plath.** Without doubt, one of the most important books to be published this year is the long-awaited edition of Plath's *The Collected Poems* (Harper), edited with an introduction and fairly extensive notes by Ted Hughes. Although she published only one volume, *The Colossus*, during her life, Plath was prolific and, as Hughes points out in his introduction, she "never scrapped any of her poetic efforts." Hughes has chosen to arrange the volume chronologically, attempting as nearly as possible to place the 224 poems in the order they were written. He begins the collection with work from 1956, which he takes as a "watershed" in that the first poems to be included in *Colossus* appeared that year. American poets seem predisposed to keep one eye on their work, the other on the rail of fame, and Plath was certainly no exception. Hughes notes that she preserved final typescripts of all her poems, and thus we can be fairly sure that the work appears throughout in finished form. Further, as Hughes argues, the fact that Plath's "evolution as a poet went rapidly through successive moults of style, as she realized her true matter and voice" makes the arrangement of the poems in the current volume even more suitable. Hughes also has chosen to include a selection of 50 "Juvenelia" from the 220 early poems which are extant, though he warns us that he's fairly sure Plath herself would have chosen to keep these poems in a drawer. Plath's admirers tend to divide into two groups—those who find the most value in the earlier, more formal poems, and those who find the intensity of the later poems the superior achievement. Regardless of which camp readers favor, however, they owe Hughes a debt for this fine attempt to give a brilliant American poet her due.

The year's two articles on Plath focused on selected aspects of her life and work. In " 'The Bland Granta': Sylvia Plath at Cambridge" (*DR* 60:496–507) Philip Gardner, who casually knew the poet during her two years at Cambridge, mixes memoir with criticism in examining a particularly productive period in Plath's life. Most interestingly, Gardner discusses the influence of Stevens and Wilbur on Plath's work during those years, which he argues "was no mere matter of titles or of language, but more importantly of shared subject matter." Lois Rosen's "Sylvia Plath's Poetry About Children: A

New Perspective" (*MPS* 10:98–115) notices that children play a major role in Plath's work, "especially in those poems that were written after the birth of her first child." Reading a number of poems and *Letters Home*, Rosen demonstrates fairly convincingly that throughout her later work (beginning with the 1956 "The Manor Garden"), "a definite progression is apparent in which the child is often not only a concrete image, but also a reflection of the poet's inner world at that point in her life."

b. Anne Sexton. In addition to Plath's *Collected Poems*, Anne Sexton's *The Complete Poems* (Houghton Mifflin) appeared this year. Like Plath, Sexton was also a prolific poet (and she lived almost 15 years longer); edited by Sexton's daughter Linda Gray Sexton, the book runs to 622 pages, collecting all the poems from Sexton's ten books, as well as six previously unpublished poems she wrote the year she died. In her introduction to the volume, "How It Was," the poet Maxine Kumin (who was Sexton's "intimate friend" and "professional ally") provides biographical information and some insight into Sexton's work habits and poetic strategies, concluding that "women poets in particular owe a debt to Anne Sexton, who broke new ground, shattered taboos, and endured a barrage of attacks. . . . Time will sort out the dross among these poems and burnish the gold. Anne Sexton has earned her place in the canon."

In "45 Mercy Street and Other Vacant Houses" (*New England Heritage*, pp. 145–65) Linda W. Wagner reads the poetry of both Sexton and Plath in her usual clear and perceptive fashion, arguing that both poets, like their precursor Emily Dickinson, eschew the "New England Tradition" of "the use of place, landscape, to reveal larger ideas" in favor of a poetry of "interiority."

c. Adrienne Rich, Diane Wakoski. Adrienne Rich's first book, *A Change of World*, was chosen by W. H. Auden for the Yale Younger Poet Award in 1951. In "Imitations and Identities" (*MPS* 10:136–58), Adalaide Morris discusses "these architecturally intricate and static poems" which "conceal" as much as they reveal about the poet. There are, Morris argues, essentially three ways to read these poems: first, we might give our attention to "their intricate and accomplished formal structures"; second, we might note "the frequent gap between poet and persona and the occasional incongruity between stated and

embedded themes"; finally, as in Rich's own description of Lawrence's early poetry, we might focus on the poems as a process,
"stress not so much the pattern in each poem as its unfolding across
poems," as Rich struggles toward the "tentative voicing of an identity" which is truly her own.

After an interesting discussion of the "critical performance" as
"always other than itself, always a dialectical relation with a poem
or play or novel as another and different presence," Evan Watkins'
"Historical Criticism and Contemporary Poetry" (*CL* 22:556–73)
examines in detail Diane Wakoski's "The Hitchhiker," paying particular attention to the poem's rather deceptive "simplicity." Watkins' meditation on the poem finds its source in the work of Antonio
Gramsci, and his piece is certainly the most serious critical attempt
to deal with Wakowski we've seen thus far.

vi. Naked on Their Goats

a. **Robert Bly, James Wright.** As a poet, translator, theorist, an-
thologist, and editor, Robert Bly has been a major influence on the
shape of postmodern American poetry, and Richard Jones and Kate
Daniels have this year devoted a massive special "double issue" of
their journal *Poetry East* (4/5) to the poet's achievement. Following the editors' brief introduction (pp. 5–7) and a "Notice" of appreciation by William Stafford (p. 8), the journal prints ten new
poems by Bly (pp. 10–24), four of Bly's Rilke translations (pp. 25–
28), and a new essay by the poet on "Form that is Neither In nor
Out" (pp. 29–34). Then come 23 "essays, memoirs, poems & documents" dealing with various facets of Bly's life and work by Donald
Hall, Annie Wright, Patricia Goedicke, Bill Lavatsky, Gregory Orr,
Larry Levis, and others. A significant collection of generally fascinating pieces, this issue of *Poetry East* is assuredly a benchmark in
Bly scholarship.

With his usual clarity, Ralph J. Mills, Jr., examines several of
Bly's more recent prose poems with reference to the poet's notions
in his "Great Mother" and "Three Brains" essays in "Of Energy
Compacted & Whirling" (*NMHR* 4,ii:29–49). Mills sees in the prose
poem especially "an effort to arrive at a more expansive, inclusive
sense of deity," which is made more accessible in a form where the
poet's "consciousness can exercise a flexibility not constrained by

problems of the line." Reading poems from *This Body Is Made of Camphor and Gopherwood*, Mills finds the book a "sequence" whose theme is, as the title implies, the body.

Two articles appeared on James Wright this year, one analytic, the other a memoir. In " 'Many of Waters': The Poetry of James Wright" (*Boundary* 9,ii:101–21) Walter Kalaidjian argues that Wright's shift to a more "personal style" in his later books is only a "surface" shift—that in fact through attention to his interest in "native landscape, particularly the locales of water," we will discover a continuity of vision. Kalaidjian begins by clearly rehearsing Wright's movement from formalist verse through a kind of surrealism, though he offers nothing much new here; later, however, he interestingly focuses on the "waterworld" as "an open-ended metaphor" in Wright's work, demonstrating how it "reflects the lifelong ambivalence and final mystification Wright felt" for America. Peter Serchuk touchingly remembers Wright in "On the Poet, James Wright" (*MPS* 10:85–90) as he describes the poet's visit to one of Laurence Lieberman's poetry workshops at Illinois in 1973.

b. **W. S. Merwin.** Aside from Cary Nelson's fine essay on W. S. Merwin in *Our Last First Poets*, two other items of interest appeared on the poet this year. Along with Roethke, Shapiro, and Jarrell, Twayne devoted a volume to W. S. Merwin (TUSAS 360) by Cheri Davis. In her preface Davis argues that Merwin "is at the vanguard in contemporary poetry and translation," which is probably an exaggeration, and that "he displays a virtuoso's agility in adopting a diversity of poetic forms and styles," which probably is not. She sees Merwin as a poet in the tradition of Stevens, that is, a poet for whom "the act of writing a poem" becomes "an entrance into a psychic state where all is incipient, unformed, and unknown"; further, for Merwin "reality without the vivid gloss the poet writes on it is insufficient. Poetry fulfills a religious need." Davis reads closely through the range of Merwin's verse, from *A Mask for Janus* to *The Compass Flower*, as well as the poet's two prose books, though unfortunately she spends little time on the translations. As the first full-length study of Merwin's achievement, Davis' book is a useful companion to the poetry. Thomas B. Byers also attends to Merwin in his "Believing Too Much in Words: W. S. Merwin and the Whitman Heritage" (*MissouriR* 3,ii:75–89). There Byers argues that Merwin's sense of language is opposed to Whitman's in that while Whitman has faith in the power of speech to "transcend difference and create relationship," Merwin searches for a speech that is "self-negating," an attempt "to reflect the *inability* to generate presence."

c. James Dickey. Can a year go by without at least one critic or reviewer playing one of our favorite literary sports—get James Dickey? Last year saw Robert Peters' witty discussion of Dickey as a "much-decorated Poetry Ace"; this year, Turner Cassity examines *The Strength of Fields* and *The Zodiac*, grudgingly admitting that "within his limits" Dickey "can be effective," and that "publicity has made Dickey one of the better poets who has ever been really popular." Cassity, however, is less generous in the rest of his comments, noting that the poet suffers from "the dread Southern urge to use eight words wherever one will do," that Dickey "thinks he is Paul Hornung," that "the debt to John Cheever" in "Lombardi" "is this side of plagiarism, but only just," and so on. Cassity reminds me of Oscar Wilde in his ability to turn a phrase, and I suspect that Wilde would share Cassity's distrust of the locker room (something he confesses during the course of his article). Unfortunately, midway through the piece he finds it necessary to admit that he finds "off-shore drilling platforms the most attractive thing in any seascape." Five years ago this comment would have been in bad taste; in our current situation, with our environment under the stewardship of James Watt, however, Cassity's aside is simply insipid, marring an otherwise not enlightening but entertaining article. Francis E. Skipp also is interested in Dickey's major poem in "James Dickey's *The Zodiac*: The Heart of the Matter" (*CP* 14,i:1–10), commenting on the importance of Pythagoras, sacrifice, and the power of the imagination to the Dutchman's quest for "the light of truth."

d. A. R. Ammons, John Ashbery, Frank O'Hara, James Merrill. As far as I can determine, A. R. Ammons and John Ashbery each attracted only two articles of note this year. Ammons' work has become progressively more formal, and along the way he has garnered some rather high-powered critical supporters, including Harold Bloom. In his "A. R. Ammons and *The Snow Poems* Reconsidered" (*ChiR* 33,i:32–38), Michael McFee remarks on the curious general dis-

Poetry: The 1940s to the Present

missal of Ammons' long poem (which is what McFee considers *SP*
to be) by these friendly critics as an aberration. He prefers to read
it as a significant achievement wherein Ammons displays his "deep
anti-formalism." Further, McFee feels that Ammons, in consciously
throwing off "the voice of the Romantic Bard or the Peeping Tom or
even the Good Old Boy," reveals more of himself here than in any
of his earlier books. Matthew Wilson is also interested in Ammons'
long poems, as he argues in "Homecoming in A. R. Ammons' *Tape
for the Turn of the Year*" (*ConP* 4,ii:60–76) that *Tape* is the poet's
"breakthrough" work, a poem wherein he discovers that "a restoration of place . . . becomes a great opening up of the world." A. Poulin,
Jr., gives us a major interview with John Ashbery in "The Experience of Experience" (*MQR* 20:242–55). Ashbery begins with an
enlightening discussion of "Leaving the Atocha Station" (a poem
which seems to be drawing progressively more attention than any of
Ashbery's others) in which he remarks of his work that "the poetry
is what's there and there are no hidden meanings or references to
other things beyond what most of us know," while further on in the
interview he dismisses the notion that he was influenced by French
symbolism. In "On the Virtues of Modesty: John Ashbery's Tactics
Against Transcendence" (*MLQ* 42:65–84) David Fite convincingly
argues that "In Soonest Mended" Ashbery defines the primary problem facing poets from the romantics on, the Cartesian duality, which
is "not so much obliterated by Ashbery as accepted, *consented to*,"
through a "repudiation of strenuous Romantic knowing." He continues with a clear discussion of Ashbery's preoccupation with absence, which finds perhaps its most realized expression in his "flux,"
"Litany."

Alexander Smith's *Frank O'Hara: A Comprehensive Bibliography*
(Garland, 1980) presents a 100-page compilation of references to
both primary works—books, pamphlets, broadsides, magazine appearances, films, videotapes, and recordings—and reviews of O'Hara's
publications; additionally, there is a selection of facsimiles of first-
edition title pages.

Judith Moffett continues her work on James Merrill with "Sound
Without Sense: Willful Obscurity in Poetry, With Illustrations From
James Merrill's Canon" (*NER* 3[1980]:294–312), an essay which
attempts to deal with Merrill's "deliberate choice not to speak his

mind." Moffett was Merrill's graduate student at the University of Wisconsin in the late 1960s, and here she takes her mentor to task for "the single important fault" in all his early poetry—"the willingness to attract and then abandon" his "devoted readers." In the later long poems, however, Moffett finds "a balance between lucidity and obscurity," which, she argues, will be Merrill's "surest way to excellence." Merrill is again taken to task in William Harmon's "The Metaphors and Metamorphoses of M" (*Parnassus* 8,ii:29–41); Harmon reviews Merrill's final volume, *Scripts for the Pageant*, of his long (and as yet untitled) poem concluding that the poet's "five or six talents are just not up to the demands of an opus that calls for twenty or thirty." Although Harmon feels that Merrill's "superlative distinction" is "as our poet of identicals and consonance," he argues that the long poem has no "shaping sense of good and evil" and thus "spends most of its time floundering in chitchat and mumbo-jumbo."

e. **Donald Justice, John Logan, Richard Hugo, Mark Strand.**   Some critics consider the literary interview to be a kind of subacademic endeavor, one on the order of writing a personality profile for *People* or *TV Guide*. In fact, some interviews are fairly superficial and do little to further our studies; others, however, like this year's interviews with Donald Justice, Richard Hugo, John Logan, and Mark Strand, do deserve our attention as they interestingly probe important issues concerning the writer's craft. Of the four, David Hamilton and Lowell Edwin Folsom's "An Interview with Donald Justice" (*IowaR* 11,iii–iv:1–21) is the most fully realized, as Justice speaks at length about his writing habits, various problems which arose in editing his *Selected Poems*, his feelings about revision, and his sense of formal prosody. The same issue of *Iowa Review* prints "A Conversation with John Logan" (pp. 221–29) by Thomas Hilgers and Michael Molloy; though not as extended as the Justice piece, Logan speaks engagingly and in detail about the genesis of his poem "Shore Scene." Thomas Gardner's "An Interview with Richard Hugo" (*CL* 22:139–52) elicits from the poet a number of comments on the writing of *31 Letters and 13 Dreams*, while Nolan Miller's two-part "The Education of a Poet" (*AR* 39:107–18, 181–93) has Mark Strand discussing both his influences as a young poet and many of his contemporaries.

vii. **Singularities, or, E. P., "This is a Darn'd Clever Bunch!"**
Because we are always more or less engaged in establishing and
revising our canon as younger poets mature and new poets emerge,
our criticism is bound to be as various as our poetry. This section tries
each year to survey the early and eclectic single essays on poets (of
all ages) who have rising reputations. This year we have a number
of interesting pieces on Dave Smith, Norman Dubie, Robert Pinsky,
Theodore Weiss, James Laughlin, Jonathan Williams, Fred Chapell,
Louise Glück, Ronald Johnson, Leslie Ullman, Charles Wright, Gregory Orr, and John Updike.

a. **Dave Smith, Norman Dubie, Robert Pinsky.**   Two fairly young
poets whose stars are on the rise are Dave Smith and Norman Dubie,
and each attracted substantial review-essays this year. In "Into the
Big Leagues" (*Parnassus* 8,ii:102–10) Michael McFee reviews *Gos-
hawk, Antelope,* arguing that this book goes beyond Smith's earlier
work (wherein he is a combination "wunderkind" and "talented
mimic"), presenting "the mature Dave Smith." Although McFee feels
that the volume is perhaps not wholly successful in that it may be
too long and at times "suffers from unrelieved abstract flatulence"
and "inferior imagination," he contends that here Smith grapples
effectively with the "Big Themes" with a genuine "fierce hopeless-
ness" which results in a "possibility of hope held in healthy tension."
Lorrie Goldensohn attempts to deal with the range of Norman Dubie's work—from *The Horsehair Sofa* (1969) to *The Everlastings*
(1980)—in "Not in the Browning Shade" (*Parnassus* 8,ii[1980]:152–
75). Dubie has published ten books and chapbooks in just 11 years,
and Goldensohn sees this prodigality as yielding "a variety of forms
in which to test his historical and literary concerns, to hone his expressionist imagery, and to extend his language." Further, in analyzing the progression from the short *Alehouse Sonnets* to the later
Browningesque long poems, she feels that Dubie has hit his stride,
his poems gaining "principally by intensifying their commitment to
story-telling, by coming up with a better, less discontinuous balance
of narrative and narrative shift."

   While this year Jonathan Holden took exception to Robert Pinsky's anti-imagist poetics, in "Explaining America: The Poetry of
Robert Pinsky" (*CR* 33,i:16–26) Jay Parini regarded Pinsky's long
poem *An Explanation of America* as a major work, one that "offers

a steadiness and wholeness of vision rare in contemporary poetry."
Arguing that, like Coleridge and Eliot, Pinsky "is determined to
create the taste by which he will be judged," Parini finds the poet's
greatest strengths to be his "modest, oddly affecting tone" and "the
way in which he moves effortlessly from abstract formulation to vivid
particulars." I would like to believe this, though I'm not sure that
Parini is in this short piece convincing, especially when he quotes
lines like "That freedom, even in a Republic, / Rests ultimately on
the right to die" as an example of a "poet in control"; or, perhaps, that
is finally the problem—unlike the long poems of Parini's earlier subject, Roethke, I feel that throughout *An Explanation* Pinsky is too
much in control. Barbara F. Lefcowitz's casual discussion of Pinsky's
"Essay on Psychiatrists" in "Ambivalence and the Bourgeois Poet"
(*ConP* 4,ii:54–60) argues that Pinsky fails in his attempt to dero-
manticize poets through the deromanticization of psychiatrists.

b. **James Laughlin, Jonathan Williams, Theodore Weiss.** James
Laughlin, Jonathan Williams, and Theodore Weiss are known primarily for their contributions to our literature as publishers and editors, though each has produced a solid body of his own work.
Laughlin once had hopes of making his primary career as a writer
of both fiction and poetry; in the mid-30's, however, while visiting
Ezra Pound in Rapallo, the older poet advised him (after reading a
few of his poems) to "do something useful . . . become a publisher."
Laughlin returned to America to found New Directions, which for
the last 45 years has certainly done more to enrich American writing
than any four or five other publishing houses combined. Still, he
continued to write poetry "for personal fun" on the side. A few of
Laughlin's own first poems and a story were included in *New Directions 1* (1936), and his first book of poems, *Some Natural Things*,
was published in 1945. *In Another Country*, ed. Robert Fitzgerald
(City Lights), selects poems from that volume and Laughlin's four
subsequent ones. In "A Portrait of the Publisher as Poet" (*Parnassus* 8,ii[1980]:194–209) Marjorie Perloff examines Laughlin's quiet
achievement as a poet; while she finds his social and political poems
wanting in their lack of "Objectivist cool," she concludes that his love
poems seem simple but are "exquisitely wrought" and that "In
Another Country," perhaps his major poem, sustains "tension"
throughout. Laughlin's own reminiscences of his publishing and writ-

ing career appear in a wonderfully lively "Interview by Robert Dana"
in a "Special *APR* Supplement" (10,vi:19–30).

Like Laughlin, Jonathan Williams has made his reputation as a
publisher, most notably of Charles Olson's *Maximus*, though he has
published many books of his own verse. Kenneth Irby surveys Williams' *Elite/Elate Poems, Selected Poems 1971–75* in " 'America's
Largest Openair Museum' " (*Parnassus* 8,ii[1980]:307–29), wherein
he discusses Williams' interest in the "interpenetration of the visual
and the aural" in poetry, his complex use of titles, and his interest
in music. Further, Irby insists that while Williams "is one of the fun-
niest and wittiest writers alive," he should not be dismissed as merely
a writer of light verse, for this would be to miss the visionary quality
of so much of his contemplative poetry. Finally, Theodore Weiss is
probably best known as the editor of the fine *Quarterly Review of
Literature*. In "Profit Under the Sun" (*Parnassus* 8,ii[1980]:83–101)
Helene J. F. de Aguilar surveys Weiss' *Views & Spectacles: New and
Selected Shorter Poems*, noting the influence of both Homer and Auden. She concludes that Weiss "is one of the most splendidly balanced
poets now writing in America."

c. Leslie Ullman, Fred Chappell, Ronald Johnson, Louise Glück.
Eric Torgersen's "Mysteriousness: The Rhetoric of the Inner Life"
(*Field* 25:46–56) takes Leslie Ullman's first book, *Natural Histories*,
to task, finding in it too strong echoes of James Wright and Robert
Bly ("mysteriousness of the most familiar sort: the *dark* bit"; "she
invokes *body* in thirteen of her poems"; "a dedicated and adroit manipulator of pronouns"). Torgersen's admonishments here are on the
order of Pinsky's, and essentially even stronger restatements of some
of David Walker's points in his essay "Stone Soup," and all three
writers have a case. And yet the final issue is not really one of counting stones or bodies and rather deipotently deciding the sources of
the "clichés"; rather, it seems to me that we must trouble to examine
how such images work in any given, specific poetic circumstance.
Certainly Ullman's early poems are apprentice work—she may or may
not emerge as an essential talent. Yet are her images flat or gra-
tuitous? Many of her lines that Torgersen quotes in derision ("Others
will find the flowers at her throat / small fires in the cave of her hair")
are certainly stronger than those I quoted earlier from Pinsky, a poet
whose rhetoric meets with, I suspect, Torgersen's approval.

Three reviews of poets who are established, though not often written about—Fred Chappell, Ronald Johnson, and Louise Glück—were of note this year. In "His Life in Mid-Course" (*ChiR* 33,i:85–91) Ellen Tucker examines Fred Chappell's *Earth Sleep*, the final volume in his poetic autobiography in four books, *Midquest*. While Tucker finds Chappell's monologues fairly unimpressive, remaining "essentially static," she regards his voice as "highly flexible" and his Appalachian portraits gifted. Ronald Johnson's first book, *A Line of Poetry, A Row of Trees* (1964), was published by Jonathan Williams, and Johnson has often cited Black Mountain (i.e., "Charles Olson out of Ezra Pound, Louis Zukofsky, and Williams") as his primary influence. In "The Poetry of a Journal at the End of an Arbor in a Watch" (*Parnassus* 9,i:217–32) William Harmon discusses Johnson's *Ark: The Foundations*, the first volume of a three-book poem in progress. Using generous (and well-chosen) quotations, Harmon argues that not all of Johnson's verse "is essential poetry," that some (like some of Pound, Olson, and Zukofsky) includes "episodes of rather belligerent quotation of moral examples"; still, he feels, Johnson has in *Ark* deepened his "wonderful, dendrological, arboricultural vision" in a "primatically concentrated succession of poems (and some prose) about the universe as a show of lyric physics, the world as a show of lyric biology, and man as a show of lyric linguistics." Finally, Louise Glück's fourth book, *Descending Figure*, was published last year, and this year Calvin Bedient reviews it in "Birth, Not Death, Is the Hard Loss" (*Parnassus* 9,i:168–86). Bedient suggests that Glück's poems "arise from protest"; specifically, he senses that "evidence of male violence dots Glück's poems like scraps of clothing dropped behind to leave a trail." He reminds us that women poets of her generation (she was born in 1943) are expected "to write polemically of men," yet he finds Glück's poetry (especially "The Sick Child") often verse of "the first intensity" for its singular "vision—groping, contradictory, excessive, obstinate, arresting, revealing."

d. Gregory Orr and John Updike.

Stanley Kunitz provides a brief introduction (pp. 5–7) to *Poetry East*'s special issue (2), *Salt Wings: The Poetry of Gregory Orr*. While Orr is relatively young (35) and a "changing poet," Kunitz feels that "his signature remains immediately recognizable." *Salt Wings* draws its 30 pages of poetry from Orr's two earlier books, *Burning the Empty Nests* and *Gathering the*

Bones Together, as well as the forthcoming *The Red House*. Charles Wright's strongest book, *The Southern Cross*, appeared this year, and it included his most fully realized poem, "Homage to Paul Cezanne," a remarkable and haunting meditation on death. Sherod Santos interviews Wright at length in *Quarterly West* (12:18–45), as the poet discusses his sense of the image and the influence of Pound, his notion of *Bloodlines* and *Hard Freight* as "put-together books, that is a single poem," and his interest in Cezanne.

Why is it that many of our best novelists (Hemingway, Faulkner, and Mailer come immediately to mind) seem compelled to attempt poetry, yet fail so miserably at it? John Updike's first book was, in fact, a charming collection of poetry called *The Carpeted Hen and Other Tame Creatures*, and since that time he has published three additional books of verse, with individual poems appearing often in the *New Yorker*. In his *The Other John Updike* (Ohio) Donald J. Greiner devotes a chapter to each of Updike's poetry collections, telling us more than we could ever want to know about the writer's poetizing. I think the primary flaw in Greiner's study is precisely that he does study at length what is finally merely ephemeral material (unlike, for example, Updike's shorter fiction and, perhaps, his play, which Greiner examines in the second half of his book). His prose is lucid and he does do a good job pointing out the novelist's central concern—his "stark awareness of mortality"; still, even after Greiner concludes, I must side with the young Updike: his poetic creatures remain as tame as ever.

In 1979 my predecessor Sandra Gilbert lamented the lack of work being done on women poets, and two years later the situation hasn't changed much. I haven't done a frequency count on this year's chapter, but I suspect the ratio is about 15 male writers discussed for every female, and even our best female critics—Marjorie Perloff, Mary Ann Caws, and Helen Vendler are examples—seem drawn generally to male writers. Further, while the quantity of criticism in our area borders on the staggering, still there are some male poets who certainly deserve more attention—Louis Zukofsky, Philip Levine, Robert Kelly, Clayton Eshleman, Paul Blackburn, James Tate, Charles Simic, Charles Wright, and the L*A*N*G*U*A*G*E poets, among others.

University of New Mexico

18. Drama

Walter J. Meserve

Jonas Barish's *The Antitheatrical Prejudice* (Calif.), which begins with Plato's rejection of the drama and goes on to trace similar reactions from ancient writers to the present, reflects a typical bias against the American theatre among scholars. Even this history of prejudice, however, ignores the large amount of antitheatrical sentiment that has existed in American society since the 17th century. Such neglect of American views may be forgiven an English Renaissance scholar, but even American literary historians give short shrift to American theatre and drama. *Early American Literature*, ed. Michael T. Gilmore (Prentice-Hall, 1980), a collection of critical essays, contains not one reference to dramatic literature. *American Literature: Colonial Age to 1890*, ed. Frank N. Magill (Salem, 1980) does not mention a single dramatist. Of the 120 people referred to in Donald Hall's edition of *The Oxford Book of American Literary Anecdotes* (Oxford) only four dramatists evidently lived sufficiently interesting lives to warrant being noted or quoted—O'Neill, Kaufmann, Rice, and Odets. It is perfectly logical to conclude from Lee Bartlett's collection of essays on *The Beats* (McFarland) that the "beats" did not write plays. Marcus Klein wrote *Foreigners: The Making of American Literature, 1900–1940* with the obvious bias that the drama is not literature. Although A. Walton Litz's *American Writers* includes essays on Odets and Baraka, the prejudice persists. Scholars interested in American dramatic literature and the theatre for which it was written find themselves tightly wedged between the indifference literary critics exude toward the drama and the director/actor/designer's singular approach to theatre as nothing but the current production.

Despite all this indifference, however, the year 1981 produced a considerable quantity of work on the theatre and the drama. There was a whole shelf of reference works, five book-length histories, another five works of general interest, an important volume of essays on the contemporary drama, and a handful of biographies. In addition, there was important work published on O'Neill, Odets, Williams, and Shepard. Also among dissertation writers there was a lot of activity. There were five historical studies on widely diverse topics, three studies of drama critics, treatments of black theatre and feminist theatre, and many dissertations focusing on individual playwrights: Simon, Hart, Williams, O'Neill, Rice, Albee, Hellman, and Odets. It may be a relief to note that there appear to be no obvious trends in dissertations dealing with topics in American drama and theatre.

i. Reference Works and Books of General Interest

Among those reference books published in 1981 which should be of inestimable value to scholars is the *Dictionary of Literary Biography*, volume 7, *Twentieth Century American Dramatists, Part I: A–J* and *Part II: K–Z*, ed. John MacNicholas (Gale), with individual essays on 78 dramatists and 12 theatres. Each essay provides a substantial review of the life and work of the dramatist and a listing of plays, a bibliography, and illustrations. The 17th edition of *Who's Who in the Theatre*, ed. Ian Herbert (Gale), appears in two volumes. Volume 1 presents brief biographies and career data on 2,200 people who were living in 1979; Volume 2, *Playbills*, gives production information (1976–1979) for theatres in London, New York, and such cities as Chichester, Stratford-on-Avon, and Stratford, as well as a listing of long-run plays since 1890. Daniel Blum's *A Pictorial History of the American Theatre, 1860–1980* (Crown) has been enlarged by John Willis for its fifth edition. This pictorial review is substantial for the 1860–1920 period and particularly effective for the period between the two world wars.

Now in its fourth year, the *American Theatre Annual, 1979–80*, ed. Catharine Hughes (Gale), provides basic information—theatre, cast, play plot, dates, a photograph, and excerpted reviews—for all plays that opened on or off Broadway before 30 April of the 1979–1980 theatre season. *Performing Arts Biography Master Index*, ed. Barbara McNeil and Miranda C. Herbert (Gale), prints in this second edition 270,000 sketches from the major biographical dictionaries of all types of performing artists. Two other works of more specialized interest, clearly for the scholar who seeks such information, are William T. Leonard's *Theatre: Stage to Screen to Television,* 2 vols. (Scarecrow), which gives the vital statistics for works produced in all three media, and *The Language of American Popular Entertainment* by Don B. Wilmeth (Greenwood), a fascinating glossary of some 3,200 terms relative to such popular entertainments as the circus, carnivals, vaudeville, burlesque, tent shows, magic shows, and medicine shows.

The American theatre, like the theatre of all countries, is a distinctive institution with distinctive people who exercise their talents, successfully or not, but seemingly always with difficulty, in a variety of places, likely and unlikely. Steven R. Wasserman attempts to provide a *Lively Arts Information Directory* (Gale) as a guide to this institution, but with its 12 sections—Organizations, Theatre Schools, Workshops, Festivals, Scholarships, Awards and Prizes, Selected Libraries, Relevant Periodical Publications, and major productions, plus others—it becomes something of a hodgepodge of selected information without a focus. In *The Vaudevillians, A Dictionary of Vaudeville Performers* (Arlington) Anthony Slide gives brief biographical information about one set of those distinctive people—some 175 vaudevillians from Abbott and Costello to Ed Wynn. Another such set is explored in *Street Performers in America: Passing the Hat* (Delacorte) by Patricia J. Campbell. This is a delightful, popular book—almost a "where to go" and "what to do" book for street musicians, jugglers, clowns, and the like. It is also a serious book with a listing of appropriate associations and additional information in an appendix. One wishes that Campbell's introduction, "Festival in the Streets," had been longer and more substantial.

Players must be ready to perform anywhere, and the fortunate ones had their names in lights on the theatre marquees. Such fortunates were *The Barrymores: The Royal Family in Hollywood* (Crown), whose exploitation of the film world absorbs the interest of James Kotselabas-Davis. For many playgoers Lincoln Center in New York means a certain kind of theatre; for the theatre person it means something different. Edgar B. Young tells the story of *Lincoln Center, The Building of an Institution* (NYU, 1980). Unfortunately, the title accurately suggests dullness, and Young explains the creation of the physical building without much comment on the people who made it or the personal and ideological problems encountered. And, of course, the theatre is only one part of Lincoln Center.

Producing America's plays has always been a business filled with incalcuable risks, one which attracts many hopeful entrepreneurs and ruins most of them. The history of American theatre is the history of disappointments, business failures, spectacular openings and dark nights, destructive fires, anxious waiting, instant success, and hastily pasted-up signs reading "closed." If starting a new religion is a quick way to financial success, starting a new theatre may be just as quick a pathway to disaster. Jan Weingarten Greenberg is a theatrical agent whose book *Theatre Business, From Auditions Through Opening Night* (Holt) attempts to explain the secrets of theatrical success. Her anecdotal approach distracts from her serious thesis, however, and her weak and casual understanding of theatre history in America creates a mediocre work, although her commentary on the Dramatists Guild is excellent. Donald C. Farber, by contrast, an attorney specializing in entertainment law, writes a straightforward and informative work on *Producing Theatre, A Comprehensive Legal and Business Guide* (Drama Book) in which contracts and contractual relationships are fully explained. For a fascinating view of practical theatre through the eyes of a playwright's agent, however, read *Represented by Audrey Wood* (Doubleday) by Audrey Wood with Max Wilk. Anecdotal in approach, this personal statement by a strong, perceptive artist and business woman is filled with comments on such dramatists as Paul Green, Dorothy and DuBose Heywood, Arthur Miller, Tennessee Williams, William Inge, Arthur Kopit, Preston Jones, and Robert Anderson. In the opinion of Audrey Wood, Inge is much underrated, and Williams is the best American dramatist of the century.

ii. Histories, Feminist Views, and Drama to World War I

There is no satisfactory history of American drama and theatre although the names of various historians are well known—Hewitt, Hornblow, Hughes, Mayorga, Meserve, Moses, Quinn, Wilson. Quinn comes the closest to writing a standard history, but his work is now nearly half a century out of date. Add another name and title to this list—Ethan Mordden, *The American Theatre* (Oxford)—and then dismiss them both. Mordden does not write the history he indicates in his preface. He knows little and appears to care less about American drama and theatre before 1900. Avoiding scholarly notation and identification of sources, Mordden writes with a lively if occasionally pretentious style, making broad statements of a generous or ungenerous nature. Having seen many plays in New York and considered them with care, he is at his best in his discussions of the drama of the 1930s but is constrained to almost meaningless listing for the three decades of American drama since World War II. Mordden has written most effectively on American musical theatre, but the new edition of *Musical Comedy in America* (Theatre Arts) with Glenn Litton's contribution, "From *The King and I* to *Sweeney Todd*," is a more nearly complete assessment. Although also lacking scholarly notation, this is a well-written book for popular tastes.

Women in American Theatre, ed. Helen Krich Chinoy and Linda Walsh Jenkins (Crown) presents another broad review of American theatre—this time from the women's perspective. An extremely ambitious work, subtitled *Careers, Images, Movements: An Illustrated Anthology and Sourcebook*, this volume has, in addition to a bibliography and lists of feminist plays and theatres, 50 essays under six major sections, each with an introduction: Female Rites, The Actress, Where are the Women Playwrights?, If Not an Actress, What . . .?, Images, Feminist Theatre. Unfortunately, it begins rather listlessly with an essay on "Sex Roles and Shamans" by Jenkins. Yvonne Shafer's "Women in Male Roles," however, is a particularly good essay in the section on the actress, which includes essays on a number of performers from Adah Isaacs Menkin to Eva Le Gallienne. The section on the playwright treats mainly 20th-century dramatists, although the most scholarly essay, "Women Open Augusta's First Theatre," written by Julia Curtis, considers the earlier period. Other topics treated in the volume are feminist theatre and a catch-all section on images, which includes a fine discussion of Susan Glaspell's *Trifles*. Women in American theatre are clearly a dominant force, but they are not well assessed at present. Perhaps they still need to be identified. Patti P. Gillespie partially fulfills that need in "America's Women Dramatists, 1960–1980" in *Contemporary Drama*, pp. 187–206.

Collections of essays published this year from the feminist point of view did not neglect women in the theatre. *Toward the Second*

Decade: The Import of the Women's Movement on American Insti-tutions, ed. Betty Justice and Renate Pore (Greenwood) included three essays. Maryat Lee, "Legitimate Theatre is Illegitimate," pp. 11–24, explained Lee's work with street actors in her Soul and Latin Theater and Eco Theater but somehow never explained her title. In "Better Than a Shriveled Husk: New Forms for the Theater," pp. 25–34, Corinne Jacker argues that "for the first time in 2,500 years a woman does not have to write as if she were a man." As if in re-sponse to Jacker, Elaine Ginsberg fears that women are writing only for women as she explores what women writers share in "Play-wrights, Poets and Novelists: Sisters Under the Skin," pp. 35–40. Gayle Kimball, editor of *Women's Culture: The Women's Renais-sance of the Seventies* (Scarecrow), published Susan Suntree's com-plaint against theatre's "three-thousand-year history of misogyny" and her rambling explanation of her experiences in producing *Antig-one Prism* with the Women's Ensemble of the Berkeley Stage Com-pany.

The structural concept of Jack A. Vaughn's *Early American Dramatists: From the Beginning to 1900* (Ungar) is basically sound: a little theatre history, brief background on 20 dramatists, and a dis-cussion of some 40 plays. It is, however, a patchwork book of stan-dard material, without new scholarship. Commentary is slight, and the title clearly reveals a prevailing bias which assumes that Ameri-can drama really started no earlier than 1900. Tice L. Miller's *Bo-hemians and Critics: American Theatre Criticism in the 19th Century* (Scarecrow), another brief work, is a much more valuable study. By identifying and briefly assessing the work of 19th-century theatre critics, Miller has provided a seminal work in the developing history of American drama and theatre. The 19th century is further explored in a few good essays. Jared A. Brown concentrates on the Theatre Royal in providing another of his enlightening comments in "A Note on British Military Theatre in New York at the End of the American Revolution" (*NYH* 65:177–87). Toward the middle of the 19th cen-tury melodrama and ethnic characters became popular theatre fare. David L. Rinear's "F. S. Chanfrau's Mose: The Rise and Fall of an Urban Folk-Hero" (*TJ* 33:199–212) is a carefully researched and well-written piece on that popular hero of several farces. If actions do not speak loudly enough, the farce heroes add distinguishing dialects, as does the Irishman, for example, in D. T. Knobel's "Vocabulary of Ethnic Perception: Content Analysis of the American Stage Irishman, 1820–1860" (*JAmS* 15:45–71). "For every smile a tear, for every tear a smile": that dictum is particularly popular in those 19th-century American plays in which women are featured and sentiment may produce both smiles and tears. Such sentiment may be associated with the "Helpless and Unfriended: 19th Century Domestic Melodrama" (*NLH* 13:127–43) by Martha Vicinus.

A. L. Lazarus and Victor H. Jones have exerted a good deal of energy in *Beyond Graustark: George Barr McCutcheon, Playwright Discovered* (Kennikat) in an attempt to show that McCutcheon, a minor Indiana novelist who wrote a number of unproduced plays, is worth consideration as a playwright. Their arguments, however, are weak, their ability to analyze plays quite deficient, and their knowledge of theatre history seriously lacking. One could never so accuse Paul T. Nolan, whose fascination with minor writers has produced many interesting and valuable essays. Nolan's latest work, *John Wallace Crawford* (*TUSAS* 378) presents an untalented playwright who took himself seriously as "Captain Jack, the Poet Scout." Crawford was always the actor, the pretender; so too, one feels, is Nolan in his assessments, but the study helps flesh out the picture of American drama of the late 19th century. Benjamin S. Lawson is much more cautious in *Joaquin Miller* (WWS 43, 1980). In a 50-page monograph he devotes less than two pages to the four plays by Miller, who is deserving of much more careful and perceptive criticism.

iii. Drama and Theatre Between the Wars

One of the most interesting essays published this year on American drama—perhaps because it flatters our sense of national pride—was written by an Hungarian, Peter Egri, "European Origins and American Originality: The Case of Drama" (*ZAA* 29:197–206). Concerned with the epic associations evoked by American drama from O'Neill to Albee, Egri argues that American playwrights have reshaped an early European influence and are now the inspiration for European dramatists.

a. Eugene O'Neill.   One of the pleasant surprises of the year was the reissuing of Doris V. Falk's *Eugene O'Neill and the Tragic Vision* (Gordian). It bears rereading. Another valuable work by a substan-

tial critic of O'Neill is Egil Törnqvist's "Strindberg and O'Neill," pp.
277–91, in *Structures of Influence: A Comparative Approach to August Strindberg*, ed. Marilyn J. Blackwell (N.Car.). Through a careful comparison of the plays of the two dramatists, Törnqvist expertly
illustrates the strong influence Strindberg held over O'Neill. *Eugene
O'Neill at Work: Newly Released Ideas for Plays* (Ungar) suggests
all of the excitement that 25 years of O'Neill's notes and ideas should
create in the mind of any critic of American drama. That excitement
is maintained in the introduction by the book's editor, Virginia Floyd,
who has so much to say that her prose becomes rambling and confused. The book presents much new material revealing O'Neill and
his plays, although far too many of his ideas are paraphrased or condensed. In the discussion of *The Great God Brown* (pp. 41–51), for
example, a limited selection of O'Neill's notes is interpreted in long
commentaries by the editor. One wonders why printing all of O'Neill's
notes was not feasible. Even with the long interpolations and the
excessive editing, however, there is an abundance of fascinating
information for the O'Neill scholar.

O'Neill usually tried to defend himself against casual comparisons, but he wrote and said too much to discourage comparativists.
Linda Ben-Zri in *"Exiles, The Great God Brown* and the Specter of
Nietzsche" (*MD* 24:251–69) argues well that the two works have
similar characters and structures. Ted R. Ellis III is less effective in
discussing Mrs. Evans in "The Materialization of *Ghosts* in *Strange
Interlude*" (*AN&Q* 19:110–14). O'Neill's prose has been frequently
subjected to abusive commentary, and one might wonder how the
dramatist would have reacted to Joseph J. Moleski's determination to
"situate it [O'Neill's work], inscribe it in a system of differences it
cannot command but whose occlusion is decisive." The curious may
read "Eugene O'Neill and the Cruelty of Theater" (*CompD* 15:
327–42).

The *Eugene O'Neill Newsletter* is becoming a dependable pub-
lication for brief and provocative comments on the dramatist, who
consistently attracts the greatest amount of attention each year
among scholars of American drama and theatre. *EON* 5,i includes
Robert Butler's "Artifice and Art: Words in *The Iceman Cometh* and
Hughie" (pp. 3–6) and Jay E. Raphael's "On Directing *Long Day's
Journey Into Night*" (pp. 7–10). "'Electricity is God now': D. H.
Lawrence and O'Neill" (5,ii:10–15) discusses the sources of *Dynamo*.

The same writer, Susan Tuck, attempts another source study in "House of Compson, House of Tyrone: Faulkner's Influences on O'Neill" (5,iii:6–10). Patrick J. Nolan continues an emphasis on influence in *"Desire Under the Elms*: Characters by Jung" (5,ii:5–10), and Joseph Petite discusses "The Paradox of Power in *More Stately Mansions*" (5,iii:2–5). Although influence studies can become tedious and limited in value for all but historians of ideas, the *EON*'s focus upon O'Neill's impact on modern literature and upon his plays as theatrical productions can be a valuable resource for scholars and artists.

b. **Clifford Odets.** Clifford Odets has another biographer. Margaret Brenman-Gibson, close friend of Odets, wife of William Gibson, and psychoanalyst in an academic department of psychiatry, has exclusive rights to Odets' papers. Dr. Brenman-Gibson, whose first volume is entitled *Clifford Odets, American Playwright: The Years 1906–1940* (Atheneum), is not a literary critic, a theatre critic, or a scholarly writer. Her quotations and sources remain unidentified, and her prose is difficult to follow. She reads Odets' plays only for revelations about the playwright and she comments excessively. It is a disappointing use of material, but the material itself is indispensable for the student of Odets who has waited 20 years for this marvelously rich source of information. Frank R. Cunningham tends to emphasize comparisons and consider Odets a writer of tragedy in his essay on "Clifford Odets" (*American Writers*, pp. 520–54). Among American dramatists he finds only O'Neill and Williams superior to Odets in "tragic form" and ranks *Golden Boy* "with the best of those American tragedies in which the actions spring from the conventions of melodrama." Unfortunately, Cunningham's theories seem to be plucked from thin air, lacking the substance of clear argument and careful use of words.

c. **Other Essays.** *Selected Letters of James Thurber*, ed. Helen Thurber and Edward Weeks (Little, Brown), bears mention because *The Male Animal*, which Thurber wrote with Elliott Nugent, ranks as one of the better comedies of its period. Another writer not particularly noted for his plays, Theodore Dreiser, receives rather perceptive comment by Helene Keyssar in "Theodore Dreiser's Dramas: American Folk Drama and Its Limits" (*TJ* 33:365–76). Keyssar ar-

gues that, as a folk writer, Dreiser lacked the proper perspective for
the stage and should have written for film. Orson Welles, erratic
genius whose exploits still occasionally attract attention, and John
Houseman provide new information in J. E. Vacha's "The Case of
the Runaway Opera: The Federal Theatre Project and Marc Blit-
stein's *The Cradle Will Rock*" (*NYH* 65:133–52) about the first production of that play.

iv. America's Major Dramatists: 1940s and 1950s

a. **Tennessee Williams.**   Critical enthusiasm for the work of Tennessee Williams does not seem to diminish with the passing of time,
in spite of the dramatist's problems in focusing and controlling his
talent. Concern for the development of his scripts reveals the serious
attitude scholars assume toward Williams' plays. The text of *The
Glass Menagerie* has been carefully studied by Lester Beaurline.
Now Drewey Wayne Gunn has recreated "The Troubled Flight of
Tennessee Williams' *Sweet Bird*: From Manuscript Through Published Texts" (*MD* 24:26–35) from three successive versions. The
essay is sensibly conceived and well written with a carefully ordered
use of evidence.

Contemporary Drama attempts a broad view of American drama
with individual essays of uneven merit on some ten contemporary
dramatists and general essays on Mexican, black, and ethnic theatre.
The varied quality of the essays appears to result from the uncertainty of the writers with regard to their audience. One essayist introduces his subject to his readers; another provides a penetrating
discussion of aspects of the dramatist's work. "Tennessee Williams,
Southern Playwright" (pp. 5–18) by Hedwig Bock is a general and
relatively uninspired survey of Williams' dramas through *The Night
of the Iguana*. Bock is contemptuous of later Williams plays. Two
other essays published this year focus on particular aspects of Williams' work. Thomas P. Adler's "Images of Entrapment in Tennessee
Williams' Later Plays" (*NMAL* 5:Item 11) discusses this idea in
Small Craft Warnings and *Vieux Carré*. In another essay of slight
importance, "The (Un)reliability of the Narrator in *The Glass Menagerie* and *Vieux Carré*" (*TWNew* 3:6–9) Adler sees Tom as an
unreliable narrator who tells of events he has not seen. Henry I.
Schvey's "Madonna at the Poker Night: Pictorial Elements in Ten-

nessee Williams' *A Streetcar Named Desire*" (*Riewald Festschrift*, pp. 7–77) discusses color symbolism and pictorial elements that relate the play to paintings. This essay should be helpful to directors and designers in producing the play.

b. **Arthur Miller.** *Arthur Miller's Collected Plays*, vol. 2 (Viking) includes *The Misfits, After the Fall, Incident at Vichy, The Price, The Creation of the World and Other Business*, and *Playing for Time*. This final item is a screenplay based on the book by Fania Fenelon. The volume includes an introduction by Miller, who comments upon his earlier radical nature, his interest in the holocaust, and his inability to discover and "settle upon a single useful style." This second volume of Miller's plays is certainly welcome, and his selective commentary is interesting in that it supports thoughts critics have entertained for some time. If Miller seems a bit hesitant in commenting on his later work, Albert Wertheim ("Arthur Miller: *After the Fall* and After," *Contemporary Drama*, pp. 19–32) does not. He finds a second flowering in the later plays and concludes, albeit in an unconvincing argument, that Miller is still developing new ideas. In another strained essay, "Miller and Things" (*LitR* 24:548–61), Marianne Boruch argues that Miller uses objects "to instruct us intuitively through their metaphoric quality."

In "The Ending of Arthur Miller's *The Price*" (*StHum* 8,ii:40–44) Milton Chaikin discusses the unanswered questions at the end of this play. William J. McGill writes a much more interesting and convincing essay in "The Crucible of History: Arthur Miller's John Proctor" (*NEQ* 54:258–64). Emphasizing the adulterous situation and the several departures Miller created from the John Proctor of history, McGill speculates intelligently on Miller's reasons.

v. Contemporary American Drama and Theatre

a. **Edward Albee.** Few people would argue with Katharine Worth's view of Edward Albee as a dramatist with a distinctive voice that is difficult to define. In "Edward Albee: Playwright of Evolution" (*Contemporary Drama*, pp. 33–53) Worth emphasizes this playwright's ability to dramatize the small changes of life. In a much more limited assessment of Albee's career, Fred M. Robinson presumes to use *A Delicate Balance* as a key to Albee's psyche in "Albee's Long Night's

Journey into Day" (*MLS* 11:25–32). Leonard J. Leff takes a different approach to Albee material in an excellent study of "Play into Film: Warner Brothers' *Who's Afraid of Virginia Woolf?*" (*TJ* 33:453–66). Using the resources of the University of Texas Library—26 boxes from the Ernest Lehman Collection—Leff has detailed the changes in scene and language necessary to transform one art into another. Language also interested M. Patricia Fumerton. In "Verbal Prisons: The Language of Albee's *A Delicate Balance*" (*ESC* 7:201–11) Fumerton carefully and convincingly details the contributions of language to the characters, actions, and meanings in this play.

b. **Poetic Dramatists.** Of the few periods in the history of American drama during which poetry on the stage was commercially attractive, the second quarter of the 19th century is the most memorable. Poetic dramatists, intimidated by the realistic prose of later 19th-century writers, seldom had their works produced on America's stages although they continued to write more plays than theatre historians are willing to remember. During the 1920s writers of poetic drama enjoyed a brief renaissance but were seemingly squelched by the Depression years.

After World War II recognized poets attempted once more to enter the commercial theatre. Archibald MacLeish had some success and perhaps more importantly forced critics to consider him and other poets writing for the stage in a more serious vein. Nila Das discusses MacLeish's best-known play as a "drama of becoming," in which the masks of Sarah and J. B. are revealed to their folly and Zeuss and Nickles cling to inner masks—"*J. B.*: Through the Masks" (*JIS* 21:67–75). For two other modern poets—William Carlos Williams and Robert Lowell—whose works have been at least recognized on the stage, critics have had opportunities to create a balanced evaluation. Paul Mariani, however, allows only three paragraphs for the production of *Many Loves* in 1959 (*William Carlos Williams: A New World Naked* [McGraw-Hill]). In an 848-page book this is not a generous allotment of time and space, and Mariani's commentary is more informational than critical: Williams wrote a play. Burton Raffel is more scholarly and convincing in his comments on *Old Glory* in *Robert Lowell* (Ungar). In his final chapter, "Half a Step into the Theater," Raffel correctly assesses Hawthorne's stories as poor material for the dramatist and provides a sensible response to Robert Brustein by doubting that Lowell was a "brilliant new dramatist."

c. Lillian Hellman. The date of Hellman's birth now seems to be established by Theresa R. Mooney, "A Note on Lillian Hellman's Birthdate" (*AN&Q* 19:148–49), who looked up her birth certificate with the following result: 20 June 1905. Two other essays dwelt upon the effect of Hellman's life on her work. Marcus K. Billson and Sidonie A. Smith make some disjointed observations on Hellman's life as revealed in her autobiographical publications but without clear reference to Hellman's plays in "Lillian Hellman's Memorial Drama," pp. 171–78 (*Women in American Theatre*), and Mary L. Broe reads Hellman's life into her plays in "Bohemia Bumps into Calvin: The Deception of Passivity in Lillian Hellman's Drama" (*SoQ* 19,ii:26–41).

d. Sam Shepard. Laurence Kitchen, an English drama critic, once stated that American drama emerged as part of world drama at mid-20th century, about the time that Arthur Miller, William Inge, and Tennessee Williams started to write. Soon Edward Albee became popular in America, but no single dramatist has since commanded the critical respect accorded these four. It is true that black dramatists such as Lorraine Hansberry and Imamu Baraka received a liberal amount of attention a decade ago, and other dramatists stimulated a few teachers and scholars to write about their plays. It has been difficult, however, to find one outstanding dramatist who could attract audiences and, at the same time, inspire students of dramatic literature. Until recently Neil Simon's popularity in the theatre kept him at arm's length from serious scholars, just as Belasco's technical successes encouraged critics to categorize him as limited. Preston Jones's reputation has ebbed and flowed in a manner similar to William Inge's. Among currently active American dramatists, Sam Shepard may be remembered as a man of the theatre who has something to say and a certain facility with language.

"The Role of Performance in Sam Shepard's Plays" (*TJ* 33:182–98) is a key to interpreting his work, according to Florence Falk. His characters, she argues, "enact their performance rituals against one or more of three metaphysical structures simultaneously"—the cosmos, the nation, the self. Shepard's hope for humanity rests upon the commitment of his characters to continue performing. Using one of Shepard's plays, *Action*, to illustrate the action-images that impel the movement forward, Gerry McCarthy contends in "'Acting it out': Sam Shepard's Action" (*MD* 24:1–12) that action-images are one of Shepard's major writing techniques. Music is another major device, according to Bruce W. Powe—"*The Tooth of Crime*: Sam Shepard's Way With Music" (*MD* 24:13–25)—who uses this play to show that music not only produces an emotional effect but a counterpoint to the spoken word. Despite his tendency to see music as pragmatic in Shepard's work, Powe cites a number of the plays to make his point in a convincing manner.

In "Sam Shepard: Today's Passionate Shepard and His Loves" (*Contemporary Drama*, pp. 161–72) Ruby Cohn reviews the playwright's work with her customary skill and insight. One of the strongest arguments of the essay concentrates on Shepard's—and Cohn's—concern for language. J. Glove's "Canonization of Mojo Rootforce: Sam Shepard Live at the Pantheon" (*Theatre* 12:53–65) is a slight if enthusiastic comment. The editor of *American Dreams, The Imagination of Sam Shepard* (Performing Arts), Bonnie Marranca, brings together 23 essays written between 1965 and 1981—14 of commentary, three on directing, two on acting, and four essays by or interviews with Shepard. Unfortunately, Marranca overplays her part by contending that, at his best, Shepard surpasses whatever has been thought possible in the theatre. Additionally, her introductory essay, "Alphabetical Shepard: The Play of Words," is a conglomeration of thoughts, irrelevant and absurd, that offers little but a bad taste for the reader. Some of the other essays, however, are fascinating. Gerald Weales, "The Transformation of Sam Shepard" (pp. 37–44), provides a perceptive review of Shepard's work. Jack Gelber makes some interesting observations in "The Playwright as Shaman" (pp. 45–48); John Lahr in "Spectacle of Disintegration" (pp. 49–56) feels that Shepard shocks his audiences. Stanley Kauffmann expresses a negative reaction in "What Price Freedom?" (pp. 104–07). Most of the essays are reprints which, in this collection, provide a general appreciation of Shepard the man and his work. The interviews with Shepard, however, and his own brief comments surely reinforce the old adage that a playwright should write plays and leave explanations of his artistry to others.

e. Assorted Playwrights. One of the best articles published this year is Gerald Weales's assessment of "Ronald Ribman: The Artist of the Failure Clowns" (*Contemporary Drama*, pp. 75–90). Taking his cue from Moko, "a failure clown" in *Harry, Noon and Night*, Weales sees Ribman as a poet, a playwright in the complete sense of that word, who writes about man, limited by his society and his own psychology and trapped between aspiration and possibility. For his essay on "Arthur Kopit: Dreams and Nightmares" (*Contemporary Drama*, pp. 55–74) Jurgen Wolter surveys that dramatist's art with emphasis upon the theme of the false dream which turns into an apocalyptic nightmare. Janet S. Hertzbach's essay on "The Plays of David Rabe: A World of Streamers" (*Contemporary Drama*, pp. 173–87) provides sharp and cogent observations on Rabe's interest in "discovering death." As a thoughtful and well-argued statement, this essay is one of the strongest in this volume. One of the weaker is Henry I. Schvey's "Images of the Past in the Plays of Lanford Wilson" (pp. 225–40), which attempts to show thematic unity in Wilson's work from *The Hot L Baltimore* to *Talley's Folly*.

The first sentence in Steven H. Gale's essay "David Mamet: The Plays, 1972–1980" (*Contemporary Drama*, pp. 207–23) reads: "David Mamet's plays are about relationships." Surely, Mamet deserves a more perceptive interpreter in this volume, and the editor of *Modern Drama* did little better in publishing Jack V. Barbera's "Ethical Perversity in America: Some Observations on David Mamet's *American Buffalo*" (*MD* 24:270–75), in which the intellectual thinness of the brief observations is matched by the arrogance of the observer: "My modest conclusion is that in satirizing such corrupt notions [businessmen who "buffalo" people] Mamet *has* written a play of intellectual content." Perhaps one had better read Mamet's "First Principles" (*Theatre* 12:50–52).

Contemporary Drama also contains two essays on Chicano drama. Both emphasize the work of Luis Valdez. Dieter Herms in "Luis Valdez, Chicano Dramatist: An Introduction and an Interview" (pp. 257–70) provides a sensible overview. The interview is particularly instructive, although the introduction provides little analysis and

is written in a very pedestrian fashion. Jack W. Brokaw quickly traces
the tradition of "Mexican-American Drama" (pp. 244–56) and deals
mainly with the work of Valdez.

Essays on black and ethnic drama complete the *Contemporary
Drama* approach to American drama. Peter Bruch's "The Quest and
Failure of an Ethnic Community Theatre" (pp. 123–40) presents the
German view. It is an unusual essay by a cultural activist who makes
a political statement while bemoaning the failure of a dream. The
black drama is presented as a list of plays, trends, and playwrights:
Winona L. Fletcher, "Consider the Possibilities: An Overview of
Black Drama in the 1970s" (pp. 144–60). But the possibilities are
not discussed. The single black dramatist featured is presented in
a sensitive and highly enlightening essay by Margaret B. Wilkerson,
"The Sighted Eyes and Feeling Heart of Lorraine Hansberry" (pp.
91–104). Highlights of this essay are the comments on *Les Blancs*
and *The Drinking Gourd*, a play written for NBC but never produced.

f. **American Plays: Produced How and Where? and by Whom?**
The critic of American or any other kind of drama considers the work
of the playwright—either in the library or in the theatre. It seems
a relatively simple approach. In the past, the playwright wrote a play
which was acted in the theatre, and the critic or historian would
work with the written play and also be aware of the interpretations
imposed by actors and actresses. Later the director emerged in the
theatrical world and created on stage through the efforts of performers and technicians an interpretation of the written play on which
assessments could also be made. The play, however, remained the
original work of the dramatist. Now that is changing. The director
frequently becomes a part of that original playwriting effort with the
result that it is difficult to distinguish which person—the playwright
or director—is responsible for the produced and published play. That
concept of cooperative work is currently being carried a step further
in the playwrights' workshops and playwrights' theatres across the
country, where the undeveloped ideas of the would-be playwright
are acted out, focused, and embellished by actors and directors who
help create the final play.

The consequence of this procedure for writing a play is important
for the critic and historian of American drama. How, by whom, and

where the play is produced and written are increasingly relevant concerns for the scholar. What is the place of the university, for example, where the workshop concept is popular? David L. Jorns, "Theatre in the Academic Community: The Place of the Art" (*Rendezvous* 16:50–56), argues that academic theatre is not fulfilling its potential for training and maintaining academic quality, and he suggests adjudication by professionals. One who has been actively engaged in academic training, Robert Brustein, recently changed jobs under pressure and wrote a book to explain why: *Making Scenes, A Personal History of the Turbulent Years at Yale, 1966–1979* (Random House). Memoirs of theatre people are frequently interesting for the voyeur, and this volume recounts what the author did at Yale and why. It is an apology of pride, however, in which with easy presumption Brustein provides an emotional response to all who disagreed with his work at Yale. "Mugged in New Haven," he writes— a bitter reaction which need not have been written. With repetition, his is a boring defense, as James W. Flannery's "An Interview with Robert Brustein" (*TJ* 33:91–104) reveals.

Most articles on the activities of the various theatres are descriptive; few are provocative. In "The Politics of Inspiration: American Theatre in Flux" (*Performing Arts Journal* 7:265–80) Ruth Mayleas, Jay Novich, and Joseph Zeigler air their tired views of contemporary conditions in the theatre. Michael Kustow, "American Theatre: An English View" (*PR* 48:518–23), finds that American theatre lacks a "public dimension," true support from the common man. Terry Helbring provides a slight history of gay themes and characters in American drama plus information on recent gay theatre companies and performers—"Gay Plays, Gay Theatre, Gay Performance" (*TDR* 25:35–46). Emily L. Sisley compares lesbian drama to feminism and "just plain theatre" in "Notes on Lesbian Theatre" (*TDR* 25:47–56). Adele Edling Shank—"The San Francisco Mime Troupe's *Americans, or Last Tango in Huahuatenango*" (*TDR* 25:81–83)—explains briefly how that theatre group creates and stages a play. "Going West: Theatre in California" (*ContempR* 238:154–58) by John Elsom deals with theatre groups in San Diego and San Francisco in a rather hurried fashion. One of the more distinctive approaches to modern theatre may be found in Bill Ellis' "The Camp Mock-Ordeal: Theater As Life" (*JAF* 94:486–505), which argues that such camping experiences as the snipe hunt are sufficiently programmed to be termed theatre even if no script exists. The line separating entertainment or entertaining events from ceremony and protocol is as uncertain for some people as that separating historical events recorded on television from historical drama or documentary drama.

"American Theater Watch, 1980–81" (*GaR* 35:597–607) is the current essay in a series of yearly reviews of the theatre season by Gerald Weales. For the many plays produced in 1980–81, Weales provides a general commentary while selecting a few for particular analysis—Romulus Linney's *Holy Ghosts*, Charles Fuller's *Zooman and the Sign*, Ron Milner's *Seasons Reasons*, and Jim Leonard's *The Diviners*. Among contemporary critics of American drama and theatre Weales stands alone as a substantial and astute scholar whose perceptive observations on plays and their place in a developing theatre provide a basis on which future historians may build. Robert Asahina's "Theatre Chronicle" (*HudR* 34:99–104), by contrast, tries to cover the entire theatre season and fails to provide carefully assessed highlights.

vi. Looking Ahead

"How Do Playwrights Make a Living?" (*TJ* 33:517–26). With difficulty, Holly Hill explains, and rarely at that. Although her information is anecdotal, she has researched very well a topic that deserves attention. That most precarious of ventures—trying to determine what will appeal to theatre audiences—links playwrights with actors, directors, producers, and the business world. To be an artist and faithful to one's belief in art and to make a living may be two distinctly different objectives. People also look for solutions to that suggested dilemma in different places. Sensitive to the situation and resulting problems, the National Endowment for the Arts, Research Division, convened an advisory group of 18 people which published *Conditions and Needs of the Professional American Theatre* (Report No. 11, May 1981). For the members of this group the answer was *money*, mainly federal money. They paid little attention to imagination and did not emphasize research. It would appear, as the hero of John Dos Passos' *U.S.A.* observes when he looks toward the sky at the end of that novel, that there are at least two worlds.

Perhaps these theatre worlds can never be joined—the artistic, the commercial, the academic, the experimental. Perhaps they should not be, and Edmund Wilson was correct with his "sick oyster" theory of art. Perhaps one need only pretend. *Pretend the World is Funny and Forever: A Psychological Analysis of Comedians, Clowns, and Actors* (Erlbaum) is the title Seymour Fisher and Rhoda L. Fisher give to their study of people who want to make others laugh and of the forces which shaped them. But this is one side of theatre fare, the side that is most readily supported by theatre audiences. The answer to the dilemma is obviously further away and involves that rare individual among playwrights, the genius who can entertain people in the theatre while stimulating them to think and feel. It takes great art to inspire great criticism and meaningful scholarship.

Indiana University

19. Black Literature

John M. Reilly

i. Bibliography

Commentary on Phillis Wheatley abounds, though more often than not references to her verse are motivated by the desire to make a point about her race, not by a critical purpose. William H. Robinson's *Phillis Wheatley: A Bio-Bibliography* (Hall) annotates a broad sampling of the most typical references from 1761 to 1979. These are arranged alphabetically within their years of publication. As preface to the secondary sources, Robinson lists the poet's published writings, including 33 nonextant poems identifiable through publication proposals. The introduction to the volume surveys common errors in dating the events of Wheatley's life and provides corrections. The representation of the poet's reputation is aided by an extensive index.

Another means of studying Afro-American literary reputations becomes available through "Alain Locke: A Comprehensive Bibliography of His Published Writings" by John Edgar Tidwell and John Wright (*Callaloo* 4:175–92). Besides his role as promoter of the Harlem Renaissance, Locke served as a representative spokesperson for black humanist values while reviewing hundreds of books for *Opportunity* and *Phylon*. These reviews are categorically listed by Tidwell and Wright, along with notices he wrote for other publications, essays on the other arts, and writings on philosophical, educational, and other topics.

The value of newspapers in establishing the intellectual and social contexts of Afro-American literature is enhanced this year by publication of Georgetta Merritt Campbell's *Extant Collections of Black Newspapers in the Libraries of the United States* (Whitston). The work was conceived as a dissertation that would extend Armistead Scott Pride's listings in *The Black Press: A Bibliography* (1968). Over 1,800 newspapers appeared in the years between 1880 and 1915. The surviving collections are presented by Campbell in Union List arrangement by state of publication. This is followed by an alphabetical listing and, as illustration of the work that remains to be done, by an index of William Monroe Trotter's *Boston Guardian* for 1902–04. Campbell's bibliography of newspapers has its counterpart in Penelope L. Bullock's study of magazines in *The Afro-American Periodical Press, 1838–1909* (LSU). Beginning with the *Mirror of Liberty*, published in New York in 1838, and concluding with *Crisis*, founded in 1910, Bullock provides discussion of the publishers and contributors for 97 magazines. Appendices give publication data, chronology, and a selected list of holdings of extant issues.

Two special issues of journals devoted to poets this year contain bibliographical aids. First is Therman B. O'Daniel's "Langston Hughes: An Updated Selected Bibliography" in the Hughes issue of *Black American Literature Forum* (15:104–07). O'Daniel prepared the original bibliography for *Langston Hughes: Black Genius* (1971). In his continuation he adds nine books and 20 dissertations about Hughes, as well as numbers of articles. The second contribution is Xavier Nicholas' "Robert Hayden: A Bibliography," contributed to *Obsidian's* celebration of Detroit poets (7,i:109–27). Writings by the poet are presented chronologically with indications of revisions and information on reprints. Reviews and other secondary materials also are noted.

Joe Weixlmann continues his excellent contributions with "Barry Beckham: A Bibliography" (*CLAJ* 24:522–28), which lists editions and reviews of separately published works, contributions to books and periodicals, printed remarks, and secondary studies. The introductory note also directs scholars' attention to an unpublished play by Beckham, *Garvey Lives!*, produced at Brown University in 1972.

The last item to note here is "The Black Arts Movement, 1965–1975: A Bibliography" by Vashti Lewis (*MV* 4,ii[1980]:37–50). The listing is derived from five easily accessible journals, and while it yields 116 items, the scope for examination is so narrow, the exclusions so many, that the result can serve only to be suggestive of the immense amount of material remaining to be recovered for scholarly study.

ii. Fiction

a. **Chesnutt, DuBois, Dunbar.** Recent criticism has regularly argued for the significance of personal experience in the evolution of

Chesnutt's literary motives. In 1981 Donald B. Gibson has plumbed that personal experience with "Charles W. Chesnutt: The Anatomy of A Dream" in *Politics of Literary Expression: A Study of Major Black Writers* (Greenwood), pp. 125–54, to describe the dialectical habit of mind that issued from Chesnutt's mulatto status. The paradox of identification with the gentry accompanied by sympathy for the peasants infused Chesnutt's melodramatic plots with contradictory values; antitheses undercut theses until in *The Colonel's Dream* he finally realized that the ordered society of aristocracy exists only in the mind and in myth. The power of tradition in Chesnutt's narratives is reinforced by the store of detail he draws upon in describing physical and social environment. Lena M. White summarizes the results of local-color convention in "Chesnutt's Chinquapin County" (*SLJ* 13,ii:41–58), the setting for some 30 short stories and three novels. P. Jay Delmar writes once again this year on Chesnutt in "The Moral Dilemma in Charles W. Chesnutt's *The Marrow of Tradition*" (*ALR* 14:269–72), but his observations on the conflict between the characters of Dr. Miller and Josh Green in the novel add nothing to critical views existing for more than a decade.

The most famous words written by W. E. B. DuBois describe the double consciousness of black Americans, the war of two ideals. Keith E. Byerman in "Hearts of Darkness: Narrative Voices in *The Souls of Black Folk*" (*ALR* 14:43–51) analyzes the manifestation of double consciousness in the very text that names it. The rational, morally confident DuBois becomes ambivalent as he writes "Of the Meaning of Progress" and reveals the personal impact of racism with even more complexity as he laments "Of the Passing of the First-Born."

Myles Hurd revives discussion of the correct interpretation of Dunbar's portrayal of the southern town and the northern city in "Blackness and Borrowed Obscurity: Another Look at Dunbar's *The Sport of the Gods*" (*Callaloo* 4:90–100). Hurd argues that Dunbar manipulates the tenets of naturalism to show the festering lives of his characters in the North, but also has the didactic purpose of demonstrating characters' responsibility for their misfortune. The result is that Dunbar cannot subordinate the double narrative to a single theme. Hurd does well to establish the interpretive problem. The next step is to explain why it exists. As part of a broader theoretical declaration, that is precisely what Houston A. Baker, Jr., attempts in

"The 'Limitless' Freedom of Myth: Paul Laurence Dunbar's *The Sport of the Gods* and the Criticism of Afro-American Literature" (*The American Self*, pp. 124–43). Challenging historically grounded literary criticism that takes each work of Afro-American writing as a report on "the state of the race," Baker proposes an orientation that refers the language of literature to mythic domains where it is not related to practical acts directly but serves as representations of those acts. In these terms Dunbar's novel becomes a discourse on the fallibility of human habits of thought, as they are embodied in the plantation tradition which Dunbar ridicules, and as they appear in the cultural taste of the migrants, whom he implicitly criticizes.

b. **Toomer, McKay, Fauset, Fisher, Bontemps.** In powerful contention with the tendency of Houston Baker's work to transcend historicism is Gibson's insistence upon analysis and evaluation that is grounded in historical reality. In "Jean Toomer: The Politics of Denial" (*Politics of Literary Expression*, pp. 155–81) Gibson argues that the thoroughgoing philosophical idealist Kabnis is the key character in *Cane*; his frustrations and the ambiguity of his position are those of Toomer, who composed his book as an evasion of the racial reality he found unbearable. Robert H. Brinkmeyer, Jr., extends this interpretation of Toomer's career by summoning secondary sources in "Wasted Talent, Wasted Art: The Literary Career of Jean Toomer" (*SoQ* 20:75–84) to describe the works after *Cane* as crippled by dogma.

Robert M. Greenberg undertakes an exposition of theory and practice in "Idealism and Realism in the Fiction of Claude McKay" (*CLAJ* 24:237–61). There is, on the one hand, devotion on McKay's part to total delineation of environment, for he held that being derives from social and historical reality. At the same time, he attempted portrayal of the exemplary common man. Greenberg properly notes the difficulty McKay had in accomplishing the second part of his task, but he directs his observations to examination of the ongoing argument within the fiction, rather than to conclusive judgment. The result is valuable.

The appreciative treatment of minor writers of the Harlem Renaissance anticipated last year apparently has begun. *Jessie Redmon Fauset: Black American Writer* by Carolyn Wedin Sylvander (Whitston) sets out to correct misapprehensions that relegate Fauset to

the status of a derivative bourgeois writer. As she conducted the research for the dissertation from which this volume evolved, Sylvander
found Fauset to be an important contributor to the renaissance by
her work as literary editor of *Crisis*. Indeed, she was more important
in this respect than DuBois. In her own fiction Jessie Fauset developed characters concerned with middle-class morality, but it is
an error, Sylvander argues, to confuse the author's perspective with
her characters'. Fauset's interest is the psychology of individuals at
odds with society's color mania. Joseph J. Feeney, S.J., has earlier
advanced a similar view of Fauset (see *ALS 1979*, 400). Now, he
contributes two items to fuller understanding. "A Small Centennial
Tribute: Establishing the Correct Birthdate and Birthplace of Jessie
Fauset, Novelist and Critic" (*MV* 4,ii[1980]:71–73) reports that the
Fauset family Bible supports 1882 as the year of the writer's birth,
April 26 as the probable date, and Fredericksville, New Jersey, as
the place. In "Black Childhood as Ironic: A Nursery Rhyme Transformed in Jessie Fauset's Novel *Plum Bun*" (*MV* 4,ii[1980]:65–69)
Feeney shows that the Mother Goose rhyme "To market, to market"
which is used to subtitle the novel has ironic application.

"'Aim High and Go Straight': The Grandmother Figure in the
Short Fiction of Rudolph Fisher" by John McClusky, Jr. (*BALF* 15:
55–59) examines elders who act as a bridge between the 19th-century
traditions of survival brought to the city by migrants and the street-
wise Harlemites whom they meet there. Nicholas Canady in "Arna
Bontemps: The Louisiana Heritage" (*Callaloo* 4:163–68) writes of
the survival of another tradition: Bontemps' memory of a granduncle
who forms the basis for characterization of Little Augie in *God
Sends Sunday*.

c. Hughes, Wright, Ellison. The Fall issue of *Black American Literature Forum* devoted to Langston Hughes includes four perspectives on his fiction. In "A Textual Comparison of Langston Hughes'
Mulatto, 'Father and Son,' and 'The Barrier'" (15:101–03) Sybil Ray
Ricks traces variations of the mulatto plot through appearances in a
play, short story, and libretto. David Michael Nifong's "Narrative
Technique and Theory in *The Ways of White Folks*" (15:93–96)
describes Hughes's experiments with a total of seven narrative points
of view. Carolyn Fowler in "The Shared Vision of Langston Hughes
and Jacques Roumain" (15:84–88) chronicles the encounter of the

American and the Haitian, indicating the sympathy Hughes's writing has for the indigenism of Roumain. Similarly, Richard Jackson outlines the impact of Hughes on such writers as Nicolas Guillén in "The Shared Vision of Langston Hughes and Black Hispanic Writers" (15:89–92).

The works of such a major author as Richard Wright are constantly subject to reinterpretation. This year is no different from others. Lucien L. Agosta in "Millenial Embrace: The Artistry of Conclusion in Richard Wright's 'Fire and Cloud'" (SSF 18:121–29) writes in response to criticism that judges the final scene of white and black unity as political wish-fulfillment. Applying a structural scheme, Agosta argues that "Fire and Cloud," and in fact all of Uncle Tom's Children, is plotted around the integral relationships of blacks and whites. The cleavages or imbalances that develop because of racism are repaired in the scene of an integrated march; thus, the book achieves closure. Jerry H. Bryant's "The Violence of Native Son" (SR 17:303–19) joins the discussion about Wright's famous novel by identifying violence as the means by which Bigger Thomas achieves self-determination, and the way Wright links the idea of mass man who represents a social threat with his own innate existentialist impulses. Bryant's interpretation is not new; rather, it must be taken as amplification of a familiar point.

Of course, novelty is not what one always seeks in continuing critical discussion. It is not novelty, for example, that makes Gibson's "Richard Wright: The Lone Marxian" (Politics of Literary Expression, pp. 21–57) stimulating. What Gibson has to offer is a comprehensive framework of interpretation, consistent in its own terms, that encourages us to appreciate an underlying dynamic for Wright's work. He locates this dynamic in the conflict between Wright's social vision and his concern with interior being. These themes reach climactic expression in The Outsider, which deals with a character who acts upon the assumption that reality is an arbitrary social construction. At the end of the narrative he declares that values exist a priori. The Outsider thus becomes anti-existentalist and Wright's later fiction shows him occupied in exploring the individualist's loci of values—consciousness and unique character.

Gibson is evidently fond of Wright, but when he comes to appraise Ralph Ellison's extension of Wright's later concern with interior being, he is harsh. "Ralph Ellison's Invisible Man: The Politics

of Retreat" (*Politics of Literary Expression*, pp. 59–98) provides a
long, careful reading of the novel as a discourse on the formation of
reality. The reading accurately demonstrates that the narrator arrives
at the point of knowing he has no fixed social identity, thus, effectively no identity at all. For Gibson, Ellison's making such individualism positive is distasteful, because the political implications are terrifying. Ellison finds more approving treatment at the hands of other
critics. Robert O'Mealley contributes the entry on the novelist to
American Writers (pp. 22–52), reiterating the discussion of Afro-
American sources and traditions that he originally developed in the
comprehensive study of Ellison's craft published last year (see *ALS
1980*, 446–47). O'Mealley does signal service to Ellison criticism by
treating the later stories as a novel in progress. Gary Marmorstein
develops this point in "Ralph Ellison's Not-So-New-Novel" (*Obsidian*
6,iii[1980]:7–21) by piecing together the six published sections of
the emerging novel to illustrate Ellison's preoccupation with narrative voice and the thematic polarities that pervade the work.

d. **Baldwin, Morrison, Gaines, Walker, Reed, Beckham, Brown.**
Critics pleased with James Baldwin's public role as racial advocate
have been uncomfortable with the religious themes in his work. Rolf
Lundén's important study "The Progress of a Pilgrim: James Baldwin's *Go Tell It on the Mountain*" (*SN* 53,iii:113–26) sets out to
repudiate the tendency to translate the Christian motifs into other
terms, and he succeeds by arguing cogently that Baldwin's first novel
centers upon Christian values and by buttressing the case with analogies to Bunyan's *Pilgrim's Progress* and *Grace Abounding*. Interestingly, Gibson's approach to social criticism permits him to make a
similar point in "James Baldwin: The Anatomy of Space" (*Politics
of Literary Expression*, pp. 99–123). This revision of an essay originally published in 1977 asserts that Baldwin's social criticism is
couched almost entirely in moral, and specifically Christian, terms.
     Two of the year's essays on Toni Morrison pursue the intricacies
of *Song of Solomon*. Charles De Arman in "Milkman as the Archetypal Hero: 'Thursday's Child Has Far to Go' " (*Obsidian* 6,iii[1980]:
56–59) advances the idea that the male protagonist in the novel
moves through rites that parallel those of a romance hero, while
Philip M. Royster in "Milkman's Flying: The Scapegoat Transcended
in Toni Morrison's *Song of Solomon*" (*CLAJ* 24:419–40) methodically

explicates the text to show increments of self-awareness associated with the progress of Milkman/Macon through the episodes of the narrative. De Arman is intrigued by Northrop Frye, Royster by the possibility of a final reading. A third critic, Norris Clark, writes "Flying Black: Toni Morrison's *The Bluest Eye, Sula,* and *Song of Solomon*" (*MV* 4,ii[1980]:51–63) to demonstrate, through a catalogue of technical devices and cultural details, that Morrison achieves literary rediscovery of black community, even though she speaks against the program of the black aestheticians who advocate such a purpose for literature. Despite its revelation of an apparent paradox, Clark's essay, like De Arman's and Royster's, restates what the intelligent reader will find but does not provide an indispensable discussion. The case is quite the contrary with Jane S. Bakerman's "Failures of Love: Female Initiation in the Novels of Toni Morrison" (*AL* 52:541–69). Bakerman joins the theme of characters searching for love and their sense of worth to motifs of initiation, amplifies her study with examination of particular causes for failures of maturation, and the result is an excellent demonstration of an interpretive thesis that illuminates the functions of plot.

Ernest Gaines's critical reputation rests largely on *The Autobiography of Miss Jane Pittman,* a novel that Frank W. Skelton suggests may not be typical of Gaines's art. Skelton's "*In My Father's House*: Ernest Gaines After Jane Pittman" (*SR* 17:340–45) attends to the fall of the leading character in Gaines's infrequently reviewed recent novel, pointing out that the reconciliations between young and old, past and present, in earlier works collapses.

Though Alice Walker unquestionably writes with deep concern for the careers and fate of female characters, reviewers of her first novel have not always noted the key role played by women; to repair the oversight Karen C. Gaston writes "Women in the Lives of Grange Copeland" (*CLAJ* 24:276–86), a study that demonstrates how women force the male protagonist to take responsibility for his actions despite their subjugation to his power. Martha J. McGowan, analyzing Walker's second novel in "Atonement and Release in Alice Walker's *Meridian*" (*Crit* 23:23–36), discerns a pattern of regeneration supplanting the previous commemoration of female suffering and compares the chief character to Camus' ideal rebel in her effort to elude or thwart tragedy. Deborah E. McDowell labels the same novel a *Bildungsroman* in "The Self in Bloom: Alice Walker's *Merid-*

ian" (*CLAJ* 24:262–75) and carefully details how the character Meridian creates an alternative to the god of American Tradition by "psychically repatriating" to the most viable aspects of black cultural heritage. Trudier Harris makes Walker a major exhibit, along with Sarah Wright and Paule Marshall, in her "Three Black Women Writers and Humanism: A Folk Perspective" in *Black American Literature and Humanism*, ed. R. Baxter Miller (Kentucky), pp. 50–74. Harris is intent upon showing the persistence of folk consciousness in the three writers. She achieves her aim ably because she carefully describes the folk tradition as a source of values exemplified by figures who refuse nihilism by expressing a humanistic philosophy in the face of their oppressive circumstances.

Marian E. Musgrave, a scholar whose essays on black literature are always informed by a comparativist perspective, pursues Ishmael Reed's parodic discounting of white mythology in "Ishmael Reed's Black Oedipus Cycle" (*Obsidian* 6,iii[1980]:60–67). Reworking myth for his own purposes in *The Last Days of Louisiana Red*, Reed plays upon classical analogues to silhouette fragmented black American society against the Theban civil war story.

Joe Weixlmann matches his bibliographical service to Barry Beckham with a first-rate critical analysis in "The Dream Turned 'Daymare': Barry Beckham's *Runner Mack*" (*MELUS* 8,iv:93–103). The bulk of the essay is given to explaining the satire of the American Dream in the novel. Weixlmann's exposition also describes the effect of narrative distancing and tone, so that the essay becomes a demonstration of narrational functions. Like other scholars noted in this survey, James W. Coleman hopes to direct our attention to neglected work. "Language, Reality, and Self in Wesley Brown's *Tragic Magic*" (*BALF* 15:48–50) concentrates on a novel heavily influenced by Ellison's *Invisible Man*, but one that is unique because of the dominance of rich, metaphorical street language and the representation of that language as the means to transcend absurdity.

e. General Criticism of Fiction. Instigation of much of the theory of black writing lies in the need to define the singular qualities of Afro-American literature. Taking all fiction by people of African descent as her subject, Bonnie J. Barthold in *Black Time: Fiction of Africa, the Caribbean, and the United States* (Yale) attempts to establish the unity of a literature separate from other modern literatures on the basis of a generalized struggle between myth and history in the minds of blacks. In her explanation this version of double consciousness derives from the victimization inherent in the forced shift from cyclic time to the linear time imposed and controlled by slave owners. Dispossession co-exists with a sense of the mythic cycle. An examination of seven Afro-American novels presents such treatments of the temporal crisis as the loss of time in Jean Toomer's *Cane*, the fragmentary experiences of time that characterize the temporal no-man's land of William Attaway's *Blood on the Forge*, and the redemption of cyclic time in *Song of Solomon*. Indeed, time is problematic for many black writers, but then, so is it for other modern writers. Barthold gives us insight, but not yet a conclusive way to define black literary singularity.

In *Black Novelists and the Southern Literary Tradition* (Georgia) Ladell Payne takes it for granted that singularity is established and seeks to associate black writers with white writers who use similar sources and themes. Concentrating on Chesnutt, James Weldon Johnson, Toomer, Wright, and Ellison, and matching features of black texts with those of white, Payne indicates, for example, prevailing concerns with identity and the theme of humanity in history. The method is more stipulative than analytic, and though it reminds us of common interests among writers it ignores the contrasting manner in which those interests are rendered into fiction. While some critics may see uniqueness in black texts that does not exist, Payne weakens his argument for redefining the southern tradition as biracial by disregarding the critical necessity to consider how differing cultural codes mediate genre and theme.

Toni Morrison's "City Limits, Village Values: Concepts of the Neighborhood in Black Fiction" (*Literature and the Urban Experience*, pp. 35–43) illustrates one way to discern difference within commonly used subjects. White anti-urbanism, she says, derives from a sense of the constraints on individualism found in the city, while black pro-urbanism has resulted from the belief that the neighborhood can be a village free from segregation's oppression. Harlem once appeared to be such a village, but recently black writers have become less enamored of the city because they find that the ancestors who provided the village connection with the past have become only parents or other adults. Yet another illustration of unique treatment of theme is presented by Richard Yarborough in "The Quest for the American Dream in Three Afro-American Novels: *If He Hollers Let Him Go, The Street,* and *Invisible Man*" (*MELUS* 8,iv: 33–59). This study addresses the paradox apparent in the fervent belief in the Dream among those who are excluded from participation by racism. The discussion is wide-ranging, including references to novels besides those named in the title, but it concentrates on the increasing difficulties black writers of the 20th century have in sustaining a belief in opportunity.

iii. Poetry

a. **Hammon, Horton, Harper, Dunbar.** In his excellent study titled "Jupiter Hammon: His Involvement with His 'Unconverted' Brethren" (*MV* 4,i[1980]:1–10) Erskine Peters demonstrates how valuable attention to "minor" figures can be. Peters' focus is the conflict between the proselytizing verse of the poet and the black audience that resisted conversion because of a sense of the contradiction between their temporal condition and the spiritual state promised by the Christianity of slave owners. In support of speculations about that resistance Peters offers detail about the ontological issue of difference between Hammon and traditional African thought, thus adding to the social history of slavery an episode of intellectual history.

John L. Cobbs's "George Moses Horton's *Hope of Liberty*: Thematic Unity in Early American Black Poetry" (*CLAJ* 24:441–50) undertakes study of another poet usually mentioned only in passing. Conceding that Horton's 1829 collection is derivative in technique, Cobbs proceeds to show, however, that the facile verses are unified by the motif of flight, an element that reveals how each poetic topic is filtered through the poet's consciousness of his own bondage.

Patricia Liggins Hill, who has written frequently on modern poets, puts her hand to a 19th-century figure in " 'Let Me Make the Songs for the People': A Study of Frances Watkins Harper's Poetry" (*BALF* 15:60–65), a categorical survey of the themes employed by the poet whose fame rests upon her public declamation of poems written for public purposes.

Emeka Okeke Ezigbo again returns to the problem of the integrity of Dunbar's dialect verse. Last year he identified a group of "positively Afro-American poems" among the dialect writings (see *ALS 1980*, 453). This year his "Paul Laurence Dunbar: Straightening the

Record" (*CLAJ* 24:481–96) broadens the approach to include treatment of the influence of James Whitcomb Riley upon Dunbar and his efforts to achieve the meticulous representation Riley prescribed. Through it all, however, Dunbar was apparently condescending toward uneducated blacks, and so he missed the opportunity to develop a black vernacular literature. Inevitably the conflict between vernacular and genteel traditions also informs the entry on Dunbar written by Charles T. Davis for *American Writers* (pp. 191–219). Davis presents Dunbar as struggling with two related problems: how to escape the claims of the genteel traditions, and how to find his authentic voice. Within their framework, according to Davis, Dunbar can be seen as selecting and rejecting options offered him from both black and white literature.

b. **Hughes, Tolson, Brooks.** The two articles on poetry in the special Langston Hughes issue of *Black American Literature Forum* are written by Dellita L. Martin and Richard K. Barksdale. Martin's "The 'Madam Poems' as Dramatic Monologue" (15:97–99) explains the portrait of Alberta K. Johnson as equivalent to that of Jesse B. Semple. Both are personae meant to illuminate urban black life. Barksdale's "Comic Relief in Langston Hughes' Poetry" (15:108–11) opens with the observation that a comic element is lacking in Hughes's verse until *Shakespeare in Harlem* (1942). From that point on, however, he cast many poems in the comic mode. Barksdale proceeds to examine the function of comedy in creation of characters such as Alberta K. Johnson, representation of experiences as universal, and the devising of techniques to embody reactions to racism.

Barksdale treats the evolution of Hughes's poetry from a different standpoint in "Langston Hughes: His Times and His Humanistic Technique" (*Black American Literature and Humanism*, pp. 11–26). There he discusses the break with the tradition of protest marked by increasing use of the folk materials called "orature" and by adoption of the monologue and blues technique. Together, Barksdale's two essays are an engaging record of the self-creation of an original poet.

Further depth is given our understanding of Hughes by three excellent articles on his adaptation of musical forms to poetry. Steven C. Tracy in "To the Tune of Those Weary Blues: The Influence of the Blues Tradition in Langston Hughes's Blues Poems" (*MELUS* 8,iii:73–98) begins with documentary evidence of the blues styles

Hughes knew, particularly the Texas and classic styles. Most important, though, Tracy brings to bear on the subject a knowledge of musical and textual structures that allows him to annotate poetic lines to demonstrate how Hughes captures on the page the spirit and pattern of performance. This is an illuminating study that provides specific technical grounding for the impressions most readers have of an intimate link between the verse and black music. Walter C. Farrell, Jr., and Patricia A. Johnson collaborate in writing the other equally excellent articles. In one, "Poetic Interpretation of Urban Black Folk Culture: Langston Hughes and the 'Bebop' Era" (*MELUS* 8,iii:57–72), they read the system of *Montage of a Dream Deferred* (1951) in relation to the musical techniques evident in the innovations of bebop. Farrell and Johnson's other article, "The Jazz Poetry of Langston Hughes: A Reflection" (*MV* 4,i[1980]:11–21), concentrates on *Ask Your Mama* (1961) as exemplary of the jazz-poetry movement that flourished on the West Coast in the mid-1950s and explains how it reflects in poetry the nationalist concerns of the musicians who created the hard bop of that era.

"What Can a Poet Do? Langston Hughes and M. B. Tolson" by Robert M. Farnsworth (*NewL* 48:19–29) recounts Tolson's expressed admiration for the proletarian sympathies of Hughes in his master's thesis on "The Harlem Group of Negro Writers" and by anecdote and comparative examination of verses traces the subsequent relationship of the two poets. Farnsworth also writes "Preface to Melvin B. Tolson's *Caviar and Cabbage* Columns" (*NewL* 47:101–02), a summary statement on the column Tolson wrote for the *Washington Tribune* between 1937 and 1944. The five specimens published with the introduction are selected from the compilation edited by Farnsworth (Missouri, 1982).

The year's work on Gwendolyn Brooks includes Larry R. Andrews' "Ambivalent Clothes Imagery in Gwendolyn Brooks's 'The Sundays of Satin-Legs Smith'" (*CLAJ* 24:150–63), an analysis of tone and imagery that project the combination of self-assertion and self-protection in the dandyism of Brooks's protagonist; George E. Kent's "Aesthetic Values in the Poetry of Gwendolyn Brooks" (*Black American Literature and Humanism*, pp. 75–94), a demonstration that the act of seeing embodies Brooks's primary aesthetic value— the idea that shared perception is the basis of human communion; and R. Baxter Miller's "'Does Man Love Art?': The Humanistic Aesthetic of Gwendolyn Brooks" (*Black American Literature and Humanism*, pp. 95–112), which presents close readings of poems in explaining how style and imagination are the means by which poetic characters prevail against determining external forces.

c. Hayden, Walker, Baraka, Knight.   Robert M. Greenberg provides the entry on Robert Hayden for *American Writers* (pp. 361–83). According to Greenberg, Hayden's poems express the tension between the irredeemable world and its possible transcendence in sensory delight, art, and religion. A different emphasis appears in Vilma Raskin Potter's "A Remembrance for Robert Hayden: 1913–1980" (*MELUS* 8,i:51–55), which stresses Hayden's coherent vision of black experience as a continuing journey. The bulk of Potter's references comes from *Angle of Ascent* (1975), but she also uses portions of the mostly unpublished *American Journal*.

In " 'The Etched Flame': Margaret Walker, Biblical and Literary Recreation in Southern History" (*TSL* 26:157–72) R. Baxter Miller gives close attention to the allusions and resonances that mark the reworking of biblical sources in what he judges to be Walker's profoundest work.

Henry C. Lacey's *To Raise, Destroy, and Create: The Poetry, Drama, and Fiction of Imamu Amiri Baraka* (Whitston) selects 1960–70 as the crucial decade in a career he considers a microcosm of the black crisis of identity and purpose. The strength of the book lies in explications indicative of the progress of the well-known career; however, since the book derives from a dissertation completed before the studies by Kimberly Benston, Werner Sollers, or Lloyd Brown were available, the interpretive discussion needs updating.

"Belly Songs: The Poetry of Etheridge Knight" by Howard Nelson (*HC* 18,v:2–11) is occasioned by the appearance of *Born of Woman*, which collects virtually all the earlier Knight poems from his previous two books. Nelson characterizes the verse as a blend of vivid lyric and narrative marked by a strong sense of verbal music that suggests in the reading the power Knight gives to it in performance. The compelling theme is relationships between and among people; consequently, 90 precent of Knight's writing can be read as love poetry, including love expressed by the prospect of racial solidarity and the celebration of heroes.

d. **General Criticism of Poetry.** This year an outstanding work of general criticism appears in the form of an anthology, *Black Sisters: Poetry by Black American Women, 1746–1980,* ed. Erlene Stetson (Indiana). In the introduction Stetson argues the existence of a black, feminist, poetic tradition marked by its own personal landscape and characteristic elements, such as the use of ambivalence as a creative strategy. The introduction to each historical section of the book uses a poet as representative. Predictably it is Wheatley for the 18th century, Frances Watkins Harper for the 19th, but then for the 20th it is Nikki Giovanni, who lends herself especially well to the ideal of the female tradition. The bibliography of anthologies, critical works, and the poets' publications, together with the notations on sources for each entry make the book a valuable resource. Above all, though, it is the conception of the book that distinguishes it. Here we have validated the principle of differential literary history with selections from 58 poets that clearly illustrate the women's voices and viewpoints that must be accounted for in our description of the black literary tradition.

iv. Drama

a. **Wright, Baraka, Bullins, Shange.** Frederick C. Stern writes "*Native Son* as Play: A Reconsideration Based On a Revival" (*MELUS* 8,i:55–60) upon a performance of the drama at the Goodman Theatre in Chicago in 1978. The heart of Wright's vision lies in Bigger's final awareness, Stern claims, but since the novelist does not resolve in artistic terms the differences between the protagonist's perception of racial injustice and his own radical sense of class struggle, it is difficult to stage the play. In addition to this block to effective dramatization there is the problem that the printed version of the play written by Paul Green dilutes the ending entirely too much, and the fact that the successful Broadway run of the play was based upon John Houseman's repair job on the Green play. Because Houseman's version is not available and Green's is too mild, production of the play is effectively discouraged.

William C. Fisher contributes the entry on Amiri Baraka to the collection *American Writers* (pp. 29–63). Like others surveying the career, he is struck by the record of intense, ongoing changes. The treatment of the plays is useful for provision of benchmarks. *A Black Mass* is a play about art, *Slave Ship* is the quintessential nationalist play, and the later Marxist works such as *The Motion of History* constitute a theatre of ideas.

"The (In)humanity of Assassination: Plays by Albert Camus and 'Kingsley B. Bass, Jr.'" (*MELUS* 8,iii:45–56) by Jack B. Moore takes up the stage history of *We Righteous Bombers*, itself a piece of theatre. Larry Neal charged that the play was stolen from Camus' *Les Justes* and shortly thereafter it was announced that Ed Bullins had written the play and attributed it to a fictitious author whom he claimed had been killed in Detroit. Moore pursues the Neal charge and demonstrates that Bullins' stagecraft transforms the contemplative original into an experience of disorientation for the audience.

Sandra Hollins Flowers responds to reviewers and critics of Ntozake Shange in "*Colored Girls*: Textbook for the Eighties" (*BALF* 15:51–54) by defending the play as a perception of the crisis in male and female relationships, rather than a diatribe against men. Careful reading implies a compassion for men as well as women, but above all the play sets the politics of relationships high on the agenda of this decade.

b. **General Criticism of Drama.** The growing list of books on black drama gains an important addition this year in Helen Keyssar's *The Curtain and the Veil: Strategies in Black Drama* (Burt Franklin). The dilemma of the black playwright arises from a conflict between the desire to reveal actuality and the demand by audiences for continued illusion. By Keyssar's reckoning the tension between play and audience, therefore, becomes as important as the situation within the dramatic text. Accordingly, she conducts her study as an analysis of persuasive techniques. Premising the investigation on theories of Kenneth Burke and Stanley Cavell, she reads the following eight plays with an eye to the relative success of strategies: Willis Richardson's *The Chip Woman's Fortune* and *The Broken Banjo*, Langston Hughes's *The Emperor of Haiti*, Theodore Ward's *Big White Fog*, Lorraine Hansberry's *A Raisin in the Sun*, Amiri Baraka's *Dutchman*, Ed Bullins' *In the Wine Time*, and Ntozake Shange's *for colored girls*. While Keyssar works from printed texts, rather than from productions, her method is nonetheless valuable because it preserves in criticism the idea of dynamic relationships between audience and performance. Appendices contain a methodological discussion of the "strategic approach," a statement on drama criticism, and a previously published bibliography of playwrights and plays (see *ALS 1975*, 413) that includes 213 authors, production, and publication dates.

v. Slave Narratives and Autobiography

The two notable articles on slave narratives from 1981 constitute corrections of previous views. Jean Fagan Yellin in "Written by Herself: Harriet Jacobs' Slave Narrative" (*AL* 53:479–86) uses a recently discovered cache of Jacobs' letters to clarify the question of her authorship of *Incidents in the Life of a Slave Girl.* John Blassingame has questioned the credibility of the work, but the letters written to Amy Post affirm Jacobs' creation of the book and define the role of Lydia Maria Child as an editor. Yellin draws upon the letters also to provide a brief biography, since the narrative, which gains significance because of its defiance of taboos prohibiting women from discussing their sexuality, is more a collection of incidents than a life writing. Frances Foster continues the excellent work she began in *Witnessing Slavery* (see *ALS 1979*, 420) with the essay " 'In Respect to Females . . .': Differences in the Portrayals of Women by Male and Female Narrators" (*BALF* 15:66–70). Slave narratives typically stereotype female slaves as sexual victims. Their children are sold at the master's will, and the women's bodies are available to the licentious masters. The truth of the popular image is undoubted, but, as Foster observes, the dominant image results from writing by male slave narrators. When women write they barely mention sexual experience and never present seduction or rape as the most profound aspect of their existence. Rather than seeing themselves as victims, such writers as Harriet Jacobs, Elizabeth Keckley, Susie King Taylor, Amanda Berry Smith, and Annie Louise Burton develop narratives showing themselves gaining control of events, becoming as heroic as men. Foster sees no contradiction between writings by female and male slaves. Instead, the point she makes is literary: writers choose to stress the events that are most useful to the purposes of their narratives.

Gordon O. Taylor seeks to establish the paradigm of an autobiographical tradition in "Voices from the Veil: Black American

Autobiography" (*GaR* 35:341–61). Racial subjugation reverberates throughout autobiographical writings, urging authors such as DuBois, Richard Wright, James Baldwin, and Malcolm X to articulate, as if for the first time, a "sensibility at once determined and precluded by history." The search for a voice leads the writers to a sense of representative self-awareness. They are the race's exemplars, their personal memory made into collective myth and their personalities arising through the presentation of a collective history. To form a tradition available to critics, Taylor's interpretation is sound and useful. Richard K. Barksdale's "Black Autobiography and the Comic Vision" (*BALF* 15:22–27) is an interesting but puzzling study of the tradition. He is drawn to the occurrence of comic distancing in the 20th-century autobiography. Earlier writers were too heavily burdened to adopt such an impersonal approach, but Hughes, Zora Neale Hurston, Nate Cobb, and numbers of oral autobiographers in this century find a comic vision of life to be congenial. Barksdale's discussion leads one to imagine he is defining a significant quality or category of life writing, but oddly he dismissively concludes by declaring that "there is no such thing as a good impersonal autobiography."

vi. Literary History, Criticism

The term "renaissance" has been an invaluable metaphor for Afro-American literary history. Used to characterize the writing of authors who came to maturity in 20th-century Harlem, it signaled, on the one hand, a liberation of black literature from the constraints of a white, and too often genteel, decorum, while on the other hand it also signified adaptation of a black, and sometimes nationalist, protest to the conditions of modern urban society. That the definition of the period has been imprecise, and the application of the term dubious to some critics, is less important than the fact that the "renaissance" has been instrumental in focusing the attention of critics upon the process of change in modern black literature. By echoing the original application of the term, William L. Andrews may help to draw attention to the dynamics that typify 19th-century black writing. His essay "The 1850s: The First Afro-American Literary Renaissance" (*Literary Romanticism*, pp. 38–60) describes the fugitive slave narrative as a form that risked fixity because of its formulaic stress upon the facts. New creativity emerged through the generic experimentation of William Wells Brown, who attempted to present a myth of history in *Clotel*, and Martin R. Delany, who linked romantic individualism to revolutionary politics in creating the black hero in *Blake*. Thus, according to Andrews' scheme of evolution, confidence in the creative self led to the rise of the black novel, while the inward-directed candor adumbrated in such narratives as Henry Bibb's and Samuel Ringgold Ward's gave rise to the black autobiography with its theme of self-development.

The theme of candid self-expression also informs the interpretation Chidi Ikonné provides for the Harlem Renaissance itself. His book *From DuBois to Van Vechten: The Early New Negro Literature, 1903–1926* (Greenwood) addresses two misrepresentations: the tendency to exaggerate the influence of whites in the creation of the "New Negro" and the opposite tendency to disregard all indebtedness while commending the movement as an uninfluenced attempt at rediscovery. Ikonné reduces the conflict between these tendencies by defining the literature as the product of the colonized black. The "New Negro" constitutes a moment in the long, continual development of racial literature, but it is not beyond white influence, as becomes evident in a survey of the rise of interest in Africa among Europeans during the 1920s. Ikonné sees the uniqueness of the renaissance in its expansive expression of black folkways, a subject that is effectively reinforced even as the black writers assimilate the forms and diction of Western literature.

We are reminded of the importance the Harlem Renaissance has for world literature in "African and Black American Literature: 'The Negro Renaissance' and the Genesis of African Literature in French" by Mbulamwanza Mudimbe-Boyi in *For Better or Worse: The American Influence in the World*, ed. Allen F. Davis (Greenwood) pp. 157–69. Black American writers established a paradigm for the expression of the racial conscience by their rehabilitation of history and art, and through their influence they made possible the present-day bipolar exchange between Africa and the black diaspora.

Jack B. Moore's study *W. E. B. DuBois* (TUSAS 399) presents a figure who cannot be classified according to the genres in which he wrote, but whose role as man of letters, interpreter of history, and black spokesperson demands for him a prominent place in literary history. Following the format of the Twayne series, Moore provides a brief biography and surveys the chief ideas and works. For *Souls of Black Folk* he has the highest praise. Its sophisticated use of persona is reminiscent of Franklin and Adams, but it is an emotionally deeper work; its subject puts it in a class with great black autobiographies, but it is more intellectual than works by Booker T. Washington, James Weldon Johnson, or Frederick Douglass. Moore examines other imaginative works in terms of DuBois' efforts to make their genres black. For treatment of the historical writings one is well advised to turn to this year's essay on DuBois written by Herbert Aptheker for *American Writers* (pp. 157–89). This is a scholar's appraisal that places DuBois' study in relationship to prevailing historiography.

Two review essays provide transition to this year's work in critical theory. In "The Survival of Black Literature and Its Criticism" (*GaR* 35:170–77) John Oliver Perry reviews Houston Baker's *Journey Back* (see *ALS 1980*, 465–66), C. W. E. Bigsby's *The Second Black Renaissance* (see *ALS 1980*, 466–67 and *passim*), and Robert Stepto's *From Behind the Veil* and *Chant of Saints* (see *ALS 1979*, 394, 423–24). Baker receives partial approval from Perry because he approaches literature with acknowledgment of the mechanisms of cultural repression. Because Perry demands a more rebellious, more bitter criticism that takes as its program the preservation of black culture, he dismisses Bigsby as a traditional academic, Stepto as a critic staking new ground for cultural colonization. Houston A. Baker himself is author of the second review essay, "Generational Shifts and the Recent Criticism of Afro-American Literature" (*BALF* 15: 3–21). The subject is *Reconstruction of Instruction*, ed. Stepto with Dexter Fisher (see *ALS 1979*, 393–94), a work Baker faults for its treatment of literary texts as though they were isolated from the systems of culture. In contrast to Perry's political program, Baker's is theoretical. The formalism he decries he also sees as the product of newly emergent middle-class professionals whose work is supplanting the Black Aesthetics fostered by the Black Arts movement, Stephen Henderson, and others. Baker proposes a new self-awareness, calling upon the critics to join in systematic formulation of theoretical problems and an approach to them that is as holistic as his conception of the anthropology of art.

Though earlier essays by Amiri Baraka such as "Myth of a Negro Literature" and "Hunting is Not Those Heads on the Wall" helped to foster dominant critical theory in the 1960s, he now stands apart from the debate outlined by Perry and Baker. Typical of his recent critical statements is this year's "Black Literature and the Afro-American Nation: The Urban Voice" (*Literature and the Urban Experience*, pp. 139–54), which revives the left-wing theory of a nation founded on the historical and material conditions of the Black Belt.

Very much involved in the debate, however, is Chester J. Fontenot, Jr. For the past two years Fontenot has been developing a theory of the combat between linear and mythic conceptions of history in black literature. This year he explains something of the method underlying his interpretations with "Angelic Dance or Tug of War? The Humanistic Implications of Cultural Formalism" (*Black American Literature and Humanism*, pp. 33–49). Fontenot is concerned to navigate the passage between a strict sociological approach to literature and a formalism that separates literature from culture. He finds his guidance in the cultural formalism of Eliseo Vivas, which he applies to black fiction in an effort to show it creating values and reflecting ideological forces.

Fontenot and a number of other critics in this report presented their views originally in a conference at the University of Tennessee. The papers have been published as *Black American Literature and Humanism*, and an account of the unpublished discussions appears in Donna Walter's "The Critics on Criticism: A Critical Summary" (*Obsidian* 6,iii[1980]:22–29). According to Walter the panel prescribed an obligation of the humanistic critic to resist the formalist habit of treating literature as primarily universal and to withstand the power of the "critical machine" to subjugate literature to technical treatment.

The inadequacy of formalism is also much on Gibson's mind in "Preface to a Social Theory of Literature," the introduction to *Politics of Literary Expression* (pp. 3–19). According to Gibson's argument there is a fundamental incompatability between formalism and black literature. Partly this is due to the conservative bias of formalist critics, but mainly it results from the inability of formalist theory to account for literature written, as black literature is, with an understanding that reality is a social formation. In Gibson's theory literature has no universal nature, but rather it has distinct character. To put it simply, the job of the critic is to describe the value system informing a work by analysis of its social dimension. But, of course, the job is not simple, nor does Gibson treat it as such. His theory has a place for expressive form as well as for the idea that literary values are grounded in history, and unquestionably his politicization of literature is highly provocative.

Eugenia Collier's "The African Presence in Afro-American Literature" (*Obsidian* 6,iii[1980]:30–55) represents an attempt to locate literary values in Africanism. As a result of blacks' enforced alienation, the African heritage persists among them in America and is available to counter European-American criticism. Among Western analogues for the inherited African aesthetics, Collier sees Plato's *Republic* paramount. Social purpose for literature and the usefulness of propaganda are common to both.

Three critical statements originally delivered to the MLA Division of Ethnic Studies belong in this survey because they attempt to distinguish contemporary black literature. In "Black American Literature: A Cultural Interpretation" (*MELUS* 8,ii:13–21) Vivian I. Davis poses the question of cultural independence. Given the broad audience for black literature, its developed myths and indigenous characters, a delivery system in place, and characteristics of a national literary language, the prospects are good for independence. Dellita L. Martin's "In Our Own Black Images: Afro-American Literature in the 1980s" (*MELUS* 8,ii:65–71) remarks an inner-directed vision in contemporary black writers. Abjuring prescriptions, including the demand to "off whitey," and protest, these writers refuse to see themselves through the eye of the "other." William J. Harris' contribution to the discussion, "The *Yardbird Reader* and the Multi-Ethnic Spirit" (*MELUS* 8,ii:72–75), describes the move from narrowly ethnocentric or mono-ethnic writing among such writers as Al Young and Ishmael Reed to a position that assumes all of American experience and literature is ethnic and, therefore, pluralist.

This report can be appropriately concluded with notation of the winter issue of *Black American Literature Forum* devoted to "Black Textual Strategies." This collection, labeled "Volume I: Theory," is guest edited by Henry-Louis Gates, Jr., who provides in the introduction a brief discussion of his own involvement in the dispute about the place of formalism in black criticism. Two of the essays in the issue relate to American fiction. One by James A. Snead entitled "On Repetition in Black Culture" (15:146–54) charts a philosophical basis for the culture that finds its characteristic shape in rhythmic performance. In another essay Jay Edwards presents an example of the method pursued by the "LSU School" in "Structural Analysis of the Afro-American Trickster Tale" (15:155–64). Like much else in the critical discourse of 1981 these essays have instrumental importance. As the renaissance metaphor drew attention to the broad pattern of Afro-American literary history, the elaboration of theory apparent in the sum of work reported for 1981 defines a new set of problems, a new level of interest among the critics of black literature.

State University of New York at Albany

20. Themes, Topics, Criticism

Jonathan Morse

An average year in most respects, 1981 did yield a number of strong contributions. Some of these demonstrate that new critical ideas are penetrating satisfactorily into the academic study of American literature; others are simply satisfying demonstrations of scholarly competence. The institution we work in is in sound shape overall.

i. Themes and Topics

a. **Thematic Studies: Monographs.** Anthony Channell Hilfer's *The Ethics of Intensity in American Fiction* (Texas) begins by using Aristotle and Irving Babbitt "to clarify the structural opposition between ethos and pathos, limitation and expansion, choice and instinct, reason and emotion" (p. 2), then goes on to identify ethos as a characteristic norm of character definition in the kind of fiction we loosely call "Victorian," and pathos as the corresponding norm in the kind of fiction we call "modern." "In the first mode character is seen as the sum of an individual's ethical choices; in the second, character is seen as the process of an individual's longings. In the first mode, a character is almost always wrong to yield to desire; in the second, a character is frequently wrong not to. An ethics of restraint tends to give way to an ethics of intensity, ethos tends to be displaced by pathos" (p. xi). Hilfer's sensitive readings chart the course of this giving way as it proceeds from *A Modern Instance* (pp. 163–64: "Howells . . . negat[es] desire to affirm the historically contingent ethical values which his own fiction puts into doubt. . . . [T]here is less energy in Howells' fiction than in the great Victorians because of his diminished confidence . . . [in] a convincing ethical base"), through "Song of Myself," several works by James and Dreiser, and Stein's "Melanctha." A concluding chapter notes that ethos has virtually disappeared from the universe of such books as *The Naked Lunch.* A disheartening progress, a stimulating body of readings.

b. **Collections.** *Memories of the Moderns* (New Directions, 1980) is a collection of Harry Levin's review-essays, most of them dating from the last decade. (A notable exception is the longest piece in the book, "Observations on the Style of Ernest Hemingway" [1951].) The other American authors discussed are Ezra Pound, T. S. Eliot, John Dos Passos, William Carlos Williams, Conrad Aiken, Delmore Schwartz, Randall Jarrell, Edmund Wilson, F. O. Matthiessen, and James Laughlin. Americanists need no introduction to the author of *The Power of Blackness;* Levin's magisterial opinions are supplemented here by personal reminiscences.

Another retrospective collection, Robert E. Spiller's *Late Harvest: Essays and Addresses in American Literature and Culture* (Greenwood), covers almost half a century of distinguished service to American literature. In 14 essays—some previously unpublished— Spiller discusses two general subjects: American literary history and bibliography from the beginnings through the early 20th century, and the discipline of American Studies. The book also includes a bibliography of Spiller's writings and a warm and generous collection of prefaces to the essays by the 85-year-old dean of Americanists.

The seven essays in *Literary Romanticism* deal with romanticism not as a period of literary history but as a state of mind—"the ability to wonder and to reflect," as Robert E. Spiller defines it (p. ix). Accordingly, these essays cover the whole history of American literature. Their subjects are Emerson (by Clarence Gohdes), Hawthorne (Arlin Turner), Afro-American writers of the 1850s (William L. Andrews), Thomas Wolfe (Louis D. Rubin, Jr.), Allen Tate (C. Hugh Holman), Walker Percy (Panthea Reid Broughton), and Richard Nixon as mythic figure (John Seelye, with excessive cuteness).

Literature and the Urban Experience is a conference volume consisting of 20 essays, plus a terrible poem by Lawrence Ferlinghetti. The essays include, inter alia, thematic studies (Alfred Kazin, "New York from Melville to Mailer"; Leo Marx, "The Puzzle of Anti-Urbanism in Classic American Literature"), autobiographical memoirs by writers (Chaim Potok, Marge Piercy, David Ignatow), studies of individual writers (Joyce Carol Oates on Saul Bellow, Helen Vendler on Robert Lowell), social-scientific studies (Joan M. Burstyn on children and public libraries, Bruno Bettelheim on "The Child's Perception of the City"), an apparently ad lib speech by James Baldwin, and an essay in literary history by Amiri Baraka which demonstrates that white liberals will sit through anything.

c. Literary History. Cambridge has reissued Warner Berthoff's *The Ferment of Realism: American Literature, 1884–1919* (orig. pub. Free Press, 1965), and a preface to the new printing allows Berthoff to reflect on the course of literary history between 1965 and the present. As it has impinged on his own sensibility, that history has, for instance, caused Berthoff to regret his failure to discuss H. L. Mencken's *A Book of Prefaces* and W. E. B. DuBois' *The Souls of Black Folk.* On the other hand, the new feminism has not changed his low opinion of Charlotte Perkins Gilman, and "it still makes sense to me to cram the later Henry James into a mere twenty-three pages and allow Charles W. Chesnutt the luxury of almost a full line." And in general—despite the Voting Rights Act of 1965, the Johns Hopkins structuralism symposium of 1966, and all the events that have directed the course of literary and extraliterary history since the first publication of *The Ferment of Realism*—"our basic picture of the historical period in question—who was important, and what publishing events mattered most—remains largely as it was."

That is, there is a recognizable canon of literary value, and our critical reading can be done without going outside the system. To revalue a book, we need only readjust our critical presuppositions with respect to canonical norms, for instance by shifting the book from one category to another. (Berthoff, p. 92: "Reissued . . . as it ought to be, [Edward Eggleston's] *The Graysons* could take on new life as a children's classic; it is at least as good a book as *The Prince and the Pauper.*") This assumption of canonicity is probably essential to the writing and reading of literary history, but of course it produces the undesirable side effects of restriction and exclusion. Some ways of alleviating these effects are examined in the 1979 English Institute volume *English Literature: Opening Up the Canon,* ed. Leslie A. Fiedler and Houston A. Baker, Jr. (Hopkins).

This collection of essays in the sociology of literature falls into two parts. One, "English as a World Language for Literature," consists of three descriptive essays about the new uses to which literary English has been put in South Africa, the Caribbean, and the Pueblo

Indian reservation culture. The primary concerns of these essays are, respectively, political, musical, and anthropological. The other half of the volume, "Literature as an Institution," comprises an entertaining fable by George Stade, "Fat-Cheeks Hefted a Snake: On the Origins and Institutionalization of Literature," a rambling address by Leslie Fiedler (who can spell neither "Gutenberg" nor "Ginsberg"), a Marxist polemic by H. Bruce Franklin consisting entirely of 1968-era clichés ("elitist," "irrelevant"), and a feminist essay which earnestly warns us on p. 132 that "If many more sessions like this one take place, the nature of the institute will irrevocably change, and such changes can legitimately be called a *lowering of standards*." Since this volume also gives us a footnote (p. 17, n. 1) which informs us that "Hurricanes ravish the Caribbean," I incline to agree.

A more practical attempt to open, or reopen, the canon is Marcus Klein's *Foreigners*. In Klein's literary history, the critical pendulum swings all the way back to its pre–New Critical position: *Foreigners* is devoted to a sympathetic revaluation of the proletarian novelists, the chroniclers of the Depression, the leftists associated with *The Liberator* and *The New Masses*, and such belated naturalists as James T. Farrell and Meyer Levin. The last section of the book is a detailed study of the life-fictions of three authors—Michael Gold, Nathanael West, and Richard Wright—who exemplify, both in the books they wrote and the authorial personas they created, Klein's thesis: "American literature of this century has been created by people who have known themselves to be marginal Americans, sometimes by an act of imagination and sometimes by right of birth" (p. 288). Klein proves his thesis in interesting detail, and what keeps *Foreigners* from being a major book is only its one-sidedness. As a collection of small readings it is a fine supplement to, e.g., Daniel Aaron's *Writers on the Left* or Malcolm Cowley's *The Dream of the Golden Mountains*, but as a history it fails to move us very far from positions that reached their maximum influence in the 1930s.

The specific reason for this is Klein's willful failure to acknowledge the importance, for good or bad, of the modernist movement. It is simply dismissed at the beginning as a conspiracy ("Like modern science, as was quite part of the general intention, literature was to require special academic training, and of course not everybody went to the university"—p. 8) on the part of "a certain class, one which might well think of itself as a dispossessed *social* aristocracy.

. . . (Gertrude Stein was Jewish, but from an old American family nonetheless. . . . Dos Passos was a bastard, but raised in such circumstances that he had standing in elevated society; he was a kind of royal bastard)" (p. 11). As to T. S. Eliot, he was just an anti-semite. And Klein proceeds to read Eliot's "Tradition and the Individual Talent," that central document of modernist epistemology, as obtusely as he has read the biographies of Stein (who was attacked by such mainstream modernists as Wyndham Lewis, not least because she was Jewish) and Dos Passos (who suffered because of his illegitimate birth, royal or not). The rest of the book is a vigorous piece of revisionist scholarship, but this initial closed-mindedness is fatal. It keeps *Foreigners* from intelligently asking the only question that matters in history: Why?

This page is probably the least unsatisfactory place to mention a many-sided theoretical study, Fredric Jameson's *The Political Unconscious: Narrative as a Socially Symbolic Act* (Cornell). This book presents a way of reading a text—or rather "less the text itself than the interpretations through which we attempt to confront and to appropriate it" (pp. 9–10)—which is controlled by a totalizing Marxism, conceived as the "'untranscendable horizon' that subsumes . . . apparently antagonistic or incommensurable critical operations, assigning them an undoubted sectoral validity within itself, and thus at once canceling and preserving them" (p. 10). The Jamesonian subsumption works by considering texts within progressively wider ideological contexts, up to and including "the ultimate horizon of human history as a whole" (p. 76). As the contexts widen, we are told, aesthetic particularities will be seen for the first time in their ultimate significance, as realizations of historical content, and texts which the passage of time has rendered spiritually inaccessible will once again be readable in all the immediacy of their meaning to history. Jameson is not afraid to apply the word "Utopian" to this project, but his utopianism is a dogma with a disturbing tendency to bare its teeth. "[H]ow is it possible for . . . a text to embody a properly Utopian impulse," Jameson asks on p. 288, "or to resonate a universal value inconsistent with the narrower limits of class privilege which inform its more immediate ideological vocation?" A predictably catholicizing answer is forthcoming, but while we wait for it we may find ourselves reflecting that that word "properly" goes far to explain the Victorian character of art produced in the socialist camp.

Benjamin Lease's *Anglo-American Encounters* is a loosely organized series of anecdotes about eight American authors who lived
in England or visited the country in a literary capacity (Irving,
Cooper, John Neal, Poe, Hawthorne, Melville, Stowe, Emerson) and
two others, Thoreau and Whitman, who attracted disciples from
England. As a critic, Lease is pre-New; he confines himself almost
exclusively to biography, plot summary, and influence study, frequently to the exclusion of any semblance of a thesis. (Yes, the grammar school in "William Wilson" resembles the school that Poe actually attended in England. So? So nothing; Lease just mentions the
fact and continues summarizing.) As a historian, Lease is unfortunately just as sketchy. He mentions only in passing, for instance,
such important matters as the copyright problem and the American
popularity of *Blackwood's*. As a result, *Anglo-American Encounters*
does not cohere. Lease opens his account in 1820 with Sydney Smith
asking, "In the four quarters of the globe, who reads an American
book?" and closes it in 1907 with Mark Twain receiving an honorary
degree at Oxford, but for all his anecdotes he fails to make clear what
happened in between.

A more successful volume, Benjamin T. Spencer's *Patterns of
Nationality: Twentieth-Century Literary Versions of America* (Burt
Franklin), "is a sequel and supplement to *The Quest for Nationality*,
which traced the evolving concepts of an American literature from
colonial times to the end of the nineteenth century. The structure and
aims of *Patterns of Nationality*, however, are somewhat different from
those of the earlier study. On the assumption that the ultimate shape
and development of 20th-century American literature are still in the
making, [Spencer has] chosen eight major authors to represent the
diverse trends of nationality during the two most recent literary
generations. The implication . . . is pluralistic" (p. ix). Spencer's eight
authors are Gertrude Stein, Ezra Pound, William Carlos Williams,
Sherwood Anderson, F. Scott Fitzgerald, Hart Crane, Edward Dahlberg, and Norman Mailer, and only the Crane essay is previously
unpublished. Each of these essays attempts to define the ways in
which the term "American literature" can be meaningfully applied
to its subject, in terms of style, subject, myth, etc. The essays are
strong—so strong, in fact, that they force Spencer's three general
chapters on "The Nature of Nationality" into a tentativeness that is
almost self-erasing. After considering a formidable range of evidence

(pp. 37–38 alone refer to Allen Tate, Hemingway, Dreiser, Faulkner, Cooper, Julian Hawthorne, Howells, James, Crèvecoeur, Whitman, Archibald MacLeish, and Frost, and allude in passing to Nathaniel Hawthorne, Jean-Jacques Rousseau, and Hippolyte Taine), Spencer here can only conclude that American literature "is a complex of several potential responses on the part of the reader. At present the term is so variously used, is charged with so many assumptions, that it is all things to all men" (p. 46). And beyond that truism Spencer will go only as far as the additional truism that "Whatever an American literature may be, we can expect its presence only as an organic part of American life" (p. 47). One of Spencer's favorite words is "difficult," and as I read these introductory chapters I found myself thinking that much of the difficulty of Spencer's task might have been self-imposed. Spencer's critical essays provide us with some ungeneralized, ad hoc, pragmatic predefinitions of what is American in American literature, and it seems possible to me that those ("Creeds and schools in abeyance, / Retiring back a while sufficed at what they are") may be all we really need.

But there is among the letters Oliver Wendell Holmes wrote to Harriet Beecher Stowe one sentence which indeed might stand as a motto for American literature: "I do not believe you or I can ever get the iron of Calvinism out of our souls." In *Rappaccini's Children* William H. Shurr, who is a theologian as well as a literary critic, carefully traces the vein of iron from its sources (the Holmes quotation is on p. 23) to its most recent manifestations. His book will be valuable as a source study. As literary criticism, however, it will have to be read with some caution. On p. 90, for instance, Shurr suggests what seems to me a brilliant integration of "The Custom-House" with the rest of *The Scarlet Letter*: "this dismal scene of Uncle Sam's pensioners, the lazy and fatuous old men for whom Hawthorne shows a distant and superior contempt, is the direct result of the theology and *mores* of those stern Puritans who held the same ground a few generations earlier, those dying generations whose begetting, birth, and dying he is about to celebrate." But on pp. 92–93 Shurr seems to me to strain very hard to establish some grounds for his discussion of the ethical problem explored in *Billy Budd*. Captain Vere resembles Thomas Jefferson in his liberal humanity; Jefferson disregarded legality in prosecuting Aaron Burr, claiming afterward that "a law of necessity and self-preservation . . . rendered the *salus populi* supreme over the written law"; "Burr" looks like "Budd"; therefore the tragedy of Captain Vere, "and what is clearly the real issue for Jefferson, is that the law, no matter how carefully constructed, can be circumvented by human ingenuity in the production of evil." I have no quarrel with this conclusion; I just have difficulty in reaching point B from point A.

The Veracious Imagination: Essays in American History, Literature, and Biography (Wesleyan) is a collection of what its author, Cushing Strout, calls "border-country pieces . . . preoccupied with the territory marked out by the overlapping concerns of fiction, history, and biography" (p. ix). Strout sometimes gets stuck on the barbed wire of his interdiscipline; for example, his detailed analysis of the failures of historical imagination in a well-intentioned period piece, Arthur Miller's political allegory *The Crucible*, seems not to have been worth the effort, either historically or literarily. (If Arthur Miller, why not Norman Corwin?) On the other hand, Strout's discussion of the achievement of E. L. Doctorow's historical novel *The Book of Daniel* (using both Aristotle and the archives, Doctorow constructed a plausible fiction about the guilt of Ethel and Julius Rosenberg; subsequent research seems to indicate that this fiction conforms accurately to the emerging shape of the historical record) makes a strong case for the "compound power" of "aesthetic and historical force, each reinforcing the other" (p. 178). Other essays deal with authors as disparate as James Gould Cozzens and William James; Strout's position throughout is the conservative one that the real (historical) and the imaginary (fictive) are complementary but separate epistemological domains.

d. Biography. *The American Autobiography: A Collection of Critical Essays*, ed. Albert E. Stone (Prentice-Hall), contains ten essays written at a generally high level of critical sophistication; they range from Anaïs Nin's meditation on the significance of her diaries, "The Personal Life Deeply Lived" (the title tells you all you need to know), to Darrell Mansell's rigorous study of referentiality and fictiveness, "Unsettling the Colonel's Hash: 'Fact' in Autobiography." *New Directions in Biography*, ed. Anthony M. Friedson (Hawaii), is a symposium volume containing three general essays of interest to *ALS*: Leon Edel's "Biography and the Science of Man," Michael Holroyd's "Literary and Historical Biography," and Margot Peters'

"Group Biography: Challenges and Methods." Of additional interest is Friedson's tabulation of the responses to a questionnaire circulated among biographers. The future of the discipline, it appears, is approaching from many directions: "[One biographer] foresees more joint works treating interdisciplinary figures or groups. [Another] thinks it likely that there will be more women writers who will do for biography what women novelists did for the novel. Other proposed developments include: group biography; the biography of the common man; biography which mixes historical figures with fictional ones—as in Solzhenitsyn's *August, 1914*; and *avant garde* biography employing such devices as have long been used by novelists—stream of consciousness; authorial uncertainty; collage and so on" (p. 96).

In *Ultimately Fiction* Dennis W. Petrie reads four biographies as paradigms of three types of the genre: the Monument of the Famous Writer (Joseph Blotner's *Faulkner*), the Portrait of the Author as a Man or Woman (Andrew Turnbull's *Scott Fitzgerald* and W. A. Swanberg's *Dreiser*), and the Vision of the Artist (Leon Edel's *Henry James*). Few critical generalizations follow from this classification, however, because Petrie's actual analyses of his chosen biographies are not much more than book reviews. (See chap. 9,*ii*, above.)

For good or bad, all three of these books testify to a continuing interest in biography as a subject for generic study. But after we have granted the value of the undertaking, the most fundamental question remains unanswered: what is biography for? In *The Life of the Poet* Lawrence Lipking provides a richly detailed answer. He proceeds by reading poems as the outcome of a life lived by a poet; he "accepts the testimony of poems as decisive evidence about the way that poets conceive, or invent, their careers. . . . Poetry . . . can tell us all we need to know about the author's ability to convert his experience into vision. Here—not in the creative process or some irrecoverable unconscious—life and poetry intersect. Thus, whatever else we know about Dante's life, we can be certain about one fact: he actually did achieve the vision recorded in the final canto of the *Commedia*. To deny it would be to deny the whole poem—and to deny his life as a poet" (p. x).

That is, Lipking (like Denis Donoghue, below, *ii,e*) does his reading with the help of an intuition that there is a transcendent source of value at the heart of what Wordsworth in *The Prelude* calls "the hiding-places of man's power." This intuition runs counter to struc-

turalist logic, but it is attractive, and its attractiveness may well be
a sign of its truth at the fundamental levels of our psychology. We
want personality to live and speak to us; we want a sign that our
selves are immortal. As Lipking points out, the man who coined the
phrase "the death of the author" is the author of an autobiography
entitled *Roland Barthes par Roland Barthes*. But to bring the author
back to life requires a strong reading of the life in the text, and here
Lipking succeeds on the ground of the poems themselves.

Lipking reads his poems in four groups: Initiation, poems of the
beginning of life as a poet; Harmonium, poems that sum up the life
that has gone before; Tombeau, poems in which the poet contemplates the legacy he has inherited from another poet; and Ending,
poems in which the poet contemplates "this open book . . . my open
coffin" (Robert Lowell, quoted on p. 184; ellipsis in original). The
lives that emerge from the readings are those of major poets: Virgil,
Dante, and Goethe, for instance (and, I note for *ALS* purposes,
Lowell and Whitman). They are lives which are well worth reading.

e. **Regional Studies.**   Western Writers (WWS) is a series of pamphlets (50 to date) from the Department of English at Boise State
University. This collection of biographical and critical essays covers
an unusually wide range; its subjects include not just Zane Grey and
Walter Van Tilburg Clark but N. Scott Momaday, Edward Abbey,
Gary Snyder, and (why not?) Jack Kerouac. Among several 1981
additions to the series are pamphlets on Scandinavian immigrant
literature (by Christer Lennart Mossberg) and on one of Henry
Adams' symbols of the failure of his age, Clarence King (by Peter
Wild).

The Past in the Present offers readings by Thomas Daniel Young
of Faulkner's *The Unvanquished*, Tate's *The Fathers*, Warren's *All
the King's Men*, Welty's *The Optimist's Daughter*, O'Connor's *Complete Stories*, Percy's *The Moviegoer*, and Barth's *The End of the
Road*. The selection of books is as thematic as the readings, for
Young's purpose is to demonstrate "the importance of a belief in
ritual, ceremony, pageantry, and manners in a world from which the
gods have disappeared" (p. xiv). Young is the biographer of John
Crowe Ransom, and it should not be surprising to hear in his thesis
the voice of *God Without Thunder*. But I was startled nevertheless
when I saw Ransom's ideas again in complete steel, virtually un-

changed, half a century after *I'll Take My Stand* and a quarter of a century after *Brown* vs. *Board of Education.* As Young retells the story, the literary South was once, at least in imagination, a domain of ritual, ceremony, pageantry, and manners—a South conscious of living in its history. As Allen Tate put it in an essay from which Young draws his book's title and epigraph, "With the War of 1914–1918, the South reentered the world—but gave a backward glance as it stepped over the border: that backward glance gave us the Southern renascence, a literature conscious of the past in the present." The clarity of that retrospective vision, however, has been steadily blurred by "modern gnosticism" (p. 2), and the result for southern literature since World War II has been the loss of its ability to realize an imaginative domain in historical terms. The South of Percy and Barth is "merely unindividualized space, not scene in the Welty sense in which place 'partakes of feeling,' precise local values being attached to feeling" (p. 24). This loss of history imperils other things as well; we cannot be gentlemen, for instance, without membership in a *gens*. And these losses have consequences that are not only historical but moral and aesthetic. For—to take Young's example of gentlemanliness, which is in turn derived from *The World's Body* —only under hierarchy can a woman be looked at in the correct way. "The woman who arouses the desire is contemplated 'under restraint,' approached through the labyrinths of a fixed code of behavior, but this procedure of indirection raises the woman to the status of a specific person and to that of an aesthetic, and therefore much richer, object" (p. 17).

Now, special economic circumstances must of course exist before a lady can be delimited from the mass of women and contemplated with appropriate ceremony—circumstances which must guarantee unhappiness for the great majority of nonladies and nongentlemen. But what fascinates me here is simply that word "object." There it stands on the page in front of you, just as if *The Feminine Mystique* had never been published—or, for that matter, *The Mind of the South,* the diaries of Mary Boykin Chesnut, or *Huckleberry Finn.* Perhaps the study of southern literature has something to gain from feminist criticism.

At any rate, Anne Goodwyn Jones makes a good case for it in *Tomorrow Is Another Day.* Consider, for example, what happens to our reading habits when the object of a textual contemplation climbs off the page and begins to talk like this about what she was doing there: "On her pedestal at the center of the South's particular romantic dream stood . . . its central symbol: the southern lady. Like the dream world itself, she was beautiful, fragile, good, and ultimately irrelevant to actuality. . . . More than—or at least differently from—Mark Twain and other southern men, therefore, southern women writers participated in the reality that they described, analyzed, and perhaps defied in their fiction. Through their authorial voices, the silent symbol spoke, and what it said, whether disguised in convention or plain and direct, was rarely fragile and good, and usually relevant to actual experience. The protagonists in their fiction, too, experience a kind of doubleness as both actual person and symbol of the South; Scarlett [in Margaret Mitchell's *Gone With the Wind*] is Atlanta, Virginia [in Ellen Glasgow's *Virginia*] is Virginia" (pp. 356–57). Feminist ideas like this provide Jones with the narrative power to unify her readings of seven widely different sorts of writers, including a romancer of the feminine fifties (Augusta Jane Evans), a failed experimental novelist of the 1920s (Frances Newman), and the creator of one of the great trash books (Margaret Mitchell). (The four others are Grace King, Kate Chopin, Mary Johnston, and Ellen Glasgow.) Some of these readings do, however, suffer from a characteristic intellectual weakness that feminism shares with other ideological criticisms: the logic of "Heads I win, tails you lose." For example, when she must deal with an appalling autobiographical statement by Kate Chopin ("I write in the morning, when not too strongly drawn to struggle with the intricacies of a pattern, and in the afternoon, if the temptation to try a new furniture polish on an old table leg is not too powerful to be denied"), Jones has her argument both ways thus: "Chopin's self-deprecation . . . may be her form of self-defense. Chopin well knew that her public would expect this sort of language from a woman writer. On the other hand, it is in fact true that she wrote at odd times. . . . Thus it is possible that Chopin here argues implicitly for the validity of a non-masculine method of and attitude toward writing" (p. 145). This is just wishful thinking, and Jones would surely heap feminist scorn on any male writer who kept himself minor by writing only when the catfish weren't running. But the large scale of Jones's large book offers many other grounds for agreement and appreciation, and I am going to recommend it highly. It is a solid piece of scholarship with a 17-page bibliography, it has an important idea at its core, and—a rarity among American books with footnotes in them—it is well written.

f. **Feminist Criticism.** In the space of 189 pages *Archetypal Patterns of Women's Fiction* (Indiana) by Annis Pratt, with the assistance of Barbara White, Andrea Loewenstein, and Mary Wyer, provides us with Jungian interpretations of more than 300 novels by American and British women. The intention, as the title implies, was to produce a literary taxonomy classified according to some characteristics of feminine psychology. That much is clear, but I have to say that the logic behind what Pratt has actually written makes no sense to me. On p. viii, in the first sentence of her preface, Pratt asserts that "During the nearly three hundred years that women have been writing works of fiction, they have constructed a body of material that manifests a considerable degree of continuity, a uniformity of concern, and an abundance of analogue in both subject and method." She goes on to claim the existence of "a core of feminine self-expression . . . at odds with [the male] world." Yet on the next page she simply throws away any chance of proving her thesis. "[I]t was for purposes of brevity as well as out of a desire to examine women's fiction totally in relationship to itself," she explains, "that I have turned away from the intriguing subject of its relationship to the male genre." The notion of examining anything in relation to itself is an absurdity, of course, and not the only one in this book. As a critic, Pratt tends to spin her readings into ineffability, thus: "Women's fiction manifests alienation from the normal concepts of time and space precisely because the presentation of time by persons on the margins of day-to-day life inevitably deviates from ordinary chronology and because those excluded from the *agora* are likely to perceive normal settings from phobic perspectives. Since women are alienated from time and space, their plots take on cyclical, rather than linear, form and their houses and landscapes surreal properties. When we add to all this the fact that feminine archetypes of selfhood have been lost from culture and even consciousness for hundreds of years. . ." (p. 11). It goes on like that. The phrase about the house with the surreal property is funny, alas.

Fortunately for Jungians, this year brings us a bigger, better book of feminist myth criticism. In *The Female Hero in American and*

British Literature (Bowker) Carol Pearson and Katherine Pope stop short of Pratt's extrapolations from texts to authors and are therefore able to express their thesis in this manageable form: "Although the experience of male and female heroes is the same on the archetypal level, it differs in important particulars because of the roles and opportunities afforded each sex in western society" (p. viii). A fringe benefit of this way of putting it is that Pearson and Pope are free to consider books written by men. In their working definitions of such important particulars as "the masculine heroic ideal" Pearson and Pope are occasionally tendentious ("Typically, characters such as Coverdale in Nathaniel Hawthorne's *The Blithedale Romance*, Huck Finn in Mark Twain's *Huckleberry Finn*, and Nick Carraway in F. Scott Fitzgerald's *The Great Gatsby* learn the folly of the masculine heroic ideal by observing the behavior of men like Hollingsworth, Tom Sawyer, and Jay Gatsby, respectively"—p. 5), but most of their many readings are stimulating.

Sally Allen McNall's *Who Is in the House?* is a psychological study of two centuries of women's fiction. Reading women's romances with the aid of Jung and Melanie Klein, McNall claims (p. 11) that these books' "inner world of fantasy is demonstrably not constructed from conflicts with the patriarchal capitalist-industrial world. It is, rather, made up of the symbols and images of pre-oedipal mother-child relation and the attempt to outgrow these. In other words, women have not written 'escape' fiction for other women all these years in an effort, conscious or unconscious, to subvert the forms of male domination. It is, rather, the far more powerful domination of the whole self by parts of the self which has been read and written about." I am not in a position to criticize this book, since I have read only a handful of women's romances, and evidently without the emotion they are engineered to evoke. (The editorial guidelines of Harlequin Books specify: "Remember, our readers enjoy 'visiting' new and unknown places (to them) and they also enjoy learning about local food, dress and customs." The condescending quotation marks and parentheses say a good deal about relations among the cultural classes in the patriarchal capitalist-industrial world.) But McNall's schematizations do look intuitively plausible.

Women & Literature, formerly a quarterly, is now an annual edited by Janet Todd (New York: Holmes & Meier). Volume 1

(1980), *Gender and Literary Voice*, contains articles discussing literary women from the Wife of Bath to Erma Bombeck, plus a review-essay by Nina Auerbach devoted to feminist criticism, and a short, strong introductory note, "Is There a Female Voice?" by Joyce Carol Oates. The American authors covered in detail are Louise Bogan, May Sarton, Edith Wharton, Lisa Alther (author of the novel *Kinflicks*), and a forgotten minor poet, Hazel Hall (1886–1924). Erma Bombeck and Marilyn French are the two American authors discussed in Judith Wilt's wide-ranging essay "The Laughter of Maidens, The Cackle of Matriarchs: Notes on the Collision between Comedy and Feminism." Volume 2 of *Women & Literature* (1981) is entitled *Men by Women*; according to the publisher's circular, "the contributors focus on male characters created by women writers and the image of men in literature and film."

Publications like *Women & Literature*, it seems to me, show feminist criticism at work at its most important task: opening up the canon, as Fiedler and Baker urge; helping us reread. As it turns the pages of our texts in its new ways, however, feminist criticism sometimes finds itself in the awkward but exhilarating position of growing several extra hands. I don't think I had ever heard of Hazel Hall, for example, until I read Marcia S. Andrews' life-and letters article about her in *Gender and Literary Voice*, but now that I have read some of her poems I have to come to terms with them—i.e., to compile a critical lexicon from the many possible vocabularies that the many-handed critical monster offers me. I have learned from Andrews that Hall was an invalid for most of her short life, and an autodidact. Her poems can therefore be thought of, if I want to think of them that way, as triumphs of the human spirit over adversity. On the other hand, another way of reading tells me that Hall has been forgotten because her poems are sentimental in conception and conventional in language. The human spirit probably shows itself more brightly in the works of some other invalid poets, major and minor: Josephine Miles, Alexander Pope. On the third hand, however, Hall as a poet is undoubtedly more tasteful and more intelligent than two of her better-known contemporaries, Amy Lowell and Carl Sandburg. Literary-historical justice is owed to Hall, but where shall the judgment come from? By forcing us to ask that question, feminist criticism is beginning to help us answer it.

g. **Science and Fiction.** The title of this section comes from Harry
Levin's essay in *Bridges to Science Fiction,* ed. George E. Slusser,
George R. Guffey, and Mark Rose (So. Ill.). *Bridges* is a collection
of ten essays in what might be called comparative generic criticism:
attempts to define science fiction by examining its central themes in
relation to Western philosophy, religion, and literature as a whole.
The quality of the essays is very high. Mark Rose's well-written *Alien
Encounters: Anatomy of Science Fiction* (Harvard) is another study
in generic criticism. Rose considers that the opposition between
human and nonhuman is what "defines the semantic space, the field
of interest, within which science fiction as a genre characteristically
operates. It constitutes what we may call the genre's paradigm. . . .
[W]e can observe the way the concern with the human in relation
to the nonhuman projects itself through four logically related categories, which I shall call space, time, machine, and monster" (p. 32).
This analysis leads Rose to draw some broad psychological inferences from his conclusion that "Science fiction is the attempt to name
the infinite. . . . [Its content may be] specified as the sense of the
infinite or, rather, as the sense of the finitude of the self, the conscious
ego, in relation to the boundlessness of the cosmos that is not the
self" (p. 191).

John Griffiths' *Three Tomorrows: American, British and Soviet
Science Fiction* (Barnes and Noble, 1980), despite its title, is not
primarily a study in comparative literature but rather a political
reading of some SF themes. As criticism it is unsophisticated, and
this unsophistication leads to some analytical bias. On pp. 20–21, for
instance, noting that some Soviet SF novels are not much more than
fictionalized science textbooks, Griffiths concludes that "Since it is
necessary for the fiction writer to demonstrate his ideological orthodoxy by frequent injections of propaganda, one way to avoid the
tedium of Marxist polemics is to stick to reading purely factual
works." But on pp. 44–45 Griffiths mentions several examples of pre-
revolutionary Russian SF which sound every bit as didactic as their
Soviet descendants. One, for instance, is called *The Self Propelled
Petersburg-Moscow Underground Railway.* What Griffiths may be
seeing, therefore, is simply a defining characteristic of many Russian
novels: a plenitude of detail and an affinity for ideas. Still, *Three
Tomorrows* is full of interesting information, such as the account
(p. 57) of an East German writer who attracted official criticism for

writing about a dictatorship on another planet in the future. All societies in the future will have become communal, the Communist party newspaper *Neues Deutschland* explained, and therefore any author who dares to conceive of the future existence of an individual dictator has "disregarded the basic laws of social development and failed to realise that even science fiction must be scientifically based on Marxism-Leninism."

This brings us naturally to the misleadingly titled *America as Utopia*, a collection of essays dealing with utopias in American (and European) literature, with primary emphases on 19th-century didactic novels and 20th-century science fiction. The book is cross-indexed, and about half of its pages are devoted to bibliography. By way of giving an idea of the wide range of this large volume, I might categorize just three of the contributions: the historically useful (Edward Bellamy's "How and Why I Wrote *Looking Backward*," rpt. from *The Nationalist* and *The Ladies' Home Journal*), the far-out (Stuart Teitler's "In Search of Zion: An Annotated Bibliography of the Ten Lost Tribes of Israel in Utopia," containing such items as Madeline Argo's *My Trip to the Ten Lost Tribes Inside the Earth* [n.p.: n.p., n.d., not in Library of Congress Printed Cards]), and the critically rewarding (Robert Plank's eloquent essay "The Modern Shrunken Utopia").

Robert Nadeau in *The New Book on Nature* and Ronald E. Martin in *The Universe of Force* are concerned with some of the scientific ideas underlying modern literature. Nadeau, after a two-chapter introduction to the metaphysical foundations of modern physics, sets out to read some books by John Fowles, John Barth, John Updike, Kurt Vonnegut, Thomas Pynchon, Tom Robbins, and Don DeLillo as "documents of culture[,] providing insights into the manner in which dramatic implications from the new physics might be assimilated into subjective experience" (p. 14). Nadeau's own assimilations, however, are, in the scientific sense of the word, uncontrolled; many of his claims have no clearly established basis for comparison. When a character in Robbins' *Even Cowgirls Get the Blues*, for example, observes that life is "a dynamic network of interchanges and exchanges, spreading in all directions at once. And it's all held together by the tension between opposites," Nadeau (p. 157) calls this fortune-cookie platitude "a statement that Werner Heisenberg could well have admired."

The Universe of Force is far more solid; in fact, it is a real contribution to the history of ideas. The idea Martin considers is that of the immutability of the force that moves the universe. As a metaphysical concept, this idea is very old; Leibniz, as we might expect, believed that "since God had created the universe perfectly, no special intervention was required to maintain its energy and motion" (p. 11), and the epigraph of Martin's book comes from Heraclitus: "All things are an exchange for fire, and fire for all things, even as wares for gold, and gold for wares." In the 19th century, however, the idea was reformulated in empirically testable terms, and the imaginative power of this new experimentalism was, as Martin shows, tremendous. Since the idea of force is connected with ideas of causality, it became possible for an English engineer, Herbert Spencer, to elaborate the first law of thermodynamics—known then as the principle of the conservation of force—into a project for knowing all that is knowable in the physical and moral universe, a cosmos conceived as an evolving interplay of measurable forces. Spencer's Synthetic Philosophy was epistemologically doomed from the start; as early as the middle of the 19th century the physicists were beginning to understand that "force" is a purely relational term—a metaphor, not a thing—and that, however they are conceived, the energies of the universe are tending inexorably toward entropy, loss of definition, death. Spencer also had methodological problems; William James, for example, pointed out that Spencer's key phrase "the persistence of force" ("one vast vagueness, of which I can give no clear account") referred to at least four different things (p. 68). But Spencer's American disciples kept the Spencerian cosmology alive for many years, and during those years it brought forth a new literary way of regarding the universe: the way of Henry Adams, Frank Norris, Jack London, and Theodore Dreiser, to each of whom Martin devotes a chapter. In Adams' case, a mind subtler than Spencer's own "was able to use [Spencer's idea of force] in the construction of a literary vision far richer and more lasting than any of its scientific or philosophical originals" (p. 98). At the opposite extreme, a wholeheartedly (though inaccurately) assimilated Spencerism provided Dreiser with the ideas around which he assembled whatever intellectual coherence his books possess. Considered as a whole in Martin's carefully documented history, the career of the Synthetic Philosophy provides support for Harry Levin's rueful generalization about the backgrounds of SF (*Bridges*, p. 21): "Our technorevolutions seem to foster, not so much a rule of reason, as an efflorescence of credulity. Perhaps the last word should be left to P. T. Barnum."

h. **Other Studies in Popular Culture.** Stephen Knight's *Form and Ideology in Crime Fiction* (Indiana, 1980) and Dennis Porter's *The Pursuit of Crime: Art and Ideology in Detective Fiction* (Yale) come to us with similar titles but different critical approaches. Knight's book, from Australia, is a study, in the English style, of the sociology of literature. The authors discussed in detail are Poe, Arthur Conan Doyle, Agatha Christie, Raymond Chandler, and Evan Hunter ("Ed McBain"), and the thesis is that crime fiction is an ideological transaction between author and readers—a transaction whose function is to reassure both author and readers that the anxieties of life in society are as curable as crime is solvable. As society changes, therefore, the genre changes with it. About this attractive thesis Knight is serious to the point of indignation. Witness his reaction to Hunter's best-known (nondetective) novel: "*The Blackboard Jungle* was very successful; it realised the disorderly state of American public schools, but finally presented a hope based on the bourgeois liberal idea of finding the conformist good naturally present in the leader of disruly adolescents." In the next three sentences Knight coins the phrases "class-aligned patterns in curricula and pedagogical systems" and "static liberal humanism" and concludes with the retrodiction that "These attitudes naturally enough led Hunter to the police story, which offered verisimilitude as a mode and optimistic problem-solving as a content; in this form he could create pragmatic liberal humanist fables about crime, the police, and the city" (pp.170 –71). But Sherlock Holmes works his familiar magic on Knight, and the only word for his discussion of Doyle is "affectionate."

Porter believes that "Detective novels provide reassurance . . . because they propose a world of fixed cultural quantities. . . . The continuing success of the detective story . . . can be explained in part by its capacity to absorb into itself the changing anxieties of the times and make them innocuous" (p. 218). That is, Porter is in general agreement with Knight about the ideology of the crime narrative. Methodologically, however, the two authors differ, for Porter is a Barthesian formalist who luxuriates in the *plaisir du texte* "in order to isolate those genre characteristics that account for [the

detective story's] popularity" (p. 4). The first section of his book
("Art") is a study in the reader-psychology of the suspense narrative;
the second ("Ideology") examines the differing ways in which
American, British, and French texts have worked out the cultural
terms of "an ideal form of policing . . . in conformity with the most
cherished behavioral norms of a given society" (p. 129). A generalizing third section reaches this conclusion (p. 236): "To read a
detective novel is to submit oneself to a sequence of experiences
planned by an author . . . to promote reader pleasure. And it is important to realize that the pleasure is not in the end but in the
process, not in the final reassertion of order but in the halting and
suspenseful approach to it. . . ." And this, as Porter goes on to point
out, is why it is less pleasurable to reread a detective story than to
reread Henry James. On the way to this conclusion, however, Porter
gives us many acute and pleasurable readings in the rhetoric of
detection.

In *Sport and the Spirit of Play* Christian K. Messenger analyzes,
categorizes, and schematizes the theme of the ludic as it is expressed
in the works of half a dozen major writers and several dozen minor
ones. Some of the minor writers are very minor indeed by ordinary
critical standards—Messenger's critique of George Jenks and his dime-
novel hero, Double Curve Dan, the Pitcher Detective, must be the
only one in the literature—and the resultant mass of detail sometimes
begins to take on a life of its own, like baseball statistics. But many
local insights do develop. I found especially interesting the thematic
variation that Messenger observes in the Frank Merriwell stories of
"Burt L. Standish" (Gilbert Patten), the Dink Stover stories of Owen
Johnson, and the school and college stories of F. Scott Fitzgerald.
From the first of Frank Merriwell's victories over the bad guys on
and off the field, to Dink Stover's discovery that the ethic of competition has not been entirely good for Yale, to the moment when Tom
Buchanan sits down to discuss the Nordic race with Nick Carraway,
there elapse 30 years: in terms of intellectual half-lives, exactly two
generations. There is something aesthetically satisfying in that fact
—and, for purposes of *ALS*, something useful for literary history.

The 16 essays in American Studies collected in *The American
Self* cover a wide disciplinary range, from straight history (Ferenc
Szasz on American religious sects between 1880 and 1915), to so-
ciology (Peter A. Lupsha, "American Values and Organized Crime:

Suckers and Wiseguys"), to regional literary studies (Marta Weigle, "The Penitente Brotherhood in Southwestern Fiction: Notes on Folklife and Literature"), to detailed studies in literary biography (George Arms on William Dean Howells' religious beliefs), to thematic essays (Sacvan Bercovitch, "The Rites of Assent: Rhetoric, Ritual, and the Ideology of the American Consensus"; Alan Trachtenberg, "Cultural Revisions in the Twenties: Brooklyn Bridge as 'Usable Past' "), to essays about Frank Capra, Paul Laurence Dunbar, women on the western frontier, the baseball autobiography of Jim Bouton, and the pornographication of American culture. Clearly, the study of popular culture is thriving this year. Reading the diversity of the books in this section was like making a fast run from the Morgan Library to the Doubleday bookstore and back again.

i. **Miscellaneous.** In *Screening the Novel: Rediscovered American Fiction in Film* (Ungar, 1980) Gabriel Miller compares eight films with the novels on which they are based. That is all he does—there is no general conclusion and only a brief introductory chapter—but in the process he makes a strong case for the reconsideration of the forgotten books behind some highly acclaimed films. In order of publication date, the novels are Abraham Cahan's *Yekl: A Tale of the New York Ghetto* (film title: *Hester Street*), David Graham Phillips' *Susan Lenox: Her Fall and Rise*, James M. Cain's *The Postman Always Rings Twice* (and its first, 1946, film adaptation), Horace McCoy's *They Shoot Horses, Don't They?*, B. Traven's *The Treasure of the Sierra Madre*, Humphrey Cobb's *Paths of Glory*, Daniel Fuchs's *Low Company* (film title: *The Gangster*), and Edward Lewis Wallant's *The Pawnbroker*. I especially liked Miller's treatment of *Yekl*, the oldest book and newest film in this list. The unheroic protagonist of Cahan's 1896 novel is an immigrant man whose marital misfortunes are intended to raise questions in the reader's mind about the human cost of cultural assimilation. By shifting the emphasis of her 1975 film from the husband to his wife, Joan Micklin Silver turned Cahan's naturalist parable into a feminist comedy. By discussing the metamorphosis in detail, Miller illuminates both the film and the book.

I lack the space this year to discuss language studies, but I would like to notice one collection of general interest to readers of *ALS*. *Language in the USA*, ed. Charles A. Ferguson and Shirley Brice

Heath (Cambridge) weighs two pounds and contains 53 essays dealing with the past, present, and future of language in a society whose
motto, *E pluribus unum*, has never been realized in linguistic practice.

ii. Criticism

a. **Collections.**   Some of the 23 essays in *What Is Criticism?*, ed. Paul
Hernadi (Indiana) seem to have been brain-damaged by the discipline's prevailing hermeticism. If she had remembered the existence outside the critical literature of Sylvia Plath or Emily Dickinson, for example, Catharine R. Stimpson would probably have felt
less enthusiastic about quoting the French feminist who asserts that
"Death . . . is a specifically male obsession. As well as essential solitude" ("On Feminist Criticism," p. 238). And Wayne C. Booth's
Arnoldian plea for a practical criticism with a social conscience and
a grounding in ethics may be just what they need to hear in the
offices of *CritI*, but out in the fresh air it amounts to not much more
than a speech in favor of goodness.[1] But this is only to say that the
architecture of the house of criticism shapes the postures of its in-
habitants. It is like all past and future architectures in that respect,
and meanwhile Hernadi has given us a guide to the institution as it
looks in 1981.

The essays in *What Is Criticism?* are grouped into four sections:
"Why Define Criticism and How?," "Criticism as Re-presentation"
(an overview of six methodological strategies, from structuralism to
reading aloud), "Criticism as Evaluation" (here Booth shares a
suite with, e.g., the Marxist Richard Ohmann and the popular-
culturist Mary Pratt), and "Criticism as Communication," which
"examine[s] the critic's discourse as personal response, communicative self-expression, textual transcoding, or the creation of works of
a secondary art" (Hernadi, p. xiii). A concluding appendix by René
Wellek is devoted to an extended historical analysis of the term "literary criticism." When they look outward, these essays tend to look

1. Booth does makes one practical suggestion: that someone should undertake "a serious study of how the increasing pressure of mass sales, produced in
part by new conglomerate publishers with no interest in books as books, have
[*sic*] affected the quality of American writing in the past three decades or so"
(p. 170). Thomas Whiteside's *The Blockbuster Complex* (Wesleyan), a good
start in that direction (*ALS 1980*, 476–77), was republished in book form this
year from its original appearance in *The New Yorker*.

in some directions more than others; Barthes, for example, is mentioned 17 times in the index, Derrida 13 times, Heidegger seven times, Freud six times, Bloom and Lacan twice each, Jung and Ransom once. But the overall presentation is well balanced. Geoffrey Hartman, who claims more uncompromisingly than any other American critic that criticism is a creative art, is represented here, but so is John M. Ellis, who complains that some contemporary critics "seem often to be trying to rival the uniqueness of literary language by their own dazzling conceptual pyrotechnics, and to display their own erudition and intellectual feats instead of the literary text's subtle individuality. . . . The result is a veritable caricature of discussion, a reduction of criticism to an entertainment for scholars . . ." ("The Logic of the Question 'What Is Criticism?'" p. 25). What we have on the whole, therefore, is a wide-ranging advanced textbook in contemporary criticism, conveniently arranged (Hernadi's introduction provides a one-sentence synopsis of each essay: a handy feature) and, at $17.50 in hardback, reasonably priced.

Reader-Response Criticism from Formalism to Structuralism, ed. Jane P. Tompkins (Hopkins, 1980) is a historically arranged anthology which takes us from Walker Gibson's "mock reader" (1950) to Walter Benn Michaels' "[fiction of] a self before interpretation or a text after" (1977). The essays in between represent the positions of eight critics whose attitudes toward the phenomenology of reading range from neo–New Critical formalism to subjectivist permissivism: Gerald Prince, Michael Riffaterre, Georges Poulet, Wolfgang Iser, Stanley E. Fish (two essays), Jonathan Culler, Norman N. Holland, and David Bleich. Tompkins contributes a detailed analytical introduction, an essay about the politics of "[t]he distinction between response conceived as meaning, and response conceived as action or behavior" (p. 206), and a large annotated bibliography. Her book fills a need very satisfactorily.

A related collection of what its editors call audience-related criticism is *The Reader in the Text: Essays on Audience and Interpretation*, ed. Susan R. Suleiman and Inge Crosman (Princeton, 1980). This book covers a broader formal range than Tompkins', since Suleiman conceives of audience-oriented criticism less as a method than as the outcome of six methodological approaches: "rhetorical; semiotic and structuralist; phenomenological; subjective and psychoanalytic; sociological and historical; and hermeneutic" (pp. 6–7). All but one of the essays in this volume are original (and that one, by Tzvetan Todorov, here appears for the first time in translation), and Crosman contributes a 26-page annotated bibliography. One essay deals with a specifically American text, "The Purloined Letter." Here Norman N. Holland matches his subjectivism against Lacan's and Derrida's deconstructions and, to my mind, loses. But his essay is worth reading, as is this collection as a whole.

Untying the Text is printed in offset from an eye-straining typescript. But it is an excellent collection, containing in its four sections ("Text, Discourse, Ideology"; "Structuralism's Wake"; "Psychoanalysis/Literature"; "Rhetoric and Deconstruction") representative works by such leading French critics as Barthes, Foucault, Riffaterre, and the Marxist poststructuralists Balibar and Macherey, and such American deconstructors as Barbara Johnson, J. Hillis Miller, and Paul de Man. The outstanding omissions are Derrida and Lacan, but these primary artists of deconstruction are discussed in intelligent detail in Young's introductory essay. At $9.95 in paperback, *Untying the Text* can be recommended to students.

The Pursuit of Signs: Semiotics, Literature, Deconstruction (Cornell) is a collection of Jonathan Culler's reviews and miscellaneous essays. One of these, a six-year-old study of Stanley Fish's critical theory, has been rendered partially obsolete by Fish's subsequent work; another, "Literary Theory in the Graduate Program," commands Ph.D. programs in English to reorganize themselves around Culler's specialty: "The exploration of textual activity is best carried out . . . when one encounters the dialectic between the literary and the philosophical. The most important contemporary example of this encounter is, of course, the work of Jacques Derrida . . ." (p. 223); still others deal with topics as diverse as the semiotics of apostrophe ("O wild West Wind") and the importance of *The Mirror and the Lamp*. As a *Gesammelte Werke* this collection is unlikely to be read all the way through by many readers, but such lucid essays as "Beyond Interpretation" make it valuable nevertheless.

William T. Stafford's *Books Speaking to Books* is a small collection of comparatist essays which fall, methodologically, about halfway between old-fashioned influence study and Bloomian antithetical criticism. This turns out to be an advantageous site to occupy; from it, Stafford can see the hazards of both the old criticism and the new, and he steers clear of them accordingly in his own excursions. It would be misleading for me to list the books Stafford goes out to see, since they are always engaged with other books, but two examples may give an idea of his method. An easy case is Stafford's comparison between black and white characters in three novels published in 1970–71: Saul Bellow's *Mr. Sammler's Planet*, Bernard Malamud's *The Tenants*, and John Updike's *Rabbit Redux*. Here the comparatist method yields chiefly the similarities that we would expect to find after conducting a comparison within a closed system: "The black/ white relationship in America . . . finally reveals itself to be an old, old story, however new the collective urgency to reconfront it and however varied the styles, voices, and tactics employed" (p. 102). But Stafford reads some other books more adventurously, and when he does his rewards are commensurately greater. Thinking about Moby Dick, Milly Theale, and Thomas Sutpen as America—not as American characters, not as symbols in any ordinary Brooks and Warren sense, but as metonyms for what Stafford calls (p. 19) "America as physical phenomenon and as idea"—earns him the right to say that "in this context the three symbolic Americas [that Melville, James, and Faulkner] conceive become very recent Americas indeed: a land that destroys those who would madly destroy it, an ideal of selflessness that may well also be self-serving, and a tragic heritage that becomes prophetically humane. Problems of American ecology, American self-righteousness, and American racism were never more with us than now" (p. 26).

b. **Generic Studies.** Walter Allen's *The Short Story in English* (Oxford) is a chronological survey of the major English, American, and Commonwealth writers in the genre, from Scott to the present—or, in American terms, from Poe to Oates. In practice, its coverage is restricted to social fiction written in the romantic, realist, or naturalist mode. Following a sensitive critical introduction, Allen settles down to summarizing representative stories, then passing judgments such as (about an Australian story whose key sentence is, "The child in the front room lay quaking with terror, dreading one of those cruel and shameful scenes which had made a hell of his childhood"), "[This] must be one of the best stories ever written" (p. 96). The secondary bibliography is short, and the book's comprehensiveness suffers from Allen's critical conservatism. Four pages are devoted to Ring Lardner and three to Erskine Caldwell, for instance, but there is nothing at all on John Barth, Donald Barthelme, Richard Brautigan, Walter Van Tilburg Clark, William H. Gass, Cynthia Ozick, or any black writer, American, African, or West Indian.

The Adventures of Augie March, Lolita, some stories by Poe, Huckleberry Finn, and The Catcher in the Rye are among the works discussed in a study in comparative literature, Pícaros, Madmen, Naïfs, and Clowns: The Unreliable First-Person Narrator (Oklahoma) by William Riggan. Not much here for specialists in American literature.

Norman Mailer, Hunter S. Thompson, Tom Wolfe, and Michael Herr are the chief subjects of John Hellman's Fables of Fact: The New Journalism as New Fiction (Illinois). The book's thesis is implicit in its subtitle: "the opposite contracts of the new journalist and the fabulator have led them to similar forms. . . . Both [Hellman's examples are Thompson's Fear and Loathing: On the Campaign Trail '72 and Vonnegut's Slaughterhouse-Five] confront their subjects with the controlling power of parody, bringing an insistent application of acknowledged artifice, comic burlesque, and bizarre fantasy to them" (pp. 67–68).

Three American books—The Confidence-Man, A Connecticut Yankee in King Arthur's Court, and The Sot-Weed Factor—are discussed in Walter L. Reed's History of the Novel, a study of the complex ways in which "the historical layers of intertextuality accumulate between the 'earliest' and 'latest' examples of a series" (p. 264)—in this case, a series of novels which descend from Don Quixote and the Spanish picaresque. With specific regard to the evidence of American literature, Reed concludes (p. 231) that "the history of the novel cannot be . . . easily delimited into evolving phases or species. Neither . . . can it be endowed with a teleology independent of the purposes of individual authors and communities of readers. Don Quixote and the picaresque are enabling examples for Melville and Twain, but they are not a necessary element of what Henry James imagined as the American writer's 'complex fate.' "

Novel vs. Fiction is a collection of essays and interviews from Genre which have been reprinted in hard covers, with an index. The subject of the volume is "a fiction being written in our time which departs from the rough but clearly understood contours of the novel" (p. 1)—i.e., specifically, the fiction of such novelists as Fowles,

Hawkes, and Barth (the subjects of individual essays), plus such critical theorists as Roland Barthes, Ihab Hassan, and (as the author of "What Are Master-pieces and Why Are There So Few of Them") Gertrude Stein.

I can give only brief mention to two specialized studies in the novel, each of which deals to some degree with American texts. Susan Sniader Lanser's *The Narrative Act: Point of View in Prose Fiction* (Princeton) uses structuralism and speech-act theory to demonstrate the complexities wrapped up in the blanket term "point of view." Marianna Torgovnick's *Closure in the Novel* (Princeton) works out a taxonomy of narrative endings—a taxonomy which has the goal of "indicat[ing] connections between literature and life established by endings" (p. 200).

c. **Monographs on Individual Critics.** I can also do no more than notice two books dealing with Continental critics whose influence on current American criticism is important but indirect. René Wellek's *Four Critics: Croce, Valéry, Lukács, Ingarden* (Wash.) consists of four short analytical monographs (less than 20 pages each) arranged in contrasting pairs. "Benedetto Croce . . . developed a critical theory in which the distinction between author, work, and reader are [*sic*] obliterated in a single act of intuition-expression. Paul Valéry . . . in contrast, keeps the three stages of the aesthetic transaction completely separate. . . . The monistic spiritualism of Croce stands against Valéry's Cartesianism. . . . Lukács conceives of literature as an index and mirror of society and reality, sees it as deeply involved and even determined by historical process and still wants it to influence the course of history. Ingarden, on the other hand . . . focuses all his attention on the work itself, which exists as a construct with a peculiarly independent mode of being" (pp. vii–viii). A much more detailed introduction to Ingarden's phenomenology, which I am not competent to discuss, is Eugene H. Falk's *The Poetics of Roman Ingarden* (N. Car.). This paragraph is also the place for me to note that I have been enjoying my introduction to the work of the polymathic Russian theorist of language M. M. Bakhtin (1895–1975), thanks to *The Dialogic Imagination: Four Essays by M. M. Bakhtin,* ed. Michael Holquist, trans. Caryl Emerson and Michael Holquist (Texas).

More directly relevant to *ALS* is *Lionel Trilling* (Ungar) by Edward Thomas Shoben, Jr., a critical biography by a clinical psychologist who knew Trilling as a colleague. This book lacks the critical sophistication of William M. Chace's *Lionel Trilling: Criticism and Politics* (*ALS 1980*, 483), but it is informed, affectionate, and, as we might expect, psychologically sensitive. It is also partisan, however, and we will have to extrapolate from Shoben's discussion of Trilling's insecurities if we want his help in thinking about any of Trilling's less appealing personal or professional traits, such as the careerism that disturbed Alfred Kazin or the orotundity that disturbed Roger Sale. The book's subtitle, omitted on the title page but mentioned elsewhere, is *Mind and Character*.

In the late 1940s, when Frederick C. Stern was an undergraduate, the moral state of American criticism could not be satisfying to any sensitive reader on the political left. In *F. O. Matthiessen: Christian Socialist as Critic* (N. Car.) Stern recalls his first encounter with *American Renaissance* this way: "My readings in other literary texts by writers who also shared my radical, left-wing concerns had provided no other such experience. When the passions seemed right to me, the literary discussions seemed forced . . . and the deck stacked toward conclusions that might please my politics but which were not literarily or intellectually convincing. When the literary scholarship seemed sound and persuasive, the conclusions were often politically conservative or even apolitical . . ." (p. 4). Matthiessen proved the great exception to this general rule, for reasons which are implicit in the subtitle of Stern's book. Stern quotes Matthiessen's credo to this effect (p. 78): "I have rejected the nineteenth-century belief in every man as his own Messiah . . . and I have accepted the doctrine of original sin, in the sense that man is fallible and limited, no matter what his social system, and is capable of finding completion only through humility before the love of God. . . . But I would differ from most orthodox Christians today . . . in that, whatever the imperfections of man, the second of the two great commandments, to love thy neighbor as thyself, seems to me an imperative to social action. . . . It is as a Christian that I find my strongest propulsion to being a socialist." But, as Stern says, "There is a difficult problem here. How does one reconcile views of life and letters as disparate as Christianity, socialism, and the 'tragic'?" Stern's reading of Matthiessen's oeuvre provides a satisfyingly nuanced answer.

d. Psychological Criticism. We Americans who read the new French criticism are faced with a major difficulty: an inability to understand what we are reading in the practical examples. We may have read the French texts under consideration, in translation or in the original, but obviously what is demanded is an assimilation of more than just the expository sense. For structuralism and its offshoots have been, before anything else, social criticisms (see Edith Kurzweil's *The Age of Structuralism* [Columbia, 1980], reviewed in *ALS 1980*, 501–02), and the American who wants truly to understand them must be not just bilingual but bicultural. This requirement holds especially true for readers of the late Jacques Lacan, TV personality, conquerer of France for Freud, intellectual entertainer of *le tout Paris*, and almost incidentally originator of a new theory of the relation between mind and language. But a party of French and American Lacanians has now landed on the shores of English and American literature, and in *The Fictional Father* the general reader of *ALS* can now begin to appreciate what the Lacanian adventure has discovered.

The title is explained by Régis Durand: "Recent Freudian theory links the emergence of language, of language as discourse, to the figure of the symbolic father. The Freudian 'primal repression' becomes with Jacques Lacan the 'paternal metaphor'; access to the order of the symbolic is gained through the agency of what Lacan calls the name-of-the-father" (p. 50). The hyphenated English phrase conceals an untranslatable verbal energy: Lacan characteristically takes seriously the fact that *le nom du père* is homonymous with *le "Non!" du père*. Using this multilayered metaphor as a guide to Melville's symbolism, Durand helps us retrace the oedipal itinerary laid out in *Moby-Dick*, chap. 114 (Davis, p. 49): "Where is the foundling's father hidden? Our souls are like those orphans whose unwedded mothers die in bearing them: the secret of our paternity lies in their grave, and we must there to learn it." The other American authors discussed are Faulkner (two essays, by André Bleikasten and John T. Irwin) and Donald Barthelme (by Robert Con Davis). Davis also contributes an essay, "The Discourse of Jacques Lacan," which summarizes the enterprise this way: "Our ideal reader . . . comes to Lacanian thought for an important perspective on how to dismantle standard presences in literature, such as father figures, mother substitutes, Christ figures, neurotics, and outsiders, and to find, instead, functions and transformations in fiction that can be examined critically in the context of their real environment—within narrative structure" (p. 184). A stimulating thought, a stimulating collection.

This has in fact been a good year for psychological studies in general. Meredith Anne Skura's *The Literary Use of the Psychoanalytic Process* (Yale) "argue[s] that the poets discovered [not just the unconscious but] *psychoanalysis* before Freud did, and that at its subtlest and most wide-ranging, this is what Freud's legacy has in common with his literary predecessors" (p. 4). Psychoanalysis, as Skura uses the term, is not a theory but a process, "a method rather than . . . a body of knowledge . . . a way of interpreting rather than . . . a specific product or interpretation. I am interested in psychoanalysis not so much for what it reveals about human nature . . . but for the way in which it reveals anything at all" (p. 5). Skura is not interested in using psychoanalysis to "strip away the surface" of a work of art; "[i]nstead, I am suggesting that we see the relation between manifest and latent meanings as a relation between two different ways of looking at the perfectly visible surface of a dream —or of *Hamlet*. The analyst is a connoisseur of strange relations, not between conscious and unconscious, but between different modes of consciousness which work both together and against each other in shaping each aspect of the material . . ." (p. 11). By way of examining these relations, Skura puts models of reading into play with specific texts: the models of literature as case history, fantasy, dream, transference, and psychoanalytic process itself. Her readings are fruitful, and her book will have wide general application.

By contrast, Walter J. Ong's *Fighting for Life: Contest, Sexuality, and Consciousness* (Cornell) is both overspecialized and overextended. This book covers an enormous intellectual range, from chess to theology, and is full of delicately provocative generalizations like this one (p. 68) about the difference in comic style between Charlie Chaplin and Carol Burnett: "there seem to be no female Charlie Chaplins. Women loners are not funny." Unfortunately, however, the book's many strong points subserve an embarrassingly shallow sociobiological thesis about the relationship between conscious culture and male competitiveness. Ong generalizes on p. 65 about the moral effects of female hormones in the uterus where a male mammal is growing ("The male mammalian organism must from the start react against its environment"), but only a few pages earlier he has been making the same kinds of points about animals that hatch out of eggs. One literary consequence of this dogged reductiveness is that a page devoted to Faulkner's "Spotted Horses" (pp. 62–63) conflates the helpless Mrs. Armstid with the self-possessed Mrs. Littlejohn in order to interpret the story as a case of "ineffectiveness of males in dealing with their own masculinity—the male clown figure, the limp phallus."

e. Formalist Studies. *Saving the Text: Literature/Derrida/Philosophy* (Hopkins) is a Derridean meditation by Geoffrey H. Hartman on the significance of Jacques Derrida's contributions to criticism, notably in his *Glas*. Three of this book's five chapters have been previously published. Meanwhile, Chicago brings us annotated translations of two of Derrida's books, both originally published in 1972: *Dissemination*, trans. Barbara Johnson, and *Positions*, trans. Alan Bass. Jonathan Culler says of the French editions, "[*Dissemination*], which contains three 100-page essays and a long preface . . . is concerned precisely with the literary, in so far as the 'literary' is our name for the effects of language which escape conceptual determination and are not reducible to a concept. . . . [*Dissemination*] . . . is Derrida's most forbidding and difficult book.

"*Positions*, on the other hand, which contains the texts of three interviews, is extremely lucid and doubtless the best introduction to Derrida that there is. The first interview, 'Implications,' is a general commentary on his work up until 1967. The second, ['Semiology and Grammatology'], is a succinct discussion of the theory of the sign and Derrida's critique of it. The last, 'Positions,' contains an account of 'deconstruction' and remarks on numerous other subjects, including history, Marxism, and Jacques Lacan" ("Jacques Derrida," in *Structuralism and Since*, ed. John Sturrock [Oxford, 1979], pp. 159–60. See *ALS 1980*, 503). Given its importance, I think it is regrettable that Chicago should charge $11.95 for this 114-page booklet.

Space has not permitted me to say much about the prose of the books in this chapter, but in any case language seems in some strange way not to matter to the production of American literary scholarship. Narrow and inaccurate in vocabulary, pretentiously obscure, flatly ungrammatical: these are the verbal traits of book after book published by some of America's leading academic presses. In *Ferocious Alphabets* (Little, Brown) Denis Donoghue looks at this language of ours with a view to curing it. Starting with small, discrete readings of such flamboyant stylists as Hugh Kenner and William H. Gass and carefully generalizing upward, Donoghue considers the ways we lay hold of language and subdivides them into two antithetical activities: epireading and graphireading. To the graphireader, there is no presence but only representation, no existence but virtuality: nothing but language—or rather, writing, a trace of meaning unconnected with anything human. Among the graphireaders Donoghue places Mallarmé and the deconstructionists. Donoghue aligns himself firmly with the epireaders, speakers of "an adversary idiom, animated by the body" (p. 210)—that is, those readers to whom the word exists as a voice, and the voice speaks as evidence of human personality. Gerard Manley Hopkins is in this group, and Georges Poulet, Paul Ricoeur, Kenneth Burke, Richard Poirier, and Harold Bloom. "The only requirement in epireading is that reading be construed as a personal encounter, the reader enters into a virtual relation with the speaker" (pp. 99–100). But of course our human relations with a speaker are also encounters with his language and its own history. That complication is both epireading's weakness and its strength. It can bring us to the verge of the intentional fallacy, but it can also make our reading strong with the strength of historical explanation.

Consider the case of F. R. Leavis. To me, separated from Leavis' Cambridge by two oceans, Leavis' criticism has always looked unattractive: cranky, provincial, and written in remarkably ugly prose. Puzzled by Leavis' reputation, I have raised these objections with some of his former students, and they have replied: Yes, but prose style isn't the point. The point turns out to be that Leavis in Cambridge was a truly great teacher, a man whose way of reading a poem really did change people's lives—specifically, the lives of many people in the English literary world. But that particular greatness died with Leavis in 1978, and its only legacy has been his books. The probate has been predictable: a writer in the *TLS* recently referred to "Dr. Leavis, of embarrassing memory." All this information must be taken into account if we are to understand Donoghue's *en passant* defense of Leavis vis-à-vis "the Cambridge manner" on p. 72. "Leavis's style has often been misunderstood," says Donoghue; "he has been widely thought to write badly." Yes, by readers who have access only to the words Leavis wrote, as opposed to the words he spoke. But finally the written words are all that can matter to readers. If many readers perceive that Leavis wrote badly, then literary history has spoken, for now: Leavis *did* write badly. That statement is based only on what Northrop Frye calls the history of taste, and it finally means only *De gustibus non est disputandum,* but it is there in our consciousness, undislodged and important. Donoghue may be overvaluing Leavis; Leavis' embarrassed ex-students may be undervaluing him; in either case, epireading presides over the critical operation. It seems to be the kind of thing that Frye warned us against.

Yet the mere fact that I react to Leavis as I do, a reader reacting not to a writing but to a writer, is an important part of my life in language. (Donoghue, p. 210: "what is the point of telling people that the self is obsolete when it is clear that, say, the Ayatollah Khomeini's self is not?") Donoghue wants to use epireading for purposes of evaluative criticism, and I don't think he will be successful. But certainly the idea of epireading has an important moral value. If we critics can learn to read for the humanity in the words, we may one day learn to listen for grace in our own speech.

A related work, less directly relevant to American institutional conditions but worth reading in its own right, is Geoffrey Strickland's *Structuralism or Criticism?: Thoughts on How We Read* (Cambridge). This antistructuralist study, which owes much to the work of E. D. Hirsch, Jr., lays out such spiritedly realist theses in its table of contents as "[A] true understanding of those whose experience differs from our own, including writers from a distant past, is always possible," "Evaluation . . . and interpretation are the same," and "The student of literature is a student of history."

This year's progress is marked by two strong studies in the philosophy of criticism. Suresh Raval's *Metacriticism* (Georgia) is a learned critique of modern critical theory, starting with its Kantian origins and moving from there to a vigorous analysis of the epistemologies of such contemporaries as W. K. Wimsatt, Norman Holland, Harold Bloom, and Paul de Man. "My purpose," says Raval on p. 11, "is to examine the logic of various critical theories, and to show the strategies by which they defend their respective positions. . . . It is part of my argument that concepts of criticism are not exactly logical because they acquire their significance in the history of a literary culture. Nor are they exactly empirical matters. . . . Yet they are amenable to a metacritical scrutiny which seeks to examine the logic of a specific critical concept and its relation to other concepts." Such a metacriticism "does not offer an indubitably true theory of criticism, for its objective is to enable us to understand the basis of literary criticism, by seeking to countervail parochial attitudes in criticism. . . . It helps us perceive the complexity of the form of critical life" (p. 241). Raval's own readings give full value to this complexity, but his elucidation of its underlying logic is admirably clear. I recommend *Metacriticism* highly.

ALS is not the place to discuss Charles Altieri's *Act & Quality: A Theory of Literary Meaning and Humanistic Understanding* (Mass.) in detail, nor do I have the expertise in philosophy to do so. I will say, however, that this book's defense of the beleaguered idea of meaning, carried out under the double aegis of Wittgenstein and Hegel, subserves a humanism which claims that "both the models and the terms for discovering actions are richest when one can discover, from pieties and historical positivities, the energy that works of genius can give to the present" (p. 3). But why defend humanism anew? Because, as Altieri says (pp. 311–12), "Full-scale defenses of the humanities provided by the previous generation of theorists have come to appear depressingly lame. . . . The blend of Arnoldian humanism and Romantic epistemology which characterizes New Criticism, for example, had by the 1960s collapsed into an academic formalism or reductive stress on original thematic readings, with no articulate sense of the significance of such enterprises. . . . One effect of this failure is that inadequately defended concepts of culture and of the mental powers employed in close reading make claims about culture and taste seem to be mere masked defenses of established social and intellectual authority." The humanism which lays claim to an intrinsic value needs rescuing from its own intellectual faint-heartedness and bad faith, and *Act & Quality* aims to bring help.

iii. Conclusion

Among the specialized studies in American literature that I read this year, the two strongest were probably Martin's *American Litera-ture and the Universe of Force* and Jones's *Tomorrow Is Another*

Day. Of the critical books I would recommend Donoghue's *Ferocious Alphabets* and Raval's *Metacriticism.* I think no clearly outstanding books were published this year in the field covered by this chapter, but the shelf of books that we have to contemplate after a year's work is nothing to be ashamed of.

University of Hawaii

21. Foreign Scholarship

i. French Contributions

Marc Chénetier

There seems to be a critical curse hanging over this chronicle: ever since I took it up major French critics have been steadily disappearing. Maurice Couturier, back in 1979, had had to bury Jean-Paul Sartre. I had to deal with Barthes' demise last year, announcing a strong French involvement with Lacanian criticism. In 1981 Jacques Lacan died. This year I would like not to name anybody and let my conscience rest. . . .

a. **Bibliography and Critical Statements.** The Montpellier-centered magazine, *DeltaES*, published its regular two issues in 1981, but one of them (xii), exceptionally, is the second fold of the original number of the series on Edgar Allan Poe and therefore does not carry a bibliography. The other one (xiii) deals with Walker Percy and does have the usual strong bibliography, compiled by Ben Forkner and J. Gerald Kennedy (pp. 177–87).

As far as general critical statements are concerned, Jean-Claude Barat (whose dissertation on American criticism was defended in 1982) wrote a theoretical piece entitled "Kenneth Burke et les 'New Critics'" (*RANAM* 12[1979]:45–64), and Marc Chénetier came up with a rather overpolemical statement on contemporary criticism of American Literature: "Even Post-Humanists Get the Blues: Contemporary American Fiction and its Critics; A Lament and a Plea" in *The American Identity*, pp. 345–62.

This year both issues of the *Revue Française d'Etudes Américaines* were dedicated to American Studies themes, and no literary bibliography or article accompanied collections devoted to fields foreign to literature as such.

b. **18th Century.** The publications of the Centre de Recherches sur l'Amérique Anglophone (CRAA) of the University of Bordeaux remain the major source of critical documents on 18th- and 19th-century America. Jean Béranger, who also edited *RFEA*, xii, dealing with "Religion in the United States," published the proceedings of his Bordeaux seminar, and four articles are devoted to the 18th century in the collections entitled *Séminaires 79* and *Séminaires 80* (Bordeaux: Maison des Sciences de l'Homme d'Aquitaine). Christian Lerat wrote two articles on Benjamin Franklin: "Benjamin Franklin et la Frontière" (*Séminaires CRAA 1979*, 35–52) sums up Franklin's views on the frontier and territorial expansion, while "Benjamin Franklin, économiste de la Frontière" (*Séminaires CRAA 1980*, 41–62) concentrates on the connections between the politician's expansionism and his long-term economic vision. In the 1979 volume of *Séminaires CRAA* Michel Fabre has a short piece on "Twasintas Seminoles, poème épique sur les marrons et les Indiens de Floride, de Alberry Whitman" (pp. 27–34). Suzy Durruty opens the 1980 volume with an article on the French author of *Miss MacCrea, a Novel of the American Revolution*, Michel-René Hilliard d'Auberteuil (pp. 11–26). Elsewhere in *Tolérance & Intolérance dans le Monde Anglo-Saxon aux 17 ème et 18 ème Siècles* (Nantes: Université de Nantes) Jean Béranger has refined our knowledge of St. John de Crèvecoeur in an article entitled "Libertés et Tolérances dans les *Lettres d'un Cultivateur Américain*" (pp. 83–97).

c. 19th Century. Using a very different angle, Noëlle Batt in a volume published by the research group in narratology of the University of Paris VIII analyzes Washington Irving's "The Legend of Sleepy Hollow." Her article, "D'un usage de la description: rivalité isotopique du narrateur et du personnage dans 'The Legend of Sleepy Hollow' de Washington Irving," in *Théorie de la Littérature et Enseignement* (Saint-Denis: Université de Paris VIII), pp. 43–54, is largely inspired by the theories of A. J. Greimas.

The 1981 harvest of French studies of 19th-century American literature is most varied indeed, both in subject matter and method. A sizable number of articles were devoted this year to neglected or little-known 19th-century figures. Jean Cazemajou's "Le Roman de l'Evangile Social: l'Exemple de *In His Steps*" in *Le Facteur Religieux en Amérique du Nord*, no. 3 (Bordeaux: Maison des Sciences de l'Homme d'Aquitaine), pp. 11–30, deals with the 1896 novel of Charles Monroe Sheldon, while Jean Bernard studies "Une oeuvre fictive de Richard Harding Davis: How I did not become a war correspondent" (*Séminaires CRAA 1979*, pp. 99–112) and Everett Carter studies "The Crisis of American Conscience in [Harold Frederic's] *The Damnation of Theron Ware*" (*Séminaires CRAA 1980*, 93–102).

Transcendentalism is also at the center of a certain number of studies this year. The general statement of Roger Asselineau's *The Transcendentalist Constant in American Literature* (NYU) ranges through several periods, but a number of particular studies make plain the variety of approaches (historical, psychoanalytical, social, textual) used by French scholars of the Transcendentalist moment properly called. Asselineau himself has added another layer to his numerous Whitmanian publications with "The Katinka Mystery, or Who Will Unknot Abbie Nott and other Knots" (*WWR*, special issue entitled *1980: Leaves of Grass at 125*, pp. 15–19). Orestes Brownson's "Catholic Republic" is the theme of Robert Rougé's paper in *Le Facteur Religieux en Amérique du Nord* (pp. 101–12), while in an article on Margaret Fuller published in the *Actes du Congrés 1978 de la SAES* (Société des Anglicistes de l'Enseignement Supérieur) (Didier), "Margaret Fuller, américaine ou romantique?" (pp. 85–98), Yves Carlet wonders where Margaret Fuller's real originality lies; her messianic attempt at making Boston "the Athens of the New World" brings her close to Thoreau, he concludes, but the latter's decision to stay in the United States separates him from the cosmopolitan colleague he could not stand.

A theoretical and excellently written article is Roland Tissot's major contribution to Thoreau studies in "Les douze échos d'économie dans *Walden*" (*EA* 34:32–43). The various semantic, phonetic, and unconscious harmonics of the word "economy" are systematically put in correspondence and enrich a text which does not thereby lose —indeed, increases considerably—its homogeneity.

Finally, three other 19th-century giants continued to attract critical attention. Guy Serratrice's essay "De l'Apparence à la Réalité: Visages du Mal dans *Huckleberry Finn*" (pp. 67–88) is a moral reading of Twain's text structures, but Serratrice hardly poses the more general questions programmed by Twain in the preamble to the novel; his thematic reading of the text relies exclusively on Huck's perceptions as they are recorded.

The second issue of *DeltaES* (xii), dedicated to Edgar Allan Poe

contains three important texts. " 'Discovery' in Poe," by A. G. Smith
(pp. 1–10) is a reflection on the meaning of this key word in "MS.
Found in a Bottle" and borrows from Irwin's and Todorov's analyses.
It deals with indefiniteness and the "semantic blankness" of the word
in Poe's tale, relating the trend to *Arthur Gordon Pym*. Claude Richard, the editor of *DeltaES* and best French specialist of Poe, proposes
a lengthy analysis of "Ligeia" (" 'L' ou l'indicibilité de Dieu: une
lecture de 'Ligeia,' " pp. 11–34), where his dominant concern with the
letter in American literature is made plain and served by a scrupu-
lously close reading of the text. Magic and alchemy are not treated
in the least in the occult manner which Viola Sachs uses in her Melville research (see below), but on the contrary from a tight linguistic
and hermeneutic point of view. For Isabelle Rieusset ("Edgar Allan
Poe poète de la connaissance," pp. 35–126) Poe's work is mostly connected with a writing practice based on a speculation on knowledge,
whence its interest and coherence. She therefore proposes a double
methodological axis in her very long article: a "discursive analysis"
in which epistemological oppositions are made salient and a search
for the structural coherence of Poe's work. Poe's "metaphysics of desire" is highlighted and her text centers on "Eureka," with heavy
borrowings from Derrida, Luce Irrigaray, and Philippe Sollers.

Régis Durand and Viola Sachs return this year with further and
entirely dissimilar analyses of Melville's creations. Durand has contributed a chapter to *The Fictional Father* entitled "The Captive
King: The Absent Father in Melville's Text" (pp. 48–72), while
Sachs wrote "Literature and National Identity: Labyrinthic Form
and Primordial Language in *Moby-Dick; or, The Whale*," in which
she argues that Melville's book "carries the quest of a national form
and language to its extreme limit (*Social Science Information* 21,i:
47–63). Sachs also has published *The Game of Creation: The Pri-
meval Unlettered Language of "Moby Dick; or, The Whale"* (Paris:
Editions de la Maison des Sciences de l'Homme). Sachs, as before
extremely concerned with myth and the occult, proposes to bring to
light "a double, ciphered text" of *Moby-Dick* "conceived as an inverted double of the Scriptures." An initiatory form is discovered
under every single detail of the text and leads her to conclude that
under the black print of the text dwells a "flow of colored dynamic
forms and elementary sounds."

d. **Drama.** This year's harvest is as thin as last year's was rich. As far as I know, only two articles came out in 1981 on American drama. One is the work of Jean-Marie Bonnet in "The 'Revels' History of Drama in English: American Drama" (*ES* 62:394–95); the other, that of Marie-Claire Pasquier, who prefaced and presented a special issue (Oct. 1981) on Richard Foreman and Kate Manheim of *Théâtre Public*: "Foreman en France: un objet qui, par définition, n'a pas de nom" (pp. 4–7).

e. **Poetry.** The event of the year in this field is probably what might be called the "William Carlos Williams explosion" in France. Numerous translations came out: *Paterson* by Yves di Manno (Paris: Flammarion), which received the first Maurice-Edgar Coindreau Award for the best American book in translation; Jacqueline Ollier published a bilingual edition of William Carlos Williams' selected poetry (Paris: Aubier-Montaigne) with a short introduction and notes; a bulky (345 pages) special issue of *In'Hui* (Centre de Recherches Nord-Américaines, Université de Picardie, Amiens) was put out by Jacques Darras, with support from the Centre National des Lettres. *In'Hui*, xiv, contains an introduction by Darras (pp. 3–5), numerous translated documents (Denise Levertov's essay, Williams' "To Elsie," excerpts from the Williams-Pound correspondence), a large number of poems in bilingual presentation, and a series of critical pieces. Jacques Roubaud's commentary on "The Red Wheelbarrow" and "The Locust Tree in Flower" opens the series (pp. 71–76), while di Manno explains his fascination with W. C. Williams' work ("pourquoi Williams?" pp. 10–17). Gérard-Georges Lemaire ("La poétique picturale de William Carlos Williams," pp. 166–75) and Jacqueline Ollier ("William Carlos Williams et le Futurisme," pp. 137–57) deal with the poet's plastic preoccupations. The texture of Williams' writing is the concern of Darras in "Grain, graine, grenat d'Amérique" (pp. 177–84), while Pierre-Yves Pétillon ("L'Ouverture des Terres," pp. 185–91) detects "the Puritan grain" in Williams' texts. Serge Fauchereau studies the relationship of "Valéry Larbaud et William Carlos Williams" (pp. 218–34). In "Le Poète et les objets de la terre gaste" (pp. 235–51) Jean Bessière dwells on the "archaeology of residues" and the reign/realm of objects in the poet's vision. In a section entitled "Testament de Williams," Laurette Véza analyzes "Asphodel, that Greeney Flower, ou le Grand Testament de William Carlos Williams" (pp. 255–61). This fat collection closes on an interview with Robert Duncan and Michael Palmer *à propos de* Williams (pp. 318–29) and a short biographical note by Darras (pp. 333–37). Jacqueline Ollier also gave a text on Williams to the *Annales de la Faculté des Lettres de Nice*: "Déchiffrage et Improvisation: Clef pour *Kora in Hell*," pp. 119–24.

Other articles on American poetry this year include Colette Gerbaud's "Le fixe, le mouvant et l'ailleurs dans la poésie de Wallace Stevens" in *Images de l'Ailleurs dans la Littérature Anglo-Américaine* (Reims: Faculté des Lettres et Sciences Humaines), pp. 123–40, and two articles by Marc Chénetier. One attempts to sum up Vachel Lindsay's conception of sign and symbol ("Sign and Symbol in Vachel Lindsay's Poetic and Graphic Work," *Poetic Knowledge*, ed. Roland Hagenbüchle and J. T. Swann [Bonn: Bouvier Verlag Herbert Grundmann], pp. 122–27); the other places Lindsay, Hart Crane, H. D., and W. C. Williams within an age-old European and American tradition of concern with Egyptian culture and hieroglyphics ("Egypt and Hieroglyphics in the American Tradition: a Sketch; with a View to Presenting Vachel Lindsay's Work as a Synthetic Step," *Traditions*, pp. 45–63).

f. **Twentieth-Century Fiction.** Several publications were dedicated this year to early 20th-century writers. Edith Wharton's first important novel was the subject of Ginette Castro's "*The House of Mirth*, chronique d'une femme et d'une société" (*Séminaires CRAA 1980*, 131–46). In "L'Histoire, la Fiction et l'Education: The Autobiography of Lincoln Steffens (1931)—Aventure Naturaliste" (*Séminaires CRAA 1979*, 67–80) Jean Cazemajou attempts an analysis of a work he himself deems somewhat bushy and monstrous. The naturalist interests of the same critic find further illustration in "Jack London, spéléologue de la misère" (*Séminaires CRAA 1980*, 77–92), which presents ill-known facets of the journalist who authored *The People of the Abyss*. But the "naturalist" group of Bordeau III has also contributed essays on Dreiser and Sinclair in this or other collections. André Muraire gave "Dear Diary: The Unpublished *Zillions*" to the *Upton Sinclair Quarterly* (5 Mar:3–6), while Michel Labarde studied "Les Apports du Journalisme dans *An American Tragedy* (*Séminaires CRAA 1979*, 81–98). Also to be noted concerning Dreiser is

Roger Asselineau's "Theodore Dreiser's Transcendentalism" appearing in *Critical Essays on Theodore Dreiser*, ed. Donald Pizer (Hall), pp. 92–103. Dealing with an author of roughly the same period is Rolande Diot's "Gullible's Dribbles: du reportage sportif au naturalisme dans les nouvelles de Ring Lardner" (*Séminaires CRAA 1980*, 119–30), where Diot's special interest in American humor finds an unexpected track. Perhaps the most important sheaf of 20th-century fiction studies published in 1981 concerns southern writers. The most important brick brought to the construction of this edifice is without a doubt the translation of Faulkner's correspondence into French by Michel Gresset and Didier Coupaye (Gallimard). This edition of a selection of Faulkner's letters accompanies the current publication in translation of all of Faulkner's works in the celebrated Gallimard collection: "La Pléiade." The second volume is being prepared by André Bleikasten, whose study "Fathers in Faulkner," a long and brilliant essay, is included in *The Fictional Father*, pp. 115–46).

There is, incidentally, a short essay on one of Faulkner's masters, Sherwood Anderson by Suzanne Galzin in "Le Mal de Vivre dans *Winesburg, Ohio* de Sherwood Anderson" (*Aspects du mal*, pp. 89–104).

The second important contribution to southern literature studies is without a doubt the issue of *DeltaES* (xiii) dedicatd to Walker Percy and edited by Ben Forkner and J. Gerald Kennedy. This abundant number (187 pages) opens on an interview with Percy by the editors (pp. 1–20) and memoirs of "A Frenchman's Visit to Walker Percy" by Gilbert Schricke (pp. 21–26). Claude Richard's "L'Exil de Binx Bolling" (pp. 27–54) is the first of two articles on *The Moviegoer*; a double reading of the text ("mediated" and "unmediated") is here suggested, which relies on the existential and fictional meanings of "exile." Robert Regan has chosen to revisit the same novel under the guise of what he takes to be a rerun: "The Return of *The Moviegoer*: Toole's *A Confederacy of Dunces*" (pp. 169–76). *Love in the Ruins* is seen from several standpoints. Max Webb's "*Love in the Ruins*: Percy's Metaphysical Thriller" (pp. 55–66) gives Percy's work the tag of "futuristic extravaganza," while Lewis A. Lawson detects in Tom More "A Cartesian Physician" (pp. 67–82). Simone Vauthier had previously studied *Lancelot* from the point of view of the theories of René Girard in "Story, Story-teller and Listener: Notes on Lancelot" (*SCR* 13,iii:39–54). The sequel to this article is "Mimesis and Violence in *Lancelot*" (*DeltaES*, xiii:83–102). Girard's theories indeed seem to apply here as they—unfortunately—do in so many other cases where violence appears as a thematic constant. "The Semiotics of Memory: Suicide in *The Second Coming*" (pp. 103–26) by J. G. Kennedy proposes that "From *The Moviegoer* (1961) onward, Percy has displayed a quasi-scientific, quasi-theological interest in the phenomenon of language," a fact indeed averred by *The Message in the Bottle*, which Frank Parker assesses further along ("Walker Percy's Theory of Language: A Linguist's Assessment," pp. 145–68). The formulation may be somewhat too broad for critical use, as the classically thematic conclusions of Kennedy's essay seem to indicate. Giving "A Rahnerian Backdrop to Percy's *The Second Coming*" (pp. 127–44), Patrick Samway does indeed accentuate the "theological" approach by suggesting that Jesuit Karl Rahner's views on the human person, mystery, and mystagogy closely apply to Percy's own vision.

To close this southern section, let me mention that William Humphrey's *The Shell*, translated by Rolande Ballorain, adapted by Alain Bosquet, was published in Paris (*Nota Bene* 4, Nov.:85–96) and that Michel Bandry, whose dissertation on poor whites in southern fiction was defended in 1982 at La Sorbonne, published a general presentation article entitled "Le 'Sharecropper Novel' des années 20" (*The Twenties*, Actes du Groupe d'Etudes et de Recherches Nord-Américaines, Aix en Provence).

There were two important articles published by Marie-Claire Pasquier on Gertrude Stein, "Gertrude Stein: l'écriture et l'exil" and "Gertrude Stein: écouter, parler, voir" (*TM* 417:1816–34; 419:2159–73). Stein's modernity is related to contemporary theatrical experiments. Pasquier also published an article on William Burroughs, "Par l'Auteur du *Festin Nu*" (*QL* 18 July:16–31), reviewing the translation of Burroughs' essays by Philippe Mikriammos and Gérard-Georges Lemaire, *Essais de William Burroughs* (Bourgois), and one on Phillip Roth, "Portrait de l'Artiste en Jeune Homme" (*QL* 16–30 Nov.) reviewing *L'Ecrivain des Ombres*, Henri Robillot's translation of *The Ghost-Writer* (Gallimard). Other translations of notable American works this year include *L'Exploit*, Nabokov's *Glory* (Paris: Julliard) by Maurice Couturier, whose excellent article, "Stratégie énonciative paramimétique: *Look at the Harlequins* de

Nabokov" appeared in *EA* 34:165–79; John Rechy's *Rush* (Paris: Presses de la Renaissance) by G. M. Sarrotte, and *Un Privé à Baby-lone*, Richard Brautigan's *Dreaming of Babylon* (Paris: Bourgois) with translation and introduction by Marc Chénetier; and *The Tokyo-Montana Express* (Bourgois), translated by Robert Pépin.

A longish article on American literature since 1970 was included in the new edition of an important French encyclopedia as "La Lit-térature Américaine de 1970 à 1980," by Marc Chénetier (*Encyclo-pédie Larousse*, pp. 237–38). Chénetier also authored an article on John Hawkes's *The Passion Artist*: "Le Réalisme Onirique de John Hawkes" (*QL* 1–15 Nov.:13–14). Most recent French contributions on contemporary American fiction now emanate from the newly born Groupe René Tadlov, based in the Maison des Sciences de l'Homme in Paris, which ambitiously aims at succeeding the Centre de Re-cherche sur la Littérature Américaine Contemporaine de Paris III, now defunct because of André Le Vot's retirement.

For science fiction specialists Jean Raynaud proposes two articles: "Oedipe et Science-Fiction: Rapport au Père et Réalité Sociale" in *Mythes, Images, et Représentations*, pp. 369–76, "La Ville dans la Science-Fiction Américaine Contemporaine" (*RFEA* 11:67–98), where he argues that science fiction, an essentially urban form of literature, seems to have recently moved "from an optimistic view of garden cities or space-stations to a gloomy depiction of cave-cities." Jacques Favier's "Getting There: Transits in Speculative Fiction" (*SJS* 7:43–55) attempts to distinguish the features that make "specu-lative fiction" similar to and different from "mainstream literature."

Numerous colleagues this year published review articles in the daily and weekly French press, which could not find their way into this report; the interest of their suggestions and reactions could not, unfortunately, outweigh the problems posed by the mass of their contributions. Most of these pieces are echoes of work in progress which ought to make 1982 a very fruitful year indeed, partly by rea-son of the European Association for American Studies Conference to be held in Paris in April 1982. The atmosphere of gestation rather than abundant production, which seems to predominate this year, may also have something to do with the theoretical hesitations and reconsiderations now taking place among French critics of American literature. A new preference for the unsystematic and the relativized seems to make rapid headway, and the variety and versatility of work to come ought thereby to be made all the greater.

University of Orleans

ii. German Contributions

Hans Galinsky

The downward trend of publications noticeable in 1980 was reversed in 1981. Book-length monographs rose from 13 to 15, essays contributed to festschrifts, collections, and periodicals soared to 100. All of them, except some not accessible to me, especially if published abroad, were inspected. There is no other way for a justifiable selection. Comparative and didactic studies kept increasing to such an extent that the latter had to be disregarded for reasons of severely limited space. In the field of periodicals and monograph series three new ventures occurred. *AAA, Arbeiten aus Anglistik und Amerikanistik*, ed. Bernhard Kettemann (Tübingen: Narr); *Forum Anglistik: Realien und Probleme der Literaturwissenschaft*, ed. Rüdiger Ahrens and Erwin Wolff (Heidelberg: Winter); TBA, Tübinger Beiträge zur Anglistik (Tübingen: Narr) have in common that none is, or will be, taking care of American literature alone.

a. **Literary History—General.** Studies in American literature in general, i.e., covering the whole or several phases of its history, embrace quite a few essays. Two of them concern American contributions to such international but chronologically limited topics as science fiction and 20th-century world literature. Of widest scope is Gustav H. Blanke's "The Imagistic Rendering of America's World Mission," *Wächtler Festschrift*, pp. 36–52. It charts the course of the images of the ark and of light from 1630 to 1865. Most of the material consists of sermons and political orations. Some of it takes in present-day writing and speeches. Continuity of Puritan uses and changes due to secularization stand out. This near-panoramic offering shrinks to an overview of 19th- and 20th-century American fiction in Walter

In this essay single quotes indicate translations from the German; double quotes enclose original quotations—*H. G.*

Hölbling's "Zeitlosigkeit und Geschichtsverlist im neueren amerikanischen Roman" (*Sprachkunst* 12:228–44). Narrative handling of time is watched from Irving's "Rip Van Winkle" through Vonnegut's *Slaughterhouse-Five*. As for the growth, in fiction, of the subjective time consciousness over against the resistance of objective historical structures of society and the final victory of the former, he distinguishes six stages: (1) Crane and Bierce, (2) Fitzgerald and Hemingway, (3) Wolfe, Dos Passos, and Faulkner, (4) Bellow, (5) Heller, Pynchon, and Vonnegut, (6) Barth, Barthelme, and Federman. Stage 6 presents the radical turn away from the mimetic tradition and its "chronology" to the insistence that linguistic articulation of contents of consciousness is the only reality. The 19th and 20th centuries once more figure jointly, though more selectively, in Armin Paul Frank's motif-oriented study "The Long Withdrawing Roar: 80 Years of the Ocean's Message in American Poetry," *Brumm Festschrift*, pp. 71–90. Taking his cue from the festschrift's title, *Forms and Functions of History in American Literature*, he thinks that "a work which employs the same *motif* as an earlier one, but is consistent in certain modifications of treatment may be said to be in a relation of tradition with the former. . . . In such a case, historical consciousness is not a consciousness of the sins or moral achievements of the fathers but of their *artistic* sins and achievements." He tests this theory by analyses of Emerson's "Seashore," Whitman's "Out of the Cradle Endlessly Rocking," and Stevens' "The Idea of Order at Key West." Results are summed up succinctly along comparative lines.

In the context of *Traditions*, pp. 187–99, Richard Martin traces "Constant Myths and Destroyed Dreams: The Nineteenth Century in the Twentieth." In his opinion "the national myths of the United States reveal a stubbornness and constancy while many of the dreams of the last century have lost their worth and credibility." Of political practitioners and theorists a host of authors ranging from Jefferson to R. Buckminster Fuller are drawn upon to corroborate his opinion. Of literary authors Emerson is relied on to "bring out clearly the growing disparity between myth and dream." Contemporary literary evidence is sampled from Coover, Sukenick, Brautigan, and Kosinski. Martin has courageously tackled an interdisciplinary subject by integrating literature with the prose of politics and criticism, both literary and cultural (e.g., Ihab Hassan, Nathan A. Scott,

Charles Reich), in order to diagnose the state of America's spiritual resources exemplified by the essential relationship of "public myths" and "private dreams." Not so much traditions but the emergence of a genre, autobiography, as practiced by native American writers is the topic of Bernd C. Peyer's "Autobiographical Works Written by Native Americans" (*Amst* 26:386–402), which surveys the genre's history from the late 18th century's Samson Occom and his incomplete manuscript autobiography through Ted C. Williams' *The Reservation* (1976) and Gerald Vizenor's "Autobiographical Myths and Metaphors" (1976). He concentrates on about 25 authors writing in English. They represent the genre's development from the apologetic and religious-didactic phase to that of the "literary autobiography." Works are studied mainly in their relation to changing policies in Indian affairs and to authors' attitudes toward white society.

Not an internal American phenomenon but a literary form type, international at least in point of reception, to whose origin and growth Americans have contributed significantly, is the subject treated by three authors in their monograph *Science Fiction: Theorie und Geschichte, Themen und Typen, Form und Weltbild* (Stuttgart: Reclam). Ulrich Suerbaum deals with its theory (pp. 8–36) and history (pp. 37–62), Ulrich Broich with its themes (pp. 63–79) and types (pp. 80–109), while Raimund Borgmeier investigates form (pp. 110–47) and world-view (pp. 148–73). Americanists will find stimulating references to a great many American practitioners of the art but also to the comic strip, the dime novel, and the Western. Of additional interest are observations on the linguistics of the genre.

Entirely confined to the 20th century but placing it in the global context of world literature is *Weltliteratur im 20. Jahrhundert*, ed. Manfred Brauneck (Reinbek: Rowohlt). It consists of four volumes of an alphabetically arranged dictionary of authors' biographies and bibliographies of their works and their German translations. Volume 5 contains integrative essays, a calendar of important dates, and a list of secondary sources. Information on American authors as supplied in the dictionary part is selective, the main stress falling on present-day literature. The essay "Literatur der USA" (vol. 5, pp. 395–422), within its limited scope, affords a condensed, though colorful, picture of 80 years of American literature. Dieter Herms, its author, provides for clarity of outline by a frank statement of his method. Literature is fitted into "political-historical categories." In their "framework, however, specific lines of the development of the literary genres have to be drawn as well."

a-1. **Colonial, Revolutionary, and 19th Century.** For the first time in several years researchers' interest in colonial literature picked up. Two monographs and three articles testify to this trend. Ursula Brumm's " 'What Went You Out Into the Wilderness to See?' " (*Prospects* 6:1–15) explores "Nonconformity and Wilderness in Cotton Mather's *Magnalia Christi Americana*." Due to its place of publication it is directly accessible to overseas readers. Not quite so easily accessible are the other pertinent items. Hans Galinsky's "History and the Colonial American Humorist: Thomas Morton and *The Burwell Papers* (*Brumm Festschrift*, pp. 21–43) examines *New English Canaan* and the *Papers* in the context of relations between history and humor in international, but specifically American, colonial history. In both texts, though in varying degree, world history, sacred and profane, factual, legendary, and mythical, is shown to serve as an armory of comical weapons. Comedy arising from Indian-English racial incongruities and from intra-English socioeconomic tensions are found to be common to both, the racial aspect in the *Papers* taking in black-white relations as well. Anne Bradstreet and her uses of the Bible, a major figure and a major problem of colonial literature, are approached in Hans-Gernot Peter's *Studien zu Umfang und Bedeutung der biblischen Bezüge im Werk Anne Bradstreets* (Füssen: Blasaditsch). Peter analyzes biblical language in Bradstreet's prose and poetry as to source, distribution, and significance. The functions that the Bible as quoted, paraphrased, alluded to, or interpreted exercises in individual poems and prose pieces are elaborated with particular care. An appendix parallels Bradstreet's uses with her sources in the Geneva and/or King James Bibles. The other monograph, by way of autobiography as their common mode of articulation, links a representative of late colonial to a main figure of late 19th-century literature. Renate Schmidt-v. Bardeleben's *Studien zur amerikanischen Autobiographie: Benjamin Franklin und Mark Twain* (Munich: Fink) juxtaposes a classic and an experiment. Part 1 of her book offers what bids fair to remain for a long time the most thorough, thematically oriented report on the theory and history of autobiography. It is supplemented by a chronological survey of critical research of both. Parts 2 and 3 analyze the two specimens as artifacts. Franklin's elitist 'image of human society,' with himself figuring as an imitable exponent of success won against formidable odds, is distinguished from Twain's inclusion of a much broader world and from his average protagonist not meant for imitation. Twain's insight into the peculiar workings of memory is duly stressed.

The two further publications in the colonial field, one of them overlooked last year, concern not individual authors but collective notions such as 'the New England conscience' and 'tradition and innovation' as applied to colonial literature. The former notion reflects the colonial age in the thought of the 19th century. The origin of the phrase, hitherto first evidenced in Henry James's short novel *Confidence* (1879), is antedated by four years in Volker Bischoff's "'The New England Conscience,' Thomas Gold Appleton, and Mrs. Vivian" (*NEQ* 53[1980]:222–25). The phrase occurs as the title and the subject of an essay by Appleton. Bischoff thinks it "likely that James was aware of Appleton and his work because of his reputation among Boston literati and his membership in the Saturday Club," joined by James, Sr. and Jr. In Hans Galinsky's "Tradition und Neuanfang als eine Grundfrage der frühamerikanischen Literatur: Koloniale Antworten, ihre literarische Nachwirkung und heutiges literarhistorisches Urteil," *Schulze Festschrift*, pp. 129–62, the question of a meaningful applicability of such antithetic but complementary concepts as tradition and innovation is held to be significant to literature in general but to colonial literature in particular. It is discussed in three ways: (1) colonial reactions to the problem, (2) the effects on later American literature, (3) 'tradition' and 'innovation' as related to terms applied to the colonial age by modern literary historians. Sub (1) John Smith's *A Description of New England*, Jacob Steendam's "The Complaint of New Amsterdam," and John Cotton's poem on Old and New Boston are drawn upon. Sub (2) the Newfoundland and Nova India motifs in Poe's "The Gold Bug," the Old World–New World themes in Fitzgerald's *The Great Gatsby* and Williams' *Paterson*, Book 2, as well as "the rebirth," "new frontier," and "Second Coming" motifs in Ferlinghetti's *A Coney Island of the Mind* are made use of. Late colonial and revolutionary emblems employed for the U.S. Great Seal and continuing in today's one-dollar bill serve as further illustrative material. Sub (3) "Colonial Baroque" as a terminological answer of recent scholarship to this problematic relationship of 'tradition' and 'innovation' in colonial literature is followed from its beginnings to its present hesitant acceptance.

As in 1980, no Austrian, Swiss, or German scholar felt attracted to subjects dealing exclusively with revolutionary or early republican literature. But a 19th-century area of even longer neglect, Longfellow's poetry, was revisited. Hans-Joachim Lang's and Fritz Fleischmann's "'All This Beauty, All This Grace': Longfellow's 'The Building of the Ship' and Alexander Slidell Mackenzie's 'Ship'" (*NEQ* 53:104–18) places lines 17–50 and 174–78 of the poem beside the article "Ship" contributed by Mackenzie to vol. 11 of Francis Lieber's *Encyclopedia Americana*. Longfellow borrows words and phrases but he also paraphrases, and, in part, follows the structural sequence of Mackenzie article. The borrowing is done with "a mastery of concentration." The presentation of external and internal evidence is as cogent as it is entertaining. With, in addition, two essays on Hawthorne, four on Poe, one on Melville, one on Dickinson, four on Twain, and one on Harte, the 19th century has increased its appeal. Its drama, however, went unnoticed. Like Lang's and Fleischmann's, Horst Kruse's essay "Hawthorne and the Matrix of History: The Andros Matter and 'The Gray Champion'" (*Brumm Festschrift*, pp. 103–19) is a source study. It examines Hawthorne's sources for his treatment of the Andros affair, i.e., Thomas Hutchinson's and David Neal's histories of New England, William Douglass' *A Summary . . . of the British Settlements in North-America*, and "several volumes" of *CMHS*. "Some very subtle parallels" between them and "The Gray Champion" as well as "some significant departures" reveal "an underlying principle," i.e., a balancing of the mimetic against the emblematic. Kruse's challenging comparison is matched by Hans-Joachim Lang's postscript appended to a new edition of a German translation of *The Scarlet Letter*. Its 1975 edition, based on an older German rendering revised by Ruth and Hans-Joachim Lang and supplemented with their own translation of "The Custom-House," has been reprinted for the paperback series *dtv Weltliteratur* (Munich: Deutscher Taschenbuch Verlag). Aside from the postscript, Hans Joachim Lang contributes annotations reprinted from the 1975 edition, a new calendar of events, and a bibliography. Put beside the 1975 one (reviewed in *ALS 1975*, 480), the 1981 postscript makes particularly instructive reading. Political, economic, and psychologi-

cal conditions of the work's production and the role of its publisher
are pinpointed.

Poe scholarship proceeded on highways and byways. Of the four
pertinent pieces two deserve brief mention. Poe's articulation of extreme emotional states, especially horror and terror, and his control
of their impact on the reader, rather than the American background
of this art, are delineated in Ulrich Broich's afterword to *Edgar Allan
Poe, Faszination des Grauens*, a selection of 11 tales, trans. Arno
Schmidt and Hans Wollschläger, *dtv Weltliteratur*, pp. 173–90. Katrina Bachinger gives her indefatigable Poe research a new direction
in "Tit for Tat: The Political Poe's Riposte to Nineteenth Century
American Culture and Society," *Salzburg Studies in English Literature: Romantic Reassessment* 87, pp. 46–90. Melville studies are represented by Lang's and Benjamin Lease's "Melville and 'The Practical Disciple': George William Curtis in *The Confidence Man*," *Amst*
26:181–91. They refute former identifications of Egbert with Thoreau. Like John Seelye before them, they detect in this novel the
presence of Curtis, yet unlike Seelye they equate not Thoreau but
Curtis with Egbert. Detailed proof is offered. In addition, they trace
Melville's use of Egbert to Ludwig Tieck's novella "Der blonde Eck-
bert," with Carlyle's *German Romance* serving as intermediary.

Emily Dickinson begins to benefit from women's studies and
returning interest in transcendentalism. Dorothea Steiner's "Emily
Dickinson: Image Patterns and the Female Imagination," *ArAA* 6:
57–71, may relate to the one, Gudrun Grabher's monograph to be
reviewed in the comparative studies section surely does to the other.
Steiner approaches "the female quality" of Dickinson's art from two
angles, that of the "poet" standing in the tradition of the "masters"
who treat "the great themes of literature," and that of the "woman
poet" "stand[ing] at the beginning of a tradition . . . of those women
who use the male tradition but modify it by adding their distinctive
perspective, or voice." Its quality is found behind "several masks,"
of which Steiner distinguishes six. They extend from "portraying the
woman in her dealings with Power, i.e. God, or an equivalent force"
to a "playful attitude toward things." "Image patterns" are shown
to correlate with these masks. They are thought to jointly "have a
structural effect on Dickinson's poetry." Persuasively put, this broad
overview deserves to be tested by interpretation of single complete
poems from their phonic to their syntactic and semantic levels.

With Twain and Harte the South and the Far West enter into a picture of scholarship decisively colored by preference for the Old East. Horst Kruse's *Mark Twain and "Life on the Mississippi"* (Mass.) links up with its German forerunner *Mark Twains "Life on the Mississippi"* (Neumünster: Wachholtz, 1970). In its new shape it is directly accessible to overseas readers. Helmbrecht Breinig's "Mark Twain—Anti-Imperialist? Clemens' Imperialismuskritik im Kontext seiner Vorstellungen von *savagism* und Zivilisation" (*Gulliver* 9:178–99) tries to correct the image of 'anti-imperialist' Twain by scrutinizing 'his attitude with respect to such related concepts as savagism and civilization, primitivism and progressivism, Manifest Destiny, and imperialism in an extended sense.' The time span covered extends from Twain's Hawaiian visit through *Fables of Man*. His 'development toward a recognition of universal equality of rights' is recognized but 'a very early dichotomy of civilization euphoria and cultural criticism' was never resolved completely. Breinig's thesis is advanced with a great many quotations, in part from sources as yet unpublished. Franz Link and Winfried Fluck fix on Twain's *A Connecticut Yankee in King Arthur's Court*, the same work to which Breinig pays a good deal of attention. As editor of a new German version, *Mark Twain, Ein Yankee am Hofe des Königs Artus* (Frankfurt: Insel), Link adds an afterword, a biography, and a selective bibliography (pp. 471–93). As in the corresponding section of his *Geschichte der amerikanischen Erzählkunst im 19. Jahrhundert* (*ALS* 1980, 531), Link views this novel in the context of Twain's life and previous works as well as in the light of the novel's original intention —'a burlesque confrontation of two mutually exclusive worlds'—and of its final results: (1) 'the present's traditional feudal structures and modes of behavior in the mirror of a time long past,' (2) a technology meant to liberate humanity from slavish drugery turning into a tool of its destruction.' For a gradual explanation of the novel's bewildering multitude of aspects Link skillfully leads the reader through a gallery of Twain's previous heroes until he realizes their common 'outsider's perspective.' In Twain's manipulation of time, which allows not only a confrontation of periods but also a pessimistic criticism of the hero's own period, Link sees a pointer toward 'a possibility of the modern futuristic novel and science fiction.' Contributing to a festschrift devoted to "Forms and Functions of History in American Literature" (*Brumm Festschrift*, pp. 134–48), Fluck is convinced that "fiction serves to reconstruct history." He is interested in "the composite character and movement of literary narrative discourse" as a "possibility that history may be said to express itself through, and inscribe itself in, the literary text." On these presuppositions he views Twain's novel. He tries to explain the problem posed by the "sudden and dramatic shift of technology" from "advancing the cause of progress and democracy" to "becom[ing] the instrument for its complete annihilation." He finds in the novel two additional "levels of discourse," (1) Hank Morgan becoming aware of his chances as businessman in a society without competition, (2) Hank indulging in fantasies of omnipotence. Self-criticism implicit in Link's view of Morgan has become explicit self-deception in Fluck's.

Twain's competitor Bret Harte is also encountered in a festschrift. Its title emphasizing the tension between tradition and innovation, the *Schulze Festschrift*, at first glance, is not the place to expect Harte, often thought a traditionalist working with merely new subject matter. Frieder Busch's "Überlegungen zu Bret Hartes Einführung einer neuen Perspektive" (pp. 179–89) convinces the reader that Harte's use of the first-person-plural perspective is fundamentally innovative in the short story. "Miggles," "Tennessee's Partner," and "The Man of No Account" illustrate its use in alternation with other perspectives, e.g., 'narrating I' (either as figure or merely as voice) and 'experiencing I/we,' with 'I' representing a group. This perspective's dissonance with formal diction is traced to traditional western humor. The perspective's relation to dialect, metaphorical use of jargon, slang, and nonverbal communication as ingredients of diction in these stories is analyzed meticulously. In the framework of the same theme of tradition and innovation Horst Brinkmann's "Zum Phänomen der Angst bei Stephen Crane and Ambrose Bierce" (*Schulze Festschrift*, pp. 191–200) presents both authors on the one hand as heirs to Poe's modes of evoking anxiety, on the other as 'significant participants' in the new beginning of a 'formal trend leading up to Hemingway.' The novelty of Brinkmann's essay lies in the method, a comparison of Bierce's "One of the Missing" with Crane's "The Blue Hotel," which so far have been analyzed only separately.

The descent into the abyss not of the psyche but of society is watched in Heinz Ickstadt's "The Descent into the Abyss: Die literarische Entdeckung des sozialen Untergrunds in der amerikan-

ischen Fiktion des späten 19. Jahrhunderts" (*Amst* 26:260–69). He
links late 19th- to early 20th-century writing, both fictional and
journalistic, by selecting Howells' *A Hazard of New Fortunes*, London's *People of the Abyss*, and Crane's *New York Sketches*. They are
meant to illustrate 'the touristic-journalistic perspective.' Alice Hegan
Rice's *Mrs. Wiggs of the Cabbage Patch* exemplifies the 'transfer of
the local color tradition to the presentation of the big-city slum.'
Crane's *Maggie* and Sinclair's *The Jungle* function as paradigms of
'naturalist melodrama,' while London's *The Iron Heel* and Norris'
McTeague represent naturalism proper. Attempts to transcend the literary and social limits imposed by the mainly middle-class observer
occur with social reformers' memoirs and fiction (Jane Addams'
Twenty Years at Hull-House, Charles Sheldon, *In His Steps*). Mike
Gold's much later *Jews without Money* and its vision of the 'community of the proletariat' opening up for ethnic subcultures a direct
way to socialism is adduced to point up the difference from *The
Jungle*'s indirect way through the historically superior Anglo-American culture. Likewise throwing his net widely, K. Dietrich Pfisterer
in "Profile und Aspekte des social gospel," *Verkündigung und Frei-
heit*, Beihefte zu *Evangelische Theologie* (Munich: Kaiser) 26: 43–
57, offers researchers of Bellamy, Sheldon, and religious poetry new
food for thought. Looking afresh on the evangelical tradition in
America and on its impact, he places Bellamy and Henry George
side by side as representatives of 'a hope of salvation ordering and
orienting their thought,' although this 'does not become a subject of
reflection in their principal works.' The influence of Bellamy's ideas
on voluntary organizations is recognized in the case of Frances Willard and her Women's Christian Temperance Union. Sheldon's *In
His Steps* emerges as a novel reflecting a community's awareness that
'conversion led to endangering and losing one's social status.' In
Frank Mason North's hymn "Where cross the crowded ways of life"
the connection of 'individual conversion' with 'social transformation'
is particularly obvious.

a-2. 20th-Century Poetry, Drama, and Fiction to 1945. The fact
that only American poetry and fiction have kept scholars' attention
whereas drama has been of interest merely in comparative, Anglo-
American, or broadly international, contexts marks a symptomatic
deviation from traditional trends of research. Of the period's poets

Pound and Eliot alone retained their spell. For the most part, previous researchers in these fields returned to them. By "A Note on 'The Apparition of These Faces . . .' in *The House of Mirth* and 'In a Station of the Metro'" (*Paideuma* 10:327) Link once more adds to Pound lore a highly probable source for the "Metro" poem in a passage of chapter 1 of Edith Wharton's novel. Probability is increased by the occurrence in the same work of such a rare name as *Paquin*, recurring in Pound's Canto LXXXI. Hans-Joachim Zimmermann's "Ezra Pound, 'A Song of the Degrees': Chinese Clarity *versus* Alchemical Confusion" (*ibid.*, pp. 225–41) elucidates an early piece of Pound's poetry. The seven poems it consists of make up "Xenia," printed in *Poetry* 3,ii (Nov. 1913). Poems III–V, republished as "A Song of the Degrees" in *Lustra* (1916), stand at the center of Zimmermann's endeavors. His exegesis is a model of erudite criticism. It encompasses Chinese culture, above all Confucianism, and alchemical lore. It is applied to a poem that is not outstanding in artistry but marks "the first emergence of the great Chinese theme in Pound's work." Section II of "A Song" serves "as a poetical illustration of Pound's programmatic creed of imagism and vorticism while section III describes all that Pound will leave behind." Appendix A reprints "Xenia," B. Richard Aldington's "Penultimate Poetry: Xenophilometropolitania" as parodistic banter on "the element of Poundian posturing in 'Xenia.'" Katrina Bachinger's objective as formulated in the title of her essay "A *Make/Made* Dialectic as a Key to Pound's *Cantos*" (*Poetic Drama and Theory: Salzburg Studies in English Literature* 65:207–24) is very ambitious. Leaning on the theory of generative grammar, she suggests that an all-inclusive description of the *Cantos*' "major form" "might be generated by considering the implications of one verb deeply buried in the epic: the verb 'to make.'" She digs it up in many passages and discovers the "dialectic" of its two prevalent forms, "make" and "made." She ranks them among the "gristly" words referred to in Pound's poetics. Of the two specimens of Eliot scholarship one exclusively, another inclusively treats of "The Waste Land." Elmar Schenkel's "Element und Krise: Überlegungen zur Funktion des Wassers in T. S. Eliots 'The Waste Land,'" *Literatur für Leser* (Munich: Oldenbourg) 4: 112–22, ties in with such motif constituents as "shore" and "ocean" in Frank's essay (cf. *a*), but on the one hand it expands so as to take in the whole image area of water 'from fish to seaside resort,' on the other it shrinks to the interpretation of 'water' and its functions in only one poem. These functions, symbolical as well as structural, are followed from the first to the last of the poem's five sections. Schenkel discovers that 'water repeats a metamorphosis which otherwise is recognizable only in the figure of Tiresias. Both represent poetic processes safeguarding the unity of the text.' From elemental reality we turn to social reality in Thomas Metscher's "Zum Wirklichkeitsbezug modernistischer Lyrik (am Beispiel T. S. Eliots)," *Englische und amerikanische Lyrik des 20. Jahrhunderts im weltliterarischen Kontext*, ed. Bruno Schrage (Rostock: Wilhelm-Pieck-Universität), pp. 36–45. Two classics, "The Love Song of J. Alfred Prufrock" and "The Waste Land," are chosen as paradigms of 'modernist poetry.' In these interpretations, the 'world-literary context' indicated in the title of this volume of collected essays is paid attention by way of brief references to Brecht, Neruda, Scottish poet MacDiarmid, and Anglo-Irish authors Yeats, Joyce, and Beckett. Of American contemporaries Pound ranks prominent. In analyzing the two poems from a Marxist standpoint, Metscher stresses Eliot's penetrating 'aesthetic perception' of the 'end' of 'the bourgeois age.' Eliot's Christian belief in salvation 'from above' is respected but considered to be responsible for 'the limits' of his 'grasp of reality achieved in his work.' The latter is held to separate him from the Marxist view of reality, while the former unites him to it as a 'humanist.'

Fiction studies focused on four customary subjects—Dreiser, Anderson, Faulkner, and Hemingway. Interest in Jewish-American writers continued as well. The appeal of William Carlos Williams as short-story writer and of Margaret Mitchell as novelist seems to be gradually increasing. Unabated curiosity about ethnic literary life prior to 1945 for the first time resulted in a fascinating inquiry into Slovak-American fiction. Dreiser scholarship yielded a useful commentary on international, mainly American, British, and German publications of the 1970s. Credit for it goes to Kurt Müller for his state-of-research report "Die Dreiserforschung der siebziger Jahre: Tendenzen und Perspektiven" (*Amst* 26:109–18). The multifaceted image of Dreiser that can be deduced from it is that of a 'representative of a determinist-naturalist world view,' an 'iconoclast' aiming at a 'cultural revolution,' a 'liberal believer in progress,' and a 'transcendental spiritualist.' New impulses are expected of psychoanalysis, social psychology, and epistemological sociology. Gratifyingly, Müller keeps putting into practice what he demands of previous researchers. "Identität und Rolle in Theodore Dreisers *Sister Carrie*, Teil II: Überanpassung und Anomie" (*LJGG* 22:209–39) continues an article reviewed in *ALS 1980*, 537–38. The first part focused on Hurstwood, the second examines Carrie Meeber. Once again are terminologies of the social sciences—social psychology, communication theory in general, and role theory in particular—drawn upon. Carrie is interpreted in terms like 'social identity,' 'discreditability,' 'impression manipulation,' 'personal facade,' 'other-directed,' 'identity diffusion,' and 'double loyalty.' Both the text and its 'biographical and historical substratum' are characterized by 'stigma,' 'social mobility,' and 'anomie.' 'The decline of Hurtswood and the social rise of Carrie on a symbolical-literary level put into a work of the imagination what David Riesman 50 years later put into a work of conceptual thought.' The presumed imaginative clairvoyance of Dreiser the creative artist and the presumed intellectual shortcomings of Dreiser the voice commenting on Carrie are juxtaposed. Their coexistence is a problem awaiting a solution. *Sister Carrie* finds a more traditional yet equally useful analyst in Rolf Högel. In "Chicago, 1880–1900: Seine Darstellung in Theodore Dreisers Roman *Sister Carrie*" (*Der fremdsprachliche Unterricht* 57:17–26) he aims 'to demonstrate the basic function of the big city for the shaping of a novel's setting as exemplified by Chicago's "cityscape" and *Sister Carrie*.' He differentiates an objective and a subjective component of the Chicago image presented in the novel. The objective one shows in '62 localities' and their names incorporated in the text as well as in Dreiser's substantial overlapping with five contemporary (1887–96) foreign, British, Italian, and French, visitors' selection of objects and data, and their reports on Chicagoans' attitude toward their city. Dreiser's subjectivity is found to appear in selections and omissions of his own. Linguistic objectivity, i.e., Dreiser's attitude toward regional, local, and social dialects, is not tested. On the whole, Anderson fares more conventionally than Dreiser. Peter Bischoff's "Zur Genese der modernen amerikanischen Short Story: Sherwood Anderson's 'I Want to Know Why'" (*ArAA* 6:261–71) reinterprets an often-analyzed minor classic. It acquires additional meaning by Bischoff's view of it as a fusion of two traditional trends, the story of initiation and an intentionally vernacular style. The author is understood 'to present, in the shape of the narrative, a poetological document of the modern American short story.' The claim is based on Anderson's "An Apology for Crudity." Jürgen Dierking in "Ein verdrängtes Dilemma: Sherwood Anderson (1876–1941)," *Gulliver* 9:66–80, outlines changes less of direction than of intensity of Anderson's political sympathies and actual engagement. Following them through the years 1913–22, 1923–29, and 1930–41, he stresses Anderson's 'function of chronicler of the machine age' in that he 'almost systematically recorded the impact of industrialization on various regions of the USA.' Williams turns up in Klaus Lubbers' "William Carlos Williams als Kurzgeschichtenautor" (*ZAL:A&E* 13:29–41). By way of genre it links up with Bischoff's and Dierking's articles. Placed in two 'concentric circles,' those of the 'situation of the American short story in the early 20th century' and of Williams' life experience, and, more especially, though connected with them, his conception of art, his short stories are represented by "The Use of Force." The autobiographical subject matter, the first-person-singular point of view, the 'reduction' of composition to a 'transcription of reality,' presentation by way of 'scene' or 'sketch,' dispensability of plot and of symbolization, miniaturization of temporal and spatial setting, and functionality of image, if any, are singled out as characteristics. The value Williams puts on 'intense vision of the facts' is seen to connect his short stories with his poetry.

Dieter Meindl's knowledgeable collaboration in the production of "Faulkner 1980: A Survey of Research and Criticism" (*MissQ* 34: 343–66), and a testimony to his independent judgment, "A Reappraisal of Margaret Mitchell's *Gone With the Wind* (ibid., pp. 414–34) should be mentioned but in passing. Both are easily available to American scholars. Hemingway could boast of three exclusive devotees. Werner Faulstich's and Hans-Werner Ludwig's "Hemingway: 'Alter Mann an der Brücke': Integrative Momente von Analysen, Rezeption und Interpretation," *Literaturwissenschaft und empirische Methoden*, ed. Helmut Kreuzer und Reinhold Viehoff, *Zeitschrift für Literaturwissenschaft und Linguistik, Beiheft* 12 (Göttingen: Vandenhoeck), pp. 226–43, uses Hemingway's "Old Man at the Bridge" as testing ground for their 'empiric method.' The elements of an original reportage and a later fiction version of the same material, which are still noticeable in the story, as well as the slight shift of perspective implied in the process of *reworking* are tested

as to their effect on reader reception and interpretation. Responses
of informants, exclusively university students, are tabulated. The
blending of reportage and fiction elements, branded by some critics
as aesthetic weakness, actually results in an increased reader incen-
tive to interpret the story as parabolic. Hudolf Haas's " 'God Bless
Tauchnitz': Some Observations on Hemingway's *Paris Sketches*"
(*Brumm Festschrift*, pp. 149–59), is the more incisive of the two
essays. As a contribution to this festschrift it too treats of history,
this time of "Hemingway's attitude towards history, politics, and culture in his formative European years after the First World War." Haas
finds that "the shortcomings and mannerisms of his fiction do show
indeed in even greater diagnostic clarity in the 'non-fiction' of his Paris
memoirs." He enumerates "the recurring reference to snob values,
the arranging of a second-hand infrastructure which is supposed to
impress the reader, the only too obtrusive insertion of foreign language items, the sardonic artifice of sophisticated irony." A relatively
new context in which to reconsider Hemingway's achievement is
provided by Wolfgang G. Müller in "Implizite Bewusstseinsdarstel-
lung im behavioristischen Roman der zwanziger und dreissiger
Jahre: Hammett, Chandler, Hemingway" (*Amst* 26:193–211). Müller claims not influence of J. B. Watson's behaviorism but 'com-
parability' between Watson's 'decidedness' in demanding 'elimina-
tion of states of consciousness as proper objects of investigation' and
the 'consistence with which the authors of *hard-boiled school* abandoned introspection,' i.e., presentation of figures as seen from within.
In this 'reductionist' view of figures in Hammett's *The Glass Key* and
The Maltese Falcon he discovers an 'essential agreement with Behaviorism's view of man.' Chandler's *The Lady in the Lake, The
Little Sister*, and *The High Window* are relied on to prove the 'modi-
fication' of Hammett's 'extremely behaviorist method.' Passages from
The Sun Also Rises and *A Farewell to Arms* are singled out to demonstrate Hemingway's suggestive omissions as indirect communications of states of mind. Müller's is a seminal essay. It calls for supplementary studies of affective epithets, imagery, and acts of memory
as indirect signals of such states.

   Twentieth-century growth of ethnic literatures is reflected in
Kurt Dittmar's "Jüdische Ghettoliteratur: Die Lower East Side,
1890–1924" (*Amst* 26:270–92). It organizes a mass of data around
three centers, (1) 'Jewish Ghetto Literature as Local Color Writ-

ing,' (2) 'Jewish Autobiographies,' (3) 'Tendentious Jewish Literature.' Around the first he assembles turn-of-the-century authors Isaac
Friedman, Herman Bernstein, and James Oppenheim, whose *Doctor
Rast* is analyzed at some length. For their 20th-century successor he
selects Konrad Bercovici. To the second center he relates the theme
of 'chances and risks of cultural change' as well as 'socio-economic
problems of Jewish ghetto life.' Predominantly women's autobiographies (Mary Antin's *The Promised Land* et al.) serve as illustrative examples. The third center of literary activity, the propaganda
novel, is documented by an even broader spectrum. It ranges from
affirmation of American values to Zionism. Ideational content is of
greater importance to Dittmar than is acculturation of literary form.
Although on a smaller scale, that of merely one ethnic author, this
holds good, too, for Gisela Birnbaum's "Eine Stimme aus dem
slowakischen Stahlarbeiter-Getto in Pennsylvanien: Thomas Bell"
(*Amst* 26:293–304). In the socioeconomic context of Braddock, Pennsylvania, and its steel industry the first Slovak-American novelist's
career is outlined by a brief examination of Bell's *The Second Prince*
(1935) and *All Brides Are Beautiful* (1936). Closer inspection is
accorded *Out of This Furnace* (1941). 'Progress of the Generations,'
'The World of the Industrial Workers,' 'Labor and Society,' 'Ethnic
World and Working Class,' 'America and Americans' form the themes
of observation. The process of integration is brought out clearly in
this pilot study.

a-3. General and Fiction since 1945. It is characteristic of this year's
activities that they did not produce an overview of the whole period
nor of all of its literary genres. Only one of them, drama, was surveyed as a whole in a volume of collected essays from several hands.
More symptomatic still, one author alone, novelist Saul Bellow, had
a book-length monograph devoted to him. A monograph on Kerouac
escaped this chronicler's attention last year and will be included here.
It took the cooperation of several scholars to bring together a volume
of collected essays on Thomas Pynchon. The post-1945 novel kept
staying in the foreground. The energy of periodical contributors was
spread across a wide area. It comprises authors born in the 1910s
like Bellow, his colleagues of the 1920s such as Mailer, as well as
later talents, especially postmodernists. Nabokov, more than a decade
older than Bellow, but like him beginning his literary career in the

early 1940s, will be discussed first. In "Nabokovs Kritik an der Stream-of-consciousness-technique" (*ZAL:A&E* 13:71–81) H. H. Müller explores a stylistic feature, the pun, its frequency, function, and affinity to other word games which make use of association, e.g., the anagram. Müller's eye for its increasing frequency in the international modern novel (Proust, Joyce, Arno Schmidt) gives the essay a comparatistic touch. Taking *Ada or Ardor* as example, he discovers whole 'chains' of puns. They function structurally not only as leitmotifs but also as 'textures' composed of them and support character presentation by serving as indices to their state of consciousness. The way characters react to them serves the same purpose. Saul Bellow is the subject of Hubert Zapf's monograph *Der Roman als Medium der Reflexion*, EurH 14,lxxxviii (Lang) as well as of Rolf Högel's essay "Gegenwart und Vergangenheit: ihre synchronische Darstellung in Saul Bellows Roman *Herzog*" (*LWU* 14:103–15). Both intersect when discussing the function of reflection in the presentation of Bellow's figures and narrative voice. They overlap in that both are based inclusively or exclusively on *Herzog*. Zapf extends this common basis by adding *Augie March* and *Humboldt's Gift*. Supported by a theory of reflection and of its reactions to the concepts of individual identity, intersubjectivity, and interaction, Zapf interprets *Augie March* as model of reflection on a 'broken individual identity.' *Herzog* furnishes a similar model as to a 'broken intersubjectivity,' with *Humboldt's Gift* playing the same role as for 'broken interaction.' Zapf considers each of these novels as corresponding to dominant 'directions of intellectual attention' in the America of the 1950s, 1960s, and 1970s. With Högel the present as subject of reflection is studied in its presentation synchronous with that of the past. He is aware that the total past as remembered by Herzog covers 'the general history of, predominantly Western, civilization of the last 2500 years.' He confines himself, however, to arranging 'the fragments of [Herzog's] past recollected' in seven 'complexes of events and persons from around 1890 to the first of June 1964.' He observes that 'the linguistic assimilation of recollected consciousness contents to the linguistic form of events occurring in the narrative present contradicts strictly realistic principles of composition,' but, according to him, it helps clarify the novel's basic conception, i.e., 'the ultimate unity of past and present.'

Not the ideational substance of post-1945 novels but the process of their creation and the criteria guiding that process are of supreme interest to the authors of the following publications. This shift of interest determines Gabriele Spengemann's 615-page *Jack Kerouac's Spontaneous Prose*, Kasseler Arbeiten zur Sprache und Literatur 6 (Lang, 1980). It combines an overview of Kerouac's critical reception with an analysis of his theory and a meticulous comparison of his practice in the two major novels which are thought to reflect his "modern prose" theory most distinctly. "Affinities" as well as "discrepancies" between the practice and the postulates laid down in Kerouac's "Essentials of Spontaneous Prose" are investigated and summed up. *Visions of Cody* is found to be more in keeping with the theory than *On the Road*.

Of the postmodernists, Barthelme, Pynchon, and Donleavy met with varying critical receptivity. Eberhard Kreutzer's "City Spectacles as Artistic Acts: Donald Barthelme's 'The Balloon' and 'The Glass Mountain' " (*ZAL:A&E* 13:43–56) excels in a detailed explication of two "paraboloid" stories laying bare and satirizing "the interaction between the artist, his work (in progress), and society" as recipient of art. Key features of the two stories are related to other pieces of Barthelme's fiction and with his poetics in general. The light the essay throws on Barthelme's connections with New York authors Koch and Ashbery, with Joyce and Poe, and on Barthelme's advocacy of "the innovative continuity of exchange between the arts" is particularly rewarding. Pynchon is the topic of *Ordnung und Entropie: Zum Romanwerk von Thomas Pynchon*, ed. and introd. by Heinz Ickstadt (Reinbek: Rowohlt). It collects 12 essays by seven American and British, and four German authors. All of these essays except one reprint articles, parts of monographs, or contributions to collections. Hence practically all of them were reviewed in earlier volumes of *ALS*. Some are more or less substantially modified. The one by Klaus Poenicke overlaps with a later version, though printed prior to the tardy publication of Ickstadt's well-organized volume. Its American and British essays have been rendered into German. Thus the general reader can gain insight into the trinational approach to a contemporary American writer whose ideas are even more provocative than his formal devices. Ickstadt's introduction, written in 1979, conveniently starts from the discrepancy between the German reading public's relative unfamiliarity with Pynchon's work and its author's 'apparent fascination, nay ob-

session with Germany and her recent history.' Tentatively he defines
Pynchon's development from *V.* to *Gravity's Rainbow* as a movement
from a 'playful and noncommitted systematization of a progressing
decay of meaning in *V.* to a growing identification with the waste of
the system, the mass of unheeded things and human beings.' Manfred Pütz, represented in Ickstadt's collection, is also met with
in Richard Pearce's *Critical Essays on Thomas Pynchon* (Hall).
The volume reprints "Science as Metaphor: Thomas Pynchon and
Gravity's Rainbow," an essay written together with Alan Friedman
and reviewed in *ALS 1974, 443.* Donleavy has a question shot at him
in Hartmut Heuermann's "Typisch amerikanisch? Zum literaturwis-
senschftlichen Problem der Nationaltypik am Beispiel von J. P. Donleavy's 'At Longitude and Latitude' " (*LWU* 13:43–56). Heuermann
cautiously reapproaches an old problem baffling outsiders rather than
insiders, to wit, whether there exist literary works that are 'typically
American.' The 'conflict of individual vs. society' is thought to be
more frequent and more intense in American literature than it is in
others. This answer is less convincing than the thorough comparison
of Donleavy's satiric parable with Defoe's *Robinson Crusoe.*

Norman Mailer figures last because unlike all the other post-1945
fiction writers he is approached not along literary but linguistic lines.
Helmut Markus' "Plädoyer für einen Roman: Die Revision eines
Übersetzungsprozesses," (*ZAL:A&E* 13:164–81) pleads for a revised
rendering of *The Naked and the Dead* on grounds of the first translation's shortcomings, some of them so severe that the novelist's
intended meaning got distorted.

a-4. **Drama and Poetry since 1945.** The post-1945 dramatists and
poets have fared less well than the fiction writers. *Contemporary
Drama* assembles 11 American and five German papers. An appended 30-page bibliography is also due to an American compiler.
The German contributions confine themselves to best-known playwrights like Tennessee Williams and Arthur Miller, besides to some
who have made a name for themselves more recently, e.g., Arthur
Kopit, Ed Bullins, Luis Valdez. The collection as a whole wants to
furnish "a useful introduction to the playwrights and dramas of the
United States during the last twenty years." Methods of introduction
vary from informative survey (Bock, "Tennessee Williams: Southern

Playwright," pp. 5–17), elaboration of an "integrated whole," i.e., the individual plays functioning as "variations on the theme of dream and nightmare resulting from identity crises" (Jürgen Wolter, "Arthur Kopit: Dreams and Nightmares," pp. 55–74), to analytical probing and sober assessment (Peter Bruck, "Ed Bullins: The Quest and Failure of an Ethnic Community Theatre," pp. 123–40). Werner Sollors' essay on another black American, "Amiri Baraka (LeRoi Jones)," needs no comment since it includes a part reprinted from the author's well-received 1978 monograph on Baraka (ALS 1978, 401–02). Dieter Herms, whose many essays on Chicano theatre were also reviewed in earlier volumes of ALS, returns to his favorite subject in "Louis Valdez, Chicano Dramatist: An Introduction and an Interview" (pp. 257–78). The interview was conducted on 14 December 1978 but is still of documentary interest. It takes in a programmatic forecast on Valdez' plans of production and organization, only parts of which have materialized in the meantime.

Poetry research did not focus on individual American poets but on a near-contemporary trend, the development from the seventh to the eighth decade. It also concentrated on 'poetry for songs' as a modern mass phenomenon. Reinhold Schiffer's "From the Sixties into the Seventies: Themes and Modes in American Poetry" (ZAL: A&E 13:9–28) renders a reliable account with an expertise rare among younger scholars. His forte, personal acquaintance with many, especially California, poets, shows to advantage in a comparison of tendencies characteristic of the 1960s and 1970s. The growing intensity of the 'natural life' impulse and the extension of ethnic-minority poetry so as to include the native American brand receive special emphasis. Gary Snyder, Simon J. Oritz, Jerome Rothenberg, Michael McClure, and Anne Waldman figure as advocates of "primitive consciousness." The American song as a species blending poetry and music, in its varieties of rock, pop, beat, country, and western, has grown so attractive to Germans that Amerikastudien saw fit to publish a detailed synopsis by way of a state-of-research report. Christoph Bode's "Neuere Publikationen zur Rock-Lyrik und Rock-Musik" (Amst 26:367–77) is a model of its kind, geared to the 1970s but retrospective enough to encompass the tradition of the popular song.

b. **Literary Criticism and Theory: Comparative Studies.** Just as in 1980, attention to literary criticism and theory was scanty whereas the appeal of comparative studies kept growing to such an extent that selection is more imperative than ever. Among the publications of the former group, two monographs and two articles stand out. In *Psychoanalytische Literaturkritik: Eine Untersuchung am Beispiel der amerikanischen Zeitschrift "Literatur und Psychologie"* (EurH 14,xcii) Waltraut Achten makes use of an American periodical to gain an insight "into what psychoanalytical criticism can and, perhaps, cannot achieve." Achten does not gloss over the 'almost exclusive' attention to 'content and meaning of literature' in psychoanalytical criticism but sees 'signs that by applying the concept of form as defense,' formal features 'need no longer be excluded.' To the student of American literature the periodical's essays on Hawthorne, Twain, Henry James, Fitzgerald, O'Neill, and Plath together with Achten's comments will be of special interest. Due to its inclusion of many non-American authors, this study has a conspicuous comparatist aspect. The same quality is even more prominent in Susanne Schröder's *Komparatistik und Ideengeschichte: 'History of Ideas' und Geistesgeschichte in ihrem Einfluss auf die internationale Komparatistik* (EurH 18,xxvii). The book bears on American literary theory and criticism in that it embraces the impact of an American school of thought, founded by A. O. Lovejoy, and of its interrelations with French and German literary scholarship in fields including American literature. Of exclusively American scope, yet like Schröder's monograph concerned with the theory of literary historiography, is Franz H. Link's "Theorien zur Geschichte der amerikanischen Verskunst" (*LJGG* 22:361–81). Restricting itself to the historiography of the lyrical genre, it renders a refreshingly critical account of theories trying to track and explain the Americanness in the history of American poetry. Link follows the formation of such theories from E. C. Stedman through Bernard Duffey. Aside from their exclusive studies he draws on inclusive ones by James E. Miller and Harold Bloom. Link shares Bloom's and David Porter's conviction of Emerson's significance but regrets that 'the historic development' evidencing it has not yet received an objective presentation. Literary theory and comparative literary studies intersect again in a study that limits itself to a formal aspect of fiction. Manfred Smuda's sophisticated "Deskriptionsmodalitäten und ihre Funktion im ameri-

kanischen und englischen Roman" (*Poetica* 12[1980]:377–96) appeared too late for inclusion in the 1980 chronicle. Smuda's theory
of literary description is indebted to Husserl's phenomenology and
Ingarden's poetics, related in its turn to Husserl. As for the theory
of narrative discourse, its links with Barthes and Ricardou are explicit. The changing proportion of description and narration in fiction and, in particular, the changing functions of description in their
mutual relationship are worked out neatly. Poe's "The Domain of
Arnheim," *The Narrative of Arthur Gordon Pym*, and "MS. Found
in a Bottle," Cooper's *The Prairie*, Norris' *MacTeague*, and James's
The Portrait of a Lady and *The Ambassadors* serve for illustration.

Comparative studies properly place American literature in greatly
varying contexts. The field is weak in multinational research pursued
historically, but strong in bi- or tri-national exploration of genres,
motifs, and sources. American-British and American-German literary
relations are in the foreground. The most comprehensive venture,
*Theatrum Mundi: Götter, Gott und Spielleiter im Drama von der
Antike bis zur Gegenwart*, a 'special volume' of *LJGG*, ed. Franz Link
and Günter Niggl (Berlin: Duncker & Humblot), opens with "Götter, Gott und Spielleiter," a synopsis by Link. It extends from Greek
antiquity to the 20th century. The "Living Theatre" concept, and
plays by O'Neill, Eliot, Wilder, MacLeish, Williams, and Miller
illustrate Link's systematic and historical survey of emergence, sub-
mergence, transmutation, and revival of an international topos. The
time span from antiquity to the present is also overviewed in Alfred
Hornung's "Sex and Art in Hawkes' Triad: The Pornographic, the
Erotic, and the Aesthetic Modes" (*Amst* 26:159–79). The topic seems
to be restricted to a postmodern novelist. In fact, however, the relations of sex and art as developed in Europe and America over the
centuries establish a background which started with Plato. "Eros
and Imagination," "Sex and Imagination in Modern Literature
(Joyce, Lawrence, Henry Miller, Nabokov)," and "John Hawkes'
Triad" make up the three sections of the essay. *The Blood Oranges,
Death, Sleep & the Traveler*, and *Travesty* are interpreted as a
paradigm each of "the erotic," "the pornographic," and "the aesthetic mode" of coming to terms with sex in the literatures of Western civilization. Greco-Roman antiquity, although to a smaller extent, yet with roots in myth and fairy tale, and with ramifications
in medieval romances of chivalry is at the basis of Dieter Schulz's

Suche und Abenteuer, Reihe Siegen: Beiträge zur Literatur- und Sprachwissenschaft 25 (Heidelberg: Winter). As indicated in the monograph's subtitle, "Die 'Quest' in der englischen und amerikanischen Erzählkunst der Romantik," the quest, a concept much discussed during the last two decades, is examined as a structural pattern. Schulz applies it to the romantic period in British and American literatures. Of American works Brown's *Arthur Mervyn*, *Edgar Huntly*, and the fragment "Somnambulism" are interpreted as examples of the quest in the Gothic novel. Cooper's *The Prairie* and Poe's *The Narrative of Arthur Gordon Pym* have one chapter each allotted to them. Another is given to Hawthorne's "Roger Malvin's Burial," "My Kinsman, Major Molineux," grouped together as 'Adventures of the Young Man,' while "The Great Carbuncle" and "Ethan Brand" figure under the common denominator 'Search for Happiness and Idealism.' *The Blithedale Romance* exemplifies 'The Utopian Quest.' Melville's *Moby-Dick* and *Pierre* are analyzed in the last, unlabeled, chapter. Continuity, transformation, and dissolution of the classic quest structure are followed through various phases. Their study skillfully synthesizes previous research and intelligently extends it to a whole literary period along lines of both impact and comparison. Tying in with Link's introductory essay, but sketching in the antique background less firmly because of its restriction to 20th-century British and American drama, Paul Goetsch's "Theatrum Mundi: Varianten im modernen anglo-amerikanischen Drama" (*Theatrum Mundi*, pp. 305–45) distinguishes five uses of the topos. As far as American dramatists are involved, they and their plays will be added in parentheses and in the order of reference: (1) 'Theatrum mundi and Christian History of Man's Salvation' (Connelly, Eliot), (2) 'Theatrum mundi as an Expression of Belief in Life' (O'Neill, Wilder), (3) 'Plays about the Insufficiency of the Gods' (MacLeish, Miller, Albee), (4) 'Theatrum Mundi: The World as a Cage in the Drama of the Absurd' (Williams), (5) 'Theatrum Mundi and the Transformation of Society' (Van Itallie, Gelber, Paul Green, Irwin Shaw, Odets). Goetsch stresses the provocativeness and malleability of the topos as stimuli for its use by modern authors. He notices its 'affinity to the epic and the absurd drama as well as to genres like poetic, religious, comical, and historical drama.'

The comparative vista shrinks from an international topos and its productivity in Britain and America to a literary genre of more recent origin, though also productive in the literature of the two countries. Ina Schabert's *Der historische Roman in England und Amerika* (Darmstadt: Wissenschaftliche Buchgesellschaft) compares British and American research of the historical novel. References to American specimens abound. They accumulate in certain sections of this well-organized monograph, e.g., in 'Fictionalization of American History and Contemporary Literature Before Cooper.' Schabert's comments on the scholarly handling of fiction about the Civil War are of particular value.

The category of source-based research of literary influence has a sound representative in Renate Schmidt-von Bardeleben's essay "Bernard Malamuds 'The Lady of the Lake': Jüdisch-amerikanische Selbstdarstellung und Britisch-englische Literaturtradition," (*Schulze Festschrift*, pp. 257–71). Results will astonish even Malamud experts. After relating the story to mainstream and ethnic minority, American-Jewish, literatures and revealing its structure as that of a 'surprise story' thematizing the self-awareness of Jewish-Americans, she explores its genesis. In this story with its Italian, Lago Maggiore, setting she unravels a network of references to Scott's verse tale of the same title. They concern subject matter, themes, motifs, and structure. Cogent reasons for Malamud's productive reception of Scott, and his *Lady of the Lake* in particular, are advanced.

Studies of American-German literary relations flourished in 1981. Hans Galinsky's "Amerikanische Dichter und amerikanisches Englisch in und aus Rheinland-Pfalz," *Universität im Rathaus*, ed. The President, Johannes Gutenberg Universität (Mainz: Universitäts-Pressestelle), vol. 1, tests the value of a regional approach toward American-German relations in literature and language. As for the former, he describes the 'take-and-give' of a region which established early Reformed Church contacts with Old and New England puritanism and was the home of most of the Pennsylvania Germans. He distinguishes the American author mediated by regional German translator (John Cotton, Maxwell Anderson, and Laurence Stallings), the American author-traveler responding creatively to the region (Jefferson, Irving, Cooper, Longfellow, Melville, Thomas Wolfe), the author traveling on the wings of fancy (Poe) on the one hand, on the other Rhineland-Palatine immigrants' contributions to American literature, direct ones like Mennonite hymns, indirect ones, i.e., mediated by oral tales about home, and handed on to Anglo- and

German-American writers (Cooper, Dreiser). Franz Schüppen's
*Charles Sealsfield/Karl Postl: Ein österreichischer Erzähler der Bie-
dermeierzeit im Spannungsfeld von Alter und Neuer Welt* (EurH, ser
1, vol. 428), a 533-page book, marks a breakthrough in Sealsfield research. Here for the first time is available a comprehensive combination of biography, analytical and historical interpretation of the
works and the literary estate, reception (though incomplete), image
of America and Europe, as well as critical assessment. Schüppen
views the whole work, its English- and German-written pieces, as
a product of "Biedermeier" times, the transitional period between
romanticism and realism. Of special appeal to Americanists will be
his first attempt, "The foundling maid," and reassessments of *Tokeah
or the White Rose*, of the immigrant's observations on American politics, history, and society, of his contacts with Cooper and the young
literature of the West, and of what Schüppen calls his 'harmoniza-
tion of American problems.' The imagological aspect, i.e., the image
of a foreign country in the literature of another, is taken up again
in Hans-Joachim Lang's "Ferdinand Kürnberger One Hundred Years
Later," *The Harold Jantz Collection: Proceedings of a Conference to
Introduce the Collection to Specialists in German-American Literary
Relations*, ed. Leland R. Phelps (Duke University: Center for International Studies), pp. 51–70. The "renewed vitality" of the Austrian
author's novel *Der Amerikamüde* (1855) is thought to be due to its
being "too good a piece of anti-Americanism to lose," and to its (immense) symptomatic value for German-American relations. The two
interconnected values are demonstrated by a penetrating analysis
of the book and its, as yet known, sources. Especially helpful is Lang's
statement that "Kürnberger writes on two different planes, a lower
plane of sensational debunking literature and a higher plane of philosophical speculation." To apply an already quoted phrase of the
author's, this essay is "too good a piece" of Germany's American literature scholarship "to lose" in the future. Another contribution to
the same conference proceedings (pp. 71–91), Hans Galinsky's "The
Current State of German-American Studies in Germany: Resources
and Research," presents an amply documented survey. As to resources, it embraces source materials, planned collecting activities,
and collections in research libraries as well as diversified research
bibliographies. The survey follows research across three areas: the
German reception of American literature, that literature's influence

on German authors, and America's image in German literature. Translation activities are included sub reproductive reception. Data of 1970–71 and 1977–78 are set side by side so as to allow trends to emerge.

One encounters only one study which deals with a trinational, American-German-Japanese relationship. Another places works of American literature in a frame of seven foreign literatures. Both of these demanding projects were accomplished by women scholars. Gudrun Grabher's *Emily Dickinson: Das transzendentale Ich*, AF 157 (Heidelberg: Winter) aims (1) to use German transcendental philosophy's concept of "the transcendental subject constituting his world" for a 'basis' on which to interpret the first-person-singular in Dickinson's poetry, (2) to define, 'in the framework of American-transcendentalism,' her 'place in the tradition of American literary history,' (3) to make her 'transcendental I,' in the context of East Asian philosophy, a starting point for a theory of lyrical poetry. The first two aims have been achieved. Judgment on the achievement of the third will have to be passed by experts on Zen-Buddhism and Matsue Bashô's haikus, which Grabher adduced for comparison. A trinational frame of reference is maintained as the hard core of her monograph but extended in Reingard M. Nischik's *Einsträngigkeit und Mehrsträngigkeit der Handlungsführung in literarischen Texten*, TBA 1 (Tübingen: Narr). This core consists of 19 American together with 20 British and 13 Canadian texts. Of more peripheral significance are Australian, French, German, Italian, and Russian specimens, narrative and dramatic. Narrative ones predominate in this selection of texts from the 13th through the 20th century. They provide the material to which Nischik applies her models of single and multiple plotting in both literary genres. The models rest on 'character,' 'place,' and 'time' as 'fundamental variables,' with 'extension,' 'arrangement,' 'theme,' 'point of view,' and 'narrative technique' as 'associated variables.' Her theory and terminology are arrived at after a comprehensive investigation of works of literary theory and criticism as well as of dictionaries of literary terms. Americanists will profit from her analyses, in terms of her models, of Jack Ludwig's *A Woman of Her Age* in part 3, of Faulkner's *The Wild Palms*, Kosinski's *Steps*, Wilder's *The Bridge of San Luis Rey*, and Hailey's *Airport*. Her systematic effort results in a more subtle and more consistent differentiation of terms. It could help unify a confusing international terminology. By relating American literature to other literatures of the world, these comparative and influence studies complement its image as mirrored in the scholarship, both traditional and innovative, in German-speaking countries of 1981.

Johannes Gutenberg Universität, Mainz

iii. Italian Contributions

Gaetano Prampolini

This report will briefly discuss or simply mention 13 items in book form and 38 shorter ones as compared to the 10 and 50, respectively, included in the report for *ALS 1980*. The year 1981 shows therefore no remarkable quantitative shift in the output of Italian Americanists. Nor does there appear to be any sensible change in quality. Two important publishing events concur, however, in giving the year a special distinctiveness. One is the inception of *RSA—Rivista di studi anglo-americani* (Brescia: Paideia), the long-awaited annual of the AISNA (Italian Association for North-American Studies), which will alternate issues containing the proceedings of the conferences of the association with issues composed of review-articles, positioning essays on wide-ranging or interdisciplinary themes, checklists, and bibliographies. The other is the appearance of the first volume of *Novecento americano* (Roma: Lucarini). Neither an encyclopedia proper nor a literary history, this work, which is directed by Elémire Zolla and planned in three volumes, aims to offer a panoramic view of the American literary culture of our century in 150 short monographs, each 15 to 20 pages long. Most of these monographs will deal with individual figures according to a set pattern (biographical sketch, analysis and critical reception of the works, extensive, up-to-date bibliographies of both primary and secondary sources). A good many, however, will be dedicated to particular aspects, genres, movements, etc. Thus, the volume already in print (which is actually the third in the whole plan) includes 42 entries on prominent writers born between 1919 and 1938 (of whom a few are not strictly literary figures, such as Barrington Moore, Jr., Noam Chomsky, Scott Buchanan), plus eight entries on such topics as the New Criticism, the Chicago School, the experimental theatre of the 1970s, contemporary Native American fiction, Chicano literature, poetic anthropology, popular fiction, and science fiction. What one is convinced of, after sampling its 767 pages, is that the choice of the materials, even though a bit idiosyncratic, is certainly shrewd and the contributors' performances—covering the whole spectrum from informative compilation to innovative interpretation—attain, almost without exception, a remarkably high level of quality. *Novecento americano* therefore may easily establish itself and remain for a long time a most serviceable tool for scholars and students alike. Our summary characterization of the year's work may end with an indication of general trends: (1) a relatively larger than usual part of the shorter contributions consists of introductions to new (or old) translations of works of poetry or fiction; (2) fiction, especially from the rise of realism to the present, and 20th-century poetry, are the fields that have received most attention; (3) among major writers Henry James gets the crown as the most studied (Melville and Pound being the runners-up). Finally, a fourth trend, which strikes one as an interesting and unusual feature, is the gravitating of a considerable number of studies toward three broad thematic areas. It is with these that we propose to concern ourselves in the first part of our report.

The first of them, one embracing contributions of markedly different kinds, may be given the generic heading of "Cultural Relationships between Italy and the United States." "American Literature in Post-War Italy" was the theme of a conference held in Bologna in 1978. The two papers presented there are now collected in *L'America e la cultura italiana* (Quaderni Ist. di Studi Nordamericani di Bologna, no. 3, Bologna: CLUEB). One (pp. 7–39), by Agostino Lombardo, has the same title as that of the whole pamphlet and follows out the whole course of the fortunes of American literature in Italy. Of the many points made in this limpid and insightful survey three at least deserve mention here: (1) the constant interest taken by Italian intellectuals in American literature has never been of a merely aesthetic nature but always a part of a wider and very keen interest in the whole of American experience in its exemplary uniqueness; (2) American literature, either because of its supposed "primitivism" and "spontaneity" or because of its democratic inspiration, was viewed and prized for a long time as an "antidote" to the excessive refinement and academism of Italian letters or to the moral and intellectual stagnation fostered by fascism; (3) after the moment

of enthusiastic discovery the postwar period has been one of medi-
tated reassessments and systematic study through which the knowledge of American literature in Italy has greatly progressed both in
width and depth. The other paper, Claudio Gorlier's well-informed
"La situazione del romanzo americano in Italia" (pp. 41–54), deals
primarily with the penetration of the American novel into postwar
Italy and shows with an array of cases in point how the choice of the
works to be translated has depended more on the publishers' often
desultory decisions and on the reviewers' too often uninformed (or
politically biased) reactions than on the specialists' scholarly expertise. "Influences," however, trace a two-way path between the two
literatures, as can be seen from two essays sharing a comparative
approach: Carla Apollonio's "La presenza di E. A. Poe in alcuni
scapigliati lombardi" (*Otto/Novecento* 5,i:107–43) and Ghan S.
Singh's "Melville and Leonardi" (*RLMC* 33,i[1980]:23–37). The
several scholars who in the past 20 years have investigated Poe's
influence on the *scapigliati* (for one of the latest efforts cf. *ALS
1980*, 576) have come to the conclusion that whatever knowledge
this Milan-based, mid-19th-century group of minor writers, occupy-
ing a middle ground between Romanticismo and *decadentismo*, had
of Poe, they must have acquired it through the French mediation of
Baudelaire's essays and translations. Apollonio confirms this and proceeds to a systematic reconnoitering of Poe's presence in the writings
of three *scapigliati*: scarce and rather vague in Emilio Praga and
Arrigo Boito, the traces of it are instead pervasive (although not always easy to distinguish from those left by other writers) in Iginio
Ugo Tarchetti, who in his stories and poems freely combines and
modifies themes, situations, and characters typical of Poe in his gothic
and most morbid vein but also in his less frequent satirical and
humoristic spells. Giacomo Leopardi (who is mentioned twice in
Clarel) in his turn may well have been a source of inspiration for
Melville's writing *The Confidence-Man*. This presents no textual evidence of the fact, but—as Singh's essay deftly shows—there is indeed
a striking affinity in the ethical pessimism and philosophical skepticism voiced by the Italian writer especially in hs *Pensieri* and
Operette morali and by the American in his satirical romance. As
experience in life and source of inspiration, Italy was very important
for both William Dean Howells and Francis Marion Crawford. In
his introduction to his own version of *Indian Summer*, the second of

Howells' novels ever translated into Italian (*L'estate di San Martino*, Pisa: Nistri-Lischi), Giuseppe Gadda Conti avails himself of his specialist's knowledge to provide a well-paced, informative, and sober account of Howells' intellectual and literary career. As to the novel, he points out the antiromanticism of its central theme and the sympathetic, penetrating depiction of Italian reality. In "Francis Marion Crawford, cittadino di Bagni di Lucca" (*Rassegna lucchese* 8:19–24) the late Rolando Anzilotti gives an equitable and elegant appraisal of the work and ideas of this prolific writer who—born in Tuscany, reared in Rome, and spending a great deal of his time in Sorrento—found in Italy not only the country of his heart but the ideal setting for so many of his best-selling romances. The literature of the Italian-Americans, finally, is the object of three interesting studies which have appeared in an issue of *Letterature d'America* (2,ix–x) dedicated to "The Italians' America." Of substantial methodological value for the study of immigrant autobiography, William Boelhower's "A Shadow in the Garden" (pp. 81–108) presents a fine structural analysis of *Soul of an Immigrant* (1921), the autobiography Constantine Panunzio wrote in a period of strong nativist feelings to prove that the new immigrant (the South-Italian, in particular) could successfully fit into American life. The "divided self" that emerges from the discrepancy between the real experience of the protagonist and the rhetorical stance of the narrator (one of the few who "have made it" in the New World) is the element, Boelhower affirms, by which immigrant autobiography enlarges but also undermines the traditional typology of American autobiography. In "Le tentazioni di Calibano: Emanuel Carnevali e il rinascimento poetico americano" (pp. 173–215) Caterina Ricciardi reconstructs Carnevali's itinerary through the poetic circles of New York and Chicago and, by attentively reading his *Autobiography*, critical writings, and correspondence with the Florentine writer Giovanni Papini, shows how his attitude toward American poetry and culture began to change from enthusiasm to an ever-growing dissatisfaction after his discovery, in 1918, of the works of Papini himself and the Italian poets of *La Voce*. It was from these that he shaped that notion of "modernity" as the expression in common language of the tragic commonplace of life on the basis of which he violently criticized such poets as Pound, Aiken, and William C. Williams for what he thought to be their too exclusive and sterile cult of technique. Ricciardi's essay makes it also clear what a pivotal figure Whitman was for Carnevali: his personality largely inspired Carnevali's autobiographical myth of the "Godlike poet"; his poetry greatly influenced the latter's verse and provided him a critical touchstone by which he could extol Sandburg as the only true American poet of the period. Whitman figures also as the major American influence on the verse of union leader and poet Arturo Giovannitti, whose years of most intense militant and literary activity in pre-World-War-I America receive sympathetic attention in Biancamaria Tedeschini Lalli's "La meta-poesia di Arturo Giovannitti" (pp. 43–79). Italian culture and American culture, middle-class extraction and working-class allegiance, art and politics are some of the dualities which coexist and are mediated in Giovannitti—and which are all epitomized, the author concludes, in his writing both in English and Italian and translating his own poems from one language into the other (hence the "metapoetic" aspect alluded to in the title of her essay). While an informative, though somewhat eulogistic, account of Giovannitti's multifaceted personality is offered by Renato Lalli's *Arturo Giovannitti* (Campobasso: Editoriale Rufus), which also contains generous excerpts from his works in Italian, his verse—along with Joe Hill's and Ralph Chaplin's—is briefly discussed in Daniela Ciani's "La poesia proletaria negli Stati Uniti: 1900–1920" (*RSA* 1:229–41), a rather hastily written survey of the poetry born in the climate of the struggles of the Industrial Workers of the World.

The poetry of these three militant "wobblies" is one of the topics Mario Maffi regrets not having been able to treat in his *La giungla e il grattacielo: Gli scrittori e il sogno americano, 1865–1920* (Bari: Laterza). But with this book we have come to the second of our thematic areas—one that may be conveniently named "Aspects and Problems of Realism in Fiction." Maffi's concern is with fiction that deals with the working class in the period between the end of the Civil War and the end of World War I. That industrial cities, industrial labor, and class struggle were realities no longer alien to America was something that did not dawn on writers until the 1880s (with the exception of Rebecca Harding Davis, whose *Life in the Iron Mills* had appeared in 1861). A full realization of those grim but irreversible realities is, however, evident by 1890 in Howells' *Hazard of New Fortunes*, which the author singles out, along with Thomas B. Aldrich's *Stillwater Tragedy* and John Hay's *Bread-Winners*, to illustrate the early phase of that ever more serious interest in the workers' living conditions and struggles which was to become so conspicuous in the literature of the Progressive Era. Its recurrent themes as well as the range of the writers' attitudes toward the working class (varying from enthusiastic sympathy to rabid hostility) are sampled in the second section of the volume where Maffi pauses to consider more closely some individual figures and works. Although neither very original nor profound, his book—written in a spirit of personal involvement and with journalistic verve—is not without merits. It clearly condenses and deftly coordinates the considerable amount of work that has accumulated on this subject and related ones (and with which Maffi is wholly conversant, as is witnessed by his detailed bibliography); it also brings to the attention of the Italian reader the achievement of neglected or little-known interesting writers such as Upton Sinclair, Ernest Poole, and John Reed, who are the objects of three of its best chapters.

Franca Bernabei's *La teoria del romanzo americano e la lezione francese (1865–1900)* (Brescia: Paideia) is instead the fruit of first-hand, careful research. Well-documented (at times overly-documented) and solidly reasoned, it studies the reception of 19th-century French fiction writers (from George Sand and Hugo to Zola and Maupassant) in the major American journals of the period where articles and reviews appeared by a group with James and Howells as its spearheads but including also T. S. Perry, C. L. Lathrop, Sophia Kirk, and many other less-known or anonymous critics. What unites and motivates them is the attempt to define the form and function of the "coming great American novel" which would express the new postwar reality. The pattern of their response comprises, on the one hand, attraction, even admiration, for the literary qualities and the experimental/theoretical thrust of the French writers but, on the other, repugnance for the use of what they considered morally corrupting and socially destabilizing subjects and for the writers' "amoral" indifference toward their materials. Nor could they understand the radical breach between the French writers' artistic preoccupations and those of the society for which they "should" have been spokesmen. The late and by no means total acceptance of Balzac, Flaubert, and Zola occurs only insofar as their works comply with the values and the "narrative model" implicit in the American critics' judgments. In her conclusion, which owes its conceptual framework and terminology to Jurij Lotman, the author speaks of a confrontation between two "cultural typologies": the American typology proves unable to relate to the French except on its own rigid terms, where the Puritan heritage and an idealistic, unhistorical conception of the relationship between art and reality combine with a proud belief in the superiority of the American Way of Life and the conviction that it is the fiction writer's task to present it in all its specificity. Bernabei's study offers a new, enlightening approach to the poetics of realism but is also interesting in that it makes us aware of the underlying continuity between James's theory of fiction and the cultural background from which he never wholly detached himself.

In *Caratteri esclusivi: Saggi sull'identitá letteraria anglo-americana* (Pisa: ETS) Francesco Binni has collected the essays on English and American literature he had published from 1965 to 1977. From the author's preface it appears that the concept of "identity" —or, more precisely, the critique of what is widely thought of today as the vanishing identity, "the loss of the self"—is a central concern of these studies. This is certainly so in one of the two essays on postmodern literature in which Binni criticizes John Barth's work as a nihilistic evasion of reality and Barth's idea of a "literature of exhaustion" as a sign of "a general atrophy of culture in capitalistic society"; and it is so, though intermittently, throughout the book. But a truer common denominator of these essays—one well becoming a critic inspired by Cauldwell, Lukács, and Marcuse—appears to us to consist, rather, in Binni's conception of the work of art as "a product of complex and dynamic relations within an ever changing social context" and his requirement that literature should cope with the real tensions and contradictions of reality. The best of the other five essays on American subjects are, in our opinion, the one on Nathanael West (*q.v. ALS 1973*, p. 451), the one on *The Bulwark* (seen as revealing "the other side of Dreiser," the mysticism he suppressed when he embraced determinism and naturalism) and the one on Ambrose Bierce (whose technique Binni defines as essentially nonrealistic and whose work he interprets as a reflection of a split in Bierce's personality—his romantic idealism vs. his cynical rationalism). Binni's breadth of knowledge and genuine concern for the relevance of literature to life are thoroughly evident in this volume. It is a pity, though, that his convoluted thinking and the uncontrolled exuberance of his writing too often severely (and, perhaps, unnecessarily) test the reader's power of understanding.

Concerned with realism, but not less with modernism (and post-modernism), Binni's book thus falls also into the third, and last, of our thematic areas, which may be termed "Modernism and Avant-garde." This area is almost entirely covered by the first issue of *RSA* containing the proceedings of the 5th Conference of AISNA, held in 1979 in Venice and having for its theme "Society and Language in Early 20th-Century American Avant-garde." The literary aspects of the theme are treated in two major papers and in two workshops. These contributions are, on the whole, of a remarkable standard, and worth therefore the attention of all future students of this subject. In his richly suggestive and methodologically significant "L'avan-guardia americana e l'avvento del modernismo, 1890–1930" (pp. 23–48) Malcolm Bradbury begins with a definition of "avant-garde" as an international phenomenon calling for a comparative approach and goes on to observe how, although modernism was not an indigenous movement in America, the Americans soon became conspicuous and active participants in it. He then divides American modernism into four phases—the 1890s, 1900–1910/12, 1912–20 and the 1920s—and indicates Stephen Crane, the later James, Dreiser, and Gertrude Stein as some of the figures whose contributions to modernism he considers crucial and pauses to examine to some length. Bradbury also connects modernism to the ongoing modernization of the Western world and specifically focuses on three famous exhibitions—Chicago, 1893; Paris, 1900; and the Armory Show of 1913—the first two visited by such a keen observer as Henry Adams, who could read in them the signs of irreversible cultural changes. In his brilliant, provocative and wide-ranging "Lo sfasamento della prima avanguardia U.S.A." (pp. 52–74) Glauco Cambon emphasizes a paradox at the heart of American avant-garde: unaware of the domestic presence of such radical literary innovators as Poe, Whitman, and Emily Dickinson (the last of whom may be safely considered an unwitting precursor of imagism), some young American writers chose to leave the *New* World "to search the new in the *Old* World." Furthermore, Cambon points out, their experiments not only appear rather limited in range and innovativeness when compared to those of their European mentors (or even to some of their unrecognized forerunners at home), but also reveal a certain obliviousness to what was going on in avant-garde circles in parts of Europe other than France. Cambon supports these contentions by an examination of the extreme and multifarious innovations realized by Italian Futurists, whose influence on Anglo-American avant-garde is much wider and deeper than it was admitted by Pound and the other Vorticists or is still acknowledged by most critics.

As to the workshops, we must limit ourselves here to little more than a listing of topics and contributors. The workshop on "Art, Literature, Language, 1900–1930" (pp. 103–59) attracted many speakers. Their papers (some of which have been unfortunately printed in their original form, as notes for oral delivery) deal with the Oriental taste of the later James (Alberta Fabris Grube); the fine arts as a guiding thread in James's major phase (Marilla Battilana); Pound and Venetian painting (Rosella Mamoli Zorzi); Pound and Futurism (Giovanni Cianci; but for a review of an enlarged version of this paper cf. *ALS 1979*, pp. 517–18); the combined influence of visual arts and Whitman on the early poetry of William C. Williams (Bianca Tarozzi); the late-1920s review *transition*, which aimed to subsume all preceding avant-garde movements (Alide Cagidemetrio); the mixed reactions of artists and writers of the 1920s to the new vertical "frontier" of the changing skylines of American cities (Renzo S. Crivelli); the rediscovery of American land promoted by Alfred Stieglitz and his "Photo-Secession" (Umberto Capra) and Paul Strand's poetics of "Straight Photography" (Michela Vanon)—but an exhaustive account of the role played by photography in renewing American culture during the first two decades of this century can be found in Vanon's introduction to her anthology from *Camera Work* (*Camera Work: Un'antologia*, Torino: Einaudi). An adjunct to this workshop, William Boelhower's "*in our time* di Hemingway, composizione cubista" (pp. 213–28) calls attention to the deep influence of contemporary visual arts (*via* Gertrude Stein) on the early Hemingway and offers a persuasive reading of *in our time* as a Cubist artifact. "American Language in Early 20th-Century Literature" (pp. 180–208) is the theme of the second workshop, to which Andrea Mariani, Caterina Ricciardi, and Marina Camboni contribute three good papers on, respectively, the language of Sandburg's poetry, the Pound-Williams controversy on the nature of American poetry and language, Williams' reflections on American language.

Finally, *Quaderni* 13 (Fac. di Lettere, Univ. di Palermo) published the proceedings of a seminar on "Formalism/Humanism"
which took place in Palermo in 1979. The centerpiece of the seminar
was "Formalism and Humanism in America" (pp. 9–54) in which
John Paul Russo thoughtfully and tersely expounds the critical principles of T. S. Eliot, Irving Babbitt, and I. A. Richards, whom he
considers both architects and representatives of the basic positions
that characterize American criticism since the 1920s.

A combination of chronological order and generic subdivisions
will be our organizing principle for the dicussion of the remaining
items. Apart from a lively and reasonable (albeit not very innovative)
overview of Anne Bradstreet's verse by Tommaso Pisanti ("Origini
americane: La poesia di Anne Bradstreet," *Critica letteraria* 9,i:62–
75), this year's only contribution to the study of literature prior to
1800 is to be found in a book by a historian. Loretta Valtz Man-
nucci's concern in her 437-page *Le radici ideologiche degli Stati
Uniti* (Lecce: Milella) is with "national ideology," as it can be seen
to take shape out of the conflicting and/or interacting views of so-
ciety-structure and power-structure advanced by members of both
colonial *élites* and lower middle classes during the years that precede
the Revolution. Valtz Manucci develops her theme mainly through
painstaking analyses of Franklin's *Poor Richard's Almanack*, John
Adams' "Ploughjogger" letters and *Journals*, John Dickinson's *Letters
from a Pennsylvania Farmer*, Paine's *Common Sense* and briefer selections from John Woolman's and Robert Rogers' journals, accumu-
lating a wealth of penetrating observations on the semantic, stylistic,
and rhetorical levels of these works. Thus it is that her book (which
might, however, have profited a great deal from a more accurate
proofreading, and also from more functional divisions and the presence of an index and a bibliography) makes rewarding reading for
the student of literature as well.

Massimo Bacigalupo's 578-page *L'ultimo Pound* (Roma: Edizioni
di Storia e Letteratura) looms large in the panorama of the studies
on poetry. But since its English version (*The Forméd Trace: The
Later Poetry of Ezra Pound*) was widely reviewed when it came out
in 1980, and since the present writer agrees in the main with the
judgment passed on it by George Bornstein in *ALS 1980* (128–29),
nothing else needs to be added here. In another item concerning

Pound, "Il poema della crisi e l'esperienza della morte simbolica: *Hugh Selwyn Mauberley* e *Le Testament de Villon*" (*Annali* [Fac. di Magistero, Univ. di Cagliari] n.s. 5,i:91–135), Mario Domenichelli may be overstating his case when he says that *Le Testament* is to *Mauberley* as the *Odyssey* is to Joyce's *Ulysses*, but he is certainly right in claiming for the French poem a larger influence on *Mauberley* than critics have so far been able to detect. At any rate, his probing reading of the two poems as Menippean satires (according to the traits assigned to this genre by Michail Bachtin) makes very persuasive sense: François Montcorbier undertook his moral reformation by dying symbolically through a self-parodic character ("Villon") who writes at the point of death a testament depicting the kind of dissolute life its author is recanting; not unlike Montcorbier, Pound celebrates his entering a new phase of his intellectual and creative growth by dying symbolically through two "parodying doubles" ("E. P." and "Mauberley") that he puts at the center of a carnival/funeral procession staging all the aesthetic and moral aberrations of the literary and cultural milieu he is turning away from. With a further turn of the screw, inspired by the Jungian journey of the self toward individuation, Domenichelli describes Mauberley/Elpenor as the ritual victim that makes it possible for Pound/Ulysses to sail on. Less persuasive (because of the reductionism implicit in them) are the author's hints at the possibility of also reading the *Cantos* as a Menippean satire.

In *Il nudo artificio: Una lettura dei sonetti di Robert Lowell* (Vicenza: Neri Pozza) Bianca Tarozzi treats her subject in five short chapters. Chapter 1 describes Lowell's books of sonnets as a complex of systems, similar to "Chinese boxes" (from the largest one, embracing the whole corpus from the three editions of *Notebook* to the sequences of sonnets (re)arranged for *Selected Poems* in 1976 and 1977, to the ever smaller systems of the single sequence, the single sonnet, the parts of each sonnet), and indicates casual, organic-like proliferation and calculated structuring, compression of form and loosening of style, as the opposite, but ever alternating and coexisting, principles that govern the poet's attempt at capturing the flux of reality. Chapter 2 sets off Lowell's primary thematic concerns in *History*, the only section of the all-inclusive system which is not segmented into sequences. Chapters 3 and 4 study two sequences strategically located at the beginning and at the end, respectively, of the whole "novel-poem": "Long Summer" of *Notebook 1967–68* and "Nineteen Thirties" of *Selected Poems*—this, the longest, most complex and ambitious sequence which Tarozzi sees as Lowell's poetic testament. Chapter 5—the best, in my opinion, along with chapter 4—contrasts "Charles the Fifth and the Peasant" from *Lord Weary's Castle* and "Charles V by Titian" from *History*, to sample two different stages in Lowell's handling of the same genre and to show the functioning of the sonnet as a self-contained unit. Tarozzi's method thus relies on selectivity and economy of treatment, but for this very reason tends to presume on the reader's capacity to span discontinuities. The author writes well (when not competing with her subject in metaphorical obscurity), with a native grasp of poetry and a solid knowledge of the Lowellian canon. Not a full-scale excavation into the rich and as yet mostly unassayed ore of Lowell's sonnets, her book is, however, an encouraging preview of it.

An unusual aspect of American poetry is the subject of Luciano Federighi's *Blues nel mio animo: Temi e poesia del blues* (Milano: Mondadori). Federighi opposes the views of those who consider the blues as primarily a music of social protest or the blues-singer as mere spokesman for communal experiences, and insists instead that the blues is essentially a lyrical and liberating expression of states of mind induced by the bluesman's personal experience of life. He substantiates this interpretation by ranging with impressive ease through the whole corpus of the blues and drawing a most detailed map of recurrent themes, tones, imagery, and metaphors. His commentary is not exempt from some redundancies and at times takes a paraphrastic turn; what are now only scattered notes on the formal aspects of the texts might have been advantageously developed into a fuller, organic discussion of language, prosody, narrative techniques, etc. (But the author may have been dissuaded from attempting this by his sound awareness that the poetry of the blues is fully released not by the written words but in the bluesman's actual performance.) At any rate, this book—which is completed by comprehensive and accurate bibliography and discography—not only serves as an agreeable introduction to the blues: it must be ranked among the few authoritative works on this topic.

On poetry there are also four shorter pieces, all introductions to as many works of translation. In *Unicorni di mare e di terra (Poesie 1935–1951)* (Milano: Rizzoli) Marcello Pagnini revises Giovanni

Galtieri's versions of 25 of Marianne Moore's poems and prefaces them with a concise and lucid description of the poet's subject matter, method, and techniques. Barbara Lanati, after outlining Robert Duncan's poetic program and achievement, concludes her introduction to Attilia Lavagno's not very accurate translation of *The Opening of the Field* (*Poesie*, Roma: Newton Compton) by stressing—in terms she derives from Julia Kristeva—the centrality of the "feminine" in Duncan's attempt to restore a communion between nature and the realm of transcendence. Francesco Binni prefixes to his own fine versions of 11 poems from Robert Creeley's *Later* (*Almanacco dello Specchio* 10, Milano: Mondadori) a long introductory note (pp. 173–79) in which he gives a well-informed and penetrating assessment of Creeley's career as that of one of the most sensitive and representative figures in the transition from modernist to postmodernist poetics. There is, finally, the editors' introduction to *La rosa disabitata: Poesia trascendentale americana, 1960–1980* (Milano: Feltrinelli), a bilingual anthology of texts and statements by 13 avant-garde poets, the best-known of whom are probably John Cage, Jackson MacLow, and Jerome Rothenberg. In their introduction Luigi Ballerini and Richard Milazzo define the kind of artifacts included in the volume as poems of the "dis-ordinary . . . linguistic objects which exceed language" (i.e., still using language but not at its communicative levels), and go on to trace the lineage of these poets (Gertrude Stein and, less convincingly, Emerson) as well as to diagram the whole range of their methods (from "deliberation" to "randomness"). Since this area of contemporary avant-garde is still relatively unknown in Italy, it is a pity that the authors' language is at times all but hermetic. (Considering the nature of some of the materials gathered in this anthology, one is also led to wonder about the usefulness, and the very feasibility, of translating them).

With an essay concerning the first American novelist of some prominence we now move on to the studies on fiction. Somewhat incoherent and lacking in focus, Paola Boi's "Personaggio et struttura in *Arthur Mervyn* di Charles Brockden Brown" (*Annali* [Fac. di Magistero, Univ. di Cagliari] n.s. 5,i:21–53) is likely to leave the reader in doubt as to its author's interpretive aims. In her last paragraph Boi suggests that Brown's praise of virtue and benevolence is to be taken as ironical in this novel. If this is meant to be the conclusion of the whole essay, it is certainly not adequately led up to by what precedes it, namely, a fairly clumsy discussion of the puzzling characterization of the protagonist and a little more incisive analysis of the narrative structure of the novel as a variation from the picaresque pattern. Under the rather cryptic title "Di un racconto incrociato" (*Paragone* 376:42–62)—which actually refers to the way several plot-lines coexist and intersect in *The Marble Faun*—Flavio Luoni performs meticulous segmentations of this text mainly to prove that nowhere are the theatrical qualities of Hawthorne's fiction so "spectacular" as in this romance. The author has no doubt well assimilated Gerard Genette's *Discours du récit* but seems somehow to have overlooked the fact that the French critic's methodological machine and terminological apparatus were in that essay subservient to an hermeneutical endeavor. There is instead nothing of this sort to be found here, behind Luoni's fine dissections.

Leonardo Terzo's *Retorica dell'avventura: Forma e significato in Moby-Dick* (Milano: Cisalpino-Goliardica) will be welcome, for one thing, as the first Italian book on Melville since 1952. In the first section of his compact, tightly reasoned study Terzo sees the complex (and to so many readers bewildering) structure of *Moby Dick* as an interfusing of comic romance (Ishmael's story), tragic romance (Ahab's story), and anatomy (the encyclopedic treatment of whaling, which frames, envelops, and connects the other two elements). Anatomy, ironical and satirical in its essence, calling all current values and established views into doubt, confers on *Moby-Dick* its unique character of unresolved epistemological quest and sets off the two protagonists as dissenters revolting against the evils of the world and seeking after a higher, reconciliatory order. On the basis of this generic description Terzo undertakes a reading of Melville's work which, although it does not sensibly alter our perception of it, possesses undoubtedly two merits: it verifies the validity of current accepted interpretations rearranging them in a very perspicuous cognitive model and, more importantly, brings out functionality as the principle everywhere at work, which can account for the presence in *Moby-Dick* of parts too often thought of as supererogatory or uselessly digressive. The second section of Terzo's book is a close rhetorical-stylistical analysis—impeccably performed and praiseworthy for depth and thoroughness—of the first six paragraphs of chapter 1. Besides confirming how carefully calculated the rich texture and the semantic ambivalence of this text are, it fully evinces the thematic homology obtaining between the macro- and micro-structure of Melville's masterpiece.

Donatella Izzo's *Henry James* (Firenze: La Nuova Italia) deserves to take precedence over the other studies dedicated to this writer. Rather than being hampered by the format of the uniform series her monograph belongs to, the author seems to have been challenged by it, to devise a strategy that would enable her to make the most of her 113 small pages. Her happy double strategy consists in concentrating only on the most significant novels and in choosing as the guiding thread for her discussion the very *raison d'être* of James's work—his uninterrupted and parallel experimentation with and meditation on the resources of fiction. An acute though necessarily summary analysis of *Daisy Miller* shows how wary James is —even in such an early and ostensibly simple work—of any naive notion of "realism," how meanings here are to be looked for not so much in the narrated matter as in the forms and style given to it, how, finally, this text possesses already a self-reflective dimension, inscribing within itself the theoretical and technical questions attending its coming into being. In the light of these fundamental elements the author then follows the ever more complex and yet intrinsically coherent developments of James's thought and art. His crucial position as both the last great novelist of the 19th century and the first of the 20th is stressed in the conclusion by Izzo's summing up his whole *iter* as one going from the realization that words cannot copy the world to the exalting, and very modern, discovery that words create worlds. Resting on the author's full and firm grasp of today's theories on fiction (to which she often refers in order to highlight the lasting value of some of James's insights), couched in incisive, terminologically precise but never abstruse language, this book can be safely recommended as one of the best short introductions to James's work ever written.

The flaws most critics have found with *The American*—says David Lucking in "Romance as Irony in *The American* by Henry James" (*Quaderni* [Fac. di Magistero, Univ. di Lecce] 2 [1980]:93–115)— depend to a large extent on their not recognizing this work for what it is (and for what James himself was to recognize it was in his *Preface*): not a "realistic" novel but a romance. It is a romance though, Lucking finely argues, in which *both* Newman and the Bellegardes must be seen as ironically conceived characters and in which their idealized, unrealistic conceptions of themselves and life, by being irremediably polarized and mutually destructive, prevent any traditional conclusion of the story in a mode of festive reconciliation. In Northrop Frye's terms adopted by the author, *The American* develops therefore the pattern not of "romantic" but of "ironic comedy." In his preface to a reprint of Sergio Baldi and Aldo Celli's translation of *What Maisie Knew* (*Che cosa sapeva Masie*, Milano: Bompiani) Sergio Perosa makes intelligent use of James's *Notebooks* and *Preface* to elucidate the narrative method and the theme of this novel. His conclusion is that Masie's moral triumph as a character coincides with her triumph as centre of consciousness of the story: it is her "range of wonderment" that saves her from corruption. Sergio Rufini accompanies his own excellent version of *In the Cage* (*In gabbia*, Milano: Il Saggiatore) with an introduction in which he explores this *nouvelle* thoroughly and penetratingly. After seeing it as a paradigmatic example of self-reflective fiction (its encoding a perfect parable of the temptations and the dangers incurred in the writing as well as the reading of any text), he investigates the manifold, ambivalent meanings generated by the metaphor of "the cage" and expands on the crucial function played by *écriture* (the protagonist's, which brings her romance to an end; James's stylistic feat is to evoke the protagonist's subconscious desire and its final unfulfillment without ever naming it). In her 20-page brochure *Lo splendore delle tenebre: "The Two Faces" di Henry James* (Pisa: ETS) Teresa M. Benussi gives this little masterpiece of the later James a sound (if not always perspicuous) reading which focuses chiefly on the importance that verbs of vision and perception have in both underlining the theme of appearance vs. reality and preparing Sutton's final illumination.

In another brochure of the same series, *Sarah Orne Jewett tra romanticismo e crepuscolarismo*, Enrica Cagnacci takes exception to the prevailing view of the Maine writer as an exponent of local-color realism, to contend that her work is instead primarily inspired by a tame, middle-class kind of *fin de siècle* romanticism. This thesis is an interesting one, but should have been supported by much fuller and more conclusive evidence than that provided here by the author's remarks on Jewett's descriptive technique and treatment of nature. A number of pithy observations (and some less convincing too) can be found in a note on "Lingua letteraria e dialetto in *Huckleberry Finn*" (*Trimestre* 13,i:133–41) where Alessandro Portelli analyzes the language of the first two paragraphs of this work to prove that they function as an index to the points of strength as well as to the contradictions of the novel as a whole. An appreciation of Edith Wharton's achievement (developed mainly through extensive plot-summaries and a bland discussion of the themes of her major works), Alberta Fabris Grube's journalistic "Una scrittrice, una societá in evoluzione" (*Donna e societá* 15:61–77) neither will change nor deepen our understanding of this writer. Mirella Billi's "Quel doppio gioco di Dashiell Hammett" (*Il ponte* 37,vii–viii:710–16) contains nothing new for the specialist, but since it is a clear, concise, well-rounded presentation of the writer, his fictional world, and the elements of his art, it will serve as a useful introduction for the general reader.

A slender monograph and five shorter items is what we have on post-World-War-II fiction. Antonio Donno's *L'intellettuale ebreo in America: Saggio su Philip Roth* (Lecce: Milella) deals with the novels of this writer insofar as they are seen to reflect the predicament of a generation of Jewish intellectuals whose efforts to become full-fledged, successful Americans begin with a rejection of their ethnic cultural heritage and end in an anguished sense of defeat, alienation, and loss of identity. *Portnoy's Complaint* is therefore indicated as the paradigm of Roth's whole production. On the other hand, from *My Life As a Man* onward, literature is seen to take on an ever greater thematic importance—as, in turn, the instrument of rebellion from Jewishness, the way to social prestige, an escape from the frustrations of life. While any consideration of the aesthetic value of these novels remains beyond the scope of Donno's sociological approach, his essay does succeed in highlighting a central aspect of Roth's work, furnishing at the same time a unified view of it.

Lina Unali, in her stimulating although somewhat rambling and journalistically written "Percorsi su carta dell'emigrato franco-canadese Jack Kerouac" (*Il ponte* 37,xi–xii:1221–28), suggests that Kerouac's French-Canadian origins and the difficulties he encountered because of them while growing up in an Anglo-Saxon environment are accountable for his sense of exile, typical of the immigrant who never feels fully at home in his new country. As signs of an attitude in which an aspiration to belonging and a pride in diversity blend, Unali points out Kerouac's flauntingly exuberant use of English, his exaltation of non-American ancestors in *Satori in Paris*, his assigning an Italian descent to the autobiographical protagonist of *On the Road*, and also his placing of "exstasy" in a southern "elsewhere." In her short introduction to the Italian version of Leslie M. Silko's *Ceremony* (*Cerimonia*, Roma: Editori Riuniti) Paola Ludovici recalls elements of Pueblo mythology which are essential for a correct understanding of the story. (She may be in error, though, when she takes the name of the protagonist as a borrowing from Melville's *Omoo*, since "Tayo" is also the protagonist of a Pueblo legend.) The "new Puritans" alluded to in the title of Alessandra Contenti's highly readable "I nuovi puritani: romanzieri popolari americani degli anni sessanta" (*La critica sociologica* 57–58:143–56) are the protagonists of the novels written by three best-seller writers of the 1960s (Allen Drury, James Michener, and English-born Arthur Hailey). Either "Builders" (the hard-working, upright, frugal leaders who found empires or pile up fortunes) or "Managers" (the dedicated, selfless, efficient administrators of the empires and fortunes confided to their care), all of them invariably embody qualities which are traditionally associated with the Puritan character. This, Contenti suggests, tells a lot about the middle-class "values" cherished by the readers to whom this kind of fiction is meant to give gratification and reassurance. In "Televisione secondo Kosinski" (*Alfa-beta* 3:22–24), an interview given to Marco Vallora in 1980, Jerzy Kosinsky, after observing how the film version of his *Being There* had been praised for the wrong reasons by TV-addict American audiences, draws a distinction between TV in itself, simply as a medium, and the socially pernicious effects of its current misuse. A fairly good idea of the kind of fiction written by Gerald Rosen and Keith Abbot can be acquired in "A Delightful City" (*Paragone* 376: 83–95), which records the conversations Franco La Polla had in 1980 with these two Californian writers.

Finally, two items on drama. In *Invito alla lettura di Thornton Wilder* (Milano: Mursia [1980]), a volume in a series intended for the student and the general reader, Floria Conta and Maria Torelli provide an unpretentious, no-nonsense, comprehensive account of the writer's life and views, his techniques as a novelist and as a playwright, the themes and motifs of his work. Intellectually more stimulating is Vito Amoruso's "Note sul teatro 'politico' americano"

(*Quaderni di teatro* 3,xii:43–51). After noticing how the contradiction between daringly experimental form and ideological tameness that Richard Schechner finds in Terry Megan's *Viet Rock* characterizes also most of the allegedly "political" theatre of the 1960s, the author affirms that such a contradiction can actually be traced throughout the American culture of this century, since criticism, however harsh, of American society is always kept in check by faith in the perfectibility of the system, a deep-seated optimism, and an unshaken trust in the resources of individualism. Amoruso's case finds corroboration in his perceptive though brief comments on two such disparate episodes of the drama of the 1930s as the Group Theatre experience and Thornton Wilder's *Our Town*.

Università di Firenze

iv. Japanese Contributions

Keiko Beppu

The output of our scholarly works on American literature for 1981 was overwhelming in volume and variety. Correspondingly, the translation of major American authors for 1981 was as productive as ever: the *Collected Works of Herman Melville* have been prepared; the similar project on Faulkner started in 1967 has brought out the 20th volume of its 25-volume series. Of special interest is the publication of Toni Morrison's *The Bluest Eye* in translation, along with the writings of Susan Sontag, Salinger, Bellow, Tennessee Williams, and Arthur Miller. Likewise, works of classic American writers such as Thoreau and Irving continue to be in print. Translation of these important literary artists, to list some names of significance, is not simply a by-product of our scholarship, but an authentic indicator of the reception of American literature in this country, and an event worthy of celebration in itself. Scholarly activity and translation work should profit from each other; each should stimulate the other.

Now the salient feature of Japanese scholarship on American writers for 1981 is a distant biographical concern observed in the books written on some 19th- and 20th-century American writers. This critical approach has resulted in excellent biographical studies on Robert Lowell, Emily Dickinson, Lafcadio Hearn, and Stephen Crane. Also reflecting the recent craze in literary criticism here and abroad, *EigoS* prepared a special number on English and American women writers with a useful checklist of the scholarship on the subject. Among the articles in the issue, the following in particular deserve a few comments. Shunsuke Kamei's "American Eves" (127: 288–90) is a quick rundown on American heroines and anticipates a new historical perspective on American literature through the plights of "American Eves." Hiroko Sato's "The Domestic Novel" (pp. 296–97) is a good survey of the genre.

Individual achievements in 1981 are grouped for the present review as follows: 19th-century American fiction, 20th-century American fiction, contemporary American fiction, American poetry, and American studies. The classification may be arbitrary and some works defy any such categorization. As has been customary with this reviewer, articles here examined are restricted with a few exceptions to those published in our major scholarly journals: *EigoS*, *SALit*, and *SELit*; and the Japanese titles for the essays are omitted.

Among 19th-century American writers, Melville and James received a concentrated critical attention in 1981: Teiji Kitagawa's *A Moby-Dick Dictionary* (Tokyo: Hokuseido Press) and Ginsaku Sugiura's *Melville: Hametsueno Kohkaisha* [*Melville: The Doomed Voyager*] (Tokyo: Tohjusha); Masayuki Akiyama's *Henry James Sakuhin Kenkyu* [*Studies in Fictional Works of Henry James*] (Nan'-undo) and Toshio Tada's *Aironii to Kyokan no Aida: Henry James Sonota* [*Between Irony and Empathy: Studies in Henry James and Others*] (Osaka: Kansai University Press).

A Moby-Dick Dictionary is a product of close reading of Melville's masterpiece and of painstaking research in relevant Melville's scholarship, especially Charles Feidelson's annotated edition of Moby-Dick (1964) and Shigeru Maeno's *Melville Dictionary* (1976). As Kitagawa explains in his foreword to the dictionary, the notes are arranged in alphabetical order, which, however, is hardly an improvement on Feidelson's *Moby-Dick*. Furthermore, the entries include such elementary idioms as "do away with" or "do wrong" (p. 67), or "take turns" (p. 228), to mention just a few examples at random. Even so, *A Moby-Dick Dictionary* is an eloquent testimony of the artist's popularity among our scholars and students, also made manifest in the translation of his collected works.

Ginaku Sugiura's *Melville: The Doomed Voyager* is a new addition to Tohjusha Series on English and American Authors. (Studies on Faulkner, Salinger, Bellow, Hawthorne, and Poe already have been reviewed in *ALS*.) *Melville: The Doomed Voyager* is a tour de force that demonstrates the critic's solid scholarship and long acquaintance with the artist. Sugiura sees Melville's opus as an organic whole and illustrates how Melville's works from *Typee* to *Billy Budd* are linked to each other, which is to show the inner mechanism of the "deeply thinking mind" that is doomed to end up in the nadir of the "mysterious darkness." The most impressive discussion is his chapters on *Clarel* ("In Search of Christ") and on *Billy Budd* ("The Doomed Voyager"); Sugiura employs his expertise in Ernest Renan, Neitzsche, Dostoevski, and D. H. Lawrence, whose *Studies in Classic American Literature* (1923) seems to have influenced him. Sugiura contends that Melville had a highly romanticized image of Christ, which colored the characterization of his protagonists. His argument is well balanced and convincing. All in all, *Melville: The Doomed Voyager* is the most valuable contribution to Melville scholarship in this country since Taizo Tanimoto's *Melville's Tragic Ambiguity and Beyond* (*ALS 1977*, 501).

Henry James has provided our scholars with numerous critical problems, yet two books on the novelist in one year is a phenomenal accomplishment. Masayuki Akiyama's *Studies in Fictional Works of Henry James* is a collection of his essays published previously in journals. The book deals with a variety of James's works in an expatiating manner: *Madame de Mauves, The American, The Portrait of a Lady* (chap. 1); *The Princess Casamassima*, and *The Bostonians* (chap. 2); *The Turn of the Screw, The Beast in the Jungle*, and *The Wings of the Dove* (chap. 3). Akiyama includes two discussions on the relationship between James and a Japanese writer, Kawabata; the connection between the two has often been made. One of Akiyama's essays, entitled "A Rapprochement Study of Yasunari Kawabata's *The Sound of the Mountain* and Henry's James's *The Ambassadors*," is written in English and hence is available to some interested readers abroad. Despite a certain clumsiness—a strategic editing could have trimmed Akiyama's ponderous work to a better advantage—the well-prepared bibliography of James scholarship here and abroad makes *Studies in Fictional Works of Henry James* a very useful guide to the students of James in this country.

Like Akiyama's book on James, Toshio Tada's *Between Irony and Empathy: Studies in Henry James and Others* is also a collection of his articles formerly published in journals. Tada's critical approach is to fathom the "precious moral" of James's works—*Confidence, The Awkward Age, The Sacred Fount, The Portrait of a Lady, What Maisie Knew,* and *The Wings of the Dove*—by examining their form and structure. His commentary on James's much-slighted *Confidence,* which constitutes an appropriate introduction, should be commended. More important and germinal to the book as a whole, however, is his essay in the appendix, an exploration of a non-American perspective on American literature exemplified in Tony Tanner's *The Reign of Wonder* (1965). The English critic's sense of wonderment before American authors becomes a governing principle of Tanner's book, which in turn serves as such for the Japanese critic. From the makeup of *Between Irony and Empathy,* it becomes evident that Tada is writing a sequel to Tanner's book, as it were, including James Fenimore Cooper (an author Tanner omitted) and adding Fitzgerald and Bellow from among contemporary writers.

In the company of the books so far discussed, Ikuko Nakazawa's *Seisho to America Renaissance no Sakkatachi* [*The Bible and American Renaissance Authors*] (Tokyo: Yamamoto Shoten) is an anomaly but well deserves comment here. *The Bible and American Renaissance Authors* is an excellent linguistic and stylistic analysis of *The Authorized Version of the Bible* (1611) and of the *New English Bible* (1961). At the same time Nakazawa examines the influences of the *Authorized Version* on the styles of Emerson, Thoreau, Whitman, and Dickinson, using abundant illustrations from their writings; her discussions of these 19th-century authors are good stylistic studies and deserve our attention. One footnote here: Kanzo Uchimura's article "Walt Whitman the Poet" (1909), which Nakazawa introduces in her book (pp. 263–81), is one of the best criticisms of the poet hitherto written by a Japanese scholar.

An interesting critical hybrid among the books in this group is Sukehiro Hirakawa's *Koizumi Yakumo: Seiyodashutsu no Yume* [*Lafcadio Hearn: The Dream of an Expatriate*] (Tokyo: Shincho-sha). *Lafcadio Hearn* is a curious combination of biography, literary

criticism, and comparative cultural study of Europe, America, and
Japan. Naturally, the book lacks unity per se, but it is sustained
throughout by the critic's passionate commitment to his subject.
Hirakawa's book is a superb critical biography of Hearn the expa-
triate, who was twice exiled, first from England and then from the
States, but his soul's home was in Japan; the profile Hirakawa makes
of the writer illuminates the inexplicable charm of Hearn's literature,
which Hirakawa identifies as Japanese literature of Meiji era written
in English. Hirakawa's expertise spawns insightful comparisons of
Hearn and Mark Twain, or Hearn and the French writer, Pierre
Loti, or Hearn and Soseki Natsume, whom Hirakawa regards as the
Japanese counterpart of Hearn the expatriate. Furthermore, Hirakawa's rendition of Hearn's works—early sketches of New Orleans,
journalistic pieces, and ghost stories based on Japanese folklores
orally transmitted to him by his Japanese wife—makes *Lafcadio
Hearn: The Dream of an Expatriate* a wonderful entertainment as
well as a serious scholarly exploration.

Articles on 19th-century American literature selected for inclusion here are: Johichi Okuda's "A Significance of Seasonal Terms in
Thoreau" (*SALit* 18:17–32); Shigetoshi Katsurada's "The Ambiguity
in Hawthorne's *The Marble Faun*" in *Evil in Literature*, a collection
of original essays, ed. Masaie Matsumura and Minoru Fujita (Tokyo:
Nan'undo); and Yukako Suga's "The Tragic Life of Madame Merle"
(*ibid.*, pp. 206–27). The last two deserve a brief comment: Katsurada's essay, subtitled "Arcadia and Death," concentrates on Donatello and his innocence that transcends the stricture of right and
wrong, even that of good and evil. Suga's discussion of James's
infamous character is a sensitive reading of her odious, dire, and
infinitely sad life.

America Bungaku no Jiko Keisei [*The Self-Formation of American Writers*], ed. Toshihiko Ogata (Yamaguchi) is the second volume
in *Studies in American Literature*—the sequels are in preparation. It
deals with representative writers of the three decades between 1890
and 1920, the period of transition between the 19th and 20th centuries in American literature. With a brief survey of the period in
the introduction, *The Self-Formation of American Writers* aims at a
certain literary history of the United States; yet, primarily it is an
ambitious collection of essays contributed by experts on the 16

American writers included in the present volume: Howells, Norris and Crane, Jack London, Cather and Glasgow, Wharton, Dreiser, Sinclair Lewis, Anderson, Pound, Eliot, William Carlos Williams, Stein, Dos Passos, and Hemingway.

The following comments sample a few chapters from the book. Kohji Oi's discussion of William Dean Howells (pp. 19–47) is a convincing refutation of some misleading interpretations of this underestimated writer. As always, his rhetoric may win a few converts. Keijiro Unoki's chapter on Jack London (pp. 91–128) is a panoramic presentation of London's life and his works, drawing upon rich biographical materials. Unoki's all-around portrait of the novelist helps to correct our naive appreciation of the writer as a mere adventure-storyteller.

In his study on T. S. Eliot (pp. 383–417) Itsuyu Iwase offers insightful observations of the poet-critic. Somewhat after the example of Canby's *Turn West, Turn East* Iwase treats the "turn East" syndrome in American artists: Henry Adams, Henry James, and T. S. Eliot. Iwase states that while James's passionate pilgrimage ends in a partial failure, if not a complete one, Eliot's urge to "turn East" comes to a successful end in his assimilation of British culture. This the critic demonstrates by a careful reading and an intelligent analysis of Eliot's poems and his critical writings. Thus, Iwase's well-planned essay catches the two birds, as it were: his observations shed light on the deeply rooted American temperament and on the understanding of T. S. Eliot the poet.

Zenichiro Oshitani's chapter on Norris and Crane in this same book (pp. 49–89) is extended into a book-length study of Stephen Crane. *Stephen Crane: Hyoron to Hihyo* [*Stephen Crane: His Life and Art*] (Yamaguchi) is a critical biography of the novelist, occasioned by his visit to Stephen Crane Pond and by an interview with old Demock, the sole eyewitness of Crane's life in the States. *Stephen Crane: His Life and Art*, the first book-length study of the writer in this country, is an unaffected biographical study accompanied by interpretations of Crane's works. As has been mentioned at the outset of this review, a biographical concern dominates our scholarship for 1981. This is true both of Oshitani's book on Crane and Hirakawa's *Lafcadio Hearn*.

Our scholarship on 20th-century and contemporary American fiction in 1981 was meager in terms of book-length studies done on

major writers such as Hemingway and Faulkner, who always enjoy
a considerable critical attention. General studies of the field are
Shunji Mukai's *Kaitakusha no Kohei: Gendai America Bungaku
Shiron* [*Descendants of the Pioneers: Studies in Contemporary
American Literature*] (Tokyo: Hokuju Shuppan) and Giichi Ouchi
and Mikio Suzuki's *Richard Wright no Sekai* [*The Fictional World
of Richard Wright*] (Tokyo: Hyoronsha). The latter is a rudimentary student guide to the writer; many of the synopses of his works
can be dispensed with. Nevertheless, the publication of the book
itself is significant because it reflects our awareness of the problems
of the blacks, as evidenced in Kitamura's *The Changing America*, surveyed later in this review.

Like many other books mentioned here, Mukai's *Descendants of
the Pioneers* is based on his previously published essay. As he explains in his afterword, Mukai's choice of his subject is determined
by his involvement in community activities. The discussion of Miller's *Death of a Salesman* in the introductory chapter is a penetrating
criticism of Japanese society. Mukai sees the tragedy of Miller's play
rehearsed by many Willie Lomans in this country. The point is well
taken, since our society follows the footsteps of her American counterpart with the lag of a decade or two. Of special note here is
Mukai's contention that Biff Loman *is* a latterday pioneer who seeks
deliverance out in the West from the rat-race in the city. Similarly,
in subsequent chapters on Hemingway, Salinger, Vonnegut, or Malamud, the author attempts to find a specific answer to the question
of our survival in the way each protagonist makes what he can of
the given situation.

Articles on 20th-century fiction are monopolized by William
Faulkner. Our Faulkner journal, *William Faulkner: Materials, Studies, and Criticism* have the following two essays: Hiroshi Izubuchi's
"Faulkner and Yeats—An Essay" (*WiF* 4,i:1–14) and Junjiro Tanimura's "Yeoman Farmers and Their Role in Faulkner's Literature"
(pp. 17–31). Izubuchi's essay is an exploration in the relationship
between Yeats and Faulkner, whose imaginative worlds are colored
by their "experience" of a civil war. Tanimura proposes to amend
the stereotyped view of the South prevalent in Faulkner criticism.
Tanimura argues that despite his aristocratic background, or because
of it, Faulkner endorsed the values of yeoman farmers and sought
in their way of living the standard of life "by which he estimates the

tragic history of the South." The only problem with Tanimura's argument is, as he himself admits, these yeoman farmers hardly ever figure in Yoknapatawpha County.

The last volume of Kenzaburo Ohashi's *Faulkner Studies* is yet to come, but a report on Faulkner scholarship in this country won't be complete without reference to his article "Faulkner and the Japanese Novel," in seven installments (*EigoS* 127:75–77, 126–28 and 141, 206–08, 252–54, 359–61, 391–93, 433–35). Summarizing the commentaries of Japanese novelists on the various volumes of Faulkner's works in Japanese translation (mentioned earlier in this review), Ohashi identifies the radical affinity between the American master and contemporary Japanese novelists. The critic's long-standing speculation is adequately documented by his close reading of Faulkner and of Japanese writers: Takehiko Fukunaga (who first introduced Faulkner to the Japanese audience), Kenzaburo Oe (his commentary is a very valuable Faulkner criticism), Kunio Ogawa, Mitsuharu Inoue, and Kenji Nakagami.

The year 1981 has registered a monumental achievement in our scholarship on American poetry: Toshikazu Niikura's *America shi no Sekai: Seiritsu kara Gendai made* [*American Poetry: From Its Birth to Present*] (Tokyo: Taishukan); Masao Nakauchi's *Emily Dickinson: Tsuvu no Hotosha* [*Emily Dickinson: The Debauchee of Dew*] (Nan'undo); *Whitman and Dickinson: Bunka Shocho o Megutte* [*Whitman and Dickinson: Cultural Symbols in Their Writings*] by Takiaki Yamakawa et al. (Tokyo: Yumishobo); and Shozo Tokunaga's *Robert Lowell: Horo to Hangyaku no Bostonian* [*Robert Lowell: An Exile and Rebel of Boston Society*] (Tokyo: Kenkyusha).

Niikura's *American Poetry: From Its Birth to Present*, an anthology of some 46 poets from Anne Bradstreet to Sylvia Plath, is unique in that the anthology is preceded by a survey of American poetry (part 1) and by discussions on the influences of American poets on modern Japanese poets (part 2). The first part is a succinct history of American poetry, in which Niikura distinguishes it from British poetry: in the country devoid of great epic tradition, American poets create just as great a tradition, the epic of modern spirit. In the second part, he offers some illuminating comparisons of Emerson and Tokoku Kitamura, Poe and Sakutaro Hagiwara, Eliot and Junzaburo Nishiwaki, and Ginsberg and Kazuko Shiraishi. The last part, two-thirds of the book, is an original anthology of American poetry; the 46 poets have one poem each, accompanied by Niikura's own translations.

The same author's *A Century of American Poetry* (1975) has a wonderful chapter on Emily Dickinson, a favorite among our scholars. (The Emily Dickinson Society of Japan established in 1980 is an eloquent testimony of the poet's popularity in this country.) Masao Nakauchi's *Emily Dickinson: The Debauchee of Dew* is an important addition to Dickinson scholarship. The book is a thoughtful critical biography of the poet which strikes a delicate balance between biographical approach and New Criticism. Nakauchi's use of previous researches done on the poet is judicious; his introduction, a convenient briefing on changes and trends in Dickinson scholarship, is based on Buckingham's *Annotated Bibliography* (1970). Yet, his critical position is firm and his own, correcting the highly romanticized image of the Belle of Amherst. *Emily Dickinson: The Debauchee of Dew* is a rounded portrait of Dickinson the poet and the woman.

Takiaki Yamakawa's *Whitman and Dickinson: Cultural Symbols in Their Writings* is the fruit of a joint project by four Whitman and Dickinson scholars, including the editor-author. Their objective is to prove the contemporaneity of these great American poets by virtue of their use of cultural symbols in 19th-century America: the railroad, the ship, and the balloon. (Inclusion of the Civil War is, as the authors admit, incongruous.) Yamakawa's introduction, "Culture in the 19th century and its Symbols," provides a solid background for this collaborative research.

Each chapter begins with remarks on the social significance of the respective inventions (cultural symbols), which clarifies the nature and purpose of their book. Naturally, the authors of *Whitman and Dickinson* dispense with many of their poetical works crucial to the appreciation of each poet's art—in this Dickinson suffers more than Whitman. On the other hand, *Whitman and Dickinson* presents a broad perspective on their works; it is an excellent study of American culture, richly substantiated by materials other than literary. And sociologists and literary historians may find the book a valuable resource.

Thus, Dickinson looms large in Japanese scholarship—a fact footnoted in Hisao Kanaseki's "Some Contemporary Women Poets in America" (*EigoS* 127:300–301): great poets must converge in Dickinson. Invariably associated with Dickinson is Sylvia Plath, which brings us to a revised and enlarged edition of Noriko Mizuta's *Sylvia Plath* (1979), which appeared last year.

Shozo Tokunaga's *Robert Lowell: An Exile and Rebel of Boston Society* is his second critical biography of the poet after the interval of a decade. Tokunaga's approach to his subject is classical: he draws upon recent scholarship—Axelrod's biography (1978) and Heyman's *American Aristocracy* (1980) in particular; he seldom goes beyond the established view of the poet. The oscillation between New England heritage and "elsewhere" characteristic of many poets is expressed in Lowell in his wavering between his indebtedness to his heritage and the public commitment he thought he owed to his time, which our biographer highly values. Besides, with the critic's careful reading of Lowell's poems in chronological order, accompanied by Japanese translations—the strategy used in his *The Frisson Nouveau: Contemporary American Poetry* (1979)—the book serves as a good anthology of the poet. *Robert Lowell: An Exile and Rebel of Boston Society* is a very readable critical biography, a relief to this liberal humanist. The book makes the poet, least known of his contemporaries in this country, accessible to beginners and even more endeared to our enthusiasts.

Two memorable achievements in American Studies for 1981 are: Nozomu Yagyu's *America Puritan Kenkyu* [*Studies in the American Puritanism*] (Tokyo: The United Church of Christ in Japan Press) and Takao Kitamura's *Kawariyuku America: Inside Report* [*The Changing America: An Inside Report*] (Tokyo: Kenkyusha). Yagyu's *Studies in the American Puritanism* is a monumental accomplishment; the book is a thorough scholarly exploration of how the ideal of "the city on the hill" endured the vicissitudes of time from the Colonial period to the American Revolution. The striking feature of Yagyu's book is the author's judicious assessment of election sermons, which continue in inauguration speeches of American presidents. Good selections from Timothy Dwight, Winthrop, Edwards, Wigglesworth, and John Norton make his work quite impeccable; the bibliography at the end comprises over 200 relevant books. *Studies in the American Puritanism* is invaluable for our researches in American literature not only of the Colonial period but of all times, since the heavily typological nature of Puritan mind has had a lasting impact on the American imagination.

Kitamura's "inside reports" on the black people in the American South serialized for over a year (1976–77) in *The Study of Current English* (a monthly published by Kenkyusha, Tokyo) are here compiled with a few additional contributions in *The Changing America: An Inside Report*. The essays by two Japanese students enrolled in American universities give the book a new dimension. The first reporter puts his finger on the question of the "reversed racism," from which he, an outsider, is free. The second article is an ironic comment on some black students the Japanese student comes to know intimately: how they work for a materialistically "comfortable life," the kind of American dream their white counterparts used to cherish. Thus, concerning the problems of the blacks, it seems that an outsider like Kitamura or the other reporters in the book can get much closer to the heart of the matter than native Americans. *The Changing America* offers us a good many insights into contemporary American life and ours. Like *Studies in the American Puritanism*, Kitamura's book is a useful companion to our studies of American literature.

Kobe College

v. Scandinavian Contributions

Mona Pers

This past year American literary criticism and scholarship in Scandinavia has been primarily concerned with 20th-century literature. An exception is a book on Henry David Thoreau. The first decades of the 20th century are represented by Henry James, T. S. Eliot, Ezra Pound, Ernest Hemingway, William Faulkner, and two less frequent subjects of literary criticism in Scandinavia, Charlotte Perkins Gilman and Ole Edvart Rølvaag. Among the writers still living and active, James Baldwin, Vladimir Nabokov, Ralph Ellison, John Barth, and Robert Coover have drawn critical attention. The only essay this year on poetry is an interpretation of a poem by Sylvia Plath.

One of two book-length studies to appear this year is Claude Gayet's *The Intellectual Development of Henry David Thoreau* (Uppsala: Almqvist & Wiksell International). In the introduction Gayet declares that his monograph "examines the main levels that constituted the dynamic whole in the thought of Henry David Thoreau." He has structured his "analytic interpretation" on four levels: philosophical idealism, metaphysics of nature, economic theory, and social philosophy. Gayet denounces the efforts of other scholars to penetrate Thoreau's thought, arguing that they have failed to see it in a "developmental perspective." However, in the main Gayet, too, fails to give a clear picture of the various stages of Thoreau's intellectual development, partly because "as a thinker, Thoreau was unsystematic," to use Gayet's own words, but also because of Gayet's way of presenting his material. In order to follow his reasoning it would be necessary for the reader to have access to all of Thoreau's writings and look up for dates the numerous references and quotations given by Gayet. In most cases, Gayet volunteers no such information. The many formal shortcomings of his book tend to cloud his main argument, which, according to the introduction, "attempts to demonstrate that the early 1850s," contrary to what others have maintained, "marked a truly progressive development of Thoreau's thought at the economic, social, and political levels." To a limited extent, his thesis does demonstrate this, although too much time is spent on elaborate analyses of Hindu philosophy and of Emerson's indebtedness to other thinkers, most of it of little help in understanding Thoreau. At times Gayet's primary interest seems in fact to be Emerson or Hinduism rather than Thoreau.

Just as Thoreau's texts often appear to be of secondary importance to Gayet, so does Henry James's short story seem to be primarily used as illustrative material for a "new" critical approach in Rachel Salmon's long and complicated essay "Naming and Knowing in Henry James's 'The Beast in the Jungle': The Hermeneutics of a Sacred Text" (*OL* 36:302–22). To understand Henry James's "The Beast in the Jungle" properly, Salmon argues, it is necessary to apply a new critical method, based on Patte's division of texts into "sacred" and "profane," and Ricoeur's theory of "hermeneutics," which rules that any text "must be accepted as 'canon' in order to produce a genuine hermeneutical discourse." Salmon decides, somewhat arbitrarily, that "the fable-like quality" of James's short story stems from the fact that it is to a large extent a "sacred" text and must be treated as such. This is in Salmon's opinion what "explicatory criticism" has failed to do in its attempts to "fill the inevitable hiatus between *naming* and *knowing*" (hermeneutical terms). Salmon spends a great deal of effort trying to explain the nature and advantages of her new critical approach but fails to demonstrate convincingly that it enhances the understanding of James's tale. The reader may gain an understanding of what the terms "hermeneutics" covers but little new insight into James's art.

The reader does not gain very much new insight into Nabokov's art, either, in Jan Holmström's short essay "Aesthetic Bliss: A Note on Nabokov's Aesthetics" (*MSpr* 75,ii:133–37). Holmström draws our attention to certain stylistic features in the author's works, concentrating on *Lolita* and *Ada*, the two novels of Nabokov's he finds especially "allusive." He points out parallels in *Lolita* to Poe's "Annabel Lee," the prevalence of parody, allusions, literary jokes, and puns in Nabokov's fiction, and concludes that "Nabakov has not in theory developed his aesthetics at length."

Aesthetics is the subject, too, of Per-Adolf Lange's essay on Hemingway," 'Prosa är arkitektur—inte heminredning': Om Hemingway och byggnadskonsten" [" 'Prose is Architecture—Not Interior Decorating': On Hemingway and Architecture"] (*Finsk Tidskrift* 1:28–39). Lange attempts to answer the question whether Hemingway learned from architecture, as he did from painting, anything of use for his writing. Lange has found no direct influence, although he sees definite parallels between Hemingway's prose style and certain types of architecture. The best of his prose is distinguished by "simplicity, solidity, utility," the same qualities that distinguish his favorite type of edifice, the Roman cathedral. Lange shows that Hemingway's novels testify to a limited interest in architecture. Certain styles, the Byzantine and the Baroque, he disliked, and he was indifferent to the modern and ancient forms. It was the Roman style cathedrals of the Middle Ages that attracted him most, and Lange demonstrates how Hemingway made use of various Italian, French, and Spanish cathedrals in his books to create a sense of place or atmosphere. His fascination with cathedrals, Lange suggests, may have an emotional rather than an aesthetic explanation: the need of a closer relation to God and the church.

The need for religion is also at the core of Rolf Lundén's essay "The Progress of a Pilgrim: James Baldwin's *Go Tell It on the Mountain*" (*SN* 53:114–26). Lundén opens his discussion by frankly stating that "critics have been uncomfortable with the religious theme" of this novel. Rather than admitting that Baldwin's theme is religious, they have offered psychological, sexual, racial, and birth-of-the-artist readings, and in certain cases declared that Baldwin's treatment of religion is ironic. Lundén is convinced that these critics "have fallen victim to their own reluctance to believe that a writer of Baldwin's caliber could write seriously about religion," to their knowledge of Baldwin's career after his conversion, and most significantly to their reading of *The Fire Next Time*. Lundén makes the interesting observation that "the interpretation of *Go Tell It on the Mountain* as an ironic account of religion appeared only after *The Fire Next Time* had been published" and draws the conclusion that all the critics from then on have used *The Fire Next Time* as a starting point for their discussion, seeking evidence that John's conversion in *Go Tell It on the Mountain* is a "gimmick," and like Baldwin's own. But, says Lundén, these critics "have found little support in the text of the novel for their theories." Lundén, on the other hand, finds strong support in the text for his conviction that "embarrassingly simple as it may seem, *Go Tell It on the Mountain* is a novel about Christianity." He assures the reader that "Baldwin presents a symbolic rendition of what happens to most people who have been convicted of their own sin." As the title of his essay suggests, Lundén has discovered that *Go Tell It on the Mountain* is "closer to Bunyan's book than we might at first expect," in its structure, theme, and universality of its characters. On solid grounds does Lundén base his conclusion that "there is no irony whatever in [Baldwin's] description of John's deliverance."

T. S. Eliot, too, has been the object of religious interpretation. In his essay "Cocktailpartyt" (*Signum* 7:217–20) Christian Braw argues that *The Cocktail Party* depicts the road to spiritual awareness and that the play is actually a love drama. The tragedy of mankind is that worldly love has gone astray. None of the characters in Eliot's play are capable of love because they all seek their own good. Braw maintains that to understand Celia it is necessary to understand the Christian concept of love, closely related to duty. In his analysis of Celia, Braw finds it useful to compare her to Hedvig in Ibsen's *The Wild Duck*. Both heroines die, but whereas Hedvig's death is a tragedy, Celia's is a victory, which illustrates, according to Braw, the difference between Ibsen's cold, humorless idealism and Eliot's indulgent, humorous spiritualism.

Apocalypse, not in an exclusively biblical sense, is the leitmotif in

Douglas Robinson's essay "Visions of *No* End: The Anti-Apocalyptic Novels of Ellison, Barth, and Coover" (*AmerS* 13:1–16). "The apocalypse is without question one of the West's most powerful cultural myths," says Robinson in the opening statement of his essay. Before plunging into his theme, he warns his readers that the term "apocalypse" has lately been applied too loosely by critics, and as a corrective he proposes a division of "the literary uses of the apocalypse" into three categories: traditional apocalyptic (virtually nonexistent in American fiction after 1800); skeptical apocalyptic (Poe, Bierce, West, and Pynchon); and anti-apocalyptical (where "apocalyptic images become the vehicle for a vision of *no* end"). An examination of the third category constitutes the theme of Robinson's essay. After having "postulated some common structures and visions found in all anti-apocalyptic fiction," Robinson proceeds to analyze and compare Ellison's *Invisible Man*, Barth's *Giles Goat-Boy*, and Coover's *The Public Burning*. Based on a somewhat sketchy examination of the three novels, Robinson's conclusion is that the "paradoxical vision of man trapped by reality but liberated by the imaginative power of story . . . [is what] joins the anti-apocalyptic novels" of these three writers, who "reject the vision of an apocalyptic end and insist upon the unrelieved continuity of history."

Another essay revolving around the concept of apocalypse is a close reading of a poem, Hans H. Skei's "Sylvia Plath's 'Lady Lazarus': An Interpretation," originally a lecture (*Edda* 4:233–43). It offers a careful analysis of Plath's poem in the context of her poetic production as a whole and of her personal life experience. Skei proceeds logically and pedagogically to explain various aspects and cryptic passages of the poem, expounding in clear terms on the stylistic, thematic, and structural idiosyncrasies of Plath's art. For the student and teacher of poetry, in particular, this essay will prove valuable. Skei has made another, even more valuable, contribution to American literary scholarship with *William Faulkner: The Short Story Career* (Universitetsforlaget), which Skein describes as a revised section of his 1980 doctoral dissertation. The extensive and thorough bibliographical investigation Skei then undertook to provide himself with a reliable basis for his interpretation he has now turned into a bibliographical and textual study of Faulkner's short stories, presented in chronological order, with emphasis on genesis, composition, revisions, and re-use. With its detailed index it will undoubtedly realize Skei's hopeful conviction and prove "useful for others," especially for those interested in Faulkner's "small-scale writings."

Of bibliographical value also is Brita Lindberg-Seyersted's "A Note on Ezra Pound as Letter-Writer" (*Edda* 4:59–60). Examining Pound's problematic "typography," Seyersted concludes that to him "letter-writing was related to poetic composition." Seyersted points out parallels in Pound's use of abbreviations, punctuation, and spelling in his poems and letters, and explains how useful Pound's choice of stationery at various periods is for the correct dating of his letters, and why "Pound's use of the fascist system of dating has proved a trap even for Pound experts."

Seyersted's "note" is informative and points the way to an area where there is room for more research. So does Orm Øverland's "Ole Edvart Rølvaag and *Giants in the Earth*: A Writer Between Two Countries" (*AmerS* 13:35–45), an encouraging sign that the writings of immigrants are finally catching the interest of Scandinavian critics. Among the Scandinavian countries, Norway leads the way in this new field. Øverland gives a presentation of Ole Rølvaag, maybe the foremost among Scandinavian immigrant writers, focusing on the personal, social, and artistic dilemma of being, emotionally, "the son of two countries." Øverland maintains that Rølvaag's main concern as an author was "the psychological and cultural cost of immigration and pioneering." He realized that for the immigrants, "the greatest loss is the tragedy of alienation" and recognized "the need for the preservation and cultivation of Norwegian language and Norwegian culture." Still there was for him, says Øverland, "no conflict between the cultivation of the Norwegian language in America and Americanization." He actually referred to the work for Norwegian culture in America as "our work for Americanization," the old enriching the new, and insisted that the literature produced by Norwegian-Americans in the United States not be termed "American literature" but, more appropriately, "American literature in Norwegian." Øverland gives an interesting account of the adventures surrounding the publication of *Giants in the Earth* and an evaluation of its literary value. Because it is a book between two countries, Øverland concludes, "a full appreciation of the novel depends on the reader's acquaintance with both the Norwegian and the American backgrounds." Still, even a reader who is not familiar with Norse lore is no doubt able to "appreciate Rølvaag's message as well as to see not only the dilemma but also the opportunity for insight of a man between two countries," to use Øverland's own words at the conclusion of the essay.

While interest in Rølvaag and other immigrant writers may have been inspired by the *"Roots* syndrome," the renewed interest in Charlotte Perkins Gilman is undoubtedly the work of the feminist movement. In "En förkvinnligad värld" (["A Feminized World"] *Finsk Tidskrift* 2/3:95–105) Dodo Norrgård outlines the background and main ideas of *Herland.* She points out certain similarities in Gilman's book to such modern writers as Ursula K. Le Guin and Marge Piercy and suggests a rereading of the Swedish poet Karin Boye's *Kallocain* for comparison and contrast to the utopian collective world of Gilman. In Norrgård's opinion, Gilman's book, although somewhat uneven stylistically, still has both "actuality and freshness."

University College at Västerås

22. General Reference Works

James Woodress

Two years ago when I wrote this chapter I had 34 reference works to examine, but last year Robbins in his survey of this genre noticed a falling off in quantity, and I think 1981 too has been a modest year. At least I have managed to see only about half as many reference books as I reviewed last time. There are some very useful works, however, this year, and they fall into five categories: handbooks, literary guides, biographical dictionaries, bibliographies, and anthologies of criticism. As usual the fountainhead of reference materials is the Gale Research Company, which continues to dominate this field of publishing.

The Literary Guide to the United States by Stewart Benedict and others (Facts on File) sounded like an interesting work from its title, but the actuality is a disappointment. It is a breezy, undocumented literary history of the United States in 246 pages and of no use to scholars. It is organized regionally into six chapters dealing with New York and Environs, New England, the Midwest, the South and Border States, the Mountain States and Southwest, and California and the Far West. Each chapter is by a different contributor. One of the announced purposes of the book is to try to grasp American writers' sense of place in an effort to provide "a fuller understanding and enjoyment of American literature." But the coverage is so superficial that it hardly provides any substance even for a nonacademic general reader. It does have a great many well-chosen and interesting black-and-white illustrations.

A work of considerable utility, however, is the third and last volume of M. Thomas Inge's *Handbook of American Popular Culture* (Greenwood). As the Popular Culture Society grows in strength and membership, this reference work provides material for helping legitimize the study of this subject. As the editor says in his introduction, "popular culture . . . is a mirror wherein society can see itself

and better understand its own character and needs." He also expects
to see in the next decade the development of popular culture programs on an interdisciplinary basis, whereas now they exist on suffer-
ance within the traditional disciplines. This volume of the *Handbook*
is the work of many hands and among its 18 chapters are essays on
such diverse topics as almanacs, jazz, magic and magicians, newspapers, pornography, and stamp and coin collecting. This is an
extremely interesting work to browse through, and the essays are
competent and documented. Each one contains an historic sketch of
its topic, succinctly written, accounts of research collections of material, descriptions of reference works, notes, and bibliography. The
whole project is well conceived and useful.

Gale Research's handsome and ambitious project, *Dictionary of
Literary Biography*, produced eight volumes in 1981. (Two of these,
devoted to 20th-century dramatists, are discussed in chap. 18.) Volume 8 of this series, which consists of two parts, covers *Twentieth-
Century American Science Fiction Writers*. Edited by David Cowart
and Thomas L. Wymer, this work serves well the growing academic
interest in science fiction. It contains biographical-critical studies of
91 authors who began writing after 1900 and before 1970. As usual,
each writer is treated by a specialist in the field and contains the
usual list of reference and primary works. Major attention is given
to such writers as Asimov, Bradbury, and Le Guin, but there are
entries for many of the lesser practitioners; and writers not usually
classed as science-fiction writers, like Vonnegut, William Burroughs,
and Jack London, also are covered. *Twentieth-Century American
Fiction Writers* also contains some useful appendices dealing with
trends in science fiction, the media of science fiction, and several
others. That this work has a place is perhaps attested to by the fact
that during the 1970s science fiction accounted for more than one-
quarter of all fiction published.

DLB, vol. 9, is devoted to *American Novelists, 1910–1945* and
comes in three parts: Louis Adamic through Vardis Fisher, Fitzgerald through Rølvaag; and Marie Sandoz through Stark Young.
Edited by James Martine, these handsome volumes contain essays on
125 writers who flourished during the first half of the century. The
quality of the essays is high; many of the contributors are distinguished scholars: Walter Rideout on Anderson, Linda Wagner on

Faulkner, Scott Donaldson on Fitzgerald, James Nagel on Hemingway, Wallace Fowles on Henry Miller, Cynthia Wolff on Wharton—to name some of the writers of major essays (c. 15,000 words). There also are eminent scholars who contributed briefer essays on lesser figures: Edward Wagenknecht on Mary Johnston; Louis Budd on Robert Herrick; C. Hugh Holman on John P. Marquand. One might question the editorial judgment that assigned only five pages to Katharine Anne Porter, three to Elizabeth Maddox Roberts, while giving T. S. Stribling six and Harry Leon Wilson six and one-half. James T. Farrell, James Gould Cozzens, and James Branch Cabell probably are not worth the major coverage they get if Erskine Caldwell and Thornton Wilder, who get minor treatment, are not. Nevertheless, these volumes are a significant reference source and a pleasure to use. As lagniappe, volume 3 contains some excellent general essays, among which are "Southern Writers between the Wars" by James Justus and "American Fiction and the 1930s" by Warren French.

The final *DLB* volume to be noticed here is the *DLB Yearbook: 1980*. The purpose of the *Yearbook*, as editors Karen L. Rood, Jean W. Ross, and Richard Ziegfeld say in their introduction, is to augment, update, and review entries published in earlier volumes of the series and to supplement the series with entries on newly prominent writers or writers previously omitted. Thus the death of Nabokov has occasioned a new entry summing up his career, three new books are discussed in a new entry on Kurt Vonnegut, and Tillie Olsen, Diane Johnson, and Gilbert Sorrentino make their way into the volume. (Further comments on this work may be found in chap. 15.)

Three more volumes appeared in 1981 in another ongoing series from Gale: *Contemporary Authors*, ed. Frances C. Locher. Volumes 97–100 (one book) rounds out an entire shelf of this work that first began appearing in 1962 and includes a cumulative index of the entire series, some 61,000 authors living or deceased since 1960. Volume 101 starts off the new century with a new format but no changes in the amount or type of material included. *Contemporary Authors: New Revision Series*, vol. 1, represents a departure from the continuous updating of this series: beginning with this volume, only entries that need revising are reprinted. Readers of *ALS* won't want to go to this volume for Steinbeck, who is more elegantly treated in *American Novelists, 1910–1945*, but anyone who wants to check on Gary Wills or Randall Stewart will find the volume indispensable.

Two more reference works in the dictionary category round out this part of "General Reference Works." *American Woman Writers: A Critical Reference Guide from Colonial Times to the Present*, vol. 3 (Li through R), ed. Lina Mainiero (Ungar), appeared this year. Designed to capitalize on current interest in women's studies, the volumes in this series contain brief sketches of a large number of women writers ranging from major to very minor. Approximately 250 writers are covered in the 522 pages of volume 3, but the sketches are too brief to be of much use to scholars. For the more important women writers the *DLB* gives more ample coverage, and for major writers such as Cather or Wharton it provides major coverage. For minor contemporary writers Gale's *Contemporary Authors* includes many more writers. The quality of the essays is better in *DLB*. The account of Katharine Anne Porter in *American Woman Writers* does not tell one the name of Porter's first husband, nor does it mention the title story in *Flowering Judas and Other Stories*.

Donald J. Winslow's *Life-Writing: A Glossary of Terms in Biography and Autobiography and Related Forms* (Hawaii) is of little use for scholars. On pp. 40–41, for example, may be found brief definitions of "sermon," "sketch," "spiritual autobiography," "table talk," "testimony," "times," and "tour," among others. Maybe freshmen who do not have access to Holman's *Handbook* or own a dictionary will find this book useful.

Among the general bibliographies that came my way in 1981 are three compilations of considerable utility: *American Prose and Criticism: A Guide to Information Sources*, ed. Peter A. Brier and Anthony Arthur (Gale); *Jewish Writers of North America: A Guide to Information Sources*, ed. Ira Bruce Nadel (Gale); and *A Bibliographic Guide to Midwestern Literature*, ed. Gerald Nemanic (Iowa). The guide to prose and criticism divides its subjects into entertainers, teachers, and reporters, a rather procrustean arrangement that puts James Thurber and E. B. White in the first group, Henry Mencken and Henry Adams in the second, and John Muir and John Gunther in the third. The major critics of the first half of the century are included in the second half of the book, from Irving Babbitt to Yvor Winters. The bibliographies are useful though highly selective.

Nadel's volume divides approximately 120 American and Canadian Jewish writers into poets, fiction writers, and dramatists, and treats them all very briefly. Major writers like Malamud or Bellow have been more adequately treated bibliographically elsewhere, but for the lesser figures the compilations here will serve a purpose. Why there was a need to single out Jewish writers for separate treatment is a question the foreword doesn't really explain, but this volume certainly makes clear that 20th-century American literature owes a great deal to the Jews. Many contributors helped compile the Midwest bibliography that Nemanic edited, and the result is a volume containing nine topical bibliographies on the region's culture, basic bibliographical data on 120 midwestern authors, and appendices covering additional authors and works of fiction. The cut-off date is 1976. Regional bibliographies present problems in a mobile society such as ours, and even though the editor required that the subject's writing "in some demonstrable way, reflect the cultural life of the region," it was not possible to omit Hemingway, who does not seem very midwestern in his total work, or Richard Wright, whose *Native Son* certainly is midwestern, but not much else. But it is useful to have a bibliography that includes Mary Hartwell Catherwood, Henry Blake Fuller, E. W. Howe, Vachel Lindsay, Booth Tarkington—all midwesterners to the core. Scholars will no doubt go elsewhere for Hart Crane or Dreiser. The general topic bibliographies are particularly valuable.

Three large volumes of reprinted criticism came out in 1981, all from Gale: *Nineteenth-Century Literature Criticism*, vol. 1, ed. Laurie Lanzen Harris, and *Twentieth-Century Literary Criticism*, vols. 4, 5, ed. Sharon K. Hall. The first supplies students without access to well-stocked libraries criticism on authors who lived between 1800 and 1900. All genres are covered as well as several national literatures. The Americans who made it into this volume are Amos Bronson Alcott, Robert Montgomery Bird, James Fenimore Cooper, Ralph Waldo Emerson, Philip Freneau, Edgar Allan Poe. The Poe section, for example, runs to 43 pages, double-columned, and begins with a review of *Al Aaraaf, Tamerlane and Minor Poems* (1830?) and ends with David Grossvogel (1979). The two volumes of reprinted 20th-century criticism also are world-wide in coverage and include 14 Americans among the 65 writers treated. To be eligible for inclusion in these volumes, a writer must have died between 1900 and 1960.

The principles of selection seem haphazard. Volume 4, for example, includes Henry Adams, George Washington Cable, Countee Cullen, Sinclair Lewis, H. P. Lovecraft, Edna St. Vincent Millay, Marjorie Kinnan Rawlings, and Thomas Wolfe.

A final item: the enormously useful *MLA Directory of Periodicals: A Guide to Journals and Series in Languages and Literatures*, compiled by Eileen M. Mackesy, Karen Matayak, and Nancy Hoover (New York: MLA), appeared in an updated edition in 1981. It contains all available information on the 3,024 journals and series currently searched for the MLA International Bibliography. At $75 MLA members can't afford it, but it's a must for libraries.

Author Index

Subject Index

DATE DUE

HIGHSMITH 45-102   PRINTED IN U.S.A.